PIMLICO

566

MICROCOSM

Norman Davies C.M.G., F.B.A. is Professor
Emeritus of the University of London, a Super-
numerary Fellow of Wolfson College, Oxford,
and the author of several books on Polish and
European history, including *God's Playground*,
Europe and *The Isles*.

Roger Moorhouse, who is a Germanist and
historian, was chief researcher on Davies's previous
books.

MICROCOSM

Portrait of a Central European City

NORMAN DAVIES and
ROGER MOORHOUSE

PIMLICO

Published by Pimlico 2003

2 4 6 8 10 9 7 5 3 1

First published in Great Britain by Jonathan Cape 2002

Pimlico edition 2003

Pimlico
Random House, 20 Vauxhall Bridge Road,
London SW1V 2SA

Random House Australia (Pty) Limited
20 Alfred Street, Milsons Point, Sydney,
New South Wales 2061, Australia

Random House New Zealand Limited
18 Poland Road, Glenfield,
Auckland 10, New Zealand

Random House (Pty) Limited
Endulini, 5A Jubilee Road, Parktown 2193, South Africa

The Random House Group Limited Reg. No. 954009
www.randomhouse.co.uk

A CIP catalogue record for this book
is available from the British Library

ISBN 0-7126-9334-3

Papers used by Random House are natural,
recyclable products made from wood grown in sustainable forests;
the manufacturing processes conform to the environmental
regulations of the country of origin

Typeset by Deltatype Ltd, Birkenhead, Merseyside
Printed and bound in Great Britain by
Clays Ltd, St Ives PLC

CONTENTS

LIST OF ILLUSTRATIONS

Silesian Landscape by Carl Friedrich Lessing, 1841 (*Kunstmuseum Düsseldorf im Ehrenhof/Landesbildstelle Rheinland*).
Lake in the Giant Mountains by Ludwig Richter, 1839 (*Nationalgalerie, Berlin*).
Prince Vratislav I of Bohemia (*SUPP, Prague*).
Bolesław Chrobry (*Muzeum Narodowe, Warsaw*).
Duke Henryk VI of Wrocław (*Jakub Kostowski*).
St Czesław (*Muzeum Narodowe, Wrocław*).
Charles IV of Luxemburg, artist unknown (*AKG London*).
Jiří z Podiebrady, engraving by J.C. Klupffel (*AKG London*).
Mátyás Corvinus, artist unknown (*Kunsthistorisches Museum, Vienna/Bridgeman Art Library, London*).
Louis II Jagellion (*collection of Roger Moorhouse*).
The marriage of Jadwiga (Hedwig), from *The Legend of Jadwiga*, c.1430–40, artist unknown (*Muzeum Narodowe, Warsaw/Bridgeman Art Library, London*).
The battle of Legnica (Liegnitz), from *The Legend of Jadwiga*, c.1430–40, artist unknown (*Muzeum Narodowe, Warsaw/Bridgeman Art Library, London*).
Duke Henryk IV of 'Pressela' as *Minnesänger* (*Handschriftenabteilung, University of Heidelberg*).
John of Luxemburg at Crécy, artist unknown (*Mary Evans Picture Library, London*).
Bohemian Hussites vs. Imperial crusaders, from the Jena Codex, artist unknown (*Narodni Muzeum, Prague/AKG London*).
St. John of Capistrano: Bonfire of Vanities (*Norbert Conrads, Historisches Institut, University of Stuttgart*).
St Vincent's Monastery on the Elbing (*reproduced from Gerhard Scheuermann, Das Breslau Lexikon, vol. 2, Dülmen: Laumann-Verlag, 1994*).
Matthäus Merian's city plan, 1650 (*Bildarchiv Preussischer Kulturbesitz, Berlin*).
Johannes Cochlaeus by Jean Jacques Boissard (?) (*AKG London*).
Johannes Hess (*Norbert Conrads, Historisches Institut, University of Stuttgart*).
Crato von Crafftheim (*University Library, Wrocław*).

Rudolf II of Habsburg (*Mary Evans Picture Library, London*).

Elizabeth Stuart (*collection of Roger Moorhouse*).

Lennart Torstenson, engraving by Jeremias Falck, after a painting by David Beck (*AKG London*).

Andreas Gryphius (*University Museum, Wrocław*).

Angelus Silesius (*Archdiocesan Museum, Wrocław*).

The *Naschmarkt*, engraving by G.M. Probst, after a drawing by F.B. Werner (*Bildarchiv Preussischer Kulturbesitz, Berlin*).

View of 'Bressla' by Hartmann Schedel, 1493 (*Bildarchiv Preussischer Kulturbesitz, Berlin*).

The defenestration of Prague, 1618, painting by Wenzel von Brozik, 1889 (*AKG London*).

Entry into Presslau of Emperor Matthias, *c.*1612 (*Ossolineum, Wrocław*).

Christian Wolff, engraving by Johann Martin Bernigeroth, 1755 (*Archiv für Kunst und Geschichte, Berlin/AKG London*).

Maria Leszczyńska, lithograph by François Seraphin Delpech, after a painting by Jean Marc Nattier (*Archiv für Kunst und Geschichte, Berlin/AKG London*).

Frederick II the Great, painting by J.G. Ziesenis (*Staatliche Schlösser und Gärten, Potsdam/Bridgeman Art Library, London*).

Bishop von Schaffgotsch, from *Portret wrocławskich duchownych* (*Archdiocesan Museum, Wrocław*).

Carl von Clausewitz, lithograph after a painting by Wilhelm Wach, *c.*1820 (*AKG London*).

August Borsig, *c.*1850 (*Bildarchiv Preussischer Kulturbesitz, Berlin*).

Heinrich Graetz (*University Archive, Wrocław*).

Ferdinand Lassalle (*Bildarchiv Preussischer Kulturbesitz, Berlin*).

The Nikolai Gate and Bridge (*reproduced from F.G. Weiß*, Wie Breslau wurde, *Breslau, 1906*).

The Ohle slums (*reproduced from F.G. Weiß*, Wie Breslau wurde, *Breslau, 1906*).

The Jesuit College (*reproduced from F.G. Weiß*, Wie Breslau wurde, *Breslau, 1906*).

The Jewish Quarter on the Karlsplatz, engraving by Steidlin, eighteenth century, after a drawing by F.B. Werner (*Bildarchiv Preussischer Kulturbesitz*).

Battle of Leuthen (Lutynia), 1757: 3rd Guard Battalion takes the churchyard in Leuthen, watercolour by Carl Röchling, *c.*1900 (*AKG London*).

Siege of Breslau, 1757, from R.S. Ben Jochai, *Die Historie des Kriegs zwischen den Preussen . . . und den Österreichern . . .*, 1758 (*AKG London*).

Love of the Fatherland 1813 by Gustav Graef: 'Ferdinande von Schmettau donates her hair' (*Staatliche Museen zu Berlin/Preussischer Kulturbesitz*).

Departure of the Volunteers from Breslau, 1813 by Adolph Menzel (*Herder-Institut, Marburg*).

Storming the Bakery in the Neumarkt by Philipp Hoyoll, 1846 (*Museum Ostdeutsche Galerie, Regensburg*).

Defending the barricades in Breslau, 7 May 1849 (*Muzeum Narodowe, Wrocław; photograph by Edmund Witecki*).

Kaiser Wilhelm II's visit in 1906 (*University Library, Wrocław*).

Opening of the *Jahrhunderthalle* in 1913 (*AKG London*).

The New Market with Neptune fountain (*University Library, Wrocław*).

The City Hall, wood engraving, *c.*1895, after a painting by Grete Waldau (*AKG London*).

The Cathedral, *c.*1911 (*Bildarchiv Preussischer Kulturbesitz, Berlin*).

The New Synagogue (*Muzeum Narodowe, Wrocław*).

The Main Square and St. Elizabeth's Church, *c.*1905 (*Kunstbibliothek, Berlin/Bildarchiv Preussischer Kulturbesitz, Berlin*).

The Main Station (*Bildarchiv Preussischer Kulturbesitz, Berlin*).

Blücher Square (*University Library, Wrocław*).

Palace Square (*University Library, Wrocław*).

Leni Riefenstahl by Eugen Spiro, 1924 (*Leni Riefenstahl and Peter Spiro*).

Girl and Cat by Balthus, 1937 (*private collection/Bridgeman Art Library, London*; © *ADAGP, Paris and DACS, London 2002*).

The Gypsy Lovers by Otto Müller (*Collection Max Lutze, Hamburg/Bridgeman Art Library, London*).

Two Women at the Table (variation) by Oskar Schlemmer, 1930 (© *The Oskar Schlemmer Family Estate and Archive, I-28824 Oggebbio (VB); photo: Photo Archive C. Raman Schlemmer, I-28824 Oggebbio, Italy*).

Wojciech Korfanty (*PAP, Warsaw*).

Róża Luksemburg, *c.*1908 (*Mary Evans Picture Library, London*).

Fritz Haber, after a lithograph by Emil Orlik (*Fotoarchiv Habermann/Bayerische Staatsbibliothek, Munich*).

Manfred von Richthofen, by Karl Bauer, 1917 (*Mary Evans Picture Library, London*).

Edith Stein (*Bildarchiv, Bayerische Staatsbibliothek, Munich*).

Helena Motykówna (*Krzysztof Szwagrzyk*).

Tadeusz Różewicz (*Grzegorz Radzki & Ewa Dessaignes/Polish Cultural Institute, London*).

Władysław Frasyniuk (*PAP, Warsaw*).

The City Hall bedecked, 1938 (*Bildarchiv, Bayerische Staatsbibliothek, Munich*).

LIST OF MAPS

LIST OF APPENDICES

To all Vratislavians,
past, present and future,
and Oscar

FOREWORD

The conception of this book goes back to early 1996, when I was introduced to the City President of Wrocław, Mr Bogdan Zdrojewski. At the time, I had just finished writing *Europe: A History* and I talked to him of my long-standing efforts to overcome the artificial division of European history into East and West. In my view, the prevailing fashion for looking at Europe's past exclusively through Western eyes, and for treating everywhere east of the Elbe as alien and foreign, formed a major barrier to contemporary aspirations to reunite Europe in the post-Cold-War period. For his part, the President talked of Wrocław's own problems of history and identity. He was the executive head of a city which for fifty years had been completely Polish, but which for centuries before 1945 had been overwhelmingly German in culture and composition. He talked of the numerous German visitors including many former Breslauers, whom he regularly welcomed to the city but whose vision of the past differed radically from that of the present inhabitants. He then said that a new historical survey was extremely desirable to further promote the present climate of reconciliation, adding perhaps surprisingly – that it could never be written 'either by a German or a Pole'. He finished by suggesting that I write the book myself.

As I remember, my first reaction was one of caution. I was well aware that the task was formidable; and, despite my established reputation as a historian of Poland, I knew my own shortcomings. In short, I was flattered and fascinated, but wary. So I responded by saying that, though the idea was tempting, it could not be realised without expert assistance in German matters. I honestly expected that the proposal would end there. But the President persisted in the most pragmatic manner. 'How could such assistance be arranged?' he asked, 'and how much might it cost?' Such was the conversation that started the project. In due course, a contract was signed between the City of Wrocław and the Ossolineum Institute, which agreed to act as the sponsoring body. A small team of local contributors was assembled. And a former student of mine and German specialist, Roger Moorhouse, was appointed as chief researcher.

In the following months the project evolved in a number of ways. Emergency financial support was provided in 1997 by the Robert Bosch Foundation, when the city's own resources were hit by the great flood of that year. Further support was generously provided by the British Academy, the Leverhulme Trust and the Alfred Krupp von Bohlen und Halbach Foundation. Numerous discussions with potential publishers helped us to define our goals more precisely and to set our sights on three separate editions of the same book – English, Polish and German – which were to appear simultaneously. After various peripatetions, contracts were signed with Jonathan Cape in London, with Znak SIW in Cracow and with Droemer Knaur of Munich. On the intellectual front, we soon realised that we were dealing with a multinational, not merely a bi-national, story. Care had to be taken to explore the Czech and Jewish perspectives, as well as the Polish and German ones; to distinguish the Austrian from the Prussian; to detach the imperial era from that of Weimar and the Third Reich; to separate the Soviet-dominated Stalinist ethos from that of the later 'People's Poland'. No less interesting were the city's connections with a wide range of international figures – with the daughter of a Scottish king, for example, or a Queen of France, a future President of the USA, a future British Prime Minister, a persecuted Macedonian refugee, a French POW, or a distinguished Australian professor. At some point, therefore, we realised that we were putting one city's experiences into a wider setting, that we were reconstructing a 'microcosm of Central Europe' (see page 10).

My cooperation with Roger Moorhouse has been extremely fruitful. In the first stage he was preoccupied with research, both in Germany and in German source material. In the second stage, under my guidance, he was able to write the first draft of many chapters and hence to contribute rather more than had been originally envisaged. In the final stages his contributions and mine became so entangled that they came to be shared, as the Poles would say, 'feefty, feefty'. Hence, there was no doubt in my own mind that Roger Moorhouse had to be promoted from chief researcher to co-author.

In a study of this sort names are extremely important. They do much more than merely identify people and places. They reveal the viewpoints and the prejudices of those who use them. Here was a problem that I had met in full measure when writing *The Isles*. One cannot say, for example, that Julius Caesar landed in England. In 55–54 BC, England did not yet exist. Nor can one say that he landed in Britain, or even in Britannia. 'Britain' is a modern English name, unsuited to the first century BC, while 'Britannia' is the Latin name for a Roman province that was created *after* the Roman conquest and not before it. So where exactly did Caesar land? To be frank, we do not know. We can only suppose that he landed among illiterate Celtic tribes who would probably have called their country by a name more akin to the modern Welsh *Prydain* than to anything known in English or

Latin. And William the Conqueror, who was a Frenchified Viking, called himself neither 'William' nor 'the Conqueror' but Guillaume le Bâtard.

By the same token, the city that is now called Wrocław has changed its name many times. One can only try to guess what its original name might have been. More than fifty variants have been recorded, each one influenced by a time, a place and a user. 'Breslau' did not come into consistent use until the late eighteenth century; and, except for Polish-speakers, 'Wrocław' was not generally established until 1945. So the two main contenders were of limited value. We found no definitive solution. But by using different forms of the city's name for successive chapters – Wrotizla, Vretslav, Presslaw, Bresslau, Breslau and Wrocław – we hope, at the very least, to draw attention to the problem.

Our 'Island City', of course, is far from unique in this respect. Europe is full of cities that have changed their ethnic and cultural connections over the centuries. And it is full of people who hold more to their collective myths than to historical reality. In my own *Europe: A History*, I pointed out the parallel experiences of Strasbourg, Wrocław, Lwów and Kiev. (Or should I have said Strassburg, Breslau, L'viv and Kyiv?) The poet and Nobel Prize-winner Czesław Miłosz, who is a Pole from Lithuania, has written of his native Wilno-Vilnius-Vilna as a city of 'semantic misunderstandings'.[1] He admits that when living there as a young man he knew little about the city's Jewish heritage, about its importance for modern Lithuania or its Belorussian connections. 'To a certain degree, I myself could serve as an example of the intellectual deformation that is caused by being raised in the spirit of nationalism. It is something from which I had later to liberate myself with difficulty.'[2] Similarly, the German writer Günter Grass, who was born in pre-war Danzig but who has close links with post-war Gdańsk, has written of his own learning curve. And he stresses the emotional complications of remembering. When he returned to his native city in 1958, for the first time since the war, an aunt who had stayed behind whispered in his ear: '*Ech waiss, Ginterchen, em Wästen is bässer, aber em Osten is scheener.*'[3] (Which approximates to: 'I know, Günter, it's better in the West, but it's more beautiful in the East.') The colour of such a statement is untranslatable – even into German – but recalling the full reality of the past is more than historians can do.

From the start, a decision was made to avoid a narrow, parochial approach and to throw the study open to as many winds and perspectives as possible. There seemed no point in strictly limiting the narrative to events that happened within the city walls. At least in outline, an attempt has been made to describe the development of the district of which our 'Island City' was the centre; to delineate the changing political, cultural and economic context that surrounded it; and to provide a selection of the triumphs and disasters which all manner of Vratislavians have encountered in their near-infinite variety. The resultant mission has taken us to times, places and people that may have been far removed from the city, but which in one way or another were closely connected with it. Shakespeare famously asked, 'What news on the Rialto?' If, instead, one were to have asked at any moment in the last millennium, 'What news on the banks of the Odra?', the answer would come from near and far: from the towns and villages of Lower Silesia, from the ruling capitals of Cracow, Prague, Vienna, Berlin, Paris, Moscow or Warsaw; from exiles in Australia, from soldiers fighting in France or in the depths of Russia, from Scottish or American travellers, from victims of Nazi concentration camps and of the Soviet Gulag, from any number of artists, academics and authors for whom the name of Wrotizla (or Vretslav or Presslaw or Breslau or Wrocław) was close to their hearts.

The choice of title caused considerable brain-racking. Given the multinational approach, it was always obvious that the book could not be called either 'A History of Wrocław' or 'A History of Breslau'. 'A History of Vratislavia – Breslau – Wrocław' would have been hopelessly clumsy, and not completely accurate. Yet there was no alternative that sprang readily to mind. In time, three candidates presented themselves. The first, 'A City of Many Names', was accurate, but somewhat colourless. The second, 'Flower of Europe' – a phrase taken from the seventeenth-century Vratislavian poet, Nikolaus Henel von Hennenfeld, was colourful, but not geographically focused. The third, *Microcosm: A Portrait of a Central European City*, was not initially promising. It reflected the sentiments of the Introduction and summarised the central concept of our endeavour, but it was thought by some to be too indefinite. Indeed, it was judged by one of our prospective publishers to make the book unpublishable. Yet gradually it grew on us, and was strongly approved of by our editors at Jonathan Cape. So hesitations were cast aside; courage was summoned. And *Microcosm* it is.

I think that I can report three distinct emotions in the aftermath of writing the book. The first of them is wonder at the extraordinary human and cultural riches that our research has revealed. The second is a strong affection not only for the city that has been the object of our study, but also for the wide variety of people of various nationalities who have passed through our sights and who often have the same sort of bitter-sweet memories. The third is undoubtedly trepidation. It is generated by the prospect of presenting this portrait to a worldwide community of Vratislavians who, inevitably, will not agree with everything that we say.

Thanks are due to a very large number of people. Leaving private indebtedness aside, we wish to pay tribute:

- to Dr Adolf Juzwenko, who has been a close friend for more than thirty years and who engineered that first meeting with the City President
- to President Bogdan Zdrojewski, whose energy and enterprise embody the virtues of the new Wrocław
- to our various sponsors, who have taken a personal interest in the project: the Urząd Miasta Wrocław, the Robert Bosch Foundation, the British Academy, the Alfried Krupp von Bohlen und Halbach Foundation and the Leverhulme Trust
- to the Ossolineum Institute in Wrocław, which kindly agreed to act as the project's host institution in Poland
- to our researchers, contributors and correspondents, including Roman Aftanazy, Dr Heinz Wolfgang Arndt, Dr Arkadiusz Bagłajewski, Dr Joachim Bahlcke, Dr Jaroslav Bakala, Gillian Beeston, Katarzyna Benda-Pawlowska, Andrzej Biernacki, Dr Ulrich Bopp, Dr Karl Brokstad, Mark Burdajewicz, Professor Norbert Conrads, Dr Rebecca Cox-Brokstad, Beata Długajczyk, Dr Mariusz Dworsatschek, Wojciech Hrabia Dzieduszycki, Dr Cyril Edwards, Professor Robert Evans, Ulrich Frodien, Dr Dan Gawrecki, Professor Józef Gierowski, Zbigniew Gluza, Dr Ted Harrison, Denis Healey, Ewa Huggins, Dr Michał Kaczmarek, Professor Maria Kalinowska, Henry Kamm, Piotr Kendziorek, Agnieszka Klimczewska, Dr Beata Konopska, Dr Maria Korzeniewicz, Dr Jakub Kostowski, Ute Krebs, Dr Karen Lambrecht, Professor Walter Laqueur, Irene Lipmann, Dr Horst Dieter Marheinecke, Dr Alison Millett, Dr Rudolf Muhs, Jane Neal, Hélène Neveu, Hanna Nyman, Professor Hartmut Pogge von Strandmann, Daša Rohelova, Joanna Schmidt, Sabine Schulenburg, Evelyn Smellie, Dr Melissa Smellie, Dr Paul Smith, Dr Beate Störtkuhl, Rupert Graf Strachwitz, Dr Krzysztof Szwagrzyk, Dr Jacek Tebinka, Michaela Todorova, Magdalena Turczyn, Dr Jakub Tyszkiewicz, Gary Wiggins, Wanda Wyporska, Dr Roman Wytyczak, Małgorzata Ziemilska-Dzieduszycka
- to my agent, David Godwin, who coordinated the final publishing package
- to our various editors and translators, notably Will Sulkin and Jörg Hensgen at Random House, Henryk Woźniakowski and Jerzy Illg at Znak, Klaus Fricke at Droemer, Thomas Bertram and Andrzej Pawelec
- to Brigadier Alan Gordon, the Bursar of Wolfson College, Oxford, who managed the project's accounts
- and to all who wished us well.

I am sure that all of them will join us in raising the toast of 'Floreat Vratislavia'.

Norman Davies

INTRODUCTION

No one can say for certain when the concept of Central Europe was born. But 1897 is probably as good a date as any. In that year, Sir Halford Mackinder, founder of the Oxford Geography School and the 'father of geopolitics', appointed the author for a key volume in the series that he was editing on 'The Regions of Europe'. The volume was entitled *Central Europe*, and it was published in London in 1903. The author was Joseph Partsch.

In earlier times, no special attention had been paid to the central parts of the European subcontinent. Generations of men educated in the Classics thought principally of the division that separated South from North: the ancient Mediterranean world from the barbarian world beyond the Roman *limes*. Others emphasised the long-standing distinction between the civilised West and the supposedly less civilised East. Both the North–South and East–West divides coincided with important cultural frontiers – between Protestant and Catholic, and between Catholic and Orthodox. Both of them undermined the notion that the lands of the Centre had much in common. Of course there had been various long-running political entities, such as the Holy Roman Empire or the Habsburg monarchy, which had dominated the area and hence had been identified with it. And Klemens Metternich, the Austrian Chancellor, had liked to talk about 'the Danubian Space'. But Central Europe was not an established concept. Nineteenth-century reference works carried entries on Central America, Central Asia and even Central Africa, but not on Central Europe.

By the 1890s, however, the recent rise of a united and extraordinarily dynamic German Empire was forcing people to think again. Germany's new-found political, economic and cultural power was sending ripples right across the map of Europe. For Germany belonged neither to the West, which had long been dominated by France, nor to the East, which had largely fallen to the insatiable appetite of Russia. It was no more part of Scandinavia than it was of Italy or the Balkans. It was looking increasingly like the key element in a central region that was distinct from all the others.

Mackinder's immediate concern was to warn the Western powers of a possible conjunction of Germany and Russia. When this danger passed, he was particularly anxious to keep Germany and Russia apart, if necessary by the creation of a cordon of strong independent states. It was in this connection that he coined his famous formula:

Who rules Eastern Europe, commands the Heartland:
Who rules the Heartland, commands the World-Island:
Who commands the World-Island, commands the World.

In each case, the crucial fault-line in European politics followed the frontier between the German and the Russian Empires. It was not surprising, therefore, that Mackinder's choice for an author on Central Europe fell on Joseph Partsch. For Partsch was Professor of Geography at Breslau; and Breslau lay less than sixty-five kilometres from the fault-line.

Partsch's study of Central Europe was a minor *tour de force*. It opens with a striking map of Central Europe in silhouette (see Appendix); and, after a systematic survey of geology, climate, ethnography and cultural development, it ends with an analysis of current strategic thinking. Like Mackinder, Partsch was particularly impressed by Russia's command of the Eurasian heartland, and hence by the danger posed to Germany from the East. 'Germany will never covet a square mile of Russian soil,' he declared, rather piously, but 'no-one can answer for it that the Russian colossus in its unceasing expansion may some day attempt once more to push its western frontier forward'.[1] He was equally concerned that France, in its efforts to recover Alsace-Lorraine, might 'conspire with the giant Empire of the East for the destruction of the German Empire'.[2] His solution to the looming problem of a possible war on two fronts was to raise the idea of a pre-emptive attack on Russia. 'The whole conditions of national defence along this eastern frontier . . .' he wrote, 'suggest that . . . serious injury can only be averted by a vigorous offensive.'[3] Partsch may well have been influenced by the location of his home in Breslau. For he had chosen exactly the opposite solution to that of the Chief of the German General Staff, Alfred von Schlieffen, whose strategic plan for Germany's defence was unveiled two years after the publication of Partsch's study and who decided that the pre-emptive strike should fall on France.

One should hasten to add that Partsch was no warmonger. He was not advocating war. His strategic speculations were offered in the same vein as those of most military thinkers in most countries, who wanted the great European peace to last for ever, but who were required to address the possibility of armed conflict. What Partsch really wanted to do was to inspire the solidarity of the peoples of Central Europe, whose predicament he had so accurately described. His book ended with an impassioned plea:

Central Europe has been the battlefield of all nations long enough to resist a recurrence of [previous] sufferings . . . May the great monument on the battlefield of Leipzig, where the criminal effort to enslave a whole continent was defeated, . . . remain . . . a warning to all ambitious tyrants in the future and an admonition to the peoples of Central Europe to remain united, to keep peace, and to command peace.[4]

For an early twentieth-century German, phrases like 'criminal slavemasters' or 'ambitious tyrants' still referred to Napoleon.

During the First World War, when Russia and Germany fought prolonged campaigns on the Eastern Front, the ominous conflict foreseen by Partsch became a reality. In Russia, an official map called 'The Future of Europe' was published in September 1914 by the Tsar's Foreign Ministry. It showed that Russia's territorial ambitions included a restored and Russian-run Kingdom of Poland stretching as far as the Oder and the western Neisse. (In essence, it closely foreshadowed the expansionist plans revived by Stalin thirty years later.) In Germany, there was every reason for alarm. The prospective loss of lands and people in the East was greater than that in the West. Indeed, an express threat had been aimed at the larger part of historical Prussia. And, with Austria-Hungary already aboard, there was little hope of finding further major allies. An urgent response was called for, in terms of both military action and strategic thinking. The military response was swiftly delivered by General Hindenburg in his crushing victory at the battles of Tannenberg and of the Masurian Lakes in August and September 1914. The strategic thinking was done by Friedrich Naumann.

Among Germany's enemies, Naumann was widely perceived as a dangerous imperialist. And since Germany was to lose the war, his negative reputation was not widely challenged. The former Lutheran pastor, and friend of Max Weber, was a long-term opponent of the British Empire. Like many people in his day, he was a 'Darwinist' who was not ashamed to talk of Germany as the fittest country of the era. He tended to talk of 'races' rather than of states and nations, even of the German *Herrenvolk*, or 'master race'. And by promoting the close alliance of Germany and Austria, his *Mitteleuropa* (1915) was viewed with great suspicion in the West, being openly denounced in France as '*une idée de guerre*'.[5] In reality, this mild Prussian was no extremist, and his call for a federation of the peoples of Central Europe had nothing in common with later Nazi calls for *Lebensraum*. Naumann was a Christian Socialist in origin and a pioneer of modern German liberalism. His sometime collaborator, Theodor Heuss, was to become both his chief biographer and the first President of the German Federal Republic.[6] Naumann was strongly opposed to the Bismarckian drive for Germanisation; he was a staunch critic of anti-Semitism; and his scheme

3

had no influence on the military leaders who pursued an *Ostpolitik* of conquest in the years after his book appeared. He was guilty of semantic confusion by variously proposing a *Staatenbund*, or 'League of States', and an *Oberstaat*, or 'Superstate'; and he probably overplayed the notion of Central Europe being a sort of exclusive reservation for German interests. Yet he was hardly the ogre conjured up by his opponents. It should have been obvious that German power and German culture were bound to predominate in any grouping of nations in the region; and Naumann, strongly opposed to a policy of annexation, was striving for a place for all.

Paradoxically, Naumann's concept of Central Europe was best publicised by those who opposed it. Figures like T.G. Masaryk, the future President of Czechoslovakia, saw Naumann as the embodiment of all the dark forces that had been obstructing the liberation of his country. Yet by drawing attention to their views on the undesirability of Naumann's scheme, they inevitably gave credence to the notion that a Central Europe of some other hue should, or even *did*, exist.

In Britain, for example, the circle of writers and politicians who launched the journal *The New Europe* in 1917 was principally concerned with the problems of Austria-Hungary and with support for the national movements there. Their leaders were Robert Seton-Watson, author of numerous works on Central Europe and Henry Wickham-Steed, sometime correspondent of *The Times* in Vienna; their champion was the future President of the Czecho-Slovak Republic. They had strong ties with the constitutionalists in Russia, with whom Britain was allied. Hence, initially, they could not show much enthusiasm for the parallel national movements in Poland or Finland. Nonetheless, their approach to the future of Central Europe was clear and consistent. It foresaw a zone of small democratic nation states, which would hold Germany and Russia apart and which would be natural clients of the Western powers. It coincided in large measure with French thinking which gave rise after 1918 to the concept of a *cordon sanitaire* against Bolshevism.[7]

In the inter-war period, when Germany was in political eclipse, the term *Mitteleuropa* became politically incorrect. It had connotations of German domination and was no more welcome to new or restored countries such as Czechoslovakia or Poland than it was to the victorious Western powers. In its place, therefore, arose a number of substitutes. One of these was *Zwischen Europa*, sometimes translated as 'The Lands Between'. It referred to a numerous group of states, which included neither Germany nor Russia. Another was 'East Central Europe'.

Although the new concept of East Central Europe overlapped to some extent with the Central Europe of Partsch and Naumann, the centre of gravity had moved far to the east and south. Prague, Vienna and Budapest were included, but Berlin and Breslau were not. Poland in the north and Yugoslavia in the south were the middle-sized keystones, while two clusters of much smaller states – one running from Finland to Georgia round the rim of the former Tsarist Empire, and the other in the Balkans – formed a flaky periphery.[8]

'The Lands Between' formed an appetising feeding ground for their predatory totalitarian neighbours. Soviet Russia began swallowing the independent republics that had formed beyond its borders during the Russian Civil War. Finland, the Baltic States and Poland resisted Soviet attacks at that stage. But a wide swathe of countries from Belorussia to Armenia was forcibly incorporated into the Soviet Union as created in 1923. A project proposed by the Polish leader, Marshal Piłsudski, for a defensive federation of border nations did not materialise. But a 'Little Entente' of democratic countries fearful of Hungary was formed under French sponsorship. The fragile peace did not last long. In August 1939, under the secret protocols of the Nazi-Soviet Pact, Hitler and Stalin divided 'The Lands Between' into spheres of influence, where each was free to act with impunity. In two years, the entire region was swallowed up. Hitler consumed eight countries: Stalin attacked just five. States that remained technically independent, like Hungary and Romania, were forced by pressure from Berlin to adopt a peculiar stance of pro-German quasi-neutrality. The limits of their sovereignty were severely constrained.

During the German-Soviet War, all thoughts of Central or East Central Europe were overtaken by the limitless ambitions of the two main contestants. For the Third Reich, all the territories to the east of Germany were designated as the *Lebensraum*, or 'living space', where German culture and settlement were to enjoy unrestricted access. For the Soviet Union, those same territories were designated for the inexorable expansion of Moscow-controlled Communist rule. The Muscovite concept prevailed. One of the few independent plans for the region's future, for a Central Europe Federation led by Poland and Czechoslovakia, was prepared by the two relevant governments-in-exile in wartime London. Thanks to the total triumph of the Soviets, it could not come to fruition. But much racking of brains was undertaken. One work, written in 1944 by a refugee from what she called 'The Middle Zone', concluded that the best solution for the people trapped between Germany and Russia was for them to join the British Empire as associate members.[9]

After 1945, the concept of Central Europe seemed to have disappeared for good. The onset of the Cold War divided Europe into two contending parts, East and West, on either side of the Iron Curtain. There was a Western Europe and an Eastern Europe. But apart from the three small and neutral states of Austria, Liechtenstein and Switzerland, there was no substantial Centre. Yet East Central Europe was a concept that *did* revive. It was well suited to the band of states that belonged to the Soviet Bloc but not to the Soviet Union; and to a large extent it replicated the membership of pre-war *Zwischen Europa*. As a result, many political commentators began to accept it as a permanent category, equally separated by its political and economic characteristics both from democratic Western Europe and from the USSR.

By the 1980s, therefore, memories of European unity were fading fast. In many quarters the status quo was beginning to be considered eternal. In the West, it was increasingly common for the term 'Europe' to be applied by members of the European Economic Community (or, later, the European Union) as an exclusive label for themselves, thereby implying that the rest of Europe was somehow not really European. In the East, the Communist authorities were using ideological terms such as the 'Socialist Camp' or the Soviet Bloc, which suggested that the European countries under Soviet rule had more in common with China or Cuba than with their West European neighbours.

Such was the highly depressing context in which a group of independent writers and intellectuals within the Soviet Bloc resuscitated Central Europe for purposes of their own. Led by the Czech novelist, Milan Kundera, they were a very diverse group expressing a variety of views and motivations. But they all feared for the traditional culture of their homelands; they all hated the artificial ideological identity that Communist rule had thrust upon them; and they all longed to re-establish close links with the cultural life of the West. In the writings of Kundera, of fellow Czech Václav Havel, the Hungarian Georgy Konrád, the Pole Adam Michnik, and others,[10] they created a spiritual zone that could not be found on the map, but which drew on all the previous variants of Central Europe to establish their views of the past, their rejection of the present and their hopes for the future. Nor, though the best-known works surfaced in the 1980s, were the ideas necessarily new. Some of them had been circulating in samizdat for decades, often in the form of half-serious jokes and anecdotes. 'Over Central Europe', declared one such Czech collection from the 1970s, 'there rises the heavy smell of boiled cabbage, stale beer, and the soapy whiff of overripe water melons . . . The frontiers are vague and irrational; and it is only the smell which permits one to identify [the region] with absolute certainty.'[11]

In the outside world, an intellectual cottage industry grew up, trying to define the new phenomenon's borders and its incoherent values. 'Central Europe is back,' wrote its principal analyst. 'For three decades after 1945 . . . the thing was one with Nineveh and Tyre . . . but in the last few years we have begun to talk of Central Europe again, and in the present tense.'[12] Yet, 'the thing' defied definition. None of its admirers could describe its geography, and none could agree about its content. There was a tangible mood of nostalgia; there was an attachment to a new form of dissident politics or 'anti-politics', which prized the role of culture, despised the state and preached non-violence; and there was a steadfast refusal to accept the world as it was. Beyond that, all discussions began and ended with the question: 'Does Central Europe exist?'[13]

Finally in 1989, when the Iron Curtain collapsed, Europe's dialectical divisions dissolved and Central Europe was free to re-emerge in the flesh once again. This time round, the criss-crossing network of links and dividing lines was anything but simple. The West, which for four decades had largely coincided with membership of NATO and the EU, put out tentacles far to the East. The EU, for example, took in Finland and established a long border directly with Russia. NATO took in Poland, the Czech Republic and Hungary, with a long list of aspirant states further afield. The East, which had long been dominated by the USSR, found that the USSR had evaporated. It was effectively reduced to the so-called CIS – that is, to the Russian Federation and the circle of struggling ex-Soviet republics, which Russia regarded as her 'near abroad'. The Centre, located as always between West and East, encompassed a company of nations from Poland to Bulgaria, which were free to choose their own identity. Though they retained many of the ideals and dreams of the 1980s, which had so discredited the Soviet monolith, they now possessed democratic systems, free-market economic programmes and optimistic prospects, which set them apart both from their former Soviet partners and from their war-torn neighbours in Yugoslavia. The former GDR, once the home of a hard-line Communist regime, entered the EU in 1990 in the context of a reunified Germany. Neutral Austria joined Sweden and Finland on the same trail in 1995. Poland, the Czech Republic, Hungary and Slovenia headed the queue of like-minded candidates. In the famous phrase of the Czech President, Václav Havel, they were all engaged in the 'return to Europe'. For Central Europeans were not only central to plans for the future. For the first time in two or three generations, they were free to take pride in their shared European heritage.

*

Notwithstanding the vagaries of changing boundaries and competing conceptions, Central Europe possesses a number of characteristics that are the natural product of conditions in a region of passage between East and West. Firstly, it has always been endowed with a rich variety of migrants and settlers. Throughout recorded history, and probably before, it has repeatedly been the scene of nomadic invasions, mixed settlements and military conquests. Among the nomads, one can count the Scythians, the Sarmatians, the Huns, the Magyars and the Mongols. Among the more permanent settlers, one notes numerous peoples with Celtic, Germanic, Slavonic and Semitic connections. Among the transient conquerors, one could list, among others, Gustavus Adolphus, Jan Sobieski, Charles XII, Peter the Great, Frederick the Great, Napoleon, Hitler and Stalin. As a result, the population of Central Europe has witnessed a profusion of languages, cultures, religions and nationalities. The ethnic kaleidoscope has been the norm since time immemorial. Yet in the age of nationalism, when every modern nation laid exclusive right to its own patch, it was most inconvenient. Central Europe inevitably became the home of perverse and competing nationalist histories, each claiming aborigineity.

Secondly, amidst the many ebbs and tides, two waves of settlement were particularly important. In the Middle Ages, after an era of westward migration, German settlers flooded eastwards across the Elbe and Oder, making huge inroads into lands, such as Poland and Bohemia, which for some time had been the domain of Slavs. This *Drang nach Osten*, or 'drive to the East', was in no sense unique. After all, the Poles pressed deep into Lithuania and Ukraine in the same period, while somewhat later the Russians '*drang*ed' their way right across Eurasia to the Pacific coast, to Alaska and even to California. For several centuries, the tide of human settlement was flowing eastwards. But then, in the nineteenth and twentieth centuries, it stopped and was reversed. The Slavic peoples reasserted themselves both separately and, under the influence of pan-Slavism, collectively. After the First World War, the Poles, the Czechoslovaks and the Yugoslavs all established sovereign states in the wake of the German and Austrian defeat. After the Second World War, the victorious Allied governments decided to expel all German people living to the east of the redrawn frontiers of Germany and Austria.

Thirdly, Central Europe became *the* great haven for European Jewry. In the centuries when Jews were deported from England, persecuted in Germany and excluded from Russia, they naturally congregated in 'The Lands Between'. One rather tenuous movement saw Jews of Chazar origin moving into Central Europe from the south and east. A much more substantial one, which reached its peak during persecutions resulting from the Black Death in the mid-fourteenth century, saw Ashkenazi Jews fleeing from the West to seek refuge in Bohemia, Hungary and especially Poland-Lithuania. These Yiddish-speaking Jews supported thriving communities not only in cities such as Vilnius, Cracow, Prague and Budapest, but in countless *shtetls* or 'little country towns', in which they emerged as the principal middle-class element and frequently as the dominant ethnic group. In more recent times, large numbers of them migrated further afield, first to Vienna, Berlin and Moscow, and later to France, Britain and the USA. In all the countries to which they moved they formed a highly assimilated commercial elite and intelligentsia. But traditional Jewish life continued back home in Central Europe until the terrible *Shoah* of 1941–5. In some eyes, the Jewishness of Central Europe was one of its defining features.

Fourthly, Central Europe's open geography combined with the ethnic kaleidoscope to form a political arena where national states were inevitably small and weak, while dynastic empires were large and strong. Already in the fifteenth century, the Jagiellonian realms, which included Bohemia and Hungary as well as Poland and Lithuania, served notice of things to come. After the fateful death of Louis II Jagiellon in 1526, the Jagiellons were replaced by the Habsburgs, who combined control of the Holy Roman Empire with their far-flung dynastic lands in the middle Danube basin. As champions of the Counter-Reformation, the Habsburgs created a special brand of Roman Catholic civilisation which in some quarters was taken to be the essence of Central Europe. Yet in the eighteenth and nineteenth centuries, their dominance was challenged by two new contenders. The Hohenzollerns of Brandenburg-Prussia, whose original eastern power-base lay outside the Holy Roman Empire, succeeded in becoming the leading force in Germany. The Romanovs of Moscow, whose career started as the self-styled Tsars of just one Russian principality, collected territory at a rate that has been calculated at 142 square kilometres per day for 150 years. By 1900 they ruled over an empire that stretched more than 8,000 kilometres, from the Bering Strait to the confines of Germany and Austria. (At Myslowitz (Mysłowice) in Silesia, there was a famous three-cornered frontier point known as the *Dreikaiserreichsecke*, or 'Three Empires Corner', where tourists could have one foot in the realm of the Hohenzollerns, the other in the realm of the Habsburgs and their fingers in the realm of the Romanovs.) The long-standing rivalry of these three dynasties came to a sudden end in 1917–18 when all three were overthrown.

Finally, Central Europe in the twentieth century had the unpleasant distinction of being subjected to a double dose of totalitarianism. Unlike Western Europe, which experienced only a brief interlude of Fascism, and unlike Russia, which experienced a much longer servitude under Communism, all 'The Lands Between' suffered in succession both from Fascism and from Communism. From Berlin to the Baltic States, from Vienna to the eastern Ukraine, from Zagreb and Tiranë to the Black Sea, a huge tract of Europe was overrun first by one or another brand of Fascist and then by one or another brand of Communist. All nationalities and all social groups were put through the grinder by one side or the other. Genocide, mass murder, 'ethnic cleansing', slave labour and social engineering were widely practised. Brave people, who dared to declare 'neither Hitler nor Stalin' were wiped out. The ordeal lasted on average for fifty years – in the case of eastern Germany, for fifty-seven years. The damage to life and liberty was incalculable. The period of recovery was bound to be long.

*

The story of Central Europe, therefore, is anything but simple. Indeed, it is extremely complex; and it is not easily explained to the general reading public. Specialist and partial studies abound, but surveys that successfully convey the flavour of the whole are, as the Poles say, 'white ravens' – rare birds.

One method, of course, is to study the history of individual cities, and through the local picture present a digest of the wider panorama. Most of the major cities of Central Europe – Vienna, Prague, Berlin, Cracow, Budapest, etc. – possess well-established histories of this sort. Yet the shortcomings are numerous. For one thing, local histories have tended to be written from a highly nationalistic point of view, which is artificially divorced from the essential multinational context. For another, the traditional genre of *Stadtgeschichte* habitually assumes a cosy, parochial focus that ignores all events and connections beyond the immediate compass of the city walls.

One also suspects that the great capitals are hardly representative of the whole. One could not study Vienna in isolation, for example, to examine the enormous range of Habsburg influence across many countries. In this sense, it might be more fruitful to look at the places that have usually found themselves on the receiving, rather than at the ruling, end.

For all these reasons, a historical portrait of a middle-ranking provincial centre has much to recommend it. Of course, the history of Silesia's main city can be seen as a fascinating tale in its own right, especially for the people who live there now or who have lived there in the past. But it is more than that. It contains a condensed compilation of all the experiences that have made Central Europe what it is – the rich mixture of nationalities and cultures; the German *Drang nach Osten* and the reflux of the Slavs; a Jewish presence of exceptional distinction; a turbulent succession of imperial rulers; and, in modern times, the shattering exposure to both Nazis and Stalinists. In short, it is a Central European microcosm.

*

The present volume has three objectives. Firstly, it aims to overcome the historiographical rivalry that has resulted in the two competing visions of 'German Breslau' and 'Polish Wrocław'. To this end, it gives prominence not only to Czech, Austrian and Jewish themes, but also to a colourful gallery of individuals from Mátyás Corvinus and Lennert Torstenson to Elizabeth Stuart, John Quincy Adams, Winston Churchill and Marshal Koniev, who belong to neither side of the German-Polish dichotomy. Secondly, it sets out to demonstrate how the political and cultural connections of the city have been transformed many times over. Thirdly, it takes great care to avoid the parochial approach, and hence to link the events and personalities of the city's history with their regional or continental setting.

One could reduce these three objectives to one overriding aim – to combat the various forms of selective amnesia that have so often marred historical descriptions. At one time, German historians regularly ignored the city's Polish connections or confined them to the remotest Piast dynasty period. Since 1945, they seem to have done the exact opposite, virtually airbrushing Breslau from all the major surveys of their own country's past. In recent years, at least, it is no exaggeration to call Breslau 'the lost city of German history'.

For their part, Polish historians have succumbed all too often to the demands of the post-war Communist regime to minimise or even to eliminate the German strand. After 1945, relentless official propaganda sought to reinforce the image of an aboriginal Polish city, which had constantly been brutally 'occupied', foully 'usurped' or cunningly 'infiltrated' by dastardly foreigners. In the conditions that have come into being through the fall of Communism, this false and xenophobic image is neither necessary nor desirable. Nowadays, at last, everyone is free to rejoice in everyone's achievements and to mourn the common catastrophes. And many Polish historians of the latest generation are doing exactly that.

As with most Central European cities, the problem of nomenclature is a thorny one. When a city has a different name for every nationality that lays claim to it, to prefer one version over another is to make a political statement and to risk causing offence. Nonetheless, a ready solution comes to hand when one realises that the choice does not lie between two stark alternatives – Breslau or Wrocław – but rather between the scores of variants which the historical sources contain. In reality, the historian has at least fifty names to choose from. So it is not too difficult to be impartial. The obvious thing to do is to use a different but appropriate name for each period of the city's history. In this way, we can emphasise one of the most fundamental historical lessons – that the past is not the same as the present. For the prehistoric period, for example, when no one knows what the city's name or names actually were, we call it the 'Island City'. For the early medieval Piast period, we call it 'Wrotizla'; for the Bohemian period, 'Vretslav'; for the Austrian period, 'Presslaw'; and for the Prussian period, 'Bresslau'. 'Breslau' is reserved for the imperial period and the Third Reich, and 'Wrocław' for post-1945 Poland. This is not to deny either that a still-greater variety of names and spellings exists or that modern forms were undoubtedly employed in particular circumstances in earlier times. Nor does it pretend that our chosen solution is above criticism. All it does is to underline the self-evident truth – that times change. Whenever we are in a quandary we use the name that was first introduced by literate Latin-speaking clergy more than a thousand years ago and which is still with us: VRATISLAVIA.

Götterdämmerung:
The Annihilation of Fortress Breslau, 1945

On the morning of 20 January 1945, a Breslau newspaper, the *Schlesische Tageszeitung* ('Silesian Daily News'), carried a calming report about military developments on the Eastern Front. Though the Second World War in Europe was reaching its climax, the Nazi Reich was feigning normality. The Soviet army had launched yet another offensive in the central sector, and the *Wehrmacht* was retreating to more defensible positions. The article promised that 'when [evacuation] becomes necessary for Breslau, the appropriate instructions will be given ... in good time'.[1] Indeed, outline evacuation plans had been formulated the previous September, but had not been given any measure of priority. The fanatical Nazi Gauleiter, Karl Hanke, had refused to accept what he viewed as defeatism. As far as ordinary Breslauers could tell, the Soviet army was still far away in the middle of Poland. There appeared to be no immediate danger.

Yet, by 10 a.m. that same January morning, the unexpected blow had struck. Loudspeakers throughout the city blared out the news:

> Achtung! Achtung! Citizens of Breslau! The Reich Defence Commissar and Gauleiter announces that Breslau is to be evacuated. There is no reason for alarm. Women and children will leave ... first. Small handluggage is to be taken with you. Women with small children are to provide themselves with paraffin stoves; the NSV [Nazi Welfare Organisation] will set up cooking points and facilities for the distribution of milk. Further information will be provided by your individual party offices. We repeat ...[2]

A later announcement was still more urgent:

> Women and children are to leave ... immediately! Go in the direction of Opperau and Kanth. Vehicles are waiting for you there. Women and children are to leave the city immediately![3]

The Nazi Party apparatus had panicked. Breslau at that juncture contained almost a million people, and an attempt was to be made to remove more than two-thirds of them in a matter of days.

The result, as described by the diarist Father Paul Peikert, was chaos:

> . . . a real panic has taken hold of the people. The railway stations are filled to overflowing all day, so that it is almost impossible to get through the crowds. Everyone is pressing themselves onto the trains, which can only accept limited numbers of the evacuees. The majority have to stay behind and try again. Most take their prams and necessary baggage and journey into the unknown along the Landstrasse.[4]

An estimated 60,000 women and children left Breslau for Kanth that day, in temperatures as low as −20°C. They joined the 600,000 Silesian refugees already choking the roads still open to the west and south. Breslau's parks began their slow transformation into makeshift graveyards. The morning of 21 January saw the bodies of forty children brought to the New Market, while the South Park took the graves of a further forty-eight.[5] By the next day, the bodies of 400 evacuees had been recovered by the municipal authorities. It is estimated that the death-march to Kanth claimed some 18,000 lives,[6] mainly of the infirm and the very young. In total some 90,000 Breslauers were to die during the entire evacuation.

Over the following days, the scenes were repeated again and again as successive groups were ordered to leave. On 21 January civil servants not eligible for the *Volkssturm* (territorial reservists) left; and four days later all remaining citizens unfit for military service. Elisabeth Erbrich was better prepared than most:

> The news was so sudden that there were terrible scenes. Many women . . . had crying fits. People ran around in the streets confused and disturbed. At the railway station refugees camped day and night with their meagre belongings, waiting for a chance to travel to the interior of the Reich. It was a heartbreaking sight that I will never forget.
>
> On Monday 22.1.45, at 10.00 in the morning, the order came to leave the city on foot as there were no other transport facilities. That day was to be the hardest of my life. With a heavy heart I bade farewell to my beloved hometown. My flight began with only the bare necessities in my rucksack, wearing as many clothes as I could put on, a pair of strong boots on my feet and a bag with a cooked chicken and food for the next few days . . . High in the sky, hardly visible, Russian fighters were dropping leaflets – 'Germans! Surrender! Nothing will happen to you!'
>
> It was icy, clear winter weather and −16°C. After a tearful farewell I set off in the direction of Zobten at 12.30. I joined a group of women with the

same destination in mind. The refugees marched like a caravan, dragging their last possessions in carts or prams, or even in cars or horse-drawn vehicles. A black line in the bright white snow, hundreds of thousands were on the move, amongst them refugees from the villages on the left bank of the Oder, who had already been travelling for days. Because of the cold and the relentless march they had many dead in their wagons that had to be abandoned by the roadside since burials were impossible in the frozen earth. Exhausted and with raw feet I arrived at Roßlingen [twenty-two kilometres from Breslau] at 16.00.[7]

One more privileged evacuee was Ilse Braun, the sister of Hitler's mistress Eva, who had lived in Breslau for a number of years. On the evening of 20 January, she found a place on a train bound for the capital. At Berlin's Schlesischer Bahnhof, the following morning, she was collected in an SS limousine and driven to her sister's apartment at the glamorous Adlon Hotel, close to the Brandenburg Gate. That evening, over dinner in the Reich Chancellery, the two discussed recent events. It soon became clear that Eva had little idea of the disaster engulfing the German 'east'. She talked cheerily of the time when Ilse could return 'home' to Breslau. Ilse's perception of events was radically different. She spoke with passion about what she had seen: the refugees, the snow, and the terror of Russian occupation. When she said that Hitler was dragging the Reich into the abyss, the conversation grew heated. Eva expressed her fury at her sister's ingratitude and said that she deserved to be shot.[8]

The ordeal of ordinary civilians was repeated among the staff of Breslau's administrative and governmental offices. On 21 January, Breslau's bishop, Adolf Bertram, departed for the safety of Jauernig in Bohemia. The sacred contents of most of the churches were removed to Kamenz in Saxony. The following day the post, telegraph and rail authorities were shifted westwards. On the 23rd, all the local concentration camps (KZ) were evacuated to Groß Rosen near Schweidnitz. The sick and injured of KZ Fünfteichen were left behind to await their fate; those of Dyhernfurth were shot.[9] Breslau's military hospitals were moved, along with sensitive SS and SD (security service) archives. The Breslau tax office was relocated to Liegnitz. The municipal administration was sent to Waldenburg. The University and Technical Highschool were transferred to Dresden. So, too, was Radio Breslau, arriving on the evening of the first RAF attack.[10]

The decks were being cleared for the final struggle. As advance Soviet units reached the Oder at Steinau, north-west of Breslau, on 22 January, all remaining men in the Silesian capital were called to arms. Gauleiter Hanke wrote, 'I call on the men of Breslau to join the defence front of our Fortress Breslau. The Fortress will be defended to the end.'[11]

*

German strategy in these last desperate months of the war is often described in Wagnerian terms: the *Götterdämmerung* – the Twilight of the Gods. As the fighting crept inexorably closer to the heart of the Reich, Germany descended into an orgy of self-immolation. The death-throes of Nazism were dragging the country and its remaining allies into the abyss. Though Hitler and the Nazi hierarchy undoubtedly entertained many wild thoughts, German military and political thinking in the final months of the war was not totally irrational. Hitler may have been increasingly detached from reality, but his critical faculties had not completely deserted him. He recognised the deep divisions among the Allies ranged against him; and his policy of creating *Festungen*, or 'fortresses', sought to exploit them. His *Fester Platz* order of 8 March 1944 outlined their purpose:

> . . . The 'Fortified Areas' will fulfil the functions of fortresses in former historical times. They will ensure that the enemy does not occupy these areas of decisive operational importance. They will allow themselves to be surrounded, thereby holding down the largest possible number of enemy forces, and establishing conditions for successful counter-attacks. Local strongpoints, deep in the battle area, will be tenaciously defended in the event of enemy penetration. By being included in the main line of battle they will act as a reserve of defence and, should the enemy break through, as hinges and corner stones for the front, forming positions from which counter-attacks can be launched.[12]

Though none of the three initial 'fortresses', at Mogilev, Bobruisk and Vitebsk,[13] had succeeded in stemming the Soviet tide, the policy was to find its high point later that year. One after another, the cities and towns of eastern Germany – Breslau, Danzig, Frankfurt an der Oder, Kolberg, Königsberg, Küstrin, Glogau, Graudenz, Oppeln, Posen, Ratibor and Thorn – were designated *Festungen*. Ideally, they would provide the platform for a future German counter-attack. At worst, they would be sacrificed in order to buy Berlin time, thereby encouraging the growing antipathy between Germany's enemies, which might conceivably cripple the Alliance. For Hitler, every day's delay was vital.

With the luxury of hindsight, the *Festung* policy appears a desperate blunder. But it should not be forgotten that Germany's predicament at the turn of 1945 was not yet terminal. Indeed, there were reasons for cautious optimism. While the Western Allies were still recovering from the shock of the Ardennes offensive and had still not crossed the Rhine, the Soviets had been stationary on their Vistula bridgeheads for some months and were still held up at Budapest. Though hugely outnumbered, German forces were now fighting in the east with shortened lines of communication against an enemy that was in danger of overreaching itself. Seen in this light, the *Festung* policy does not appear quite so unrealistic. The ultimate Soviet success was not a foregone conclusion.

*

The Soviet Vistula–Oder offensive had been launched at 5 a.m. on Friday 12 January. A one-and-three-quarter-hour rolling artillery barrage destroyed everything in its path. Around midday, tanks began to move off from the Vistula bridgeheads. Soviet forces there were divided into four 'fronts': the 3rd Belorussian Front, under Chernyakovskii, headed for the Baltic coast; the 2nd Belorussian Front, under Rokossowski, moved in parallel; the 1st Belorussian Front, under Zhukov, held the centre; and the 1st Ukrainian Front, under Koniev, left the Sandomierz bridgehead in the south. It was Koniev who had Silesia in his sights.

Soviet numerical superiority on the Vistula was estimated by the German High Command at fivefold in manpower, fivefold in armour, sevenfold in artillery and seventeenfold in air power.[14] Koniev and Zhukov could field eight infantry armies, two tank armies and an air army, containing just under 2,250,000 men. Facing them was Harpe's Army Group A, consisting of the 9th and the 17th Armies, plus the 4th *Panzer* – in all just 400,000 men.

Though bad weather prevented the exploitation of Soviet air power, freezing conditions on the ground, with little snow, were ideal for the rapid advance of tanks. By the first evening Koniev had already penetrated the German defensive line to a depth of nineteen kilometres along a forty-kilometre front. Kielce fell on the 15th and Częstochowa three days later. From then on, it became clear that Koniev's target in Silesia was to be Breslau:

> . . . intelligence assessments confirmed that any Soviet thrust due west would be met by heavy German defence on well-defended lines. To guarantee speedy success with the breakthrough operation and the subsequent westerly drive, Zhukov proposed that his armies strike first for Łódż and then shift their attack towards Poznań. Stalin agreed . . . and the revised attack assignments for 1st Belorussian Front were duly affixed to the master plan. Once this decision was accepted, the need to adjust Koniev's attack to the north disappeared and Breslau rather than Kalisz became the prime target for the 1st Ukrainian Front.[15]

The Soviets effectively completed their Vistula–Oder operation by the end of January. Their troops had penetrated deep inside the borders of the old

Reich. Königsberg, Posen and Thorn were surrounded; Upper Silesia had been overrun. In Lower Silesia, two bridgeheads across the Oder had been secured at Steinau and Brieg; Militsch, just fifty kilometres to the north-east, was occupied as early as the 23rd; and Breslau itself was coming under artillery fire from Soviet emplacements on the Trebnitz hills.

However, the Soviet advance had slowed considerably. Having covered the 300 kilometres from the Sandomierz bridgehead in eight days, the Soviets took a further eight days to apply pressure on the Silesian capital. The reasons are clear: Soviet planning for the next stage of the advance had not yet been completed. Some hesitation following the swift establishment of the Oder bridgeheads was to be expected. And the speed of the advance was endangering the lines of supply. The forward units that had crossed the Silesian border at Namslau, for example, were running short of ammunition and fuel.[16] Moreover, the 'highway of ice' that had facilitated the offensive was starting to melt. The resistance of the German defenders stiffened as they fought for their own towns and villages. In Berlin, and perhaps in Breslau, it may well have appeared possible that the *Festung* policy might yet bring results.

*

The first *Festungskommandant*, General Johannes Krause, had arrived in Breslau in late September 1944, but comparatively little was done to prepare for a siege. The forces directly available amounted to just one division. And the disparate groupings – *Wehrmacht*, *Luftwaffe*, *Waffen SS* and *Volkssturm* – were due to pass under combined command only in an emergency. As if to complicate matters further, Gauleiter Hanke, who assumed the title *Reichsverteidigungskommissar* (Commissar for the Defence of the Reich), persistently interfered with Krause's preparations. Only when Soviet units crossed into Lower Silesia near Namslau on 20 January was the imminent threat appreciated.

Breslau was to be defended in the first instance by an outer perimeter, mainly of earthworks, encompassing Trebnitz, Oels, Ohlau and Kanth. This formed part of a wider defensive network which, under the codename 'Operation Bartold', had been constructed by forced labour during the previous months. In late January barricades were erected using, among other things, gravestones and trams. Flak and artillery batteries were established in the Botanical Garden, in the New Market and in the garden of the Archbishop's palace. Machine-gun nests were set up in church steeples.[17] The Oder bridges were wired with explosives.

The regular forces inside the city totalled some 30,000 men organised into eight regiments.[18] Three infantry regiments (Hanf, Sauer and Mohr) were mainly composed of reservists and cadets from the military academy at Frankenstein. The Besslein regiment was made up of *Waffen SS* reservists from nearby Deutsch Lissa, and the Wehl regiment consisted of *Luftwaffe* ground troops. The 609th Division comprised a further three regiments of infantry under the designations Kersten, Reinkober and Schulz. But this was no more than a scratch formation, having been raised in Dresden just a few weeks earlier. Only two of its staff officers had experience of service at divisional level.[19] In addition, the *Festung* possessed some 200 Italian soldiers, pressed into German service, various Hitler Youth and *Volkssturm* elements and a regiment of pioneers. Most significantly, however, it received two battalions of paratroopers, or *Fallschirmjäger*. Those troops, the 2nd and 3rd Battalions of the 25th Paratroop Regiment, almost 4,000 men in all, were airlifted into the city in late February. They would be the last group of the famed *Fallschirmjäger* to see combat in the Second World War. Altogether the *Festung* possessed some 45,000 soldiers of varying usefulness.

Frontline support was provided by an artillery regiment with some thirty-two assorted artillery pieces, a *Panzerjägerabteilung* (tank-destroyer battalion) with nineteen self-propelled guns of various types, and a trainload of 'Goliath' remote-controlled midget tanks. Military and civilian supplies had been stockpiled for some months and, in theory at least, should not have posed a problem. Whether the *Festung* command could deliver them when needed was, of course, another question.

On paper, at least, Breslau was a formidable fortress. Yet the quality of the garrison was very uneven. Hardened SS veterans were mixed with raw recruits. A lack of basic training was commonplace, even among regular units. Hugo Hartung, conscripted in September 1944 at the age of forty-two, noted the shortcomings:

> Orders are countermanded. Training in anti-tank measures, which we have not yet had, is timetabled and then cancelled again. Instead we have to pack and make ready to move out immediately. But even this order is amended. We receive live ammunition and have to occupy the northern perimeter of the airport. General Confusion is in command.[20]

The *Volkssturm* was the subject of caustic Soviet propaganda. A leaflet dropped on Silesia in December 1944 ridiculed Himmler's last 'wonder weapon' in biting verse:

> . . . Come on then, all that creeps and crawls,
> In the schoolyard and Kindergarten!
> With dripping pants and dripping noses!
> The Volkssturm calls and cannot wait.[21]

German accounts were scarcely better. Otto Rothkugel kept a diary in the *Volkssturm Kampfbatallion 46*:

> When I registered with my Company, I saw what a motley mob it was. I received an old Italian rifle and ten bullets, but I didn't know what to do with them. Everything looked so disorganised. And the Russians were on the other side of the Oder . . . Anyway I was now a Volkssturm man with the Peschke Batallion No. 46. In the state we were in, the Russians would simply walk all over us. I was pleased, since it meant that we might get out of there alive.[22]

The overall strength of the German forces is hard to assess. Breslau was far from defenceless, but its military capability would be hindered by the large numbers of civilians still in the city. The day before the Soviet ring was closed, German estimates put the number of remaining civilians at some 80,000. This was, to say the least, a conservative estimate, and other commentators have put the figure closer to 200,000.[23] In the circumstances, it is surprising to note that a British military historian could conclude that Breslau had transformed itself in a short space of time into 'a fortress of astonishing resilience and extraordinary tenacity'.[24]

*

By early February 1945 the Soviets' Vistula–Oder operation was complete. The *Wehrmacht*'s Army Group Centre had collapsed and Berlin stood tantalisingly within reach, yet the Soviet advance had slowed. Some Soviet commanders wanted to drive on and bring a swift end to the war. But Stalin reluctantly urged caution. The broad salient of the Soviet frontline was to be straightened by the systematic reduction of the islands of continued resistance – at Königsberg, Küstrin, Posen and Breslau. The prize of taking Berlin was to be contested between the 1st Belorussian Front under Marshal Zhukov and the 1st Ukrainian under Marshal Koniev. There had long been keen rivalry between the two commanders. Overshadowed by Zhukov for much of his career, Koniev passionately wanted to take Berlin first. Yet any advance on Berlin was dependent on the left flank holding Silesia and neutralising the threat of a German counter-attack.

Koniev's plan was a complex one. He had originally hoped to entice the defenders out of the urban areas and eliminate them in open battle, a policy that had brought some success in Upper Silesia. But the formation of *Festungen* such as Breslau forced him to rethink. After consolidating the Oder bridgeheads at the end of January, he now planned to push on to the west, while encircling centres of enemy resistance wherever necessary. His strategy, and the central importance of Breslau was made plain in his memoirs:

> It was perfectly clear to me that our three armies, forming an arc of almost 200km, would be riveted to the spot until we had completely encircled Breslau. On the other hand, if we did encircle the city it would at once enable the 5th Guards and the 21st Army to reach the level of the Front's right flank. If we managed not only a swift encirclement, but also the capture of Breslau, all of the 6th Army could be placed in the Front's reserve and be made available for subsequent use depending on the situation.[25]

Hence, when German resistance at the Steinau bridgehead was abandoned on 7 February, the Soviet offensive resumed immediately. Once again rapid gains were made. Ohlau and Brieg fell, to be followed by Kanth and Neumarkt on the 9th and Liegnitz and Haynau on the 11th. Breslau, meanwhile, was invested by two Soviet armies in a pincer movement starting from the north-west and south-east. Soviet T-34 tanks were first spotted from the Schöngarten airport on 9 February. This meant that the last railway line, which had linked Breslau westwards to the outside world, was now cut. As the danger grew, the German 8th and 19th *Panzer* and the 254th Infantry Divisions were thrown into the fray.[26] But the desperate defence did not suffice. The Soviet pincer was biting through the ever more slender threads of communication which kept the garrison of the *Festung* in contact with Army Group *Mitte* in Bohemia. On 13 February, the two arms of the pincer met at Domslau. At that point the main German units not assigned to the *Festung* were ordered to withdraw. On 15 February, Soviet troops captured the Sudeten mountain passes, thereby blocking the route of any prospective relief column. Breslau was cut off.

The siege of Breslau sealed the fate of Dresden, which until then had been largely unaffected by the fighting. Dresden had served as the primary base for reinforcing the Silesian front. As a result, it stood high on the list of bombing requests that Moscow made to the Western Allies. On the eve of the Yalta Conference, an air raid there was perceived as a necessary demonstration of inter-Allied cooperation. Hence, on 25 January, Winston Churchill pressed his Secretary of State for Air on the plans that RAF Bomber Command might have for 'basting the Germans in their retreat from Breslau'.[27] The outcome was to be Operation Thunderclap – the saturation bombing of Dresden – which was to inflict the most intense firestorm of the war and a toll of casualties of the same order as the A-bomb at Hiroshima. It happened on 13 and 14 February, just as the escape route from Breslau was sealed. Dresden's streets were clogged with Silesian refugees. Churchill's grizzly metaphor was to prove all too appropriate.

Koniev left three armies besieging Breslau: Gluzdovsky's 6th, Zhadov's 21st and the 5th Guards. He made doubly sure by sending the 3rd Guards Tank Army, under Rybalko, to stiffen the ring. With his left flank thus secured, he was now free to release his centre and right flank and drive them forward into Saxony and the approaches to Berlin. In Breslau, the German military command changed hands. General Krause's ill health and his failure to prevent the encirclement cost him his post. He was replaced by Major-General Hans von Ahlfen.

At first sight, the situation on the Western Front may have seemed to resemble that in the East. The outlying districts of the Rhineland around Aachen were already in Allied hands. British and American forces were pouring into Germany. Yet, in many respects, the contrast between West and East was stark. While the Soviets had crossed the last of the natural obstacles before Berlin on the Oder, the Western Allies were still a month away from crossing the first of the great German rivers at the Rhine. What is more, they were not facing the same level of desperate resistance. Although the overall balance of forces in the West was fairly even – seventy-eight Allied divisions were deployed against seventy-nine German ones[28] – the raw statistics were deceptive. All three German Army Groups in the West had been pared to the bone to supply reserves in the crucial battle for Berlin. All were seriously under strength.[29] And none was disposed to fight to the last man. German soldiers in the West knew that they would be reasonably treated if they surrendered. In the East, they had no such assurances. They were facing an implacable enemy, which showed no concern even for the welfare of its own men and rarely bothered to take prisoners. The nature of the war in the East was infinitely more savage than anything the Western Allies could imagine.

Once the ring around Breslau was closed, the frontline ran in an oval aligned from north-west to south-east. From the line of the River Weistritz, where the Besslein regiment faced the 181st and 294th Soviet Guards, it ran through Lohbrück, Opperau and Klettendorf, where the Hanf and Wehl regiments faced the 359th and 309th Guards. To the south-east, Herzogs-hufen and Brockau were held by the Kersten, Reinkober and Schulz regiments against the 218th and 273rd Guards. To the north, the front ran approximately along the line of the River Weide from Weidenhof to Burgweide. It was held by the Sauer and Mohr regiments against the Soviet 294th Guards.

Inside the fortress, the opening fortnight of the siege gave a grim foretaste of what was to come. The Deputy Mayor, Dr Wolfgang Spielhagen, having

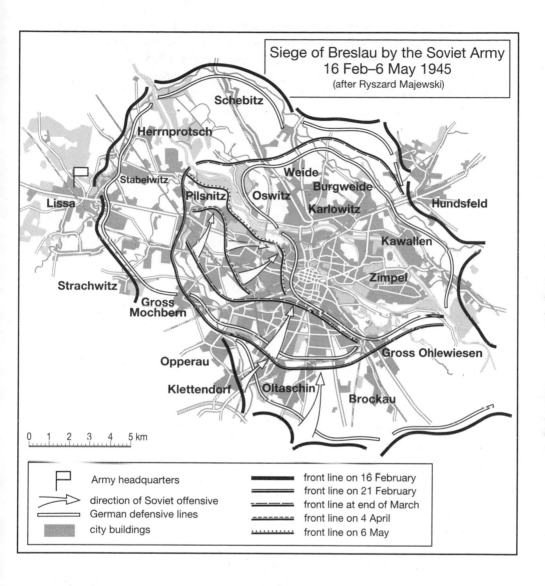

**Siege of Breslau by the Soviet Army
16 Feb–6 May 1945**
(after Ryszard Majewski)

Army headquarters

direction of Soviet offensive

German defensive lines

city buildings

front line on 16 February
front line on 21 February
front line at end of March
front line on 4 April
front line on 6 May

returned on 26 January from taking his family to the comparative safety of Berlin, was publicly executed on the Market Square by firing squad. It was known that he had been a persistent critic of Hanke and the *Festung* policy, and it seems that he had sought a transfer. The Gauleiter was settling a personal score, but he was also removing his only potential rival. Four more executions of officials followed. By early February the first shootings of civilians were being reported. On 2 February, five men were shot for alleged theft and looting. Four of them – Kowalenko, Korban, Bratulin and

Schagraf – were described as 'foreigners'.[30] They were almost certainly forced labourers.

The following day, the last German Mass to be held in the Sandkirche preceded a night of almost incessant Soviet shelling. The psychological and physical toll was enormous. Burials in the Gräbschen cemetery during the first three days of February numbered twenty-five, sixty-eight and fifty-seven;[31] sixty suicides were registered in ten days.[32] Horrific tales of the fate of German civilians in East Prussia did little to calm nerves, though some erroneously considered such stories to be Nazi propaganda.

The first Soviet attack, which was launched from the south, caused panic. It dramatically disproved the popularly held belief that the Soviets would concentrate on surrounding Berlin. But it also upset military calculations, which had assumed that the northern district of Hundsfeld would bear the brunt of any Soviet operation. The *Festung* command had ordered the resettlement of civilians from the north-eastern suburbs to the southern suburbs. The appearance of Soviet tanks in the South Park meant that these refugees were obliged to undergo emergency resettlement for a second time. It was effected by the SS, in their own inimitable style.

Initially the Soviet attackers made rapid advances. They had the space to make their numbers tell and the frontline to the south shrank swiftly. By the 24th, the Hindenburgplatz just four kilometres from the city centre was already the scene of bitter house-to-house fighting.

The fall of Breslau's outer villages and suburbs brought home to its inhabitants the realities of Soviet occupation. After four years of warfare, the Soviet soldiery had been thoroughly brutalised. Spurred on by propaganda and by the complicity of their superiors, they committed numberless atrocities. Aleksandr Solzhenitsyn, then an officer in East Prussia, recalled their attitude:

> All of us knew very well that if the girls were German they could be raped and then shot. This was almost a combat distinction. Had they been Polish girls or our own displaced Russian girls, they could have been chased round the garden and slapped on the behind.[33]

Some witnesses would contest the finer distinctions. Apparently even fellow Soviets were not spared. The treatment of Soviet citizens 'liberated' in the Reich in 1945 is a subject which could not be discussed in the post-war Soviet Bloc. But it certainly interested the NKVD officers who controlled the rear areas. One lengthy report written in February by one Tsiganov, the deputy chief of the Political Department of the 1st Ukranian Front during the siege of Breslau, was sent to the Central Committee of the Komsomol in Moscow. It lists the nightly gang-rapes and shootings perpetrated against former slave-labourers in the district of Bunzlau. 'I waited for days and nights for my liberation,' a young Soviet woman called Maria Shapoval complained, 'and now our [own] soldiers treat us worse than the Germans did. I am not happy to be alive.' In one incident on 14/15 February, for instance, a Soviet *shtraf* company, or 'penal unit', under the command of a senior lieutenant, surrounded a village, where confiscated cattle were being herded, shot the Soviet Army guards, broke into a women's dormitory and started an organised mass-rape.[34] In theory, liberated Soviet citizens were supposed to be sent to screening camps where their loyalties could be tested. One such camp certainly operated in Cracow. Yet, in practice, many of the would-be candidates for screening never made it. On 7 March, for example, the Swedish military attaché heard that 250 liberated Soviet workers were summoned by the NKVD to a political meeting in Oppeln, then simply gunned down by their compatriots.[35] The prevailing proposition, which had been fomented by the NKVD earlier in the war to counter the wave of desertions, held that any Soviet citizen who was sent to Germany either as a slave labourer or as a POW and who had failed either to commit suicide or to join the partisans, was *ipso facto* a 'Traitor of the Motherland'. According to Solzhenitsyn, this betrayal 'was the foulest deed in Russian history'.[36]

In such circumstances, German civilians could expect little mercy. A report from Opperau, to the south-west of Breslau, confirmed the harsh realities:

Suddenly in the hall of the house, we heard loud screaming. A Russian appeared with a girl whom he was brutally beating. He took the weeping child into a neighbouring room. Again and again, we heard screaming and pleading . . . but the pleading was to no avail. The whimpering grew quieter, then everything went silent. Soon after the Russian left the room. Some brave women then went next door to have a look. It was a horrific scene. A thirteen-year-old girl lay bleeding on the floor – completely naked – and dead.[37]

The other staple of the Soviet soldiery was looting. The above report from Opperau noted that no one was immune:

Countless German soldiers lay side by side. And we had to observe, over and over, how even the Russian dead were not spared. Their uniforms were torn open, watches and wallets were taken and rings were torn from their fingers. We stood paralysed with fear. How terrible this war was! In the last few hours we had all experienced such terrible things that we had forgotten how to weep.[38]

That same day, news of the fall of *Festung* Posen reached *Festung* Breslau.

Nonetheless, the Soviet attack ground to a halt. The line of the railway embankment, encircling the city to the south-west, was a formidable barrier. By 12 March, the frontline had moved only a few hundred metres to an area near the Höfchenplatz. Once in the suburbs, the Germans changed their tactics. Reserve units were established to back up each frontline battalion, while other units sought to create *tote Räume*, or dead space, forming a free field of fire for the defenders. Sentimentality played no part: churches and historical buildings were sacrificed. The conduct of the *Entrümpelungs-kommandos*, or 'clearance squads', of the Pioneer regiment, who cleared each block prior to its demolition, was viewed by the civilian population as being on a par with the work of the Soviets:

> Without informing the evacuees . . . the apartments are entered [and] all furniture, crockery, pictures, and household equipment thrown onto the street below. Everything is thrown onto the street. Even religious items and family mementoes, so dear to their owners . . . On the road everything is covered in fuel and burnt . . . How often do people tell me, sobbing and weeping, that they have lost everything . . .[39]

Thereafter, the fighting progressed literally from room to room, floor to floor and block to block. Soviet superiority in numbers was minimised. Soviet tactics switched either to burning each contested block, so as to flush out the defenders, or to storming the ground floor before fighting their way upwards. A member of the SS Besslein regiment wrote a letter to his son to explain:

> We brought our artillery into position behind a wall 30m from the Russians . . . and fired nine shots into their position, which was on the first floor of three houses. We couldn't get into the cellars to blow them up as they were already on fire. As the raiding party advanced, I had to go with them. Ivan had retreated from two of the houses because of the artillery fire, but he was still firing from the third. We threw our hand grenades through the window frames, but he persisted. Through this we suffered some injured. I got a scratch on the right hand and a piece of shrapnel hit the hand grenade in my pocket. But such things only make one fiercer. When even our Panzerfaust failed to flush them out, there were 6 more shots from our artillery and my men and I stormed the first floor with hand grenades and revolvers. The 7 Ivans that we didn't get fled across the road. But two were floored by our flanking machine gun. The position was cleared.[40]

The effectiveness of German tactics is confirmed by the fact that the defenders scored some notable successes. In March, they drove Soviet forces from the towns of Striegau and Lauban to the west of Breslau. Goebbels was delighted and distributed Iron Crosses liberally. German counter-attacks using elite troops (*Waffen SS* and paratroopers) succeeded in holding the Gandau airfield, where the contribution of the garrison's armoured remnant was vital:

> I crawled as far as a felled tree . . . [and] peered cautiously through the branches. At 150 or so metres we spied a massive armoured vehicle standing in an avenue . . . We got back into our own machine as fast as we could and drove on until the avenue lay before us . . . I ordered the driver to incline to the left. The gun was already loaded, and it was only a matter of seconds to lay it on the target . . . I duly ordered: 'Fire!' By now the Russians had noticed us, and they began to depress their barrel, which had been pointing up into the trees. It was too late. The crack of our gun was almost painful, but it was reassuring as always, and I saw the red flash of a strike immediately to the left of the barrel. We had hit with our first round . . . the Russian vehicle was already blazing to high heaven.[41]

The Soviet advance in the southern suburbs was also checked. A telling example of stubborn resistance occurred in the block bounded by Höfchenplatz/Gabitzstrasse/Opitzstrasse/Hohenzollernstrasse. Though relatively small, this single block was contested for some eight days before finally falling on 13 March. In bitterness and brutality, if not in scale, the struggle for Breslau bore many comparisons with Stalingrad.

The international conventions of warfare were routinely ignored on the Eastern Front by both sides. But, in their terminal desperation, the Germans appear to have pushed the limits to the utmost. In early March, for example, they were reported to have fired torpedoes mounted on trolleys into the Soviet lines. They also made maximum use of the remote-controlled crewless miniature tank, known as Goliath, which had been available throughout the war, but had not been frequently deployed, except against the Warsaw Rising. On 29 March, a counter-attack by German paratroopers at Breslau-Schmiedefeld was accompanied by a form of chemical warfare. Containers, affectionately known to the German troops as *Pissbeutel*, or 'piss bags', were filled with a yellow-green liquid (probably the nerve gas 'Tabun') and hurled into an enemy-held cellar. The after-effects of this 'tear-gas that destroys the lungs'[42] were such that the position could not be entered without gas masks for days afterwards.

Grim humour was not entirely absent. A Dutch *Gruppenführer* in the SS Besslein Regiment noted that German and Soviet troops had taken a drink together on one section of the frontline before continuing the battle. And the author Hugo Hartung recounted the tale of a German contingent playing records on an abandoned gramophone during a lull in the battle, only to hear Red Army soldiers on the floor below applauding and making requests.[43] In spite of the fighting, life went on. One SS soldier sent to a Red Cross station wrote:

> We made our way under incessant enemy artillery fire and over mountains of smoking rubble. In the rear, my three colleagues and I found a sort of pub that was still partly in business. There we were served by a girl and drank a thin beer. It was strange – here were a few people peacefully having a drink, and a few streets further we had to cross the road at the double, under fire from Russian artillery. Dead soldiers and civilians lay in the bomb craters, yet here people were laughing and drinking.[44]

Life for the non-combatants also continued. A report[45] from Kletschkau Prison told of a new type of inmate; the *Bunkerliebchen*, or 'bunker sweetheart', usually charged with prostitution, who wore flowers in her hair and cavorted with the soldiers at the front, sharing schnapps, rations and brief encounters. Even the more restrained inhabitants were infected by the feeling of *carpe diem*. On 15 March, a religious service was held in one of the camps for foreign forced labourers, and in a former school building on Clausewitzstrasse, twelve weddings and two christenings were performed.[46] The following day a giraffe was born in the zoo during a Soviet artillery attack.

The Ausländer-Auffanglager on Clausewitzstrasse contained some 3,000 foreign prisoners – Czechs, French, Ukrainians, Serbs, Bulgarians and, above all, Poles. Like the fifteen other camps that kept operating during the siege, it was formally a sub-branch of the KZ Groß Rosen, with which it had lost contact. These prisoners formed roughly one-quarter of the non-military population left in the city, although the distinction with other civilians was much reduced after mid-March, when all able-bodied persons were made liable to conscription into militarised work brigades. Discipline was ferocious. Since the *Festung* was a frontline area, *Drückebergerei*, or 'shirking', was a capital offence and all cases were judged by summary courts martial. The Gestapo still had time to interrogate people who were caught in possession of an unauthorised piece of sausage. Daily lists of the executed appeared in the only newspaper available, the *Frontzeitung der Festung Breslau*.

Given that Breslau was physically cut off, the problem of transport and supplies was vital. The task of supplying the estimated 200,000 soldiers and civilians of the *Festung* fell to the *Luftflotte 6* of the *Luftwaffe*. In the seventy-six days of the airlift, from 15 February to 1 May, almost 2,000 flights were carried out by Junker 52s, Heinkel 111s and Messerschmitt 109s, principally via the Gandau airstrip. They flew in some 1,670 tonnes of supplies, predominantly ammunition, and evacuated some 6,600 wounded. On one representative day, 22 March, forty Ju 52s, twenty-four He 111s and six Me 109s departed from bases in Bohemia and Bavaria. Of these, sixteen Ju 52s and one He 111 were lost. But the *Festung* received 54.3 tonnes of supplies.[47] The material and psychological impact of the airlift was immeasurable. One diarist noted with pride: 'Germany has not forgotten its besieged Breslau'.[48]

The aerial defence of the *Festung* was consigned to the 2nd Night Fighter Squadron (II/NJG). A long-established unit flying mainly Messerschmitt 109s and 110s, the II/NJG had seen service in the Low Countries and France, and had counted the fighter ace Heinz-Wolfgang Schnaufer among its pilots. Its presence over Breslau was to be short-lived. It was transferred to Görlitz on 23 February, owing to the demands of protecting the approaches to Berlin. That day, British Intelligence learned via Enigma intercepts that night-fighter operations over Breslau had been officially cancelled.[49]

When Breslau's main airfield at Gandau began to look threatened, a new runway was needed. General von Ahlfen was already pessimistic about Breslau's chances. He was reluctant to commit more elite forces to the defence of Gandau and unwilling to countenance Hanke's plan to blast a runway through the city centre. His lack of enthusiasm caused Hanke to replace him on 5 March with General Hermann Niehoff, who was left in no doubt about his responsibilities. He was warned by his superior, the fanatical C-in-C of Army Group A, Ferdinand Schörner, that he and his family would answer personally for the continued defence of Breslau. 'If you fail,' he was told, 'you will answer for it with your head.'[50]

Later that month, Niehoff received orders from Berlin for the construction of a runway along the Kaiserstrasse from the Scheitniger Stern to the Kaiserbrücke. The street, which was lined with numerous administrative and university buildings and by the Canisius and Luther Churches, was to be razed with explosives and cleared by gangs of labourers, including children as young as ten. Once work started, the Soviets responded by strafing the workers. Soviet aircraft – the Ilyushin 2 (known to the Germans as the 'Black Death') and the Polikarpov 2 (known as the 'sewing machine' because of its peculiar engine note) – are estimated to have caused some 3,000 casualties. One worker on the airstrip summed up the situation: 'We sleep like rabbits. With open eyes. And wait for death.'[51]

Late in March, the Soviet besiegers were joined by 90,000 men of the Second Polish Army of General Karol Świerczewski, which was deployed to the north of Breslau in the vicinity of Trebnitz–Oels. Unlike Berling's First Polish Army, which had been formed by the Soviets in 1943 from Poles in Russia, the Second Polish Army had been raised in 1944 in Poland under the auspices of the Lublin Committee. It could be fairly described as the main military arm of the political circles that were in the process of seizing control in Poland. Naturally, it could only have operated with Soviet approval and under higher Soviet command, but its political activities were one step removed from direct Soviet supervision. And its appearance before Breslau had very obvious, though unspoken, political connotations. Świer-czewski himself (pseudonym 'Walter') was a highly political soldier, who had fought both in the Russian Civil War and in the International Brigades in Spain. (He was destined to be killed in the dirty post-war campaign against the Ukrainian underground.) His orders in March 1945 clearly indicated that he and his men were intended to participate in the liberation of Breslau, yet the orders were changed at the last minute and the Second Polish Army was redeployed to the Western Neisse.[52]

The circumstances that underlay this change of plan have never been clarified. Of course, it is perfectly possible that Marshal Koniev decided for purely military reasons that it was more important to throw every possible man into the battle for Berlin than to accelerate the fall of Breslau. On the other hand, it would be a very strange coincidence if the decision had not been connected in some way to an important political development that occurred at the same time. On 14 March 1945, the Council of Ministers of the so-called Provisional Government in Warsaw had passed a resolution authorising the establishment of administrative cadres for Lower Silesia.[53] In other words, with or without the consent of Moscow, the new Polish regime was preparing to take over Breslau as soon as it had fallen. Indeed, an advance party of would-be Polish administrators, headed by Bolesław Drobner, reconnoitred the outskirts of Breslau shortly after the Second Army had left. One can only assume that the Soviets had no wish to see their military operations complicated by a premature *coup de main*. At a juncture when the battle for Berlin had not yet been won and when no final inter-Allied decision about the future of German territory had been taken, Stalin could not have favoured a démarche that would have given his Western Allies genuine grounds for complaint.

After an almost imperceptible hiatus, the Soviet advance intensified again over the Easter weekend. It restarted at 6 p.m. on the evening of 31 March, when Soviet artillery launched a six-hour barrage. It was aimed at the western perimeter, with the immediate target of taking the Gandau airfield. It was supported by a large-scale air offensive, which concentrated on bombing the city centre and strafing the workers on the Kaiserstrasse airstrip. On 7 April, more than ninety Soviet aircraft were in action. The next day it was 160. In early April, as news of the fall of the Glogau *Festung* arrived, Breslau suffered its most intense bombardment. The Cathedral, the Sandkirche and the Mauritiuskirche all fell victim. Corpses littered the parks and open spaces. Commandant Niehoff abandoned his command bunker on the Liebichs Höhe and joined Hanke in the basement of the University Library. The few people who were not already living in cellars were forced underground by the downpour of bombs. As a *Volkssturm* man recorded, movement above ground was all but impossible:

> Easter Sunday . . . We leave Matthiasplatz in a break in the fighting. But after a few minutes all hell breaks loose. We run crouching, heads covered, tight against the wall and dive into cellar after cellar. In one . . . there is a woman screaming like a lunatic. Outside, a terrible roar as the block opposite collapses . . .[54]

The appearance of German planes in the skies brought a brief moment of renewed hope, soon dashed. They were captured German aircraft – and they too were being used to bomb and strafe the defenders. Hugo Hartung despaired:

> Now . . . German bombs are falling from German planes onto the unhappy city, destroying its people, its houses, churches and bridges, its altars, libraries and art treasures. As in the Bible, fire is falling from the heavens.[55]

However, 'friendly' aircraft were still to be seen by the defenders. For despite Soviet air superiority and the loss of Gandau, the German airlift continued. The Friesenwiese and Oderwiese meadows served as makeshift airstrips, while on 10 April, a Ju 52 landed on the Kaiserstrasse[56] runway and evacuated twenty-two wounded.[57] In the first two weeks of the renewed Soviet offensive almost fifty-one tonnes of ammunition were delivered to Breslau daily. How much of it reached the German forces is unknown.[58]

By the end of April the Soviet grip had tightened considerably. Gains in the west, including the Linke-Hofmann works, brought the frontline to Striegauer Platz and Tschepiner Platz, barely a kilometre from the Market Square. Despite Hanke's exhortations on the occasion of the Führer's birthday on 20 April, it was becoming clear that the promised relief was not going to materialise. On 1 May, as the airlift finally ground to a halt, word spread of the death of Hitler. Berlin radio presented the event as a last act of heroism:

From the Führer's headquarters it is announced that our Führer, Adolf Hitler, fell for Germany this afternoon at his command post in the Reich Chancellery, fighting against Bolshevism till his last breath.[59]

Hanke, named in Hitler's testament as successor to Himmler as *Reichsführer-SS*, demanded continued sacrifice, 'to save as many Germans as possible from Bolshevism'.[60] But, as Hermann Nowack observed, civilian morale was failing:

I went over the piles of rubble towards the Kaiserbrücke. Everything destroyed. Garve to Stanetzkistrasse: ruins; Mauritiusplatz: ruins; Brothers' Monastery: badly damaged; Brüderstrasse: largely burnt out; Tauentzienstrasse completely burnt out; my son's house . . . burnt out down to the cellar. Not even a plank, just black walls. Goebbels said, 'We have to be hard.' Now as I stand here, I am turned to stone.[61]

As popular discontent with the *Festung* policy mounted, the terror of the Nazi regime increased in parallel. The apparatus of Nazi 'justice' had operated throughout the siege, but now the screws were tightened. Any minor misdemeanour – anything that aroused suspicion – could have fatal consequences.

One of the many victims was a British RAF sergeant and POW by the name of Cyril Harlestrap, who had been part of a work detail from the Ohlewiesen camp. He had absconded in mid-December 1944, and in late January 1945 had reappeared at the home of one Martha Gessner, who offered him refuge in her cellar. When German soldiers joined them in the makeshift shelter, Harlestrap pretended to be Greek, drinking and playing cards with the German officer. His pretence came to an end on 27 February, when he was caught listening to British radio transmissions. He was taken to the Gestapo headquarters on Tauentzienstrasse for interrogation and, on 4 March, was shot in the yard of the police headquarters, 'whilst trying to escape'.[62]

Discontent swelled into active resistance. The existence of a secret anti-Nazi group was revealed in mid-March when a clandestine newspaper, *Der Freiheitskämpfer* ('The Freedom Fighter'), was distributed. Leaflets appeared denouncing the work of the *Brandkommandos* and the demolition of buildings. General Niehoff was lampooned as a 'Nero raging in Breslau'. Two Nazi Party offices, in the suburbs of Gneisenau and Elbing, were bombed by saboteurs. The priest Paul Peikert eloquently expressed the hatred felt by ordinary citizens:

No government has used the word 'people' more than this one, but never have the rights of the 'people' been more crushed under foot than by these brutes here in Breslau. In their eyes only the enemy and themselves exist. The people are like air. The people are bullied and terrorised. For [the Party] the people have become just an object and this leads to the senseless frenzy of destruction against everything that is dear to them . . .[63]

Cilli Steindörfer experienced the arbitrary nature of the Nazi terror at first hand. After her home had been overrun by Soviet soldiers, sixteen-year-old Cilli was taken in by a Red Army major. When she was subsequently recaptured during a German counter-attack, she was assumed to be a Soviet spy. She was executed by the Gestapo in the garden of the *Sicherheitspolizei* prison on 25 March.[64] That same day another sixteen-year-old was shot, this time for alleged desertion: while serving in the *Volkssturm*, 'Horst' had broken down and left his post during a Soviet assault.[65] A month later, on 27 April, a full-scale revolt broke out in the suburbs of Zimpel, Carlowitz and Bischofswalde. Waving white flags, an estimated 1,500 civilians (mainly women) besieged the party offices and stoned military command posts, demanding an end to the fighting. Of the 100 arrested, seventeen alleged 'ringleaders' were executed by the *Sicherheitsdienst*.

A young Polish woman, a forced labourer who had the good fortune to be employed in a food store, managed to keep a diary:

Wednesday, 28 March: German soldiers set up quarters in our cellar, which is turned into a hospital . . .
Friday, 30 March: In our courtyard, a so-called *Versorgungsbombe* [supply pod] is found: a red parachute with white strings and ammunition in it.
Saturday, 31 March: A great Russian attack from the East. The building hit twenty times. Our boss had to flee his bath . . .
Easter Sunday, 1 April: Bombardment starts at 9 a.m. Wounded brought to the hospital . . . Matthiasplatz in flames.
2 April: Air raids all day.
3 April: Air raids again. I tried to visit Witek. But his house was just a heap of rubble. Dead horses and makeshift graves on the streets . . . A grenade kills 6 people opposite us. I saw the bodies, mutilated and covered in dust . . .
4 April: A common cart picked up the dead from yesterday. They are thrown in like chunks of meat. Afternoon bombing.
5 April: On fire watch with Frau Vogt. The Russians use megaphones to call on the German soldiers to surrender.
6 April: Soldiers living in our house take my photo.
Wed. 11 April: A *Nähmaschine* flew over dropping incendiaries.
Fri. 13 April: Disappointed. Everyone had said the fighting would end today: but the struggle goes on . . .

Sat. 14 April: Learned from the paper that Roosevelt is dead.
19 April: Terrible firing. Witek was lucky. The shrapnel hit a pen in his breast pocket, so didn't pierce his heart . . .
Thurs. 20 April: Refugees on the University Bridge run hither and thither carrying their belongings. It reminded me of [1939] when we Poles had to flee the Germans. A plane overhead was playing with them, chasing them to and fro . . . On night watch, hear the Russian loudspeakers saying that Berlin has fallen . . .[66]

Berlin had not fallen. But the end was obviously nigh when the SS came round and told the foreign workers, 'Remember to say that we treated you well.'

After the death of Hitler, popular resistance to the *Festung* gradually found echoes among the German military. As late as 4 May, Niehoff was spurred on to further resistance when he was awarded the Oak Leaves and Swords to his *Ritterkreuz*, the highest German military decoration. But that same day, he was visited by a joint delegation of the remaining religious leaders, who demanded an end to the fighting. Father Ernst Hornig posed the decisive question: 'Is continuing the defence of Breslau something which you could justify to God?'[67]

Over the previous four to six weeks, the military arguments for defending Breslau had withered. Once the 17th Army's *Panzer* reserves had been sent off to fill gaps in the defences of south-eastern Bohemia, Breslau had no possible hope of relief. The issue was raised, therefore, concerning what exactly sustained the defenders' determination. The Catholic priest Johannes Kaps believed the answer lay neither with the Nazi terror, nor with propaganda, but rather with 'some deeper sentiment . . . of which they were hardly conscious':

> Perhaps they were stirred by the knowledge that this city, which was now at the mercy of the enemy from the vast plains of Asia, had been German for more than seven hundred years . . . that it had defended itself once before when surrounded by the hordes of Genghis Khan, and that it represented the very heart of European culture and Christianity on the threshold of the vast Asiatic plain . . .[68]

The priest's psychological observations may have been accurate. He knew his flock. But he was not strong on cultural geography. Unknowingly, he was revealing the faulty mental map that had so often led Germans astray throughout his lifetime.

As a soldier, General Niehoff would not have needed reminding about the comprehensive military catastrophe that Germany was suffering. In the fourteen weeks during which Breslau had been under siege, the overall

34

predicament of Germany's proud *Wehrmacht* had been inexorably under-mined. In mid-January, it had been able to assume a stance of stoical defiance; at the beginning of May, it was sliding into the abyss of terminal collapse. The prospects had always been worse than the Nazi command had admitted. It turned out that Cracow as well as Warsaw had fallen before the Breslau *Festung* had even been implemented. The horrific destruction of Dresden, a city of similar size to Breslau, showed that the superior air power of the Western Allies could no longer be effectively contested. The extraordinary rapidity of Zhukov's drive on Berlin demonstrated that the predominance of Soviet ground forces was far greater than anyone had imagined. The meeting of the 'Big Three' at Yalta, which reiterated the demand for Germany's total surrender, showed that differences within the Allied coalition could not be exploited. The fall of Budapest on 13 February, after Hitler had sent it the lion's share of the remaining reserves, showed that his strategic priorities had been faulty. As a result, March saw Western armies surging across the Rhine, while the Soviets built up their positions for the final shattering assault on Berlin. On 3 April, Vienna fell, thereby severing the *Anschluss* that had created the Greater German Reich. Three weeks later, on 25 April, Marshal Koniev, whose reputation was all too familiar in Breslau, pulled off two startling achievements in the space of a single day. On the one hand, his troops linked up with Zhukov to the west of Berlin, thereby completing the encirclement of the Reich's nerve-centre. On the other, they linked up with the advancing Americans at Torgau on the River Elbe, thereby cutting the Reich clean in two. (These facts would have filtered through to the defenders of Breslau by radio, but it would be interesting to know if anyone in the city was made aware that in distant San Francisco, also on 25 April, the founding conference of the United Nations had convened, on the assumption that the Allied victory in Europe was a foregone conclusion.) Berlin surrendered to the Soviets on 2 May; Hamburg to the British on the 3rd. On the 4th, the day when General Niehoff was contemplating capitulation, American troops from Bavaria met American troops from Italy on the summit of the Brenner Pass. With one exception, all the capitals of Europe were now in Allied hands. The German garrison in Prague, threatened both by a popular rising and by Soviet encirclement, was the very last to hold out. Though not far distant, it had no conceivable means of offering assistance to Breslau.

Such were the straits in which General Niehoff was obliged to make his decision. Though wary of crossing either Schörner (now C-in-C of the *Wehrmacht*) or Hanke (now *Reichsführer-SS*), Niehoff made arrangements for a ceasefire. Negotiations began in the morning. Notwithstanding a renewed civilian demonstration in Zimpel, they were not without difficulty, for not all of the military was in agreement. Whilst a short-lived football game was improvised on the frontline between Soviet and German troops,[69] certain SS elements preferred to barricade themselves into the *Jahrhunderthalle* rather than face surrender.[70] Others attempted in vain to break out to the south-west. The commander of the *Volkssturm*, General Otto Herzog, committed suicide. And Soviet threats to raze the city forthwith if it did not capitulate sowed confusion. Niehoff's negotiator, Herbert von Bürck, then stepped on a mine when being led blindfold through the frontline and was seriously wounded.

Hanke was furious. He visited Niehoff in the command bunker late on 5 May. He raged about betrayal and threatened to impose dire punishments on defeatists. But, when Niehoff calmly reiterated his decision to capitulate, his theatrical performance collapsed. Hanke asked what he should do. He parried the suggestion of suicide and refused the offer of false papers, fearful that he would be betrayed. He then found his own solution. That night he commandeered a pilot and a Fieseler Storch light aircraft and was flown to the Sudetenland.[71]

Before the *Reichsführer* had departed, Niehoff issued a statement to his troops:

> Hitler is dead, Berlin has fallen. The allies of east and west have shaken hands in the heart of Germany. Thus the conditions for a continuation of the struggle for Breslau no longer exist. Every further sacrifice is a crime. I have decided to end the battle and to offer the enemy, under honourable conditions, the surrender of the city and the garrison. The last shot has been fired – we have done our duty, as the law demanded.[72]

At 7 a.m. on 6 May, Breslau's artillery ceased firing. A general ceasefire by German troops followed at 1 p.m. After that they were only permitted to return incoming fire:

> About 9 o'clock, there were a few explosions from the front. The pessimists reckoned it would start again. Then silence. Ceasefire. Thank God.[73]

A radio message was received from the headquarters of the German 17th Army in the Sudeten mountains. It read:

> It is with feelings of pride and sorrow that the banners of Germany are lowered in tribute to the steadfastness of the garrison and the self-sacrifice of the people of Breslau.[74]

The *Festung* had fallen.

*

The 'honourable conditions' secured by Niehoff from Gluzdovsky included a guarantee of safe conduct, medical care, the retention of personal property by the garrison and civilian population and the immediate repatriation of prisoners at the end of the war.[75] None would be honoured.

Soviet troops entered the city centre at dusk. The German defenders had been required to lay down their weapons. They assembled in order to be herded into the former Nazi concentration camps at Fünfteichen and Hundsfeld. In due course they were shipped to the Soviet Union to feed the Gulag. Few of them would ever return.

Most of Breslau's cultural monuments bore terrible scars. Almost all the churches had suffered extensive damage. Seventy of the university's 104 buildings were destroyed. Tactical strongpoints, such as the Palais Hatzfeld (Hanke's *Oberpräsidium*), the Sternloge (SS headquarters), the University Library (*Festung* command) and the New Market (site of a large flak battery), were heaps of rubble. Yet the devastation was indiscriminate. An estimated 20,000 houses had disappeared. The central, southern and western suburbs were disfigured by the fragile, blackened shells of the homes and businesses that had once stood there. But some buildings and districts remained intact.

The population had been reduced to a residue of refugees, prisoners and invalids. Though exact figures will never be known, it is plausible that German military casualties exceeded 60 per cent, including 6,000 dead and 23,000 wounded. Estimates of the civilian dead range between 10,000 and 80,000, including 3,000 suicides.[76] Estimates of Soviet casualties were as high as 65,000, with around 8,000 dead. If this is correct, the Soviets experienced a more favourable casualty ratio in Breslau than was usual on the Eastern Front.

The surviving Breslauers, emerging from their cellars into a scarcely recognisable world of shell holes and rubble mountains, faced an uncertain future. They had shown extraordinary stamina. They had hoped that their sacrifice would delay the Soviet thrust into the heart of the Reich. But the Soviets were too strong to be deflected. The siege had lasted eighty days and had tied down some seven Soviet divisions.[77] Breslau had surrendered four days *after* Berlin and was thus the last fortress of the Reich to fall. Indeed, it was one of the very last parts of Germany to surrender. For this dubious honour, it had experienced *Götterdämmerung* to the full. In May 1945, it was virtually impossible to imagine that 'the Flower of Europe' would ever bloom again.

ONE

Island City:
Archaeology and Prehistory to AD 1000

The City was the offspring of the River and the Plain. It was conceived at a point where people moving up and down the River met others who were following trails across the plain. Historians do not usually recognise events for which there is no definitive evidence, but it is reasonable to deduce that some time long before recorded history a small settlement came into being at the river crossing. In fact, there are many circumstantial indications to suggest that the site was repeatedly, if not permanently, occupied from very remote times. There is also good reason to assume that the first settlers were not connected in any way with the Slavonic and Germanic peoples who would later dominate. The earliest trace of Stone Age habitation, about half an hour's stroll from the left bank of the river, has been dated to more than 300,000 years ago.[1] The first substantial prehistoric settlement, which has been identified on the right bank of the river, dates from the eighth century BC.[2] Two rich prehistoric hoards have played an important role in scholarly ruminations. One of them, from the first century BC, discovered about five kilometres to the south-west, contained no less than 2.75 tonnes of Baltic amber.[3] The other, discovered about three kilometres to the north-east, came from a princely gravesite of the fourth century AD. It contained an extraordinary collection of utensils and jewellery fashioned in gold, silver, bronze and fine glass.[4]

Archaeologists have drawn very conflicting conclusions from the fragmentary information that is available. Yet most would agree that a marked decline in human activity occurred around the middle of the first millennium of our era. In the region as a whole, the population fell to perhaps one-quarter of the preceding level. According to a recent opinion, life on the middle reaches of the River 'virtually stopped'.[5] If this is correct, one must accept that the new wave of settlers who began to make their presence felt in the sixth to seventh centuries AD had little in common with their many predecessors. Equally, the urban community, which henceforth was to enjoy an unbroken history, could not be seen as a simple continuation of earlier settlements on the same site. It would not be out of place to talk of a new beginning.

*

Historical geography underlines two crucial factors in the early stages of development. The first relates to the intersection of the two ancient trade routes – one on the east–west axis of the Plain linking Western Europe with the Black Sea, the other following the north–south alignment of the River from the watershed of the Danube Basin to the Baltic. The second factor relates to a much more specific and local feature. Immediately upstream of a long, marshy and impassable stretch of the River, a cluster of perhaps a dozen riverine islands provided a natural crossing point and refuge for the graziers and fishermen who frequented the riverbanks. Of course, it is impossible to say whether the crossing point was manned by an unbroken series of ferrymen from the days of the amber hoard to those of the earliest medieval dwellings. But it is not inconceivable. What is certain is that the riverine islands would have proved more attractive than other locations in the vicinity. It is the islands that lent this place its most outstanding characteristic. (The siting of Paris on the islands of the Seine is but one of many parallels to prove the point.)

The presence of the nearby mountains exercised a powerful influence. Subalpine in character, the highest ridge in the 'Giant Mountains'[6] rises to a height of 1,602 metres at the peak of 'Snowy Head',[7] some 100 kilometres to the south-west. Icebound for half the year, it forms a formidable barrier that can only be crossed with ease through one or two passes. At the same time, it encourages life-giving falls of rain and snow on the Plain below. Importantly, too, the rocks of the mountains contain an unusual variety of valuable minerals. Deposits of iron, which first attracted the Celts, are matched by a rich coal basin, and by numerous mines yielding lead, tin, copper, gold and silver. In addition, there are several famous mineral springs, whose waters have brought in a continuous stream of visitors, from nature worshippers in prehistoric times to modern health tourists. All these attractions are situated within eighty kilometres, or two to three days' walk, of the City, which naturally became the focus for related trade and transport. At a similar distance to the north lies a lower range of limestone heights, the 'Cats Hills',[8] which became an important source of high-quality stone in the age of permanent building. Most interesting of all is a curiously isolated peak,[9] which rises magnificently from the surrounding plain less than forty kilometres from the City, and which lent its name to the province. A holy mountain and a cult centre from the earliest times, it added a sense of the sacred to the district over which it presides.

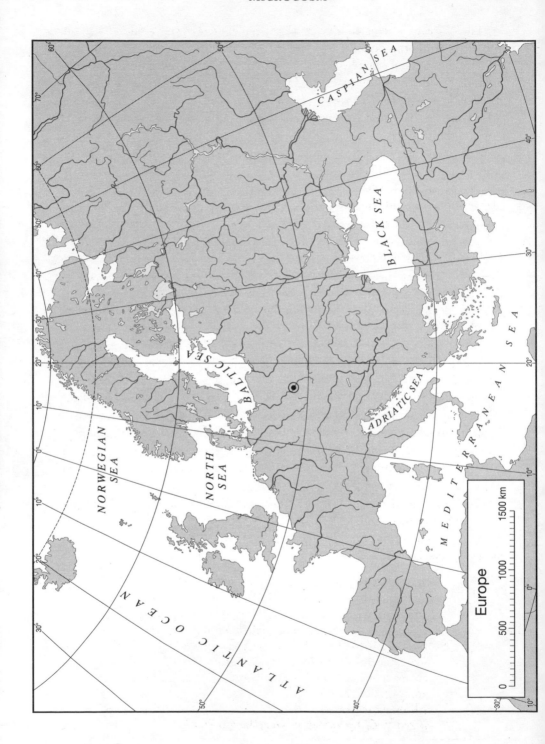

The Great Northern Plain, Europe's largest geographical feature, stretches from the oceanic seaboard to the heart of Eurasia, a distance of many thousands of kilometres, broken only by rolling hills and broad rivers. One of those rivers, the Odra (or Oder), rises in the mountains of Central Europe at a height of 640 metres, initially flowing north-east through the Moravian Gate, before turning north-west and forming the main artery of the province of Silesia. On approaching the Baltic Sea, it adopts a northerly course, crossing the lowest and flattest expanse of the Plain and finally reaching the coast through the arms and lagoons of its delta.

Given that the River flows through flood plains for most of its length, it is generally slow and shallow, possessing an average velocity of only 3.6 kilometres per hour and an average depth of only one metre. Along its 854-kilometre course it is joined by numerous left- and right-bank tributaries, including the Mała Panew (Malapane), the Nysa (Glatzer Neisse), the Oława (Ohlau), the Bystrzyca (Weistritz), the Widawa (Weide), the Barycz (Bartsch), the Bóbr (Bober), the Western Nysa (Neisse) and the Warta (Warthe). Positioned close to the confluence of three important tributaries, the Island City stands at a mere 110 metres above sea level, although the sea is more than 400 kilometres distant. At that point, the River has traversed only half its length, though it has already fallen 80 per cent of its total gradient. As a result, a sudden spring thaw in the mountains can bring an onrush of high water, while heavy precipitation in the upper reaches of the basin can cause floods of catastrophic proportions. In historical times, seriously destructive floods were recorded in 1179, 1454, 1464, 1501, 1515, 1595, 1729, 1736, 1785, 1804, 1813, 1829, 1834, 1854, 1903 and 1997 (see pages 495–6). During hot summers, in contrast, the water level can fall low enough to obstruct regular navigation.

Watching the River's flow, whether turbulent or lazy, has been the preoccupation of countless generations. It invariably inspires reflection on the human condition. One poetess watched the swans swimming serenely between the islands and expressed a deep sense of calm:

> patrzę jak zabitą rzeką odpływają dwa łabędzie
> jakby unosiły moją wiarę i ludzkie milczenie
> znów nie wierzę że się nauczyłam tylko rozstawania
> dyktowanego ludziom przez ich naturalną śmierć
> pozwól mi trochę nad tym brzegiem pobyć
> nie czuję się wygnańcem ani tułaczem
> ani panem czasu ani niewolnikiem
> zdążę gdy zawołasz
> jak ongiś matka
> przed nocą by zasnąć w szczęśliwym śnie[10]

(I watch as a pair of swans glide down the murdered river
as if they were carrying off my faith amidst human silence.
Once again, I can't believe that I have only learned about the
separation
to which people are condemned by their natural death.
So let me just stay on this bank for a while.
I don't feel to be either an exile or a wanderer
nor master of my time, nor yet a prisoner.
I'll come when you call
As once my mother called
Before the night, to send me into a happy sleep.)

Another poet, observing the same spot in the midday heat of summer, feels the earth stand still, as a pair of lovers embrace, oblivious to their surroundings:

Die Kirchen haben sich ausgestreckt
im breiten Mittagsschlaf.
Die Oder steht reglos um diese Zeit.
Ein Liebespaar auf der dritten Bank.
Im Sonnenbruch flimmert die Luft.[11]

(The churches have stretched themselves out
in an afternoon siesta.
The Oder is motionless for a moment.
On the third bench sit a pair of lovers.
The air shimmers in a shaft of sunlight.)

Unfortunately, nothing is known about the City's original name. One can only say with confidence that the present name, which probably derives from that of a tenth-century ruler, is very unlikely to have been the first one. After all, cities do not usually enjoy royal patronage until they are well established. In this situation, historians face an acute dilemma. They can either use the later name for the earlier period to which it is inappropriate, and thereby face charges of anachronism. Or they can use their imagination to invent a name which, in the nature of things is unhistorical, but which may nonetheless be closer to historical reality. In this spirit, one might dare to talk of the 'Island City'.

River names, in contrast, are well known to be the oldest items in the toponymy of any landscape, and the Odra/Oder is no exception. Of course, there can be no definitive solution. But modern attempts to establish either Germanic or Slavonic origins must be viewed with some scepticism. So, too, must the ingenious idea that the modern name is a Germano-Slavonic hybrid. The earliest written reference comes from Ptolemy in the second century AD. But that reveals little beyond the fact that a recognisable form of the modern name – Οὐιαδου[12] – was already in existence 1,800 years ago. Two hypotheses appear to carry the greatest weight. One suggests that Odra/Oder derives its name from Irano-Sarmatian roots. The Old Iranian word *adu*, meaning 'stretch of water', has connotations with the Adriatic Sea. The other suggests a Celtic derivation. This has not found favour in recent times, although scholars in the early twentieth century were eager enough to explain the toponymy of Silesia in Celtic terms.[13] After all, the earliest inhabitants to have their ethnic links verified were Celts, and the area to the south and south-west has numerous Celtic names. The standard proto-Celtic word for 'river' is reflected in the modern Welsh word *dŵr*, meaning 'water'. It recurs in river names across Europe wherever ancient Celtic settlements were established, and in forms as varied as *Douro* (Portugal), *Dordogne* (France) and *Derwent* (England) – that is, 'White Water'. So it is not unreasonable to suppose that Odra may belong to the same series. One should also take note of the curious figure called Odras in Celtic mythology. The prehistoric Celts spurned all forms of writing, but the legend of Odras has survived in Ireland. There, she is presented as a wayward nymph who, having offended the vengeful queen and deity, Morrigan, is changed into a pool of water.[14]

Thanks to the shifting channels and extensive marshes of the valley floor, the best arable land has always lain near the surrounding hills, especially to the west. In modern times, the continuous strip of fine farmland running parallel to the mountains and the River became known as the *Langental*, or 'Long Valley'. It is beautifully irrigated by the mountain-fed streams and enjoys a microclimate that is markedly milder than places further east. At the same time, it is warmer and wetter than the districts further north, which are rendered especially infertile by large expanses of sandy soil. Nonetheless, much of the original forest cover has remained intact; broad stretches of heath and scrub are common; and to the present day the River flows in its middle reaches between alternating landscapes of cultivated fields and of dense, lonely wilderness.

At 51° 7′N, the Island City is situated midway on the latitudinal line joining Brussels with Kiev, and at 17° 2′E midway on the longitudinal line between Uppsala and Taranto. In consequence, it lies well inside the Continental Climatic Zone, which is marked by four distinct seasons, including hard, freezing winters and hot, sunny summers. But it is far removed from Eurasia's most severe extremes, and is on the right side of the vine line, at a point where many sorts of fruit can ripen abundantly. Its low-lying position in the Odra valley can encourage mists and fogs. Yet it is well sheltered from the harshest effects both of turbulent depressions from the west and of icy winter winds from the east.

The importance of the Island City as a river crossing is underlined by the fact that it lay at the intersection of some of Europe's oldest trade routes. The main Amber Route running south from the Baltic coast, for example, crossed the Odra before negotiating the Moravian Gate and finishing at Aquileia at the head of the Adriatic. This was one of four routes linking the eastern Baltic to the Mediterranean. Tacitus, in the second century AD, opined on the importance of amber to the Baltic tribes of his own day:

> . . . they are the only people to collect the amber – glaesum is their word for it . . . Like true barbarians, they have never asked or discovered what it is or how it is produced. For a long time, indeed, it lay unheeded like any other jetsam, until Roman luxury made its reputation. They have no use for it themselves. They gather it crude, pass it on unworked and are astounded at the price it fetches.[15]

In displaying his Roman disdain for the 'barbarian' tribes of the East, Tacitus was almost certainly wide of the mark. Amber had been widely used since the early Stone Age as ornamentation, and as a cure for a multitude of illnesses, including asthma and rheumatism. It has been found both at Stonehenge and at Mycenae. Its value was recognised by the peoples of the eastern Baltic, and its use long pre-dated the coming of 'Roman luxury'.

Trade from the Scythian steppes was carried westwards along the so-called Salt Route, crossing the Odra en route for Germania and Gaul. Salt became invaluable in prehistoric Europe, when its use as a food preservative made it a prerequisite in the shift from a nomadic to an agricultural society. It was produced on the salt pans at the mouth of the Boristhenes (Dnieper) and was later mined in quantity at Wieliczka in the Carpathian foothills. The lucrative salt trade spurred the growing exchange of many other commodities.

By 1500 BC these trading routes already formed an extensive network. And while they were not roads in the modern sense, the pathways were often improved using logs and primitive drainage in damp or marshy areas. Exactly how the Amber and Salt Routes looked in the vicinity of the Island City is unknown, but later medieval roads in the area were strengthened by timber fixed with iron stakes, and similar techniques had been known much earlier.

The procession of nameless prehistoric peoples who settled in, or passed through, the environs of the Island City is a long one. It began in the late Stone Age, and continued for several millennia until the early centuries of our own era. Neolithic sites to the south of the City,[16] and the 'Corded

Ware' sites to the east and west,[17] are proof of Stone Age settlement. One of the latter,[18] a complex of fifty-seven individual graves, including rich finds of bulging, black-brown pottery with crude lugs and diagonal ornamentation,[19] has given its name to an archaeological culture.

Following the Neolithic, the region passed through two Bronze Age cultures – the Uňetice (*Aunjetitz*) (*c*.1800–1400 BC) and the Lusatian (*c*.1300–400 BC). Uňetice Culture, which took its name from a site in neighbouring Bohemia, has been described as 'the classic image of the Bronze Age'.[20] It left rubbish pits and barrow burials in Silesia, and demonstrated the prominence of metallurgy, personal ornamentation and a patriarchal, sun-worshipping society. Though especially prevalent in the area between the Odra and the Ślęża mountain (Zobten), it was also present in the Vistula valley and in Moravia.

Lusatian Culture was a similar hybrid of Vistulanian and Bohemian influences, and predominated in the region for some 800 years. With an emphasis on stock breeding, metallurgy and innovative decorated pottery forms, it spread north into the valley of the Noteć (Netze), where its most famous stronghold, dating from the fourth century BC, consisted of an oval island built on elaborate ramparts of timber and pilework, with more than 100 south-facing houses.[21] There is reason to suppose that something similar could conceivably have been constructed on the islands of the Odra.

With the advance of the Iron Age around 700 BC, ultramontane influences from the South returned to the fore. Late Lusatian times had been heavily influenced by the so-called Bylany Culture from central Bohemia, and many symbolic and ornamental elements of Bylany origin were adopted into Lusatian pottery designs. By around 350 BC, the trickle became a flood, to the point where the middle Odra was once thought to have been the scene of an 'invasion' of Celtic warriors, craftsmen and farmers. Modern historians prefer the concept of cultural expansion to that of physical invasion.

Nonetheless, the large-scale presence of Celts in ancient Silesia is beyond question. It is thoroughly supported by numismatic, archaeological and toponymic evidence. Although it would be denied by ideologists of the Nazi and Communist regimes, who were not averse to using state censorship to suppress it, serious scholars have confined their debates to differing assessments of its duration and extent. Celtophile enthusiasts would argue that Celtic civilisation was dominant in the area from the mid-fourth to the late second centuries BC, and that its influence lingered on for a lengthy period after that. Sceptics argue that the Celts and their culture were 'temporary visitors' among the long-standing aboriginal proprietors of the territory. Certainly, the Celts had relatively few friends among the scholars who first attempted to reconstruct the prehistory of Silesia in modern times.

Both the Prussian School, which led the field from c.1850 to 1945, and the Polish Autochthonous School, which predominated in the years 1945–90, promoting the Slavonic character of the aboriginals, had other priorities in mind. Even so, the subject has never completely succumbed to political pressure and its devotees include some very reputable names.[22]

Celtic civilisation spread into Silesia from Bohemia, which was contiguous to its principal area of concentration between the mid-Rhine and mid-Danube. The opening phase of so-called Hallstatt Culture did not expand significantly northwards. But the second phase of La Tène Culture reached both the Odra and the Vistula. Its earliest manifestation near the Island City was at a hill site, which has yielded typical torques of an early vintage, as well as glass jewellery and hand-fashioned pottery.[23] A much larger site nearer to the River produced twenty-three warrior graves replete with iron weapons.[24] Hoards of Celtic gold coins have also been unearthed well to the west of the River,[25] while several important skeletal burial sites attest to the persistence of the Celtic population as late as the second century BC.[26] A tall Celtic stone column still stands guard not far from the holy mountain of Ślęża.[27]

Ślęża has inevitably attracted the lion's share of scholarly dispute. No one doubts that the mountain-top was used for prehistoric ritual or religious purposes. The only questions are 'by whom?' and 'when?'. Early German scholars were less resistant to the Celtic tag than later Polish Stalinists were. The latter were apt to negate the Celtic presence outright. Of course, it is definitely possible that the stone-built ramparts, like the ceremonial walkway leading to the summit, were of pre-Celtic provenance. But that conclusion would only indicate that the Silesian Celts inherited their shrine from some shadowy predecessors. And it would militate against the possibility that the site was of post-Celtic, even of Slavonic origin. Nowadays, however, the most visible part of the sanctuary has been firmly attached to the Celtic legacy. A complex of stone cult circles marks out the sacred area of a Celtic *nemeton*, or 'temple', from which a further circle can be viewed on a neighbouring peak some three kilometres distant. Five enigmatic stone figures – now known as 'the Bear', 'the Boar', 'the Monk', 'the Mushroom' and 'the Girl with a Fish' – were all unearthed here at various times and are inscribed with the mark of the crooked cross. (They aroused feverish interest in the 1930s.) There has even been a suggestion that the Slavonic name of Ślęża derives from a Celtic word for 'sun'.[28]

After perhaps some 300 years, the day of the Celts drew to a close. Some experts maintain that traces of their culture can be observed in modern Polish folklore, such as the Cracovian ritual of the *Lajkonik*, or 'hobby horse'.[29] That is a far cry indeed. But it can be observed in the coins first collected by Aloysius Haunold (1634–1711), and in those enigmatic stone figures that have parallels in several ex-Celtic countries as far afield as Spain and Portugal. The notion that Celtic practices persisted long after the Celts had been absorbed by their successors is supported by the medieval chronicler Thietmar. Writing in Latin in the early eleventh century, he noted not only that the 'Mons Silensis' had given its name to the surrounding province, which he designated *pagus Silensis*, but that 'the accursed pagan cult' was still being practised on 'the holy mountain' in his own time.

Meanwhile, the Odra basin passed into its so-called Venedian stage (*c*.200 BC–AD 600), the Venedian being another archaeological culture allegedly with 'paramount' Celtic content. The Venedian and the subsequent Przeworsk Culture, unearthed at numerous locations around the Island City,[30] revealed a rapid development in iron-working and the production of weaponry. The changes coincided with the onset of a long period of troubles.

Central Europe emerges somewhat from the darkness of prehistory in the work of the Greek geographer Strabo and of the Roman historians Pliny and Tacitus. A dim picture was constructed of relatively sedentary populations surviving the comings and goings of tribal migrations, often attended by violence. The Scythians were the first of these migrants. A semi-nomadic people of Central Asian origin, they moved on to the Black Sea steppes in the eighth century BC and were famously described by Herodotus as a fearsome race of horsemen, who scalped their victims, blinded their slaves and held their women in abject subservience. They stormed into Silesia around 400 BC, thereby hastening the decline of the Lusatian Culture. The second phase of Scythian expansion, this time involving more protracted settlement, occurred around AD 100.

The Sarmatians, a Caucasian people, followed in the steps of the Scythians. Tacitus wrote of them, and of their influence on the native Venedians, with undisguised distaste: 'The Venedi have borrowed largely from Sarmatian ways; their plundering forays take them over all that wooded and mountainous country.' But he added caustically that '. . . [the Venedi] are a squalid and slovenly people; the features of their nobles get something of the Sarmatian ugliness from intermarriage.'[31] This was not a good advertisement for the later claim of the Polish nobility to Sarmatian ancestry. Yet the Sarmatian peoples had much to offer. A gravesite discovered in 1886, to the north-east of the Island City, contained three stone-lined burial chambers, covered with timber roofs, buried some two metres beneath the surface. Though the bodies themselves (thought at the time to be those of a local prince, his wife and child) had disintegrated, the grave goods made it one of the most spectacular archaeological finds of the period. In addition to gold and silver jewellery, vessels of bronze and coloured glass, Roman coins, Sarmatian-type buckles and objects of North Pontic origin all came to light. Not surprisingly, since imperial German archaeologists were eager to find evidence of early Germanic settlement, the long-dead prince and his family were initially classified as Vandals.[32]

Germanic incursions began as early as the fourth century BC. Weapon finds and incinerated villages indicate considerable local resistance.[33] Goths and Burgundians were present on the middle and lower Odra at the turn of the millennium, as were the Marcomanni of Bohemia. Like the Sarmatians before them, the Germanic tribes migrated sporadically over a long period of time, combining peaceful settlement with less-than-peaceful raiding and looting. Their advance started in piecemeal fashion. The Marcomanni, themselves refugees from Roman expansion further west, probably subjugated both the lower and the middle Odra in the early first century AD.

Some decades later, a tribe arrived that was of prime significance for the City's early history. By general consent, the Vandals originated in northern Jutland, in the district still known as Vendsyssel. By the third century AD, they had migrated via the lower Vistula into the valley of the middle Odra, where Roman authors recorded them under the headings of the *Silingi* and *Asdingi*. From their 'capital' at Niemcza (Nimptsch), the Vandals developed practices that belied their reputation as heathen destroyers. Their sojourn in Silesia coincided with the maximal phase of Roman economic penetration and, in exchange for slaves and amber, they acquired quantities of Roman glass, coins and enamel beads. The process of partial acculturation was further speeded up by the influx of 'barbarian' auxiliaries into the Roman army. The delicacy of the filigree jewellery found at local gravesites[34] bears witness to the skill of Vandal goldsmiths, while the multitude of Roman coins dating from Hadrian (r.AD 117–38) to Claudius Gothicus (r.268–70) points to a lucrative trade 'beyond the Imperial frontiers'.

Nevertheless, like its predecessors, the Vandal sojourn was not to last indefinitely. In AD 406, under pressure from the next wave of migrants, the Vandals joined the Goths, the Suebi and the Alans in a daring winter invasion of the Empire across the frozen Rhine at Mainz. After a lengthy stay in the Iberian peninsula and the founding of a kingdom in North Africa, they sacked Rome in AD 455, only to be destroyed by the Byzantine general Belisarius some eighty years later. According to the historian Procopius, the remnant of the Odra Vandals sought to contact their North African brethren in the sixth century, but without success.[35] Thereafter they disappeared, giving way to, or being absorbed by, the next components of the Silesian kaleidoscope.

The Huns had first stormed into south-eastern Europe in AD 370. They extended their power over many of the Slavonic and Germanic peoples of eastern Europe and eventually attacked the Roman Empire. Before their final defeat in AD 455, they inspired fear across Europe through a combination of dazzling horsemanship and unparalleled ferocity. Their possible presence in Silesia was hinted at by the discovery of a Hunnish bronze cauldron on the outskirts of the Island City. More importantly, the disruption engendered by the Huns hastened the widespread depopulation already mentioned. The theory gains support from Procopius in his report on the migration of the Heruli tribe in AD 512. '[The Heruli] . . . passed through all the lands of the Sclavenians,' he wrote, 'then wandered through much unpopulated land and finally reached the so-called Vareni.'[36] Though the identification is not certain, that 'unpopulated land' could well have included Silesia.

*

At this point, a brief recapitulation may not go amiss. By the middle of the first millennium AD, the list of culture groups, tribes and assorted peoples who are known to have lived in or near the Island City was approaching a score. It included the Corded Warers, the Jordanovians, the Uñeticians, the Lusatians, the Bylanians, various unspecified Celts, the Venedians, the Przeworskers, the Scythians, the Sarmatians, the Marcomanni, the Silingae and Asdingi (the Vandals), the Goths, the Huns, the Gepids, the Heruli and various unspecified Slavs. If the sources were more plentiful, the list would certainly have been longer. At each stage, the newcomers mixed and mingled, and ultimately obliterated their predecessors. One description of the fifth-century population of the Odra valley talks of 'a hybrid of Hunnic-Alanian, Gotho-Gepidian and Scandinavian elements'.[37] Though the details are often disputed, the overall picture is one of incessant evolution and constant admixtures. It is hard to believe, therefore, that serious scholars can support schemes that lay exclusive claim to these territories in the name of just one nation. But they have repeatedly done so. And they still do. German historians of the imperial vintage loved to look back to the Germanic Goths and Vandals and to sidestep the others. Polish historians of the nationalist Autochthonous School decided not only that the prehistoric Lusatian Culture was created by 'proto-Slavs', but also that the descendants of those allegedly Slavonic Lusatians were the only 'natives' of the region. Of course, there exists a very strong human instinct to reinforce one's present identity by tracing – or where necessary by inventing – one's ancient roots. But this encourages the sort of exercise where an impartial view of historical reality is the first casualty.

The selective mechanisms that have recommended aboriginal theories to insecure modern communities can easily be spotted. Yet the essential thing to realise is that the game can be played by all interested parties. The Polish Autochthonists might imagine that their belief in the proto-Slavonic character of prehistoric Silesian settlement could somehow justify the return of Polish rule in the mid-twentieth century. But, if so, they could hardly object if Czech apologists argued that Bohemian rule over Silesia before 990 justified the return of Bohemian rule after 1335, or if German apologists justified the medieval *Drang nach Osten* by reference to the activities of the Goths and Vandals. Modern Celtophiles could no doubt dream up claims on Silesia by the Welsh or the Irish. Far better to resign oneself to the fact that the concept of 'historic right' is a dubious fiction.

The outpourings of the poets and folklorists of the Romantic age, who with no pretence at objectivity or academic accuracy squeezed prehistory for whatever tales or legends attracted them, are there to be enjoyed, but not to be taken literally. Nearly two millennia after the passage of the Goths, for example, a latter-day poet born in the Island City could still revel in their exploits:

> Erschlagen lag mit seinem Heer
> Der König der Goten, Theodemer.
>
> Die Hunnen jauchzten auf blut'ger Wal;
> Die Geier stießen herab zutal.
>
> Der Mond schien hell; der Wind pfiff kalt;
> Die Wölfe heulten im Föhrenwald.
>
> Drei Männer ritten durchs Heidegefild,
> Den Helm zerschroten, zerhackt den Schild.
>
> Der erste über dem Sattel quer
> Trug seines Königs zerbrochenen Speer.
>
> Der zweite des Königs Kronhelm trug,
> Den mittendurch ein Schlachtbeil schlug.
>
> Der dritte barg mit seinem treuem Arm
> Ein verhüllt Geheimnis im Mantel warm.
>
> So kamen sie an die Donau tief,
> Und der erste hielt mit seinem Roß und rief:
>
> 'Ein zerhauener Helm, ein zerspellter Speer –
> Vom Reiche der Goten blieb nicht mehr!'
>
> Und der zweite sprach: 'In den Wellen dort
> Versenkt den traurigen Gotenhort!

Dann springen wir nach dem Uferrand –
Was säumest du, Vater Hildebrand!'

'Und tragt ihr des Königs Kron' und Speer,
Ihr treuen Gesellen, ich habe mehr!'

Auf schlug er seinen Mantel weich:
'Hier trag' ich der Goten Hort und Reich.

Und habt ihr gerettet Speer und Kron',
Ich habe gerettet des Königs Sohn.

Erwache, mein Knabe, ich grüße dich,
Du König der Goten, Jungdieterich!'[38]

(Slain there lay amid his host
Theodemer, King of the Goths.

The Huns bayed from their bloody wall,
Upon their prey the vultures fell.

Bright shone the moon, cold whistled the wind.
The wolves howled in the woods of pine.

Three warriors bold rode across the fields,
Hacked to shreds their helms and shields.

The first upon his saddle bore
The broken spear of his slain king.

The second his crown-encircled helm,
Riven in two by an axe's blow.

The third clasped in his loyal arms,
A mystery in his cloak so warm.

To the Danube deep they came.
There the first halted, loud exclaimed:

'A riven helm, a broken spear –
Of the Gothic realm no more remains!'

The second said: 'Into the foam
Let the Goths' sad hoard be thrown!

Then let us leap for the further strand –
Why linger, Father Hildebrand?'

'You bear our monarch's crown and spear –
Here, loyal comrades, I hold more!'

He opened wide soft folds of cloth:

'Here is the hoard and the realm of the Goths.

Whilst you have rescued spear and crown,
I have rescued the king's own son.

Awake, my boy, 'tis thee I greet:
King of the Goths, Young Dieterich!')

In a similar way, Polish Romantic writers of the nineteenth century often looked back with nostalgia to the prehistoric era of the early pagan Piasts as to a lost Golden Age. In his mystical epic *Król-Duch* ('King Spirit'), for example, the incomparable but near-untranslatable Juliusz Słowacki recalled the legendary Piast, founder of Mieszko's line, and the charms of Silesia's magical mountain. Piast was remembered as a simple, good-hearted peasant free of all the envy and pretensions with which 'civilisation' would encumber later generations:

Kmieć Piast, przed chatą dobrego wieczora
Używał, stary kmieć pełen dobroci:
A wtem skrzypnęła domowa zapora
I weszli do wrót Aniołowie złoci . . .[39]

(One fine evening, the old peasant Piast was basking
Before his cottage, full of good will,
When the gates of the house creaked open,
And golden angels walked up to the door . . .)

If Piast was more than simply a figure of legend, he would have lived in the ninth or early tenth century. And it is interesting to note that when Słowacki goes on to describe the Ślęża mountain and its ghostly visitors in that period, the historical setting correctly envisages a princely pilgrim who is not a Pole but a member of the Přemyslid dynasty:

Była w Słowiaństwie wówczas – osławiona,
Zober nazwana – czarodziejska góra:
Skalny szczyt miała – na buków ramiona
Włożony – w chmurach wisiała – jak chmura.
Na niej pustelnia stała postawiona,
Ubrana w osty – i w paproci pióra;
I trzej mieszkali, mówią pustelnicy
Pod strażą – orła, gadziny i lwicy.

Świętopełk, niegdyś – król Czech i Morawy,
Po stracie wojska – zniknąwszy cudownie,
Gdy wiatr go porwał w oczach – za hełm krwawy

I uniosł jako palącą się głownię . . .
Ow król bez grobu, człowiek wielkiej sławy.
Mówią . . . nawiedzał skały tej lodownie
I pustelnicze groty . . . i las wonny
Odwiedzał – jako mieszkaniec pozgonny.[40]

(In those days, famed throughout Slavdom,
There was a magic mountain by name of Zober.
A rocky peak soared above its beech-covered shoulders,
And, like a cloud, it hung among the clouds.
On top, a hermitage had been built,
Clothed in thistles and feathery ferns.
Three hermits, so they say, resided there,
Guarded by an eagle, a lizard and a lioness.

Once upon a time, a figure of great renown
Sventopelk, King of Bohemia and Moravia,
Miraculously disappeared, having lost his army.
Torn away on the wind by his bleeding helmet,
Lifted off before his very eyes like a flaming brand.
The graveless monarch, or so they say,
Haunted the rocks of that icy place, residing,
After death in the hermits' grotto and the scented woods . . .)

Słowacki's literary fancies can only be deciphered by the most advanced of exegetists. But no historian can fail to notice that the great Polish bard called the Ślęza mountain by a form of its Germanic name – 'Zober'.

*

The earliest Slavonic migrants appear to have arrived in the Silesian basin in the late fifth or early sixth century AD. They would have trickled in as part of a process of small-scale tribal movements, as had been the case with earlier phases of the *Völkerwanderung*.

The more definite presence of 'White Croats' has been fixed in the Odra valley from the first half of the sixth century. It may be surprising that the first recognisably Slavic pioneers may have been Croats rather than Poles or Czechs. Yet the existence of a sixth-century 'White Croatia', encompassing the north-western Carpathians, Galicia, Silesia and eastern Bohemia – though shrouded in mystery – is confirmed not only by contemporary Arab historians, but also by the Byzantine Emperor Constantine Porphyrogenitus, and even by Alfred the Great.[41] Around AD 635 these 'White Croats' were invited into the Byzantine Empire by the Emperor Heraclius in order to expel the Avars, who were overrunning the Adriatic coast. One speculation is

53

that they may have been Slavicised Sarmatians.[42] If correct, this would be a further buttress to the legends about the Sarmatian origins of the Poles.[43]

The departure of the 'White Croats' paved the way for the intensified migration of other Slav groupings. Within a century or so, the Odra basin was occupied by seven or eight such tribes, whose names have somehow survived either in Latin or Slavonic forms. The new settlements were often formed on old sites, using natural defensive features, such as hilltops and islands, and were frequently surrounded by ramparts of wood and earth. The central district, which encompassed both the Island City and the Ślęża Mountain, was taken over by the Ślężanie (Slenzanians). Traces of what was taken to be their original fort were found in 1875 during building excavations near Breslau's Botanical Gardens. Bones and animal remains were discovered around a cluster of pile-supported dwellings beside the riverbank. Whatever the exact date of its foundation, this Slavonic *gród* was established around a castle and was broadly oval in shape, with dimensions of approximately seventy by fifty metres.

The Silesian tribes were not to remain uncontested, however. The first challenge to their supremacy came with the growth of Greater Moravia in the late ninth century. Emerging initially under Prince Mojmír (r.830–46), Moravia briefly became the dominant force in Central Europe. By the reigns of Mojmír's successors – Rastislav and Svatopulk – it had expanded into Bohemia, Slovakia, 'Hungaria' and the lands to the north of the Carpathians.[44] Though destroyed by the inroads of the Magyars, which started in AD 895, Moravia lasted long enough to be Christianised; and it may have left a Christian legacy. The Byzantine mission of Sts Cyril and Methodius had arrived in Moravia from Constantinople in AD 863, sending numerous disciples into the surrounding countries, including one 'Oslaw', who was reportedly sent to Silesia.[45] Slavonic princes from beyond the Carpathians were received in the Moravian capital at Nitra, where they were baptised. Yet the decisive step in the general acceptance of Christianity in these parts was to come not from Constantinople but from Rome. Even so, there is good reason to assume not only that the initial impetus came from the Byzantine mission, but that Byzantine influences could have lingered for some centuries. Certainly, Orthodox and Uniat Christians in the Island City a thousand years later were eager to claim that their forebears, and not the Roman Catholics, were the founding fathers of the faith.[46]

After the collapse of Greater Moravia, the power vacuum was filled partly by the influx of the Magyars and partly by the rise of the Bohemian dynasty of Přemyslids. Bohemia was politically consolidated under Prince Boleslav the Cruel (r.929–72), the brother and murderer of Prince Wenceslas, Bohemia's patron saint. Closely associated with the infant Holy Roman

Empire and hence with Roman Catholicism, Bohemia acted as the natural heir to the Great Moravian state. After the defeat of the Magyars on the Lechfeld in 955, in which Boleslav fought alongside the Holy Roman Emperor, its rule was extended to many former Moravian lands, including Slovakia, Silesia and Moravia proper. The oldest Bohemian archaeological find in the Island City, which consists of coins bearing the legend *Vratsao*, and which has been dated to Prince Boleslav's reign, conforms to this chronology. Yet in all probability the Bohemian presence began two or three decades earlier during the reign of Prince Vratislav I (*r.*915–21), who would not have missed the strategic potential of the Slenzanian castle on the Odra island as a sentinel for his northern border. Prince Vratislav is the likeliest source, in some unrecorded antique form, of the Island City's modern name.

Though Bohemian rule is usually judged to have taken the form of a loose political hegemony, it was nevertheless to have some profound consequences. These included the spread of German influence and the consolidation of Christianity. German influence in Central Europe radiated from the Holy Roman Empire, newly consolidated in the tenth century under the Saxon emperors. Christianisation was pursued in a three-cornered contest between the missionaries of Germany, Byzantium and Rome. While the example of Moravia showed that the Byzantines had been welcomed in reaction to the heavy-handedness of previous German missionaries, the Papacy apparently aimed to reserve the Slavic lands beyond the Carpathians as a sphere of direct papal control. For behind the rhetoric of saving pagan souls lay the very real threat of a Christian crusade and of forcible conversion. As St Methodius himself had once noted, it was 'better to embrace Christianity voluntarily and to retain your independence than to be forcibly baptised in foreign captivity'.[47]

Bohemia had long balanced itself between Latin and Greek Christianity. Yet after the Moravian demise and the subsequent murder of St Wenceslas, German religious influence took a dominant hold, culminating in 973 in the establishment of a bishopric at Prague, subordinated to the metropolitan of Mainz. This step matched political developments. In 950, Prince Boleslav was obliged to recognise imperial suzerainty. Germanisation and Christian-isation marched hand in hand. To become a Christian was the only way to be accepted by one's neighbours as a civilised ruler. But to become a German Christian was a sure way to lose one's independence.

The same conundrum was undoubtedly faced by the next Slavonic ruler to come under pressure. Mieszko I, Prince of the Polanians on the River Warta, held court at Poznań. Only by courting the Pope directly, and by receiving Christianity from Bohemia, could he hope to avoid the unwanted corollary of subordination to the Empire.

As the first documented prince of the Piast line, Mieszko (r.c.963–92) is one of the heroes of popular Polish history. He emerges from the mists of prehistory through his defiance of the German monarch Otto I in the 950s and his marriage in 965 to Dubravka, daughter of Boleslav of Bohemia. Christian baptism was an adjunct to the political alliance. According to the late-medieval annalist Jan Długosz, Mieszko took the new religion very seriously, imposing it on his subjects by force.[48] The German chronicler Thietmar of Merseburg saw him as little more than a glorified heathen.[49] Nonetheless, it is clear that Mieszko had learned from the fate of the martyred St Wenceslas, never thinking to shed his martial virtues. Under his rule the Polanian Principality jealously guarded its independence from the Empire, while engulfing many of the surrounding territories. The conquest of Pomerania was completed, and both Cracow and Silesia incorporated, before 991. *Polska* (Poland), which had started its life as the tribal territory of the Polanians, was turning into something far more powerful. The accession of Cracow was particularly significant for the future. Prior to 990, Cracow, like the Island City, had lain in the Bohemian realm, subjected presumably to the same Celtic, Germanic and Czech influences. Yet from 990 onwards it was to become an essential partner for Polanian Poznań. In due course, it was to form the centre of Małopolska (Lesser Poland), a province whose name reflected its subordination to Mieszko's own homeland, which in turn took the name of Wielkopolska (Greater Poland). Together they formed the lasting core of a united Polish state.

In or around 991, Mieszko's chancellery drew up a document, the *Dagome Iudex*, to inform the Holy See of the boundaries of his extended realm and to give them papal protection:

> [take] . . . all of one civitas, called SCHINESGHE [Gniezno], with all that belongs to it, within boundaries that begin with the seashore, continue by the border of Prussia as far as the place called Rus, then follow the border of Rus as far as CRACCOA [Cracow] going on from CRACCOA as far as the River ODDERE [Odra] right up to the place called ALEMURE. Thence from ALEMURE to the land of MILZE, and from the boundary of the MILZE keep inside the ODDERE, then follow the River ODDERE back to the civitas of SCHINESGHE.[50]

A new regional power had been born. Despite the Slavic brotherhood implied by Mieszko's Bohemian conversion, the rise of the Polanians most immediately threatened the dominance of Bohemia.

Even so, the Bohemian–Polanian alliance prospered for a season, thanks to the person of St Vojtěch. As a member of the ruling Bohemian circle, Vojtěch – who is equally known by his baptismal name of Adalbert – had the highest connections not only in Bohemia but also in Germany and Poland. Yet as Bishop of Prague, he despaired of the murderous political intrigues surrounding him; and he set off on a missionary journey to convert the pagan Prussians. Travelling through the Polanian lands in 997, quite possibly via the Island City, he reached the Pomeranian coast at Gdańsk and took ship for Prussia. Within a short time he was dead, brutally murdered, another martyr of the faith.[51] Given his high status, he gained rapid canonisation, which brought developments of which the Island City would be a major beneficiary.

The year AD 1000 aroused enormous fear and expectations. All over Christendom people believed that it would bring the Day of Christ's Second Coming. The most devout confessed their sins and awaited the end of the world in hope and trembling. In contrast, Prince Mieszko's successor, Bolesław Chrobry ('Boleslas the Brave', r.992–1025), used the occasion to enhance the standing of his nascent kingdom. Lord by now of all the territory between the mountains and the sea, the one thing he lacked was widespread international recognition, and the recently martyred saint was to provide the means for him to obtain it. For Vojtěch Adalbert had once been tutor to the new Emperor, Otto III; and the Emperor, the highest secular authority in Western Christendom, held the power to invite Bolesław into the inner circle of Catholic princes.

Prince Bolesław prepared the ground well. The previous year, he had bought back Vojtěch's body from the Prussians, and had buried it before the high altar of his new church in Gniezno. 'St Wojciech' had been designated patron saint of his adopted country, so that in the spring of 1000, when the young Emperor came to Gniezno on a pilgrimage in the company of his Byzantine Empress, the stage was set for a ceremony of immense significance. The Emperor greeted Bolesław as his 'brother', confirmed the text of the *Dagome Iudex* and announced the elevation of Gniezno to the status of a metropolitan See. In addition, he proclaimed the creation of three bishoprics – one at Cracow in the south, one at Kołobrzeg (Kolberg) in the north and one at 'Vratislavia' in the west. In this way the Island City entered the historical record at the same moment that 'Polonia' entered the recognised community of Christian principalities.

All that remained was the elevation of a united Poland to the rank of a kingdom. In this too the Emperor was obliging. 'It would be unworthy to honour such an important and powerful man as just another prince, duke or count,' he said, 'rather, he must be raised to a royal throne and adorned with a crown.'[52] With this, Otto III placed his own crown on Bolesław's head and handed him a nail from the True Cross and the lance of St Maurice. In return he received a reliquary containing the arm of St Adalbert. Bolesław had to wait twenty-five years to receive his own royal crown. It was finally granted by Pope John XIX in the final year of his reign.

Following its establishment, the bishopric of Vratislavia included most of the later province of Silesia, with the exception of some south-eastern districts from Kłodzko (Glatz) to Pszczyna (Pless), which were left in the Moravian bishopric of Olomouc. It coincided with seventeen secular administrative areas, each run by a castellan. In some places, as at Otmuchów (Ottmachau), the Bishop of Vratislavia combined his spiritual role with the temporal one of castellan.

In the feudal order of AD 1000, the rule of the Bishop was felt far more immediately than that of the Bishop's lord, the King. The average subject's loyalty to the King of Poland came at the end of a long list of much more urgent obligations – to his family, to his lord, to his Bishop and to his tribe. One can hardly speak of a Polish 'state' in the modern sense, only of a Polish *patrimonium* and the obedience of its subjects. The bland statement that 'Silesia became part of Piast Poland in the late tenth century' requires some qualification. Medieval kingship was precarious and impermanent. Its authority often extended only sporadically beyond the confines of the court and the heartland. The Central European 'states' of the early medieval period – Greater Moravia, Bohemia and Piast Poland among them – waxed and waned according to their military strengths, their geography, their internal quarrels, their dynastic fortunes and the random irruptions of nomads. In the event, the Piast hold on Silesia was to prove hardly less transient than that of its predecessors. Indeed, the transience of political rule was destined to be one of the principal characteristics of the Island City's history.

Naturally, given the later turbulence, the ethnic origin of the first Vratislavians has exercised many minds. Yet archaeology is notoriously unable to attach national labels to material cultures that leave so few ethnic clues. Nevertheless, the archaeological cultures of Silesia have all been recruited at one time or another, and usually on the most tenuous of evidence, as witnesses to the struggles of German and Polish 'national' archaeology. Thus the Lusatian Culture has been variously described as 'pre-Slav', Germanic and 'Illyrian'[53] and was once even considered to be Thracian,[54] while the Venedian Culture is simultaneously ascribed 'East Germanic' and 'proto-Slavic' characteristics. Yet a simplistic bipolar approach, where Germanic battles Slavic, cannot begin to describe the complexity of Silesia's prehistory. Other elements were always present and, in some cases, dominant. Late Przeworsk culture, for example, is considered to have had a pronounced Sarmatian character,[55] whilst the Iron Age cultures betray a more or less insistent Celtic flavour. Perhaps, most typically, the later Dobrodzień Culture displays such a rich mixture of disparate cultural signatures that the adjectives 'Germanic' and 'Slavic' are but two among many.

The contrast between the evolutionary view of Silesian history and the view of the Polish Autochthonous School is striking. If one assumes, as adherents of the latter do, that from 2500 BC onwards Silesia was continuously inhabited by right of sole possession by proto-Slavs and proto-Poles, then every event of prehistoric times has to be trimmed to suit the basic assumption. Hence, at some unidentified time, the proto-Slavs are magically transformed into real Slavs. A 'mist of secrecy' is often conveniently said to cover the period of transformation. After that, the Slavs are said to be Poles-in-the-making, and all non-Slavs or non-Poles are explained away as 'predators and intruders'. The Greater Moravians of the ninth century and the Bohemians of the tenth century had no right to be in Silesia. Mieszko I, in contrast, who takes over in 990, is simply recovering his own. When the Czechs do the same sort of thing in 1037–50, or on a more permanent basis in the fourteenth century, the idea that they too were simply recovering their previous losses in unthinkable.

Happily, the latest generation of academics has rejected the inflexible positions of their predecessors. As a Vratislavian specialist has recently stated, the old Polish-German confrontations were not so much academic discussions as a 'form of political and ideological warfare'. 'The real point is that it is only in the early medieval period that proof can be found to confirm the presence of a Slavonic population in the Polish lands.'[56]

One may conclude that the ethnic labelling of prehistoric cultures is often unnecessary, unhelpful and ultimately meaningless. Modern studies show that cultures can migrate without the large-scale migration of people. There is no need to believe either in the ethnic purity of prehistoric communities or in the fiction of 'national territorial rights', which supposedly reserved one piece of land for the eternal and exclusive use of one nation. The old German idea of *Blut und Boden* – the eternal bond of Blood and Soil – is surely redundant. The most convincing interpretation holds that prehistoric peoples constantly intermingled, thereby creating a succession of multi-layered hybrid cultures. The old fixed nationalist archetypes must be rejected in favour of a shifting, multicultural kaleidoscope.

The early chroniclers and historians throw little light on the issue of ethnicity. Tacitus, for example, deemed that the Venedians were 'to be classed as Germans, for they have settled houses, carry shields and are fond of travelling'.[57] While this statement makes a valid comparison to the largely nomadic Sarmatian peoples, it does little to aid a more precise identification. On this basis, all non-Roman Europeans, with the exception of the nomads, would have been classed as Germans!

One must be equally alert to the danger of reading history backwards and of endowing West Slavs of the tenth century with the same degree of particularity that applies today. Very little is known in detail about, for example, the pre-literate phase of the Slavic languages. But it stands to reason that the degree of divergence between, say, Czech, Polish, Lusatian and Pomeranian was much narrower than it became in later centuries. Indeed, there is almost no evidence one way or the other to indicate whether Czech or Polish would have diverged sufficiently by AD 1000 to be regarded as separate languages. In all probability, the Slenzanian dialect of Vratislavia would have been as close to the Bohemian dialect of Prague as to the Polanian dialect of Poznań. If, and when, Bishop Vojtěch stopped over in the Island City, he would have had less difficulty in making himself understood than a contemporary Czech tourist in Wrocław.

What the early chroniclers *do* make clear, however, is that Silesia, like all points on the European Plain, lay open to the periodic surges of mass migration. It may have been German historians who invented the expressive term *Völkerwanderung*, but the wanderings applied just as much to the Celts, to the Slavs and to others as to the Germanics. Though the first recognisably Slavic migrants may have been entering a comparatively empty land, it is sensible to assume some continuity of occupation in the Island City itself. The descendants of those mid-first-millennium citizens, whose ancestry was already richly varied, would have been overlain in the following centuries by successive waves of newcomers. By the time of the City's cession to Mieszko's principality in the late tenth century, the residents of Vratislavia – like most of Europe's inhabitants – would, in the last analysis, have been largely 'alien, mongrel immigrants'.[58]

TWO

Wrotizla between the Polish, Czech and German Crowns, 1000–1335

Local histories are usually written with scant regard to the wider political framework within which a particular city or district developed. Yet the wider framework is one of the key determinants. The early history of Silesia and its capital city is inseparable from the fluctuating three-sided arena where the Polish Piasts, the Czech Přemyslids and the German Emperors competed.

In this regard, the moment that the Island City first reached the historical record is quite telling. In the spring of AD 1000, in the newly built basilica at Gniezno, a Polish King and a German Emperor presided over the consecration of the bones of a Czech martyr. A papal bull was read, decreeing the diocesan structure of the new Polish See, with its bishoprics at Cracow, Kołobrzeg (Kolberg) and Wrotizla:

> With no further ado he [Otto III] made an archdiocese there [at Gniezno], which I do hope was legal, since he had no consent for it from the actual diocesan superior for all this region [Archbishop of Magdeburg], but he gave it over anyway to Radim [Gaudentius], the martyr's brother, subjecting to him Reinbern, bishop of the church in Salsa Colberg, Poppo in Cracua and John in Wrotizla. But Unger of Posnania was left out of the arrangement; and there [at Gniezno] an altar was made, wherein he laid with all honour the relics of the saint.[1]

The Island City was immortalised as *Wrotizla* in a chronicle account of the event, written in late 1013 by Bishop Thietmar of Merseburg. By the turn of the first millennium, it had belonged to Bolesław's realm for a decade. That first Polish kingdom bore remarkable territorial similarities to its successor at the turn of the second millennium. In addition to the heartland of Wielkopolska, both states incorporated Pomerania, Mazovia, Małopolska and Silesia, and broadly occupied the territory between the Baltic and the Carpathians, the Odra and the Bug. Both, too, were bordered by a unified Germany to the west, by the Bohemian lands to the south and by the fragmented lands of the Balts and the eastern Slavs to the north and east.

Yet such geographical coincidences signify little. Only a few years on either side of AD 1000 the map would have shown a very different picture. The Piast realm, like most medieval polities, was in a state of constant flux. Its borders changed from year to year as the military power of the ruler waxed and waned. Bolesław Chrobry is said to have delineated Polish territory by driving iron stakes into both the River Saale near Halle and the Dnieper at Kiev. But this is mere literary bravura. Only a decade earlier, in 990, Silesia had belonged to the Bohemian crown, to which it would return in 1039. Bolesław himself raided deep into Saxony and even managed in 1003 to take temporary control of Prague. In those days there was no such thing as a national territory.

Much that is known about Piast Silesia derives from the Cracovian chronicler and historian Jan Długosz, or 'Longinus' (1415–80). Although many other earlier chroniclers, such as the Anonymous Gaul (d.1116), made vital contributions, Długosz paid special attention to Silesia, because he saw it as part of Poland's lost inheritance. Moreover, as a great collector of charters, scrolls and legal documents, he had unrivalled access to original sources. He was not infallible. But it is possible that he was able to draw on extensive material from a chronicle, or chronicles, since lost.[2]

The ecclesiastical See of Gniezno proved to be far more durable than Bolesław Chrobry's kingdom. The Polish Primacy, as established *de facto* in 1000, has enjoyed an almost continuous existence to the present day. The diocesan structure remained intact until the nineteenth century, and was restored as soon as Poland regained her independence in 1918. The bishopric of 'Wrotizla' retained its place within the Polish See until 1821, thereby upholding the ecclesiastical link with Poland long after the political link had been broken. It returned to the Polish fold after the Second World War.

The problems of feudal fealty often compounded territorial insecurities. The political structure of medieval Europe consisted in theory of a pyramid of loyalties and duties, running from the peasantry at the bottom, through the nobility, clergy and princes, to the crowned monarchs, Emperor and Pope at the top. Yet feudal homage was valid only in so far as claims could be enforced. Therefore, Polish rulers, who enjoyed comparative isolation both from Rome and from the imperial court, were often free to play with the rules to suit themselves. Like their counterparts in England at the other end of the continent, they paid homage to Pope or Emperor only when obliged to do so or when seeking some specific benefit. The exact relationship of Piast Poland to the Empire was frequently disputed at the time and has since been frequently disputed by historians. In reality, it was infinitely malleable, lurching from decade to decade between partnership, subservience and independence.

The formal title of the earliest Piasts is equally open to misunderstanding. Their traditional designation as *Dux*, or Duke, is sometimes taken to correspond with a rank in the feudal hierarchy, which implies subordination to the Emperor. Yet it might just as well be interpreted as 'commander' or 'war-leader'. No contemporary documents explain it. It must remain appropriately ambiguous.

Hence, though Bolesław I Chrobry underwent a crowning ceremony at Gniezno in AD 1000, he had to wait some twenty-five years for an official coronation that was approved by the Pope and possibly by the Emperor. In 1032, his successor, Mieszko II (r.1025–34), paid homage to the Emperor Conrad II at Merseburg, thereby – at least theoretically – making Poland a fief of the Empire. In 1076, Bolesław II Szczodry (the Bold, r.1058–79) had himself independently crowned King of Poland, exploiting Emperor Henry IV's absence at Canossa.

The ill-defined nature of Poland's relations with the Empire encouraged numerous outbreaks of warfare, which inevitably thrust Silesia into the frontline. Imperial incursions in 1005 devastated both Głogów (Glogau) and Wrotizla, while the invasion of 1109 foundered on the resistance of those two same towns. Głogów held off a siege, while Wrotizla witnessed the defeat of the imperial and Bohemian forces on the east bank of the Odra. Jan Długosz swelled with pride at the victory of Bolesław III Krzywousty (the Wry-Mouth, r.1102–38) over the Emperor Henry V:

Bolesław has assembled as large a force as he can, and makes it appear larger than it is by swelling its ranks with peasants. With this he sets off after the Emperor in a forced march that continues day and night. When he has nearly reached the Emperor's camp a mile from [the city], he draws up in a line of battle, harangues his troops to bolster their courage and make them eager for the fray, and attacks. The two armies close with tremendous shouts. It is morning, and the battle continues until the afternoon. Many fall, and there are times when the Poles almost think of running, but Bolesław is always there where the need is great, encouraging and fighting alongside his men. When the battle is at its height, Bolesław sends in the Saxon unit he has been holding in reserve. This charges one wing of the Emperor's line, crumples it and makes an opening for the others to get in among the enemy, who, realising what is happening, take fright. Seeing his troops wavering, the Emperor himself turns to escape, first throwing away the imperial insignia lest these betray him. The battle then becomes a slaughter. The Germans run in all directions. Many are caught and brought to Bolesław, who, as always, is considerate and grants them their lives. There are so many corpses on the battlefield that every dog for miles around is attracted and it becomes unsafe to walk anywhere near except in a largish group.[3]

The site of the battle has been known ever since as Psie Pole (Hundsfeld), 'The Field of Dogs'.[4] Sceptics think that Długosz turned a skirmish into a great battle. Some even dispute that the battle took place at all.

Though imperial interest in Silesia was temporarily dampened, the ambitions of the Bohemians were far from thwarted. Silesia became the touchstone of Polish-Bohemian relations and was invaded at the slightest sign of Polish weakness. So it became Bohemian once again between 1039 and 1054, being returned to Poland at the Peace of Quedlinburg in exchange for an annual tribute. Subsequent Bohemian invasions in 1062, 1093 and 1133 were prompted by Polish lapses in payment.

Poland's Piast monarchy was constantly disturbed by internal dissension. A weak ruler, the death of an heir or the emergence of rival claimants was enough to provoke civil war. The first of several such episodes occurred in the 1030s during the last years of Mieszko II. The King's apparent insanity and squabbles with the Empire led to a temporary collapse of the monarchy and to a pagan revolt, which shook the nascent ecclesiastical organisation to its foundations. This was to be the Bohemians' best opportunity. The invasion of Břetislav I took them as far as Gniezno, where, as legend has it, on starting to loot the churches they were miraculously struck blind and unable to capture the relics of St Adalbert. During the fifteen-year Bohemian occupation of Silesia, the Bishop of Wrotizla seems to have taken refuge at Smogorzów (Schmograu) and later at Ryczyn (Ritschen), which had remained in Polish hands.

In 1037, the royal seat of Poland was moved from Gniezno to Cracow. Nothing much changed in the way that Wrotizla was governed. But Cracow was more distant than Gniezno, and Małopolska had different priorities from Wielkopolska. Cracow lay less in the shadow of the Empire, and its southern neighbour was not Bohemia but Hungary. Over the years, therefore, Silesia's political predicament experienced some subtle shifts. One of these could be found in the growing tendency to escape from royal control. Another, with some delay, was the eventual reassertion of Silesia's links with Bohemia.

Notwithstanding the efforts of Kazimierz Odnowiciel (the Restorer, r.1034–58), the unity of the Piast realm came under threat once again in the late eleventh century. In 1093, the machinations of a royal palatine, Sieciech of Cracow, provoked a rising, which was based in Wrotizla and led by the

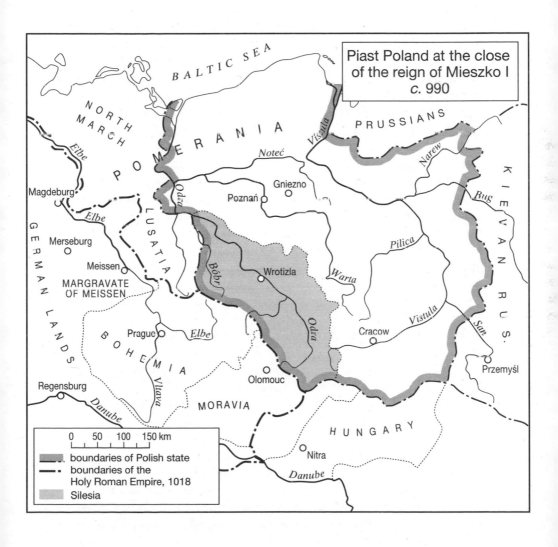

Piast Poland at the close
of the reign of Mieszko I
c. 990

BALTIC SEA

NORTH
MARCH

POMERANIA

PRUSSIANS

Elbe

Magdeburg

Elbe

LUSATIA

Noteć

Vistula

Narew

Gniezno

Poznań

Bug

K
I
E
V
A
N

R
U
S.

Merseburg

Meissen

MARGRAVATE
OF MEISSEN

Bóbr

Wrotizla

Pilica

Warta

G
E
R
M
A
N

L
A
N
D
S

B
O
H
E
M
I
A

Prague

Elbe

Odra

Cracow

Vistula

San

Olomouc

Przemyśl

Regensburg

Vltava

Danube

MORAVIA

H U N G A R Y

Nitra

Danube

0   50   100   150 km

boundaries of Polish state
boundaries of the
Holy Roman Empire, 1018
Silesia

castellan of the city, Magnus. The revolt aimed to replace the ruler King Władysław I Herman with his illegitimate son, Zbigniew, but it foundered when the King sent a force to subdue it:

> Władysław . . . assembles a force and . . . advances on [the town] . . . All those living in the outskirts compete to proclaim their loyalty, and, when he reaches the city itself, he is met by a procession of clergy, monks and citizens, headed by the Bishop . . . and is conducted into the city with all due respect. The castle gates stand open and Magnus and his knights receive the Prince humbly and with all due deference.[5]

Despite Wrotizla's unwillingness to fight, the first stirrings of regional particularism had surfaced. They were to be greatly accelerated in Bolesław III's testament of 1138.

The role played by Magnus signalled the emergence of a powerful class of magnates, who were rising to provincial and then national prominence through the support of old and wealthy clans. Scholars have speculated as to whether Magnus belonged to the Powała clan or to the Turzynitas, with whom St Stanisław, Bishop of Cracow, was connected. One has linked him to King Harold III of England. But his authority as '*comes Vratislaviae*' was self-evident. So, too, was the crucial factor of royal favour. Magnus resurfaces in the first decade of the twelfth century as *comes* (count) of Mazovia. Other magnatial clans who held sway in Silesia were the Łabędź, to which the castellan of Wrotizla Peter Wlast belonged, and the Odrowąż, from whom Saints Jacek and Czesław were descended. Many of them had links with Moravia. The Rawita clan is especially interesting in that it started off as Czech and ended up as Polish.

The reign of Bolesław 'the Wry-Mouth' supplied the lull before a very long storm. It was initially dominated by the repeated intrigues of the King's exiled brother Zbigniew, which dragged the country into frequent contests with Bohemia and the Empire. But the victory at Psie Pole assured Polish independence for a quarter of a century, and during that time the King could concentrate on the suppression and conversion of the pagan tribes of Pomerania. By the end of his reign, Poland's relations with Bohemia were effectively regulated. At the 'Whitsun Peace of Kłodzko' (Glatz) in 1137, the common border was settled. Silesia's southern and western frontier became one of the most stable in Europe.

The major innovation of Bolesław's reign – the seniority system – was to be less durable. According to Długosz,[6] it had first been mooted in 1097 as a means of satisfying the ambitions of quarrelling heirs. Indeed, the idea was an ancient one, having been relatively widespread among pre-Christian societies. The Árpáds of Hungary, for example, had practised seniority succession prior to the accession of King Stephen in AD 1000. The particular system devised by Bolesław, however, was to be a compromise between primogeniture and equal distribution among all male heirs. It was designed to satisfy individual ambitions, while maintaining the essential integrity of the kingdom. It provided that Wielkopolska, Mazovia and Sandomierz were to be held in hereditary domain by each of the King's younger sons, while the senior son was to receive Małopolska, Silesia and Pomerania and was to rule as Grand Prince. Despite its good intentions, this system was to foster the very rivalries and jealousies that it sought to assuage. As a result, it ushered in the period that is generally known as the 'Age of Fragmentation'. In a little over 150 years Piast Poland had effectively come full-circle.

The centrifugal forces started to multiply soon after Bolesław's death. The senior son, Władysław (later 'the Exile'), clashed with his brothers. By 1146 he had been forced out in the so-called 'Revolt of the Juniors'. His presence at the German court once again focused imperial attentions on Poland, and imperial offensives in 1146, 1152 and 1157 eventually obliged Bolesław IV Kędzierzawy (the Curly), the Exile's brother, to recognise the Emperor's overlordship. Yet turbulence persisted. The next Piast senior, Mieszko III Stary (the Old, r.1173–7, 1194–1202), sought to strengthen his position vis-à-vis his rivals, but only provoked his own expulsion. His return to the throne, following the seventeen-year reign of a younger brother, Kazimierz Sprawiedliwy (the Just), caused yet more internecine conflict. By the time of Mieszko's death the seniority system was virtually defunct. The Piast princes had little desire for the resurrection of a unified crown, and a further round of territorial splintering ensued.

In the early part of these vicissitudes Silesia remained intact. But it was divided between Władysław's sons following the imperial invasion of 1157: Bolesław I Wysoki (the Tall) became Duke of Wrotizla, and Mieszko Plątonogi (the Tangle-Footed) took the neighbouring Duchy of Opole (Oppeln). However, their incessant infighting soon caused them too to be expelled and Emperor Frederick I forced a second submission in 1163 to re-install his protégés. Such were the circumstances in which the separate line of Silesian Piasts was born. In the eyes of some German historians, this was also the moment when Silesia was judged to have become a separate imperial duchy, thereby ending its status as an integral province of Poland. Needless to say, few Polish historians would agree (see pages 89–90).

Counting from Władysław the Exile, eleven Piast princes were to rule in Wrotizla in the two centuries between 1138 and 1335. They claimed the right to rule all of Silesia, even when the territory of the Duchy of Wrotizla shrank. They did not avoid the usual family feuds, and they were repeatedly disturbed by endless fighting over seniority. Yet their line displayed remarkable persistence and continuity. For eight generations, the ducal palace in Wrotizla passed from father to son or, on three occasions, from the ruling prince to his brother. The average length of tenure was nearly eighteen years.

Several of these Silesian Piasts were especially long-lived and influential. Bolesław the Tall (r.1163–1201), who had served as a youthful knight in Ruthenia and Italy, dominated the last decades of the twelfth century. His son, Henryk I Brodaty (the Bearded, r.1201–38), ruled for nearly forty years and was married to the future St Jadwiga (see below). He was the founder of the so-called 'Henrician Monarchy', which controlled most parts of Poland and formed a reunited kingdom in all but name. His great-great-grandson, Henryk IV Probus (the Righteous, r.1267–90), led the last attempt by the Silesian Piasts to win control of the whole of Poland. Having formed a broad coalition of princes that conquered Cracow in 1288, he was negotiating with the Pope to recognise his royal title when he was felled in his prime by poison. His body was buried in his own foundation, the Church of the Holy Cross in Wrotizla, and remained there in a magnificent sarcophagus until disinterred by the Nazis 650 years later for the purposes of 'racial measurement' in the Institute of Anthropology. No decision about the true extent of Probus's 'Germanity' had been reached before the Institute and all its contents were pulverised by the Soviet bombardment in 1945.

Several other dukes enjoyed less glorious reputations. Henryk II Pobożny (the Pious, r.1238–41) was killed on 9 April 1241 in the great victory of the Mongol Horde at Legnica (Liegnitz). His head was carried off on a Mongol lance and his mother was forced to identify the mangled corpse by his six toes. Bolesław Łysy (the Bald, r.1241–66) was a troublemaker, a chief of robber barons. He is remembered in Polish history as the author of a shameful deal in 1249, which ceded the territory of Lubusz to the Brandenburgers, thereby opening the gateway for German expansion. The heirless Henryk VI (r.1311–35) formally ceded the Duchy of Wrotizla to the King of Bohemia in 1327, reserving for himself the lifetime governorship. Though other Piast princes continued to hold various Silesian duchies, he was the last Piast of the Vratislavian line.

Silesia mirrored the wider scene during Poland's 'Age of Fragmentation'. Over the decades, the principle of equal male inheritance was introduced and inexorably divided the province into ever-smaller territorial units. At the death of Duke Henryk II of Wrotizla in 1241, there were two Silesian duchies, Wrotizla and Opole; a generation later there were four. By 1289 there were nine, from north to south: Głogów, Żagań (Sagan), Legnica, Jawor-Lwówek (Jauer-Löwenberg), Wrotizla, Opole, Koźle-Bytom (Cosel-Beuthen), Racibórz (Ratibor) and Cieszyn-Oświęcim (Teschen-Auschwitz).

Two decades after that, less than a century after the start of the process, the number had reached eighteen, later reduced to seventeen. Seeing such chronic instability, no one would have predicted that the Silesian Piasts were to outlive their senior Polish cousins by some 300 years.

The Mongol invasion of April 1241 served as a brief distraction from the Piasts' dynastic navel-gazing. To contemporary Christians, the Mongols of Batu Khan were the 'horsemen of the apocalypse', the 'soldiers of the Antichrist'. Having razed Kiev and besieged Cracow, they advanced on Silesia. Their practice was to send raiding parties in advance to test the strength of the forces ranged against them – a wise strategy, as Mongol armies carried wives, children, supplies and booty with them in an extended caravan. Even so, their reputation for brutality and destruction preceded them and they revelled in it. Wrotizla prepared for Armageddon:

> Leaving Cracow, Batu moves off towards [Wrotizla]. Finding the bridges destroyed, the Tatars, who, if they cannot ford a river, swim across it, do just that . . . [The Duke of Opole] attacks one isolated Tatar unit . . . but when the rest of the Tatar army comes up, he escapes to Legnica . . . The Tatars move swiftly . . . They find the town deserted, for its inhabitants have all fled with their treasures and provisions, and the knights have removed whatever was left into the castle, before setting fire to the town in order to deprive the Tatars of loot and shelter. The Tatars lay siege to the castle: during the siege Czesław, the Dominican prior of the priory of St Wojciech, a Pole, saves the castle with his tears and prayers: for a pillar of fire appears above his head and illuminates the whole city with an indescribable brightness. This so frightens the Tatars, that they abandon the siege and withdraw.[7]

Despite the miraculous efforts of Czesław, the Mongol Horde had overrun the left-bank suburbs. It then rode off to the west, leaving the smouldering ruins behind. Outside Legnica, Henryk II prepared his hastily assembled coalition of Polish, Silesian and Teutonic knights to face the invaders. But when the Duke of Opole fled with his retinue in the thick of the battle, the end result was no longer in doubt. Henryk himself is said to have muttered *'Gorze się nam stało'* ('Now we have had it'). His men were slaughtered and he was decapitated, his head being brought before the commander as proof of victory. The Mongols departed as rapidly as they had arrived. Silesia's nobility lay dead; its capital had been destroyed.

The battle of Legnica offers one of those rare moments where local events assume a European, not to say world-historical, perspective. For the Mongols, having galloped victoriously from Central Asia to Central Europe, would clearly have been capable of pressing on westwards. It has been suggested that this was only prevented by the death of the Khakhan Ogatai, which obliged all the lesser Khans to return to Karakorum to elect a new supreme leader.[8] One is entitled to wonder whether their decision to return home via the Danube Basin did not save nascent 'Western Civilisation' from extinction. (There is a wonderful problem here for the devotees of 'counter-factual' history.) However, there is no evidence that the Mongols had anything more in mind than delivering a devastating blow to the rulers of Poland and Hungary and preventing them from interfering in the Mongol conquests further east.

Descriptions of the battle contain much local interest. Apart from the princes and their retinues, the Christian combatants included *crucesignati*, or 'crusaders' (probably Knights Hospitallers), volunteer goldminers from Złotoryja (Goldberg) and a large contingent of 'Vratislavian barons'. The slaughter that followed the defeat was terrible. For example, accounts of local provenance state that one single clan, which was based at the manor of Strachowice near Wrotizla, lost no fewer than fourteen of its knights. The family, which was descended from the sole male survivor of that clan, and which from 1285 would take the name of von Strachwitz, continued to play a conspicuous role in Lower Silesian society for the next 700 years.[9]

The course of the campaign also contains much to excite military historians. The outcome at Legnica seems to have been decided principally by the supremacy of Tatar archers over Polish crossbowmen. Considerable speculation surrounds St Czesław's alleged deployment at Wrotizla of a miraculous 'fireball'. It centres on the possibility that the Mongols could have imported a consignment of 'Greek fire', which then exploded prematurely. According to Długosz, they were not above using a dastardly concoction of chemistry and witchcraft at Legnica:

> Among the Tatar standards is a huge one with a giant X painted on it. It is topped by an ugly black head with a chin covered in hair. As the Tatars withdraw some hundred paces, the bearer of this standard begins violently shaking the great head, from which there suddenly bursts a cloud with a foul smell that envelops the Poles and makes them all but faint, so that they are incapable of fighting. We know that in their wars, the Tatars have always used the arts of divination and witchcraft . . . Seeing that the all but victorious Poles are daunted by the cloud and the foul smell, the Tatars raise a great shout and return to the fray, scattering the Polish ranks that have hitherto held firm, and a huge slaughter ensues.[10]

Taken together, St Czesław's 'fireball' and the secret weapon used at Legnica suggest that the Silesians may have been the first Westerners to witness, experience and suffer the consequences of the military use of gunpowder.

The so-called 'Vinland Map' was one indirect consequence of the Mongol invasion. Still the subject of intense academic controversy, it is thought to have been drawn around 1440, and was incorporated into the encyclopaedic *Speculum majus* of Vincent of Beauvais. It constituted the first cartographic attempt to show the extent of the then known world. With an oversized Europe at its centre, the map shows the Japanese islands to the east and a truncated Africa to the south. Most notably, however, it shows the island of 'Vinland' to the far west, under the heading 'discovered by Bjarne and Leif in company' – evidence, if one accepts the map's validity, of the Viking discovery of the New World. Much of the material for the map was gleaned from the Carpini diplomatic mission to the Mongols of the 1240s, which began its work in the Silesian capital. Accordingly, though the map itself was drawn up some two centuries later, it shows the names of only two European cities: Rome and 'Breslauia' – Wrotizla.[11]

Closer to home, the Mongol invasion had more immediate repercussions. It spelt the end of the Henrician monarchy and, with that, of Silesia's effective control of Poland. But it also signalled the strengthening of a growing factor in Silesian politics – Germanic settlement.

*

The reassertion of Bohemian influence was an essential aspect of the development of Silesia and Wrotizla. Bohemia, of course, had played a more or less constant role in Silesian affairs throughout the Piast period, mostly as a dependency of the Empire and as a potential beneficiary of imperial generosity. In this way, it gained partial or temporary control over Silesia a number of times, only to find its long-term ambitions for the province blocked by the Polish loyalties of the Silesian nobility and by the distrust of the imperial establishment. By the mid-thirteenth century, therefore, the tactics were changing. In place of the earlier heavy-handed diplomacy, the new goal was to exploit the widening dissensions between the lesser Piast princes, to court the vulnerable and to detach Silesia by stealth.

Otakar II, King of Bohemia and Margrave of Moravia from 1253, was the main architect of this tactical shift. One of his first campaigns was conducted in Prussia in 1255, where he helped the Teutonic Knights anchor their Prussian conquest to the Baltic. They named their fortress and town 'Königsberg' in his honour, though, as Długosz sourly noted, he was not their king. Otakar was the rising star of the Central European firmament. After securing a collection of territories that stretched from the Silesian border to the Adriatic, he wooed his Silesian neighbours. He made Władysław (younger brother of Henryk III of Wrotizla) Archbishop of Salzburg, while educating the future Duke Henryk IV at his court in

Prague. His guardianship of the young duke was rewarded by his appointment as Henryk's heir and by the promise of assistance in his campaigns against the Austrian forces of Rudolf von Habsburg.[12] Henryk in turn profited from the demise of his mentor in 1278 by adding the district of Kłodzko to his duchy.

The developing 'special relationship' between Silesia and Bohemia survived the death of Otakar. It received something of a setback when, twelve years later, Henryk IV broke faith with Otakar's successor, Václav II, to whom the Duchy of Wrotizla had been promised, by preferring the claims of the Duke of Głogów. Václav avenged himself by retaking Kłodzko. But Otakar's wooing was already bearing fruit. In 1289 Kazimierz II of Koźle-Bytom became the first Silesian prince to recognise Bohemian overlordship. Eleven years after that, Václav succeeded in having himself crowned King of Poland in Gniezno, as Wacław I.

The striking success of the Bohemians was quickly undermined by the King's premature death in 1305 and by the murder a year later of his sixteen-year-old successor, Václav III (Wacław II of Poland). This dynastic misfortune undoubtedly dampened the enthusiasm of the Silesian dukes for the Bohemian connection. But the succession in Prague, in 1310, of the influential House of Luxemburg revived the rationale of the alignment, while the resurgence of a reunited Polish realm gave it redoubled urgency.

Throughout the thirteenth century the lives and times of the Dukes of Wrotizla supplied a rich fund of intrigue and adventure. In 1213, the cathedral received a golden crown from the testament of Queen Gertrude of Hungary, who was the sister of St Jadwiga and who had been foully murdered by one of her husband's barons. Gertrude was also the mother of St Elizabeth of Thuringia, sometime 'Princess of the Wartburg'; and it was through these family connections that the ruling circle in Wrotizla was put in touch with the world of German courtly love. Queen Gertrude's crown was melted down to make a golden chalice. Later, in 1238, when Duke Henryk the Bearded died, he and his wife, St Jadwiga, had been living separate, celibate lives for thirty years. At his burial at Trzebnica (Trebnitz), it was said, 'Jadwiga is the only woman there to refuse him the last honours, and whose eyes remain dry.'[13]

Ten years after that, the first of several wars broke out among members of the ducal family. Hiring a force of Saxon mercenaries, Bolesław of Legnica declared war on his brother Henryk III of Wrotizla and invaded the duchy. At Środa (Neumarkt), 500 men and women, who had taken refuge in the church, were burned alive. Although Wrotizla had only recently been refounded after the Mongol invasion, it successfully withstood a three-month siege.

In 1254, Duke Henryk III's other brother, Conrad, abandoned his career in the Church and attacked Wrotizla in conjunction with his Polish in-laws from Poznań and Kalisz. They avoided the city, but wreaked havoc on the villages around Oleśnica (Oels) and, finding a ford across the Odra only half a kilometre from Wrotizla, carried off a huge quantity of cattle unimpeded. Duke Henryk was ambushed, put under arrest and forced to accept a redivision of the brothers' inheritances.

The same feud was still going on twenty-three years later, with a new generation of dukes eagerly joining the fray. War broke out between Legnica and Wrotizla after Duke Henryk was taken hostage once again, after being dragged from his bed by his brother's men. This time both sides called in allies – Legnica from Germany and Wrotizla from Poland – and a bloody battle between them ended in stalemate. The citizens of Wrotizla appealed to Otakar of Bohemia, who mediated a settlement, at the cost of taking the town and castle of Kłodzko for himself.

The death of Henryk IV Probus in 1290 illustrates the extreme fragility of medieval political fortunes. The Duke, who had returned to Wrotizla to die, had just achieved his greatest success by winning Cracow and had only missed seizing his chief rival as future King of Poland after Łokietek had escaped in the guise of a Franciscan friar. His death, in Wrotizla, started yet another round of confused conflict punctuated with a surfeit of Henries. One group of citizens supported Conrad of Głogow's son Henryk, the designated heir, while another group supported Conrad's nephew, Henryk of Legnica. The Legnician proved stronger, and forced a surrender. Whereon, even Długosz lost the thread. 'Conrad is afraid of being imprisoned', he wrote, 'and leaves the city by one gate as Henryk enters by another at the head of the knights and townspeople.'[14] No matter that in reality Conrad was already long dead. It is comforting to find that famous chroniclers, no less than modern historians, can sometimes be defeated by the medieval labyrinth.

To no one's surprise, the Legnician victory was short-lived. The Glogovian party took their revenge with the help of a young man called Lutek, whom the new Duke took into his service even though he had earlier put Lutek's father to death. The blow fell when the Duke was bathing by the river near Wrotizla castle:

Lutek's men surround the Duke's tent . . . and drag him naked from his bath . . . The assailants set him on a horse and make him ride for a day and a night to Sadowel, where he is handed over to [his rival], who promptly casts him into the dungeons, chained in an iron cage with only two tiny openings, one through which he can breathe and be fed, the other through which he can empty his belly. In this cage, he can neither sit, stand or lie; his shoulders and thighs suppurate and his body is covered in vermin . . . At the end of six months, seeing that no effort is being made to effect his release, he makes a pact . . .[15]

The final fragmentation of the Duchy of Wrotizla therefore came about through an amicable agreement. Rather than fight each other, the three sons of the late Duke decided to create three separate duchies for themselves and to arrange for financial compensation against the resultant inequalities. One of them took Brzeg (Brieg) and a payment of 80,000 marks, the second Legnica at the cost of 32,000 marks and the third, who was able to borrow 48,000 marks from his knights and burghers, emerged with the top prize and the title of Duke Henryk VI of Wrotizla.

At this juncture, it is essential to realise that the centre of gravity of Poland's interests was moving to the north and east. Two developments were responsible. In the north, the military order of the Teutonic Knights had founded a dynamic new state, which was steadily becoming the premier force on the Baltic coast. In 1308, the Knights captured Gdańsk (Danzig), robbing Poland of its principal seaport and giving notice of a major struggle to come. In the east, the Grand Duchy of Lithuania, the last great pagan country of Europe, was engaging in a dramatic spurt of massive expansion. Starting from their native homeland on the Niemen, and exploiting the chaos caused by the Mongol invasions, the Lithuanians were busily absorbing the Ruthenian principalities that separated Poland from Muscovy. Mińsk and Kiev would both enter a Lithuanian realm that was rapidly filling the enormous space between the Baltic and the Black Sea. The Polish kings could hardly stand idly by. Once Władysław I Łokietek (the Elbow-High, r.1320–33) had restored a strong Poland, the next monarch, Kazimierz Wielki (Casimir the Great, r.1333–70), would face a strategic choice of capital importance – to re-enter the old arena of competition with Bohemia and the Empire or to concentrate on the new challenges posed by the Teutonic State and by Lithuania. He chose the latter. So the Poles went east. It was a natural corollary that Polish power in the west would wane. Soon after his accession, Kazimierz was to abandon Silesia as a deliberate act of policy.

The fate of two cities embodied the implications of this new constellation. The Polish Piasts set their eyes on the city of L'viv, the capital of Red Ruthenia, which would pass permanently into Polish hands in 1349. As Lwów, it was due to develop as the bastion of Polishness in the east. At the same time Wrotizla was allowed to drift apart. As Breslau it was destined to develop as a bastion of Germanity. Not for the last time, the destinies of Lwów and Breslau were closely linked together (see Chapter 8).

Some historians have expressed surprise that Silesia in general, and Wrotizla in particular, did not welcome a resurgent Poland more positively.

Yet the reservations are easy enough to understand. For one thing, Władysław Łokietek had battled his way to the Polish throne at the expense first of the Silesian Piasts and then of the Bohemians. His defeated rivals were predisposed against him. For another, the increasingly Germanised ruling circles of Silesia probably felt a greater affinity with the Germanised elite of Bohemia than with the Polish court in Cracow. The burghers of Wrotizla were already making overtures to the King of Bohemia several years before their Duke was persuaded to do the same. Church–state relations also played a vital part. Silesia remained part of the Polish See, and an energetic Polish king was asserting the rights of the Church and the Papacy. It can hardly have been an accident that the decision of Duke Henryk VI of Wrotizla to accept Bohemian suzerainty in 1327 was taken amid acute tensions between the burghers and the Bishop. In the same year the burghers reacted angrily to the arrival of a papal legate, Piero d'Alverni, and to his attempt to re-impose the traditional ecclesiastical tax of Peter's Pence. The legate was chased out of Wrotizla and the cathedral looted. Several of Bishop Nanker's retainers were killed and the Bishop himself fled to Nysa (Neisse). The move to join Bohemia, therefore, went hand in hand with a reluctance to meet the increased demands of the Polish Church.

By the early fourteenth century Silesia had devolved into a score of petty, and often petty-minded, duchies. Pursuing their own squabbles and facing ever-more ambiguous attitudes from Cracow, many of them sought protection by turning to the new Bohemian King, John of Luxemburg. Skilfully and unscrupulously manipulated, they successively switched their allegiance. After the Dukes of Wrotizla and Opole had acknowledged Bohemian suzerainty in 1327, Legnica, Brzeg, Oleśnica, Żagań and Ścinawa (Steinau) followed suit in 1329. Głogów defected two years after that and Ziębice (Münsterberg) in 1336. The formal recognition of Bohemian rule in Silesia was made at the Treaty of Trencin in 1335:

> In the name of the Lord, Amen . . . King John of Bohemia and his first born son, the illustrious Charles, Margrave of Moravia . . . have freely renounced all rights . . . [and] legal title to the Kingdom of Poland that they were entitled to . . . They exclude however the noble Princes and Dukes named below, their vassals and duchies, lands, [and] possessions . . . They exclude the territories of [Wrotizla] and [Głogów] and all accompanying lands and titles. The Dukes and Duchies mentioned are these: Duke Boleslaus of [Legnica] and [Brzeg], Henry of Sagan [Żagán], Konrad of [Oleśnica], Johann of [Ścinawa], . . . Bolko of [Opole], Bolko of [Niemodlin (Falkenberg)], Albert of [Strzelce Opolskie (Groß Strehlitz)], Wladislaus of [Koźle] and [Bytom], . . . Leszko of [Racibórz], Johann of [Oświęcim] and Wladislaus of [Cieszyn].
>
> . . . The King of Poland will be well-disposed towards the King of

Bohemia and the Margrave of Moravia with regard to the rights, titles and assets that they have or assert to have over the above named Dukes and Duchies . . . Moreover the King of Poland renounces . . . all rights of the King or his successors to the named Dukes and Duchies.[16]

The House of Luxemburg had achieved in a quarter of a century what the Přemyslids had failed to achieve in three centuries. Silesia had returned definitively to the Bohemian fold for the first time since the days of St Adalbert. And Wrotizla had taken the lead. Most strikingly, Poland's renunciation of Silesia – though long regretted – had been entirely voluntary.

*

The economy of Wrotizla developed in the orbit of three distinct but interrelated centres: the court, the merchants and the Church. From the earliest ducal presence, the city required an infrastructure of services and supplies to satisfy the court's needs. Prior to the reorganisation of the city after 1241, numerous outlying settlements were established to meet the demand. The village of Sokolnice started life as a settlement of falconers, and Nabitin, further west, was a settlement of Odra fishermen. According to one source, the origins of Psie Pole, to the north-east, had nothing to do with the battle of 1109, but could be attributed to the location of the Duke's hunting kennels.[17]

The merchant community of Wrotizla grew in proportion to the city's emergence as a nodal point of both local and long-distance trade. The tradesmen's quarter of the medieval town lay to the south of the river in the vicinity of the present city centre, where Polish, German, Ruthenian and Jewish traders ran depots and stalls for domestic and imported wares, including leather, wax, hemp and animal skins. In 1214, or possibly 1232, the city was granted a major privilege – that of holding an annual eight-day market, during the Feast of St John in June. Much of the long-distance trade lay in the hands of Jewish merchants who bridged the gap between the principal commercial cities in Germany, especially in the Rhineland, and those in Poland, such as Cracow and Lublin. In 1247, a Franciscan friar reported meeting a compatriot from Wrotizla in Kiev.

The economic influence of the Church should not be underestimated. It was at the heart of the regional economy. Some of the earliest monastic immigrants, such as the Premonstratensians and the Benedictines, were engaged in agriculture and trade, thereby amassing a considerable fortune. In time they attracted new immigrants. The Walloons were called in by Bishop Walther in the mid-twelfth century. They came with a complement of Augustinians from his home town of Liège and settled around the

Church of St Mauritius, some distance from the town centre. Though long identified as a distinct community of aliens, they were absolutely committed to making their living in their new home. And, it would seem, they prospered there. Their primary trade, brewing, became a Silesian speciality and the foundation of many a family fortune.

The Church was also active in granting mining rights in Silesia.[18] As early as 1136, Pope Innocent II gave the Archbishop of Gniezno '*item villa ante Bitom*' – presumably the right to exploit mineral wealth. But it was the great monasteries that often took the lead. The Cistercian abbey at Lubiąż (Leubus), for example, was the first to obtain the Duke's permission for mining gold and copper in the vicinity of Złotoryja. Monastic sheep-farming provided the stimulus for the growth of textile manufacture, which first started at Lwówek. Small towns thrived on the specialised economic activities that they fostered, which also help to explain their precocity in the realms of guilds and legal incorporation. The specialised textiles produced at Lwówek were displayed in the magnificent cloth-market, an architectural treasure that survived until 1945. An alleged riot among the plebs of Złotoryja during the reign of Henryk the Bearded was an event to arouse the passions of Marxist historians in a later age.

The community of artisans, tradesmen and merchants serving the court and Church in Wrotizla was initially little affected by the advent of new immigrants. The newcomers imported iron ploughs, the three-field system and forestry skills; they caused a steady growth in population, while adding variety and efficiency to the existing economy. Major change came only in the aftermath of the Mongol invasion.

Wrotizla – refounded, relocated and repopulated (as far as was necessary) – showed itself remarkably adept at picking up where it had left off, and moved almost immediately to a new stage of its existence. It was soon the site of not one but three towns, and the suburbs were beginning to develop their own specialisations. In short, it rapidly came to require the new commercial privileges appropriate to its status. The 'Mile Right' of 1272 decreed that no independent markets were to be held within a mile of the city. This meant that the Abbey of Trzebnica had to abandon the market that it had long patronised within the city walls. The 'Warehousing Right' of 1274 ensured that all goods in transit had to be offered for sale in the city for a minimum of three days. To facilitate increased trade, three separate market squares – the Ring (Market Square), the Salt Market and the New Market – were laid out.

The continuous influx of colonists, however, had far-reaching cumulative consequences. In the thirteenth century, German settlers established numerous new communities and expanded countless existing villages in the districts surrounding Wrotizla. The city was bound to respond to the needs of the thriving region of which it was now the hub.

*

Little is known of the bishopric of Wrotizla at its foundation in AD 1000, beyond the name of its earliest incumbent, one Johannes or Jan. One may presume that it benefited, both spiritually and materially, from its location on the pilgrimage route from Bohemia to the shrine of St Adalbert in Gniezno. But its fragility was self-evident, and was to be vividly demonstrated by the pagan revolt of the 1030s. During those years the diocese was either transferred to the jurisdiction of Prague or allowed to lapse entirely. It is an open question, of course, whether the conversion of Silesia and the foundation of its bishopric had been 'consensual' or 'compulsory'. Yet there is little evidence to suggest that the common people participated in the decisions. All the indications are that the bishopric of Wrotizla was founded purely as an act of princely policy. One must also face up to the possibility that Bishop Johannes never actually took up his See. The earliest local source, the twelfth-century *Liber Fundationis* from Henryków (Heinrichau), clearly states that Hieronymus, the cleric appointed to Wrotizla after the pagan revolt, was 'the first bishop'. This would suggest that the bishopric's previous existence was for some reason not locally known or recognised.

Whatever actually happened, the bishopric henceforth enjoyed a continuous career. Bishop Hieronymus (r. 1051–62) built a small wooden cathedral on the site of its modern successor. Yet the successful restoration was not a foregone conclusion. Kołobrzeg, on the Baltic coast of Pomerania, for instance, had been given a bishop at the same time as Wrotizla. But, lacking royal support, the experiment soon lapsed and a new Pomeranian bishopric had to be established in the mid-twelfth century at Wolin (Wolin).

Nonetheless, with the gradual spread of the faith beyond the confines of court and Cathedral, Vratislavian Christianity grew more secure. By the early twelfth century, the Church of St Giles (Aegidius) had been built close to the cathedral, while beyond the islands the Church of St Adalbert was consecrated in 1112. The Church of St Mauritius was built in the 1130s. Monasticism also arrived. A party of Benedictines, who were brought from Cologne via Tyniec near Cracow, established a monastery on the Ołbin (Elbing) in the mid-twelfth century. They were followed by the Premonstratensians and by Augustinian Canons Regular, the former moving into the Church of St Martin and the latter to the Abbey of Our Lady on the Sands. The Benedictines were replaced by the Cistercians in 1193.

The period of the most enthusiastic church-building is synonymous with the name of Peter Wlast. As castellan of Wrotizla, Wlast is said to have founded some seventy-seven religious institutions in total, nineteen of which were in the town, including St Adalbert, Our Lady on the Sands and the Abbey of St Vincent, where his own sarcophagus was to lie. The total is undoubtedly exaggerated, and it remains a moot point where he found the funds. According to some sources, Wlast had 'inherited' the Danish crown jewels,[19] others suggest that he had profited from his marriage to the Ruthenian princess, Marija Svyatopolkovna.[20] Wherever the money came from, he was a most generous patron.

Wrotizla possessed a personality of similar prominence in Walther de Malonne. Born near Liège around 1120 and educated in France, Bishop Walther had worked at Płock in Mazovia and allegedly was already fluent in Polish when he was appointed to Wrotizla in 1149. His twenty-year tenure saw the confirmation of the bishopric's territorial possessions by the English Pope Adrian IV, and a forceful campaign against the lapses of his fellow clergy. Most notably, the foundation stone of a new cathedral was laid in 1158. Dedicated, like its wooden and stone-built predecessors, to St John the Baptist, it was modelled on the cathedral of Lyons, with a triple nave, a semi-circular apse and a subterranean crypt.

The dedication of the cathedral to St John the Baptist was well suited not only to the first Bishop's baptismal name, but also to the pioneering mission of the Silesian Church. It laid the symbolic foundation-stone of Wrotizla's identity. Prague had St Wenceslas; Cracow was to have St Stanisław; but Wrotizla had the Baptist. Henceforth, for generation upon generation of Vratislavians, the key text was to be found in the Gospel account of the *vox in desertibus*:

> The voice of one who crieth in the wilderness, Prepare Ye the way of the Lord . . . Every valley shall be uplifted, and every mountain laid low: the crooked made straight and the rough places plain.[21]

St Jadwiga (Hedwig), the wife of Duke Henryk I of Wrotizla, was possibly Silesia's most prominent ecclesiastical patron. Born into the House of Andechs-Meranien (Merano), she married Henryk in 1186 at the age of twelve; she contributed fully to the spiritual life of the province. According to later tradition she helped establish the Cistercian monastery of Henryków, named after her husband, as well as the Augustinian priories at Nowogród and Kamieniec (Kamenz) and the Cistercian nunnery at Trzebnica, where she would herself be buried in 1243. Soon after her canonisation in 1267, her tomb became the place of pilgrimage that assured her universal acceptance as the patron saint of Silesia.

St Jadwiga was personally acquainted with at least three other saints: St

Elizabeth was her aunt, St Czesław (Ceslaus) her confessor and St Jacek (Hyacinth) was Czesław's brother. Jacek and Czesław were Silesians from the Odrowąż clan in the district of Opole, and they had received the habit of the newly formed Order of Preachers from St Dominic himself. They were charged with missionary work in Poland, Prussia and Lithuania. Jacek – known as the 'Apostle of the North' – founded priories at Prague, Cracow, Sandomierz and Kiev and led missions in Prussia, Russia and Scandinavia. Czesław meanwhile came to Wrotizla via Cracow and Prague, founding a priory and being promoted to the position of Provincial of Poland. According to legend, he single-handedly defeated the Mongols outside Wrotizla in 1241,[22] was reputed to have raised four persons to life[23] and to have had the ability to walk on the Odra.[24]

Wrotizla's link with the Dominicans was surprisingly persistent. The very first Polish Provincial – Czesław's predecessor – was a native Vratislavian: *Frater Gerardus, nacione Wratislaviensis, studens Parisius.* Brother Gerard sent out Czesław, Jacek and the others to establish priories as far afield as Gdańsk and Kamień (Kammin) in Pomerania, and probably became the first Latin Bishop of Ruthenia. Later Vratislavian Provincials included Gosław de Breslau (r.1275–9, 1291–3), Piotrus de Chomiąża (r.1354–70, 1382) and Jean de Brzeg (r.1370–82).[25] The Franciscans also came in force, becoming especially active in the proliferation of female convents.

The military orders followed hard on the heels of the mendicants.[26] The Knights of the Red Star came first. They were originally founded in 1217 in Prague, where the Blessed Agnes confided two hospitals to their charge. From there her sister, the Duchess Anna, facilitated their move into Silesia. By 1247 they were well established in Wrotizla, under a certain Merotonius[27] or Merboto, who created a hospital and a monastery and took over the Church of St Elizabeth. Enjoying ducal patronage, they subsequently spread their activities to Kluczbork (Kreuzburg), Bolesławiec (Bunzlau), Ziębice, Świdnica (Schweidnitz) and Legnica.[28]

Next came the Hospitallers – the Knights of the Hospital of St John of Jerusalem. Count Vincent of Pogarel had travelled to Outremer as a Hospitaller with the Third Crusade. His family and others had established houses of the Order on their estates, where in due course the Order had succeeded them. The Hospitallers then obtained the parish churches of Lwówek, Złotoryja, Brzeg and Dzierżoniów (Reichenbach), but were unable to gain a foothold in Wrotizla until 1273, when they settled on a site close to the Świdnica Gate, south of the Old Town. There they established the Holy Trinity Hospital, a monastery and, around 1320, the Corpus Christi Church (where the 'Maltese Cross' can still be seen in the masonry). This impressive complex of buildings, with a raised gallery spanning the roadway, would have dominated the southern entrance to the city.

The Teutonic Knights were also present in Wrotizla. The Order had been established at Acre in 1198 to serve German crusaders and pilgrims in the Holy Land. But following the disintegration of the Crusader Kingdoms, it had sought a new mission and, after an abortive sojourn in Hungary, accepted a commission from Duke Conrad of Mazovia, in 1230, to subdue the heathen Prussians. Its connection with Wrotizla was a close one. Duke Henryk I participated in the Order's crusades against the Prussians,[29] and many of the Order's knights fought alongside Henryk's son at Legnica in 1241. Almost a century later, in 1329, all the brother dukes of Silesia were admitted as *confratres* of the Order, apparently in recognition of their hostility to the King of Poland.[30] The Order also maintained a house in the city. Situated on the Altbüßergasse, the building was known as the 'Preußische Herren Steinhaus' and was probably the Order's hospice.

The thirteenth century saw the consolidation in Wrotizla of a fully fledged parish network. Parish churches were evidently functioning prior to 1226, when Bishop Laurentius founded the Church of St Mary Magdalen as a replacement for the Parish Church of St Wojciech, which he handed to the Dominicans. But the system was only then in the process of completion. A learned academic controversy thrives on the subject of Polish medieval parishes. One school of thought holds that they were created by the bishops, principally through the donation of tithes.[31] At all events, the assignation of tithes proved a frequent source of dispute between the Bishop and the assignees. One such dispute sparked the bitter quarrel between Bishop Laurentius and Duke Henryk the Bearded. Another, in 1255, involved Bishop Tomasz I and the Hospitallers.

The power and influence of the Church were not restricted to religious matters. In the fourteenth century, for example, the Bishops of Wrotizla, following the example of the Archbishops of Gniezno, purchased nearby Silesian principalities to boost their income and status.[32] In so doing, they fanned a growing conflict between the temporal and spiritual authorities. The friction, essentially a reflection of the investiture contest as played out between the Emperor and the Pope, ran long and deep. It was often sparked by a financial dispute, either in the payment of the Peter's Pence or in the taxation of Church property. More ominously, given the growing Germanisation of the citizens and the continuing association of the bishopric with Poland, it increasingly took on national overtones.

In this conflict, the Church's ultimate weapon was excommunication, and the bishops were not shy of using it. Duke Henryk IV was put under interdict in 1284, as was the entire diocese between 1319 and 1321. It is even suspected that Duke Henryk I, husband of St Jadwiga, had died excommunicated in 1238.[33]

The row in 1284–5 between Duke Henryk IV Probus and Bishop Tomasz II had started with the Duke's high-handed demands for financial assistance in his bid for the seniorate. When the Bishop declined, his castle at Otmuchów (Ottmachau) his town of Nysa were promptly sequestrated. What is more, the Duke ordered that all tithes in the duchy were to be paid to him. The Bishop then complained to the Primate of Poland, Archbishop Świnka, who called a synod at Łęczyca to hear the complaints:

> The upshot is . . . that the Archbishop imposes heavy ecclesiastical penalties on Duke Henryk and all who supported him, and places an interdict on the town of [Wrotizla] and all other places in the duchy. This is observed by all the churches and monasteries in the diocese, except that of the Minor Friars of the Order of St Francis which publicly flouts it. The Duke and the city fathers, who support the Duke, expel the Bishop and all the clergy including the Dominicans . . . who all go to other Polish dioceses until the storm subsides. Meanwhile Bishop [Tomasz] goes to Lyons to attend a synod, but fails to get support . . . because Duke Henryk's procurators arrived ahead of him . . . and got the interdict lifted. So the Duke neither repays the Bishop nor provides any compensation for the hurt suffered. The Bishop returns to Poland a saddened man and lives in Racibórz as the guest of Casimir, Duke of Opole.[34]

The conflict reached a peak with the appointment, in 1326, of Oksa Nanker as Bishop of Wrotizla. A vigorous defender of Polish interests in the city, Nanker was to clash with Silesia's new Bohemian king, John of Luxemburg.

Over a period of 300 years Christianity had, therefore, made tremendous strides in Wrotizla. The last overt remnants of paganism had disappeared. The Church had grown into an organisation of enormous financial and political power. Whether or not its prelates followed the humble Gospel of Christ was a different matter.

*

In medieval Latin Christendom, cultural life was divided between the religious and the secular. The former may be further divided into the universal and the local or particular; the latter into the courtly, the patrician and the popular. The various forms have not survived in the record in equal measure, but all are represented.

Wrotizla's cathedral, churches and abbeys were monuments to the triumph of mainstream Roman Catholicism. Their architecture, symbolism, religious furniture and Latin rites would have been totally familiar to a visitor from England, France or Italy. St Vincent's Abbey on the Ołbin was reckoned to be the largest monastery in Poland. Local accents were provided first by the cult of St Adalbert and later by the cult of St Jadwiga.

Yet the city was increasingly exposed to cultural imports from Western Europe – from the Low Countries and northern Italy. It naturally took some considerable time for trends and fashions to filter through, but they did. The acculturation of Silesia was spearheaded by scholars who travelled to study at foreign universities. Since distances were long and the costs high, the number of Silesians studying in France or Italy was always small, but they represented the cultural elite. Most of those who studied abroad in the twelfth and thirteenth centuries had some connection to the bishopric. Two of the city's clerics, Canon Jakob and Bishop Tomasz I, held doctorates in canon law. Bishop Tomasz I, who held office from 1232 to 1268 and was fifteenth in the line of Wrotizla's bishops, was the first to possess a substantial biography. A member of the Rawita clan, he may well have acquired his 'Christian' name when taking orders, as the cult of St Thomas Becket was then popular in Cracow. He was certainly a skilled lawyer, who remained in close touch with papal procurators. A series of Hospitaller bulls from 1249, for example, which have survived in a number of variants, all issued within the space of a few days, indicate the skill and cunning with which Wrotizla's interlocutors operated in the papal court.[35]

Religious occasions provided some respite from the drudgery and despair of medieval life. Quite apart from their religious content, they were a form of popular theatre. After the canonisation of St Jadwiga, for instance, an immense crowd gathered at the convent of Trzebnica to watch the translation of the saint's body, performed by the Abbots of Lubiąż and Kamieniec and the canons and priests of Wrotizla:

> [They] raise the bones of the saint from her sarcophagus and wash them in wine. The more important bones are placed in a specially prepared case and are given to the Cathedral [of Wrotizla] and other Polish churches. When the skull is raised the brain proves to be completely undamaged and healthy . . . They discover three undamaged fingers of the saint clasping a tiny ivory figure of the Blessed Virgin, which she had . . . always carried with her. She once dropped it, and to her great grief, was unable to find it; but a pig discovered it and brought it to her in its snout while she was praying in church. After this, she always clasped it in her hand, even during meals and when at work.[36]

In Wrotizla itself, schools were opened in the early thirteenth century to educate the sons of clerics and burghers.[37] The Cathedral school, first mentioned in 1212, was the pioneer. A few decades later, it was already teaching a broad curriculum of Latin, Greek, Hebrew, grammar, logic, philosophy and physics. A second school was established on the left bank of the river in 1267, thereby saving its pupils two daily river crossings. The School of St Mary Magdalen, sanctioned by the papal legate Guido of Lucina, added rhetoric and dialectics to the standard educational fare. A third parish school, that of St Elizabeth, opened in 1293.

Municipal education was matched by the provision of rudimentary care for the sick and aged. Since the international hospital Orders did not usually maintain hospitals in their European possessions, the gap had to be filled from the charitable impulses of either the city council or the parishes. The earliest healthcare was provided by the Abbeys of St Vincent and Our Lady on the Sands. As from 1214, the latter established the Holy Spirit Hospital to tend to the needs of the poor. Both the Czech-based Order of the Red Star and the Polish-based Order of Miechów were active in Silesia, but the exact nature of their operations in thirteenth-century Wrotizla has not been ascertained. The Lazarus Hospital took in lepers from 1312. The Order of St John, which had made a number of property deals in the city, did not engage in hospital foundation until the 1330s. Though such hospitals were as much concerned with the well-being of patients' souls as with their health, they encouraged medical and anatomical expertise. Wrotizla's first apothecary's shop – a business under the name of 'Heinrich' – opened its doors in 1331.

With some delay the innovations of the so-called 'Twelfth-Century Renaissance' were reaching Silesia. In the field of the natural sciences, for instance, Wrotizla could boast one of the most important scientists of the age. Witeło (Vitellio, c.1230–80), born near Legnica and educated in Wrotizla, Paris and Padua, described himself as a 'son of Thuringia and Poland'.[38] He was probably the child of a German father and a Polish mother. A philosopher, mathematician and scientist, he was employed as a diplomat by King Otakar II of Bohemia. For a time he was a canon of Wrotizla Cathedral, and he travelled widely in Italy with the son of Duke Henryk III. But he is best remembered for a groundbreaking treatise on optics, the *Perspectiva*, which drew on the work of the Arabic scholar Alhazen and developed the ideas of Robert Grosseteste. It was written around 1270, but not published for some 300 years. A philosophical letter sent to Witeło by his friend Ludwik of Lwówek on the subject of the nature of devils has also survived.

The international character of Wrotizla's educated elite is well represented by the career of Władysław (c.1237–70), the youngest son of Duke Henryk II the Pious. Destined from boyhood to be a cleric, he spurned the quarrels of his brothers – Bolesław the Bald and Henryk III – and rose rapidly through the ecclesiastical ranks, becoming successively Vicar of Vyšehrad, Bishop-elect of Passau, Chancellor of Bohemia and Archbishop of Salzburg. Yet he never turned his back on his native city. In 1261, he joined his brother in confirming Wrotizla's incorporation under Magdeburg Law; and in the last four years of his life, being both guardian of his under-age nephew and deputy of the exiled Bishop, he ran the duchy and diocese of Wrotizla in tandem. He is buried in Salzburg Cathedral.

In the secular sphere, chivalry was an essential ingredient of aristocratic culture. It was represented in the person of Duke Henryk IV, who has been described as 'one of the most dazzling knights of his age'.[39] Raised by King Otakar II in Prague, Henryk was no stranger to courtly poetry and, of course, to accompanying ethos. The ideals of courtly love had spread across Europe in the twelfth and thirteenth centuries from Provence. No mere source of entertainment, they advocated a brand of restraint which, as illustrated by princely troubadours, was thought to demonstrate their suitability to rule. In the German lands they inspired the so-called *Minnesänger*, a group of poet-musicians whose songs spoke of high-minded romance and chivalrous deeds. Rightly or wrongly, Duke Henryk IV has been identified with the 'Heinrich von Pressela' who was the author of two *Minnelieder* from the late flowering of courtly culture. They are to be found in the contemporary collection, *Die Manessische Liederhandschrift*:

> Ich klag' dir, Mai, ich klag' dir, Sommerwonne,
> Ich klag' dir, lichte Heide breit,
> Ich klag' dir, augenblendender Klee,
> Ich klag' dir, grüner Wald, ich klag' dir, Sonne,
> Ich klag' dir, Venus, sehnend Leid,
>   Daß mir die Liebe thut so weh.
> Wollt ihr mir helfen streben,
> So hoff' Ich, daß die Liebe mög ergeben
> Sich einem minniglichern Wesen.
> Nun laßt euch fein verkündet meinen Kummer,
>   Bei Gott, und helfet mir genesen.[40]

> (I complain to you, O month of May, and summer's joy;
> I complain to you, the bright, broad heath;
> I complain to you, the eye-piercing clover;
> I complain to you, the forest green, and to you, the sun.
> I complain to you, O Venus, of my languishing sorrows –
>   How love causes me such pain.
> If all of you help to plead my case,
> I trust that Love may pass judgement
> On one charming creature whom I know.

Hear now the full tale of my trouble!
God have mercy on me! And find me a remedy!)

Even if the identification of the author is mistaken, one is left with an example of the sort of entertainment that lords and ladies could have enjoyed at the court of Wrotizla in the late thirteenth century. If the identification happens to be correct, it shows that Poland as well as Wrotizla was briefly ruled by a none-too-brilliant German poet.

*

The ethnic composition of Piast-ruled Wrotizla can be sensibly discussed only when certain misconceptions have been laid to rest. It is wrong to assume, for example, that all the subjects of the Piasts were Poles. It would be equally wrong to assume that a homogenous Polish nation in the modern sense had yet been formed. By the same token, it would be a mistake to imagine that all the subjects of the Holy Roman Empire were Germans, or that the various brands of German felt any degree of common identity. The phrase *regnum Teutonicum* was only cautiously being adopted by the imperial court from the twelfth century,[41] and the inhabitants of that *regnum* still identified themselves as Saxons, Swabians, Frisians and Bavarians, rather than as uniform Germans. Similarly, it would be wrong to assume that the Kingdom of Bohemia was homogenous. Given that it included both Cracow and Wrotizla until 990, and numerous German-speaking districts until modern times, it is obvious that medieval 'Bohemians' were far from being the same thing as modern 'Czechs'. No subject is more in need of that wise warning: 'The past is a foreign country.'

At the turn of the millennium, the Vratislavians were almost certainly – and almost exclusively – ethnic Slavs. Yet in the absence of any records relating to the vernacular speech of the city, it is impossible to say whether the local Slavonic dialect leaned more to the Czech, to the Polanian or to the Wendish. Modern claims that the streets of early Wrotizla echoed to 'the Silesian dialect of Polish' are based on the anachronistic suppositions of nineteenth-century Romantics. Nobody really knows. One can only surmise that in the eleventh century, when Bohemian and Polish influences both remained strong, the local variant of West Slav speech would have displayed the same sort of mixed characteristics that prevailed elsewhere on the Czech–Polish borders. One may also surmise that in the decades after 1050, when Silesia was returned to Piast rule and was more closely linked to the new capital in Cracow, the Polish colouring of the citizens and of their language strengthened.

In the twelfth century, the Polishness of Wrotizla would probably have been further bolstered by the successful wars against the Empire. Under

Peter Wlast (see below), whose own native language is also a subject of speculation, Silesia was a fully integrated province of the Polish kingdom. At the same time, however, the Polish Church was subject to several foreign imports and influences. Like the contemporary chronicler, the Anonymous Gaul, Bishop Walther de Malonne was probably a Francophone cleric who strengthened links with the West by patronising the cults of both St Geneviève and St Rémy. Bishop Heymo (r.1120–6) is also assumed by some to have been of French or Francophone origin. No doubt there were others. The settlement of Walloon weavers – from a non-German province of the Empire – became a long-lasting feature.

Nothing better illustrates the fluid state of the ethnic landscape than the career of Jaksa of Kopanica, also known as Jaxa von Köpenick (fl.1150). Jaksa was probably a Lusatian Wend or Sorb, an ancestor of the once-extensive Slav nation that still survives in the enclave of Budišyn, or Bautzen, in Saxony. He lived at a time when Slavonic Lusatia extended far to the north, when his people were still resisting Christianisation and when the district where Berlin was later built still lay within the Wendish realm. Like nearby Spandau, Jaksa's home town of Kopanica (Köpenick) was one of two Slav forts on the site of the future Berlin, which held the advancing Saxons at bay. A silver coin minted in 1150 bore the legend 'Jacza de Copnik' and showed Jaksa sitting in his fortress, wearing a helmet and clutching a gigantic sword.[42] Tradition holds that he had personally accepted Christianity from the Polish Bishop of Lubusz (Lebus) – a diocese immediately to the north of Wrotizla – and that his army contained a large contingent of Poles. At all events, as the chroniclers confirm, Jaksa captured Brandenburg from the Saxons in 1154 and was only driven out by Albert the Bear after a bitter three-year war. Albert took the title of *Markgraf* and founded the city of Berlin as capital of the Mark Brandenburg. Jaksa, defeated, took refuge in Wrotizla.

His exploits have often been dismissed as colourful legend, although they have regularly been resurrected, whether in hostile or friendly guise, by people interested in the origins of Berlin. Jaksa became 'the noble savage' – the Caractacus of the March – against whom the civilising mission of the Brandenburgers could be contrasted. His true identity is shrouded in mystery.[43] To Długosz, he was a Duke of the Sorbs; the chronicler Henry of Antwerp described him as a Pole; other sources portray him as a Pomeranian, a Silesian or even a Serb. Furthermore, Jaksa is commonly cited as the son-in-law of Peter Wlast in Wrotizla.[44] But there is a second Jaksa to confuse matters. Jaksa of Miechów (d.1178) was one of the earliest Polish pilgrims to the Holy Land and was castellan of Köpnitz in Małopolska. For some, the two Jaksas are one and the same person.

Jaksa's stay in Wrotizla is equally problematical. He has been credited with the foundation of St Vincent's Abbey, which was also said to have been founded by Peter Wlast. Scholars trying to square the circle have produced some strange conclusions. Perhaps Wlast and Jaksa were one and the same man. Or Wrotizla had two abbeys dedicated to St Vincent. Or St Vincent's was founded by Wlast and refounded by Jaksa. The biggest surprise came in 1962, more than 800 years after Jaksa's arrival, when, during renovation work at the Arsenal, a twelfth-century tympanum was uncovered, which had been transferred from its original position above a portal in the Abbey of Ołbin. There, cast in stone, was the name of Jaksa.[45]

The most radical changes, however, attended the influx of German settlers and the consequential spread of German culture. The first signs would probably have been manifest in the court circles of Władysław the Exile and especially of his German-educated sons. But the critical shift cannot be dated before the last quarter of the twelfth century. The Cistercians of Lubiąż were Saxon monks imported from Pforta, near Bolesław the Tall's sometime place of exile in Altenburg. At first they were an isolated German community in Silesia. But in 1175 they obtained the right to settle agricultural colonists on their lands. What is more, in 1180, the Polish Benedictines of St Vincent's Abbey on the Ołbin in Wrotizla were supposedly replaced by Premonstratensians from the Empire. Their new abbot, Cyprian, was German-born. In the following decade, he was promoted to become Wrotizla's first German bishop.

In the thirteenth century, the process of Germanisation accelerated. In Wrotizla it is often associated with the reign of Duke Henryk I, who succeeded in 1201. As the son, grandson and husband of German princesses, Henryk has been described as 'a blond Polish Duke with a German heart'.[46] Both the Polish and German languages were used at his court. Alongside his wife, the future St Jadwiga, he surrounded himself with German relatives, German advisers, knights, monks and nuns, and thus – consciously or otherwise – laid the foundations of the later German province of *Schlesien*. German settlement in Wrotizla also dates from the reign of Duke Henryk I, having begun around 1214.[47]

Silesia is viewed by some as the classic example of German eastern expansion.[48] In the conventional interpretation, settlers, predominantly from Saxony, Thuringia and Bavaria, were attracted by preferential conditions of tenure, by the promise of fertile land and by the opportunities for improvement. They were settled in a network of towns spread at approximately twenty-kilometre intervals over the countryside.[49] Where Slavic villages already existed between the colonial settlements, laws and customs were adjusted to those of the newcomers. Importantly, there is little evidence that the native Silesians proved hostile.[50] Silesia, once a bulwark against German influence, thus became one of its most reliable conduits.

The destruction of Wrotizla, in 1241, only increased the pressures for change, and German merchants gradually gained the upper hand in the Silesian capital. They feared another round of dynastic conflict, and sought to protect themselves by adopting German municipal and legal models. At their instigation, the city was rebuilt by Duke Henryk's widow, Anna. Reconstruction and administrative reform encouraged the continuing influx of immigrants, which was to be sustained for the remainder of the century. Once Magdeburg Law was introduced, German became the official language of administration. As a result, ever-widening sections of the indigenous Slavonic population were Germanised. Similar German inroads were made into the Polish Church. After Lubiąż and St Vincent's, the abbeys of Henryków and Kamieniec became bastions of German culture. The convent of Trzebnica was taken over by German nuns from Bamberg. In 1274, the Franciscans of Wrotizla transferred to the Saxon province of their Order. These processes would eventually lead to the emergence of German 'Breslau'.

In modern German historiography it is not unusual to find 1163, the date of the division of Silesia between Władysław's fractious sons, presented as the date of Silesia's separation from Poland[51] and its effective secession to the Empire. This interpretation holds that the Silesian Piasts, raised in the imperial court and restored by Barbarossa, sought to escape the backward and treacherous life of the Kingdom of Poland by allying themselves with the Empire. It is generally justified by the Germanisation process, which was begun by Bolesław the Tall but was predominantly associated with his son – Henryk I of Wrotizla. It assumes that the continuing Germanising activities of Henryk's successors led naturally to the re-establishment of the city under German law, and ultimately to the cession of the province to the Empire's Bohemian ally.

Though at first sight persuasive, this argument contains some dubious assertions. For, even if the Silesian Piasts pursued conscious policies of Germanisation, they did not necessarily aim to join the Empire. The Polish state, though fractured and weak in the 'Age of Fragmentation', was by no means beyond recall. Both the dynastic loyalties of the princes and the kingdom's unified ecclesiastical structure continued to give it cohesion. Indeed, the close relationship between Wrotizla and the Polish Church was self-evident. Wrotizla often played host to Polish synods and served as a secondary residence of the Archbishops of Gniezno.[52] Furthermore, the dukes' alleged intention of planning to secede from Poland sits uneasily with their unbroken involvement in Polish affairs. The Silesian Piasts did not cease to be closely involved with their Polish relatives. On three occasions in the thirteenth century, the throne of the senior prince in Cracow was graced by Silesian princes in the persons of Henryk I, Henryk II and Henryk IV.

In this light, Germanisation need not be seen as the symptom of a desire to secede from Poland. It is more likely to have been an instrument to promote Silesian Piast ambitions *within* Poland. The deliberate importation of German settlers served to strengthen not only Silesia, but also the Silesian Piast case for ruling in Cracow as the senior princes of Poland. Only when the Silesian princes had been definitively thwarted in Cracow did the trajectory of the province change direction. The Polish Crown only lost the Silesian dukes when the Silesian dukes lost their grip on the Polish Crown.

Moreover, Germanisation generally proceeded smoothly. It has been described as a 'peaceful penetration . . . without serious friction or bloodshed . . . [and] without racial or national antagonism'.[53] This comment may be over-optimistic. Conflicts did arise, especially within the Church. German settlers in Silesia were collectively excommunicated in the mid-thirteenth century for following a different version of the religious calendar. Half a century later, Bishop Heinrich von Würben (*r.*1302–19) was excommunicated by the Archbishop of Gniezno for favouring the German interest. Nor was the conflict confined to Poles and Germans. Fighting in the city between Poles and Czechs was recorded in 1314.

It would be particularly out of place to assume that the Polish element was decimated. The villages on the right bank of the Odra remained solidly Polish, while Polish names such as Baran or Cebula figured regularly, even among the city's patricians. The secular clergy remained predominantly Polish, as did some of the religious Orders, especially the Dominicans.

Much reliance was once put by historians on the prevalence of German names in the records. From the mid-thirteenth century, all the names of Wrotizla's office holders and leading citizens are known and the great majority of them are indeed German. Yet the dangers of equating ethnicity with particular names should be obvious. It was very easy for a German-speaking scribe to inadvertently exaggerate the German element, by changing Polish names into their (to him) simpler German equivalents during transcription. Studies based on German patrician families reveal little about important issues such as bilingualism or the identity of the illiterate lower classes.

Some indications of the complicated ethnic and linguistic make-up of the city and duchy emerge from the *Liber Fundationis* of the Cistercian Abbey of Henryków, some sixty-five kilometres to the south of Wrotizla. Written in two parts, one dating from 1268 to 1273 and the other from *c.*1310, the book consists of a collection of abbatial documents interspersed with elaborate commentaries. It provides a colourful picture of the relations between the largely German monks and the surrounding Polish peasantry. At one point, the Latin text incorporates what was claimed to be the very first sentence ever recorded in the Polish language: 'DAJ, AĆ JA POBRUSZĘ A TY POCZYWAJ.' The sentence has puzzled scholars ever since it was published in 1854. It means something like: 'Let me do the turning [or stirring] and you take a rest.' What exactly was being turned, or stirred, is unclear. But the stirrers were talking in Polish.

Wrotizla's Jewish community clearly pre-dated the earliest records of its existence. Jewish merchants had been active in Central and Eastern Europe from Khazar times. One of the first descriptions of the Slav lands was written in the 960s by Ibrahim ibn Jakub, a Jew from Cordoba in Moslem Spain, who definitely stayed in Prague and possibly in Cracow. And it has been contended[54] that a Jewish community functioned in Poland from the tenth century onwards, stimulated by a Jewish presence to the east in the former Khazaria. Jewish residence in Wrotizla might conceivably date from the late eleventh century, when Jewish refugees left Prague during a spate of forced conversions.[55] But hard evidence does not precede the late twelfth century. Some sources recall a gravestone belonging to a certain Rabbi Ahron, who died in 1177.[56] More recent authorities rely on the oldest-surviving Jewish gravestone in Wrotizla, which was cemented into the wall of the old cemetery and was made almost thirty years later:

> This stone is / the funeral monument of David / of the sweet voice, / son of Sar Shalom, / who joined (his ancestors) / in the 2nd day of the week / and the 25th day of the month aw / in the year four thousand and 800 / and 163 from the creation of the world. / His soul has been tied in the knot of life.[57]

David's 'sweet voice' indicates that he was a professional cantor. His father's name, Sar Shalom, is thought to be oriental in origin. The date of his death, 25 aw 4963, is equivalent to 4 August 1203.

In that same year, two Jews, Joseph and Haskiel, sold the lease of the suburban village of Sokolniki to Duke Henryk the Bearded. The supposition is that the lease had been granted as collateral against a loan and that it was surrendered as soon as the loan was repaid. It confirms that the principal occupation of Wrotizla's Jews – or perhaps just the best-recorded – was moneylending.[58]

Jewish butchers were fairly numerous. In the early fourteenth century, no fewer than twelve of the city's ninety-two slaughterhouses were Jewish-owned. This does not indicate that 13 per cent of the population was Jewish, since Jewish butchers could have supplied certain categories of meat to Christian customers.

Judaic law, however, forbade Jews to live in close proximity to Gentiles, so physical segregation would have been the norm. Though formal ghettos were never introduced in Poland, Jewish families would have occupied a distinct quarter with immediate access to their synagogue, ritual bathhouse and kosher food market. In the thirteenth century the Jewish community of Wrotizla was located close to the ducal castle to the north-west of the town (the name Rabbinergässel, or 'Rabbi's Alley', survived into modern times). Shortly after the Mongol invasion, a permanent Jewish cemetery was organised outside the walls in the Oława (Ohlau) district to the east of the city. A charter that gave Wrotizla's Jews fixed rights, the so-called *Schutzprivilegium*, or 'Protection Privilege', was granted in 1267. This followed close on the similar charter that had been issued two years earlier in nearby Kalisz and which acted as a precedent for many cities under Polish rule. By the early fourteenth century, the Jewish community in Wrotizla possessed a school (*yeshiva*) in the centre of the city, a teacher of the Talmud and an official administrator.

Segregation, of course, well suited the prejudices of the Christian majority. Jews were not admitted to the city's guilds, which required the usual Christian qualifications. In consequence, they kept to their own commercial and craft organisations. They were not permitted to hold municipal offices, to sell kosher meat to Christians, to supply wet-nurses or to appear in the streets during Christian processions. In line with other cities operating under German law, Jews would have been required to wear the *Judenfleck* (a yellow patch signifying a Jew). They were also exposed to sporadic hostility and even violence. Although the occurrence of an alleged pogrom in Wrotizla in 1219 has been disproved, there can be little doubt regarding the intolerant attitude of some elements, especially among the burghers and clerics. One reaction to the charter of 1267 was expressed by a diocesan synod held in the same year. 'Since the Poles are a new plantation in the soil of Christendom,' it read:

> we must continually be on our guard lest the Christian population here, where the Christian religion has not yet taken deep root in the hearts of believers, succumb to the influence of the counterfeit faith and evil habits of the Jews living in their midst.[59]

The Church authorities made every effort to keep the two communities apart, not least by banning mixed marriages and irregular sexual liaisons. In this, they mirrored the similar restrictive attitudes of the Jewish elders.

In theory, the Jews were directly subject to the Duke. But as time passed, the City Council intervened on its own account. In 1302, for instance, they tried to limit Jewish horse-trading by insisting that every sale had to be witnessed by one Jew and one Christian. They also introduced special taxes, on the pretext that Jews did not participate in the municipal militia. Attempts were made to limit the business of Jewish bakers, and to establish a Christian monopoly in the cloth trade.

In 1319, tensions heightened by a year of famine and a major fire resulted in the temporary expulsion of the Jews from Wrotizla. The traditional involvement of Jews in trade and finance made them particularly vulnerable in times of economic hardship, and superstitious people often blamed the Jews for natural disasters. Not for the first or the last time, they were turned into a scapegoat for other people's woes. According to tax records, the number of Jews in Wrotizla returned to the preceding level within seven years.

Special regard must be given, therefore, to the ways in which the Jewish community fitted into the fragmented jurisdictions of the medieval period. Expulsion from the city was not equivalent to total banishment. Decrees of *De non tolerandis Judaeis* were not equivalent to generalised persecution. Jews forced out by the City Council could usually take refuge with one of the neighbouring jurisdictions. They often sought the protection of sympathetic nobles, for example, who disliked the city's restrictive practices on their own account, who themselves were not permitted to reside in the city or who were happy enough to use Jewish services and to give Jewish traders access to land in the immediate vicinity of the city gates. In the period before the jurisdictional unification of Wrotizla, they could simply move across the Oława from the Old City to the New City. Hence, despite moments of tension, the settled coexistence of Christians and Jews in and around Piast Wrotizla was a fixed feature of life.

*

The administration of Piast Silesia, and of its chief city, passed through several phases. In the eleventh and early twelfth centuries, the King's deputy – in the form either of a senior *wojewoda* or palatine, the *Comes Palatinus* or 'Count of the Province', or of a more junior *kasztelan* (*castellan*) – ruled supreme over all secular matters. The Bishop and his courts controlled the clergy and all ecclesiastical affairs. After the pagan revolt of the 1030s, the royal establishment in Wrotizla was able to consolidate its direct hold over a score of *castellani* in the surrounding districts. In due course, most of these positions turned into hereditary offices, thereby confirming the emergence of a regional aristocracy. For the time being, there was no parallel development within the city.

Peter Wlast (Vlast), also known as Piotr Włostowic or Peter of Denmark (d.1155), served as Palatine in Wrotizla under both Bolesław Krzywousty and Władysław the Exile. Magnus apart, he is one of the very few high officials of the era about whom something is known. Once considered to have been a Dane, or even a Viking,[60] he is more likely to have been a knight of Danish descent who entered royal service during the Pomeranian wars. Polish sources stress his connection with the magnatial Łabędź clan, while his Ruthenian wife, Marija, was a close relative of Krzywousty's own consort, Princess Zbysława. Thanks to numerous military exploits for his master, such as the capture of Prince Volodar Rostislavovich in Kiev, Wlast was rewarded with huge grants of land in various parts of Poland. As a result, he controlled the resources to become a major ecclesiastical patron (see above). His political downfall occurred in 1145, when he was blinded on the orders of Władysław the Exile. As Palatine, he could not have avoided the internecine wars between 'the Exile' and his sons; and it is generally assumed that Wlast was condemned for some unspecified act of treason. Yet a local source suggests otherwise. In the Latin poem, the *Carmen Mauri*, which was composed in Wrotizla some time after Wlast's death, the Palatine's maiming was the product of an incautious jest. While out hunting with 'the Exile' in the forest, Wlast had supposedly cast aspersions on the virtue of his prince's jealous wife, Agnes von Babenberg. So the wife's honour was redeemed with the Palatine's eyes.

In the 'Age of Fragmentation', the Dukes of Silesia assumed *de facto* independence, although they never formally renounced the nominal supremacy of the senior Piast princes in Cracow. Indeed, both Henryk II and Henryk IV established themselves in Cracow as well as in Wrotizla and were briefly rulers of the whole of Poland in all but name. After 1202, however, the Silesian Piasts refused to recognise Leszek Biały's seizure of the seniorate. Henceforth, right down to Łokietek, they regarded all the Cracovian seniors as usurpers.

The long-running conflict between the Dukes and the Bishops of Wrotizla gave further expression to the centrifugal forces at work. The first hint of trouble came in 1155, when Bishop Walther de Malonne appealed to the Pope for protection of his possessions. The papal bull sent to Wrotizla on that occasion is one of the oldest documents relevant to the city. It served as a prelude to the general settlement between Church and state in Poland reached at the Synod of Łęczyca (1180), whereby the Church recognised the Senior Prince's possession of Cracow and the state recognised the Church's right to retain diocesan property after a bishop's death. The power of the bishops, in fact, was growing rapidly. In Wrotizla, the tensions between the Duke and the Bishop repeatedly broke into open warfare. Henryk Brodaty, who insisted on maintaining traditional controls on the Church, drove

Bishop Tomasz I (r.1232–68) into exile. In 1256–7, the same prelate found himself imprisoned by Bolesław the Bald. Under Henryk Probus, Bishop Tomasz II (r.1270–92) refused to surrender some seventy vills which the Church had founded on ducal land, and was duly expelled. Followed from the city by much of the Polish clergy, he responded by excommunicating the Duke. A long-standing political division had opened up in which the Duke could count on the German burghers, while the Bishop (and behind him the Polish Archbishop and the Roman Pope) were supported by the Polish element.

These fractures within the existing order gradually created the space for the rise of municipal self-government. Yet here one meets a historical controversy of some delicacy. When the subject was first examined more than 100 years ago, German historians placed near-exclusive emphasis on the legal issues and, in particular, on the various acts of municipal incorporation. They created the impression firstly, that, nothing worth mentioning had ever happened in the city prior to its incorporation and, secondly, that incorporation at a stroke brought all of Silesia's cities into being as ready-made model communities – inhabited by Germans, practising German law, and observing German norms. Since then, numerous studies have shown that urban institutions evolved slowly and irregularly over a much longer period of time. No simple scheme can be applied. With the possible exceptions of Złotoryja in 1211 and Lwówek in 1217, no Silesian cities were planted *ab initio* in the wilderness. Nearly all had a long history before the arrival of German settlers and only adopted the main organs of self-government in stages.

The Bavarian Geographer of the ninth century, for instance, had mentioned fifteen fortresses in the lands of the Slenzanie alone. The papal bull of 1155 lists a score of Silesian towns, which had all existed for the best part of a century or more before the main wave of incorporations. These included Bytom, Głogów, Legnica, Milicz (Militsch), Niemcza (Nimptsch), Otmuchów and Strzegom (Striegau). The Anonymous Gaul, writing in c.1100, distinguished *castra* or 'fortresses' from *urbes* and *civitates*. He put Wrotizla and Głogów in the last category, together with Poznań and Cracow.

In the case of Wrotizla, the historical record is complicated both by the absence of a foundation charter and by the very ambiguous chronology of events. It used to be thought that the incorporation of the city had been caused by, and immediately followed, the Mongol invasion of 1241. Numerous pieces of evidence now indicate that the Mongols merely interrupted a series of developments that had started some decades previously. A city praetorius (*Schultheiss/soltys*) appears on the scene already in 1214, implying that a judicial official of that sort could well have been part of a wider organisation. Similarly, a document of 1242 from the Abbey of Trzebnica, which describes nearby Wrotizla as an incorporated city, implies that some form of incorporation had taken place sometime previously. One may also argue that if the great Market Square was laid out in the early 1240s, plans for such a major undertaking must surely have been prepared in the 1230s. All of this points to the probability that the act of incorporation, supposedly authorised by Duke Bolesław the Bald in March 1242, was neither the beginning nor the end of the story. Certainly in the definitive act of reincorporation of 16 December 1261, there are references both to the annulment of former privileges and to 'irregularities' that had occurred during Duke Henryk III's childhood. In the 1260s, when Duke Henryk was ruling in tandem with his brother Władysław acting as episcopal administrator, a systematic code of *ius municipale*, or *Weichbild*, was received from Magdeburg, and Wrotizla moved definitively into a far-flung network of similar urban communities.

In that era, Wrotizla exercised considerable influence on other cities in Silesia and beyond. Professional 'locators' from the city were active in the incorporations of Bochnia (1253), Cracow (1257) and Lwów (1356). A fourteenth-century collection of Vratislavo-Cracovian *ortyli* or 'legal judgements' provided a guide to the interpretation and practice of urban codes. Yet the overall pattern was by no means homogenous. The town of Środa (Neumarkt), for example, which lay only twenty-five kilometres to the west of Wrotizla, took its law not directly from Magdeburg but from Halle, which had developed its own variant of the Magdeburg code. Środa's contacts with Halle went back to 1210 and its incorporation appears to have been completed before 1223. The Law of Neumarkt envisaged only limited municipal autonomy where authority was exercised either by a *scultetus* (*Schultheiss/soltys*) or by a hereditary *advocatus* (*Vogt/wójt*) and by their accompanying bench of magistrates. It was suited to small settlements, and was consequently adopted by more than 500 localities, both urban and rural, throughout medieval Poland. Indeed, it so closely resembled the set-up in Wrotizla preceding the reincorporation of 1261 that one is tempted to wonder whether Wrotizla had not modelled itself first on Środa before turning to Madgeburg at the second attempt. (Środa itself, though not its numerous brood, transferred to Vratislavian norms in 1362.)

Wrotizla was prevented from developing the full-blown institutions of municipal authority for several decades. The City Council, which appeared in the 1260s, did not initially enjoy plenary powers. But, in 1326, it bought out the rights of the hereditary advocate – *Schertilzan* – for the modest sum of forty marks. Thereafter the city's executive and legislative functions, including those of the advocate, were gradually taken over by the merchant-elected City Council (*Rat/rada*) and, with some delay, by a mayor chosen by the council. At the same time, special privileges were granted to the city's Jews, and the important commercial monopoly of storage was established.

Duke Henryk Probus had earlier granted the city the right to introduce a system of guilds. From 1272, every resident Christian merchant or craftsman was obliged to belong to an appropriate guild, whose elders regulated the activities of its members and swore obedience to the City Council. By 1327, twenty-nine separate guilds were in existence, though specialisation would multiply that number much further. The most important included the clothiers, the tailors, the butchers, the bakers, the blacksmiths, the tanners and the brewers. Each had its own meeting-place, its own church or chapel, its own street or quarter, and its own rules and regulations. Within a very short time the more prominent elders were forming a permanent patrician elite. Their families intermarried among themselves and the provincial nobility. They dominated the Magistrates' Bench and the City Council, often turning their municipal offices into lifelong or hereditary positions. Though they could never dominate completely, the system that they founded was due to remain intact until the nineteenth century.

The exact sequence of events in the slow evolution of Wrotizla's self-government is almost impossible to establish. But some clues may be found in the known changes and additions to the building of the City Hall, which had started life in the 1240s as a Merchants' Hall on the new Market Square. The earliest mention of the *Consistorium*, or 'seat of the municipal administration', dates from 1299. At about the same time the Advocate's Chamber was added, while the Councillors' Chamber did not take shape until 1328. The Świdnica Cellar, which was gradually transformed from the office of the city's wine and beer monopoly into the main city treasury, was first mentioned in 1331. Certainly, by the end of Piast rule in Wrotizla, arrangements were settling down into the pattern that would last until the imposition of Prussian rule some 400 years later. Elections and re-elections to the City Council took place every year on Ash Wednesday. The councillors varied in number from six to twelve. Whether individually or collectively, they supervised the city's courts and magistrates, regulated trade and weights and measures and controlled the city's finances. The city's Great Seal – which bore an image of its patron, John the Baptist, and the words WRATISLAVIAE SIGILLUM CIVITATIS – came into regular use in 1292 at the latest. It overlapped with, and then replaced, an earlier seal bearing an image of the crownless Piast eagle, undoubtedly used by the Advocate.

Many details of Wrotizla's early medieval government have survived. The names of the chief officials were listed, at least partially, from as early as 1214:

1214 Godinus scultetus
1229 Alexander scultetus de Wratislavia
1248 Advocatus noster Henricus Wratislaviae
1257 Heinrich, Vogt von Breslau
1261 Advocatus Henricus et Alexander filius eius[61]

The entry for 1261 seems to indicate that the Advocacy had become hereditary. The series ends in 1326 with the laconic comment '*vendidit*' (he sold it).

The names of the City Councillors were recorded from 1266:

Consules Wratislaviensis
1. Albertus de Banz
2. Godefridus Albus
3. Herdegnus
4. Albertus de Ciraz
5. Siffridus de Gorliz
6. Helevicus de Bolezlaw[62]

Despite several early breaks, this series continued until 1741.

Wrotizla's great Book of Accounts is known as the *Henricus Pauper*, or 'Poor Henry', from the signature of its first, self-deprecating bookkeeper. It meticulously recorded the city's income and expenses. The earliest-surviving entry relates to the very last year of the thirteenth century:

Anno domini 1299 prime mee collecte magistri Petri. Et illo anno fuerunt tantum quattuor collecte, et fuit tota summa de omnibus his collectis:
– Summa de prima collecta quam collegit Gothscalcus ante me 3 centum marc et 15 marc
– Summa de secunda collecta 200 marce et 70 minus 1 marc . . .[63]

'Master Peter' reports that four tax collections had taken place in that year, one of which represented his own debut. The total collected by his predecessor, Gottschalk, in the first round was 315 marks. The total collected in the second round was 269 marks. There follows a long list of contributors. Among them, *Judei dederunt 16 marc* (the Jews gave sixteen marks). At the end, a statement of responsible stewardship:

Residua pecunia posita est ad universos usus civitatis, videlicet ad pontes, ad murum, ad propugnacula, et ad alia necessaria.

(The balance of the money has been put at the disposal of the general purposes of the city, whether for the bridges, the wall or the barbican or for other necessities.)[64]

As for the Law of Neumarkt, the entire codified register of crimes and punishments was recorded in a set of volumes long preserved in the town archive of Głogów. The volumes were probably taken there in the mid-fourteenth century, when Środa transferred to Magdeburg Law. For what it is worth, the punishment for rape was decapitation.[65]

Nonetheless, the evidence shows that the competencies of municipal self-government were spreading. As the authority of the Piast dukes faded, the cities of Silesia were steadily learning to run their own affairs and to stand on their own two feet.

*

From its ancient focus on the Odra islands, Wrotizla expanded in the eleventh and twelfth centuries into a complex of five separate settlements. Tumski Island hosted both the original royal fort and the Cathedral Church of St John. The wooden castle, in which Bolesław Chrobry would have stayed in 1017, was enlarged and enclosed by a stone palisade in the 1220s. The first stone cathedral began to rise in the mid-eleventh century. Under Henryk the Pious, the castle was doubly extended and joined to a new octagonal chapel (now the Church of St Martin). This was the refuge into which many of Wrotizla's inhabitants successfully fled during the Mongol invasion of 1241.

Nearby Sand Island, known from medieval Latin sources as *Arena*, was the site of the principal Odra crossing, and was linked to each bank of the river by bridges first mentioned in 1149. Peter Wlast installed the Augustinian Canonry there, together with the magnificent Church of the Blessed Virgin, giving the canons the income of the nearby tavern and slaughterhouse. A convent of Augustinian nuns appears in the records from 1229.

The right-bank settlement of Ołbin was also developed by Peter Wlast, who built there both his own magnatial palace and the Benedictine Abbey of St Vincent, which absorbed the adjoining Church of St Michael in 1139. Transferred to the Premonstratensians in 1195, the whole complex was surrounded by defensive walls and remained one of the principal sights of Wrotizla until its demolition in 1529.

The left-bank district, destined to become the heart of medieval Wrotizla, stayed relatively open until the mid-thirteenth century. The Parish Church of St Adalbert (Wojciech), dating from 1112, was handed to the Dominicans in 1226. The Church of St Mary Magdalen was founded in the same year to

99

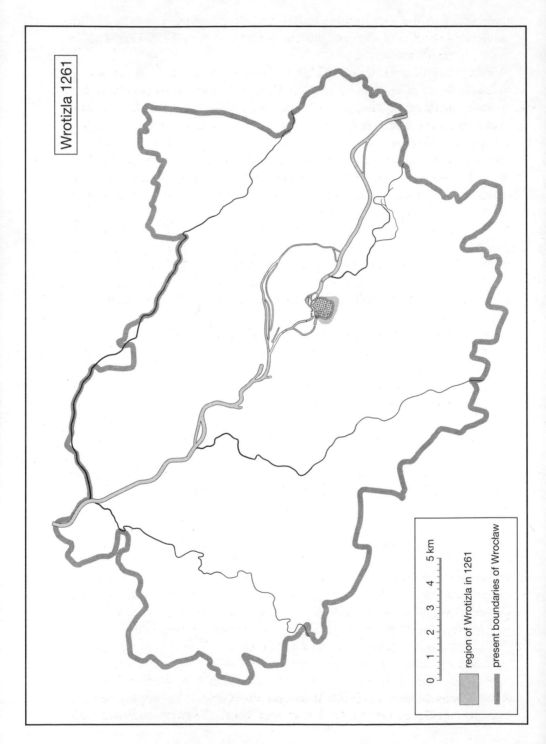

Wrotizla 1261

0 1 2 3 4 5 km

region of Wrotizla in 1261

present boundaries of Wrocław

undertake parish duties. Informal markets had undoubtedly been held here since early times, and German sources talk of a *deutsches Kaufhaus* built in the early thirteenth century.

The immediate result of the destruction of Wrotizla in 1241 was a veritable frenzy of building. The main Market Square was laid out, together with the smaller Salt Market to its south-west side. The City Hall was also begun, with the erection of a single-storey stone building with a long, low cellar. Further to the east, the New Market was established, whilst a separate New Town was founded in 1263. Occupying an island framed by the Odra and the Oława, the latter was initially settled by clothworkers and maintained its own administration and town hall until unified with the rest of the city in 1327.

Elsewhere, church-building continued apace. The Churches of St Adalbert, St Nicholas, St Mary Magdalen, St Elizabeth and the Cathedral of St John were all reconstructed in stone. Elsewhere, brick was widely used. The later decades of the thirteenth century saw the founding of the Churches of St Christopher, St Barbara and, from 1288, the magnificent Church of the Holy Cross. Following a fire on the left bank in 1272, Duke Henryk decreed that in future houses should not be built of wood.

Fortifications were planned to protect the developments. Initially they merely consisted of a ring of double palisades circling the town to the south of the river, but in the 1260s these were further strengthened by the addition of eight-metre-high walls and towers.[66] Access was guarded by five wooden gates. This was soon to be the strongest fortress in the Kingdom of Poland. Such costly measures were financed by a special tax imposed in 1274. The Jewish community was especially hard hit, being obliged to donate gravestones as well as funds for the construction effort. In 1291 the palisades and walls were complemented by a moat. The effect was achieved by diverting the 'White Oława', a tributary of the Odra, around the walls to rejoin the main arm of the river to the west. Though the New Town and Walloon quarter remained beyond the walls, the fruits of fifty years of reconstruction were secured.

Naturally, several new bridges had to be provided. The first bridges had been linked to wooden roadways which crossed the Sand Island and Cathedral Island on piles. In the late thirteenth century they were joined by the so-called 'long bridge', approximately on the site of the later University Bridge. The redirection of the White Oława also required the construction of numerous additional wooden crossings to link the town to its southern hinterland. Mikołaj Mikora (d. *c*.1175), a magnate whose residence once stood alongside that of Peter Wlast on the Ołbin, was responsible for building a bridge across the River Widawa (Weide). Liberally endowed with brick-built churches, stone houses, regulated waterways and permanent bridges, Wrotizla was visibly turning into 'a Venice of the North'.

Several self-contained villages sprang up nearby. To the south-east, beyond the River Oława, lay the Walloon settlement of St Maurice, variously recorded in early sources as the *platea gallica* or the *vicus b. Mauritii*. To the west, on the road to Legnica, lay the village of Sokolniki. Further out lay Szczepin (Tschepine), a village of fishermen centred on the Church of St Nicholas.

Further afield, the countryside was being transformed no less than the city. Monasteries and castles were springing up on all sides, each of them acting as a focal point for the domestication of the surrounding wilderness. Among the monastic houses, Lubiąż (1175) was the oldest; Trzebnica (1202) was the closest to Wrotizla; and Henryków the most productive of dependent foundations. The Benedictine monastery at Krzeszów (Grussau), for example, which stands at the foot of the Karkonosze mountains, was founded in 1242. It was taken over in 1292 by the Cistercians from Henryków, who were to remain there for 518 years.

Many of the castles of Lower Silesia were built on commanding heights by local magnates in the eleventh, twelfth or thirteenth centuries and remained in the hands of the founders for generations. The castle of Świny, or Schweinhaus, for instance, was mentioned in the Cosmas Chronicle in 1108 as 'Zwini in Polonia'. It was the seat of the Schweinichen family throughout the Middle Ages.[67] The history of Siedlęcin, or Boberröhrsdorf, is not unsimilar.

As Piast authority in Silesia fragmented, however, many castles became the strongholds of the multiplying duchies. The Piast castles at Legnica, Strzegom, Jelenia Góra (Hirschberg) and Bolków (Bolkenhain) all fit into this category. So, too, does the spectacularly sited castle of Książ – Schloss Fürstenstein – which started life in the thirteenth century as the home of the Dukes of Świdnica and which dominates the valley of the River Pełcznica. Once described as the *clavis ad Silesiam* or 'the key to Silesia', it was repeatedly modified and restored, most notably in the sixteenth century by the Hochbergs and in 1941 by Adolf Hitler (who never moved in).[68]

Hence, by the end of Piast rule, medieval Wrotizla had effectively taken shape. The urban centre had moved to the newly developed left-bank site, with the Market Square at its heart. Ołbin to the north, the *platea gallica* to the south-east, the Nikolaus quarter to the west and the New Town to the east were all established satellites forming part of the whole. The city already bore the hallmark of its distinctive shape, framed by the river on one side and the moat on the other. It would not exceed these bounds in any significant way until the nineteenth century. Moreover, it was already the service centre of a thriving region, whose inhabitants had been putting down roots that were no weaker than its own.

*

Many years were to pass before Poland fully resigned herself to the loss of Silesia. Yet the Polish monarchs had too many distractions elsewhere to reassert their former claims. In his final years, Łokietek was fully preoccupied with campaigns against the Teutonic Knights, whilst his son Kazimierz the Great (r.1333–70) involved himself ever more deeply in Ruthenia and Hungary. At the Treaty of Trencin in 1335, which coincided with the death of Duke Henryk VI of Wrotizla, Kazimierz reluctantly agreed to renounce his rights in Silesia in return for a renunciation of Bohemian claims to the Polish throne. But he did so only verbally, and the treaty was not formally ratified until 1339. Two years later, Polish forces entered Silesia from Wielkopolska, occupying Wołczyn, (Konstadt) Kluczbork and Byczyna (Pitschen). An extended Polish-Bohemian war, in which the Czechs raided close to Cracow and the Poles rode up to the gates of Wrotizla, was only brought to a close by the Treaty of Namysłów (Namslau) in 1348. Even then, peace was slow to follow. In the 1350s, further Polish-Bohemian tensions saw goods from Wrotizla excluded from the Black Sea route. The tensions subsided after an exchange of territory, the Poles surrendering their footholds in Silesia in return for the Duchy of Płock. In the 1360s, King Kazimierz married a Silesian princess, Jadwiga of Żagań, for his third wife, and was preparing for a renewed confrontation with Bohemia when he died. The Silesian question was not really closed until 1372 when the new King of Poland, Louis of Anjou (r.1370–80), formally undertook to maintain the status quo.

In the last analysis, Wrotizla's fate had been decided by the much-reduced proportions of the duchy and the consequent vulnerability of its last, heirless duke. Yet it is well worth pondering the alternatives that existed at the critical time in the 1320s. If Duke Henryk Probus had succeeded in holding on to the seniorate in Cracow, there is no doubt that Wrotizla could have developed as one of the major political and commercial centres of a reunited Poland. In that case, it would have been perfectly possible for the dominance of German culture in Silesia to have been reversed, as it was in late medieval Cracow and Poznań. However, Poland was not reunited by the Silesian Piasts, but by one of their fiercest rivals, Władysław Łokietek, Duke of Kujawy. As a result, Duke Henryk VI was driven to seek protection from another powerful sovereign. In the first instance, he attempted to tie himself to the Empire. In 1324, four years after the Kujavian's coronation in Cracow, the Vratislavian paid homage to Louis of Wittelsbach, King of the Germans, who renewed the decree recognising Wrotizla as an imperial fief. The move simply did not work. Rejected by the Pope, and preoccupied by his interests in Germany, the Wittelsbach could offer no practical assistance. Łokietek was meddling in the nearby statelet of Namysłów-Oleśnica, while most of the other Silesian duchies were falling to John of Luxemburg. In the circumstances, Duke Henryk VI had little choice. He could hardly have allied himself with Łokietek, since the alliance would have left him in an exposed position surrounded by territory controlled by Bohemia. So, on 6 April 1327, after lengthy negotiations, he drove the best bargain available. He formally surrendered all his rights in the Duchy of Wrotizla to John of Luxemburg. In return, he received the governance and income of the duchy for life. This time, the arrangement held. When Henryk VI died, the King of Bohemia took direct control of the duchy, which by feudal law he had already possessed for eight years.

After 1327, therefore, Wrotizla, for all practical purposes, had cut its political links with Poland. It maintained close commercial ties with its Polish neighbours, especially with Cracow; it continued to shelter a distinct, but shrinking, Polish community; and it upheld its association with the Polish Church. But Poland did not forget its prodigal son. Writing in the fifteenth century, the historian and chronicler Jan Długosz penned a nostalgic entry, which made a bold prophecy: Wrotizla 'used to be part of the Kingdom of Poland and will return to it when God takes pity on the Polish people'.[69] One can only admire his far-sightedness.

THREE

Vretslav in the Kingdom of Bohemia, 1335–1526

In the late Middle Ages, Central Europe became an arena for the competing ambitions of several powerful international dynasties. In the fourteenth century, no one family had yet established hereditary control over the Holy Roman Empire, while in Hungary, Bohemia and Poland each of the native dynasties died out – the Árpád line in 1301, the Přemyslid line in 1306 and the senior Piast line in 1370. As a result, the rumbustious nobles of the orphaned kingdoms, who held the right of confirming the royal succession, 'danced an elaborate gavotte' with the representatives of their would-be foreign rulers. 'They resembled nothing so much as the shareholders of old-established companies who seek an association with one or more of the stronger multi-national conglomerates.'[1] For their part, the multinationals, having gained a foothold in one kingdom, pursued a policy of extending their control over each of the others in turn. The House of Luxemburg, for example, which gained Bohemia in 1310, took control of the Empire from 1347 and of Hungary from 1387. The House of Anjou, which moved into Central Europe by winning the throne of Hungary in 1308, extended its realm to include Poland in 1370–86, but thereafter fell out of the race. Throughout the fifteenth century the Lithuanian House of Jagiello appeared to be winning. Having established themselves in Poland in 1386, they took over Hungary in 1440 and Bohemia in 1453. Yet it was the House of Habsburg that eventually scooped the jackpot. The Habsburgs hailed originally from the valley of the Aar, now in Switzerland. Their first bid to control the Empire (1273–1308) failed. But their second attempt, which started in 1438, proved long-lasting. And in 1526 they took both Bohemia and Hungary from the Jagiellons. They would remain the dominant force in Central Europe until 1918.

Silesia, which joined Bohemia in 1327, shared each of Bohemia's vicissitudes for 200 years. Ruled first by the Luxemburgs and then by the Jagiellons, with two Hussite and Hungarian intervals, it finally fell to the

Holy Roman Empire	Bohemia	Hungary	Poland
		⬇ Arpad Dynasty	⬇ Piast Dynasty
H Rudolph I von Habsburg* (1273–91)	**P** Vaclav II (Wenzel) 1278–1305 (Wenceslas Wenzel)		
Adolf of Nassau (1292–8)		Andrew III	
H Albert I	**P** Vaclav III (1305–6)	**P** Vaclav III 1301–5	**P** Vaclav III 1300–5
	Rudolph (1306–7)	**W** Otto von Wittelsbach	
Henry VIII* (1308–13)	Henry of Carinthia (1307–10)	**A** Carobert of Anjou 1308–42	
	L John of Bohemia 1310–46		Władysław Łokietek 1320–33 (Władysław I)
W Lewis of Bavaria Wittelsbach* (1314–47)			Kazimierz I 1333–70 (Casimir the Great)
L Charles IV* (1347–78)	**L** Charles 1346–78	**A** Louis of Anjou 1342–82	
			A Louis of Anjou 1370–82
L Vaclav (Wenzel)* (1378–1419)	**L** Vaclav IV (1378–1419)	**A** Maria 1382–7	**A** Jadwiga 1382–6
(Sigismund** 1410–19)		**L** Sigismund 1387–1437	**J** Jagiełło of Lithuania 1386–1433 (Władysław II)
L Sigismund* (1419–37)	**L** Sigismund (1419–37)		
H Albert II* (1438–9)	**H** Albert 1437–9	**H** Albert 1437–9	**J** Władysław III of Varna 1433–44
H Frederick III (1440–93)	**H** Ladislas Posthumous 1440–57	**J** Władysław 1440–44	
		J Ladislas 1445–57	**J** Kazimierz Jagiellonczyk 1445–92
H (Maximilian** 1486–93)	George of Podiebrady 1458–71	Matthias Corvinus Hunyadi 1458–90	
	J Władysław Jagiellonczyk 1471–1516		
H Maximilian (1493–1519)		**J** Władysław Jagiellonczyk 1490–1516	**J** Jan Olbracht 1492–1501
			J Alexander 1501–6
H (Charles 1516–**)			**J** Sigismund I 1506–48
	J Louis 1516–26	**J** Louis 1516–26	
H Charles V 1519–56		**H** Ferdinand von Habsburg 1526–56	

H Habsburg	**W** Wittelsbach	**A** Anjou	* Holy Roman Emperor
P Přemyslids	**L** Luxemburg	**J** Jagiellon	** King of the Romans

Habsburgs. Its capital city, whose name was recorded in 1327 as Wretslaw (after the old Czech Vretslav), lay in the thick of the troubles.

The transfer of Silesia to Bohemian rule involved Vretslav in the political and cultural life not only of Bohemia but also of the wider Holy Roman Empire. For the first two decades the duchy simply became a personal fief of the Bohemian King. As of 1355, however, it was incorporated into the Bohemian crown lands, thereby becoming one of four constituent elements – Bohemia, Moravia, Silesia and Lusatia. In formal terms, it was to retain this status until 1741 – a period of 386 years.

The Empire, of which the Kingdom of Bohemia was a part, had once been the most powerful monarchy in Western Europe. It comprised a kaleidoscope of states – lay and ecclesiastical, large and small – and encompassed much of Central Europe, stretching from Provence, Alsace and Holland in the west to Pomerania and Moravia in the east. Its early Emperors, the Ottonians and Hohenstaufen among them, had been seen as successors to the Emperors of Rome and had presided over the strongest state and the most magnificent court of the period. By the late Middle Ages, however, this former grandeur was waning. The Empire had become a collection of territories that recognised the pre-eminence of the elected Emperor, some only nominally. It was decentralised and disorganised.

The Empire's elective constitutional arrangements were also ossifying. In 1338, the Electoral College definitively rejected the long-standing papal claim to confirm the appointment of an Emperor, and in the Golden Bull[7] of 1356 the mechanics of election were fixed for the duration. Henceforth, the Emperor was to be the prisoner of his subjects, and in particular of those who elected him. Frankfurt am Main was to be the site of all imperial elections. A majority of votes among the seven named Electors was to be decisive. The seven Electors were to be the Archbishops of Cologne, Mainz and Trier and the Dukes of Bohemia, Brandenburg, the Rhine-Palatinate and Saxony. The Emperor Karel (Charles) IV, who formulated the Golden Bull, was bowing to reality. In Lord Bryce's famous pronouncement, 'he legalised anarchy and called it a constitution'.[3]

Bohemia, meanwhile, had grown into one of the leading powers in Central Europe. Its relationship to the Empire was profoundly ambivalent. Though its earlier dukes had paid homage to the Emperor and in 1212 had been made hereditary kings, it was not directly subject to the Empire. The Emperor had no sovereign rights in Bohemia, could exact no military levies and could raise no taxes. The core territories of Bohemia and Moravia, including the city of Prague (soon to boast an archbishopric and a university), as well as Kutná Hora, Plzeň, Olomouc and Brno, formed the heart of the traditional Czech homeland. Lusatia was the homeland of the

Slavonic Sorbs. Yet the influx of Germanic immigrants had already created a thoroughly multi-ethnic state by the time of the accession of the Luxemburgs in 1310. As in Silesia, the Germans and Flemings had brought more advanced farming methods, had begun to exploit mineral resources and had strengthened the realm economically. Their arrival had also sown the seeds of ethnic unrest. Nevertheless, Bohemia possessed one of the best-organised and most efficient state administrations of medieval Europe.

From the dynastic point of view, the realm of the Bohemian Přemyslids had grown from its Czech core to include not only the Austrian duchies, but the Kingdoms of Hungary and Poland. Though this conglomeration came to an end with the extinction of the dynasty in 1306, it was to see renewed expansion under the Luxemburgs. At its greatest extent, during the reign of Karel IV, it encompassed Bohemia and Moravia, Upper and Lower Lusatia, the Upper Palatinate and Brandenburg, including the small provincial town of Berlin. The jewel in the crown, however, was to be Silesia.

Following the cession of the Silesian duchies, engineered by King Jan (John), Silesia began its career as a Bohemian province, shifting thereby from Poland's western periphery to become the north-eastern outpost of the Crown of St Wenceslas. Vretslav became, after Prague, Bohemia's second city. But the circumstances of the cession have aroused controversy ever since. While later German historians would describe it as 'Henry VI's greatest service',[4] Jan Długosz complained that 'No neighbour of Poland has ever been so envious or hostile as have the Silesians.'[5] Nor was the coming of the Luxemburgs welcomed by all of Vretslav's citizens. The first demonstration of discontent came in 1333 when the clothworkers rose in revolt. Four years later, further opposition came from Vretslav Cathedral – the opening salvoes in a lengthy ecclesiastical and political struggle (see below). Vretslav was destined to have as much influence on Prague as vice versa.

The Luxemburgs had originated, not surprisingly, in the imperial county of Luxemburg. They had risen to prominence with the elevation, in 1308, of Count Henry IV as Holy Roman Emperor. Thus empowered, Henry was able to find an advantageous throne for his son Jan, who came to Prague as King in 1310, ending a protracted and bloody interregnum. With Jan's arrival, the Luxemburgs became leading dancers in the aforementioned 'dynastic gavotte' that was to dominate Central Europe throughout the fourteenth and fifteenth centuries. They left the stage in 1437. The final act of the drama came in 1526, when the premature death of Louis Jagiellon caused both the Bohemian and the Hungarian crowns to pass to the House of Habsburg.

The Bohemian kings of the Luxemburg dynasty were a very mixed bag.

Beyond the City: *Silesian Landscape* (1841) by Carl Friedrich Lessing.

Beyond the Plain: *Lake in the Giant Mountains* (1839) by Ludwig Richter.

Prince Vratislav I of Bohemia (*r. c.* 930).

Boleslaw Chrobry (*r.* 992–1025),
King of Poland.

Henryk VI (*r.* 1311–35),
last Piast Duke of Wrotizla.

St. Czesław (*c.* 1200–42),
Dominican miracle-worker.

Charles IV of Luxemburg (*r*. 1346–78), King
of Bohemia, Holy Roman Emperor.

Jiří z Podiebrady (*r*. 1458–71),
King of Bohemia.

Mátyás Corvinus (*r*. 1458–90),
King of Hungary, conqueror of Bohemia.

Louis II Jagellion (*r*. 1516–26),
King of Bohemia and Hungary.

The marriage of St. Jadwiga (Hedwig) (1186).

The Mongol invasion: the battle of Liegnitz (Legnica), 9 April 1241.

Duke Henryk IV of 'Pressela'
as *Minnesänger*.

The death of the blind John of Luxemburg: Crécy, 26 August 1346.

Bohemian Hussites versus
Imperial Crusaders (*c.* 1430).

St. John of Capistrano: the bonfire of the vanities (1453).

St. Vincent's Monastery on the Elbing, destroyed 1529.

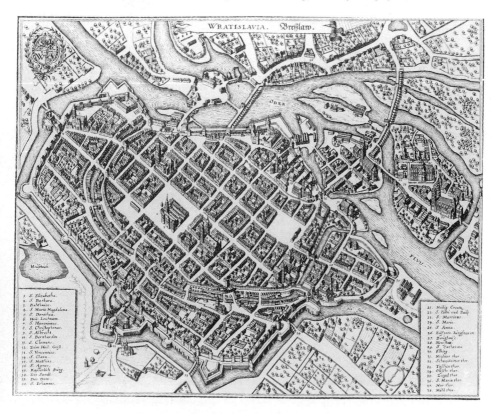

Matthäus Merian's city plan, 1650.

Johannes Cochlaeus (1479–1552),
theologian.

Johannes Hess (1490–1547),
reformer.

Crato von Crafftheim (1519–85),
humanist.

Rudolf II of Habsburg (1576–1612),
Emperor.

King Jan (John) (r.1310–46) was essentially an absentee. 'Vain, profligate and pleasure-seeking',[6] he felt little for Bohemia and was responsible for its general neglect. Hamstrung by concessions made to the Czech nobility, he was forced into the Domažlice Agreement of 1318, whereby he agreed to dismiss all foreign advisers and exclude all foreign troops. Thereafter, obsessed with chivalry, he led the life of a 'knight errant', crusading with the Teutonic Order in Lithuania or assisting the French kings in Languedoc, and returning to Bohemia only to collect taxes and knights. His adventures did benefit Bohemia territorially, however. In addition to his Silesian gains, aid to the Emperor at the battle of Mühldorf in 1322 won him the strategically valuable Chebsko (Egerland). A disputed succession delivered the Duchy of Upper Lusatia in 1319, and Tyrol was gained by marriage in 1335.

King Jan was to die fighting for the French against the English at the battle of Crécy in 1346, where the blind and ageing 'knight errant' was to experience the eclipse of European cavalry at first hand. As a later schoolboy history gasped:

> The blind king of Bohemia was led into the battle with his horse tied to the horses of two brave knights, his vassals. 'I pray you,' he cried, 'to lead me so far into the fight that I may strike one good blow with this old sword of mine!' And with eager shouts they plunged together into the thick of the fight, and fell among the heap of wounded and dying and dead.[7]

Though cut down by the massed ranks of Welsh archers and English infantry, they were accorded the greatest honour. Jan's broken body was laid to rest in the tent of the 'Black Prince', Edward, Prince of Wales. As a mark of respect, his arms and his motto *Ich Dien* were adopted by all future Princes of Wales. Incongruously, they remain in use at St James's Palace in London to this day.

Given his prolonged absences, King Jan's greatest contribution to his adopted kingdom must be found in the career of his son Karel (Charles) IV (r.1346–78). Karel had been installed as governor of Bohemia prior to his father's death and later ruled as *de facto* regent. As King, he oversaw the regeneration of the Bohemian realm, which, after his election as Emperor, became the centre of imperial life. Germany was ruled for a season from the Karlštejn Castle near Prague. A polyglot and a man of letters, Karel was described as being German by birth, French by education and Bohemian by inclination. In his autobiography *Vita Caroli*, he noted rather immodestly that 'We could speak, write and read not only Czech, but also French, Italian, German and Latin . . . so there was no difference in using any one of them.'[8] As a result, his rule possessed a strongly cosmopolitan flavour, as he sought to steer a middle course between the predominant Germanity of the Empire and the predominantly Czech character of the kingdom. Suppressing the banditry that had characterised his father's reign, he provided the peace and stability that allowed his kingdom to flourish both economically and culturally. Moreover, he presided over an outbreak of building fever, which began with the construction of St Vitus's Cathedral in Prague in 1344. He was also a frequent visitor to Vretslav, which he described as 'his most beautiful city'.[9] An entry by the chronicler Nikolaus Pol for the year 1353 took pride from this fact:

> Emperor Charles was very favourable to [Vretslav], he called it his and his father's beloved and loyal city, as it had always remained faithful to them. He thought so much of it that he even wrote to the Council in his own imperial hand, desiring to know how they were as he was concerned about them.[10]

After Prague and Nuremberg, Vretslav was the third most common destination of the Emperor's travels,[11] being granted an estimated thirty-one visits in thirty-two years. It saw enormous developments during Karel's reign, whence many of its finest examples of Gothic architecture can be dated.

Karel's eldest son, Václav (Wenceslas) IV (r.1378–1419), was the least successful member of the Luxemburg dynasty. By reputation a sadist and a drunkard, he is often referred to in German historiography as 'Wenceslas the Lazy'. Indeed, in 1400 the 'useless King'[12] was deposed by the Electors of the Holy Roman Empire for his indolence. His record as King of Bohemia was little better. By failing to deal with the growing ethnic conflict, he encouraged persistent interference from his overmighty relatives, suffered periodic imprisonment at the hands of the Czech nobles and finally, between 1396 and 1402, endured the rule of a baronial Council. In religious affairs, his protracted struggle to control the Church produced the Bohemian patron saint, St Jan (John) Nepomuk, who in 1393 was allegedly tortured by the King's own hand, before being thrown in a sack into the River Vltava.

In Vretslav, the uncertainty and lawlessness of Václav's reign contributed to the 'Beer War' of 1380–2, and to a protracted constitutional struggle that culminated, in 1418, in a full-scale revolt of the guilds. By the end of his reign, the political capital so painstakingly accumulated by his father had been thoroughly spent. Václav was incapable of dealing with the pressing challenge of Hussitism (see below), which he had initially supported. In 1419, he sought to quell the discontent by strengthening the German

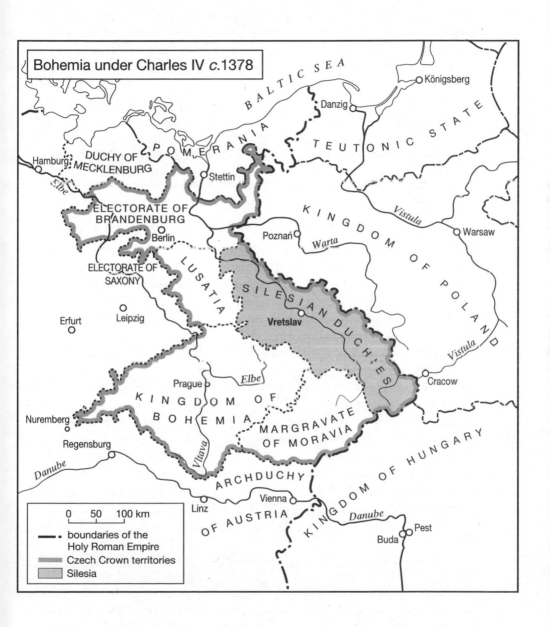

Bohemia under Charles IV c.1378

BALTIC SEA

Königsberg

Danzig

P O M E R A N I A

TEUTONIC STATE

Hamburg

DUCHY OF
MECKLENBURG

Stettin

Elbe

ELECTORATE OF
BRANDENBURG

Berlin

ELECTORATE OF
SAXONY

Poznań

Warta

K I N G D O M

Vistula

O F

Warsaw

P O L A N D

Erfurt

Leipzig

L U S A T I A

S I L E S I A N   D U C H I E S

Vretslav

Vistula

Prague

Elbe

Cracow

K I N G D O M   O F

Nuremberg

B O H E M I A

MARGRAVATE
OF MORAVIA

Regensburg

Vltava

Danube

ARCHDUCHY

K I N G D O M   O F   H U N G A R Y

Linz

Vienna

OF AUSTRIA

Danube

Pest

Buda

0   50   100 km

boundaries of the
Holy Roman Empire

Czech Crown territories

Silesia

element in the Prague City Council. The Czech population rose in revolt and stormed the City Hall, hurling ten German magistrates out of the window on to the pikes of the mob below. Václav was so shocked that he died of an apoplectic stroke, to be succeeded by his half-brother Zikmund (Sigismund).

Affable, generous and highly educated, Zikmund (r.1419–37) was a man of a very different stamp. A veteran of the Turkish wars, Holy Roman Emperor from 1410 and King of Lombardy from 1431, he possessed no mean talents. But his reign coincided almost exactly with the rise of the Hussites. In 1415, as Emperor, he had been implicated in the betrayal of Jan Hus at the Council of Constance; and as King of Bohemia after 1419 he was to lead the crusades against the Hussite Revolt. The prospects for an early conclusion of the conflict were slim. The Hussites would have submitted to Zikmund, had he allowed their Four Articles of Prague, but he was not disposed to compromise. Instead he retired to his second city, Vretslav, called an Imperial Diet, and planned the reconquest of his kingdom. In the Silesian capital he signalled his determination in brutal fashion. In March 1420, after a brief trial, he had twenty-four leaders of the recent Guilds Revolt beheaded on the Fruit Market. His harshness was not welcomed, however. Walking incognito in the city, he entered the council offices in the Schweidnitzer Keller and listened to the talk. Upon hearing numerous uncomplimentary remarks about his own person, he was moved to write in chalk across the table: '*Wenn mancher Mann wüßte, wer mancher Mann wär, gäb mancher Mann manchem Mann manchmal mehr Ehr.*' Freely translated, this means: 'If some people knew who some people were, some people would sometimes show some people more respect.'

During that same visit of the Emperor to Vretslav, the Church authorities examined a certain Jan of Prague, known as Krasá, and condemned him to death. In the eyes of his admirers, Krasá was a 'great lover of the Truth', who was persecuted in a 'godless, unjust and wrongful manner'. When it was put to him that the Council of Constance had been legally convened and that it had put the religious reformer Jan Hus to death (see below) in a proper and holy way, Krasá was caught in a trap:

> Unwilling to approve the statements put to him by those unworthy pharisees, that is by the bishops, doctors and monks, he was sent to the meanest of deaths. He was racked and tortured, dragged through the streets by horses, drenched with manure and finally burned at the stake. Though invited to deny the truth, he faithfully stood by our beliefs, a true strongman of God, praying for his enemies and bearing their insults, their curses and the laughter unbowed . . .[13]

From his base at Vretslav, Zikmund headed four imperial crusades against the Hussites. Thoroughly unsuccessful, they did little but sow profound hostility between the Czechs and Germans of the kingdom. Atrocities became commonplace as the conflict took on an increasingly 'national' complexion. The majority of the German population of Prague was expelled, while at Kutná Hora the German citizens killed around 5,000 Czechs, of whom some 1,600 were simply flung to their deaths down the mineshafts. Nonetheless, under the inspirational leadership of Jan Žižka and Prokop the Shaven, the Hussite *tabory* or 'war wagons' not only defeated Zikmund's crusaders but also carried their revolution through Slovakia, Lusatia and Silesia as far as the Baltic coast. But Silesia, and specifically Vretslav, was their most important target. In the spring of 1428, they launched an offensive. Troppau and Ottmachau (Otmuchów) were besieged and ravaged before the invaders entered the lands of their arch-enemy, Konrad of Oels (Oleśnica), Bishop of Vretslav. The fortress of Brieg (Brzeg) was taken without a fight. The Hussites then skirted round to the west to take Steinau (Śinawa) and the fortress of Glogau (Głogów). In late March they stood at the gates of Vretslav itself. As Nikolaus Pol wrote:

> . . . Haynau [Chojnów], then Neumarkt [Środa], four miles from here, were attacked and plundered. The monasteries, churches and houses were ruined by fire. On the same day they also devastated the small town of Kanth [Kąty] . . . in the suburbs of [Vretslav] the church and priory of St Niklas and many houses were burnt out. The statues on the stone chapel and the stone bridge were decapitated and mutilated, with only the crucifix being spared, as is still visible. Between here and Strehlen [Strzelin] and around Schweidnitz [Świdnica], they robbed, plundered and burnt many priories, churches and villages and smashed the [statues of] saints.[14]

In those weeks the city had effectively become an overcrowded refugee camp, yet its hastily completed fortifications refused to yield. The Hussites, unprepared for siege warfare, were reluctant to attack the walls and contented themselves with decapitating the icons in unprotected churches, before withdrawing laden with loot.

After this initial failure, five more Hussite campaigns followed. But Vretslav remained intact. The conflict gradually stagnated, although, with the Hussites holding fortresses such as Ottmachau, skirmishing and spasmodic raiding continued for many years. Eventually a compromise allowed Zikmund to return to Prague as King. But he was to enjoy very little time on the throne for which he had fought so hard. He died without a male heir, the last of the Luxemburgs, in December 1437.

Like all religious conflicts, the Hussite Wars summoned up the ugliest elements of human nature. The savage penalties meted out to 'heresiarchs' invited savagery in response. The Hussite bands attacked Catholic churches and monasteries with studied fury, especially when joined by drunken peasants in search of loot. In 1425, for example, they burned the monastery of Bardo in southern Silesia, together with its prior. In 1428, when they reached the walls of Vretslav, they also occupied Mount Zobten (Ślęża), whence they were dislodged only with great loss of life. In 1432, they burned both the Abbey of Leubus (Lubiąż) and the Convent of Trebnitz (Trzebnica), from where they stole the bells and the lead from the roof. For their part, the Vratislavians showed little mercy. In January 1429, when they recovered Ohlau (Oława) in a night raid, 'they filled the wells with dead heretics'. Captured heresiarchs like Henryk Peterswalder were handed over to the Inquisition. In 1430, an unfortunate Silesian officer, suspected of betraying the Bishop of Vretslav by not defending his castle at Ottmachau with sufficient vigour, was decapitated. Fighting in the locality of Vretslav continued until 1433–4. On 13 May 1433, the Catholic forces under Duke Nicholaus of Ratibor (Racibórz) gained a decisive victory near Trebnitz; and the following May, the most active Hussite leader in the region, 'Peter the Pole', *Starosta* of Nimptsch (Niemcza), was captured and brought to Vretslav in chains. Yet a settlement was in the offing. In December of that year, Alesz, the royal governor of Bohemia, arrived in Vretslav in the company of the Bishop, Konrad of Oels. Peter the Pole was released. Czechs and Vratislavians sat down to a hearty meal provided by the Dean of the cathedral.

In the years after the Hussite Wars, Bohemia sank further into chaos. Devastated, impoverished and depopulated, the once proud kingdom reached its lowest ebb. Decades of international isolation had dented its cosmopolitan character and upset the balance of domestic politics in favour of the Czech nobility. The years of Hussite turmoil had resulted in the 'outer' lands, Moravia, Silesia and Lusatia, being left to their own devices. Political stability was difficult to restore. The royal accession of Zikmund's son-in-law, Albrecht V of Habsburg, was not recognised by the Czech nobles, and he died before his claim could be enforced.

The Czechs then accepted as successor Albrecht's son, Ladislav Pohrobek (Ladislas the Posthumous, *r.*1453–7 – so called because he was born after the death of his father), though a long minority loomed. In the meantime, a Czech regency council was to rule; and from 1448 it came under the control of Jiří z Podiebrady (George of Podiebrady), a former moderate Hussite leader. When the young King died in late November 1457, aged only seventeen, suspicions were therefore rife in places opposed to Podiebrady's rule. Many suspected that the King had been poisoned. Vretslav's chronicler, Peter Eschenloer, wrote, 'Who wants to believe that such a strong young man in the best of health could be killed in so short a time by a natural disease?'[15] Other chroniclers linked the King's suspicious death with his frequentation of brothels, among them those in Vretslav's 'Venusberg'.[16] The truth was more prosaic. Scientific analysis of Ladislav's skeleton, carried out more than 400 years later, established that he had died of juvenile leukaemia.

Podiebrady (r.1458–71), the former regent, succeeded in having himself crowned King in March 1458. He rapidly soothed international concerns with a series of agreements and marriage treaties, and was even mentioned as a possible candidate for Emperor.[17] Domestically he enjoyed no such success. He ruled over a vastly different kingdom from that of fifty years before. As a Hussite, he found it very difficult to portray himself as leader of all his disparate subjects: Czechs and Bohemian Germans, Silesians and Lusatians, Catholics and Hussites. The list of opponents to his accession was long. Moreover, his relations with the Papacy were always stormy. The balancing act that he sought to maintain between outward conformity to Catholicism and his own unorthodox inclinations eventually brought excommunication and, in 1466, the proclamation of a crusade against him. The stability for which he strove was always precarious.

Moravia, Lusatia and much of Silesia had all refused to accept Podiebrady's accession. Their hesitations are often explained as a straight-forward Catholic reaction to his Hussite background, but there was more to it than religion. The national issue also played its part. The early decades of the fifteenth century had not been kind to the areas of German settlement. In 1410, the Teutonic Knights had been roundly defeated by the armies of Poland-Lithuania at Grunwald, while the Hussite Wars of 1419–37 had destroyed many of the German towns of Bohemia and Silesia. It must have appeared that the tide of German influence was turning. As the largest and arguably most Germanised city of Silesia, Vretslav was well placed to sense the danger. Its aversion to Podiebrady verged on the fanatical.[18]

Vretslav's anti-Hussitism provided the background to the Jewish pogrom of 1453 (see below). But it was to find more conventional expression after Podiebrady's accession in 1458. Initially, resistance to the new King meant that Vretslav was technically at war with the rest of the kingdom.[19] Amidst rising friction, much pressure was applied to the resisters to back down. They were eventually persuaded to be obedient and promised to pay homage in February 1463. However, abetted by the Church, the City Council failed to keep its promises and sought help to remove the 'heretic king'. For his part, Podiebrady had little thought of taking retaliatory action.

Increasingly frustrated, he refrained from confrontation, hoping that the hard-liners would tire. But tire they did not. Spurred on by the papal legate, Jerome of Crete, and by the Canon, Johannes Kitzinger, their hostility increased. In the spring of 1463, they sent an invitation to King Kazimierz of Poland to assume the throne and envoys to the Pope to plead for Podiebrady's removal. Though the other Silesian duchies had all been cowed into submission, Vretslav stubbornly refused to yield. The resultant stalemate persisted for more than a decade.

In the autumn of 1462, Pope Pius II took Vretslav under his special protection. Four years later, his successor, Paul II, excommunicated Podiebrady and called for a crusade. First to respond, of course, was the Silesian capital. In May 1466 an army of nearly 3,000 men took the field against the principality of Münsterberg (Ziębice), which belonged to Podiebrady. In quick succession, the town and castle of Münsterberg and the monastery at Kamenz were taken. The thorn in the King's side was beginning to fester. Soon, greater powers answered the Pope's call. Podiebrady's own son-in-law, Mátyás Corvinus, King of Hungary (r.1458–90), rallied to the cause more out of territorial greed than religious conviction. He invaded Bohemia in 1467 with a mixed force of 20,000 Hungarians and Croats and, after some desultory warfare, defeated the forces ranged against him. In May 1469, he was crowned in Olomouc by Czech and Silesian Catholics before hurrying to Vretslav to declare himself its saviour. In the eyes of the Hussites, he was no better than a foreign usurper.

Having ruled Hungary since 1458, Mátyás Corvinus was one of the most illustrious figures of late medieval Europe. He regained a position of power and glory for his country which far surpassed that of Bohemia. As a patron of the arts and of Renaissance scholarship, he established his court as a haven of humanist culture. He was the founder of the University of Bratislava and of a great library in Buda, the *Corvina*, whose treasures were surpassed only by those of Florence and the Vatican. In military matters, with his feared 'Black Army' of mercenaries, he held his own against the Empire, campaigned against the Turks, crusaded in Bohemia and in 1485 drove the Habsburgs from Vienna, which he promptly proclaimed as his capital.

Warmly welcomed in Vretslav, Corvinus was honoured with the best food and wines and with magnificent church services. It soon became clear, however, that any political honeymoon would be short-lived. His presentation of a bill to the city to pay for the costs of its liberation demonstrated an uncompromising stance. Moreover, as head of a strongly centralised Hungarian state, he was unwilling to accept Vretslav's claims to autonomy

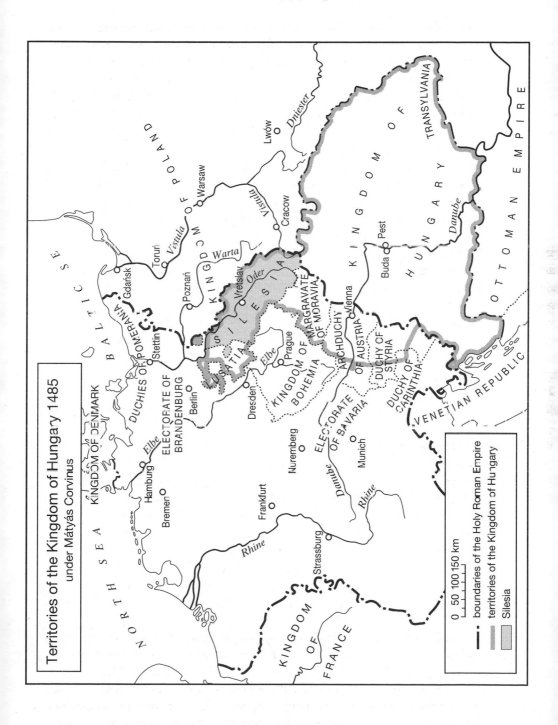

Territories of the Kingdom of Hungary 1485
under Mátyás Corvinus

boundaries of the Holy Roman Empire
territories of the Kingdom of Hungary
Silesia

0 50 100 150 km

or to allow the council to participate in the city's government. His attitude towards his new conquest was made plain by his aide, Georg von Stein, who cautioned:

> You must not take such liberties in future; to fight against Kings, to be disobedient to Kings, to call Kings heretics. It is for the Pope to identify heretics, not for you peasant of [Vretslav].[20]

With the death of Podiebrady in 1471 Corvinus appeared to have gained the upper hand, but his position of strength was illusory. He had in fact been outflanked by Podiebrady's appointment of Władysław, the son of King Kazimierz of Poland, as his heir. Rather than facing the Czechs alone, Corvinus now faced a Czech-Polish alliance, which threatened his new-found gains. Following a Polish thrust into Silesia in 1474, he reappeared in Vretslav with his 'Black Army', to face a joint force besieging the Silesian capital. He was soon to learn that his men had as many enemies within the walls as beyond them. His army's reputation for cruelty and ill discipline had preceded it throughout Central Europe, and had moved the city councillors to invoke the *Ius praesidii* and call out the militia. Corvinus's men were thereafter confined to the north bank of the Oder, where they were forced to face the besiegers from outside the walls. That winter they were even prevented from gaining access to the city they were defending, when the Vratislavians broke the ice on the river.

Corvinus himself spent the siege in more pleasant surroundings. He reputedly fell in love with the daughter of a councillor, one Maria Krebs. Three centuries later, an otherwise forgettable playwright put the romance on the stage. In the finale, Corvinus is seen leaving Vretslav and bidding his love farewell:

> Mátyás: Marie! We must part . . . I do not wish to be the enemy of your peace, the destroyer of those precious days that you hope for. So I lift my hand and commend you to heaven! Friendship! Until our souls are reunited there!
>
> Marie: Friendship until death! Friendship until the grave divides us, you noble man![21]

In reality, when Corvinus returned to Buda, he took Maria Krebs with him. Unable to marry her, he kept her in a secluded wing of the Royal Palace for the duration of their six-year affair. She was to bear him his only son and heir, János.

Meanwhile at the siege of Vretslav, the Polish army was persuaded to accept a truce, having suffered hunger, disease and a fire that destroyed most of its camp. During the subsequent negotiations, the mutual dislike between Corvinus and Władysław was such that they reportedly refused to look at each other. But agreement was eventually made in Buda in September 1478. The Bohemian lands were divided – Corvinus took Silesia, Lusatia and Moravia while Władysław retained the rest.

The arrangement was to last for another twelve years, until the death of Corvinus enabled Władysław Jagiellon (r.1490–1516) to reunite the divided lands. Władysław was famously indecisive. His habit of agreeing to every proposal with the words '*bene, bene*', caused him to be known to history as 'King Bene'. During his long reign he could not prevent the Czech magnates from steadily accumulating power, property and privilege. Accepting the vacant Hungarian throne, he moved his court to Buda. In Silesia, the loss of a strong ruler and the waning of centralised power resulted in a dramatic upsurge in lawlessness. A certain nostalgia was even felt for the 'despotism' of Corvinus.

Władysław was succeeded by his ten-year-old son, Louis II Jagiellon (r.1516–26). Feeling insecure as a minor, Louis agreed to a double marriage pact, to strengthen the position of his dynasty and detach the House of Habsburg from its alliances. In 1522, he was married to Maria of Austria, sister of the Emperor Charles V, while Ferdinand of Habsburg was married to Louis's sister Anne. Despite this masterstroke, the young King was still hamstrung by the continued dominance of the Bohemian nobility. An object of ridicule in his own court, he was apparently forced by straitened circumstances to pawn his jewels to pay for the food and clothing of the court. Faced with a Turkish invasion, he led a weak and demoralised Hungarian force into battle against the Sultan at Mohács in August 1526:

> In this pitiful defeat, the unfortunate King fled on his heavy warhorse. Near Mohács he came to a marsh into which the Danube flowed. As he tried to jump to the bank, the back legs of his horse stuck fast and he stumbled. In that marshy place, in full armour and without assistance [he] was wretchedly crushed and choked to death.[22]

The consequences of that unexpected death were to set the House of Habsburg on the road to Central European hegemony.

*

By the time of the Luxemburgs' accession, Vretslav was already a commercial centre of international standing. In the next two centuries it consolidated and to some extent expanded its position. There were good times and lean times. But in that time the population nearly doubled, from an estimated 12,000 in 1327 to about 22,000 in 1526. The inhabitants lived primarily from trade, both local and long-range, enjoying regular contact with numerous cities and countries. The historian Barthel Stein (1476–1522), describing Vretslav in 1512, noted the presence of merchants from all over Central and Eastern Europe: 'Russians, Wallachians, Lithuanians, Prussians, Masurians and the inhabitants of both Great and Little Poland'.[23]

Vretslav had enjoyed numerous commercial privileges since the later thirteenth century, which provided a solid legal framework for its prosperity. Markets were held twice weekly, on Thursdays and Saturdays. And the annual trade fair, which opened on St John's Day, rivalled similar events held in Leipzig, Poznań and Lublin. A second St Elizabeth's fair was added in 1337; and a third, in October, from 1374. Merchants from the east mingled with their counterparts from Flanders, western Germany and Italy. The three market squares provided huge open spaces for the exchange of eastern raw materials, such as furs and hemp, for western and local products, such as finished textiles and luxury goods. According to Barthel Stein,[24] the tradition developed whereby merchants from east or west would rarely cross the river, but would simply offer their wares for sale in the city before returning homewards.

From 1387 to 1515, Vretslav belonged to the Hanseatic League, yet it did not greatly benefit from its membership. The Hansa was in marked decline in the fifteenth century, and from 1474 Vretslav ceased to participate actively. To compensate, merchant circles were formed in the city with members from Leipzig, Nuremberg and Augsburg. Individual banking houses also came to prominence – notably the Fuggers of Augsburg and, in 1515–21, to complement their presence in the cathedral, the Thurzós of Cracow.

The economy of Silesia and of Vretslav benefited little from the reign of King Jan. He was the first of several predatory monarchs who took more than they gave. Though increased political stability and strengthened imperial contacts were to bring long-term advantages, his absenteeism and heavy-handed methods proved unsettling.

Under Karel IV, in contrast, the Kingdom of Bohemia experienced an economic boom. Viticulture and fruit farming were developed and native industries blossomed. The silver mines of Kutná Hora, for example, assumed a central importance. Large mints were established there and it grew to rival Vretslav as the second city of the realm. Indeed, it has been estimated that the Kutná Hora mines accounted for fully one-third of medieval Europe's silver production.[25]

Vretslav, in the Caroline Age, experienced similar growth. It developed close commercial contacts with Cracow and Toruń and, alongside Prague and Nuremberg, became a major centre of the Empire's trade network, with links to the Low Countries and the Venetian Republic. Indeed, given Prague's less favourable location, it has been contended that Vretslav was the most important commercial city of the Bohemian crown.[26]

On 29 February 1360, the Emperor Karel IV granted Vretslav the right of minting imperial gold coins (though no such coins actually appear to have been struck during his reign). Two years later, he authorised the additional right of minting silver hellers. These privileges greatly increased the city's prestige and were reconfirmed by Václav (from 1416), under Zikmund (from 1422) and under Podiebrady (in 1460–2). Low-grade hellers bearing the inscription MONETA WRATISLAVIENSIS were struck throughout the fifteenth century, sometimes in conjunction with the town of Schweidnitz. The quality of municipal groschen, half-groschen and hellers improved markedly in the 1470s under Corvinus. Medieval Vretslav possessed two mints: the main one, to the east of the New Market, had previously belonged to the Duke and was run by the City Council from 1360 to 1662; a smaller mint, which closed down before 1500, was located on the present-day Ulica Mennicza (Mint Street).

Silesian brewing developed from a small-scale clerical undertaking to a highly profitable civic enterprise. One of Vretslav's most notable products in the later Bohemian period was a brand of beer called 'Schöps'. First mentioned in 1392, Schöps superseded the popular Schweidnitzer beer in the late fifteenth century and, according to one commentator, was to be found in every local tavern as well as being exported to Dresden, Nuremberg and Leipzig.[27]

In theory, Vretslav was well placed to benefit economically from the political and religious upheavals of the early fifteenth century. As the Hussite conflict was kept at arm's length, it was able to profit to some extent from trade normally bound for Prague. On the other hand, the extension of the Hussite Wars into Silesia demonstrated that Vretslav was no less vulnerable than the capital itself. The severe disruption suffered in this period led to the Bohemian lands being eclipsed by other, more stable trading centres.

Later in the fifteenth century, Vretslav's resistance to Podiebrady served only to delay the city's re-entry into lucrative trading networks. Under Mátyás Corvinus, a currency reform and reorientation of commerce towards Hungary brought a measure of prosperity. But Corvinus's insatiable territorial ambitions meant that all his subjects groaned under taxes which largely offset any benefits that his accession had brought.

By the end of the fifteenth century, Vretslav was increasingly being challenged by the rise of rival trade centres in Leipzig, Cracow and Toruń. At the Hanseatic Assembly of 1469, its representative complained of the restrictions imposed by the League, noting that 'those in the Hansa are fettered and are condemned to decline, whilst those outside the Hansa are free to prosper'.[28] Yet independence also had its dangers. Growing friction with Poland led, after 1485, to a thirty-year tariff war with Cracow and in 1511 to a general boycott of Vratislavian goods ordered by the Polish King Jan Albrecht. For Vretslav, trade with Poland was the key to its success, but the city was in danger of killing the golden goose. It had been trying not only to enforce the legal monopoly of storage within its own jurisdiction but to extend it to all Polish cities with which it traded. This ambitious claim would have established effective control over the trade routes leading to the Baltic coast, to Lithuania and to the Black Sea. But the plan backfired. The Polish trade boycott, and the establishment of stores at Kalisz, Cracow and Poznań to offset the loss of trade from the Silesian capital, forced the city into a humiliating climbdown. The trade war with Cracow had seemed to foreshadow the end of the city's prosperity. In these circumstances, Stein wrote his *Descriptio Vratislaviae* in 1512 almost as a eulogy for what he considered a dying city. In it he noted sadly that Vretslav 'used to exercise such a power that it dominated the whole province, playing kings and lords off against each other'.[29] Three years later, Stein's nightmare became a reality. Vretslav was forced to surrender its warehousing privilege.[30]

Efforts to revitalise economic life included the dredging of the Odra in 1494 to facilitate river traffic and the establishment of a lottery in 1517 to improve municipal finances. After almost a century of setbacks, the city was finally solvent and was beginning to grow again. By the time of Mohács, it was recovering its place as one of the foremost commercial cities in the imperial network.

*

The late-medieval Church experienced a protracted and debilitating crisis, which can only be described as institutional sclerosis, and which threatened to lay it low. It was beset by schism, by so-called heresies, by clerical excesses and, above all, by an inability to reform abuses that all intelligent believers regarded as scandalous. From 1309 to 1377, the Popes fled from the intolerable politics of Rome to the 'Babylonian Captivity' of Avignon. From 1378 to 1419, during the Great Schism, Popes and anti-Popes struggled for supremacy in a hopeless morass of incompetence. For almost two centuries, the conciliar movement sought to address the problems by appealing to the authority of General Councils of the Church. But few such councils were called and none achieved the fundamental goal of harmony. The Council of Constance (1414–17) succeeded in restoring the Papacy, but did not realise more important reforms. It gravely compromised its standing as a forum of Christian principles by ordering the execution of the reformer, Jan Hus. Prior to the great Council of Trent (1545–63), no other assembly gained general support. Thanks to the delay, the Protestant Reformation intervened in the early sixteenth century and a wound was inflicted that has never been healed.

The distress at the heart of the Roman Church was reflected at all levels. The factions and quarrels that preoccupied the centre were multiplied throughout Christendom. What is more, religious differences increasingly took on a 'national' colouring. In the ethnically mixed cities of Central Europe, this was potentially explosive.

In Silesia, the first such conflict erupted in 1337, between King Jan and the Polish Bishop of Vretslav, Oksa Nanker. It was rooted in a row over the payment of Peter's Pence, a papal tax that was raised in Polish but not Bohemian sees. Its immediate cause was the King's seizure of the strategically important castle at Militsch (Milicz), to the north of Vretslav, which was the property of the Bishop. Bishop Nanker then confronted and excommunicated the King, to which the latter merely commented that the Bishop wanted someone to make him a martyr.[31] The episcopal residence was moved to Neisse (Nysa), and Vretslav was placed under interdict. For four years no official church services were held. In 1339, Bishop Nanker summoned one John of Schwenkenfeld, the Inquisitor of Heretical Faults, who sought to convince the City Council to relent. According to Długosz, the Inquisitor 'left the City Hall pursued by curses, insults and the grinding of teeth' and 'was lucky not to have been assaulted'.[32] His efforts were fruitless, and he was murdered soon afterwards. Only with Nanker's own death in 1341 did the city return to the bosom of the Church. The King retained the castle at Militsch, but the Church retained its right to Peter's Pence and its subordination to Gniezno.

In the early fourteenth century, Waldensian teachings entered Bohemia and Silesia, surfacing for the first time in troubles at Schweidnitz in 1315. Emanating from the valleys of Savoy, Waldensian doctrines took root primarily in the German-inhabited districts. They taught a new fundamentalism, accusing the Church of doctrinal indolence. The Waldensian storm blew over, but it was followed by the more serious threats of the Lollards and the Hussites.

The Lollards were followers of the English religious reformer John Wycliffe (c.1330–84). They protested against the worldliness of the established Church and preached a return to the asceticism of early Christianity. They believed that the Bible was of divine inspiration and ought to be available to everyone in the vernacular. Though suppressed in England, Lollardy had already spread to the Bohemian lands, via court contacts established with the marriage of King Richard II of England to Anne of Bohemia, a sister of King Václav. Its penetration of Bohemia is well demonstrated by the arrival in Prague in 1409 of a Lollard preacher named Peter Payne[33] and by the earlier presence in Vretslav of a certain 'Stefan', who described himself as a Lollard and a former student of Wycliffe at Oxford. Others described him as a 'militant, poor priest'[34] and a 'heresiarch':

> In that same time when Father Ludolf was Abbot of Sagan [Żagań], a certain heresiarch by the name of Stefan was held in the prison at [Vretslav]. It was known of him that he erred on fifty or more articles of faith . . . Firstly, he dared to affirm that he possessed the Holy Spirit, though he was a layman . . . or similarly, that dead children are saved without baptism . . . or again, that any honest layman can forgive sins and celebrate the Eucharist . . . He could not have cared less about the laws of the Roman Church, [maintaining] that evil prelates have no authority and that excommunication should not be allowed . . . since he refused to admit any arguments that were not drawn from biblical texts, he put quite a few learned men to shame . . . I think he must have been a peasant, having little grammatical skill in his speech . . . This same Stefan stated that in Oxford he had been imprisoned three years for heresy but that for all that time it could not be proved . . . when he was cornered by Father Ludolf and Master Jan, however, and did not agree with their proposals, he was condemned by the Inquisitor of Heretical Faults and burned in the year 1398.[35]

It was the start of a period of deep conflict when Catholics were all too ready to brand opponents as 'heretics', and the 'heretics' took the Catholics to be heretical. There ensued a savage century of reciprocal persecution.

Taking his cue from Wycliffe, Jan Hus (c.1370–1415), Dean of the philosophical faculty of the University of Prague, led a similar challenge to the established Church in Bohemia. He sparked a revolt that was to develop into one of the gravest crises of medieval Central Europe. Hussitism soon became part of a power struggle between the German and Czech elements within Prague University. Religious and ethnic issues dovetailed when the German element of the university called for a denunciation of Lollardy, which the Czech followers of Hus could not accept. Excommunicated in 1410, Hus was called five years later to the Council of Constance and asked to explain his continued protests. There, despite a guarantee of safe conduct from the Emperor Zikmund, he was condemned as a heretic. He was charged with holding beliefs that he steadfastly denied were his own. Stripped of the priesthood, disfigured and crowned with a dunce's cap bearing three demons, he was handed to the secular authorities with the words, 'O cursed Judas . . . we commit your soul to the Devil.'[36] He was then tied to a stake and set alight. He expired singing. As Hus had said,

'When thou speakest the truth, they break thy head.'[37] Truth was his watchword. 'Therefore, faithful Christians!' he exhorted his followers, 'seek the truth, listen to the truth, teach the truth, love the truth, be true to the truth, hold to the truth, and defend the truth to the death.'[38]

Hussitism, however, came in more than one variety. The central issue concerned the claim that the laity should be allowed to follow the practice of the clergy and partake of Holy Communion in both kinds – that is, bread *and* wine. As a result, the mainstream followers of Hus took the name of Utraquists. Their emblem was the chalice; their motto was '*Pravda vítězí*' ('Truth prevails'). Yet there were further demands. When war broke out in Bohemia in 1419–20, the Hussites adopted 'The Four Articles of Prague':

- Communion was to be administered to clergy and people alike in both kinds.
- The Word of God was to be freely preached.
- The worldly possessions and property of the clergy was to be abolished.
- Sinful conduct was to be publicly exposed and punished.[39]

The more radical demands led to the creation outside Prague of an armed camp of militants, which took the biblical name of Tábor. A third centre was established at Oreb. One branch of Hussitism, the Adamites, were nudists. But it was the Taborites who produced the most uncompromising 'warriors of God' – the one-eyed Jan Žižka (d.1424), Prokop Holý (Procopius the Shaven, d.1434) and Jan Roháč of Duba (d.1437) – and who soon came to blows with both the Catholics and the Utraquists. After the death of Žižka, they spawned the super-militant 'Brotherhood of Orphans'. They rejected the compromise enshrined in the Compacts of Basel (1433), which represented a slightly modified version of the Four Articles and which were to carry the force of law in Bohemia until the mid-sixteenth century. They held out in their stronghold of Tábor until 1452. Since Prague was dominated by the Utraquists, and much of Bohemia by the Taborites, the second city of the kingdom, Vretslav, became the natural headquarters of the Catholics and the Luxemburg loyalists.

Vretslav would play its part in another long-running controversy, which rumbled on for several decades. At the Council of Constance, representatives of the King of Poland laid charges against the Teutonic Knights of Prussia for conducting their activities in a manner that was inconsistent with Christian principles. The Polish advocate, Professor Paweł Włodkowic (Paulus Vladimiri, c.1370–1435), Rector of the Jagiellonian University, was a philosopher, theologian and jurist. The principal charge concerned the violent campaigns of sequestration and extermination, which allegedly accompanied the Knights' mission of converting the pagans of the North. But it raised other issues regarding the rights of non-Christians to their lands and property, their right of resistance and the need for some form of international tribunal to regulate the resultant disputes. The high-minded arguments of Paulus Vladimiri were undoubtedly inspired by the politics of Poland's long-standing wars with the Knights, but they constitute an early contribution to the theory of international law. And they hardly deserved the crude response that they evoked. For Paulus Vladimiri's chief opponent, the Dominican Johann Falkenberg, did not content himself with a reasoned confutation. He also published a wild satire in which the Poles were presented as 'odious heretics', 'shameless dogs', sacrilegists and 'idolators of Iagel'. '*Ceteris paribus . . .*' he commented, ' – all things being equal – it is more meritorious to kill Poles and their King than to kill pagans.' In this climate, there was little chance of an impartial hearing. Poland's grievances were deferred to the arbitration of the imperial *Reichstag* or Diet.

The Diet assembled at Vretslav during the winter of 1419–20. Paulus Vladimiri was again present. But the Emperor's decree, issued on 6 January on the territorial aspects of the dispute, supported the status quo. It was immediately appealed against, both by the Knights and by the Polish King, and hearings proceeded inconclusively in Rome over the next four years. There would be no satisfactory resolution. The Knights renewed the war against Poland in 1431, thereby breaking the 'Perpetual Peace' that had been called while the lawyers argued. Paulus Vladimiri died without seeing any tangible reward for his travails. Even so, he is remembered not merely as an advocate of the Polish cause but as a champion of conciliarism. The arguments that he put forward at Vretslav in 1420 left no trace in the local record, but his writings certainly deserve the thoughtful attention of Vratislavians of a later age:

> To remove the danger of warmongering under the guise of lofty principles, Vladimir[i] put forward the idea of an international penal code and of an international tribunal to deal with . . . crimes committed by one state against another. In this respect, he was the first to demonstrate the inhuman and un-Christian character of killing, exterminating, expelling or enslaving a nation, or national group, for ideological, racial or other reasons.[40]

The Vretslav Diet is notable for many reasons. It was the only such meeting ever to take place east of the Elbe. And for a winter, Vretslav stood at the centre of European diplomacy, the focus of imperial and papal politics. But it also marks a minor turning point in European history. At the Diet, Zikmund somehow persuaded other rulers to support his anti-Hussite crusades, though opinion had long been turning against them. The movement begun by Pope Urban II at Clermont in 1095 was morally bankrupt. Vretslav witnessed the crusaders' last hurrah.

The Church's counter-offensive against the multiplying challenges to its authority came in various forms. For one thing, the Inquisition was strengthened. As early as 1420, the Archbishop of Gniezno ordered all parish priests to inform on anyone with heretical tendencies, male or female, religious or lay; and various individuals in Vretslav were required to supply written references of their orthodoxy.[41] For another, encouragement was given to cults, such as that of the Czech Catholic martyr Jan Nepomuk, which emphasised the moral supremacy of the Church. But none made a greater impact than the strange and disturbing episode provoked by John Capistrano (1386–1456).

'Brother John' was a sixty-seven-year-old Franciscan and former governor of Perugia who had been sent to Bohemia as 'Inquisitor General' to stamp out heresy. Long active in Moravia and expelled from Prague, he was invited to Vretslav in 1453 and received a rapturous welcome. Finding virtually no Hussites there, he turned his invective on the ostentatious wealth of the burghers. He preached in St Elizabeth's Church, and then, from the window of his lodging at No. 2 Salt Market, watched as his congregation dragged out their luxuries to be burned. According to the chronicler Nikolaus Pol, the cadaverous monk – dressed in a simple grey cloak and wooden sandals – held an open-air sermon on 22 February on the Salt Market, where he 'strongly condemned the vices and excesses in clothing, eating and drinking'. As a result, 'mirrors, masks, boardgames, dice and playing cards were burnt on a great bonfire'. Pol concluded that, on that day, Capistrano 'awoke an especial devotion in the people'.[42] It was a performance worthy of Savonarola in Florence. Capistrano would later be honoured as the patron saint of jurists. His spiritual stock rose even further when it was claimed that he had raised thirty persons from the dead, restored hearing to 370, speech to thirty-six, sight to 123 and had made 920 of the lame and crippled walk.[43]

Capistrano preached three times daily in Vretslav between 14 February and 27 April 1453. He probably spoke in Latin with the help of a German interpreter. His passion was no doubt increased by the knowledge that the Ottoman Turks had surrounded the last remnant of the Roman Empire at Constantinople and that news of its fall could be expected any day. (In fact, the Turks launched their decisive attack on 2 April, Easter Monday, when Capistrano was preaching 'On the Resurrection'. News of their victory, which occurred on 29 May, would not have arrived until sometime in June.) The content of the sermons, whose texts have survived in their entirety, was not very surprising. It included all the standard subjects of a Christian revivalist drive: 'On the Last Judgement', 'On the stages of Perfection', 'On Contrition', 'On Confession', 'On the Articles of Faith', and so forth.[44] Catholic commentators have concentrated on the resultant 'renewal of religious morale in the city'.[45] They are not telling the whole story.

For Capistrano's activities were not confined to good works. He regularly denounced three dangers – from Turks, from Hussites and from Jews. But with few Turks or Hussites in the town, it was the Jews who bore the brunt. In May, Vretslav's Jews were rounded up and Jewish property was confiscated. Accused, among other charges, of poisoning the water and 'desecrating the host', the prisoners were tortured until suitable confessions had been extracted. It was said that Capistrano took an active interest in their 'interrogations'. Sentenced to death, a first batch of fourteen victims was tied to wooden boards on the Market Square. Their flesh was removed with red-hot tongs and thrown into pans over hot coals. They were then quartered alive. For the remainder of the condemned, the choice was to convert or be burned. Some, including the Rabbi, committed suicide, but another forty-one people were burned on the Salt Market on 4 July. By medieval standards, as Hus had discovered, the penalties for religious dissidence were severe. By modern standards, they reveal a very specific, and pathological, concept of Christian revivalism.

Capistrano's excesses inflamed Vretslav's diehard anti-Hussitism. It resurfaced, amid another flood of sermonising, in the refusal to recognise King Jiří z Podiebrady. It even undermined the Bishop. The Czech prelate Jodok z Rožmberka (Jost von Rosenberg, 1430–67) was appointed to Vretslav in 1456, shortly before Podiebrady's accession. Despite his impeccable Catholic credentials and later role as a founder of the anti-Hussite League of Grünberg, he was not forgiven for accepting Podiebrady and was swamped by outpourings of anti-Czech feeling. In one exchange, he came to blows with the papal legate, Jerome of Crete, after quoting the words of St Paul to Titus: 'The Cretans are always liars, evil beasts and slow bellies.'[46] As a result of such tensions, he was a rare visitor to Vretslav, preferring the safety of his family seat at Český Krumlov, whence he attempted to mediate and to preach moderation. Though he was a tireless opponent of Hussitism, his death in 1467 was greeted in his bishopric with celebrations and derogatory ditties:

> One wolf does not bite another wolf; the Bohemians are villains.
> The Christian Bohemians are not called Christians, but heretics.
> Bishop Jost, the old wolf, taught the other wolves how to eat geese.[47]

Thirty years after Bishop Jost, Vretslav received a prelate of particular distinction. Born in Cracow, Jan Thurzó (r.1506–20) came from a prominent Hungarian family that had made a career in Poland, but whose connections stretched from Cracow to the Bishoprics of Olomouc and Oradea, and to the Fuggers in Augsburg. Like Copernicus, a student first in Cracow and then in Padua, Thurzó had served as Rector of the Jagiellonian University, having previously studied at the Cathedral School in Gniezno. He built a summer palace at Janová Hora, near Javorník, on the Bohemian side of the mountains, but is best remembered for the open mind with which he welcomed the intellectual and religious innovations of his day. He corresponded with Erasmus, Melanchthon and Luther, and collected pictures by Cranach, Dürer and others. From Vretslav he used his wealth and influence to sponsor promising academics or attract learned teachers. He also helped to establish the first printer in the city, and numerous publications were subsequently dedicated to him. Described by some as the 'sun of Humanism', Thurzó was to serve as a catalyst in the transfer of the new thinking to Silesia.[48] He was given to signing himself 'Johannes Turzó, Episcopus Vratislaviensis, Polonus'.

By the early sixteenth century, the Church in the Kingdom of Bohemia appeared to have weathered successive storms of heretics and Hussites. But the new learning of the humanists was foreshadowing fresh struggles. The coming decades were to bring a shock from which the Church has never truly recovered – the Protestant Reformation. Vretslav had taken a lead with its spirited defence of the Church against Hussitism. It would now play a leading role in the propagation of Martin Luther's beliefs and would become a bastion of the Protestant faith. The irony is that it became predominantly Protestant in the very same years that it passed under the rule of the Most Catholic House of Habsburg.

*

Late medieval culture remained essentially theocentric, and religious concerns dominated all aspects of the sciences and the arts. One can point to important shifts, such as the growth of vernacular literature or the appearance of Renaissance art, but one cannot escape the fact that the new trends were largely subjected to established religious priorities. Dante Alighieri wrote his sublime *Divina Commedia* in the dialect of his native Florence, yet he used it to portray an unorthodox but nonetheless deeply religious vision of Man's progress through Hell, Purgatory and Paradise. The Renaissance, one must emphasise, was not the same thing as the Enlightenment.

Cultural life in Silesia, as elsewhere, changed very slowly. Painting, sculpture, architecture, music – all remained firmly entrenched in the religious sphere. Most literary works were still written in Latin and addressed devotional subjects. Secular culture, in contrast, took the form of a three-cornered contest between influences emanating from Bohemia, Germany and Poland. In Bohemia, for example, the Czech nobility fought very effectively against the form of German culture imported by the Luxemburg dynasty, winning notable victories, such as the Agreement of Domažlice (1318), which restricted foreign influences.

The Caroline Age signalled an important stage in this contest. Karel's strict even-handedness towards the rival Czech and German constituencies prompted the general advance of vernacular culture. The Czechs benefited most. Having escaped from the ecclesiastical influence of the Archbishopric of Mainz, Prague was granted a university in 1348, the first seat of higher learning east of the Rhine. Its mission was to educate the 'four nations' of Bohemians, Silesians, Bavarians and Saxons.

The new self-confidence was reflected in a surge of development in the Czech language. The Dalimil Chronicles (1314), the allegorical verse of Smil Flaška and the later philosophical writings of Tomáš of Štítné (c.1331–c.1401) demonstrated that Czech was already a stable literary language. A Czech translation of the Bible, appearing in the 1360s, pre-dated the first French and English translations and was only preceded by the Italian translation. Czech–Latin dictionaries appeared; and an encyclopaedia, with entries by Karel IV himself, followed. Czech found its way into the other lands of the crown of Bohemia, especially into Upper Silesia, where it was reportedly facilitated by the relative closeness with Polish.[49]

Yet as Czech national consciousness began to sprout in Prague, so too did a rival German consciousness. A leading figure in this development was Johann von Neumarkt (1315–80). As Chancellor to Karel IV, he undertook a reform of the use of the Latin and German languages at the Bohemian court. His efforts to regulate syntax and vocabulary were to make him one of the most important influences in the evolution of medieval High German.[50] Soon after his death, his labours bore fruit. The remarkable dialogue entitled *Ackermann aus Böhmen* ('Death and the Ploughman', c.1400) penned by Jan z Teplé, the town scribe of Žatec (Saaz) in northern Bohemia, is a recognised treasure of German medieval literature.

Parallel developments occurred in Silesia. The link with the Holy Roman Empire, the service of many Silesians at Karel's court and the opportunities offered by the University in Prague, undoubtedly contributed to the delineation of a specifically Silesian identity. *Toutes proportions gardées*, the Emperor's own literary work, the autobiographical *Vita Caroli*, was mirrored in Vretslav by the Hedwig's Codex, a hagiographical celebration of the life of St Jadwiga, which was written for Duke Ludwig I of Liegnitz (Legnica) in 1353, but whose illustrator had been trained in Prague.[51]

St Jadwiga provided one of the primary cultural wellsprings of the period. Canonised in 1267, she soon developed a local cult following, with her tomb at Trebnitz becoming a pilgrimage site of the first rank. She inspired numerous devotional offerings. The Jadwiga Triptych, a series of scenes from the life of the saint, which once graced the Bernardine Church in Vretslav, was painted in 1430. The 'Freytagshandschrift' of 1451, which comprises a collection of sixty illustrations on the same theme, was commissioned by a city councillor, Anton Hornig.

Silesia, and Vretslav in particular, experienced strong Bohemian influences. It was, after all, the second city of the kingdom. There was constant traffic between the Silesian capital and Prague. Bohemia had developed into one of Europe's cultural bastions, and by the turn of the fifteenth century the road to Prague carried Vretslav's principal line of cultural communication to the West.

The Bohemian connection can be seen in such works as the Glatz (Kłodzko) Madonna and the Vratislav Holy Trinity (c.1350), but Petr Parléř (1332–99) was its most famous representative. Born in Swabia, he rose from obscurity to become court architect to Karel IV. He created many of Prague's late-Gothic masterpieces: St Vitus's Cathedral, the Charles Bridge and the Old Town Gate. His influence spread throughout the kingdom and it is likely that he visited Vretslav. Certainly his style can be seen there in the Church of St Dorothy (c.1381) and, according to some, in the tomb of Bishop Przecław of Pogarell (r.1341–76).[52]

After the outbreak of the Hussite Wars, however, new cultural signatures became manifest. Experts observe a native Silesian style in the Jadwiga Triptych, while the altar of the Church of St Barbara, from 1447, reveals Dutch elements. German craftsmen and German styles dominated. The Nuremberger Hans Pleydenwurff (1420–72) supplied the altarpiece (1462) for the Church of St Elizabeth in Vretslav, and the sculptor Peter Vischer (1460–1529), also from Nuremberg, created the tomb of Bishop Johannes Roth in 1496.

Much of Vretslav's medieval art is no longer in place. Time, plunder and changes of taste have all wrought their destructions. In this respect, the Second World War caused enormous losses, not only from physical damage but from the depredations of successive regimes. The National Museum in Warsaw possesses several masterworks from Bohemian Vretslav, now displayed – like the altarpiece from St Barbara's – as prize examples of medieval Polish craftsmanship. Yet discoveries are still coming to light. One of these was the remarkable series of late-medieval wall-paintings, both religious and secular, which were fully revealed by restoration work in the 1990s. The predominant motifs are floral. Although they are not of the greatest artistic value, they help the modern visitor to imagine the rich coloration of medieval interiors that have long since lost their hue.[53]

Vretslav was quick to clamber on to the newfangled bandwagon of printing. The first press was established there by Caspar Elyan (c.1435–86) in 1475, a year after Cracow. Born in Glogau, Elyan had learned his trade as a printer in Cologne. Late in life he was nominated a Canon of Vretslav Cathedral. In the decade after 1473 he produced nine known *incunabula*, all in Latin. The first was a religious text on the history of Our Lord's Transfiguration. The second, precisely dated to 9 October 1475, was an impressive sixty-four-page volume, the *Synodical Statutes of the Bishops of Vretslav*, which contain the earliest examples of Polish texts in print, including the Lord's Prayer, the Hail Mary and the Credo. Later items included both poetry and prose. Elyan was not alone. There was a print-shop from 1480 in Liegnitz and from 1521 in Neisse; and others in Vretslav. Conrad Baumgarten of Rotenburg, who had worked in Venice and Olomouc, arrived in Vretslav in 1503. His copper-printed copy of the fourth woodcut edition of *The Legend of St Jadwiga* (1504), a masterwork of its type, marked the founding of a 'State Printworks' that would operate for 300 years and more.[54] Above all, Vretslav's first historians found their way into print. The town clerk, Peter Eschenloer (c.1420–81), published his *Historia Wratislaviensis* in 1472, and Barthel Stein followed suit with his *Descriptio totius Silesiae et civitatis regie Vratislaviensis* in 1512.

One consequence of the Hussite Wars was that Vretslav renewed and revitalised its cultural contacts with Cracow. Once the Charles University had been taken over by Utraquists, the Jagiellonian University in Cracow became the more usual destination for young Vratislavian men seeking a higher education. Especially between 1433 and 1510, the ties were very close. Hundreds of Vratislavians studied in Cracow, many of them going on to become teachers, priests and professors. Hundreds of Cracovians, like Bishop Thurzó, came to live and work in Vretslav. Mikołaj Tempelfeld, for example, a famed preacher at St Elizabeth's in Vretslav, was (after Vladimiri) yet another Rector of the Jagiellonian to feature in Silesian life. His contemporary, Mikołaj Kopernik (1473–1543), who had graduated from Cracow, held a canonry at the College of the Holy Cross in Vretslav for thirty years as a form of scholarship for further study. It is assumed that he stopped over there on his way to Italy in 1501.

In 1505, the city fathers of Vretslav sought to launch a university of their own. They obtained a charter from King Władysław Jagiellon, and duly took possession of several buildings centred on Holy Cross College, which was to house the new foundation. But the approval of the Pope could not be obtained. Dastardly intrigues by Cracovian agents in Rome were suspected.

By the late fifteenth century, humanism was spreading throughout Western and Central Europe. It supported the humanities, rather than logic or metaphysics, as the centre of intellectual and artistic endeavour. Quite naturally, given their level of education, many of its most important patrons were churchmen. In Vretslav, Bishops Rudolf von Rüdesheim (r.1468–82), Johannes Roth (r.1482–1506) and Jan Thurzó (r.1506–20) had all benefited from study in Italy and served as catalysts in the transfer of the new thinking to Silesia.[55]

Caspar Ursinus Velius (1493–1539) was one of Thurzó's most brilliant protégés. Born in Schweidnitz, he had entered the University of Cracow at the amazing age of twelve. At fifteen, he was already a poet of note and had attracted the attention of the Bishop in Vretslav. In 1517, still only twenty-four, he was made Poet Laureate to Maximilian I in Vienna. Though he was to become one of the most important German humanist poets, and a friend of Erasmus, his relationship to his mentor, Thurzó, remained strong. Touchingly, after the Bishop's death in 1520, many of Velius's poems were found among his valuables.[56]

Two other Vratislavian humanists, who were exact contemporaries, had close links with Cracow. Lorenz Rabe, better known as Laurentius Corvinus (1460–1527), was born in Neumarkt, studied and worked at the Jagiellonian University, knew Copernicus and is generally regarded as one of the pioneers of literary humanism in Poland. He wrote Latin verse, a theoretical textbook of poetics and studies of Polish monarchs. In the twenty years after 1502, he twice served as City Secretary in Vretslav. His poems sang the virtues both of his adopted Poland and of his native province. His *Hortulus Elegantarum* or 'Little Garden of Refinements' (1512), for example, is a hymn of praise to Cracow:

> Has tibi Sarmaticum: doctissima Craca sub arem
> Corvinus iero mittit ab orbe notas
> Hinc ubi bella potens in edibus inclyta saeria
> Menia preruptis tollit ad astra iugis
> Scilicet alma meum rude pectus mater alebus
> Enati primitas excipe quaeso tui.
> Duas mens et bereo non sat madefactus ab ymba
> Sole nec Apbrico parturit rustus ager:
> Dum mihi castellani sunder plus roris Apolli
> Et mea sub tepida rura calore coquet.
> Ipse sub autumni tibi sidere vitibus hortum
> Plenas maturis setibus arura dabo.[57]

> (Learned Cracow, let these verses
> bring my Sarmatian plot to you;

I have come to an earth-bound space,
where the banks of mighty buildings
reach to the stars; here, Corvinus
broadcasts his beat to the planet,
but it was my alma mater
who gave this yokel wings to soar.
I glory in my dappled moods,
As a field grows gold when no more
soaked in the sun that doused with shade.
The task of my keepers has been
to husband Apollo's juices
and warm my earth gently; I own
the duty to render, come autumn,
both the first fruits and the mature vintage.)

Michael Falkener (1460–1534), in contrast, left his native Vretslav to become a lifelong professor of philosophy in Cracow. Under the name of Michael Wratislaviensis, he published numerous works on scholastics, mathematics and astronomy, and exchanged polemics with Martin Luther. He also wrote hymns and made collections of psalms, and thereby demonstrated that Renaissance humanism was by no means incompatible with religious devotion.

The cultural landscape of Jagiellonian Vretslav was probably more diverse than that which obtained both before and after. The dominance of German culture, as established in the fourteenth century, had been successfully challenged first by Czech and then by Polish elements. After the Reformation, and under Habsburg rule, the German element would increasingly return to the fore.

*

Vretslav was a multi-ethnic city in the Middle Ages. Its ethnic composition moved in an endless state of flux, changing with each political and cultural ebb and flow to which it was exposed. The first tide, from the beginning of the fourteenth century, brought German influences flooding through Central Europe, spreading into new areas such as Little Poland and western Slovakia and consolidating previous gains in districts such as the Böhmerwald. In places such as Bohemia, Germanisation was contested with success. Elsewhere, as in Lower Silesia, it threatened to overwhelm the Slavonic element completely.

The Poles of Vretslav had long-standing roots, but by 1400 probably numbered no more than a couple of thousand. Their status had been brought into question by Bishop Nanker's squabble with King Jan, which in one dimension can be seen as a rearguard action to preserve the sinking

Polishness of the province. In the aftermath, tensions persisted between the Poles and the German burghers, prompting the visits of Kazimierz the Great and Karel IV to Vretslav in 1351, when the Church of St Dorothy was founded as a symbol of reconciliation. Soon there were fresh problems. The Poles were prominent in the 1418 revolt, which had started from the Polish Church of St Clement, in the New Town. And in 1462, they were apparently so impoverished that a foundation was set up to provide for the maintenance of the Polish clergy. Nonetheless, they stayed. They were certainly still in Vretslav in 1493 when Schedel's *Weltchronik* described the city as being 'of considerable note to the German and Sarmatian peoples'.[58]

Vretslav's Poles, therefore, could largely be found among the Catholic clergy, whose appointments were still ultimately controlled from Gniezno, among the poor and among the growing number of migrants from the countryside. But in the sixteenth century, Polish surnames appear with greater frequency than previously among the masters of guilds and the owners of property. Polish noblemen became a common sight in Vretslav's streets.

Nonetheless, one has to wonder how far modern concepts of nationality can be applied to late medieval Silesia. Germanity and Polishness were not exclusive categories. Bilingualism must have been common, especially in the oral sphere; and Latin was the normal vehicle of communication between all educated people. Multiple identities were the norm. What, for example, was the nationality of Bishop Thurzó or of Laurentius Corvinus? And in what language did the Bishop and the City Secretary converse when they met? There can be no simple answers.

Elsewhere in the province there is evidence of a gradual re-Polonisation. With the notable exception of the urban strongholds, the German majority of Upper Silesia was undermined by a concerted Polish 're-colonisation'. The German population of Beuthen (Bytom), for example, fell between 1350 and 1500 to just 53 per cent.[59] The change was confirmed by Stein, who noted in 1512 that Silesia was divided by the River Oder into its two 'national halves' – German and Polish. Vretslav lay astride the dividing line.

As the second city of the Kingdom of Bohemia, Vretslav also supported a considerable Czech community. Though few of the Czech residents have appeared in the historical record, there are sufficient examples to demonstrate their presence. It is known, for example, that in the second half of the fourteenth century, a quarter of the canons of the cathedral chapter were of Bohemian origin.[60] More tangibly, there is Jan Krasá. This unfortunate Czech, murdered in Vretslav at the height of the anti-Hussite hysteria, has variously been described as a merchant, a member of the Prague Senate and a fanatical Hussite. There is also the Rožmberka (or

Rosenberg) family. Originally from the district of Český Krumlov (Böhmisch Krumau) in southern Bohemia, they had already supplied generations of royal clerics and administrators, before they extended their influence into Silesia in the fifteenth century. Two brothers, Jindřich (d.1457) and Jan (d.1472) of Rožmberka, served successively as *Hauptmann*, or royal representative, in Silesia. Their brother Jodok went one better, being appointed Bishop of Vretslav in 1456.

The Bohemian connection was a two-way street. The University of Prague, founded in 1348, was the closest academic institution to Silesia until the re-establishment of the Jagiellonian University at Cracow in 1400. Among its students, Silesians made up the third-largest group, comprising about 10 per cent of the total. Karel IV took many Silesians into his service. His adviser and Archbishop of Prague, Arnošt of Pardubice (*c.*1300–64), had close connections in Glatz, where he is buried. Johann von Neumarkt, Chancellor to the Emperor for nearly two decades, was born in Neumarkt near Vretslav. He became one of the most important figures in Karel's circle, accompanying the Emperor on his foreign travels, and was a correspondent of Petrarch. He was appointed successively Bishop of Naumburg, Litomyšl and Olomouc, before being made Bishop of Vretslav in the final year of his life (though he was to die before taking up the position). Similarly, Karel's third wife was Anna of Schweidnitz, the only child of Duke Heinrich of Jauer (Jawor) and heiress to the sole surviving independent Silesian duchy. Such figures provided a graphic demonstration of Silesia's new allegiance.

One family demonstrates Vretslav's Central European, cosmopolitan connections better than most. Johannes Thurzó (1437–1508), a Hungarian entrepreneur from Levoča, had settled in Cracow in 1463. Though established there as a city councillor, his primary business interest was in mining and, in association with the Fuggers of Augsburg, he established a near-monopoly in the supply of Carpathian copper. His resultant wealth brought him the title of 'Lord of Bethlenfalva' and enabled him to smooth the careers of several relatives. Among them, two sons became Silesian landlords: Lords of Pless (Pszczyna) and Wohlau (Wołów), a third was made Bishop of Olomouc, and, of course, Jan, was appointed Bishop of Vretslav (see above). A nephew became Bishop of Oradea (Großwardein) in Transylvania. Such contacts, including a double marriage into the Fugger family, made the Thurzós one of Central Europe's most powerful and influential families.[61]

Old prejudices died hard, however, and outsiders were not always welcome. From its origins in the first half of the twelfth century, the Jewish community of Vretslav had grown by the mid-fourteenth to number some seventy families, possessing its own school, two synagogues and a cemetery beyond the city walls. Under King Jan, it was generally left in peace, being granted a new charter of protection in 1327, reconfirmed in 1345. Thereafter, it experienced the familiar ills of sporadic harassment and overzealous taxation. The King's change of heart appears to have coincided with the failure of his Jewish doctor, Abraham, to cure his blindness. The luckless physician was drowned in the city moat.

In an age of superstition, natural phenomena repeatedly sufficed to spark hostility towards the Jews. In 1337, as Nikolaus Pol reported, outbreaks of violence were caused by the sight of a comet in the night sky:

> In June a comet appeared in the shape of a sword, to the north soon after sunset. It lasted until the month of August. This, alongside other troubles, resulted in the Jews being accused of many bad things particularly of poisoning the wells; and many people died as a consequence. Before the month was out, another comet appeared which lasted for three months.[62]

The complexities of the Jews' predicament, however, can best be seen from the developments of 1345 when the King first confirmed Jewish liberties and then permitted the council to levy a special tax on the Jewish community. He had recently raised a 'voluntary loan' from the municipality, and the tax on the Jews seems to have been a device to enable the council to recover its interest payments on the borrowed money. This is a good example of the type of medieval practice whereby Jews were inhumanely reduced to being 'the mere object of financial operations'.[63] What is more, the tax was designed with the proviso that those who did not pay were to assist physically in the construction of the city walls and that Jewish gravestones were to be confiscated for use in the fortifications and building works.[64] It took fifty workmen ten days to clear the Ohlauer cemetery, only recent burials being left intact.[65]

The Black Death of 1349 was to make such measures look positively benign. Throughout Germany it was widely blamed on the Jews. In Vretslav it prompted a large-scale pogrom, which left only a fraction of the community untouched. The immediate cause appears to have been a fire, which broke out on 28 May. The Jewish houses and synagogues were systematically attacked, and only five or six from more than sixty Jewish families survived. The Emperor demanded that the murderers be punished. But in a letter to the Emperor, the council blamed the episode on a group of itinerant flagellants.[66]

At the end of the next decade, either in 1359 or 1360, another fire sparked another pogrom. This time, several of the intended victims were saved by accepting baptism, among them '*Elze, die getuufte Jodinne*' (Elze, the baptised Jewess).[67] Writing 100 years later, Długosz was well aware of the irrationality and wickedness of such reactions:

> On July 25 fire breaks out in [Vretslav] and, because the citizens are too lazy to extinguish it straight away, it spreads and becomes a blaze that no one can put out. Almost all the dwellings in the city are destroyed and the city itself is reduced to ashes. The citizens vent their anger on the Jews, then quite numerous, and cruelly slaughter them, irrespective of age, sex or status, as if they had caused the fire, robbing them of their belongings and expelling the survivors . . .[68]

A Jewish poet bracketed the lamentable atrocity in Vretslav with similar events in Salzburg:

> Salzburg und Breslau, und die es bewohnt,
> Hat der Freche verheert und keinen geschont;
> So hat er uns Treue und Tugend belohnt.[69]

> (In Salzburg and Vretslav: the cruel oppressor
> persecuted their inhabitants and spared no one
> thus repaying their Loyalty and Virtue.)

Neither the King nor the council made any move to apprehend the perpetrators. To modern sensitivities, the mindless cruelty of the citizens, and the persistence of the Jews, who regularly returned from their refuges, is hard to comprehend.

After 1364, only one Jewish family was officially permitted to reside inside Vretslav. But in around 1400, new Jewish liberties were granted and new Jewish immigrants moved in. In 1446 and 1450, new edicts of toleration were issued. The Jewish commune was formally reconstituted with Rabbi Salomo at its head as *Judenmeister*, or 'Master of the Jews'. But the respite was brief. For in February of 1453, John of Capistrano appeared. And when Capistrano had finished, the entire Jewish population of Vretslav had been converted, expelled or burned (see page 128). King Ladislav subsequently confirmed the expulsion of the remaining Jews and ordered that all Jewish children under the age of seven be fostered in Christian homes. In 1452, he granted Vretslav the 'privilege' *De non tolerandis Judeis*. The aim was that no Jew would ever live within the walls again.[70] A cross was erected in the Salt Market on the spot where the stakes had stood. It was to remain in place for 400 years until replaced by the statue of Marshal Blücher.

*

In common with most medieval cities, Vretslav experienced the whole gamut of natural disasters. Fires were commonplace, and in the fourteenth century large sections of the city centre were destroyed on at least four occasions: in 1344, 1349, 1360 and 1379. Floods were also a perennial menace. The inundation of 1464 caused damage far and wide:

> At Lissa, the water was three yards over the bridge; . . . the Olaw [Oława] and all the surrounding rivers were so high that houses and mills in the villages were swept away. All the ponds overflowed; many people were ruined and many more animals killed. At Neumarkt, they had to be ferried from their houses. At Schweidnitz, the stone bridge was washed away; at Striegau the hospital was lost. In Bolkenhain, many people were drowned; in Liegnitz a large section of the city wall was knocked down . . . the rivers were all so high that the people were amazed.[71]

More unusually, an earthquake shook Vretslav on Christmas Day 1384.

Leprosy was a constant scourge. It prompted the establishment both of the Lazarushospital, apparently founded in 1312, and the 'Hospital of the Eleven Thousand Virgins' in 1400. Medical treatment of the disease was non-existent, and the control measures were often those set out in the Bible. The afflicted were subjected to a symbolic burial, their clothing was burned and they were permanently ostracised. They were forbidden to enter public buildings, drink from streams or fountains or touch children.

Plague visited Vretslav repeatedly. After 1349 the outbreaks recurred at roughly ten- to fifteen-year intervals, of which those of 1496 and 1516 were the worst (the former claimed 3,000 lives, the latter 2,000). When the plague struck, the council did not meet, trade was suspended, taverns shut their doors, and church services, if held at all, took place in the open air. All sections of society were affected indiscriminately, but clergymen and doctors were especially vulnerable. Wearing masks of pimpernel against infection, they could do little for the sufferers. Mass graves were dug beyond the walls. Many prominent victims were claimed in the outbreak of 1464, including the *Landeshauptmann*, the chairman of the *Schöffen* and a leading councillor. Peter Eschenloer was both shocked and bewildered:

> In [Vretslav] especially, mainly young people died; and women; and all on the third day and in good spirits . . . I do not know what to say about this Pestilence; many fled and died and many fled and survived. I think the Pestilence is a chastisement of God, by which all those whom He has determined must die. They flee or stay, [but] when they are all dead, then the Pestilence will stop.[72]

Shortly afterwards, the 'French disease' – syphilis – made an appearance. Its historical origins are obscure, but it is often considered to have returned with Columbus from the New World. In Vretslav, it was first diagnosed in a woman who had returned from a pilgrimage to Rome in 1496. Fear of its spread, particularly via the city's brothels, led to a swift response. Already by 1500, numerous hospitals had been set up to care for its victims, including the Hiobshospital and the Lazarushospital, which switched from the treatment of leprosy.

Witch-hunting was yet another late medieval affliction that Vretslav did not escape. Though it would reach its peak in the sixteenth century, its earliest instance in the Silesian capital, resulting in the drowning of two women in the Oder, occurred in 1456.[73] There were to be another eight cases before the end of the century. Numerous folk tales of witchery punctuate the Bohemian period. The legends of the 'Kottwitzer Virgins' and the 'Twelve Dancing Beauties' illustrated the perils incurred by young women who did not go to church. But the so-called 'Poor Sinner' was probably Vretslav's most famous witch. Reputed to live (along with the obligatory broomstick) on the bridge connecting the two towers of the Church of St Mary Magdalene, she was condemned to sweep it for all eternity in punishment for her dissolute life. The usual punishment for witchcraft in Vretslav, though, was either drowning or banishment. Unlike many German cities, Vretslav apparently did not burn its witches at the stake.[74]

The punishments imposed for murder, in contrast, were savage. The tale of an unfaithful wife demonstrates the point. After administering poison to her husband on eight occasions, the wife of a Vretslav innkeeper had slept with the serving boys and had conspired with them to murder him:

> The woman was brought to the Main Square. In front of her house, where the murderous deed was done, her right hand was hacked off. She was then buried alive and a stake was driven through her body. The serving boys were then dragged around the Square where their right hands were cut off. Their flesh was torn by glowing tongs. Then they were quartered and their bodies placed on the wheel.[75]

The corpses would have been displayed on the city's approaches as grizzly reminders of Vratislavian justice.

At least one murderer, however, seems to have aroused the sympathies of the citizens. He was the city bellmaker who, in 1386, had killed an apprentice for interfering in the delicate process of casting a bell for the Church of St Mary Magdalene. According to legend, after confessing his crime, he found the bell to have been perfectly cast. His last request before execution was to hear the bell toll. His story was made famous by the romantic poet Wilhelm Müller:

> War einst ein Glockengießer zu Breslau in der Stadt,
>   Ein ehrenwerter Meister, gewandt in Rat und Tat,
> Der hatte schon gegossen viel Glocken, gelb und weiß,
>   Für Kirchen und Kapellen, zu Gottes Lob und Preis.
>   Doch aller Glocken Krone, die er gegossen hat,
>   Das ist die Sünderglocke zu Breslau in der Stadt . . .
>
> 'Laßt mich nur einmal hören der neuen Glocke Klang!
>   Ich hab' sie ja bereitet, möcht wissen ob's gelang.'
> Die Bitte ward gewähret, Sie schien den Herrn gering,
>   Die Glocke ward geläutet, als er zum Tode ging.[76]

> (In Breslau town, there dwelled a caster,
>   Of his craft a canny master:
> His bells of metal white and gold
>   In churches and in chapels tolled.
>   But of all the bells he cast, the crown
>   Was the Sinner's Bell in Breslau town . . .
>
> 'Let me hear the new bell ring –
>   I made her, let me hear her sing!'
> So to his wish they gave assent:
>   It tolled as to his death he went.)

The 'Sinner's Bell', as it became known, was rung thereafter to announce the sentencing of criminals and, from 1526, before all executions.

The condemned usually met their fate at ten o'clock in the morning on the 'Old Scaffold' south of the City Hall. Other sites were the 'Raven's Stone' (*Rabenstein*), close to the Schweidnitz Gate, and the 'Heretic's Hill' (*Ketzerberg*) to the east of the city. Those convicted of lesser misdemeanours would be punished on the pillory, erected to the east of the City Hall in 1492. The total number of victims is unclear, as few precise records have survived. But it has been calculated that 454 persons lost their lives for heresy or witchcraft in the eight decades between 1445 and 1525.[77] This would mean that an execution took place every two months on average.

The identity of the executioners was often shrouded in mystery. Across Germany they were generally referred to under the name of 'Master Hans'. In Vretslav, only one name – that of Niklas Pucker – has reached the historical record. He is thought to have held his grizzly office around 1350. A century later, Vretslav was the scene of a curious event. It had been chosen as the meeting-place of executioners from all over Germany, who were pressing for improved recognition for their work. But the arrival of fourteen executioners caused widespread rumours that a mass execution was being planned. The meeting was stormed by an angry mob, and the executioners, including Vretslav's own 'Master Hans', were driven out. For much of the late fifteenth century, the city was left without an executioner and was forced to rely on the unprofessional efforts of pardoned criminals.[78]

As if such tribulations were not enough to cause sleepless nights, it seems that the trials of the Hussite period also left their scars. Legend holds that Jiří z Podiebrady's nickname of 'Jirsik' came to mean a 'bogey-man'. Vretslav's unruly children would be cowed and silenced by the news that 'Jirsik is coming!'[79]

*

The City Council – the *Rada* or *Rat* – dominated the government of Vretslav throughout the Bohemian period. It met intermittently and in private. It was responsible for trade, taxation and municipal justice and was headed by an elected chairman, comparable to a mayor, who held the key to the coffers. The other councillors, who varied from five to ten in number, held positions of lesser importance, such as keeping the document archive or the municipal seal. Though election to the council was theoretically open to any Vretslav citizen, in practice only the most prominent and wealthy patrician families were represented. The list of councillors, which was kept from 1287 to 1742, often shows successive generations of the same families, such as Borg, Dompnig and Rehdiger. The apparent nepotism and the image of the council as a self-serving, closed society were the main reasons for popular discontent, especially from the guilds. The legal arm of the administration centred on the *iuratus* (*Przysięgli, Schöffen*), who were legal advisers, and the *advocatus* (*Woojt, Vogt*), a lawyer appointed to protect and represent the citizenry. The advisers (between eight and twelve in number) were often required to attend council meetings and held their own meetings in public. The *advocatus*, usually a hereditary position, maintained offices within the City Hall.

Vretslav's system of government steadily evolved throughout the fourteenth century. The office of Mayor developed into that of a representative head, while the competence of the City Council was also extended. The involvement of the advocates had been increasingly resented, and after the hereditary office was bought, it was occupied thereafter by a compliant member of the council. The right to fortifications was granted in 1350, and the right to mint coins a decade later. Yet Vretslav's effective independence was not completed until 1434, when the grant of the *Ius praesidii* gave it the right to refuse the imposition of garrisons from outside.

The Silesian Estates operated alongside the City Council. They formed a typical provincial assembly, which met at irregular intervals to discuss issues of general interest. They were subdivided into three *curia* – those of the princes, the knights and the cities – and numbered in all some forty members. Vretslav, as the most populous city in Silesia, assumed a special position in this constellation. After 1357, when it took responsibility for the office of 'Regional Governor' or *Landeshauptmann* for the duchy, it effectively turned itself into a city-state, governed by the council and carrying one of the strongest voices in the Estates alongside the Silesian princes.

In the same period, the guilds strengthened their position. Membership was compulsory for anyone wishing to exercise a craft, and apprenticeships could only be accepted under their auspices. At the head of each stood a small number of masters wielding responsibility for the guild's rules and their enforcement. Though obliged to swear an oath of loyalty to the council, they resented their subordination, and latent conflict was a constant ingredient of Vretslav's medieval politics. In 1418, the simmering tensions erupted into open revolt.

The council's troubles had begun in 1380 through a squabble with the Church over the sale of beer, which became known as the Vretslav Beer War. The council had traditionally imported a popular local beer from Schweidnitz and sold it in the 'Schweidnitzer Keller'. However, it began to be increasingly undercut by unsanctioned sales of beer by the Bishop's agents. The council complained to the Bishop, but to no avail. Then it ordered that a shipment of the Bishop's beer be confiscated until the matter was satisfactorily resolved. In the resultant confrontation, the city was placed under interdict. This state of affairs continued until the summer of 1381 when the new King, Václav IV, arrived to receive the city's homage. He requested that the Bishop raise the interdict for the duration of his stay, so that the necessary church services in his honour could be held. When his request was refused, he was furious and ordered his soldiers to sack the cathedral, the Bishop's residence and various monastic houses. Thereafter his drunken soldiers roamed the city, dressed in looted clerical garb, trying to sell their booty, but the Bishop remained unmoved. The conflict ended when a compromise was reached allowing the Bishop to supply beer to his own dependents, while the council kept its lucrative monopoly on sales to the public. The Beer War had vividly demonstrated Václav's unpredictable nature, but also showed the strength of the City Council, which had been able to oppose the might of the Church with relative impunity.

Nonetheless, by the early fifteenth century, discontent was increasingly directed against the council. It was the product of ongoing constitutional uncertainties, combined with the heavy taxation of Václav's reign and a general decline of law and order. The artisans were particularly aggrieved, feeling themselves pushed to the limits of solvency, yet persistently denied a voice in the city's government. After one abortive revolt in 1406, they again resorted to violent means twelve years later. At dawn on 18 July 1418, a group of disgruntled guildsmen, mainly butchers and textile workers, gathered at the Church of St Clement in the New Town. Absolved in advance from the sins they were about to commit, they stormed the City Hall, where the council was in session:

> One, named Jakob Kreuzberg, a cooper, battered open the door to the tower; Matthes Hengesweib, a brewer, rang the bell. On the main square, in front of the stocks, they executed the mayor; Nikolaus Freiberger, Hanns Sachsen, Heinrich Schmieden, Johann Stille; three advisors, and Nikolaus Fäustling and Nikolaus Neumarkt. Georg Rathburg, a cobbler, chased his own cousin, Johann Megerlin, who had taken refuge in the tower, and threw him . . . onto the pikes of the rebellious mass gathered on the Fish Market below.[80]

The Mayor and six councillors were executed with Karel IV's ceremonial sword, a gift from the Emperor himself, and in the chaos, priceless artefacts and documents were lost. A five-day stand-off ensued before order was restored. As a concession to the rebels, a new council was elected giving representation to the guilds. In reality, power remained firmly in the hands of the patrician families, and the issue of genuine guild representation was not addressed until almost two decades later. In the meantime, the Emperor Zikmund had thirty of the ringleaders executed when he came to Vretslav for the Imperial Diet of 1420. Fearing the reaction of the populace, he had the streets leading to the gallows closed. Observing the executions, he expressed his admiration for the 'fearlessness' of the condemned, and their 'brave and indomitable bearing'.[81] As was customary, the rebels' heads were boiled, tarred and mounted on pikes on the city walls. The headless bodies were buried in unmarked graves in the churchyard of St Elizabeth.

The list of the condemned, as published in the Emperor's decree of 26 March 1420, mentions the men's names and, in some cases, their trade:

Johann Schultheiss (butcher)	Nicolas Stelczner (carter)
Kaspar Münchof (inn-keeper)	Arnold (ploughman)
Bartosz Wigandsdorff	'Red' Jorge (knife-grinder)
Nikolaus Kastner	Heckler the painter's son
Jan Donin	Egrer (mason)
Peter Bursnicz	Burkhard (needlemaker)
Hackenteufel (plumber)	Heinrich Steynmüller

Francis Döring
Nikolaus Kolkamer
Nikolaus Seder (mason)
Bartosz (mason)
Polkewicz (butcher)
Esscher
Jan (knife-grinder's boy)
Mikołaj Polan

Nikolaus Schönbrücke (tanner)
Feyngenest
Joh. Polan
Pawel (butcher)
Brumhoz
Teufel (tailor's boy)
Johann, the stuttering weaver
Jörge

In addition, a similar number were exiled for life, banned from coming within eight kilometres of the Emperor's realms: Stewbel (wineseller), Taschner (tanner), Wojciech (taverner), Mönch (journeyman), Quittenberg (weaver), Mertin (shieldmaker), Thomas (glovemaker), Johann Muhlheim (furrier), Frankenstein (maltster), Hugwicz (wheelwright) . . .[82]

Since the 'revolt' or 'rising' of 1418–20 coincided with the beginnings of the Hussite Wars, later historiography with Marxist leanings was to make much of a scheme whereby the German conservative establishment was royalist and pro-Catholic, while Hussitism attracted only the urban poor, the peasants and the lower clergy. In fact, the picture was not so simple. Both the landed aristocracy and the patricians were divided into warring factions. At least one of the Silesian Piast princes, Bolesław of Oberglogau (Głogówek), known as Wołoszko (d.1461), was a high-profile Hussite, as was the Lithuanian duke Bolesław Swidrygiełło. It is doubtful whether the peasants who joined the Hussite bands, or the mob that attacked the City Council, did so from ideological motives. It is certain that when the population of Vretslav opposed 'the heretic king', Jiří z Podiebrady, the common people were just as aroused as their betters.

Of course, the patrician families were more involved in higher politics than ordinary citizens were. In the 1420s, Vretslav's stance was largely decided by the fact that Bishop Konrad of Oels had been appointed Royal Viceroy of Silesia and that the majority of the patriciate backed him. In the 1430s, in the war of succession after the death of Zikmund of Luxemburg, Vretslav supported first Albert of Habsburg and then Albert's widow, Elizabeth of Luxemburg. In the latter phase of that struggle, the Bishop found himself pitted against his own brother, Duke Konrad the White of Oels. Twenty years later, in 1459, Vretslav alone in Silesia refused to accept Podiebrady. Yet the solidarity of the citizens' resolve was remarkable. When two of the councillors dared to hint at a compromise with Podiebrady, they were charged with treason and forced to flee. They were replaced by two leaders of the anti-Czech party. When Podiebrady's forces approached the walls on 1 October 1459, the citizens rushed en masse to man the defences.

A similar situation occurred in 1467. The military defeat of the Catholic army at Frankenstein (Ząbkowice) convinced a couple of Vretslav's councillors that they should sue for peace. They were instantly removed and this time they were not replaced. A 'Committee of Ten' was appointed to keep an eye on council policy. The citizens controlled the council no less than the council controlled the citizens.

Mátyás Corvinus put the council to the sternest of tests. Having 'liberated' Vretslav from Podiebrady in 1468, he made a number of important changes to the administration. Following the revised constitution of 1475, he decreed that he himself would appoint the Chief Councillor, while the council was to be elected by a committee of citizens. The instruments of his rule in Vretslav were to be Heinz Dompnig and Georg von Stein. They enforced royal despotism, enriching themselves in the process and provoking popular anger with their harsh and inconsiderate rule. Their end came after Corvinus's sudden death in April 1490. Stein wisely fled to Brandenburg, but Dompnig merely requested that the council release him from office. He then settled into a brief and uneasy retirement before being caught smuggling incriminating documents from the City Hall. His torture and execution followed in July 1490, just two months after the death of his master. Corvinus's constitution died with him. By the time of Vretslav's cession to the House of Habsburg, the council was firmly back in uncontested control.

*

In 1335 Vretslav had consisted of the 'Old Town' and the separate 'New Town'. It occupied an area of some 133 hectares and was one of the largest in contemporary Central Europe, equal in size almost to Prague. Confined in the north by the arms of the River Oder and in the south by the protective moat, the inner Ohlau (or Oława), it possessed an additional ring of brick walls on the south side with seven fortified gates. Beyond the inner Ohlau lay another moat, the outer Ohlau, which had been created in the early fourteenth century. The land between the two provided space for expansion. This area was home to the malt merchants. According to Nikolaus Pol, the Emperor Karel IV was personally responsible for the developments:

> . . . He improved the city with neat and delicate houses and buildings, extending it with a large area beyond the Ohlau to the south, which was filled with houses, the built-up district having previously only reached to the Ohlau. The streets were so tidily divided off that the beautiful houses were equal to anywhere in Germany, whilst its straight little streets were often superior.[83]

The New Town, which merged with the Old Town in 1337, was situated on a virtual island to the east and was populated predominantly by textile workers. The Mauritius quarter, on the other hand, beyond the outer moat to the south, still housed the descendants of the Walloon immigrants of the twelfth century. To the north of the river lay the so-called 'Polish side', where the Polish population was concentrated in a rambling district whose roads led to the frontier of the Polish kingdom some fifty kilometres away.

Formal subdivisions were decreed during the reign of Emperor Karel, principally to facilitate the collection of taxes. Vretslav was divided into four 'quarters': the 'Ruthenian Quarter' in the south-west, the 'Butchers' Quarter' in the north-west, the 'New Market Quarter' in the north-east and the 'Furriers' Quarter' in the south-east. A fifth district – the 'Venusberg' – also deserves mention. Situated to the north of the Old Town, it possessed numerous taverns and 'bathhouses' where prostitutes plied their trade. As elsewhere in medieval Europe, the prostitutes were not merely tolerated, but were protected, licensed and regulated by law, providing a considerable source of public revenue. The indulgence shown to them would be changed only by the advent of syphilis and of the Reformation.

Early fourteenth-century Vretslav was predominantly built of wood. Nonetheless, it already contained some fourteen stone-built churches as well as the religious houses maintained by the Knights Hospitallers, Franciscans, Dominicans and Augustinians. It was to flourish further in the Caroline Age. Mid-century fires helped reconstruction in stone or brick, and much of the finest Gothic architecture dates from the subsequent period. Under Karel's influence, and that of his court builder Petr Parléř, a great deal of religious building was undertaken. Notable additions included the Church of St Dorothy, founded in 1351, expansion of the Churches of the Holy Cross and of Our Lady on the Sand and the rebuilding of the Church of St Mary Magdalene.

The City Hall was also enlarged.[84] An upper floor was added to the original single-storey *consistorium* after 1328. Three decades later another floor was added. The tower was then raised and in 1367 was graced with a mechanical clock. The bay window on the south-east corner was constructed in 1483 and the middle bay on the south façade followed two years later. Around 1500, the decorative east gable was completed. In the interior, the original beamed ceilings were replaced throughout by vaulting in the second half of the fifteenth century. By 1526, Vretslav's most famous building possessed a form that would have been instantly recognisable to its modern-day admirers.

The houses on the Main Square would have displayed similar, though less exuberant, medieval styles. Indeed, since the old ducal palace on the riverfront was already run-down, they often served as temporary royal residences. The Emperor Albrecht V stayed in the 'House of the Golden Cup' in 1438. He apparently fell down the stairs there, causing him to limp for the rest of his life.[85] The original 'House of the Golden Sun', on the west side of the square, housed King Władysław Jagiellon during his visit in 1511. The 'House of the Golden Crown', on the east side of the square, belonged to Bishop Jan Thurzó.

Many practical improvements were made in the realm of utilities. A municipal water system was introduced, and a new defensive wall was begun inside the outer moat. The condition of the streets and squares was also addressed. A special tax imposed by King Jan in 1331, the *Pflastergeld*, required every wagon to pay a penny on entering the city and thereby fund municipal roadworks. By 1450, the main thoroughfares were completed, and the old muddy tracks were replaced by constructions of wooden planks known in German as *Knüppelbrücke*. The feature survived until modern times in the names of two well-known streets – the Schuhbrücke (Szewska) and the Schmiedebrücke (Kuźnicza).

In the fifteenth century Vretslav continued to grow. By 1403, its population had risen to an estimated 17,000, and by 1470 to 21,000. Expansion into the belt of land between the moats was well advanced. Indeed, overcrowding was becoming a problem. Already in 1404, the council decreed that no more privies were to be built over the inner moat and no more sewerage was to be directed into the river. The citizens evidently enjoyed the same none-too-fragrant surroundings that prevailed elsewhere in medieval Europe.

Within the walls, fresh foundations included the Church of St Christopher (*c.*1400), the Church of Corpus Christi (*c.*1450), the Dominican Church of St Catherine (*c.*1459) and the Bernardine Church, which was erected in the New Town from 1463 by demand of the followers of John of Capistrano. Beyond the walls, the Leprosy Hospital and Church of the Eleven Thousand Virgins[86] appeared to the north of the river in 1400, while the Church of St Nicholas in Szczepin was rebuilt after being destroyed by the Hussites in 1428.

The towns and villages in the former Duchy of Vretslav were changing no less than the city itself. Schweidnitz, for example, lost its former independent status, as Vretslav had done, when the last heiress married Emperor Karel IV in 1353. But for the next two centuries it continued to compete with the Silesian capital both in wealth and size. It was a major commercial centre in its own right, and it could afford to adorn itself with some fine buildings. The Gothic Church of Sts Stanisław and Václav, judiciously dedicated to the patrons of both Poland and Bohemia, was founded in 1330, but remained under construction throughout the fifteenth century. Its altarpiece was the work of Veit Stoss (Wit Stwosz), and its spire of 104 metres was the tallest in Silesia. The early-sixteenth-century town square at Schweidnitz, with its Renaissance town hall and its sturdy burgher houses, reflected on a smaller scale the glories of its Vratislavian counterpart.

Further afield, the environs of Vretslav gave rise to numerous architectural treasures, both religious and secular. Many of the most representative Gothic churches of the Bohemian period were destined to be remodelled during the Counter-Reformation. But excellent examples survived in the fourteenth-century Church of Sts Peter and Paul at Striegau (Strzegom), the Church of St Nicholas (1390–1410) at Brieg and the fifteenth-century Church of St James at Neisse. Late medieval castles were built at Gröditzberg (Grodziec) and at Hermsdorf (now a suburb of Jelenia Góra). Monuments to municipal energy and pride can still be seen in the fortified walls and gates of Patschkau (Paczków), the 'Silesian Carcassone'; in the remarkable bridge across the Nysa at Kłodzko (Glatz), which is highly reminiscent of the Charles Bridge in Prague; and in the Town Hall at Lwówek (Löwenberg). At Wohnwitz (Wojnowice), west of Vretslav, an impressive Renaissance country palace was built in 1513 by Nicholas Schebitz, sometime governor of the district. In a literal sense, though, the most attractive locations from the Bohemian era must be identified with the growth of the mountain spas. Bad Warmbrunn (Cieplice Zdrój) began to flourish after 1288; Bad Landeck (Lądek Zdrój) around 1400.

By the time of the Habsburg succession in 1526, Vretslav filled the entire space inside the moats and walls. The splendid plan made by Barthel Weihner, some forty years later, shows a city perfectly encircled by water and demonstrates its wonderful defensive position. Though the Ottoman armies were on the march not far to the south, no enemy was going to capture Vretslav with ease.

*

Most people live their lives absorbed in local affairs and in their personal problems. In the Middle Ages, when communications were so poor and slow, such parochiality was one of the established features of everyday life. Yet, despite the barriers, there were undoubtedly people who scanned the wider horizons and reflected on the turn of events. In the days of the last Duke, for example, there would have been individuals who had walked on pilgrimage to Rome for the Jubilee Year of 1300, who had marvelled at the glories of the Eternal City and who joined the million-strong crowds from all over Christendom. In the following decades, they would have shaken their heads in disbelief at the exile of the Popes to Avignon and would have bemoaned the inability of their Pope and their Emperor to establish the harmonious union of the 'Two Swords'. A hundred years later, at the end of the Hussite Wars, there would have been Vratislavians expressing similar laments. Having thrown in their lot with the Catholic-imperial party, they would have rejoiced at the restoration of a united Papacy. But they can only have wept at the failure of the Church to put its Christian principles into practice, and of the Emperor either to convert or defeat the Hussites. The advance of the Turks, the catastrophe of the Varna Crusade of 1444 and the fall of Constantinople, which cut the last link of continuity with the Roman world in which Christ had lived, must have seemed especially threatening.

In the days of Bishop Thurzó in the first quarter of the sixteenth century, the Jagiellons were at their magnificent height. From the Vratislavian perspective, the King, Władysław II Jagiellon, ruled over both Bohemia and Hungary while his brother, Zygmunt Stary Jagiellon, sometime Governor of Silesia, ruled over both Poland and Lithuania, from the approaches to Vretslav to distant Kiev and beyond. Yet a number of changes occurred in those years, which were pregnant for the future and which must surely have caught the attention of any well-informed person who was watching the rush of the water under the Oder bridges and musing on the passage of time. Firstly, Martin Luther's 'Protestant Revolution' was launched in 1517 at Wittenberg in Saxony, in the province adjacent to Silesia; 'Brother Tetzel' had been selling indulgences as close to Vretslav as Görlitz. Secondly, in 1519, the imperial electors chose another Charles, Charles V of Habsburg, who, in addition to his Central European titles, was King of Spain and Lord of the new-found Americas. For the first and last time in its long history, Vretslav found itself in a vast, worldwide empire 'on which the sun would never set'. Thirdly, in 1525, having secularised the Teutonic State in the wake of the Lutheran Reformation, the last Grand Master and first Duke of Prussia, Albrecht von Hohenzollern, paid homage to the King of Poland to hold his Prussian lands in fief. No one at that point could have foreseen the consequences. But it must have been obvious to all that a fresh, potential rival to the Habsburgs and Jagiellons had entered the stage. Lastly, having crossed the middle Danube, the Ottoman Turks were still on the march in Hungary, only 250 miles away. And they were getting closer.

Any one of these recent events would have been enough to persuade the more open-minded conversationalists in Vretslav's squares and taverns that the old world was about to change. Taken together, they would have given grounds for serious anxiety and excitement.

FOUR

Presslaw under the Habsburg Monarchy, 1526–1741

Fortes bella gerant, ran the slogan, *tu felix Austria nube* ('The strong wage wars, but you, happy Austria, arrange marriages'). The Habsburgs were well aware that their startling change of fortune in the early sixteenth century was in large part due to their fertility. They knew that they might never have overtaken the Jagiellons in the race for supremacy in Central Europe, but for the fact that one line of the Jagiellons had been heirless. In the short term, the most important consequence of the battle of Mohács must have seemed to be the first advance of the Ottoman armies to the gates of Vienna. In the long term, it became evident that Mohács had created a golden opportunity for the Habsburgs, from which they would benefit for the next 400 years.

The Habsburg realm had grown spectacularly around the turn of the sixteenth century. By means of dynastic speculation, prudent marriages and sheer good luck it had expanded to encompass lands as distant as the Philippines and Peru, and in Europe as varied as Spain, the Netherlands and Austria. In a very short space of time, the Habsburgs had become the first 'world power'. The prime beneficiary of this serendipity was the Emperor Charles V (*r.*1519–56), a devout Catholic and a polyglot, who famously spoke 'Spanish to God, French to women, Flemish by choice and German to his horse'. By 1520, he was already King of Aragon and Castile, Holy Roman Emperor and Duke of Burgundy. Two years later, following the election of a sympathetic Pope, his ideal of a universal Christian monarchy appeared to be close at hand. However, tormented by the distractions of Turks, Protestants and Frenchmen and seeking to concentrate on his more lucrative Spanish possessions, he divided his realm in 1522, giving his younger brother Ferdinand I the hereditary Habsburg lands of Upper and Lower Austria, Styria, Carinthia, Carniola and the Tyrol. Thereafter, though means were sought to repair the division, the Spanish and Austrian lines of the Habsburg dynasty would stay for ever separate, and the ideal of a universal Habsburg Empire was lost. It was to Ferdinand, therefore, that the Hungarian and Bohemian crowns fell after the death of Louis Jagiellon at Mohács in 1526.

Though born and raised in Spain and initially speaking no German, Ferdinand was destined to be the virtual founder of the Central European Habsburg monarchy. With his acquisition of Bohemia and Hungary, and the separation between the Austrian and Spanish Habsburg lines, a recognisable Austrian Habsburg block emerged that was to last until the First World War. At the outset, however, the new dynasty stood on shaky ground. With his coterie of strictly Catholic Spanish advisers and his attempts to restrict the power of the princes of his new lands, Ferdinand was distinctly unpopular. Despite claiming his new thrones by right of treaty and succession through his brother-in-law Louis Jagiellon, he was only reluctantly recognised by the nobility of Bohemia and Hungary. Moreover, the advance of the Turks, the spread of Protestantism in Germany and the deep divisions in both Bohemian and Hungarian society would not have filled him with confidence.

In Silesia, the advent of the Habsburgs altered little. The province was still composed of some sixteen principalities. After 1526, only six of them were ruled directly from Vienna, the others enjoying varying degrees of autonomy. Silesia had twice before fallen under Habsburg rule – in 1306 and 1437 – and neither of those attachments had brought any lasting consequences. Moreover, since Ferdinand had received his Bohemian crown on the basis both of election and of succession, he was obliged to confirm the traditional privileges of his new subjects.

The Silesian capital, whose name was recorded as Presslaw in 1620, probably viewed the prospect of Habsburg rule with rather less alarm than it did the continued advance of the Turks. In practice, this equanimity was borne out. The city's traditional privileges were duly confirmed and extended. Even in the realm of religion, few of the expected negative consequences surfaced. After all, Presslaw had become a Protestant city under a Catholic king; and some sort of outburst might have been forecast.

In practice, there was a growing diversity of belief in the Habsburg lands. All shades of Reformed Christianity were represented: Silesian Lutherans, Bohemian Utraquists and Moravian Anabaptists and, in due course, Hungarian Calvinists and Transylvanian Unitarians. Given the Turkish threat, Ferdinand was unwilling to allow any religious persecution that might jeopardise the loyalty and martial spirit of his subjects. Thus, despite his profound suspicions towards Protestantism, he was forced to tolerate it. One of the conditions demanded of Ferdinand by the Bohemian nobles had been that he promise to respect their right to worship as they pleased. This 'Austrian clemency' was not ideological; it was pragmatic. It was born not of sympathy, but rather of a genuine concern for the unity of the Habsburg realms. Though he was later to expel the Anabaptists from Moravia and to encourage Jesuit operations in all his lands, Ferdinand stopped short of any move towards the violent suppression of Protestants.

Presslaw emerged from the rabid conformism of the fifteenth century to become one of the most active centres of the Lutheran Reformation. In the spring of 1518, only months after the publication of Luther's ninety-five Theses, it saw the Bishop himself, Jan Thurzó, forbidding the sale of indulgences. Thereafter, it was to rank alongside Nuremberg, Magdeburg and Bremen as one of the earliest Reformed cities in Germany. Its Catholic bishopric, facing a largely Lutheran population and a determined City Council, was almost reduced to the role of a powerless spectator.[1] Its Catholic king was confronted by the new faith on his first visit to Presslaw in the early summer of 1527. At the end of a magnificent reception, he was petitioned by the council with an appeal that he recognise their adherence to the Reformed religion. Though the request was not explicitly granted, it was not refused.

The Habsburg realm saw further Protestant advances following the accession of Ferdinand's son, Maximilian II, in 1564. The hereditary lands were largely Protestant and the faith was accelerating into the other territories. In Hungary, the Church was virtually dead on its feet – bereft of spiritual life and staffed by placemen – and the 'new broom' of Lutheranism threatened to sweep all before it. In Bohemia, the anti-Roman traditions of the Hussites favoured change. Silesia, too, was proving a fertile breeding-ground for Protestantism.

The new Emperor, Maximilian (r.1564–76), may well have aided the Protestant cause. He was a faltering Catholic, who was referred to by the Spanish court (where his wife Maria had been raised) as the 'Heretic Spouse'.[2] The precise nature of his beliefs has long been disputed. Though outwardly conforming to Catholic practice, he described himself as being 'neither Catholic nor Protestant, but a devout Christian'.[3] It is said that he refused extreme unction on his deathbed and even that he had converted to Protestantism. His persistent ill health opened the door to further influences. Through his doctors, some of whom (such as Johann Crato von Crafftheim) were members of the Presslaw humanist circle, he gave the seal of respectability to their wide-ranging spirit of experiment and inquiry (see below).

Under his successor, Rudolf II (r.1576–1612), the humanist trend was extended, though it was not accompanied by religious tolerance. Rudolf was one of the most fascinating monarchs of the early modern age. In a sense there were three Rudolfs – the feeble, unstable monarch whose inheritance unravelled in his later years; the generous benefactor of the arts and sciences, who patronised the astronomers Tycho Brahe and Johann Kepler; and the obsessive occultist, who dabbled in alchemy, magic and the cabbala and was, by his own confession, 'a man possessed by the devil'.[4] Rudolf would have liked to eradicate Protestantism. He gave encouragement to the Jesuits and sought to restrict Protestant political power. The ever-present Turkish threat, however, forced him to temper his religious policy with moderation. His religious tolerance was directly proportional to the scale of the Turkish threat. The perception that the Turks might have been more tolerant of Protestantism than the Habsburgs was hardly conducive to an energetic defence of Habsburg territory. So, in the 1570s, he granted religious freedoms and confirmed traditional privileges in several Habsburg provinces – though often at a price.

Such considerations may have been paramount when, in 1577, the Silesian capital planned the reception of its new Emperor. In one corner of the main square, a fantastic and elaborate gateway was constructed in the style of Constantine's triumphal arch in Rome, replete with statues, cherubs, inscriptions and mechanical figures (Rudolf was fascinated by automata). Through it the massed ranks of Silesia's nobility and clergy paraded, until finally, after 2,073 riders had passed, Rudolf's entourage of 660 horsemen made their entry. Not surprisingly, the bill was substantial. The City Council's estimates for the kitchens alone included: 21 oxen, 900 chickens, 240 geese, 240 ducks, 1,888 carp, 584 pike, 8 tonnes of butter, 1 stone of almonds and 1 stone of raisins.[5] Notwithstanding, Rudolf still demanded 200,000 thalers from the council to ease his confirmation of their privileges.

Even so, Rudolf continued to patronise Presslaw's predominantly Protestant humanist circle. Intellectuals such as Johann Crato von Crafft-heim, Johann Jessenius von Jessen, Peter Monau and Johann Wacker von Wackenfels were all to grace the imperial court in Prague, thereby supplying a welcome antidote to the growing intolerance of the age.

In Rudolf's later years, his regime began to disintegrate. He was increasingly reclusive and evidently mentally unstable. It is said that he personally ceased all religious practice after 1590 and apparently lived in fear of the sacrament.[6] He remained unsympathetic to both Catholicism and Protestantism and took no direct part in the persecution of Protestants. Yet other family members were not so restrained. His brother Matthias and his cousin, the Archduke Ferdinand, began to clamp down on Protestantism in the late 1590s, encouraged by a lull in Turkish hostilities. Thereafter, the rising political and religious tensions, coupled with the Emperor's apparent mental incapacity, led to the so-called *Bruderzwist* or 'brothers' feud'. Rudolf apparently sought to use magic spells to rid himself of his rival while

Matthias resorted to more conventional means – securing the support of his relatives. In 1608 he arranged to be recognised as King of Hungary, aided by a reluctant tactical espousal of religious toleration. Three years later, he added the title King of Bohemia. In 1612, after Rudolf's death, Matthias was crowned Emperor.

Matthias (r.1612–19) was now troubled by his previous advocacy of religious tolerance. A strict Catholic, he had once viewed toleration much as Ferdinand I had – as a necessary concession. Once in power, however, he saw it as a nuisance, if not as a sin, and sought wherever possible to promote the Counter-Reformation. Received in Presslaw in September 1611, he was pointedly reminded of the religious concessions made by his predecessor. He lodged at the House of the Seven Electors, but left again in October, shortly after receiving the city's homage. He may have ruled in a climate of sharpening religious conflict, but it was to be his successor, Ferdinand II, who presided over open revolt.

Ferdinand (r.1619–37) was a Jesuit-educated champion of the Counter-Reformation, who had once asserted that it is 'better to rule a desert than a land full of heretics'.[7] Having ascended the Bohemian throne in 1617 with a promise of religious toleration, he cheerfully reneged on the deal, violating the religious freedoms enshrined in the *Majestätsbrief* (Letter of Majesty) of 1609. As a result, two of his governors, Vilém Slavata and Jaroslav Martinic, faced a hastily improvised trial before the Bohemian Estates. Together with the secretary of the Royal Council, they were thrown from the windows of the Royal Chancellery in Hradčany Castle, in a deliberate replay of the act that had launched the Hussite Revolt 200 years earlier. Unlike their predecessors, however, the trio were unhurt. Their supporters claimed that angels swooped from the heavens to break their fall, while their opponents claimed that they landed on a dungheap. Whichever was the case, the signal had been given for the start of the Bohemian Revolt and, with it, the Thirty Years War.

The complex series of conflicts that ravaged almost all parts of the Holy Roman Empire, between 1618 and 1648, consumed a whole generation. From its origins in the defenestration of Prague, it shifted through Danish, Swedish and French phases, as foreign powers took up the conflict against the Catholic-Habsburg-imperial forces, before concluding at the Peace of Westphalia. Silesia, as a largely Protestant territory ruled by the Catholic Habsburgs, was condemned to play an important part. Having been a fortress of loyalism during Bohemia's political and religious revolt of the fifteenth century, it now turned rebel. It supported the Protestant Elector Palatine Frederick as a rival King of Bohemia, supplied troops for the White

Mountain campaign of 1620 and suffered in the aftermath, being exposed to the full force of the Counter-Reformation.

Presslaw shared the initial enthusiasm for the new King of Bohemia. In February 1620, it played host to Frederick V and his Scottish queen as they rode to the now Protestant Church of St Elizabeth to receive the city's homage. The royal pair were to return some ten months later after the catastrophic defeat at White Mountain. Travelling over the snow-covered hills from Prague, they arrived late in November. Elizabeth Stuart, 'the Winter Queen', who was pregnant, penned a letter to her royal father, King James VI and I, pleading for his help in their distress:

> Sire,
> I do not wish to importune your Majesty with a very long letter. The Baron de Dona will not fail to inform your Majesty of the misfortune that has befallen us, and which has compelled us to leave Prague, and to come to this place, where God knows how long we shall be able to remain. I, therefore, most humbly entreat your Majesty to protect the King and myself by sending us succour; otherwise we shall be brought to utter ruin. It is your Majesty alone, next to Almighty God, from whom we expect assistance. I most humbly entreat [your Majesty] . . . to send us sufficient succour to defend ourselves against our enemies; otherwise I do not know what will become of us. I, therefore, again entreat your Majesty to have compassion on us, and not to abandon the King at this hour, when he is in such great need. As to myself, I am resolved not to leave him; for if he should perish, I will perish also, with him. But whatever may happen, never, never shall I be other than,
>
> Sire,
> Your Majesty's
> Most humble and most obedient
> Daughter and Servant
> ELIZABETH
> Bresslau, 22 November[8]

As it turned out, she did leave him, departing from Presslaw in late November, while the King spent Christmas in the city. The couple were reunited in late January 1621 at the fortress of Küstrin (Kostrzyn) in Brandenburg, where their son Maurice was born the following month.[9] They themselves were heading for a life of exile and obscurity, but were to have their revenge on history, for their youngest daughter Sophia was to become the matriarch of the House of Hanover and protoplast of the British royal family.

Despite the initial setback, Presslaw managed to avoid the worst consequences of the imperial wrath. It maintained a delicate balancing act, professing neutrality and periodically being besieged by one side or the other, or even by both. Though peripheral to the main theatres of war, Silesia offered an easy route for the northern Protestant powers to attack the southern strongholds of the Habsburgs. Thus, in 1626, the forces of Christian IV and Count Mansfeld marched through Silesia en route to Transylvania. The following year, the Saxon Field Marshal Hans Georg von Arnim led a successful advance into the province, thereby inspiring a Silesian deputation to Vienna, which appealed for greater protection. In 1632, he repeated the exercise, bringing his new Swedish allies with him, capturing Lausitz, Sagan (Żagań), and Glogau (Głogów) and besieging Presslaw. Though comparative newcomers on the European scene, the Swedes had lofty ambitions. The *Inventarium Sveciae*, published that year in Frankfurt, already presented Silesia as a Swedish possession.[10] Their presence in Presslaw was short-lived, however. They stabled their horses in the churches and hurried to plunder the suburbs before being driven off by imperial forces. But they would return.

Swedish troops targeted Silesia once again in 1642. Under their inspirational commander Lennert Torstenson, they renewed their advance. By now they were accomplished looters: Their 'wolf-strategy' meant that the army of mercenaries plundered as they marched, leaving cities, towns, villages and farms ravaged. When there was no booty left, they ransacked monasteries, smashing the tombs of the abbots and cutting beringed fingers from the corpses.[11] The soldiers lived off the land like so many locusts; but they lived in fear of their commander. Carried on a litter, Torstenson kept the rabble in line with the whip and the noose. He was hated, but he gave his men the right to plunder. And they gave him victory. He would be lauded as Sweden's greatest military tactician:

> Torstenson goes forth to accomplish his task . . . Sweden requires his services, and all is sacrificed to the Fatherland . . . The enemy believes him still in the arms of death, but already he is in Silesia; Glogau is besieged, and in three days taken. The enemy, exasperated . . . by the sagacity of Torstenson, unites and advances to encounter him . . . The walls of Schweidnitz [Świdnica] are witnesses of his victory. The enemy, vanquished and put to flight, abandons the field of battle to the conqueror, and leaves upon it their commander wounded and a prisoner . . .[12]

Invalided by gout, Torstenson pursued the defeated imperial army to Vienna, while his troops maintained a presence in Silesia that was to last for six years. From the outset, he placed Presslaw once again under siege.[13] Then, following an assault on the suburb of St Mauritius and a skirmish with the militia, he opted to accept the defenders' professed neutrality. With his troops controlling the entire left bank of the Oder, he was not bothered by Presslaw's nominal independence. Eventually, however, Torstenson was forced to act. In 1647, the Vratislavians gave aid to cavalrymen from the imperial garrison at Elbing (Ołbin) and compromised their neutrality. So they were besieged once again, and subjected to artillery bombardments and a determined blockade. Still they refused to yield. The following year, an agreement was reached. Swedish troops were permitted to trade in the suburbs, but Presslaw's neutrality was to be respected. Torstenson withdrew, and his erstwhile hosts were left to nurse their wounds.

By the Peace of Westphalia, Silesia returned to the *status quo ante*. It was handed back to Habsburg rule while retaining its crucial right of Protestant worship. In thirty years of warfare and disease, its population had been reduced by one-third. That of Presslaw had been reduced by 40 per cent and did not regain the level of 1618 until about 1700. The population of Glogau had been decimated. In Schweidnitz only 118 houses were left standing. The Silesian poet Friedrich von Logau, whose family estate at Nimptsch (Niemcza) had been destroyed by enemy troops, summed up the futility of war:

> Die Welt hat Krieg geführt weit über zwanzig Jahr,
> Nunmehr soll Friede sein, soll werden, wie es war.
> Sie hat gekriegt um dass, o lachenswerte Tat!
> Was sie, eh sie gekriegt, zuvor besessen hat.[14]

> (The world has warred for twenty years and more –
> Peace will now prevail, all will be as was before,
> The joke is this: all that it's been fighting for,
> It already owned before it went to war.)

Nonetheless, the blood-letting of the Thirty Years War did not remove all the dangers. The Ottoman threat on the Danube remained, as did the possibility of religious conflict. In the decades after the battle of Mohács, and the first siege of Vienna in 1529, the Ottomans posed a constant menace on Austria's south-eastern flank. Apart from some gains under Rudolf II, the Habsburgs remained on the defensive. Presslaw, though not directly involved in the fighting, shared the Catholic passions. It was threatened in the sporadic Ottoman attacks of the early seventeenth century and again when the combined Turkish and Hungarian armies of Imre Thököly raided into Moravia and Silesia in 1682. But it was never attacked. Nonetheless, fears of a general Ottoman invasion were rife and were fuelled by the lurid accounts of travellers and soldiers, who talked of massacres of Christians, and even of cannibalism. They prompted the thorough modernisation of the

Austrian Habsburg territories *c*.1648

NORTH SEA

BALTIC SEA

KINGDOM OF DENMARK

Königsberg

DUCHY OF PRUSSIA

SWEDISH POMERANIA

Gdańsk

Hamburg

Stettin

Toruń

Vistula

UNITED PROVINCES

Elbe

ELECTORATE

Berlin

COMMONWEALTH OF POLAND-LITHUANIA

OF BRANDENBURG

Poznań

Warta

Warsaw

Cologne

Rhine

ELECT. OF SAXONY

S

I

L

E

S

I

A

Presslaw

Oder

Vistula

Dresden

Frankfurt

Elbe

Prague

Cracow

Nuremberg

KINGDOM OF BOHEMIA

MARGRAVATE OF MORAVIA

Strassburg

Danube

ELECTORATE OF BAVARIA

ARCHDUCHY

Vienna

KINGDOM OF FRANCE

Munich

OF AUSTRIA

KINGDOM OF HUNGARY

Pest

Rhine

SWISS

COUNTY OF TYROL

DUCHY OF STYRIA

Buda

CONFEDERATION

DUCHY OF CARINTHIA

OTTOMAN

DUCHY OF KRAINA (CROATIA)

EMPIRE

VENETIAN REPUBLIC

Danube

0 50 100 150 km

▬▬·▬ boundaries of the Holy Roman Empire

▨▨▨ Austrian Habsburg territories

▨ Silesia

city's defences and the tradition of the *Türkenglocken*, or 'Turkish bells', which were to warn of the advancing infidel. When the bells sounded, the militia was mustered and citizens were required to stop work and hurry to church to pray for deliverance. As Nikolaus Pol recorded:

> Bakers and Cobblers were to tidy their things, the herb-women were forbidden to sell their wares and had to go to Church with the others. The farmers . . . were to dismount from their horses, remove their hats and pray. If anyone was caught working, they were to be punished.[15]

The critical point was reached in 1683 with the renewed Ottoman advance on Vienna. In that year, the armies of King Jan Sobieski of Poland passed through Silesia on their way to take command of the imperial forces at Vienna and raise the siege. As a result, copies of the so-called 'Sobieski Madonna', the icon presented by a grateful Pope to the victorious King, became an item of special veneration among Silesian Catholics. Deliverance finally came in 1699, when at the Treaty of Carlowitz the Ottomans admitted defeat. Austria received all of Hungary, Transylvania, Croatia and Slavonia. Silesia could relax. The *Türkenglocken* fell silent.

Yet the Habsburgs continued to be tormented by the presence of Protestants. In this, the Emperor Leopold I (*r.*1658–1705) was typical. He was a learned, cultured and deeply devotional man – the personification of the *pietas Austriaca*, or 'Austrian piety'. He abhorred Protestantism and rejected all compromise on the issue of religion, which he saw as the litmus test of loyalty to the monarchy. Aided by the Jesuits, he aimed to enforce religious uniformity in the Habsburg lands. The veneration of saints was encouraged, Commissions of Reform were sent to the Protestant areas and Calvinist clergy in Hungary were given the choice of exile or death. Silesia was specially targeted. Though partially protected by clauses in the Peace of Westphalia, it was not spared a Catholic offensive, spearheaded by more than thirty Catholic religious Orders. Protestant Presslaw was swimming against the tide.

To add to its troubles, the House of Habsburg faced a prolonged succession crisis. Under Leopold's sons, Joseph I (*r.*1705–11) and Charles VI (*r.*1711–40), the problem of the Habsburgs' future loomed ever larger. After Joseph's premature death, Charles VI was forced to abandon his efforts to secure the Spanish throne and return to Vienna. From then on, his main preoccupation was to uphold the undivided Austrian inheritance. Still childless, he prepared the 'Pragmatic Sanction' in 1713, providing for the succession of a female, and four years later he was given a daughter, Maria Theresa. He now redoubled his efforts. The Pragmatic Sanction was renewed in 1724 and formally accepted by the Estates of the monarchy. In 1731, it was guaranteed by an imperial Diet. The assent of the European powers was won, but the crisis was not averted. With Charles's death in October 1740, the flimsy nature of his efforts was revealed. The unhappy Habsburgs were attacked by Prussia and the resultant wars were to cost them not only the city of Presslaw, but much more besides.

*

By the sixteenth century, the Silesian economy was thoroughly integrated into that of the Bohemian realm. It was well placed to benefit to the full from Bohemia's rich natural resources, its copper and silver mining, its textiles and agriculture. Yet, primarily through geographical factors, it was less well integrated into the wider imperial economy. Silesia's rivers all encouraged trade with Saxony, Brandenburg and Poland. The relative ease of transporting goods to Poznań, Cracow, Berlin or Dresden contrasted sharply with the difficulties of reaching Vienna or central Germany. Such difficulties would increase with the outbreak of the Thirty Years War. Nonetheless, the Habsburg connection *did* bring advantages. It offered a large market, and the conflict with the Ottomans furnished a long-term incentive to develop Silesia as a strong and secure agricultural base.

These considerations bore fruit in the expansion not only of agriculture in general, but especially the production of flax and madder. From the early sixteenth century, Silesian flax supplied one of the major ingredients of linen manufacture throughout the Empire. Though it was often exported to Western Europe as unworked fibre, it was increasingly being used for local purposes. As a result, Presslaw became an important centre for linen weaving, which used the waters of the Oder for washing and dyeing. Madder was another commodity in which Presslaw specialised. Known in German as *Krapp*, and locally as the *Breslauer Röte* or 'Presslaw blush', it was cultivated for the red dye, alizarin, obtained from its roots. After harvesting, the roots would be laid on wooden drying frames in rooms heated by a kiln, then pounded into a fine powder. Madder was first evidenced in Presslaw in 1504,[16] when regulations on the drying process were passed. It flourished throughout the sixteenth and seventeenth centuries. Also produced at Liegnitz (Legnica), Ohlau (Oława) and Strehlen (Strzelin), it was considered to be inferior to the variety grown in the Netherlands, though it compared well to products from further east.[17] After initial successes in the German markets, it was usually prepared for export to Russia, notably to the fairs at Nizhny Novgorod. It became one of the staples of the regional economy. Indeed, the increased agricultural yields and general prosperity of Silesia in the early sixteenth century may have been one factor in Vienna's decision not to tamper with the province's constitutional status. By the end of the Habsburg period, production was

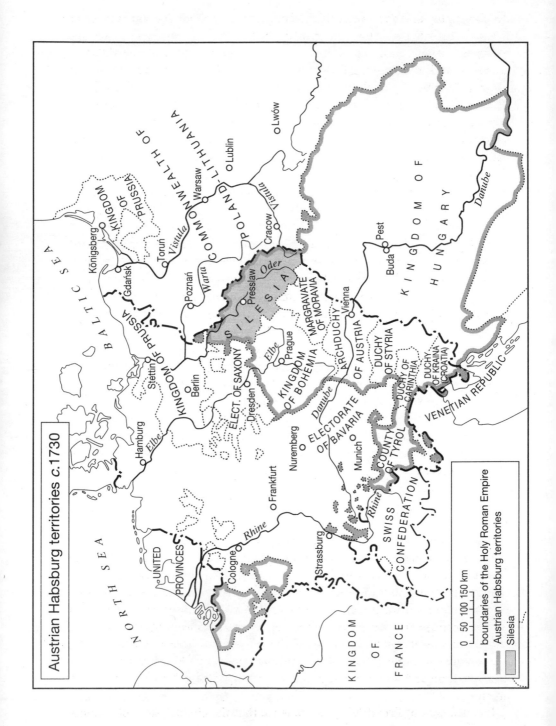

Austrian Habsburg territories *c*.1730

NORTH SEA

BALTIC SEA

KINGDOM OF PRUSSIA

KINGDOM OF PRUSSIA

Königsberg

Gdańsk

Torun

Stettin

Hamburg

Elbe

Berlin

Poznań

Warta

Vistula

COMMONWEALTH OF

LITHUANIA

Warsaw

oLublin

oLwów

POLAND

Vistula

Cracow

oLublin

KINGDOM OF SAXONY

ELECT. OF SAXONY

Dresden

Elbe

Prague

KINGDOM OF BOHEMIA

SILESIA

Presslaw

Oder

MARGRAVATE OF MORAVIA

Danube

ARCHDUCHY OF AUSTRIA

Vienna

Pest

Buda

KINGDOM OF HUNGARY

Danube

DUCHY OF STYRIA

DUCHY OF CARINTHIA

DUCHY OF KRAINA (CROATIA)

VENETIAN REPUBLIC

Nuremberg

ELECTORATE OF BAVARIA

Munich

COUNTY OF TYROL

Frankfurt

Rhine

Cologne

Rhine

UNITED PROVINCES

Strassburg

SWISS CONFEDERATION

KINGDOM OF FRANCE

0 50 100 150 km

boundaries of the Holy Roman Empire

Austrian Habsburg territories

Silesia

declining and in 1737 competition from Saxony forced the authorities in Presslaw to ban the export of madder shoots.

On the wider economic scene, the rise to prominence of the Atlantic seaboard and the influx of Peruvian silver had far-reaching effects on Central Europe. Though European trade continued to grow during the sixteenth century, a gradual downturn became evident as business shifted to new centres on the North Sea and Atlantic coast. For some countries, the shift was fatal, coinciding as it did with the loss of traditional Eastern markets through the Turkish wars. The Bohemian silver mines, for example, were marginalised and many of their investors were ruined. The inflation of the 'Price Revolution' was also detrimental. On average, prices rose fourfold during the century while purchasing power remained stagnant.

In Presslaw, the downturn was offset to some extent by improved contacts with the Low Countries, but it was not avoided. It can be witnessed in the relative strength of various guilds. Historians have shown[18] that the most populous guilds in the sixteenth century were those providing food, metals and textiles. They have concluded that the city's merchants were primarily concerned with meeting regional and domestic demand, and that long-range trade was relegated to secondary importance.

By the early seventeenth century, a capitalist economy was clearly in the making. In Silesia it was demonstrated by a cottage textile industry producing export goods for Germany and Hungary, and by the further development of mining. But progress was to be shattered by the Thirty Years War, which wrought tremendous devastation. Two decades after the Treaty of Westphalia, many Silesian towns had still not recovered. Schweidnitz counted just 350 of its former 1,800 inhabitants; Löwenberg (Lwówek) just 200 out of 1,700.[19] Economic recovery would be delayed by permanent shifts in trading patterns. That it recovered at all was due largely to a continuing demand for Silesia's traditional products: flax, linen and minerals.

Though not totally immune, Presslaw was insulated against the swings of the regional economy thanks to its involvement in the international network. Commercial links to the east had been damaged by the Ottoman advance, but ample compensation derived from a lucrative reorientation towards Hamburg and Antwerp. Presslaw remained a marketplace for the whole of Central Europe through the import of Western European and colonial wares.[20] It was also able to spearhead the recovery of Silesia. By the 1670s, when many of its neighbours were still depressed, it had largely recovered its population and was taking the lead in reviving the local trade in wool and linen.

It was a sign of Presslaw's pre-eminence that the city's system of weights and measures was adopted far and wide. From 1630, for instance, the 'Presslau Mile' was adopted throughout Silesia. This enormous unit of length was established by running a wooden wheel over the roads and eight bridges separating the Sand Gate and the suburb of Hundsfeld (Psie Pole). It worked out at a distance of 10,282 metres. It was roughly equivalent to $6\frac{1}{2}$ English miles or 10 kilometres.

Presslau's coinage also gained wide acceptance. The city minted its own gold ducats in 1517–78, 1611–22 and 1630. They portrayed the municipal coat of arms, with the head of St John the Baptist prominent in the centre. Silver coins were also minted. After the Thirty Years War, the Habsburg authorities enforced the monopoly of imperial money.

The theory of mercantilism thrived in response to the rise of a Europe-wide trading bloc. It held that trade meant power, and that international trade was a 'zero sum game'. If one country's trade was to expand, it could do so only at the expense of its rivals. Special emphasis was placed on the exploitation of natural resources. Precious metals were deemed indispensable to a nation's wealth. Trade balances had to be 'favourable' – that is, an excess of exports over imports.

In the early decades of the eighteenth century, the government in Vienna was hastily introducing mercantilist policies into the Habsburg lands. Currencies were reformed. Excise on domestic products was lifted. Imports were heavily taxed. Commerce Commissions were established in Prague and Presslaw to foster industrial enterprise. Silesia benefited from a renewed emphasis on mining. Its gold, silver and lead mines were expanded, drained by steam power, and made more efficient. Wool production also increased and yields improved by as much as 100 per cent. The province was rapidly becoming the richest and most productive of the whole monarchy. Its inhabitants were also the most heavily taxed. One million or so Silesians paid 22 per cent of the total Habsburg tax burden,[21] while representing only 11 per cent of the monarchy's taxpayers. A corollary of their success was that they began to attract covetous glances from neighbouring powers.

*

The primary religious phenomenon of the early modern age was the transformation of Presslaw from a citadel of militant, anti-Hussite Catholicism into a bastion of anti-Catholic Lutheranism. The reasons for this were numerous. Firstly, the city was already a centre of humanist ferment from the late fifteenth century. Secondly, a strongly anti-clerical sentiment had developed. In 1512, Barthel Stein noted that one in fifty of the population was a clergyman and Presslaw supported some forty churches and eleven monasteries. Thirdly, Lutheranism undoubtedly benefited from its wide-spread identification as the 'German' religion. Lastly, one commentator[22] has cited the popular reaction against earlier anti-Hussite fanaticism.

Johannes Hess was the main instigator of the Reformation in Presslaw. Sometime secretary to Bishop Thurzó, he had studied in Bologna and Wittenberg, where he had made contact both with Luther and with Melanchthon. He received holy orders from the Bishop on 2 August 1520 and was appointed preacher at the cathedral. His own public adherence to Luther's doctrines came early in 1522, when he preached at his home town of Nuremberg. Soon afterwards, he received a letter from Luther stating, 'I am happy to hear that you have become a preacher of the gospel.'[23] Like Luther, Hess's initial objective had been to expose what he saw as abuses committed in the name of the Church – in his words, 'cautiously and responsibly to modernise the church without provoking a rift within it'.[24] But the rift was already looming. His appointment as priest to the vacant parish of St Mary Magdalenee in June 1523 was the critical step. When he was called to answer for his beliefs the following April, in the Church of St Dorothy – at the so-called 'Presslaw Disputation' – Hess opened the breach that he had sought to avoid. That September, the City Council called upon all preachers to follow his example. Numerous Lutheran appointments followed. Ambrosius Moibanus was made parish priest of St Elizabeth's and Andreas Winkler was appointed rector of the influential St Elizabeth's School. From that point on, there would be no Catholic parishes in the city centre until 1707.

For the remainder of the sixteenth century, Silesia benefited from the 'Austrian Clemency' – the reluctance of the Habsburgs to enforce religious discipline. The largely consensual nature of the Silesian Reformation was undoubtedly connected to this. A peculiarly tolerant Melanchthonian approach promoted the peaceful coexistence of Lutheran and Catholic faiths, which were even to take turns sharing churches on Sundays.[25] Presslaw demonstrated similar latitude. The 'Presslaw Disputation' began with a Mass and ended with a *Te Deum*. And Hess combined evangelical preaching with Catholic worship. He and his colleagues fostered a 'reasonably harmonious mixture of a Catholic bishop, Lutheran burgherdom and a crypto-Calvinist, if not thoroughly unorthodox intelligentsia'.[26] For their part, the local Catholics were equally prepared to take a moderate line. They long resisted the introduction of the Jesuits and, while welcoming the Lutherans' declaration of loyalty to the Habsburgs, were able, with imperial support, to restrain their more militant co-religionists.

It was odd, therefore, that Presslaw was chosen as the scene of a disturbing religious hoax. In 1528, details were published there of a secret alliance which aimed to eradicate Lutheranism by force. The signatories were listed as Ferdinand, Holy Roman Emperor, the Electors of Mainz and Brandenburg, the Archbishop of Salzburg, the Bishops of Bamberg and Würzburg and the Dukes of Saxony and Bavaria.[27] Though all those involved hastened to disassociate themselves from it, the pact brought the Empire to the brink of war. But it was a forgery. Its author was one Otto von Pack, an assistant to Duke George of Saxony, who had invented the story to make money. After years on the run, he was finally arrested and executed in Brussels.

As if to reconfirm its tradition of toleration, Protestant Presslaw became the home of Johannes Cochlaeus (1479–1552), Luther's leading opponent and his first Catholic biographer. One of the most polemical Catholic theologians of the age, and once a leading humanist, Cochlaeus had been present at the Diet of Augsburg in 1530 and was a veteran of several disputations with Luther. Exiled from Saxony, and increasingly alarmed at the progress of the Reformation, he found refuge as a canon in Presslaw in 1539, whence he pursued his very personal crusade. His last public appearance was at Regensburg in 1546. He penned his peculiarly bilious *Commentaria de actis et scriptis Lutheri* in 1549 before retiring to Presslaw. After a career of invective, it was said that Cochlaeus was greatly calmed in his retirement by the tranquillity of Cathedral Island.[28]

The career of the Catholic bishop Martin Gerstmann (r.1581–5) exemplifies the paradoxical conditions that had emerged. The Bishop was the son of a Protestant burgher family, who had converted to Catholicism. Despite the decrees of the Council of Trent (1545–63), he steadfastly declined either to attack his Protestant neighbours or to intervene when Protestant princes persecuted their Catholic subjects. A blatant case of such persecution occurred at Brieg (Brzeg) near Presslaw, and the Bishop's inaction incurred the wrath of his own people.

In this context, it is essential to recognise that the coexistence in Presslaw of Lutherans and Catholics was rather exceptional in its day. The religious settlement in the Holy Roman Empire, reached in 1555 at the Peace of Augsburg, did not establish universal freedom of conscience or worship. On the contrary, it established the notorious principle of *cuius regio eius religio* – that is, the right of the political authorities of each state or city to introduce religious uniformity within their own jurisdiction. The norm was for Catholic rulers to demand a monopoly for Catholicism and for Lutheran rulers to demand the same for Lutheranism. A city like Presslaw, where the Lutheran majority did not expel the Catholic minority, has to be regarded as a fortunate aberration. At the same time, one should not have any illusions, for neither Catholics nor Lutherans cared much for the modern spirit of Christian tolerance and ecumenism. They were united in the stiff-necked belief that no other religious denominations but themselves should be admitted. As a result, early modern Presslaw did not tolerate Calvinism, just as it did not tolerate radical sects like Anabaptism, and just as it did not tolerate Judaism.

Fifty years after the Reformation, the half-hearted policy of the Habsburgs had run its course and was replaced by a more concerted effort at reconversion. In Silesia, the change was first made manifest in Oppeln (Opole), Ratibor (Racibórz) and especially Neisse (Nysa), which became known as the 'Silesian Rome'. In Presslaw, the advent of Bishop Andreas von Jerin (r.1585–96) signalled a reduction of religious cooperation. A Catholic parish was set up across the river, in the wooden Church of St Michael, on the former site of the Abbey of Elbing. Monasteries were to be reformed and married priests sacked. The Jesuits were imported for the duration. But the Protestant backlash was not slow in coming. The theory spread that the Turks were more tolerant of Protestantism than the Habsburgs – the slogan ran 'rather Turkish than Papist'.[29] The brief Habsburg conquest of Transylvania in 1604 seemed to confirm this idea, when it was accompanied by a brutal enforcement of Catholicism. In Presslaw, Protestant protests arose over the appointment as Bishop in 1608 of a member of the ruling dynasty, Archduke Karl von Habsburg, who was forced to relinquish his secular powers. The day after Christmas in that year, a Lutheran mob assaulted the Dominican Priory of St Wojciech (Adalbert), and amid shouts of alleged immorality forced the prior to leave. Yet the overall outcome of the tensions was positive. Struggling with similar disturbances in Bohemia, the Emperor Rudolf issued a *Majestätsbrief* for Silesia on 9 July 1609, in which he recognised that the Lutheran Augsburg Confession should enjoy equal standing with Catholicism. After eighty-six years of legal uncertainty, the Lutherans of Silesia had finally obtained official recognition.

From Luther's time onwards German Protestants were to enjoy a wonderful musical tradition. Indeed, Luther composed their very first hymn book, which was to lay the foundation for a corpus of sacred songs and cantatas that culminated in the sublimities of J.S. Bach. Yet simple metric melodies of great power and dignity formed the bedrock of the tradition. One of these was first recorded sixty years before Bach's birth, and was printed in Leipzig in a collection entitled *As hymnodus sacer* (1625). Slow and stately, it was called 'Breslau':

Revived and revised by Felix Mendelssohn in the mid-nineteenth century, this would become a standard item in the Protestant repertoire. In English, it is best known in the version that was set to the words of Charles Everest:

> Take up thy cross, the Saviour said,
> If thou wouldst my disciple be;
> Deny thyself, the world forsake,
> And humbly follow after me . . .
>
> To thee, great Lord, the One in Three,
> All praise for evermore ascend;
> O grant us in our Home to see,
> The heavenly life that knows no end.[30]

During the Thirty Years War, Silesia escaped serious religious conflict. Having stood squarely behind the Bohemian Estates in defence of religious freedom, it might have expected, after the battle of the White Mountain, to feel the full force of the Counter-Reformation. But it was treated leniently. In 1621, it was granted a guarantee of religious freedom by the Dresden Accord, in return for a declaration of loyalty to the Habsburgs and a payment of 200,000 florins. And it was spared the compulsion that was employed elsewhere. In places, the Liechtenstein Dragoons stamped out all traces of Protestantism by force. Generally speaking, though, the onslaught was successfully resisted. The semi-independent Piast and Podiebrady princes of Lower Silesia mounted a dogged defence of the Protestant cause. And Presslaw became a *cause célèbre*.

Religious duality in Presslaw was first enshrined, at Saxon insistence, in the Dresden Accord. It was repeated at the Peace of Prague in 1635 and again at the Peace of Westphalia in 1648, when both Saxony and Sweden insisted on a reconfirmation of the earlier concessions. Thanks to its powerful allies, the city held out against the might of the Catholic Empire, even when the remainder of Silesia suffered.

The Peace of Westphalia also allowed for the construction of Protestant *Friedenskirchen*, or wooden 'peace churches', which were to be built beyond the walls of Schweidnitz, Jauer (Jawor) and Glogau. Yet it stopped short of declaring religious freedom for all. And it did not prevent the re-introduction of Catholicism into those regions not explicitly protected. As soon as the Swedes withdrew, Silesia was again exposed to the advance of the Counter-Reformation. Success was swift. From 1653, Protestant clergymen were systematically replaced. Within a year, closures and expulsions had overtaken 650 churches.[31] By 1660, Upper Silesia had been completely cleared of Protestant churches and clergy.[32] In the province as a whole, only 200 of 1,500 Reformed churches survived to the end of the century.[33]

The Society of Jesus formed the vanguard of the Catholic offensive. Founded by St Ignatius Loyola in 1540, its members placed emphasis on education and missionary work and fostered a militant brand of piety. In Silesia, they scattered Marian shrines around the countryside, while founding schools and colleges in the towns. The Jesuit mission to Presslaw is of special interest, not only because it provoked much hostile comment from the local Lutherans, but because the missionaries themselves were all too conscious of fishing for souls 'in a sea of Protestantism'. It operated in two distinct periods: 1581–95 and 1638–1776. Prior to 1659, it lacked an institutional base and confined its activities to catechism, private teaching and preaching by invitation in the cathedral, in the two remaining Catholic convents of St Clare's and St Catherine's and in the Churches of St Vincent and St Matthew. The fathers were well prepared, both theologically and linguistically. Many of them had been trained at the Jesuit colleges at Dillingen and Ingolstadt in Bavaria, which regularly attracted high-born Polish pupils and produced a constant stream of suitably bilingual graduates. According to their own records, they took pride in victories scored over local pastors in set-piece pulpit duels. In 1591, for instance, a Lutheran preacher was said to have boasted about 'winning Purgatory from the Catholics'. The next Sunday, a Jesuit preacher in the cathedral performed with such brilliance on the subject of Purgatory that his opponent 'did not dare to raise the subject again'.[34]

After a brief absence, the Jesuits re-entered Presslaw in 1638, when Johannes Wazin and Heinrich Pfeilschmid were spirited in by the Bishop, wearing false wigs. Their primary aim was the reconversion of the

Protestant Churches of St Mary Magdalenee and St Dorothy. In the meantime, they gradually increased their presence, especially after the granting of imperial sanction at the Recess of Linz in 1645. In 1659, the Society of Jesus received the chapel of the old royal castle for its use. Sunday sermons were preached at 9 a.m. in German, at 1 p.m. in Polish and in the afternoon, for students, in Latin. On average, some 400 sermons were delivered each year. Finally, in 1698, the Jesus Church opened its doors on the Schuhbrücke, and in 1702 established the Jesuit College, which was to become the university. Throughout these years, the Jesuits in Presslaw were great publishers. One of their earliest publications was a twenty-four-page pocket-sized Canisius Catechism. Later publications included the *Leopoldus Auster Austriae Salutaris* (1674), dedicated to the Emperor and, in 1740, a volume celebrating the centenary of the Marian Congregation, which was printed in 4,000 copies.[35]

The Jesuits promoted processions in Protestant districts with the slogan 'Watch today, stand at attention tomorrow, participate the day after'.[36] In 1662, the procession for the Feast of Corpus Christi was held in Presslaw for the first time in 140 years. It was headed by the prominent Silesian spiritualist writer and Catholic convert Johannes Scheffler (1624–77), better known as 'Angelus Silesius'. The son of a Polish Lutheran nobleman, Scheffler had converted in 1653 and had entered the monastery of the Knights of the Cross. Writing of his motives, he confessed:

> I want to carry the cross through the city with a crown on my head, so that I resemble Christ, who carried the cross through [Jerusalem], with the crown of thorns on His holiest of heads. Thus will I earn the conversion of all those that mock me . . .[37]

The reconversion that Scheffler hoped for was still some way off.

The most active phase of the Counter-Reformation began with the appointment of Sebastian von Rostock as Bishop of Presslaw in 1664. Combining the bishopric with the political office of *Oberlandeshauptmann* for the first time since 1608,[38] he brought a new vitality to religious politics in Silesia and substantially strengthened the Catholic cause. All the main Catholic Orders were settled in Presslaw in the later seventeenth and early eighteenth centuries, beginning with the Capuchins in 1669 and ending with the Brothers of Charity in 1711.

Yet Silesia's Protestant guardian angels swooped again to her defence. In 1707, facing a two-front war and fearful of Swedish intervention, the Emperor Joseph I agreed to the second Treaty of Altranstädt, in which he pledged to respect religious freedom in Silesia and to return those Protestant churches reconverted since 1648:

> His Imperial Majesty promises: . . . that the churches and schools in the duchies of Liegnitz, Brieg, Münsterberg [Ziębice] and Oels [Oleśnica], as well as in the city of Presslaw and the other cities and villages, which were taken after the Westphalian Peace, should be either cleared of Catholics or closed. They should be returned to their previous condition . . . with all relevant rights, freedoms, incomes and lands and property within six months at the most . . .[39]

In effect, Silesia was exempted from the Counter-Reformation. The treaty prevented forced conversions and expulsions, restored more than a hundred Protestant churches and allowed for the erection of six *Gnadenkirchen*, or 'mercy churches'. It was not fully honoured, however. Under Charles VI, old plans for an enforced religious unity were dusted off and restrictions on Protestant worship reappeared.

In subsequent decades, the religious climate stabilised and inter-confessional conflict mellowed into a state of grudging mutual acceptance. Nonetheless, dissatisfactions continued. Presslaw's Lutherans never created the monopoly for themselves that the citizens of many Lutheran states in Germany enjoyed. It is not difficult to appreciate that the vast majority of Silesian Protestants viewed the Prussian invasion of 1740 as a liberation.

*

In the sixteenth century, Presslaw came to prominence as a cultural centre of major renown. Thanks to the efforts of Bishop Thurzó and others, it already enjoyed a strong humanist tradition, and the presence of such figures as Johann Crato von Crafftheim and Laurentius Scholz caused it to be described in some quarters as the 'home of humanity'.[40] In 1557, Philip Melanchthon was moved to express the most lavish praise:

> The greatest virtues of [Presslaw] are the erudition and learning of its citizens, the care and fairness of its government and the prudence and humanity in its management of local custom.[41]

As Melanchthon suggested, education was central. Presslaw possessed a generation of teachers who were enthusiastically spreading the new ideas. Among them were Laurentius Corvinus, rector at the school of St Elizabeth (Elisabethschule) and Ambrosius Moibanus at the school of St Mary Magdalene (Magdaleneeum), where Greek and Hebrew were first taught.[42] The school of St Elizabeth played a primary role. It had been quick to adopt Protestantism, especially through the rectors Andreas Winkler and Petrus Vincentius, the latter having studied under Luther at Wittenberg. It was also the first to be raised to the status of a *Gymnasium* in 1562. The cathedral school (Domschule) in contrast, where Barthel Stein taught, remained steadfastly Catholic.

The city was provided with an excellent library by Thomas Rehdiger (1540–76),[43] who had studied at both Wittenberg and Padua. The benefactor returned seldom to his birthplace, having adopted a peripatetic life, wandering between northern Italy and the Low Countries. But on his premature death he bequeathed his collections of coins and books to Presslaw. According to his will, his valuable library was to be given to his family, on condition that it be displayed for public use. It included 300 volumes of documents and 6,000 books and took five years to be transported from Cologne. Its formal establishment as a public institution was repeatedly delayed by administrative squabbles. It finally opened for business in 1661, eighty-five years after its founder's death.

One of the greatest treasures of Rehdiger's library – and of all the libraries to which his collection was subsequently bequeathed – was an original copy of the Second Quarto Edition of Shakespeare's *Hamlet*:

THE
Tragicall Historie of
HAMLET
Prince of Denmarke
By William Shakespeare
Newly imprinted and enlarged to almost as much
againe as it was, according to the true and perfect Coppie
AT LONDON
Printed for I [James] R[oberts] for N[icholas] L[ing],
And are to be sold at his shoppe under Saint Dunstan's Church in
Fleetstreet 1605[44]

The Second Quarto, printed in 1604, could not have been collected by Rehdiger himself. Unlike the First Quarto Edition of 1603, which was pirated, it contained the first authorized text of the play that had been staged two years earlier. The copy that somehow found its way to Presslaw carried a substituted title page dated 1605 (by the end of the twentieth century, it would be one of only seven such surviving copies, and carried an estimated value of ten million US dollars). The Bodleian Library in Oxford, which opened its doors in 1602 with upwards of 2,000 volumes, was never fortunate enough to obtain a Second Quarto of its own.

The educated elite of Presslaw had access to several universities. They lost out on plans to create their own seat of higher learning, but were specially well represented in the Universities of Cracow (founded 1400) and Frankfurt an der Oder (founded 1498). In 1526–30, Liegnitz briefly possessed its own Protestant University, the first in Europe, but it closed after only four years due to religious and financial controversy.[45] Despite Presslaw's change of religious allegiance, the Jagiellonian University of Cracow continued to educate the majority of Presslaw's sixteenth-century schoolmasters.[46]

The humanist circle that gathered in Presslaw around Crato von Crafftheim (1519–85) exercised an extensive influence on the Habsburg court. Its reputation for Calvinist leanings was no more than skin-deep, and its strength lay in its openness to all manner of bold ideas and experiments. It included the poets Jakob Monavius and Andreas Calagius, the astronomer Andreas Dudith, the philanthropist Thomas Rehdiger (see above) and the botanist Carolus Clusius, official plant collector to Maximilian II. The court historiographer to both Maximilian and Rudolf II, Johannes Sambucus, as well as Rudolf's adviser, Johann Wacker von Wackenfels (1550–1619), also figured prominently. The concentration of talent was impressive. The Dutch philosopher Justus Lipsius described his three friends. Crato, Monavius and Dudith, as '*tres stellae in una iam urbe*' – 'three stars in this one city'.[47]

Even so, the group's fame rested largely on that of its physicians. Three Vratislavians served as court physicians to the Habsburgs for the best part of fifty years. Crato von Crafftheim was the first. He studied under Luther at Wittenberg and completed a doctorate in Padua, before returning to Presslaw in 1550 to work on an investigation into the transmission of the plague. His pioneering study, *Ordnung oder Präservation zur Zeit der Pest* (1555), was a landmark of medical science. From 1560, he was successively appointed *Leibarzt* to Ferdinand, to Maximilian and to Rudolf II, maintaining his position until his retirement and return to Presslaw in 1580. He was succeeded by another Vratislavian, Peter Monavius, brother of the poet, who held the post for eight years. The last of the three was Johann Jessenius von Jessen (1566–1621), who was called to the imperial court in Prague in 1600 to treat the astronomer Tycho Brahe. He served as *Leibarzt* from 1602 until Rudolf's death in 1612. Of course, medical science in the sixteenth century had a very wide remit. In the fashion of Paracelsus, it was concerned with 'the whole person', without having any great knowledge of the body's mechanisms. All the physicians of the Presslaw circle believed that astrology and alchemy were just as relevant to their profession as herbalism or anatomy.

Contrary to what might be supposed, the Renaissance and the rise of humanism did little to stem the superstitions prevalent in the medieval world. Indeed, sixteenth-century Europeans frequently believed in magic, witchcraft and the supernatural, and a paradigm case of late Renaissance superstition surfaced in the 'Affair of the Golden Tooth'. In 1593, a seven-year-old boy from Weigelsdorf (Ostroszowice) near Reichenbach (Dzierżoniów), one Christoph Mueller, was found to have a tooth at the back of his lower left jaw that appeared to be made of gold.[48] He was repeatedly examined, first by Bishop Jerin's doctors, by Laurentius Scholz, and then by a visiting professor of medicine who gave him lunch to see whether the tooth performed normally. Soon, the boy had become a travelling curiosity, being reported not just in Silesia, but as far afield as Prague, Frankfurt and London. The affair was made public in 1595 by Jakob Horst of Helmstedt[49] and was thereafter discussed by prominent doctors, academics and alchemists, being variously described either as a hoax or as the work of the devil. News of the phenomenon spread rapidly through Central Europe until 1599, when the alchemist Andreas Libavius declared the pigmentation to be natural. Thereafter the controversy faded. Historians of dentistry have speculated whether they were dealing with a precocious example of a gold crown, yet the most interesting aspect of the episode undoubtedly lies in the coincidence of the new empirical scientific tests and of old superstitions. Mueller was fortunate not to have been burned as a warlock.

The explosion of religious and political tensions after 1618 put an end to frequent communication between one part of the Empire and another. Yet Silesia produced such an impressive crop of writers and poets that the period is often referred to in the history of German literature as 'the Silesian century'. Foremost among them was Martin Opitz (1597–1639). Though born in Bunzlau (Bolesławiec), Opitz was educated at the Magdaleneeum in Presslaw and, after numerous travels, returned to Silesia in 1623 as a Privy Councillor in the Duchy of Liegnitz. Increasingly prominent as a poet, he published the *Buch von der deutschen Poetery* (1624), which became the basic theoretical textbook of German Renaissance poetry. He was named Poet Laureate by Ferdinand II a year later. Though a Protestant, he continued his political career as secretary to the notoriously fanatical Catholic administrator Karl Hannibal Graf von Dohna, who implemented the Counter-Reformation in Presslaw. Opitz later secured the post of historiographer and secretary to the court of Władysław IV Vasa in Warsaw. He died of the plague in Danzig (Gdańsk) in 1639. His beautiful ode to innocence, *Ein rein Glas* ('Unblemished Glass', 1632), is indicative of his style:

> Freylich, freylich ist ein Glas
> Edle Jungfraw alles das,

Was in ewrer besten Zier
Als die Sonne leuchtet für
Schaut wie schön die Sternen all
Leuchten auß des Himmels Saal
Wie der Mond sein bleiches Haar
Außgebreitet gantz vnd gar
Wie die grosse weite Welt
Schläfrig in die Bethe fellt
Wie die Wasser stehen still
Wie sich nichts bewegen will
Eh der Vögel Lobgesang
Wiederthrönt mit hellem Klang
Eh der liechte Venus Stern
Sich läst sehen weit vnd fern
Eh die schöne Morgenröth
Auß dem süssen Schlaf vffsteht
Vnd entdecket jhren schein
Wirdt das Glas zubrochen sein.[50]

(Verily, verily, a glass you are,
Noble Mistress, standing there,
Shining in your best array,
Like the sun at break of day:
See how the stars in harmony
Glitter in Heaven's canopy,
How the moon lets dangle there
Every lock of her pale hair,
See then how the great wide world
Sleepily in bed is curled,
How the still, calm waters stand,
Nothing stirring in the land –
Before the sweet note of the bird
Once again in hymn is heard,
Before the fair Venusian star
Meets the beholder from afar,
Before the beauteous, rosy Dawn
Is from her sweetest slumber torn
That her radiance she may see
Ere then – the glass will broken be.)

Opitz is seen by literary scholars as the founder of the 'First Silesian School', which imitated his strict and mechanical poetical style. Among his acolytes were the Catholic Vratislavians Angelus Silesius (1624–77) and Andreas Scultetus (1623–47), the epigrammatist Friedrich von Logau

(1604–55), and, most prominently, Andreas Gryphius (1616–64).

Born in Glogau and orphaned as a boy, Gryphius travelled widely as a pupil and teacher until the generosity of a patron enabled him to attend the University of Leiden. Returning to Silesia in 1647, he was soon appointed *syndikus* (administrator) in his home town, where he stayed until his death. Yet he made his name as a poet and dramatist. Pervaded by melancholy and fervent religious tension, his work reflects the depths to which Germany had sunk through the ravages of the Thirty Years War. His *Vanitas* ('Vanity') is typical:

> Die Herrlichkeit der Erden,
> Muss Rauch und Asche werden,
> Nicht Fels, nicht Erz bestehn.
> Das, was uns kann ergötzen,
> Was wir für ewig schätzen,
> Wird als ein leichter Traum vergehn.[51]

> (All of this world's splendour must,
> Turn to ashes and to dust,
> Neither stone nor bronze hold sway.
> All that can afford us pleasure,
> which we deem eternal treasure,
> Will, like a daydream, fade away.)

As a playwright, Gryphius dealt with themes of stoicism and martyrdom. His best-known drama, *Carolus Stuardus* ('Charles Stuart', 1657), portrayed the recently executed King Charles I of England as a latter-day Christ dying for his people. It contained the memorable scene of a choir of the murdered Kings of England crying for revenge on the regicides:

> Erscheine Recht der grossen Himmel!
> Erschein' und sitze zu Gericht,
> Und hör ein seufftzend Weh-getümmel,
> Doch mit verstopfften Ohren nicht.

> Willst du die Ohren ferner schliessen
> Siehst du nicht wie man Throne bricht;
> So lass doch dieses Blutvergiessen,
> Gerechter ungerochen nicht.[52]

> (Appear now, Justice, from the skies,
> Take your place at court, appear!
> Hear the clamour of sorrow's sighs
> Ring out, and do not stop your ears.

176

For if, Just Spirit, your ears stay deaf,
You will not see how thrones are broken;
Do not let this blood be spilled,
Without your vengeance being spoken!)

Yet the versatility of Gryphius was not confined to literature. In 1658 he was asked to perform a post-mortem on three Egyptian mummies, once a part of the collection of the humanist Laurentius Scholz, which had somehow found their way to a Presslaw apothecary.[53] Gryphius is said to have studied anatomy in Leiden and recorded his findings in *Mumiae Wratislavienses* (1662).

The 'Second Silesian School' recruited a later generation of Vratislavians, including Christian Hofmann von Hofmannswaldau (1617–79), Johann Christian Hallmann (1640–1704) and Daniel Casper von Lohenstein (1635–83). Like Gryphius, Lohenstein worked as a *syndikus*, this time in Presslaw, writing dramas in his spare time. Though he produced only six plays, all on historical themes, he has nevertheless been described as the best German dramatist before Schiller.[54]

Christian Hofmann von Hofmannswaldau was a product of St Elizabeth's school in Presslaw and had studied at Danzig, where he had met Opitz. After extensive travels he returned home to an administrative post in 1646. His amateur poetry, which gives full rein to the eroticism and stylistic extravagance of the High Baroque, has won the epithet of 'the lowest level to which German lyric ever sank'.[55] His contemporaries would have disagreed. At his funeral, Lohenstein began the oration with the words 'The great Pan is dead . . .'

The work of philologist Valens Acidalius (1567–95) aroused similar controversy. After an education in Padua and Bologna, he found a patron in Rudolf II's adviser, Johann Wacker von Wackenfels of Presslaw, in which city he became rector of the *Gymnasium*. During his short life, Acidalius earned a considerable reputation as a critic and Latin poet. But he found notoriety in 1595, when he was revealed as the editor of the infamous *Disputatio nova contra mulieres, qua probatur eas homines non esse* ('A new disputation against women proving them not to be human beings'). In his defence, he protested that he had given his publisher a copy of the facetious disputation in haste, considering it harmless. The true authorship of the tract, strenuously denied by Acidalius, was never established.

Painting flourished, too. The restoration of many monasteries and churches, after the reconversion of Silesia, led to a huge demand for painters of murals and frescos. The most prominent was Michael Willmann (1630–1706). Born in Königsberg (Kaliningrad), Willmann had learned his trade in the Low Countries and had worked in Berlin and Prague. After a brief sojourn in Presslaw in 1650, he was employed restoring the Abbey of Leubus (Lubiąż). Hc devoted the next forty years to the Abbeys of Leubus and Grüssau, which had been destroyed by the Swedes during the Thirty Years War. His most famous works, the frescos in the Church of St Joseph at Grüssau, still stand. His paintings also graced the Cathedral of Presslaw and the Churches of St Elizabeth, St Anna and St Ursula. His *Judgement of Solomon* (1664) hangs to this day in the City Hall. Willmann earned the title of 'the Silesian Rembrandt'.[56]

As his career demonstrates, much art of the period was generated by the Counter-Reformation. This was specially true of sculpture. The creation of Marian shrines in Silesia occupied many unnamed sculptors and stonemasons. The creator of the Marian statue near the cathedral, for example, is unknown. But three men succeeded where others failed. Johann Albrecht Siegwitz (1700–66), Johann Georg Urbanski (*fl.*1725) and Franz Joseph Mangoldt (*fl.*1731) created much of the baroque sculpture in Presslaw that survives. Siegwitz and Urbanski are disputed as the authors of the two surviving statues of St John Nepomuk. Siegwitz is known to have carved the figures of the 'four cardinal virtues' that adorned the main entrance of the university. Mangoldt is credited with the sculptures that appear to float within the university's Aula Leopoldina (1731–2).

The Enlightenment in the natural sciences coincided with the baroque period in the plastic arts. Its concern for the application of reason and the pursuit of objective inquiry brought spectacular results. The Vratislavian Philipp Jakob Sachs von Löwenheim (1627–72) was one of its champions. Educated at Leipzig, Paris and Padua, he had already made a name for himself when he returned to his home town shortly before his death to take up the post of city physician. He was a member of the German Academy established in Schweinfurt in 1652 and founder of the snappily titled scientific journal, *Miscellanea Curiosa Medico-Physica oder Ephemerides Academiae Naturae Curiosorum*, which was published in Presslaw.[57] Under his influence, it is said that the Presslaw group of the academy, which alone contributed thirty-five members, became its most influential section.

Caspar Neumann (1648–1715) was one of that group. Born in Presslaw and educated at Jena, he had worked as a preacher and tutor before being appointed Deacon of the parish of St Mary Magdalenee in 1678. Apart from his career as a Protestant cleric, he was a scientist of note. He corresponded with Leibniz and kept detailed statistics on the city's population. Soon he was put into contact with the Royal Society in London, which sought to use his data in an examination of life expectancy. His statistics appeared in 1693 in a study authored by the astronomer Edmond Halley entitled *An estimate of the Degrees of Mortality of Mankind, drawn from curious Tables of the Births and Funerals at the city of Breslau.* In it Neumann was congratulated for the 'exactness and sincerity' of his work. His data comprised one of the first attempts to relate mortality to precise calculations of age. It is no exaggeration to describe him as the father of demography.

Of course, the concept of culture cannot be confined to the conventional categories of religion, letters or the arts. Presslaw's baroque period witnessed some interesting new developments, which included drama, music, sport and a mania for parades and processions.

In the sixteenth century, drama did not yet feature in regular public performances. But it was present in masques held either in the street or in patrician houses, and it found an early place in education. The Jesuits, in particular, were to encourage their pupils to write plays and perform them in school. The performance of a *Singspiel* by Gryphius in 1653 to celebrate the coronation of the Emperor's son was cited as the first dramatic event in Presslaw outside school premises. Presslaw's first dedicated theatre building, the Ballhaus, opened its doors in 1677 on the Elbing under the patronage of Count Herberstein. It was soon replaced by another more convenient building on Albrechtstrasse, rebuilt in 1703 after a fire. The actors were supplied with repertory companies, which toured all the main cities of Germany from about 1650 onwards. A printed programme, which has survived from 1692, shows the company of Johann Veltheim offering a series of plays, including Shakespeare's *King Lear* and a musical pastiche entitled *Die getreue Olympia.* The theatre offered every sort of show, from tragedies to acrobatics; in lean times, when it had no bookings, it was used as a storehouse for salt. It passed into the possession of the City Council in 1727.[58]

Musical life had its origins in the churches, where choirs, organs and instrumental groups were well established throughout Habsburg times. Lutheranism, in particular, possessed a very strong musical tradition; and at a later stage the Counter-Reformation was second to none in this regard. Presslaw's Italian Opera, in contrast, appeared only in 1725. It was launched on the initiative of the imperial Viceroy, Count Franz Anton von Sporck, whose residence at Karlsbad was famed throughout the Empire for this branch of entertainment.[59]

'Recreation' did not form part of medieval life. However, as soon as a modicum of prosperity was achieved and 'free time' became available, the idea began to attract city dwellers. In Presslaw, archery contests and chivalrous tournaments provided popular forms of entertainment.

Presslaw's penchant for parades derived partly from the rivalry of the City and Church authorities and partly from the competition between

Protestants and Catholics. The municipality was regularly moved to lay on a parade for every state occasion, whether it was the coronation of an Emperor, the entry of a high official or the visit of a prominent foreigner. Each of the guilds staged an annual parade of its members, while church processions were held many times a year. The Lutherans marked each of the main Christian festivals, while the Catholics went in additionally for saints' days and passion plays. Elaborate costumes, solemn music and colourful props boosted the impact. Carnival, during the days preceding Lent, was a time for general rejoicing.[60]

There remains the issue of Presslaw's links with Polish culture. Later Polish historians have sometimes taken the line that 'the political frontier . . . did not prevent Presslaw from being an integral part of Poland's literary and scientific sphere'.[61] They point to the large numbers of Polish books that continued to be printed in Presslaw, to the unbroken presence of the spoken Polish language and to the very strong ties that bound the Catholic cathedral and the cathedral chapter to the Polish Church. They produce long lists of distinguished Polish clergymen, from Erazm Ciołek to Bernard Wapowski and Wacław Grodecki, who worked and resided on Cathedral Island. Yet they ignore three cardinal facts: firstly, that Lutheranism, to which at least 75 per cent of the citizens adhered, had cut the city off from its pre-Reformation roots; secondly, that the great majority of Vratislavians, being monolingual German-speakers, had no ready access to foreign culture; and thirdly, that Cathedral Island was, quite literally, a tiny island of Polish influence in a cultural landscape of overwhelming Germanity. What *can* be said is that Presslaw's educated elite possessed a much greater knowledge of things Polish than their counterparts in subsequent centuries. After all, most of them were classically educated, and they shared the Latin-based culture that also flourished in the upper reaches of Polish society. Many of them had been educated in Cracow, and through their studies at the Jagiellonian University would have come into intimate contact with Polish art, science and letters. All of them would have been aware that the Commonwealth of Poland-Lithuania was still a very large country – larger than the Holy Roman Empire – which might yet recover from the ills that beset it. At least one-third of all news items in the Presslaw press of the late seventeenth and early eighteenth centuries were dedicated to Polish affairs. Neither Poland nor Polish culture was yet the beleaguered creature that it would soon become.

Despite decades of warfare, therefore, Silesia had developed into one of the most abundant cultural wellsprings of the Habsburg monarchy. Its writers, scientists and poets were achieving international renown, and it is tempting to imagine how they might have fared, had the province not attracted the attentions of Berlin. And yet, in a sense, it was already semi-detached from Austria. It was perhaps the religious and cultural divisions of Silesia that lent Presslaw its cultural dynamism under the Habsburgs. After all, the Protestant poet Martin Opitz served a re-Catholicising extremist. Both Angelus Silesius and Michael Willmann were ex-Lutheran Catholic converts, and Caspar Neumann was a Protestant priest at loggerheads with the Jesuits. Whatever its origins, that dynamism is indisputable.

Presslaw's culture was in fact driven by many different elements. No single group dominated:

> The decline and revival of the city's economy, austere Lutheranism and the triumphant Counter-Reformation, Viennese absolutism and patrician self-government, the ostentation of ennobled merchants and the penury of the ordinary workers, German, Polish and Bohemian elements and pan-European influences – all were interwoven into one.[62]

Under Habsburg rule, the German predominance in Presslaw's ethnic make-up was markedly enhanced. The Habsburgs were themselves a German dynasty, who in the Czech lands of Bohemia had promoted the German element. Although their handling of Silesia was less conflictive, they encouraged a social ethos where German norms were favoured by the court, the nobility and the urban patriciate. As Prague ceased to control its own destiny, so the administrators sent to Silesia were more likely to be German nobles from Bohemia than Czechs. After 1648, Poland too hit hard times, and it ceased to exert the influence abroad that had prevailed in the Jagiellonian era. The intensity of Silesia's relations with Poland declined and, with the exception of political refugees (see below), the number of Poles coming to Presslaw decreased. The resident Jewish element had all but disappeared. To all intents and purposes, Habsburg Presslaw was a thoroughly German city.

It would be wrong to suppose, however, that Presslaw's Germanity was in any way monolithic. The inhabitants did not form a homogenous mass. For one thing, the worlds of Catholic and Protestant Vratislavians were connected with different centres of gravity. The Catholics were linked to Vienna and to an increasingly Germanised Prague. The Protestants were connected more with northern Germany and the Low Countries. People, as well as ideas, were interchanged. Three Presslaw bishops of the period were Habsburg archdukes. Presslaw's Lutheran divines were more likely to be imported from Saxony or the Rhineland. For another thing, Silesia was 'opened up' during the Habsburg period. Contact with Western Europe – through the 'Grand Tour' or a university education – became the norm for its educated elite. Between 1597 and 1740, around 800 Silesians studied at the University of Leiden, Andreas Gryphius being foremost among them. Silesians like Martin Rehdiger and Laurentius Scholz went west; and Westerners like Johann Wacker von Wackenfels or Valens Acidalius came east. Moreover, the people of 'Germany' inhabited a kaleidoscope of petty principalities in the sixteenth and seventeenth centuries and were wracked by periodic civil wars. Describing them all simply as 'Germans' implies a sense of community and a unity of purpose that were almost wholly absent. Germans coming to Presslaw from Franconia (like Johannes Hess) or from Prussia (like Michael Willmann) not only felt different from each other, but must have felt profoundly different from the 'Old Germans' of Silesia and from the Germanised Slavs whom they met on arrival.

With regard to an age that preceded both censuses and modern national consciousness, it is impossible to make an accurate estimate of Presslaw's Polish population. But numbers clearly dwindled further from the low level already reached in late Bohemian times. They were recharged to some extent by the constant stream of transients, merchants and work-seekers from the adjacent Polish provinces, but at the same time, they were constantly reduced by the inexorable progress of Germanisation. In the sixteenth and seventeenth centuries, few families in the upper and middle strata of Vratislavian society cultivated their Polishness, even if they had Polish antecedents. Successful immigrants who established themselves in the city would usually adopt the language and customs of the German majority. What is more, the reassertion of the Catholic Church in Presslaw from the mid-seventeenth century onwards actually encouraged Germanisation by increasing the incidence of intermarriage between Polish Catholics and German Catholics. It is simply not true to present Vratislavian society as one divided into a German Lutheran majority and a Polish Catholic minority. As time went on, the Poles formed a distinct minority, even within the Catholic minority.

The result was a small Polish community living on the margins of Presslaw, both geographically and culturally. They continued to be connected to 'the Polish side'; the right bank of the river, but were less connected to the Catholic hierarchs on Cathedral Island than they were to one or two lowly parishes on the periphery, where Poles congregated and the Latin Mass was interspersed with Polish hymns and prayers. Their communal leaders were obscure priests, such as Brother Stanisław Bzowski of the Order of Preachers (1567–1637) and Father Michał Kusz (1600–54), who addressed their flock in their native tongue, who struggled to keep their tiny schools in being and whose very existence would hardly have been noticed in the gilded chambers of the Rathaus. But despite its continuing subordination to Gniezno, even the clerical community of Cathedral Island lost its Polish character. Karol Ferdynand Waza (r.1625–55), son of the Polish King, was the last Pole to occupy the See of Presslaw until 1956.

Strictly speaking, the Jewish community of Presslaw ceased to exist after its expulsion in 1455. And the legal prohibition was to remain in force for three centuries. Nonetheless, it did not amount to a total ban, and various categories of privileged Jews were allowed to take up residence. Others were permitted to visit for limited periods or for particular purposes. Generally speaking, the imperial authorities were concerned to ease the restrictions, while the City Council, under pressure from the guilds, was determined to keep them in place.

From the early days of Habsburg rule, Jewish mint-masters worked in Presslaw under special licence. In the 1540s, Isaak Meyer, a Jew from Prague, was recorded as the *Breslauer Muenzer*, or leaseholder of the mint. One of his coins, the so-called *Juden Heller*, caused a storm of protest over its size and poor metal content. In time, the Jewish minters seem to have been employed on work on the imperial (as opposed to municipal) coinage, and in particular as importers of bullion. A seventeenth-century successor to Meyer, Lazarus Zacharias, arrived in 1657 under the terms of an imperial patent. His private house became the first place of Jewish worship in Presslaw since the Middle Ages.

Jewish merchants were always free to enter the city and to ply for trade during Presslaw's three annual fairs, but they were subject to close supervision. In 1577, they were required to wear a yellow disc for identification. Jewish *Parnasei ha-Yarid*, or 'fair treasurers', were appointed to levy the municipal taxes, and a *Va'ad ha-Yarid*, or 'fair committee', organised the dietary and accommodation requirements of the visitors.[63] The punishments for failing to leave on time could be severe.

Much of Silesia's trade with Poland remained in Jewish hands, and the imperial authorities were aware that Presslaw's obstructive stance was harming commerce. In the early seventeenth century, therefore, steps were taken to lift the harsher restrictions. From 1630, a number of Jewish families were finally given a licence to reside in Presslaw for specific periods. And from 1637, the Council of the Four Lands – the autonomous body that regulated Jewish affairs in Poland – sent a permanent official to Presslaw to smooth relations with the City Council and to head the *Judenamt* or 'Jewish office'. Other officials followed. By 1696, they represented the cities of Prague, Krotoschin, Cracow, Lvov, Glogau, Zülz (Biała), Poznań and Lissa (Leszno). These *szamesi* or *Schamessen* became a fixed feature and formed the nucleus around which a restored Jewish community began to develop.

In the late seventeenth century, Jews increasingly congregated in or near Presslaw in defiance of the regulations. Some of them lived beyond the city limits in the parishes of St Matthias or St Vincent, where kosher butchers operated. Others gave the Karlsplatz its popular name – the 'Jewish Market'. By 1700, some 500–600 Jews were present. Several synagogues, such as the Lissaer and the Kalischer, had been established in private houses.

The municipal *Judenordnung* of 1702, followed by an imperial Edict of Toleration in 1713, gave retrospective approval to the existing state of affairs. But restrictions continued. Jews still could not legally reside in Presslaw without prior registration, nor could they be buried there. Instead, they found their final resting place in the cemeteries of Dyhernfurth (Brzeg Dolny), Krotoschin or Zülz. When numbers kept on rising, the City Council took fright. In 1738, it ordered all 'unprivileged Jews' to leave forthwith, under threat of a fine of 1,000 ducats per head. One hundred families left.

All of this begs the question whether Presslaw's Jews formed a separate ethnic group or just a religious community. In fact they were both. They were certainly not the sort of assimilated or semi-assimilated Jews who would appear in future times. Most of them came from Poland. They spoke Yiddish at home, Hebrew in the synagogue and both Polish and German in the marketplace. They practised Orthodox Judaism, whose 613 rules of everyday conduct, including an absolute ban on intermarriage, kept them strictly apart from their Gentile neighbours.[64]

*

Silesia sheltered numerous prominent Polish refugees in the second half of the seventeenth and early eighteenth centuries. Politicians who had enjoyed Habsburg support in Poland naturally made for Habsburg-controlled territory when events turned against them at home. In 1655, for example, King Jan Casimir Vasa (*r*.1648–68), sometime Spanish admiral, Portuguese Viceroy, French prisoner and Roman cardinal, fled to Silesia in order to escape the Swedish invasion of Poland. He was granted the former Piast duchies of Ratibor and Oppeln in lieu of unpaid Habsburg dowries, and set up court at Oberglogau (Głogówek). From Oppeln in 1656, he issued the ringing *universał*, or 'General Declaration', urging all his loyal subjects to resist the Swedish invaders to the last.

A decade later, the famous *Rokoszanin* or rebel 'Confederate', Jerzy Lubomirski (1616–67), twice set up his political base-in-exile at Presslaw. Grand Crown Marshal and Field Hetman, Lubomirski was bitterly opposed to the Polish monarchy's pro-French tendencies, and in 1664 he was formally banished for the treasonable activity of planning a royal election while the old King was still alive. First in 1664–5 and again in 1666–7, his agents and supporters used their refuge in Presslaw to foil French plans in Poland, to disrupt the Sejm (parliament) and to undermine the royal party's efforts at restoring unity. Diplomatic missions were sent to seek assistance in Vienna and Berlin. Contacts were established with Moscow and even with the Tatars of Crimea. Recruiting teams were dispatched to all of Poland's far-flung provinces to rally noblemen to the confederate cause. And an expedition marched off to confront the King in a campaign that ended in the bloody fratricidal slaughter of the battle of Mątwy (July 1666). Despite his nominal reconciliation with the King, Lubomirski returned to Presslaw to renew his scheming. His unexpected death was caused by a stroke aggravated by inept medical treatment. As a pro-French opponent commented, '*Trois médecins ignorants ont plus fait que toute les armées du Roi de Pologne*'[65] ('Three ignorant doctors achieved more than all of the King of Poland's armies').

One of Lubomirski's many emissaries active in Presslaw was his son, Stanisław Herakliusz Lubomirski (1642–1702). Poet, dramatist and diplomat, Lubomirski Jr took great pride in his father's defiance. '*Cała Rzeczpospolita*', he declared, '*na koniu przy moim ojcu*' ('The whole of the Commonwealth is in the saddle with my father'). A few years earlier he had been sent on an embassy to Versailles. In February 1665, he travelled from Presslaw to the imperial court at Vienna. He wrote much poetry and many letters, but is best remembered for a couplet in his work *De Vanitate* ('On Vanity'):

> Żyłem źle, żyłem dobrze, dałem przykład z siebie
> To sztuka: zażyć zycia, a przecie być w niebie.[66]
>
> (I lived evilly; I lived well; I made myself an example
> But it's an art – to live life to the full, and still reach Heaven.)

In 1675, the last of the Piast princes, Georg Wilhelm of Liegnitz-Brieg, died at his seat of Ohlau. It was the end of a line going back to the previous millennium. After his death, Ohlau passed to the Habsburgs, and with some delay was handed to another family of Habsburg clients from Poland. Between 1691 and 1737, the baroque palace at Ohlau, fifteen kilometres to the south of Presslaw, belonged to Jakub Sobieski, the Polish King's son.

Sobieski received Ohlau thanks to his marriage to the Emperor Leopold I's sister-in-law. But, connections apart, he was one of life's losers. He made more failed attempts at more thrones than his father fought glorious battles. He spent many vain years trying to gain control of Moldavia. And in 1697, he was the well-beaten, Austrian-backed candidate in the Polish royal election. For years after that he was chosen by Charles XII of Sweden to oust the Russian-backed Elector of Saxony from Poland. This scheme came to a sudden end in February 1704, when a posse of Saxon cavalrymen appeared at Ohlau under an officer called Kospoth, kidnapped its owner in broad daylight and carried him off for a lengthy period of incarceration in the Königstein near Dresden.

Maria Leszczyńska, known as 'Marynka' (1703–68), was the daughter of one of Jakub Sobieski's rivals, who actually succeeded in clambering on to the Polish throne while Sobieski languished in the Königstein. Historians disagree about her birthplace, but one of them states that her pregnant mother travelled to Presslaw from Poznań to consult a physician 'who refused to quit Presslaw'. Another states that she was born near Presslaw *im Polnischen Dorf* – which has been identified as the village of Polska Wieś, a property of the Abbey of Trebnitz (Trzebnica), where the baby's aunt was a nun. At all events, Marynka grew up and travelled further and higher than any of her contemporaries. After decades of wandering, in Sweden, Prussia and Alsace, she became, against all expectations, the bride of Louis XV, *'Reine de France et de Navarre'*. Her father, Stanisław Leszczyński, ex-King of Poland, became *Le Bon Roi Stanislas*, Duke of Lorraine. Marynka's grandson was Louis XVI, the principal casualty of the French Revolution.

Marynka's good fortune constituted one of the social sensations of the age. By persuading the young Louis XV to snatch her from obscurity, the Regent, Philippe of Orleans, perfected every poor girl's dream:

> Par l'avis de son Altesse
> Louis fait un beau lien;
> Il épouse une princesse
> Qui ne lui apporte rien
> Que son mirliton . . .[67]

> (On the advice of his Highness
> Louis makes a fine match;
> He is marrying a princess
> Who brings him nothing
> Except her petticoat . . .)

But nothing could teach Marynka's new French subjects to spell her name properly. Learned authorities variously labelled her Leczinska, Lezczynska or even Leckzinska.

Maria Clementina Sobieska (1701–35), who was brought up at Ohlau, was struck by the same sort of extraordinary fortune that met Marynka. Aged seventeen, she learned that her hand was being sought in marriage by the Chevalier de St George, the Jacobite 'Old Pretender' to the British throne. A year later, having escaped the clutches of Hanoverian spies on her way to

Italy, she was married by proxy in Ferrara to become the titular, but legitimate, 'Queen of Great Britain' and 'Queen of Ireland'. Her husband, James Edward Stuart, never restored his family's rightful position. Nor did his son, Charles Edward Stuart, 'Bonnie Prince Charlie', who – unbeknown to most of his British subjects – was a French-born prince whose mother-tongue was Polish.

The moment when Clementina learned of her destiny was preserved for posterity by one of those present. The place was the Palace of Ohlau. The time was February 1718. The observer was Charles Wogan, an Irish soldier of fortune, who had once cheated the death sentence by breaking out of Newgate Prison in London, and who had now been dispatched by the Jacobite high command in Paris to break the news. His account was published four years later in London in a work entitled *Female Fortitude: Exemplify'd in an Impartial Narrative of the Seizure, Escape and Marriage of the Princess Clementina Sobieska . . . now published for the Entertainment of the Curious*. Having been warmly welcomed at 'Olaw in Silesia', Wogan saw his chance:

> It seems that the young Princess when a child affected to be called by her Playmates, Queen of England; and that the Ladies of Court, seeing her extremely pleased with the Title, still continued to call her so. Which Mr Wogan observing, artfully closed with the opportunity . . . and told her. She had hitherto enjoyed only an Imaginary Title, but he was now sent to offer her a Real One.[68]

Such, at least, was Wogan's version. The consequence was that Clementina set off from Ohlau some weeks later on her secret journey to Italy, only to be intercepted at Innsbruck on British-Hanoverian instructions and held captive in a monastery. The dashing Wogan had to be sent out for a second time to effect a midnight rescue and spirit his charge over the snow of the Brenner Pass. He was rewarded by the Pope with the title of Roman Senator and with a colonelcy in the Spanish army.

During Poland's 'Saxon Era' between 1697 and 1763, when the Wettins ruled simultaneously as both Electors of Saxony and Kings of Poland, Silesia filled the territorial gap between the two parts of their joint realm. As a result, a constant stream of royal-electoral agents, diplomats and courtiers passed through Presslaw in transit between Dresden and Warsaw, or Warsaw and Dresden. Of course, the strategic rationale of the Polish-Saxon Union was to outflank the dynamic pretensions of Prussia. If the union had prospered, Prussia could conceivably have been checked. As it was, the union faltered. Russia established control over Poland. Saxony retreated into its shell. And Silesia was swallowed by Prussia.

*

It is perhaps ironic that, despite two centuries of unprecedented progress, the people of Presslaw still lived largely at the mercy of nature. Floods recurred, most notably in 1729 and 1736. Fires remained a common threat. The south tower of the cathedral burned down on two occasions – in 1540 and 1633. The 'west-end' of the Old Town was burned out in 1584. The New Market was destroyed in 1628. The Church of St Dorothy succumbed in 1686; the Church of Our Lady on the Sand in 1730.

Presslaw, like many other cities, was also still afflicted by periodic outbreaks of the plague. The worst of these occurred in 1542 (claiming 5,913 lives), 1568 (9,251), 1585 (c.9,000) and 1599 (3,000). A chronicle recorded the scene in 1585:

> Many Breslauers fled, were strewn here and there, and were so despised that one could have bought ten of them for a penny. They suffered hunger and sorrow. In sum, they were scorned, people ran from them, as if from Turks.[69]

Epidemics continued well into the seventeenth century: 1613, 1623, 1625 and 1668 were all plague years, and that of 1633 claimed 13,231 victims. Death must have seemed ever-present. Indeed, a legend of 1680 has Death riding through the city on a white horse, stopping on the squares and streets to collect the dead:

> On the Main Square, he said:
> > 'Come out, ye sick and well, come out,
> > Come out ye young and old,
> > Tis large enough the square hereabout,
> > The dance of death to hold.'
>
> On the Schmiedebrücke, he said:
> > 'Swing heartily with your hammer high!
> > My horse is wanting new-forg'd schoon,
> > I'm riding to my grave to lie,
> > Whither you will follow soon.' ...
>
> On the Judengasse, he said:
> > 'To Jew or Christian, I am blind,
> > To Moses and Prophets all,
> > For each that comes from womankind,
> > At my feet shall surely fall.'[70]

'Death' visited the city for the last time in 1709.

If medical advances failed to protect people from the plague, philosophical advances failed to protect them from superstition. The blossoming of humanism coincided almost exactly with an upsurge in prosecutions for witchcraft. While the works of Erasmus were permeating the nascent book market, the bible of witch-hunters, the *Malleus Maleficarum*, went through some twenty-eight editions. Presslaw was equally receptive to both trends. Already, in the late fifteenth century, it had shown itself to be at the forefront of the witch craze. However, where culprits had formerly been drowned or banished, punishments were stiffened after 1532 to include burning at the stake. Prior decapitation was practised in cases that required leniency. The criminal code of the Holy Roman Empire recommended the application of torture to suspects thought to have taught witchcraft or to have associated with witches. It prescribed death by burning for all witches who had caused actual injury or damage. Protestant attitudes were no different. The Protestant champion of witch-hunting, Revd Benedict Carpzov, who operated in nearby Saxony, is thought to have been responsible for the deaths of 20,000 women. The number of trials gradually declined in Presslaw in the late sixteenth century, but some sensational cases still arose. One was that of the so-called '*Zuckelhese*', a ninety-seven-year-old woman tried in August 1559. In time-honoured style, she was condemned to drowning in the Oder. When she failed to sink – a sure indication of her guilt – she was battered to death by the executioner.[71] In another case, a spinster living in the Catterngasse (Katharinengasse) was accused, around 1580, of practising bestial sodomy with her English mastiff. After denunciation and interrogation she was duly decapitated and burned. The unfortunate dog, unable to answer the charge that it was the devil incarnate, was burned with her.[72]

Devils and demons were a fact of life. They were everywhere, glimpsed on dark nights and heard whispering on the wind. They were the subject of learned treatises, one of which was written by King James VI and I of Scotland and England. Another, the *Homo-diabolus* (1617), was penned by Caspar Dornavius (1577–1632), a historian and prolific author connected to the circle of Crato von Crafftheim. Peculiar and unexplained events would habitually be attributed to demonic influence. Insanity, epilepsy or even excessive body-hair would suffice to bring the innocent before the Inquisition. Even children were not spared. In 1580, a peasant woman left her eight-day-old infant sleeping while she gathered the harvest on the outskirts of Presslaw. When she returned the child was crying incessantly and would not be calmed. The woman was naturally concerned and sought advice. She was informed that the infant was a changeling – a substituted child of the devil – and that a sound beating would ensure the return of her own. She complied and beat the infant with birch rods. Legend has it that the devil himself duly appeared, exchanging the babies with a withering glance and the words *'Da hast's'* – 'There you are'.[73]

By the seventeenth century, Presslaw seems to have been tiring of witch-hunts. Its index of criminal cases, the *Malefizbücher*, shows no examples after 1609 and a solitary case of sorcery in 1612.[74] Nonetheless, the Inquisition continued to find miscreants in rural Silesia and especially in the foothills to the south. In 1639, in the towns of Neisse, Ziegenhals (Głuchołazy) and Freiwaldau (Gozdnica), 242 women were burned. Fifteen years later, the district became specially notorious:

> In the Silesian town of Neisse, the executioner went to the trouble of constructing a huge oven in which, over a period of nine years, he roasted over a thousand witches, some as young as two years old; in 1651 alone, forty-two women and girls were put to death in it.[75]

Obviously one needs to exercise a degree of scepticism with regard to unsubstantiated or exaggerated reports. The study of witchcraft did not reach academic circles until the late nineteenth century. Even so, two things are abundantly clear. The scale of witch-hunts in early modern Europe was horrendous. And Polish society, hardly less than German society, was deeply implicated.

*

At first, the accession of the House of Habsburg changed little in the municipal life of Presslaw. Traditional rights and liberties were confirmed, and the Emperor Ferdinand's desire to restrict the powers of his new provinces was widely evaded.[76] The Habsburgs directly ruled only six of the sixteen Silesian principalities. The remainder, which enjoyed varying degrees of autonomy, were ruled by their former feudal overlords, including various lines of Piasts, Podiebradys and Hohenzollerns. Presslaw was governed by the constitution approved by the Luxemburgs, and its privileges were jealously protected. At the outset, the Habsburgs were forced to adopt the existing administrative structure of the Kingdom of Bohemia. The key organ for governing Silesia was the 'German Chancellery', which met in the royal castle in Presslaw and served both Silesia and Upper and Lower Lusatia. Though subordinate to the Bohemian Estates and to the 'Bohemian Chancellery' in Prague, it afforded an added degree of autonomy until its abolition in 1616.

In time, however, Vienna sought to extend its control over the provinces. The result was the Silesian Provincial Council, the *Schlesische Kammer*. Established in 1558, the council also met in the royal castle in Presslaw, but answered directly to the Habsburg court. These measures were strengthened by the office of *Oberlandeshauptmann*, or 'Governor', usually the Bishop of Presslaw, who oversaw the government of the province. The highest spiritual and temporal authorities in Silesia were thus united in the hands of a single appointee of the Emperor. As the demands on the provincial administration grew, however, the office of *Oberlandeshauptmann* was absorbed into that of the *Oberamt*, or 'Supreme Governor'. The competence of all such bodies did not extend to territories directly subordinate to Vienna.

So the semi-independent duchies retained substantial freedom of manoeuvre until the upheavals of the Thirty Years War provided an opportunity for imperial action. Silesia was not subjected to the punitive Bohemian Constitution of 1627, but the remaining islands of autonomy were annexed. And the 'Bohemian Chancellery' was moved to Vienna. In 1621, the Duchy of Jägerndorf (Strzelniki) was seized. Münsterberg followed suit when the Podiebrady dynasty died out. With some delay, Vienna was apt to redevolve its acquisitions. Münsterberg was granted in 1654 to the Auersperg family, while the Duchies of Ratibor and Oppeln were mortgaged between 1645 and 1666 to the King of Poland. In these cases, the residual autonomy was strictly limited. Interestingly, when the Habsburgs took over the Duchies of Liegnitz, Brieg and Wohlau (Wołów) in 1675, they overstretched themselves. The duchies had been bound by private treaty to pass to the House of Hohenzollern on the extinction of the native Piasts. Sixty-five years later, their annexation by Vienna was to give Frederick the Great the legal claim on which the invasion of 1740 was supposedly based.

Presslaw was inevitably involved in the changes. The concentration of provincial institutions in the city, which had begun under Mátyás Corvinus, continued under the Habsburgs. In 1535, the City Council decreed that all meetings of the Silesian Estates should only be held in Presslaw. Two decades later, a supreme financial authority for the province was set up. In other words, Presslaw was beginning to flex its muscles. Increasingly it referred to itself as *Vratislavia, Silesiae metropolim* – 'Presslaw, metropolis of Silesia'. The City Council was able to impose its wishes on rival jurisdictions. Its strength is amply demonstrated by the circumstances of the Reformation. Johannes Hess was appointed against the express opposition of the Bishop. The city fathers claimed that '. . . we have learned through Holy Scripture . . . that it is up to us to rebuild and restore the Holy Christian Church, which has been brought so low by numerous abuses and lack of faith'.[77] They took similarly forceful action in the demolition of the Abbey of St Vincent's in 1529, when they decreed that no potential strongpoint for an invading Turkish army must be left. The Bishop protested, but he was in no position to resist.

One feature of Habsburg rule lay in the monarchy's reliance on the military and political support of the grand, landed aristocrats. The essential link between the court in Vienna and their subjects in the provinces was maintained by a dense network of intermarried, landed and loyalist families whose leading members headed the nobility of their home areas, whose palatial seats acted as focuses of provincial social life, and whose power and influence were apparent both in the central offices of state and in local administration. Since Catholicism was the watchword of the Habsburgs, the great majority of these aristocrats remained Catholic, even when the Protestant Reformation overran the inhabitants of their lands. Silesia was no exception. Even when the main cities, like Presslaw, had mainly gone over to Lutheranism, the great princes, counts and barons, such as the Hohenlohes of Waldenburg (Wałbrzych), the Dohnas of Wartenberg (Syców) or the Hatzfelds of Trachenberg (Żmigród), continued to swan along in the devout and luxurious manner to which they were accustomed.

Moreover, a particular aspect of Silesian aristocratic life made a particular impact on Presslaw. Under pressure from the City Council, the Silesian Estates had resolved that Presslaw was to be the one and only place where the provincial estates would meet. As a result, the province's most prominent families established a routine of spending part of the year at court in Vienna, part of the year in the country and part in Presslaw. To this end, they acquired or built their own town houses, which gradually assumed the size and style that their owners' status demanded. In time, the palaces of Catholic aristocrats vied with those of Protestant patricians, and wealthy patrons were found to finance the schools, churches and monasteries which the Catholic community in the city had previously lacked. The process would continue well into the nineteenth century. But it was one of the reasons why the City Council of Presslaw, despite its strong Lutheran associations, was never able to introduce religious uniformity. In this sense, the city (like the province) was subject to a sort of diarchy, in which neither party could exert absolute control.

In the sixteenth century, a distinct sense of 'civic pride' was cultivated.[78] It manifested itself both in historiography and in poetry. The earliest municipal histories by Eschenloer and Stein had been written around 1500. But by the time of the Habsburg succession, the genre was developing into the ultimate 'must-have accessory' for all self-respecting cities. The *Origines Wratislaviensis* of Franz von Köckritz, which had been commissioned as a collection of important legal documents and privileges, was completed in 1555. The contribution of Crato von Crafftheim, his *Historiae urbis Vratislaviae synopsi*, was delivered in 1584. The *Schlesische und der herrlichen Statt Breßlaw General Chronica*, by Heinrich Rättel, was published in Frankfurt am Main the following year.

'Poems of praise', or *Lobgedichte*, flowed thick and fast. The City Council did not hesitate to mobilise local talent and to commission suitable works.[79] The high point was reached in 1613 with the publication of the *Breslographia* of Nikolaus Henel von Hennenfeld, in which the author contended that 'if this part of Germania were a ring, then Vratislavia would be its gemstone'. He then produced a list of epithets describing Presslaw as 'the eye of the light', 'the sun of Silesia' and 'the flower of Europe'.

Yet the prize for stilted sycophancy must undoubtedly go to Valens Acidalius for his *Ad Solem* ('To the Sun'):

> Phoebus (Apollo), Father, dear eyes of the world,
> Your progress brightens the uttermost ends of the earth.

> Have you ever, anywhere beneath your gleaming axle,
> seen a city more fair than is Breslea?

> What say you, Father? Does any such lie below your head lamps,
> as you sweep aside the night, where I cannot see?

> I understand! How could you judge whose light is brightest
> and yet remain untouched by jealousy?

> Behold Phoebus! Your ancient light, your halo, burns about you,
> yet your spokes could not bear the radiance of our town.

> Her refulgent rays are your rivals that reach to displace the stars,
> And wield a flail so strong that it scourges yours.

> And is it not unfriendly, almost we might say an act of jealousy,
> when, whitening, you draw a mask of cloud about your face?

> So, proud progenitor of the golden-headed deity, break free
> from the Indies' confining cage to seek your ancient ways,

> Bend your wings hither, and here at last begin to rise:
> Knowing the place and time, bring in the beauteous day![80]

It is not recorded whether or not the City Councillors were pleased.

Hence, despite their absolutist pretensions, the Habsburgs were obliged to share rule in Silesia with others. They were forced to accept limitations on their power by their subjects' stout defence of traditional privileges. In 1720, they asked the Silesian princes and Estates to ratify the Pragmatic Sanction, hoping to guarantee the unity of the Habsburg lands and the succession of Maria Theresa. In Presslaw City Hall, on 25 October, their request was solemnly granted. The treaty was signed and sealed in red wax. But it did not serve its purpose, for two decades later, one of the signatories of the Pragmatic Sanction would march on Presslaw in open defiance of its provisions. He would treat the city's long-defended privileges with similar contempt.

*

For a variety of reasons Presslaw experienced relatively little urban spread in the early modern period. In fact its most notable developments of the early sixteenth century were the demolition of existing districts, either for defensive or medical reasons. Enclosed behind its ageing walls and moats and obsessed by the Ottoman threat, the city had little incentive to grow beyond its medieval limits. Indeed, when the Turks were besieging Vienna in 1529, the Vratislavians were sufficiently concerned to engage in some sporadic fortification-building. But their most obvious reaction was to condemn the area on the north bank of the river. St Vincent's Abbey and St Michaelis Church on the Elbing and the Church of the Eleven Thousand Virgins were all destroyed to prevent their capture in a possible attack. Some historians have observed a religious motivation in these decisions, given that all the lost institutions were Catholic, but this is open to question. Other sacrifices were less controversial. Fears about the spread of venereal disease led to the razing in 1551 of the Venusberg, whose inhabitants merely moved to the streets behind the cathedral, where business was resumed, undeterred by the protests of the clergy.

Presslaw was evidently regarded as highly attractive. As Ferdinand of Habsburg was to attest in 1538, 'He who has not seen Presslaw, has not seen a beautiful city.'[81] When measured in 1561, Presslaw was also shown to be larger than the Habsburg capital in Vienna. It was celebrated by the production of numerous maps, most notably that of Barthel Weihner of 1562, which still hangs in the City Hall. In 1558, it was further graced by the placing of one of the earliest botanical gardens in Europe, on the Reuschegasse, to the west of the Main Square. The later and more famous botanical garden – that of Laurentius Scholz – was established between 1585 and 1590 in the south-east of the Old Town. It contained curiosities from the New World and exotica from the East.

The City Hall was also given its finishing touches. The tower was adorned with a cupola in 1559 and the clock faces were added a decade later. The astronomical clock on the east façade was completed in 1580. With these additions almost three centuries of endeavour were complete. Future modifications would not introduce any significant changes.

Much of the surrounding Main Square found its final form at this time. The spectacular Griffin House was completed in 1589, by the city architect Friedrich Gross, and was the largest patrician house in the city. The House of the Seven Electors followed in 1672, with the addition of its frescos. The

House of the Golden Eagle dates from the early decades of the eighteenth century. Such opulent buildings often accommodated prominent guests. The House of the Seven Electors, long an unofficial residence, housed the Emperor Maximilian II in 1563. Rudolf II stayed in the House of the Golden Sun in 1577. The House of the Blue Sun, No. 5 on the Main Square, had one of the most impressive guest lists. It was completed in 1574 and long served as a coaching house. It twice housed King Władysław IV of Poland, in 1619 and again in 1624. Sigismund III Wasa is also said to have lodged there with his future wife, Anna of Austria. As a result it came to be called the 'Polish Court'. And No. 21 was for many years the residence of the Fuggers.

The renovation of Presslaw's defences was largely left to two later military architects, Hans Schneider von Lindau (1550–1608) and Valentin von Saebisch (1577–1657). Von Lindau had rebuilt the defences of Danzig before coming to Presslaw, where he renewed the bastions to the south and east. Saebisch was appointed Master of Fortifications around 1606. He began with a thoroughgoing '*Reglement*', which detailed the tasks that each guild was to fulfil. Even the clergy were not exempt. He modelled the fortifications on those of Palma Nova near Udine, a fortress considered to be a benchmark of its type. In time, Saebisch produced an impressive defensive system of bastions, trenches, ravelins and casemates. It would soon be put to the test.

The outbreak of war in 1618 acted as a further brake on expansion. Presslaw withdrew behind its defences, sporadically besieged by both imperial and Swedish armies. Nonetheless, it was never sacked, though its good fortune should be attributed as much to shrewd negotiations as to any supposed impregnability. When the islands were finally retrieved from the Swedes, the churches and cathedral library were found to have been looted and used as stables. Compared to events elsewhere, this was not the greatest catastrophe. A poem by Andreas Scultetus from 1641 emphasises Presslaw's fortunate position compared to the surrounding countryside:

> O herbes Schlesien, du liebes Vaterland,
> Mein Leben, wie dich noch der blinde Kriegesbrand
> Nicht hatte so verzehrt; Mein Tod zu diesen Zeiten.
> Wer feindet dich nicht an? Wer steht auf deiner Seiten?
> Man sucht dich in dir selbst. Wo deiner Väter Lust
> Und Aufenthalt geprangt, liegt jetzt lauter Wust.
> Bloß Presslaw blüht noch auf. Hier find ich was zu lieben.
> Hier ist ein Schlesien fast einzig überblieben.[82]

(O bitter Silesia, beloved fatherland, you were

My very life, until war's blind breath
So raged through you now you're my death.
Who is not your foe? Who stands by your side?
We don't recognise you. Where your fathers' pride
And joy once sojourned, wasteland alone remains.
Only [Presslaw] still thrives. Here love I find –
For, here, and nowhere else, Silesia has survived.)

Urban growth in the seventeenth century was further hampered by demographic losses. In 1633, Presslaw's population was reduced by more than one-third by an outbreak of the plague and it has been estimated that population levels did not fully recover for fifty years. Even so, the belated arrival of the Counter-Reformation initiated a spate of new building after 1659. The Jesuits, in particular, lost little time in magnifying the Catholic presence. In the final decade of the seventeenth century three churches were added to the Presslaw cityscape, all of them masterpieces of the baroque. The Church of St Anna was built in 1687 to house the female choristers of the Church of Our Lady on the Sand. The Church of St Anthony arose in 1685 to the design of the master builder, Matthäus Biene. And Biene was engaged again in 1689–98, this time to build the Church of the Holiest Name of Jesus, later known as the University Church or St Matthew's. Modelled on 'Il Gésu' in Rome, it was an archetypal edifice to the greater glory of the Jesuit Order. The vast painted ceiling was created by the fresco specialist, Johann Michael Rottmayer. Secular buildings of the same general vintage included the Matthias Hospital (1675), the Orphanotropheum (1702–15) or 'Orphanage', and the Jesuit-run University (1728–40).

One could argue, of course, that the finest achievements of the baroque were to be found in its elaborate funerary monuments. High on the list in this category would be two chapels in the cathedral – one, the 'Cardinal's Chapel' (1680–86) dedicated to Prince-Bishop Cardinal Friedrich of Hesse-Darmstadt (r.1671–82), and the other, the superb Borromini-inspired 'Elector's Chapel' (1716–24), built by J.B. Fischer von Erlach for Franz Ludwig (r.1683–1732), Elector of Mainz and Bishop of Presslaw. The latter was adorned with illusionist frescos by Carlo Carlone, plasterwork by Santino Bussi and sculptures by the Bohemian master, F.M. Brockhoff. In 1693–9, the medieval tomb of Duke Henryk VI in the Church of St Clare was extended and enlarged to form the grand mausoleum of the Presslaw Piasts. In 1715, a splendid baroque funerary chapel by Benedict Müller was added to the old Dominican Church of St Adalbert.

The influx of landed aristocrats into Presslaw led to the erection of several magnificent palaces. Among the older examples were the House of the Oppeln Piasts from 1532, and the House of the Liegnitz-Brieg Piasts, which arose in various stages up to 1675 and possessed an impressive Renaissance façade. Among the more modern examples, four deserve mention. The Spaetgen Palace was built in 1710 for Heinrich Baron von Spaetgen and was destined to become the residence of Frederick the Great. A decade later, the Schreyvogel Palace was built for the Vienna banker, Christian von Schreyvogel. It was to serve General von Tauentzien as a headquarters in his defence against the Austrians in 1760. The original Hatzfeld Palace was built in 1722 by the court architect to Vienna, Christoph Hackner, for Duke Franz Philip von Hatzfeld-Trachenberg. Eight years later, the imperial representative in Presslaw, Duke von Lamberg, ordered his Lamberg Palace to be built, again in the Viennese style.

Amid such opulence, the walls of the dilapidated imperial castle were finally torn down in 1728. A new building was begun, which was to include the baroque masterpiece of the 'Aula Leopoldina' (1731). Lastly, just before the end of Habsburg rule, a Neptune fountain was erected in the New Market in 1732. It was christened the '*Gabeljürge*' – 'the chap with the fork'. It was a fitting reminder of the lighter side of the Habsburg era, which was now to be superseded by something distinctly heavier in tone.

In the countryside around Presslaw, Protestant church-building took rather more demonstrative forms than in the city itself, where by and large the Lutherans simply took over existing places of worship. At Reimswaldau (now Rybnica Leśna) near Waldenburg, for instance, a rare example of a *Schrotholzkirche*, or 'timber church', dating from 1557 still stands. Built from rough-hewn timber with a free-standing belfry and rustic paintings in the interior, it is highly evocative of the simple devotion of the early Protestant rural communities. In the mid-seventeenth century, by special provision of the Peace of Westphalia, the Protestants of Silesia were awarded the right to erect a number of *Friedenskirchen*, or 'peace churches', which were to be built outside the towns entirely of timber or clay, with no nails. A fine example from 1654–5 stands near Jawor (Jauer) on the road to Świdnica (Schweidnitz), designed by the military engineer, von Saebisch. The Holy Trinity Church (1657–8), in Świdnica itself, is another. Fifty years later, at the Treaty of Altranstädt (1707), the Habsburg Emperor was obliged to concede that his Protestant subjects in Silesia would be allowed to construct a series of *Gnadenkirchen*, or 'grace churches'. One half-timbered example survives at Milicz, fifty kilometres to the north-east of Wrocław.

The Catholic Church, in contrast, indulged itself with baroque piles of colossal size and theatricality. Most of the ancient medieval abbeys of the region – Trebnitz, Leubus, Heinrichau (Henryków) and Grüssau – were completely transformed. Leubus, for one, was remodelled in the eighteenth century along the lines of the most grandiloquent baroque monasteries in

Austria, and it must surely be one of the largest ecclesiastical structures in Europe. Another marvel of the Counter-Reformation was created in the mountains at Albendorf (Wambierzyce) near Glatz (Kłodzko), where a complex Way of the Cross was constructed in 1716–21 on the orders of Daniel Paschasius von Osterberg. This 'Silesian Jerusalem' centred on a miracle-working statue of the Virgin, and became Lower Silesia's most frequented pilgrimage site. Approached up a broad flight of steps, the altarpieces in its sequence of chapels were the work of Michael Willmann.

In many ways, the smaller towns of the province mirrored developments in Presslaw – though on a smaller scale. There was an enormous amount of rebuilding to do after the Thirty Years War. A town like Striegau (Strzegom), on the road to Liegnitz, for example, was not put properly back on its feet until it was resettled in 1713 by veterans from the War of the Spanish Succession. Liegnitz itself was embellished in the first half of the eighteenth century with many monuments and buildings reminiscent of a minor capital. The choir of the former St John's Church was turned by Carlo Rossi into an octagonal chapel for the mausoleum of the Liegnitz Piasts. The ducal sarcophagi are surrounded by historical paintings. Next to it, the new St John's Church was built for the Jesuits in 1714–21. Outside the town, the lavishly decorated St Jadwiga's Church (1727–31) was designed by Kilian Ignaz Dietzenhofer to the orders of the Abbot of Bohemian Broumov. Its oval dome, twin towers and hexagonal nave are as striking as the paintings of Cosmas Asam, Franz de Becker and Wenzel Reiner. Inside the town, the final phase of Habsburg rule saw the appearance of the Abbey of Nobles (1708), the Palace of the Abbots of Leubus (1735–45) and, in the marketplace, the late-baroque City Hall.

The landed aristocracy vied with the Church hierarchy in the ostentation of their architectural taste. As their medieval castles became militarily obsolete, they were revamped, reconstructed or replaced by country palaces. In the sixteenth century, superb Renaissance houses were put in place by the Hochbergs at Fürstenstein (Książ), the Talkenbergs at Plagwitz (Płakowice) and the Piasts of Liegnitz-Brieg at Ohlau. Yet nothing outshone the baroque splendour either of Gross Peterwitz (Piotrkowice) near Trebnitz, which was built after 1693 by Count Colonna, who had married the local heiress, or of Goschütz (Goszcz) near Wartenberg, which was built in 1730–40 for Count Heinrich Leopold Reichenbach.

Early modern Silesia had nothing to compare with the châteaux of the Loire, or the villas of the Roman Campagna, or indeed with the most princely piles of Poland or Lithuania. Yet its architecture, both inside and outside Presslaw, aspired to standards far above provincial mediocrity. It was created by well-established schools of architects, artists and craftsmen, it displayed high levels of design and workmanship, and it possessed not just charm, but real élan and great diversity.

*

The citizens of Habsburg Silesia can have had little inkling of the fate that awaited them. As the various Piast mausoleums attested, their particular brand of Germanity had been built on Slavonic foundations. For hundreds of years they had belonged to the Kingdom of Bohemia. They took pride in their large degree of self-government, which their Habsburg masters had not disturbed. It is very doubtful whether many of them would have viewed 'the barbarians of Berlin', who were newcomers to the neighbourhood, as serious challengers to the might of Austria. The optimists would have hoped that the long-prepared Pragmatic Sanction would ensure a smooth succession and a prolongation of the status quo. The pessimists would have predicted trouble, possibly an international challenge to the Habsburgs' hold on the Empire. But no one was to claim later that they had correctly foreseen what actually happened.

FIVE

Bresslau in the Kingdom of Prussia, 1741–1871

The rise of Prussia was one of the primary political phenomena of early eighteenth-century Europe. At the time of the coronation of Frederick I as 'King in Prussia' in 1701, his dominions, which consisted of little more than the core territories of Brandenburg, Eastern Pomerania and East Prussia, did not rate as a great power. Yet by the outbreak of the Seven Years War in 1756, virtually the whole of the European continent was in arms against a Prussian agglomeration that had become the dominant force in northern Europe. The chief architect of this meteoric rise was Frederick (Friedrich) II (r.1740–86). His dynasty, the Hohenzollerns, was destined to eclipse the previous leader among the German princes – the Habsburgs.

An accomplished flautist and correspondent of Voltaire, yet described as ruthless, malicious and misanthropic, Frederick succeeded to the Prussian throne at the age of twenty-eight. His youth had been an eventful one. Persecuted by his father for an apparent lack of interest in things military, he had sought to flee the court in 1730 in the company of two friends, Lieutenants Katte and Keith. Following his arrest, Frederick was forced to witness the execution of Katte and, during solitary confinement in the fortress of Küstrin (Kostrzyn) on the Oder, to endure the prospect of his own execution. He languished at Küstrin for about fifteen months, during which he studied military theory and the workings of the Prussian administration. By 1733, he had regained his father's esteem. He was to become 'perhaps the ablest tactician of military history'.[1]

On his accession in 1740, Frederick is said to have recognised that Prussia could not stand still, that she either had to advance to greatness or accept the lot of a second-rank player. So, backed by sound finances and a well-trained army of some 100,000 men, he resolved to abandon his father's cautious policies. The opportunity for action was to present itself five months after his accession. When the Russian Empress Anna Ivanovna, and the last of the male Habsburg line, Emperor Charles VI, died almost simultaneously, Frederick sensed the vulnerable position of the young Maria Theresa in

Vienna and the confusion in St Petersburg. Despite the Pragmatic Sanction (see page 160), he saw his chance to seize the richest of the Habsburg provinces: Silesia.

The Hohenzollerns had been eyeing the Silesian duchies for a long time. A treaty of 1537 had secured them the succession to the duchies of Liegnitz (Legnica), Brieg (Brzeg) and Wohlau (Wołów) on the extinction of the native Piasts. The Great Elector had sought to press these claims in 1648 and had contemplated military action twenty years later.[2] But when the Piasts died out in 1675, their duchies were taken over by the House of Habsburg. So Frederick had a grievance to nurse. Yet, in reality, his actions in 1740 had little to do with legal niceties and everything to do with opportunism and power politics. He saw the invasion of Silesia as his personal 'rendezvous with fame'[3] and, at another level, as the first step on Prussia's rise to greatness. As he would candidly confess in his memoirs, 'it was a means of acquiring a reputation and of increasing the power of the state'.[4]

The first Silesian campaign of 1740 might reasonably be described as a precursor of the *Blitzkrieg*. Prior to the invasion, utter secrecy was maintained and every strategy of diplomacy exploited. Several regiments were sent on an elaborate feint to the south-west of Berlin and, on the eve of the invasion, a masked ball was staged in the capital. The King disguised his advance, which began on 14 December, as a preventative measure, claiming that Austria was on the brink of collapse. Yet, seen from his point of view, it was full of risk. Prussia itself was not yet the major respected power into which Frederick was to transform it:

> His officers were considered as mere adventurers . . . his soldiers as vile mercenaries; and the name of 'Prussian' seldom occurred without some contumelious jest . . . The country itself formed an undescribed species of hermaphrodite monarchy, which partook rather of the meanness of an electorate than the dignity of a kingdom.[5]

What is more, though all precautions were taken, the outcome of the march could not be foreseen with any certainty:

> At noon on 14 December, Frederick reached Krossen [Krosno], the last town in Brandenburg . . . The superstitious townspeople were in a state of some alarm, for the King's advent coincided with the fall of the bell in the great church. But Frederick assured them that the omen was auspicious, signifying the collapse of the House of Habsburg.
>
> On 16 December, Frederick and the leading troops marched through a woodland zone and crossed the Silesian border . . . The King was met just

inside Austrian territory by two black–cloaked figures who stood at the roadside like crows. These were Protestant clergymen from Glogau [Głogów], come to beg Frederick to spare the heretical churches in case of bombardment. The King greeted them as the first of his Silesian subjects.

Frederick spent that night in a baronial house in Schweinitz [now Świdnica near Zielona Góra] and wrote to Berlin: '. . . I have crossed the Rubicon with flying colours and beating drums. My troops are full of enthusiasm . . . and our generals are avid for glory.'

. . . Bad weather set in on 18 December. The baggage and artillery dragged far behind, and the soldiers marched in mud and water up to their knees, ruining their white gaiters. Glogau proved to be rather better defended than . . . expected, and . . . the Prussian invasion threatened to bog down . . . Frederick was all the more anxious to press on to Breslau because he knew that the city authorities . . . were engaged in talks to admit an Austrian garrison. He accordingly left Glogau under blockade . . . and on 28 December set off for [Bresslau] with the advance guard . . .[6]

As he proceeded through Silesia, Frederick bargained with Vienna on the move. He offered to maintain the Pragmatic Sanction and to vote for Maria Theresa's husband, Francis of Tuscany, as Emperor, if Vienna would meet his terms. He received the Habsburgs' refusal at the gates of Bresslau on New Year's Day 1741. On that freezing day:

Frederick and his grenadiers arrived outside the massive ramparts of [Bresslau]. The main gates were shut against them, but the wickets were open, and a stream of tradesmen's lads made for the lines of brass-capped Prussians, bearing wine, bread, fish and meat, and dragging casks of beer behind them on little sledges.[7]

Inside the fortress, the tension was tangible. Already burdened with refugees, the citizens had watched the Prussian advance with an unease that foreshadowed unrest. Though not overtly pro-Prussian, the majority of them were not demonstrably pro-Austrian either. Discontent with Vienna, stemming from economic and religious grievances, was common.[8] On 10 December, when an order had arrived stating that imperial troops were to be sent, it was not welcomed. If the long-cherished privilege of self-defence, the *Ius praesidii*, was about to be compromised, the population also feared for their other liberties, not least for their freedom of worship. So on 14 December, the council's proposed acceptance of the order had sparked a large-scale revolt. Some 600 men, led by a cobbler named Johann Döblin,[9] had stormed the City Hall and symbolically manned the defences. Their action prevented the entry of imperial troops. But their boldness collapsed as soon as the Prussian vanguard appeared at the end of the month.

Frederick II's attack on Silesia inspired one of those wonderful pieces of dramatic writing on which young historians were once invited to base their style:

Yet the King of Prussia, the anti–Machiavel, had already fully determined to commit the great crime of violating his plighted faith, of robbing the ally whom he was bound to defend, and of plunging all Europe into a long, bloody and desolating war; and all this for no end whatever, except that he might extend his dominions and see his name in the gazettes. He determined to assemble a great army with speed and secrecy, to invade Silesia before Maria Theresa should be apprised of his design, and to add that rich province to his kingdom . . . It was the depth of winter. The cold was severe, and the roads heavy with mire. But the Prussians pressed on. Resistance was impossible. The Austrian army was then neither numerous nor efficient. The small portion of that army which lay in Silesia was unprepared for hostilities. Glogau was blockaded; [Bresslau] opened its gates; Ohlau [Oława] was evacuated. A few scattered garrisons still held out; but the whole open country was subjugated; no enemy ventured to encounter the King in the field.[10]

For three days the Prussians camped on the Oder islands while royal and municipal officials negotiated. It was then agreed that no Prussian garrison would be imposed, so long as neutrality was maintained and the Austrians were excluded. Frederick preceded his assent with the phrase 'in the present circumstances and for as long as they prevail' (they were to do so for seven months). It was also agreed, on that same morning of 3 January 1741, that Silesia's new ruler should perform a ceremonial entry:

Just before noon the royal train entered by way of the Schweidnitzer Tor. Frederick's table silver was first through the gate. It was borne on pack-horses which were draped with hangings of blue silk, all a-dangle with gold tassels and little bells. Frederick himself was mounted on a mettlesome steed. His blue silken cloak was bedaubed with the falling snowflakes, but he repeatedly uncovered his head to acknowledge the greetings of the crowd. He descended at the house of Count Schlangen-berg in the Albrechtstrasse, and twice appeared on the balcony in response to the continuing applause.[11]

The royal party tarried for three days, during which time the good behaviour of its troops did much to make the annexation more acceptable. A communiqué sent to the Minister of War, however, betrayed a less peaceful tone. 'I have [Bresslau],' Frederick wrote, 'and tomorrow I shall advance against the enemy further.'[12] What he did was to blockade the Austrian fortresses of Glogau and Brieg, attempt the bombardment of Neisse (Nysa), billet his troops in winter quarters in the towns and villages of Silesia and then ride home. 'This monarch surely has some great project in mind,' commented the Danish envoy to Berlin. 'He will not be content with conquering a province, but will strive to become the arbiter of the German Empire.'[13]

Early in 1741, desultory warfare prevailed in Silesia. Hungarian hussars in Austrian service, who specialised in raids and ambushes, took to kidnapping Silesian nobles who had welcomed the Prussians. In March, an Austrian force under General Neipperg crossed the hills and overran the southern districts, linking up with the fortress at Brieg. This time it was Frederick who was taken by surprise. He hurriedly returned to Bresslau, gathered his scattered troops together and marched out to do battle. The clash of arms took place on the afternoon of 10 April 1741 on the snow-covered fields at Mollwitz (now Małujowice) near Brieg. The two sides were evenly matched. The Austrians had the advantage in cavalry, the Prussians in infantry. Frederick ceded command to the veteran Field Marshal Schwerin, who had fought alongside Marlborough at Blenheim and alongside Charles XII at Bender. In the heat of intense fighting, when defeat looked imminent, Schwerin ordered the King to leave. Snatching some state papers and mounting a powerful English grey, Frederick galloped far from the field, only to learn that the well-drilled Prussian infantry had rallied and carried the day without him. It was a near squeak. The Austrians had come within an ace of forcing the Prussians to surrender and hand Silesia back. Frederick would never again leave a still-disputed battlefield.

The consequences of Mollwitz were manifold. The horse that had saved Frederick's skin, *der Mollwitzer Schimmel*, was given honourable retirement in the Lustgarten at Potsdam, where it lived for another twenty years. At an international level, France, Spain and Bavaria joined Prussia in an alliance against Austria, thereby starting the War of the Austrian Succession. At a local level, Bresslau lost its autonomy. In the summer of 1741, political agitation by Prussian agents coupled with extraordinary taxation sowed confusion, and Frederick finally elected to make a move. Prussian troops entered Bresslau at six o'clock on the morning of 10 August, accompanied (as stipulated in the neutrality agreement) by the city militia. However, they moved swiftly to secure the fortifications and the City Hall; and by midday both the militia and the City Council had sworn allegiance. Reportedly the only injury was a clipped ear sustained by a recalcitrant guard on the Ohlauer Tor. The incident was reflected in a contemporary refrain recorded in the diary of one Johann Steinberger:

Glogau bei Nacht,
Brieg mit Macht,
[Bresslau] mit Lachen,
Neiße mit Donnern und Krachen.[14]

(Glogau by night,
Brieg by might,
Bresslau with laughter,
Neisse with crashes and thunder.)

After 480 years of semi-independence, the Silesian capital had now been subordinated to a centralised state. There was still no single established way of spelling its name. But the form 'Bresslau', which was recorded at this time, marked an apt, midway stage between the 'Presslaw' of the past and the 'Breslau' of the future.

In all probability, Frederick II's intentions in all this were quite limited. Yet he had provoked what has been called 'the first world war'. For the War of the Austrian Succession and the Seven Years War – of which the two Silesian wars would form only a part – were to have worldwide repercussions. Lord Macaulay could not find words strong enough to express his outrage:

> Had the Silesian question been merely a question between Frederick and Maria Theresa, it would be impossible to acquit the Prussian King of gross perfidy. But when we consider the effects which his policy . . . could not fail to produce, we are compelled to pronounce a condemnation still more severe . . . The plunder of the great Austrian heritage was indeed a strong temptation . . . But the selfish rapacity of the King of Prussia gave the signal to his neighbours. His example quieted their sense of shame . . . The whole world sprang to arms. On the head of Frederick is all the blood which was shed in a war which raged during many years and in every quarter of the globe, the blood of the column of Fontenoy, the blood of the mountaineers who were slaughtered at Culloden. The evils produced by his wickedness were felt in lands where the name of Prussia was unknown. And, in order that he might rob a neighbour whom he had promised to defend, black men fought on the coast of Coromandel and red men scalped each other by the Great Lakes of North America.[15]

One wonders how many people in Bresslau recognised the power of the shockwaves radiating from the political earthquake at whose epicentre they stood.

For the next year, Silesia came to terms with its new status. Military operations moved into Bohemia, where, in May 1742, two further defeats persuaded the Austrians to sue for peace. The Treaty of Bresslau, on 11 June 1742, promulgated from the balcony of the House of the Golden Sun on the Main Square, brought the First Silesian War to a conclusion. Austria recognised Prussia's annexation of Silesia. Prussia undertook to uphold the rights of Silesian Catholics.

Mindful of Maria Theresa's successes on other fronts, Frederick re-entered the fray. He started the Second Silesian War with a re-invasion of Bohemia in August 1744 and the capture of Prague. But an Austrian counter-manoeuvre forced him to retreat to Silesia. The campaigning season of 1745 opened with Frederick staying at the Abbey at Kamenz (Kamieniec), seeking to tempt the Austrians and Saxons down from the hills. When they eventually descended on to the Silesian plain near Striegau (Strzegom), their commander, the Prince of Lorraine, was unaware how close the Prussians' main force lay. On 4 June at Hohenfriedeberg (Dobromierz), therefore, Frederick was able to advance under cover of darkness. He took the enemy flank by surprise in the early morning, picked off the Saxons and Austrians separately, then finished off all resistance with a sensational charge by the Bayreuth Dragoons – one of the most celebrated episodes of the Silesian wars. By 9 a.m. the battle was over. Austrian losses outnumbered those of the Prussians by three to one. Further Prussian victories at Soor and Kesselsdorf convinced Maria Theresa to sue again for peace. The Treaty of Dresden, signed on Christmas Day 1745, renewed Austrian recognition for Prussia's annexation of Silesia. Frederick, who in five years of intermittent warfare had earned the sobriquet 'the Great', remarked that he would not, in future, attack 'even a cat'.[16] In reality, his sergeants were brutally impressing Saxon prisoners into Prussian service. One Saxon carabineer who escaped declared that he 'would more willingly serve the King of Poland for twenty years than the King of Prussia for one'.[17]

Prussia, materially exhausted, welcomed the interval of peace. Yet peace was all too fleeting. The third round of the struggle for Silesia, the Seven Years War, broke out in 1756. Following the formation of a fresh anti-Prussian alliance comprising France, Austria, Russia, Sweden and Saxony, Frederick was obliged to return to war. He began with a pre-emptive strike against Saxony and an advance into Bohemia. But defeats at Kolin in June 1757 and at Moys in September brought operations back into Silesia. On 22 December the armies met on the outskirts of Bresslau. Heavily out-numbered, the Prussians under the Duke of Braunschweig-Bevern lost a quarter of their number and were driven off. The city's garrison surrendered two days later.

Frederick, however, was not prepared to concede defeat. Adding Braunschweig's survivors to the small detachment that had marched with him from Berlin, he created a combined force of some 33,000. At Parchwitz (now Prochowice near Legnica) he addressed them, unusually, in German and appealed to their patriotism:

> The enemy hold the same entrenched camp of [Bresslau] which my troops defended so honourably. I am marching to attack this position . . . I fully realise the dangers . . . but in my present situation, I must conquer or die. If we go under, all is lost. Bear in mind, gentlemen, that we shall be fighting for our glory, for the preservation of our homes, for our wives and children. Those who think as I do can rest assured, if they are killed, that I will look after their families. If anybody prefers to take his leave, he can have it now, but he will cease to have any claim on my benevolence . . .[18]

He then moved off to face an Austrian army of 82,000 – more than twice his strength. He found it near the village of Leuthen (now Lutynia), drawn up on a wide front, some sixteen kilometres west of Bresslau.

The battle of Leuthen (5 December 1757) finds a place in all the military textbooks. Apart from deciding Bresslau's fate for the next two centuries, it was Frederick's 'most celebrated day'. Napoleon was to call it a 'masterpiece of manoeuvre',[19] which showed how speed, surprise and strategic skill could give victory to the lesser battalions. As he advanced to the town of Neumarkt (Środa Śląska) on the Sunday afternoon, Frederick had learned from some peasants that the main body of Austrians was bivouacking nearby in the undulating, snow-covered countryside. They were stationary, and therefore vulnerable. He rose before dawn on the 6th, climbed a small hill, the Schönberg, whence he observed the Austrian camp on a plateau, and carefully laid his plan. It worked to perfection. The Prussians approached at right-angles. The Austrians steadied themselves for a frontal attack. But some way short of their apparent destination, the Prussian infantry turned sharp right into a shallow defile, running for a few kilometres hidden from view and parallel to the front. They then emerged, not against the well-prepared Austrian centre, but against the bewildered and exposed left wing. From there, they could roll up the flank while denying the enemy the advantage of their numerical superiority. Resistance was fierce and numerous confused actions ensued. The Austrians recovered and re-formed their lines. Leuthen village was not carried until the late afternoon. But the verdict was not in doubt. When Frederick led the pursuit towards Lissa (Leśnica) in the dark, snow was falling again on the 10,000 dead and on the lines of prisoners. He lodged in the Castle of Lissa with the Baron von Mudrach, displacing bemused Austrian officers with a polite 'Bon soir, Messieurs!'. That night, as his army marched into the night, singing 'Nun *danket alle Gott*', he confided to his host, 'You know what *Va banque* is? That's what I played today.'[20]

In Bresslau, meanwhile, the Austrian garrison was not in surrendering mood. The Commandant, von Bernegg, erected a gallows on the Main Square to deal with defeatists. Yet five days of bombardment finally persuaded him to surrender; 17,000 Austrians, including seventeen generals, joined the 13,000 captives from Leuthen. Frederick was present on 21 December to watch them streaming through the Schweidnitzer Tor 'in a seemingly endless column'. He was escorted by a small party of officers, an easy target for any Austrian sniper who might have thought of shooting him. 'God be thanked,' he remarked, 'I have removed this terrible thorn from my foot.'

Despite the success at Leuthen, Frederick's grip on Silesia was far from secured, and 1759 was to be his blackest year. His army had already lost 100,000 men and could not replenish its reserves. In August at Kunersdorf (now Kunowice, near Frankfurt-an-der-Oder) it suffered its greatest ever defeat, losing a further 19,000 men and 172 guns.

In the summer of 1760, therefore, the Austrians and Russians closed on Bresslau yet again. On 30 July some 50,000 Austrian troops appeared under Gideon von Loudon, a general who had once been rejected by the Prussians. Frustrated by a flooded moat, he threatened that neither children nor pregnant women would be spared. His opponent, General Friedrich von Tauentzien, replied furiously from behind decrepit fortifications, and with a mere 5,000 defenders, that 'I and my soldiers are not pregnant!'.[21] While directing operations beside the bastion to the south of the Schweidnitzer Tor, he narrowly escaped an Austrian cannonball. He silently covered it with his hat and expressed the desire to be buried where it had come to rest. His spirited resistance was to be rewarded. On 4 August a Prussian relief force arrived, setting the scene for the conclusive confrontation of the Silesian campaigns.

The battle of Liegnitz (15 August 1760) reran some of the remarkable features of Leuthen. An army with a numerical superiority of three to one was repulsed with heavy loss, thanks to the speed and skill of Prussian manoeuvring. On this occasion, Frederick had been marching along the Katzbach in order to join up with his beleaguered forces in central Silesia. The clash took place in the early hours by the village of Panten to the north-east of Liegnitz. The Austrian Field Marshal Daun had set troops in motion during the night, only to find that Frederick had vacated the camp that was due to be attacked and had taken up position on the commanding plateau that Daun himself had aimed to occupy. After that, the Prussians were able to deal a fatal blow at Loudon's corps without ever facing Daun's main body. The engagement was over so quickly that a Turkish spy in the Austrian camp, working in the guise of a Greek baker, did such a brisk trade in baklava among the troops that he missed the battle and was unable to make his report. In due course, Schweidnitz (Świdnica) was relieved. Bresslau never had to withstand a direct Austrian challenge again.

The general settlement, however, was slow in coming. With the fall of Berlin in October 1760 and the subsequent union of Austrian and Russian forces in early 1761, Prussia was outnumbered by three to one. Frederick was cut off at his fortified camp of Bunzelwitz (now Bolesławice) north of Schweidnitz. Fortune appeared at last to have deserted him. Only the death of the Russian Empress Elizabeth in January 1762, which was to break the allied coalition, saved Prussia from destruction – the so-called 'Miracle of Brandenburg'. Europe was tired of war. At the Treaty of Hubertusberg in February 1763, Austria agreed to return to the *status quo ante*. Prussia's possession of Silesia was finally confirmed.

Frederick had, in fact, condemned Silesia to a generation of war. Prussia had had to defend itself from the repeated attacks of its indignant neighbours for nearly a quarter of a century, and the contiguous territories of Silesia, Saxony and Bohemia were fought over time and again. Between 1740 and 1763 there were only seven years of peace. Frederick regularly set up his winter headquarters in Bresslau, and four of the set-piece battles that were the hallmark of the period – at Mollwitz (1741), Hohenfriedeberg (1745), Leuthen (1757) and Liegnitz (1760) – were fought in the vicinity.

Frederick II's Bresslau winters were times for reflection, correspondence and, sometimes, despair. In 1757–8, he wrote to Maria Theresa stating that, had they been allies, they could have made all of Europe shudder. In 1758–9, he complained to his friend, the Marquis d'Argens:

> I am sick of this life . . . I have lost everything in this world that was most dear to me. [He instructed the Marquis to] eat oysters and crayfish in Hamburg; empty the chemists' pillboxes . . . and enjoy the delights of the spirits in paradise . . . [but] do not forget a poor, cursed man condemned to make war for all eternity.[22]

In 1761–2, installed in the Spaetgen Palace with no prospect of a solution and no firewood, he contemplated suicide. That winter he wrote again to the Marquis d'Argens:

> I seek escape from all this by looking at the world as if from a distant planet; then everything appears to me very small and I feel sorry for my enemies who take so much trouble for so little.[23]

It was at Bresslau that he learned of the 'Miracle of Brandenburg'.

During the remaining decades of Frederick's reign, Silesia experienced renewed economic growth, repopulation and a state-sponsored policy of industrialisation and reconstruction. The Prussian statesman Karl Svarez (1746–98) was associated with many of these developments. He was born in Schweidnitz and had studied law in Frankfurt-an-der-Oder before practising briefly in Bresslau. Appointed to the City Council in 1771, he masterminded the reform of the Silesian credit and education systems, before being called to Berlin in 1780. His main works, the *Allgemeines Landrecht* and the *Allgemeine Gerichtsordnung für die preußischen Staaten*, completed a thorough reorganisation of the antiquated Prussian legal system. Many of the effects of war had already been alleviated by the 1780s. Silesia became progressively more integrated into the Prussian state. Observing this 'Prussification', the Bresslau philosopher Christian Garve noted at the end of the eighteenth century that the Silesians were hardly discernible from the other 'nations' of Prussia.[24]

During the reign of Frederick the Great, the Kingdom of Prussia increased in size from 119,000 to 195,000 square kilometres. Excluding its Rhenish and Westphalian possessions, it formed a territorial complex that stretched from Magdeburg to Memel and from Stettin to Beuthen (Bytom). Its population had grown from 2.2 to 5.8 million. It had benefited from the collapse of Swedish power in the Baltic and from the weakness of Poland, which Frederick had done much to provoke. By the time of his death in 1786, Europe again stood on the brink of major upheavals, but Prussia's place in the constellation of European powers was secure.

Unfortunately for Prussia, his successor, Frederick William (Friedrich-Wilhelm) II, (r.1786–97) was not of the same mould. Easy-going and intelligent, yet a 'frank polygamist' and inclined to mysticism, he did not possess the qualities to guide Prussia unscathed through the Age of Revolution. His reign was notable for the influence of one Johann Christof Wöllner, a Rosicrucian who pushed policy in the direction of religious bigotry. Despite well-meant reforms, the economy went into decline. More seriously, Frederick William had little taste for military affairs, and his establishment of a supreme college of war (*Oberkriegs-Collegium*) did nothing to improve Prussia's readiness for it. Though he presided over phenomenal territorial expansion during the Second and Third Partitions of Poland (1793–5), the acquisitions markedly increased the numbers of Catholics and non-Germans in the kingdom, thereby promising instability. The annexation of Warsaw in 1795 brought Europe's largest Jewish community under Prussian control.

King Frederick William II's connection with Bresslau might be seen as

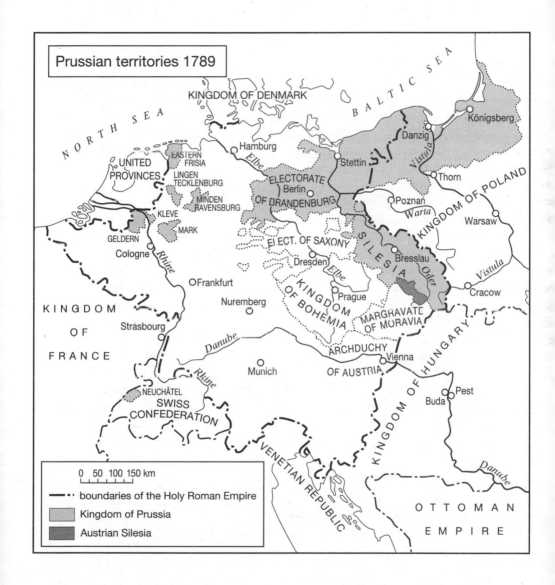

Prussian territories 1789

KINGDOM OF DENMARK

BALTIC SEA

NORTH SEA

Königsberg

Danzig

Hamburg

Stettin

Thorn

EASTERN FRISIA

UNITED PROVINCES

LINGEN TECKLENBURG

MINDEN RAVENSBURG

ELECTORATE OF BRANDENBURG

Berlin

Poznań

Warta

KINGDOM OF POLAND

Warsaw

KLEVE

MARK

GELDERN

Cologne

Rhine

EI ECT. OF SAXONY

SILESIA

Bresslau

Oder

Vistula

OFrankfurt

Dresden

Elbe

Cracow

Nuremberg

KINGDOM OF BOHEMIA

Prague

MARGRAVATE OF MORAVIA

KINGDOM OF HUNGARY

Strasbourg

Danube

KINGDOM

OF

FRANCE

ARCHDUCHY OF AUSTRIA

Vienna

Rhine

Munich

NEUCHÂTEL

SWISS CONFEDERATION

Buda

Pest

Danube

0 50 100 150 km

VENETIAN REPUBLIC

OTTOMAN

EMPIRE

- ·- boundaries of the Holy Roman Empire

Kingdom of Prussia

Austrian Silesia

symbolic of his shortcomings. Of only two statues of him erected in Prussia, one – in the style of Trajan's Column in Rome – was raised on the occasion of the King's visit to Bresslau in 1786, in the newly established Scheitnig Park. But it was too high for most people to recognise the personage at the top. It was known as 'Old Mr Scheitnig'.[25]

Even-tempered and free from the vices of his father, Frederick William III (r.1797–1840) had the makings of a model king. He began well, cutting expenses, dismissing ministers and rectifying the most oppressive abuses. Yet he was drawn out of his depth by his dealings with revolutionary and Napoleonic France. Neither his diplomacy nor his generals were effective. After the defeats at Jena and Auerstädt and the punitive Peace of Tilsit (1807), Prussia lost its earlier territorial gains. French exactions strained the economy to the limit.

French troops first appeared before Bresslau in November 1806. Their task was formidable:

> Always one of the most significant fortresses of the land, [Bresslau] had gained in strength through the efforts of Frederick II. Her streets and markets hid themselves behind three strong walls, of which the main wall . . . inspired respect even from afar. Her broad and deep moats were filled by the Ohlau and the Oder. There was no hill which could dominate her; only the extended suburbs could offer the besiegers any sort of advantage.[26]

The siege began on 6 December with the destruction of the Oder bridges and the Nikolai suburb. Four days later the Ohlau suburb was razed. From these positions, the fortress was to be bombed into submission:

> Many good [Bresslauers] sought refuge underground. People began to creep into the cellars . . . We moved into a small flat in the Hatzfeld Palace, the seat of the government . . . since our Minister-Viceroy had thought it sensible to remove himself . . . The bombs buzzed and hummed above us; there was a ceaseless racket of crashing, exploding and cracking. I got used to it very quickly, the others too, I think. The cannonades on both sides were sometimes so heavy, that I imagined I was going deaf, as the walls and the floor groaned in protest . . .[27]

Negotiations were started when a Prussian relief force failed to break through. Surrender came on 5 January 1807. The siege had taken more than 160 lives and had destroyed some 150 buildings in the Old Town. The suburbs had been almost completely reduced to rubble. The French garrison, headed by Jerôme Bonaparte, Napoleon's youngest brother and

King of Westphalia, remained for almost a year. During this time the fortifications were dismantled to be replaced by boulevards, and the Tauentzienplatz was built.

The dark years of Prussia's humiliation saw the launch of a reform programme in Berlin. Led by Stein, Hardenberg, Gneisenau and Scharnhorst, the administrative and military machinery of the Prussian state was restored. After Napoleon's retreat from Moscow in 1812, it gave Prussia the means to assume leadership of Germany's War of Liberation.

On 3 February 1813, King Frederick William III was advised to leave Berlin for Bresslau to avoid seizure by French troops. Once there, he came under the influence of the 'war party' and reluctantly placed himself at the head of the developing public mood for action. His timidity was summed up by a popular saying. The official line ran: 'The King called and everyone came.' This was turned around to: 'Everyone called and the King finally came too.'[28] Professor Henrik Steffens of the University of Bresslau was one of those at the forefront of demands for war. His speech on 10 February gained many adherents. He later summed up the local mood:

> How often did you complain that you had rushed off to this far corner of Germany . . . and now it has become the moving, inspiring centrepoint of everything. A new epoch of history is starting here, and you can express what is stirring the surging masses.[29] . . . I was seized by the thought – it is up to you to declare war, your position allows it, regardless of what the Court decides.[30]

The King responded by introducing conscription, forming *Jägerabteilungen* or 'troops of chasseurs'. He also allowed his commanders, Lützow, Sarnowski and Petersdorf, to form irregular *Freikorps*, which were to attract non-Prussian Germans into units designed to form the nucleus of a new German army. Discussions with the Russians dragged on for weeks, and only on 10 March did Frederick William finally burn his bridges. Then, from his residence in Bresslau, he promulgated the decree *An mein Kriegsheer* ('To my army'), urging it to fight for the independence of the Fatherland. He also founded the Order of the Iron Cross, to honour service in the forthcoming war. On 17 March, he made the proclamation *An mein Volk* ('To my people'), calling for the overthrow of the Napoleonic yoke:

> You know what you have endured for almost seven years; you know what your sorry fate will be if we do not end this struggle honourably . . . It is the last decisive struggle, which we are waging for our existence, our independence and our prosperity. There is no solution, other than an honourable peace or a glorious defeat.[31]

Apart from Steffens, the resultant rush of volunteers to Lützow's *Freikorps* included the ardent nationalist Ernst Moritz Arndt, the poets Joseph von Eichendorff and Karl Theodor Körner and the 'father of gymnastics', Friedrich Jahn. Ferdinande von Schmettau typified the spirit of sacrifice felt by those who could not fight. She sold her hair for the cause, gaining two thalers, which she donated to the war effort. When held up as a symbol of patriotism by the authorities, she fashioned her hair into trinkets, thereby raising an additional 196 thalers.[32] Facing such determined opposition, Napoleon withdrew to the Elbe, leaving isolated rearguard units at Danzig (Gdańsk), Thorn (Toruń), Stettin (Szczecin), Küstrin and Frankfurt an der Oder.

The campaign of 1813 inevitably affected Silesia. Napoleon had been defeated in Russia and was withdrawing from Poland. But he still had large contingents at his disposal, and at every point of contact he proved himself tactically superior. The unpredictable movements of his forces, and those of his pursuers, threw all the eastern parts of Germany into turmoil. In May, for example, having drawn the Russians and Prussians deep into Saxony, Napoleon twice turned on them and pushed them back into Silesia. On 21 May, he outflanked the Russo–Prussian camp at Bautzen, killed 18,000 in a fierce engagement and drove them in disorderly retreat over the River Neisse. In the course of the follow-up, he lost his closest comrade, Michel Duroc, who had been with him since the siege of Toulon twenty years before:

> The cavalry general, Bruyère, a fine officer, had both legs carried away and died of the dreadful injury; but the saddest event of the day was the result of a cannonball which, after killing General Kirgener, mortally wounded Marshal Duroc, Napoleon's oldest and best friend ... The Emperor who was at his side showed signs of the greatest grief [and] parted from him in tears having given him a rendez-vous 'in a better world'.[33]

Soon the French were back at the gates of Bresslau. A skirmish occurred on 31 May and the Prussian garrison was panicked into withdrawal. Thereupon a deputation, headed by the Mayor, August von Kospoth, met Napoleon at Neukirch (now Nowy Kościół) near Goldberg (Złotoryja) to beg for mercy. The Emperor replied:

> It would break my heart if I were not in a position to grant that request. War is a terrible evil and brings suffering and misery with it. I will endeavour to keep it to a minimum, especially in such a beautiful land as Silesia.[34]

Despite Napoleon's reassurances, Bresslau lived through some anxious days in June 1813 when the French, the Russian and the Prussian armies were all in the neighbourhood and a major battle between them seemed likely. Napoleon, with 40,000 men, had set up camp at Neumarkt, and the Russians were drawn up in massed ranks only a kilometre to the east of the city. The French, whose troops were bivouacked on the streets, observed good discipline and prevented looting except in the outer suburbs. They did not exact any financial contributions, but they did make a compulsory purchase of rice for the sum of 10,000 thalers. They built palisades in front of the east-facing gates and armed them with cannon, because Cossack patrols had been raiding right up to the walls:

> The most terrible night was the one when people living in the suburbs were ordered by the French to gather up their belongings and take them into the city. It was said that the suburbs were about to be torched and that a great battle was being prepared. A truce put an end to all those [false rumours] . . .[35]

The French were not seen again in Bresslau except as prisoners of war.

The year of 1813 brought Bresslau enormous prestige. Not only had the city served as the launchpad of the War of Liberation, but it had given birth both to the Iron Cross, the most famous German military decoration, and to Germany's national colours, of black, red and gold, which were first used by the Lützow *Freikorps*.[36] As Steffens had claimed, Bresslau really did become the 'inspiring centrepoint of everything'.

Frederick William III's reign lasted for another generation. But it was spent following the reactionary political lead set by the Austrian Chancellor, Metternich, who demanded that the popular forces unleashed by the War of Liberation were to be suppressed – if necessary by force. So the Prussian King reneged on the promise of a constitution and called instead for the formation of *Landtage*, or 'provincial Diets'. Contrary to the original intention, these assemblies were overwhelmingly dominated by the land-owners. They met in private and acted in a purely advisory capacity. As one German official admitted, their establishment was 'the safest way to bring calm and happiness to [the King's] subjects'.[37] National-liberal hopes had been dashed. The first Silesian Diet met in Bresslau in 1823.

Frederick William IV (r.1840–58) did not live up to the popular hopes invested in him. He relaxed press censorship, reversed his father's ecclesiastical policy and stopped the campaign of Germanisation in Prussia's eastern provinces. Yet he refused to promulgate the long-postponed constitution, justifying his decision with the words 'no piece of paper should come between me and my people'. A romantic idealist and a believer in the principle of divine right, he had little grasp of political realities. As a result, the 'United Diet' that opened in Berlin in 1847 was no more than the congregation of the unrepresentative provincial Diets that had been initiated by his father. By that time, liberal frustrations were combining with acute economic and social grievances to create revolutionary tensions.

The 'Prussian Revolution' of 1848 was foreshadowed by persistent unrest. In 1843, the radical journalist Wilhelm Wolff (1809–64) had published a disturbing article in the *Breslauer Zeitung* detailing the miserable conditions endured by the city's prisoners. The next year, a revolt of Silesian weavers found a powerful echo, especially when Prussian troops en route to suppress the rising, were attacked in Bresslau by an angry mob.

The events of 1848–9 were triggered in Prussia by news of the February Revolution in Paris. Bresslau, in fact, responded before Berlin did. On 17 March, a 'sanguinary collision'[38] was reported by the *Silesian Gazette* and troops were temporarily withdrawn. The inhabitants were fully armed, and neither police nor soldiers were on the scene. Later that month, when the rebels were attacked with customary brutality, they fought back. Repeated confrontations resulted in the resignation both of the Chief of Police, Heinke, and of the Governor, von Wedell. By the autumn the Citizens' Militia had occupied all the municipal offices and was blocking tax payments to Berlin. The clampdown finally came in the spring of 1849. On 7 March, the dispersal of a popular meeting sparked widespread unrest. A body of rioters descended on the City Hall and erected barricades; they were met with bayonet charges and musket volleys. That evening, the military commander declared a curfew and a state of siege.[39] In the aftermath, nineteen lay dead and sixty-five injured. An outbreak of cholera claimed the lives of a further 3,000.

No event during 1848–9 was more pregnant for the future than the German *Parlament* which convened at Frankfurt am Main. Intended as the constituent assembly of a unified German state, it did not realise its main aims. But in twelve months of passionate debate it aired many of the issues that were to come to the fore in the following decades. Silesia sent a total of fifty-five parliamentarians to Frankfurt, among them four representing Bresslau – Bruno Abegg, Eduard von Reichenbach, Wilhelm Wolff and, as the leader of the Bresslau Security Committee, Heinrich Simon (1805–60). The Bresslau historian, Gustav Stenzel (1792–1854), also attended as a member of the Catholic Party, as did the Prince-Bishop of Bresslau, Melchior von Diepenbrock, as a representative for Oppeln (Opole). The Bishop did not find the discussions in Frankfurt to his taste and promptly returned home. But the others, especially Wolff, Simon and Stenzel were extremely active. Unlike the representatives from the neighbouring duchy of

Posen, the Germanity of whose constituents was called into question, the Bresslauers were less concerned with the national issue than with constitutional and social matters. On one side stood Stenzel. He joined his fellow historian, Richard Roepell (1808–93), in demanding a constitutional monarchy and – as a supporter of the *Kleindeutsch* concept, which excluded Austria – opposed Polish sovereignty on the grounds that it would somehow increase Russian influence. On the other side stood Simon and Wolff. Simon demanded the abolition of the nobility, and also wished to see the restoration of an independent Poland. Once the *Parlament* was dissolved, he became one of the five 'Reich-Regents'. Soon afterwards, he was condemned *in absentia* by the Prussian courts and departed for a lifetime's exile in Switzerland.[40] Wolff was a radical schoolmaster and journalist, who shared Simon's democratic views and joined him in calling for a German republic. He followed Marx and Engels into exile in England, where he died in 1864. Engels later wrote of Wolff: 'With him, Marx and I lost our most faithful colleague and the German revolution a man of irreplaceable worth.'[41] Marx dedicated the first volume of *Das Kapital* to Wolff, as 'an unforgettable friend' and the 'intrepid, faithful and noble champion of the Proletariat'.[42]

The years after 1848 were something of an anticlimax. Frederick William IV presided over a phase of economic recovery and the beginnings of German economic union. But internationally he tamely submitted to Austrian plans at the Punctuation of Olmütz in 1850, thereby abandoning Prussia's distinctive vision of Germany's future. Having once paraded through Berlin wrapped in the revolutionary tricolour, he now sided decisively with the forces of conservatism and reaction. Moreover, he soon proved to be inconsistent and unbalanced to the point of insanity. He took no further interest in wider German politics. His brother Wilhelm, who was Regent from 1858, succeeded to the throne three years later.

Under William (Wilhelm) I (*r.* 1861–88) and his 'Iron Chancellor' Otto von Bismarck, Prussia seized the initiative and led Germany to unification. Three wars were fought, against Denmark (1864), Austria (1866) and France (1870–1), which swiftly secured Prussia's uncontestable supremacy among the German states.

Bresslau inevitably took a front-row seat in the Austro-Prussian War of 1866. When the conflict loomed in May, the recovery of Bresslau was known to be a 'primary war-aim' of the Emperor Franz-Joseph.[43] For its part, the City Council sent a loyal address to Berlin, expressing in the most fervent terms their willingness to fight for Prussia. In his response, King William noted with satisfaction that 'the spirit of 1813' was still alive and promised full support. As a result, the strongest of the three Prussian armies facing Austria was sent to central Silesia. Crown Prince Frederick set up his headquarters in Bresslau on 28 May. During the fighting, which took place in the summer, the Austrians, weakened by their simultaneous operations against Italy, were forced to abandon all thoughts of invading Silesia. Nonetheless, the Crown Prince's Second Army made slow progress crossing the mountains into Bohemia; and it arrived very late in the day, like Blücher at Waterloo, to deliver the decisive blow in the driving rain at the battle of Sadowa (3 June 1866). At the end of the campaign, both the King and the Crown Prince stood together in Bresslau to take the salute at a march-past of the Silesian Corps, and to thank the citizens for their steadfast loyalty to the Prussian cause.

Less than five years later, the novelist and playwright Gustav Freytag accompanied the Crown Prince during the Franco-Prussian War. He noted with gloomy foreboding the growing passion of the Hohenzollerns for the idea of Empire and the trappings of power. The German Empire, he thought, would corrupt Prussia:

> A certain Spartan simplicity and rigour has maintained discipline in the civil service, the army and the people. The new Imperial dignity will change that ... The splendour ... the pomp ... the costumes and decorations ... will claim greater and greater importance ... Courtliness and servility will creep in.[44]

These things, Freytag believed, had no place in 'old Prussia', and their influence would destroy her. At the end of that campaign, after the defeat of France, Freytag was a witness in the Hall of Mirrors at Versailles as the King and the Crown Prince stood together once again, this time presiding over the declaration of the German Empire.

*

Once Bresslau had been annexed by Prussia, its long-term economic prospects rose significantly. In the initial period, when Bresslau had to adapt to the loss of its traditional markets in Austria and the Empire, and when war caused much disruption, conditions looked less rosy. But as soon as the teething troubles could be overcome, a bright future beckoned. In the decades after 1741 Prussia made enormous territorial gains. The Prussian market was growing for anyone who could exploit it. The Partitions of Poland gave Prussia enormous new provinces. The acquisition in 1793 of Great Poland (which was renamed 'South Prussia') and of so-called 'New Silesia' was particularly advantageous for Bresslau. Prussia's military establishment had a voracious appetite for the goods that Bresslau already produced, while Silesia's rapid industrialisation created new sectors of manufacturing and trade. In 1815, Prussia acquired hugely valuable lands in western Germany on the eve of the Railway Age. The movement of goods from east to west was increased to unheard-of volumes and speeds.

In the eighteenth and nineteenth centuries, therefore, Bresslau progressed from a provincial economic centre with well-established international connections to a major centre of both national and continental significance. But success did not come overnight. Every gain seemed to be matched by a setback. Silesia in 1740 had a population of about one million, which it more than supported by its own agricultural production. The economic jewel in the Habsburg crown, it thrived on extensive sheep farming as well as spinning and weaving, and it possessed an entrepreneurial nobility. In Upper Silesia, zinc, iron, lead and silver were mined, though the region's main mineral resource – coal – was yet to be exploited in earnest. Frederick II had ambitious plans. As he wrote to the Bishop of Bresslau in 1741, 'I have taken it upon myself to make Silesia the most thriving and happiest of my provinces.'[45]

Silesia was now to be treated as an integrated economic unit. The old Habsburg economic system was swiftly removed. The arcane taxation system was abolished. So too was the tax office in Bresslau. The tax burden for the majority of Silesians was actually reduced. Yet the wars of the 1740s caused a great deal of destruction, and the fragile growth of trade foundered on the punitive tariffs instituted by Austria and Saxony. Hard times returned. Silesia had lost its traditional markets, but was unable as yet to reap the advantages of the reorganised Prussian system. As a result, new measures had to be devised to stimulate its growth. In addition to Merino sheep-breeding, the promotion of potato-growing and the attempted introduction of tobacco, vineyards and mulberry trees, it benefited from a state repopulation policy and from the opening of state grain stores. The native aristocracy was also very active. Count Heinrich von Reichenbach, for example, had inherited the lordship of Goschütz (Goszcz) to the north-east of Bresslau in 1727. He founded villages, established paper mills and promoted weaving. His son, Carl Heinrich, added furnaces, glassworks and brick kilns.[46] By 1748–9, Silesia was producing a trading surplus of 4.7 million thalers.

Renewed hostilities during the Seven Years War promptly wiped out the successes. Economic growth was also inhibited by the obstructiveness of Vienna and Dresden. By 1770, Silesia was probably in a worse economic situation than it had been thirty years before.[47] Fortunately, the government in Berlin was proactive. Coal-mining was promoted and a six-month tax exemption was granted. The King made three million thalers of his own funds available, for the relief of famine and hardship. Such measures were desperately needed. In 1765, peasant unrest had erupted on a massive scale in Leobschütz (Głubczyce) in Upper Silesia, sparked by a dispute over labour services. But, fuelled by hunger, it threatened to spill over into Lower Silesia. Only the presence of the King himself, and a substantial detachment of Hussars, sufficed to keep order.

Bresslau fared better than the rural districts around it. In addition to the production of traditional wares, such as madder and beer, it continued to service the regional economy. Its four annual markets were extended to include a Silesian trade fair. With a population growing again after a generation of warfare and stagnation, it emerged as one the largest cities in the kingdom, being granted the official status of a *Residenzstadt*, or 'royal residence'. By the end of the eighteenth century, it was the capital of Prussia's most dynamic province, which was producing 45 per cent of the country's exports and consuming 44 per cent of its imports.[48]

Nonetheless, renewed unrest broke out. Conditions were especially bad in Upper Silesia. In 1780, labour services were refused in Pless (Pszczyna) and two years later a widespread strike hit Neustadt (Prudnik). In 1784, seventy-six villages in the county of Glatz (Kłodzko) were in dispute with their lords. When Frederick visited, he avoided the troubled districts for fear of unleashing a general rebellion.[49] In the following years, tensions would be further heightened by the French Revolution and by the promised abolition of serfdom in Poland, whither many Silesian peasants fled. In 1793, the tailors of Bresslau rose in protest against working conditions. In the ensuing chaos thirty-seven were killed and seventy-eight injured.

During the Napoleonic Wars, Silesia's economy suffered repeated dislocations, though demand from within Prussia was sufficient for its nascent industry to survive. But the arrival of the French did not improve matters. In 1807, peasant revolts in Trebnitz (Trzebnica) and Striegau were brutally suppressed by the French army. Four years later, 'a veritable peasants' war' broke out in Ratibor (Racibórz) and Pless. The rebels attacked with scythes, but were beaten off with heavy losses; 300 of their number were arrested and flogged.[50] Yet it was the post-war period that posed the greatest economic challenge. The Silesian textile industry was hit especially hard, being pushed into a permanent crisis by a decline in demand and by mechanised competition from the Rhineland and from Britain. Innovation provided the only glimmer of hope. Rapeseed and hops were sown, and the world's first beet-sugar factory was built in Wohlau in 1802.

The response of the provincial authorities was to develop technical education, improve communications and encourage manufacturing. From 1818, the road network was renovated with stone surfaces, while two schools opened in Bresslau for the training of industrial and agricultural apprentices. These enterprises soon bore fruit. In 1819, the Heckmann factory opened for the production of sugar-refining equipment. In 1833, Gustav Ruffer established a machine shop, which within three years was employing 200 workers and producing textile machinery and steam engines. In 1844, the established metal-working shop of Gottfried Linke turned its hands to locomotives, constructing the very first home-built wood burner for the Silesian railway. Rolling stock was destined to be one of Bresslau's major industries.

August Borsig (1804–54) was a product of the new system. After training in Bresslau as a joiner, he opened an iron foundry and machine shop in Berlin in 1837, using 8,500 thalers of loaned capital. Four years later, his firm produced Prussia's first locomotives. In seventeen short years, he produced some 500 engines in the largest locomotive factory in continental Europe and succeeded in beating off British competition in Germany. His biographer was moved to admire 'the greatest and most successful industrialist and genius . . . that Germany has ever produced'.[51]

It might almost be said that Germany's railway revolution began in Bresslau – at least in embryo. In 1816, nearly ten years before the opening of the Stockton and Darlington Railway in England, a rail link was proposed between Bresslau and Zabrze in Upper Silesia. It did not materialise and the honour of the first German railway went, in 1835, to the line between Nuremburg and Fürth. But Bresslau was not far behind. On 22 May 1842, the *Silesia* left Bresslau on a twenty-six-kilometre stretch of track for Ohlau. A second stretch was added in 1843 in the opposite direction as far as Freiburg (Świebodzice), and a third in 1844 to Liegnitz. By that time, Bresslau possessed three railway stations, one for each line – the Freiburger, the Niederschlesisch-Märkische and the Oberschlesische. In 1846, the connection to Berlin was completed. The following year, Vienna and Dresden and Cracow could all be reached. The 1850s saw the connection to Posen (Poznań) and the building in Bresslau of the first Hauptbahnhof in Germany. By 1871, it had become one of the busiest and most important railway junctions in Central Europe.

Bresslau's trade was greatly enhanced by the rapprochement with Great Poland, and numerous convoys of goods continued to arrive from the East, even from Russia and Romania. But political changes in Poland resulted in new tariff barriers. The creation in 1815 of the Congress Kingdom was not advantageous, although a loophole was energetically exploited via the independent Republic of Cracow, which acted as an important entrepôt both for the Congress Kingdom and for Galicia. When the republic was summarily abolished in 1846, a protest delegation was sent from Bresslau to Berlin, and the Mayor of Bresslau travelled in vain to Vienna.

One source of salvation was found in the wool trade, where a remarkable surge took place in the first decades of the nineteenth century. It was due both to the expansion of sheep farming in Silesia and Great Poland and to the greatly improved means for importing raw wool from Austria and Hungary. The annual turnover of the Bresslau wool-market leaped from about 20,000 centners in 1810 to 43,000 in 1823, 88,000 in 1836 and a peak of 132,000 in 1862. Woollens gradually replaced Bresslau's previous textile speciality which had consisted of printing fine cotton percale.

Banking developed rapidly during the same period. Before the Napoleonic Wars, Bresslau's only banks consisted of the state-owned Royal Bank and the two private firms of Eichborn and Molinari. After 1815, they were joined by several dynamic newcomers, notably the house of Heimann, which was destined to outpace all competitors. The bankers invested heavily in the wool trade and, at a later stage, in the railways. Their operators were assisted after 1834 by the founding of the German Customs Union.

Despite these advances, the Prussian economy of the early nineteenth century was still predominantly agrarian and dependent on circumstances that could neither be predicted nor controlled. The failed harvests of 1816–17 caused shortages, while the bumper harvests of the 1820s caused a collapse in grain prices. The uncertainties fuelled growing discontent, which merged with political demands for representation and produced a near-revolutionary atmosphere. Open unrest resurfaced in the Silesian Weavers' Revolt of 1844. Later to be immortalised in Gerhart Hauptmann's play *Die Weber* ('The Weavers'), it centred on the village of Peterswaldau (Pieszyce), near Reichenbach (Dzierżoniów). One of Hauptmann's characters expresses the futility of the weavers' existence:

> You can fight to the last, but in the end you have to give in. Poverty gnaws at the roof over your head and the floor under your feet. In the old days, when you could still get work at the factory, you could just about carry on in spite of the worry and hardship. But I haven't been able to get work for over a year. Basket-weaving is finished too; you can barely scrape a living at it. I weave into the night and when I fall into bed I've earned one groschen and six pfennigs. You've got education, you tell me. Is that enough with everything going up? I have to throw three thalers away in house tax, one thaler in ground rent, and three in interest. I can count on earning fourteen thalers; that leaves me with seven thalers for the whole year. With that I have to cook, eat, dress myself, get shoes and mend my clothes. I have to have a place to live in and God knows what else. Is it surprising when there isn't enough to go round?[52]

In the eyes of their critics, the weavers had targeted wealthy merchants by demanding higher payment for their labour. So when the Provincial

President dismissed them as part of a 'universal assault of the poor against the rich', a brutal 'pacification' by the military ensued. Eleven weavers were killed and twenty injured.

This episode, and another in Hirschberg (Jelenia Góra) in 1845, were but preludes to the Europe-wide outbreaks of 1848, and the extent of purely economic motives in the Silesian troubles has attracted some examination. Growing industrialisation and urbanisation had certainly caused Bresslau to exhibit some of the worst social conditions in Germany. The housing crisis, for instance, was much more acute than in Berlin. Some commentators[53] have contended that Bresslau's relatively advanced industrialisation under-lay a radical movement which opposed the 'bourgeois revolutionaries' and pressed demands that were more social than national or liberal. Indeed, the presence of proletarian protesters who could later be described as 'Marxist elements' is witnessed by the reports of the *Schlesische Zeitung*. Their radicalism was demonstrated by the activities of the '*Katzenmusiker*', or 'cats' chorus', a group of 'flying pickets' who would surround a building and then chant and jeer until they achieved the desired result, such as the resignation of an official or the revocation of a law. In the countryside, peasants looted manor houses and tax offices.

After 1848–9, economic recovery was somewhat ambiguous. Silesian industry benefited from its steady integration with the wider Prussian economy, but social discontent rumbled on. The dramatic expansion of the Prussian rail network brought tremendous benefits. Upper Silesia, in particular, had been waiting for the railway. As a dense network was put in place, it opened up to outside investment and gained access to a much wider market. The river remained a secondary carrier, with only one modest commercial steamer plying the Oder from Bresslau to Stettin from 1856 onwards. Towards the end of the nineteenth century, Silesia was producing nearly 40 per cent of Germany's coal and fully one-quarter of the country's yield of zinc.

In 1852, Bresslau hosted the first Exhibition of Silesian Industry (*Schlesische Industrieausstellung*), which generated a measure of local pride. But a reporter from *The Times* of London was not impressed:

> The example of the Crystal Palace is about to be followed in Silesia, where there is soon to be an exhibition of Silesian manufactures under a glass roof. This is much more appropriate than its projectors have probably apprehended, for the whole linen manufacture of Silesia, which is the produce of hand-weaving, is a hothouse plant, that is only kept from immediate extinction by heavy import duties on the far superior productions of Manchester ... Silesia remains the Ireland of Prussia.[54]

Salomon Kaufmann, a cotton producer from Schweidnitz, echoed these sentiments. The year before, he had travelled to the Great Exhibition in London and had been shocked by the marked superiority of the machine-produced competition. After an extended visit to Manchester, he collected as many patterns and samples as possible and returned home to introduce the new methods into his own factories.[55] Full-scale industrialisation was only just beginning.

*

Prussia annexed Silesia in the early phase of the Enlightenment. Europe was turning its back on the religious bigotry of the preceding period and was entering the so-called 'Age of Reason'. What is more, Prussia was one of the more tolerant of the German states. It did not permit the same degree of religious liberty that had been practised in neighbouring Poland until the late seventeenth century, but equally it did not profess the same sort of religious partisanship that surrounded the Habsburgs. The Hohenzollerns of Berlin had welcomed Huguenot refugees from France and had found a *modus vivendi* between Lutherans and Calvinists.

Yet religious life in Prussian Silesia would not lack controversy. The annexation of a predominantly Catholic province by a predominantly Protestant kingdom was to bring special problems. On entering Bresslau in January 1741, Frederick II ordered thirty Prussian cavalrymen to guard the Jesuit College from the wrath of the Protestant mob. It was said that the Prussian soldiers, when approaching a quiet corner outside the Jesuit College, had heard the sound of moaning and, after fruitless investigations, had decided to knock the wall down. Inside they discovered an old grey-haired man, living in his own filth, with a piece of bread and a jug of water that had evidently been passed to him through a hole in the wall. When asked who he was, he replied that his name was Jakob Sturm, a preacher from Liegnitz, and that he had written a number of tracts against the Jesuits. He had counted twenty-six winters since his arrest, and he died ten days after his release.[56] This, of course, was a Prussian tale. But it says something about the reigning tensions.

Though a religious sceptic himself, Frederick recognised the social importance of religion. Initially, he maintained a distance from both confessions in Silesia. The restrictions on Protestant worship in some Catholic districts were lifted and the rights of Catholics were respected in Protestant ones. In 1742, he allowed the Bishop of Bresslau, Cardinal von Sinzendorf, to return to his post, on condition that the Vatican be kept at arm's length and that he become a 'Prussian Pope'.[57] Yet, mindful of the divided loyalties of Silesian Catholics, the King could not resist interfering. His tool was to be Philipp Graf von Schaffgotsch (1716–95), a Jesuit-educated Silesian who had been accepted into the priesthood in Vienna. In 1740 he had defected to serve Prussia and had been rewarded with rapid promotion. Three years later, he became Frederick's favoured candidate for the post of coadjutor in Bresslau in a blatant contravention of the Church's own right of appointment. The King communicated his desire to the Bishop, in inimitable fashion:

> The Holy Ghost and I are agreed that Prelate Schaffgotsch should be co-adjutor of [Bresslau] and that those of your canons who resist him shall be regarded as persons who have surrendered to the Court in Vienna and to the Devil, and, having resisted the Holy Ghost, deserve the highest degree of damnation.[58]

The Bishop replied in kind:

> The great understanding between the Holy Ghost and Your Majesty is news to me; I was unaware that the acquaintance had been made. I hope that He will send the Pope and the canons the inspiration appropriate to our wishes.

In this case, the King was unsuccessful. A compromise solution had to be found whereby the papal nuncio in Warsaw was charged with Silesian affairs. But, in 1747, the King tried again and Schaffgotsch, aged only thirty-one, was duly appointed Bishop of Bresslau. The démarche was to be short-lived. With the outbreak of war in 1756, Schaffgotsch defected again and went off to serve Maria Theresa. When he returned to Silesia in 1763, he was forbidden to enter Bresslau and was exiled to the episcopal residence of Johannisberg at Jauernig in Austrian Silesia. The affairs of the bishopric were managed by two suffragan bishops, notably by Johann Moritz von Strachwitz (1721–81).

In the late eighteenth century, Catholicism in Prussia entered a period of intellectual crisis. The dissolution of the Society of Jesus in 1774, the humiliating partitions of Catholic Poland and the vibrancy of Protestant universities such as Halle all combined to magnify Protestant prestige. No one better personified this pre-eminence than the most important theologian of the age, Friedrich Schleiermacher (1768–1834). Born and educated in Bresslau, Schleiermacher became Dean of the Theological Faculty of Berlin University. Through his efforts to win over the educated classes and his emphasis on feeling as the basis of faith, he was to have a profound influence on Protestant thought. As a proponent of the Union of Protestant Churches in Prussia, he also wielded political influence. His principal works were *Über die Religion* ('On Religion', 1799) *Die Weihnachtsfeier* ('Christmas Celebration', 1806) and *Der christliche Glaube* ('The Christian Faith', 1821–2). On his death, it was said that 30,000 people joined the funeral procession through the streets of Berlin.

The Union of Prussian Protestant Churches, effected in 1817, joined the Lutherans and Calvinists of Prussia into one 'Evangelical State Church'. The use of the word 'Protestant' was forbidden. In 1822, a new common liturgy was introduced. Dissenters could be labelled as heretical. For Bresslau's Lutherans, the reorganisation was not insignificant. For nearly three centuries they had been a self-governing community. Unlike most Lutherans in Germany, they had not been subject under Habsburg rule to the state authorities or to the religious inclinations of the ruling dynasty. But now they were obliged to relinquish all aspects of their autonomy. The King of Prussia was *summus episcopus* of the state Church, just as Henry VIII had made himself 'Supreme Governor' of the Church of England. His Protestant subjects, who could no longer call themselves Protestant and who were no longer straightforward Lutherans but hybrid Luthero-Calvinists, were simply expected to obey. They were asked to adapt to a major confessional and liturgical shift. Some would say that they had suffered a major defeat.

Not surprisingly, a prominent group of dissenters, that of the 'Old Lutherans' emerged in Bresslau. Its leader, Johann Scheibel (1783–1843),[59] another Vratislavian born and bred and a Professor of Theology at the university, had headed the protests against the Union. Having petitioned both the City Council and the King, he managed to delay its official recognition in Bresslau, thereby creating a 5,000-strong congregation. In the following years, the movement suffered persistent persecution. Many of its members emigrated, establishing communities as far afield as Adelaide in South Australia.[60] The Old Lutherans of Silesia were only granted recognition as a tolerated non-conformist Church in 1845.

Catholicism, too, had its dissenters. The German Catholic Movement, which emerged in the 1840s, was protesting against its perception of the Roman Church as superstitious and fanatical. It was founded in Bresslau in 1845, by, among others, Johannes Ronge (1813–87), a former chaplain in Grottkau (Grodków). Having publicly polemicised against the cult of 'Christ's Coat' in Trier, Ronge was excommunicated. But, freed from Church control, he only widened his attacks. In an open letter to the Bishop of Trier, he wrote, 'Already the historians are taking up their pens and are covering your name with all the contempt of this world and the next; they describe you as the Tetzel of the 19th century.'[61] Ronge's followers were no less trenchant. They rejected the primacy of the Papacy, confession, celibacy, indulgences, fasting, pilgrimage and the cults of saints and relics. Welcomed by the Prussian authorities, their numbers grew rapidly, reaching some 259 communities and 100,000 members by 1848. Ronge became a celebrity, lauded by Protestants and sympathetic Catholics alike, and fully engaged on lengthy speaking tours.

Nonetheless, mainstream Catholic life in nineteenth-century Bresslau was changing as well. In 1811, for example, in the middle of the Napoleonic Wars, the state authorities in Prussia implemented their plan for dissolving all religious Orders and confiscating their property. At a stroke fifty-six monasteries and seventeen convents in Silesia were closed and sequestrated, many of them in Bresslau. The Catholic community was robbed not only of the educational, medical and pastoral services of the Orders, but also, perhaps more fundamentally, of the irreplaceable devotional flavour that only dedicated monks and nuns could contribute. Admirers of Prussian state power called it modernisation. Many believers thought it retrograde, not to say heartless. The only exceptions to be made were for religious institutions caring for the incurably sick or the mentally ill. Apart from that, everything had to go. The St Matthias Hospital became a secular school. The Dominicans' Library became a state library. The ancient Abbey of Trebnitz was turned into a factory.

Another important reorientation took place as a result of the Concordat of 1821, when the Catholic Diocese of Bresslau was detached from its historical links with the See of Gniezno (Gnesen). To a large extent, the step was a natural consequence of the partitions of Poland. Gniezno itself lay inside the territory taken by Prussia, while most of its ecclesiastical province had fallen under Russian or Austrian control. The Polish Primate at Gniezno was unable to exercise his duties. The solution in Prussia was to create a new archbishopric of Posen-Gnesen to administer the former Polish provinces, and to raise the princely bishopric of Bresslau into an independent see directly subordinated to Rome. The status of the Vratislavian diocese was undoubtedly enhanced, not least because its authority now ran from the Baltic to Bohemia, and included Berlin. For the first time in 800 years, it was also fully drawn into the German sphere. All its Prince-Bishops in the subsequent era were Germans:

1747–95	Philipp Graf von Schaffgotsch
1795–1817	Joh. Christian, Prince of Hohenlohe-Bartenstein
1824–32	Emanuel Schimonski
1836–40	Leopold Sedlnitzky
1843–4	Josef Knauer
1845–53	Melchior Baron von Diepenbrock
1853–81	Heinrich Förster.

The incidence of Polish names on the episcopal list is misleading. The only prelate with any Polish sympathies was Bernhard Bogedein, a suffragan bishop in Bresslau in 1858–60, who supported the preservation of Polish primary schools and who is now described as 'a moderate Germaniser'.

Judaism returned to Bresslau with the Jewish community, which was officially readmitted in 1744 after an almost 300-year absence (see below). But the Jews, too, had their religious conflicts. They moved into a Bresslau where industrialisation was in progress and where they quickly formed part of the educated middle class. In other words, they encountered conditions that favoured the tendencies associated with Reformed Judaism. It was in this context that the rivalry of Rabbi Abraham Geiger and Chief Rabbi Salomon Tiktin turned sour. After Tiktin's death in 1843, his son Gedaliah pursued the feud. By the time of the foundation of the Bresslau Jewish Theological Seminary in 1854, the Reformist-Orthodox division had ossified into two divided communities with separate rabbis, separate schools and separate synagogues.

The ideas of Abraham Geiger (1810–74), and their role in the formation of Reformed Judaism, had a bearing on events far beyond Bresslau – indeed, far beyond Germany. They were first formulated in the 1830s in a series of lectures presented in his native Frankfurt, but were elaborated and published in various works when he worked in Bresslau between 1838 and 1866. The English translation of his *Judaism and its history* (1866) had a great effect on the evolution of American Jewry. In the practical sphere, Geiger shared the laurels with Samuel Holdheim as one of the co-organisers of the three rabbinical conferences – Braunschweig (1844), Frankfurt (1845) and Bresslau (1846) – where Reformed Judaism was launched. He had two main concerns. One was to modify Jewish ritual so that practising Jews could participate fully in the political, social and cultural life of the country (in this regard, he even toyed with the idea of moving the Jewish Sabbath to Sunday). The other was to open up Judaism to the full rigours of intellectual and theological debate. He firmly believed that much of the tension between Christians and Jews was born of mutual ignorance and that both sides must engage in dialogue. He had no illusions about the superiority complex of many Christians and of Christianity's pretensions of being 'an ecclesiastical world power'. On the other hand, he saw signs of hope. 'Christianity had been intolerant,' he wrote, 'but intolerance is not a trait that is essentially Christian.' And 'The drama is not yet concluded . . . the time will come . . . Judaism has not yet fulfilled its mission.'[62] In 1866, Rabbi Geiger left Bresslau to take up the office of Chief Rabbi in Berlin.

The Jewish Theological Seminary, the first of its kind in Europe, owed its foundation to the cooperation of Rabbi Geiger with the prominent Jewish theologian Zacharias Fränkel (1801–75) and to funds donated by the Bresslau businessman, Jonas Fraenckel (no relation).[63] Its founders recognised not only that traditional rabbinical training required modernisation, but that the principles of Judaism could not escape critical examination. When the seminary opened its doors in August 1854, the omens were not good – a cholera epidemic was raging and only twenty-one students and four lecturers attended. But, under Fränkel's directorship, it developed rapidly, doubling student numbers within four years and becoming one of the most important centres of Jewish scholarship in the world. Its celebrated library and its journal, the *Monatsschrift für Geschichte und Wissenschaft des Judentums*, were to rival those of Berlin, Paris and Vienna.

Nevertheless, one of the primary religious developments in nineteenth-century Bresslau derived from the dynamic growth of the Roman Catholic population. Between 1817 and 1849 the Catholics of the Bresslau area grew from 26 per cent to 39 per cent of the total, driving the Protestant share down from 72 per cent to 59 per cent (the Jewish community, though increasing in absolute numbers, declined proportionally from 1.3 per cent to 1 per cent). It is reasonable to assume that the increase came mainly from Catholic immigration from other areas of Silesia, Bohemia or Poland. By 1871, when the German Empire was proclaimed, the old, Protestant character of Bresslau was being transformed into that of a more cosmopolitan, multi-denominational metropolis.

The coexistence of three religions, each with their dissident wings, exposed nineteenth-century Bresslau to a rich ferment of argument and debate. In this sense, Bresslau became 'the Hyde Park Corner of Prussia'. Liberals and conservatives battled it out on all fronts. From 1811, the University of Bresslau had two separate Faculties of Theology. The larger of them was Catholic, inherited from the old Jesuit College. The other, imported through the merger with the University of Frankfurt an der Oder, was Protestant. Each argued with the other; and both argued with the members of the Jewish Seminary. Competition was rife. Publications proliferated. The poaching of professors from one side to another was an open game. Conversions in all directions were not uncommon. Religious life at this level was nothing if not exciting.

Debate became particularly intense in the late 1850s over the rights and wrongs of ultramontanism and the principle of papal infallibility. The Roman Catholic Church struggled to maintain doctrinal discipline:

28 April 1860.
We read in the *Silesian Gazette* that the Prince Bishop of Bresslau has withdrawn the licences of two members of the Catholic Theological Faculty. Dr Baltzer, a canon [of the cathedral chapter] has temporarily

lost the right of *missio canonica* [right to conduct mass:], whilst Dr Bittner has permanently lost his *venia legendi* or [permission to conduct lectures]. The [Faculty] noticeboard displays the following announcements:

'I allow myself to inform my colleagues and students that, as the result of a decision by His Princely-Episcopal Eminence, I am temporarily unable to present my classes, until such time as the academic position contained in my pro memoria to the Holy See regarding anthropological dogmas has been resolved. Prof. Dr Baltzer.' . . .

'I allow myself to report to attenders of my lectures in the Catholic Theology Faculty that in accordance with a decree of the Prince-Bishop of the 8th inst., which does not question my proven loyalty to the Church, I shall not be presenting any further classes. *Veritatem laborare nimis saepe aiunt, extingui nunquam* (Livy XXII, 39). Bresslau, 26 April 1860. Prof. Dr Bittner.'[64]

Canon Johann Baptiste Baltzer (1803–71) was suspended by the Vatican in 1862 and joined the independent 'Old Catholics' the year before he died.

*

After 1741 Bresslau was immediately drawn into the cultural life of the Prussian kingdom. Not surprisingly, since the King had claims to be an enlightened philosopher, philosophy came to enjoy special prominence. Christian Wolff (1679–1754), born in Bresslau, taught mainly at the University of Halle. Known as 'the German spokesman of the Enlightenment', he argued in his *Vernünftige Gedanken* ('Rational Ideas') that every occurrence must have an adequate reason for happening. His philosophy was to hold sway in Germany until displaced by that of Immanuel Kant in the late eighteenth century. Unlike Wolff, Christian Garve (1742–98) studied in Frankfurt and Halle, but spent most of his adult life in Bresslau. His main interests lay in ethics and psychology, and he was a pioneer in the study of the role of the individual in society. A correspondent of Goethe and Schiller, he was a scholar who greatly helped to popularise the German Enlightenment.

Education was strongly promoted in Prussia. Despite the nominal introduction of compulsory elementary schools in 1717, schooling had varied in both quality and extent. Yet in the second half of the eighteenth century, it was significantly improved through increased government spending and regulation. In Bresslau, as elsewhere, the state sought to exploit the pedagogical skills of the Jesuits. After the dissolution of the Order in 1773, they were ordered to change their dress and name, but to proceed with their activities in the educational sphere, as the *Gesellschaft der Priester des Königlichen Schulinstituts* (Society of Priests of the Royal School

Institute). In the nineteenth century, several city schools were housed in former monastic buildings.

The resultant growth in literacy supplied a readership avid for news. The Jesuit-sponsored *Schlesischer Nouvellen-Courier* had been produced in Bresslau since 1708. But in 1742, its place was taken by the state-sanctioned *Schlesische priviligierte Staats- Kriegs- und Friedens-Zeitung*, generally known as the *Schlesische Zeitung* ('The Silesian News'). The new paper's publisher was Johann Jacob Korn (1702–56), a Brandenburger who had settled in Bresslau in 1732. Korn was granted the privilege to produce the *Schlesische Zeitung* and received articles written by the royal hand, under the pseudonym 'a high-ranking Prussian officer'. His publishing enterprise flourished. By the end of the century, its list included the works of Garve and Svarez and numerous Polish-language editions of German works.

The Langhans family, which had deep roots in Silesia, achieved prominence in the development of German architecture. The elder Langhans, Carl Gotthard (1733–1808), began his career by designing the new Hatzfeld Palace, whose construction he oversaw between 1766 and 1774. Thereafter, as Head of the Building Department of the regional Prussian administration (*Chef des Bauamtes der Bresslauer und Glogauer Kriegs- und Domänenkammern*) he is credited with a number of other Bresslau landmarks, including the Prussian Garrison on the Bürgerwerder and the Bresslau Theatre (Schauspielhaus). Appointed Director of the Prussian *Oberhofbauamt* in Berlin in 1786, he ended his career in glory after designing and constructing the Brandenburg Gate.

The younger Langhans, Carl Ferdinand (1781–1869), was destined to become, alongside Gottfried Semper, one of the leading architects of the next generation. Like his father, he began work in Bresslau, with the new Church of the Eleven Thousand Virgins (1821) and the 'Stork Synagogue' (1827–9). In Berlin, he designed the elegant residence of King Frederick William III, the Palace of 'Unter den Linden' (1828).

The Prussian army brought a huge influx of soldiers and administrators to Bresslau. Among them was the military theorist Carl von Clausewitz (1780–1831), who arrived in 1830. Having seen combat at the tender age of thirteen, Clausewitz had enjoyed a fascinating career. He had served as military tutor to the Prussian Crown Prince before entering Russian service in 1812 and fighting at Borodino. He was then instrumental in negotiating the Convention of Tauroggen, whereby Prussia reneged on its French alliance. Returning to Berlin, he was reinstated and promoted to General. In 1830 he was appointed Chief of Staff of an Army of Observation stationed in Bresslau to watch the border during the November Rising in Poland. Though successful in organising a sanitary cordon to prevent the spread of cholera into Silesia, he succumbed to the disease in his lodgings on the Schweidnitzer Strasse, and was buried in the Bresslau military cemetery. His monumental study *On War* (1853), a bible to military theorists, was published by his widow.

Military duties also brought the Lessing family to Bresslau. Gotthold Ephraim Lessing (1729–81) arrived in 1760 as secretary to General Tauentzien. In his spare time he studied philosophy and aesthetics in the city's libraries, and produced the treatise *Laokoon, oder über die Grenzen der Malerei und Poesie* ('Laocoon; or, On the Limits of Painting and Poetry', 1766), in which he took issue with Winckelmann. While stationed in the barracks on the Bürgerwerder, he wrote the play *Minna von Barnhelm*, a drama of manners set during the Seven Years War, which marks the birth of classical German theatre. Lessing's family remained in the city after his departure for Berlin in 1765. His younger brother, Karl Gotthelf, became director of the Bresslau Mint, and the latter's grandson, Carl Friedrich Lessing (1808–80), became a noted artist of the Romantic Movement (see below).

J.W. Goethe (1749–1832) came to Bresslau in the autumn of 1790 at the invitation of his patron, the Prince of Saxe-Weimar, whose regiment of cuirassiers happened to be stationed at Schweidnitz. He attended a ball at the Royal Castle organised by King Frederick William II, and in the course of his travels he twice stayed at the Rote Haus Inn on Ruska Strasse. On his way back to Weimar, he stopped at Hirschberg, climbed the Schneekoppe and drank the waters at Bad Warmbrunn (Cieplice Zdrój). Goethe did not like Bresslau. In a letter dated 11 November 1790, he described it as 'noisy, dirty and smelly'.

One of Germany's most exquisite lyric poets, Josef Baron von Eichendorff (1788–1857), was a pupil at the St Matthias Gymnasium in Bresslau in 1801–4. His family seat was at Lubowitz (Łubowice) near Ratibor, but he retained many connections to Bresslau, including a spell in 1816–19 in the Silesian provincial administration. Eichendorff's simple melodic lines evoking giant hills, dark forests and moonlit nights frequently provided the inspiration for songs by Schubert, Schumann, and Wolff. His chosen themes of *Lust* (Desire), *Heimat* (Homeland) and *Waldeinsamkeit* (Loneliness in the Forest) evoke the very soul of Silesia:

> In einem kühlen Grunde
> Da geht ein Mühlenrad,
> Mein Liebste ist verschwunden,
> Die dort gewohnet hat.
>
> O Täler weit, O Höhen,

O schöner grüner Wald,
Du meiner Lust und Wehen
Andächt'ger Aufenthalt!

Im Walde steht geschrieben
Ein stilles ernstes Wort
Vom rechten Tun und Lieben,
Und was des Menschen Hort.

　Bald werd' ich dich verlassen,
　Fremd in die Fremde geh'n,
　Auf buntbewegten Gassen
　Des lebens Schauspiel seh'n.

(In the cool and gentle valley
The mill-wheel still is turning.
But my sweetheart has departed,
And will not be returning.

　O valleys broad! O soaring crags,
　And fair green woods below!
　My refuge for reflecting
　On all life's joy and sorrow . . .

Deep in the forest stands engraved
The quiet, telling truth
Of how aright to live and love,
Of where lies man's real wealth . . .

　Yet, I too, soon must leave you.
　A stranger in a stranger's land,
　I'll watch on some packed avenue
　The world's immodest pageant.)[65]

In 1811, the Jesuit-founded Leopold University of Bresslau was secularised and merged with the Viadrina University of Frankfurt an der Oder to form the 'Friedrich-Wilhelms-Universität zu Bresslau' or *Academia Viadrina Wratislaviensis*. It assumed a unifying role in intellectual life, bridging the gulf between the Protestant and Catholic communities. Its students, inspired by the nationalist resurgence, organised themselves into *Burschen-schaften*, or 'scholars' societies', which sprouted almost everywhere. Three such groups had been formed in Bresslau by 1817: the German *Raczek* and *Germania* and the Polish *Polonia*. Despite the police suppressions marshalled by Metternich, they taught a doctrine that could not be contained. The nationalist genie could not be returned to its bottle. By the 1840s, the generation that had joined the Lützow *Freikorps* and the *Burschenschaften* were fully employed as journalists, university lecturers and schoolteachers.

The artist Adolph Menzel (1815–1905) was typical of this growth of national sentiment. Born in Bresslau, he emerged as probably the finest illustrator of his day, and his work was often directed to the patriotic themes of the time. He was called on to illustrate Franz Kugler's *Geschichte Friedrichs des Grossen* ('History of Frederick the Great', 1842), before producing numerous illustrated works on the soldiers and uniforms of the Frederician era. Though almost entirely self-taught, he later earned a reputation as a noted painter, and has found a place alongside Caspar David Friedrich as one of the most important German artists of the nineteenth century. The breadth of his work is demonstrated by the ethereal beauty of *The Balcony Room* (1845) and the monumental *Coronation of William I at Königsberg* (1861–5).

The Vratislavian artist Philipp Hoyoll (1816–*c*.1875) had quite different interests. He had studied at the Düsseldorf Academy before returning to Silesia in 1839 to make a living as a portrait painter. Caught up in the *Vormärz*, the prelude to the 'springtime of the nations', he painted his masterpiece *Zerstörung eines Bäckerladens* ('The Destruction of a Baker's Shop') in 1846 (see illustrations). A depiction of the shooting of starving rioters, the scene is apparently set on the Bresslau Neumarkt, but is in fact a pastiche of events during the Weavers' Revolt two years earlier. Nevertheless, it is a powerful symbol of Bresslau of 1848–9. Hoyoll himself became a noted pamphleteer, publishing under the pseudonym 'Kilian Raschke'. Like many veterans of 1848, he died in exile in England.[66]

Carl Friedrich Lessing (1816–80) was Hoyoll's exact contemporary. A Vratislavian who had studied in Berlin before joining the Düsseldorf School, he was deeply influenced by Caspar David Friedrich, specialising in historical scenes and evocative Silesian landscapes. His later work drew on a fascination with Hussite themes and produced a series of paintings: *Hussite Preacher* (1835), *Hus before the Council* (1842) and *Hus at the stake* (1850), which evoked Bresslau's Bohemian past. Unlike Hoyoll, he avoided politics and died in honourable retirement in Karlsruhe.

The writer Willibald Alexis, whose real name was Georg Häring, shared both the cultural milieu of Menzel and his fascination with Frederick the Great. Though born in Bresslau, he spent much of his life in Thuringia. Specialising in romantic historical novels and short stories, he produced some pretty dubious Fredericiana:

> Friedericus Rex, unser König und Herr,
> der rief seinen Soldaten allesamt ins Gewehr,

zweihundert Batallions und an die tausend Schwadronen
und jeder Grenadier kriegte sechzig Patronen.[67]

(Fridericus Rex, our monarch and lord,
He called out his soldiers to take up the sword,
He summoned at least two hundred battalions
and of grenadiers, some thousand squadrons.)

Two middle-ranking Silesian poets of the early nineteenth century, both of
whom died young, had close connections to Bresslau. Friedrich von Sallet
(1812–43), born at Reichau (Zarzyce), made the headlines more than once.
In 1830, when an army officer, he was court-martialled and cashiered, and
then reprieved by the King, for writing satirical poems. Ten years later, he
published a highly eccentric interpretation of Christianity, the 'Layman's
Gospel' or *Laienevangelium*, composed in blank verse. He lived in Bresslau
after leaving the army, and wrote several volumes of poetry on subjects
varying from 'Young Love' to 'Pantheism'. In an age when the sense of
Germanity was rising, Sallet was not slow to ask what being German really
meant. And he answered in biting satire:

> ... Wir wollen auch echtdeutsch erzittern
> vor jedem Polizei-Gendarme
> Echtdeutsch uns krümmern vor den Rittern
> Und vor dem Bureaukratenschwarm.[68]

(As true Germans we want to tremble
before every Policeman and Gendarme
As Germans bow down to the nobles
and to the bureaucratic swarm.)

Moritz, Count von Strachwitz (1822–47), born at the family seat of
Peterwitz (Stoszowice), was a student at Bresslau before going to Berlin and
joining the literary circle of the *Tunnel über der Spree*. His lyrical, historical
and patriotic ballads were written in the few short years before his death.
Some of them, like *Richard Löwenherz' Tod* or *Das Herz von Douglas*, were
very popular in their time. He was a Prussian for whom the ideas of
'Homecoming' and 'Fatherland' were indissolubly linked with Silesia:

> Sei mir gegrüsst am Strassenrand
> Mein alter Wartenstein!
> Ich fahre in mein Vaterland
> Mein Vaterland hinein. ...

Du aber bist noch, herziger Schatz,
Wie immer schön und süss,
Und alles steht am alten Platz,
Da, wo ich's stehen liess.[69]

(Greetings from the roadside
Beloved Wartenstein!
I'm travelling to my Fatherland
Dear Fatherland of mine . . .

But you are still, my dearest love,
As ever, sweet and kind,
And everything is in its place,
Just as I left behind.)

Strachwitz also possessed a profound, if peculiar, sense of 'Germania':

Land des Rechtes, Land des Lichtes,
Land des Schwertes und Gedichtes,
        Land der freien
        Und getreuen,
Land der Adler und der Leuen,
        Land, du bist dem Tode nah',
        Sieh dich um, Germania![70]

(Land of justice, land of light,
Land of sword and lyric,
        Land of liberty
        And fidelity,
Land of Eagles and of Lions,
        Land, your end is surely nigh,
        Guard thyself, Germania!)

František Ladislav Čelakovský (1799–1852), who spent most of the 1840s in Bresslau as the first professor of Slavonic languages, illustrates the great difficulties that the non-German cultures of Central Europe were facing in his time. The leading poet of the Czech National Revival, he had been expelled from the University of Prague only to find that many of his lectures in Bresslau had to be abandoned for lack of students. His devotion to the Czech national movement won him little sympathy from German colleagues, while his support for pan-Slavism set him apart from Polish circles. In 1848, when the Czech cause surfaced in Prague, Čelakovský was surrounded in Bresslau by people with completely separate interests. Prague was physically close, but culturally distant.

Elizabeth Stuart (1596–1662),
'The Winter Queen'.

Lennart Torstenson (1603–51),
Swedish general.

Andreas Gryphius (1616–64),
playwright.

Angelus Silesius (1624–77),
poet.

The *Naschmarkt*: the north side of the Main Square (eighteenth century).

View of 'Bressla' by Hartmann Schedel (1493)

The defenestration of Prague, 1618, by Wenzel von Brozik.

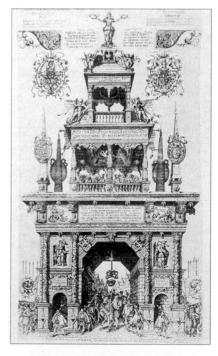

Entry into Presslau of the
Emperor Matthias (*c.* 1612).

Christian Wolff (1679–1754),
philosopher.

Maria Leszczyńska (1703–68),
Queen of France.

Frederick the Great (*r.* 1740–86),
King of Prussia.

Philipp von Schaffgotsch (1716–95),
Bishop of Bresslau.

Carl von Clausewitz (1780–1831),
theorist of war.

August Borsig (1804–54),
industrialist.

Heinrich Graetz (1817–91),
historian of the Jewish people.

Ferdinand Lassalle (1825–64),
pioneer of socialism.

The Nikolai Gate and Bridge, demolished in 1820.

The Ohle slums, redeveloped in 1866.

The Jesuit College (completed in 1738), now the University.

The Jewish Quarter on the Karlsplatz (*c.* 1700).

Prussian attack: the battle of Leuthen (Lutynia), December 1757.

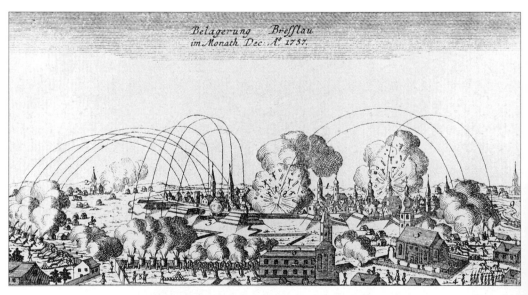

Austrian defeat: the siege of Bresslau, December 1757.

By that time, Bresslau was emerging as a cornerstone of Germany's liberal-national movement. Its thinkers, politicians and pamphleteers drew heavily on the symbolism of 1813 and sought to reawaken the national solidarity of the struggle against Napoleon. Heinrich Hoffmann von Fallersleben (1798–1874) was foremost among them. Prior to his forced exile in 1841, he had been Professor of Philosophy at Bresslau and a versatile author. He penned some well-loved nursery rhymes:

> Alle Vögel sind schon da,
> Alle Vögel alle!
> Welch ein Singen, Musiziern,
> Pfeifen, Zwitschen, Tirilieren!
> Frühling will nun einmarschiern,
> Kommt mit Sang und Schalle.
>
> (All the lovely birds are here,
> All the birds, yes, every one!
> What a singing, music-making!
> Whistling, chirping, twitter-making!
> Spring will soon be marching in,
> Coming with its song and din.)

He also penned the most famous of German anthems, the *Deutschlandlied*, which he composed on the British crown territory of Heligoland:

> Deutschland, Deutschland über Alles,
> Über alles in der Welt.
> Wenn es stets zu Schutz und Trutze,
> Brüderlich zusammenhält.
> Von der Maas bis an der Memel,
> Von der Etsch bis an der Belt.
> Deutschland, Deutschland über Alles,
> Über alles in der Welt.
>
> (Germany, Germany above all else,
> Above everything in the world.
> As always for protection and defence
> We stand together as brothers true.
> From the Maas to the Memel,
> From the Etsch to the Belt.
> Germany, Germany above all else,
> Above everything in the world.)

To all Vratislavians with a sense of history, it must have been ironic to hear that Hoffmann's anthem came to be sung to a Haydn melody called 'Austria'.

The novelist Gustav Freytag (1816–95) was Hoffmann's former student and fellow lecturer at Bresslau. While editing the leading journal of German liberalism, *Die Grenzboten*, Freytag wrote *Soll und Haben* ('Debit and Credit', 1855), one of the archetypal social novels of the century. In this *magnum opus* he used the experiences in Bresslau of his two protagonists, the Gentile Anton Wohlfahrt and the Jew Veitel Itzig, to extol the virtues of liberal constitutionalism, middle-class values and enlightened Protestantism:

> Already the sun was low in the sky, as the two wanderers arrived at the first houses of the [Silesian] capital. First solitary small buildings, then dainty summerhouses set in flourishing gardens, then the houses became closer together, the street closed in on either side, and with the dust and rattling of the carts, uneasy thoughts settled in the hearts of our heroes.[71]

Adolf Anderssen (1818–79), another graduate of the university, found fame as a chess master, and is widely credited with popularising the game throughout Germany. Appointed as the representative of the Berlin Chess Society (*Berliner Schachgesellschaft*) for the London International Tournament of 1851, he astonished the chess world by defeating the favourite, the Englishman Howard Staunton, and emerging as champion. For a time Anderssen was considered the strongest player in the world. His strength lay in his ability to force rapid decisions. One of his contests was dubbed 'the immortal game'. In 1861, in Bristol, he played in a match against Ignác Kolisch, in which time limits were first employed, using sandglasses. He won the second London Tournament in 1862 and the Baden-Baden Tournament in 1870. Despite his international repute, he continued teaching mathematics and German at the Friedrichs Gymnasium.[72]

Bresslau developed all the cultural institutions required by a modern city. The Botanical Garden was established in 1811 on a section of drained riverbed east of the former Cathedral Island. The Merchant's Hall (Zwinger) provided a site for musical performances and balls and staged a concert by Chopin in 1830. The Theatre and Opera House (Stadttheater), built by Carl Ferdinand Langhans, was completed in 1841 and later gained a reputation as a home for 'Wagnerian nights'. The Art Gallery was opened in 1853, and five years later the Silesian Museum of Antiquities followed. In 1862, the old Scheitnig Park was restored by the German horticulturist, Peter Josef Lenné, who had designed the gardens of Sanssouci at Potsdam and the Berlin Tiergarten. The nearby Zoological Garden was established the following year.

University life showed signs of extraordinary dynamism. Scientific research, then in its infancy, blossomed. In 1840 the first Physiological Institute in Germany was opened at Bresslau under the leadership of the renowned Czech physician, Johannes Purkinje. The chemist R.W. Bunsen taught at the university in the 1850s before taking a chair at Heidelberg, where he made his name. The physicist G.R. Kirchhoff lectured at Bresslau in 1850–4, while the father of German zoology, Karl Siebold, taught there from 1850 to his retirement. The historians Theodor Mommsen (1817–1903), Gustav Stenzel (1792–1854) and Richard Roepell (1808–93) headed an illustrious list of alumni. Mommsen, after his passionate support for the 1848 Revolution, came to Bresslau in 1854 to teach Roman history and law, before moving to Berlin and becoming a prominent member of the Prussian and National Parliaments. Stenzel, who had come to Bresslau University in 1820, was a member of the Frankfurt Parliament of 1848 and the foremost nineteenth-century authority on Silesian history. And from 1841, Roepell occupied the Chair of Slavistics in Bresslau, the first of its kind in Germany. He had begun his career by authoring the first history of Poland in German in 1839. As a specialist in Polish history, he was one of few German scholars to devote themselves to the study of Germany's immediate eastern neighbour, an exception to a deplorable rule that has never been properly overcome. His reputation drew numerous students from partitioned Poland and served to strengthen the Polish presence both at the university and in the city at large.

The Department of Slavistics started by Roepell was a remarkable institution from several points of view. It was not just an institute of *Polonistyka*. Frantisěk Čelakovský was one of its leading lights, and it took a broad interest in philology, comparative literature and history. When Roepell advanced to university rector, the directorship fell to Professor Wojciech Cybulski (1808–67), a Posnanian and specialist on Mickiewicz, who defied the convention of the day and lectured in Polish. A Slavonic Literary Society (TLS) served to open the university's doors to the non-academic public. Most importantly, the professors of the department were deeply involved in cultural politics. Čelakovský had lost his job at the University of Prague for protesting against Tsarist policy in Poland. Cybulski was a real live patriotic insurrectionary, who had fought in the November Rising, had survived exile in Arctic Russia and for good measure had been imprisoned at Schweidnitz by the Prussian authorities. The chief initiator of the TLS, then a medical student, Teodor Matecki (1810–86), was twice imprisoned for Polish conspiratorial activities. He was tried in Berlin in 1846 and escaped from the Moabit Prison in 1848 when it was stormed by the mob. The other students must have loved it.

In this regard, one has to pay attention to the many adversities with which Polish culture was contending. In the mid-nineteenth century, every European state was intent on promoting a single state language. Despite the solid body of Polish speakers in Prussia, Prussian officialdom had no more love for Polish culture than British officialdom had for Welsh or Gaelic, or French officialdom for Breton. Multiculturalism was a movement of the distant future. What is more, the Partitions of Poland had created a climate in which everything Polish was widely taken to be doomed. There was no Polish state, so there was no point in preserving Polish language and culture. The policy of Germanisation in Prussia, like Anglicisation in the British Isles or Russification in the Tsarist Empire, was being adopted not by reactionaries but by progressives. In an era when various forms of vulgar Darwinism were taking hold, the world was thought to be divided into 'historic nations', which had a natural right to political and cultural independence, and 'unhistoric nations', which did not. To put it bluntly, Poland was generally considered to have squandered its right to be counted among the historic nations. The Poles had to fight a heroic campaign over nearly two centuries to prove that assumption wrong.

Manifestations of Polish culture in Bresslau, therefore, were much more likely to emanate from visitors and temporary residents than from locals. Prussians in particular, who had fed on the corpse of old Poland, were less sympathetic to the Poles than other Germans were. In the 1830s, for instance, the citizens of Dresden and Leipzig in neighbouring Saxony held meetings in support of refugees from the Russo-Polish War and composed *Polenlieder* or 'Songs for Poland', in their honour. Few such episodes were recorded in Bresslau. Even so, the number of Polish contacts remained high, and the Polish undercurrent should not be neglected.

Józef Wybicki (1747–1822) lived in Bresslau from 1802 to 1806. At the time, he was coming to the end of a lengthy exile caused by the Third Partition. He was a distinguished reformer, constitutionalist and writer, with several plays and operas to his name. Most importantly, he had just spent several years in the service of Napoleon's Polish Legions, and was already the author of the famous *Pieśń Legionów*, ('The Song of the Legions', 1797)

> Jeszcze Polska nie zginęła
> Póki my żyjemy
> Co nam obca przemoc wzięła
> Szablą odbijemy.
> Marsz, marsz, Dąbrowski!
> Z ziemi włoskiej do Polski!
> Pod Twoim przewodem
> Złączym się z narodem.

(Poland has not perished yet
So long as we still live
That which alien force has seized
We at swordpoint shall retrieve.
March, march, Dąbrowski!
From Italy to Poland!
Let us now rejoin the nation
Under thy command.)

At the end of 1806, when Napoleon was reorganising Central Europe after Austerlitz, Wybicki left Bresslau for Berlin to meet the Emperor and to join the commission charged with forming the Duchy of Warsaw.

Maria Czartoryska, Princess of Württemberg (1768–1854), a highly educated and well-married aristocrat of the Napoleonic generation, holds a special place in Polish literature. One of the few women of her time to gain fame as a writer, she ran a prominent literary salon in Warsaw during the French occupation and, as the author of *Malwina* (1816), introduced Poland to the influential genre of sentimental writing derived from Laurence Sterne. It was a genre where even the most trivial emotions and reactions were analysed *ad nauseam*. She passed through Bresslau on her way to take the waters at Karlsbad:

Lidia and I were chatting so beautifully, it was a shame that no-one else could hear us and that the sight of [Bresslau] interrupted so fine a conversation.
[Bresslau] drove out all other thoughts. I was expecting to find my mother there. We alight at our well-known auberge. I step down [from the coach] and walk to the stairs. Oh! How my heart is beating with joy!
– Why are you weeping, Malvina? Lidia asked, seeing the letter which I held in my hand.
– My mother is feeling faint and is still in Warmbrunn: She won't be coming; I won't be able to see her . . .
– So let's go to Warmbrunn, Lidia declares . . . We'll go straight away and leave tomorrow at dawn.
Lidia's words seemed to be spoken by a guardian angel and lifted the burden from my heart. Why could I not think of such a simple solution for myself! I just don't know. There must be some reason why my good intentions always seem to be overtaken by unwanted preoccupations. But more of that later. Now, we're leaving for Warmbrunn.[73]

Juliusz Słowacki (1809–49), the most romantic of Poland's Romantic poets, spent two months in Bresslau in the early summer of 1848. A wandering, tortured and tubercular exile, he had earlier travelled from Paris to Posen to encourage the revolutionary events; he had come to Bresslau in the hope of meeting his mother. Most of his greatest works lay behind him. And in eight frustrating weeks of waiting in May and June, having taken lodgings under a false name in the Neue Schweidnitzer Strasse, he daily expected to be expelled by the Prussian police. He spent his time visiting the post office to look in vain for his mail, composing – or at least thinking about – some of the rambling mystical verses that would be added to the published version of *Król-Duch* ('King Spirit') after his death, and writing a constant stream of instructions to his friends and family in Poland on how to find him. His mother was to drive in her carriage from Lemberg to Cracow, and then take what he called the *cug* from Cracow to Bresslau:

1 When you set off, send me a letter ahead so that I can wait for a couple of evenings on the debarquardère of the railway.
2 Address all your letters to Madame Sophie Mielęka, Tauentzienstrasse, No. 69.
3 If by some chance you miss me on the debarquardère, get someone to take you to the Hotel Weisser Adler, then send the man there, who has my visiting card, to come and fetch me.
4 Send him to Neue Schweidnitzerstrasse no. 3 (second floor, right-hand doorbell); and if I'm not there, tell him to leave your card.[74]

Even Romantics must attend to details. His mother came in early July, a passenger in the very first season of the Bresslau–Cracow line. He left on the 8th and never saw her again.

Many lesser Polish figures were connected to Bresslau either through birth or education – Bandtkie, Elsner and General Langiewicz. Still more Poles, from Mniszek, Skarbek and Kościuszko to Kołłątaj, Kraszewski and Lenartowicz passed through in transit. Słowacki's Romantic rival, Zygmunt Krasiński (1812–59), stayed in Bresslau no fewer than eight or nine times. Polish interest in the city was rising. Romantic authors and publicists searching for *Staropolska*, or 'Old Poland', began to write about their 'Polish brothers' in Silesia and their 'grievous loss' of Bresslau. Luminaries such as Stanisław Staszic and Julian Ursyn Niemcewicz contributed to a growing body of literature, which ranged from poetic eulogies of Poland's lost lands to scientific studies of regional dialects. Wincenty Pol spanned both ends of the spectrum, but his *Pieśń o ziemi naszej* ('Song of our Land', 1843) was typical of the former:

A od ruskich rzek wybrzeży
Aż po Tatrów pierś jałową
Po dziedzinę Krakusową,

Tam po Odrę, po Żuławy,
Stara ziemia Piasta leży –
I lud gnieździ starej sławy,
A w pośrodku Wisła bieży![75]

(And from the banks of the Ruthenian rivers
To the barren breast of the Tatras,
Through the realm of Krakus,
There, along the Oder, and in Żuławy
Lie the old lands of the Piasts –
where the people of ancient fame dwell,
and the Vistula flows through their heart.)

Yet it is interesting to see how many Poles who might otherwise have settled in Bresslau decided to leave. Jerzy Bandtkie (1768–1835), who had studied and taught at St Elizabeth's Gymnasium and who became a leading authority on Silesian culture, chose to move to Cracow. The composer Józef Elsner (1769–1854), who went to school at the St Matthias Gymnasium and who became Chopin's teacher of piano, spent virtually his whole career in Warsaw. The actor and fertile dramatist Karl von Holtei (1798–1880), a German with exceptional Polonophile proclivities, spent his childhood and retirement in Bresslau, but not the bulk of his career. It is hard not to conclude that the cultural climate of Prussian Bresslau was no more than lukewarm for such people.

Bresslau's secular musical life, already well established in the eighteenth century, went from strength to strength. It gained no small prestige from the three-year stay between 1804 and 1807 of Carl Maria von Weber, composer of *Der Freischütz*. Thereafter it was a regular destination for leading performers on the circuit between Vienna, Prague and Berlin. The high point, according to many, was the visit in July 1829 of the violinist Niccolo Paganini:

During his 8-day stay, he gave two concerts in the Aula and two by general request in the Theatre. He was received with enthusiasm and constant applause. During one of the rehearsals, a group of students broke down the door and pushed their way in by force, just to hear the master play. Their disorder was broken up by the police. Several reviews appeared, the most important by Panoffski in the Bresslau Gazette nr 180 . . . The greatest praise was offered to the effect that Paganini played with unequalled charm and wizardry . . . No-one played like him before; no-one plays like him at present; and no-one will play like him again.[76]

*

Prussia in the eighteenth and nineteenth centuries was a dynastic state, which demanded loyalty from its subjects but was not very interested in national or ethnic matters. Indeed, until a radical change of heart in the 1860s, it was firmly opposed to the German national movement. It was still a supranational entity, where service to the crown was the only decisive factor. As Frederick the Great noted in 1752:

> I have done everything possible to spread the name 'Prussian', in order to teach the officers that, whatever province they came from, they were all counted as Prussians, and that for that reason all the provinces, however separate from one another, form a united body.[77]

The very idea of 'Germany' in the eighteenth century was so vague that it was almost meaningless. No two definitions of it would be the same. The Habsburg lands further clouded the issue. Which of them could be counted as German? The radical solution of excluding them all, as in the later 'Kleindeutsch' idea, surfaced only in 1756, at the Treaty of Westminster. It is important to remember that the Holy Roman Empire stayed in existence until 1806 and that the Kings of Prussia, who were imperial electors, had every reason to keep it going. It was only after Napoleon intervened that the framework changed. It was Napoleon who determined that the Holy Roman Empire should disappear, that the Habsburg crown lands should be transformed into a completely new 'Austrian Empire' and that the Kingdom of Prussia should be reconstructed as a separate entity. Prior to 1806, the Habsburgs and the Hohenzollerns were uneasy partners in the same overarching entity. After 1806, they were independent competitors for control of a future 'Germany' that was still to be conceived.

The issue of language was largely irrelevant. Frederick the Great spoke French by preference and, though he understood German, he said that it compared unfavourably to the neighing of his horse.[78] In the 1770s, when the First Partition gave his kingdom a sizeable Polish population, he decreed that any future Crown Prince should gain a working knowledge of Polish. This particular tradition persisted right down to the minority of William II, a hundred years later.[79] For a brief time between 1795 and 1806, when Warsaw lay in Prussia, the Polish population reached 40 per cent. Fleetingly, it looked as if Prussia would become a Germano-Slav state.

In Bresslau, therefore, anyone who was a good Prussian would feel at home. German and Polish were common currency in the streets; Latin and Hebrew were present as sacred languages; and French was the language of the royal court. Local and religious affiliations were strong. But the stark national divisions, which developed in Silesia later between German and Pole, would barely have been understood.

By 1815, German nationalism was on the rise, but its influence should not be exaggerated. Frederick William III's speech *An mein Volk* had made no mention of 'Germans'. It referred exclusively to the peoples of Prussia as 'Brandenburgers, Prussians, Silesians, Pomeranians and Lithuanians'.[80] Only the frustrations of the decades after 1815 encouraged more exclusive forms of national identity. The triumph of the German national cause was not complete before the declaration of the German Empire at Versailles in 1871.

Thanks to the lack of an effective census, the size of the Polish population of Bresslau is very difficult to ascertain. But it was certainly growing. The opportunities for work and study made the city a haven for Poles not only from nearby Upper Silesia and from the Duchy of Posen, but also from more distant parts of partitioned Poland. In 1817, some 16 per cent of students at the University in Bresslau were Polish,[81] many of them enrolled in the Faculty of Law. Primed by their studies under Roepell and others, or by membership of the TLS they were to figure prominently in the Polish national risings of 1848 and 1863.

Bresslau evidently bore a complex and cosmopolitan make-up. Rapid industrialisation was beginning to attract economic migrants from the south – from Croatia, Serbia, Slovakia and Romania – as well as from the east. Several eye-witnesses left their impressions. A description from 1840 is especially illuminating:

> Breslau is a remarkable city: made up of different elements. The Prussian-Silesian one prevails, but alongside it there is a Polish and . . . an Austrian-Silesian one. Of the 15–20 couples that one meets here, at least one pair speaks Polish. At our tavern table, where we were only 30 in total, were seven men and women who were Polish speakers. They even have their own inns: the White Eagle, . . . the Wiżianowsky . . . The Austrian element is noticeable mainly in the dialect . . . certain tools and dishes have Austrian or corrupted Bohemian names. After fourteen years away from Austria, I had almost forgotten the dialect and the jolly tone of speech, but here I was reminded of it in a flash. Of course, after a few days . . . the idiom appeared less Austrian and more Prussian – rather a mixture of the two. The common incidence of the German and Polish languages reminded me of Prague . . . But Breslau is a thoroughly German city, the Poles are guests here.[82]

The attitude of German Bresslauers towards their Polish 'guests' was not uniform. A few were unashamedly fascinated by all things Polish. In 1829, Karl von Holtei produced an operetta about Tadeusz Kościuszko, called *Der alte Feldherr* ('The Old General'). Others did not greet the Polish presence quite so enthusiastically. It is interesting to see that, while Poles had long complained of 'Germanisation', Germans were now complaining ever more vociferously about 'Polonisation'. Indeed, a nasty, supercilious anti-Polish streak had taken root in the Prussian make-up ever since Frederick the Great, whose thoughts on the Poles were less than kind:

> La même encore qu'à la création,
> Brute, stupide et sans instruction,
> Staroste, juif, serf, palatin ivrogne,
> Tous végétaux qui vivaient sans vergogne.[83]

> (The same today as at the creation,
> Crude, stupid and without instruction,
> Lord, Jew, serf, and drunken palatine,
> All beasts living entirely without shame.)

In 1848, the Prussian government saw fit to expel all Polish migrants from Bresslau ostensibly for fear of revolutionary sympathies. It prompted an impassioned response from a Pole in the Democratic Club, known only as 'Stanislaus S——i':

> The Polish nation is already too used to suffering and sorrows of all kinds to tolerate today's humiliation . . . [it] looks with contempt on the death throes of a government which seeks to extend its sorry life . . . through the destruction of a crowd of refugees. Sirs! You have seen the atrocity committed today . . . And what is the crime that we have committed? It is the love for our unhappy fatherland which sighs for deliverance. That is what drove us through cannonfire . . . to your hospitable city, to lay our troubled brows amongst you and await the hour of our rebirth. The action of your government has destroyed all our hopes at a stroke.[84]

The ban did not last long. Nonetheless, the novelist Gustav Freytag was complaining about the Polish presence in 1857. 'On the whole,' he wrote to a friend, 'Breslau is very much polonised and lacks the desired purity and other symptoms of education.'[85] His lack of enthusiasm was well demonstrated in his poem *Der polnische Bettler* ('The Polish Beggar'), published in 1845:

> In Breslau vor dem Dome stand einst ein Bettelmann
> In grauem, leinenem Kittel, mit vielen Lappen d'ran.
> Die Rechte hielt ein Säckchen, die Linke den Knotenstab,
> Das weisse Haar hing zottig ihm über die Stirn hinab,
> Und traurig sah'n die Augen in's Gotteshaus hinein,

Er legte Stock und Ranzen bedenklich auf einem Stein
Und wischte mit schmutzigem Ärmel sich ab der Thränen Thau:
'O heilige Mutter Gottes, du braune von Czenstochau!
Hier steh' ich in fremden Landen, ein elender armer Wicht,
Und wenn ich polnisch bitte, verstehn mich die Leute nicht,
Und wenn ich polnisch bete, hier hören die Heiligen nicht,
Du braune Mutter von Polen, hilf deinem armen Sohn,
Du liebe heilige Mutter, ich zittre vor Hunger schon!' . . .[86]

(By Bresslau Minster a beggar once stood,
His smock in patches, like his linen hood,
His left hand held a staff, a scrip in his right,
His hair hung from his brow in tufts of white.
Into God's house his sad eyes strayed,
Staff and scrip on a stone he laid,
With a dirty sleeve he wiped away the tears:
'Lady of Czenstochau, hear my cares!
In foreign lands, in misery, I stand here –
If I beg in Polish, the people won't hear me,
If I pray in Polish, the saints won't heed me;
Brown Lady of the Poles, help your wretched child,
I shake for hunger, dear Holy Mother Mild!')

In time, the Polish 'guests' appeared to become more accepted. Another commentator stated that the inhabitants of Bresslau 'are partly German and partly Slavic [but] on the right bank of the Oder, they speak mainly Polish'.[87] The Polish historical novelist, J.I. Kraszewski (1812–87), who stayed in Bresslau regularly between 1858 and 1879, was still more emphatic. 'To this day,' he wrote in 1860, 'Germanisation has not managed to erase the traces of [Bresslau]'s Slavonic origins. Indeed, one could say that the city is still half-Polish. One can hear our speech at the very gates of the Silesian capital; and [the district immediately] across the river is even known [to its inhabitants] as "Poland".'[88] If this was accurate, nothing much had changed since the days of Barthel Stein, 350 years before.

By the nineteenth century, Jews formed the second prominent minority in Prussian Bresslau. After the Prussian annexation, the regulations on Jewish residence had been eased. In 1744 Frederick II promulgated his *Allergnädigste Deklaration* ('Most merciful Declaration'). Twelve Jewish families were permitted to reside permanently in Bresslau. Only one son from each family could marry and settle. All the other children were permitted to return for a three-day stay on payment of a fee. The concession was not overly generous.

Nonetheless, under the leadership of Rabbi Benedix Reuben Gomperz of

Wesel, Bresslau's Jewish community had prospered. In 1761, it gained its own cemetery on the Claasenstrasse to the south of the city. Yet despite his self-proclaimed enlightenment, Frederick shared many prejudices of the age. In 1779, when visited by a Jewish delegation seeking greater liberties, he responded tartly:

> Those [liberties] which are connected to your trade you can keep. But, it's just not on that you bring whole hordes of Jews to Bresslau and want to make a new Jerusalem out of it.[89]

By Frederick's death, the Jewish population of Bresslau numbered some 2,500. In 1790 a new decree restricted numbers to twenty-four privileged and 160 semi-privileged families. At the same time the Neue Königliche Wilhelms-Schule, or 'William's School', was established in the Jewish quarter in the south-west of the Old Town. Like the later Mädchenschule für arme Töchter, or 'School for Poor Girls', it adhered to the principles of the Jewish Enlightenment, or *Haskalah*, and strongly promoted assimilation. It inevitably met resistance from Orthodox Jews.

In 1812, Prussia granted Jews legal equality, thereby encouraging a further rise in numbers. The Jews of Bresslau soon acquired all the accoutrements of permanence. In 1829, the 'White Stork' Synagogue was built in the heart of the Jewish quarter. Fifteen years later, the Fraenckel Hospital opened to care for the sick. More schools followed. In 1856, a new cemetery was established on the Lohestrasse. By 1871 the Jewish population of Bresslau had risen to 13,916, some 7 per cent of the total.

The Jewish community participated fully in Prussia's blossoming cultural life. Three academics deserve special mention. The botanist Ferdinand Julius Cohn (1828–98), a Bresslauer by birth, was appointed Professor at Bresslau University in 1859 and came to be recognised as the father of bacteriology. The astronomer Johann Galle (1812–90), discoverer of the planet Neptune, headed the Bresslau Observatory from 1851. And Heinrich Graetz (1817–91), Professor at Bresslau from 1853, was the foremost Jewish historian of the nineteenth century. His eleven-volume *History of the Jewish People* (1853–75), which is said to have been buried with him, set a benchmark for the future study of the subject. Though Graetz might have objected, such men were every bit as German as they were Jewish. Assimilation was proceeding apace.

*

Vratislavian society underwent considerable change during the Prussian period. A new ruling class was installed, which looked towards Protestant Berlin rather than Catholic Vienna. It abandoned the old tradition of municipal self-sufficiency, aligning the city much more closely to the state than previously. At the same time, a prolonged agrarian crisis in Silesia supplied a constant stream of migrants from the countryside, who manned the early experiments in industrialisation and who foreshadowed both demographic growth and social upheaval. Until the end of the eighteenth century, however, the population of Silesia remained fairly stable, and that of Breslau grew only modestly, from 49,000 at the Prussian takeover to 55,000 in 1790. The explanation would seem to be that neither the state repopulation policies of the late 1700s nor the influx of rural migrants made much impression on the very high death rates caused by poverty, disease and malnutrition. Bresslau did not start to grow dynamically until the mid-nineteenth century.

Conditions were grim for the majority living on the land in the eighteenth century. Though the royal domains generally protected their peasants from undue exploitation, state intervention on the remaining estates was rare. There, the lord of the manor was still all-powerful. He could buy and sell his peasants, demand unlimited labour services from them and refuse them permission to marry. On 'review days' the peasants were obliged to present their children to him so that he could choose his new servants.[90] Disagreements were rarely settled in the peasant's favour. In cases of dereliction of duty, corporal punishment was the norm – the lash being common. On one estate in Silesia, recalcitrants were locked in a wooden box, barely a metre square, in which they could neither stand nor lie, 'nor see sun nor moon'.[91] The large-scale flight of Silesian peasants across the border into Poland or to the towns was not surprising. However, the nascent industrial sector could, as yet, provide only limited employment. Many peasants merely exchanged a life of oppression in the village for an equally distressing one of exploitation or neglect in the city.

Life for the middle and upper classes was considerably more spacious and gracious. Even for them, however, child mortality remained high throughout most of the Prussian period, while poor hygiene encouraged endemic diseases such as tuberculosis, as well as the epidemics of cholera. But ownership of property guaranteed an educated existence of relative ease. What is more, social attitudes were breaking the traditional routine of church and family. The rise of Freemasonry, for instance, was driven as much by the revolt against stultifying social mores as by any coherent new ideology. The first Masonic Lodge in Bresslau, '*Aux trois squelettes*' (The Three Skeletons), was established in May 1741. It was followed in the later eighteenth century by a number of rival lodges as the movement reached its peak of popularity and influence. Some lodges were socially exclusive and politically conservative, others were more open. But all spread the attitudes of the Enlightenment, attracting 'the great and the good' of Bresslau society.

Their appeal is demonstrated by the fact that two successive Bishops of Bresslau, Philipp Graf von Schaffgotsch (r.1748–95) and Joseph, Prince of Hohenlohe-Waldenburg-Bartenstein (r.1795–1817), were Freemasons, even though they risked excommunication through their membership.

Serfdom was abolished in Prussia in stages between 1811 (during the French occupation) and 1848. The change most frequently took the form of 'rentification' – that is, the imposition of rented tenancies in place of traditional labour dues. Since the rents were fixed at a high level and the earnings of agricultural workers or tenant farmers were very low, it often proved less than a blessing, especially for the poorest peasant families. It provoked a new 'flight from the land', which in turn put pressure on towns and cities, like Bresslau, to provide rural refugees with work and decent shelter. In very many cases, the need could not adequately be met. Serfdom was not abolished in the Russian-ruled Kingdom of Poland, adjacent to Bresslau, until 1864. But thanks to the complicated politics of the Polish Risings, it took place under relatively favourable terms, which usually left the peasants in ownership of their land. Nonetheless, it released yet another wave of rural migrants, who made their way to the Prussian cities, first as seasonal workers or temporary domestics and then in due course as permanent residents.

Until the early nineteenth century, Bresslau was still bounded by the line of its old walls. But around 1830, the trickle of urbanisation became a flood. While the population of Silesia as a whole increased twofold between 1800 and 1871 to 3.5 million, that of its capital topped 100,000 in 1849 and then more than doubled by 1871 to 207,000. For the mass of newcomers, no social comforts were provided. In the slums of the Weißgerbergasse, or in the poorer areas of the Nikolai and Oder suburbs to the north and west, overcrowding was acute. More than 20 per cent of Bresslauers lived five to a room, and more than 10 per cent of them in cellars. Disease was rife. Pneumonia, tuberculosis and diphtheria were a constant threat. Cholera claimed well over 1,000 lives in 1831 and again in 1837. It recurred in 1848, 1849 and 1855. In 1866, more than 4,000 Vratislavians succumbed to the disease. 'Cholera cemeteries' proliferated, and yet the migrants were not deterred. Cities like Bresslau 'killed their inhabitants in such numbers that they depended on a continuing flow of migration from the surrounding areas'.[92] The appeal of a new urban life did not easily fade. Yet many unfortunates were driven to desperation. In 1854, one Caroline Reichelt killed her two young children 'in despair at her poverty'.[93]

From the mid-nineteenth century a new middle class emerged in Germany. Often associated with the homely 'Biedermeier' culture, it consisted of bankers, merchants, entrepreneurs and factory owners. In

Bresslau, they lived in the elegant streets around Tauentzien Platz or in the Schweidnitzer suburb. They were educated, literate and in touch with the cultural and artistic trends emanating from Paris or Berlin. Some were also politically active, as members of discussion groups or professional bodies. They were bound by their shared belief in property, diligence and the rule of law.

Nonetheless, the juxtaposition of rich and poor contributed to a marked increase in crime. The numbers of robberies and physical assaults grew. In Bresslau, there were some notorious murders. At 10 a.m. on the morning of 21 January 1853, August Langer killed his wife with a double-barrelled pistol. She had refused to come back to him after a domestic quarrel and he had shot her in public, in the middle of the butter market. He attempted to take his own life, but was arrested, put on trial and sentenced to death.[94]

The executions of criminals passed for popular entertainment and in Bresslau were said to attract as many as 15,000 spectators.[95] The chance of witnessing a botched job was probably part of the appeal. In 1811, a spectacularly clumsy decapitation in Bresslau contributed to a change in Prussian law. The executioner, from Liegnitz, was considered to be a master with the sword:

> His first stroke went far too high and only caused a little blood to flow; his second missed altogether [detaching no more than] the offender's blindfold. As the [man] tried to look round, the third stroke was struck and missed again. At this point the [Bresslau] executioner snatched the sword and carried out the fourth stroke, which finally separated the head from the rump to the extent that it only needed a fifth stroke to complete the severance.[96]

It was said that the Liegnitz executioner had to be protected from an angry mob. That same year, execution with the sword was replaced in the Prussian legal code by the use of a 3.6-kilogram axe.

The year of 1848 heralded the Communist Manifesto, and much would be made by Marxist historians of the revolutionary climate of that era. Certainly the heady mix of social, constitutional and national discontent built up to produce a scatter of eruptions across the European continent. In Silesia, the repeatedly violent protests of weaving towns signalled deep distress, while demands for varying degrees of constitutional reform and for German or Polish aspirations were voiced. Yet the fact is that the different strands of protest never coalesced, and the crisis was contained. There was no Silesian Revolution in 1848–9. Bresslau twice exploded in reaction to news from Paris or Berlin, but on each occasion revolt was effectively suppressed. On the social front, the working class did not present a uniform stance. On the contrary, the representatives of the old craft industries, like the hand-weavers, were simply overtaken by those of the new manufacturies, where neither the entrepreneurs nor the factory workers had any interest in prolonged protest. The rise of industrial Bresslau was to bring new social problems of its own. But it was too dynamic to be held back. It raced ahead after 1848, as memories of the 'Springtime of the Nations' were left behind.

*

Until the mid-eighteenth century, Bresslau was a semi-independent city-state, enjoying ancient privileges and freedoms. Its political alignments had always come about by consent. It had never been captured by enemy forces. One commentator lauded this prized 'virginity', though he conceded that 'in truth . . . the seductions were never particularly . . . dangerous'.[97] Frederick the Great would rob Bresslau of its innocence. After his arrival, its ancient freedoms were doomed.

Already in January 1741, before the Prussians had made a formal annexation of Silesia, its administration was being reorganised. The old Habsburg bodies, the *Oberamt* and *Schlesische Kammer*, were replaced by a military Field Commissariat. The following year, the commissariat was itself replaced by two *Kriegs- und Domänenkammern*, or 'War and Domain Chambers', one in Bresslau and one in Glogau. These were in turn subordinated to a Provincial Minister for Silesia, reporting directly to the King, who was to be the monarch's 'eyes and ears'. The Silesian Estates, meeting in Bresslau's Rathaus, swore their allegiance on 7 November 1741. The municipal administration was also reorganised. Frederick noted that he deprived the Silesian towns of their traditional franchise 'for fear of their filling the councils with men who are devoted to Austria'.[98] Within two years of the Prussian conquest, Bresslau was governed entirely by Prussian officials. In effect, the old 'Republic of Bresslau' was suppressed and replaced by a system run entirely by royal appointees. A royal Regulation of January 1748 confirmed the arrangements. The executive Magistrature was to consist of twenty persons, made up of a Director, a Vice-Director, a Mayor, ten city councillors, four guild councillors, two legal syndics and one secretary. The three leading figures were to be named personally by the King from a shortlist drawn up by the War and Domain Chambers. The Minister for Silesia was to exercise overall control.

Despite some welcome changes, such as the establishment, in 1743, of the Prussian postal system, the general enthusiasm surrounding the Prussian occupation faded. The economic downturn cast long shadows and Bresslau's diminished political status rankled. The introduction of the Prussian military system proved especially burdensome. The quartering of some

35,000 troops in private households throughout Silesia aroused much anger, and the introduction of cantonal recruitment quotas (from which Bresslau was exempted) is estimated to have driven some 10,000 Silesians over the border into Bohemia and Saxony.[99]

Prussian rule was not fully accepted until the long sojourn of Count Karl von Hoym as Provincial Minister for Silesia from 1770 to 1806. Hoym (1739–1807), of Saxon-Pomeranian lineage, had entered Prussian service in 1762 and had quickly caught the eye of the King. He was cultured, diligent and affable, never letting status or rank obstruct common courtesy. Under his guidance, Silesia blossomed. Bresslau too recovered its smile and grew to love its King. Frederick was more sceptical. On his final visit in 1785, he received a rapturous welcome. But when a courtier remarked how much the Vratislavians loved him, he replied that 'one could put an old ape on a horse, and lead it through the streets, and the people would cheer all the same'.[100]

The short French occupation of Bresslau in 1807 heralded several new developments. One was the restoration, at least in part, of the city's self-government. According to the Prussian *Städteordnung* of November 1808, a 200–strong elected council was instituted. A Magistrature of fifteen persons assumed the powers of a local executive. It was headed by an *Oberbürger-meister*, or 'Chief Mayor', whose deputy held the lesser title of *Bürgermeister*. The territory of the city was divided into wards, each administered by officials whose work was supervised by the council. The regulation of health, education, religion and municipal finance all became matters for local competence. The state reserved overall control, and the property qualifications for electors remained absurdly high. Even so, the citizens were given a sense of their own value, and stability was ensured by the twelve-year term envisaged for the Chief Mayor. The City Guard returned to its ancient watch.

The post-Napoleonic reform era had two notable results in Silesia. Firstly, the last remnant of regional autonomy was abolished when the Minister for Silesia became a mere cog of the Prussian bureaucracy and was no longer required to report directly to the King. Secondly, through the dissolution of numerous religious institutions in 1810–11, Silesia's social connections to Berlin were strengthened. Many of the former ecclesiastical estates were granted to prominent Prussian officials and generals, such as Blücher at Krieblowitz (Krobielowice) and Yorck von Wartenburg at Klein Oels (Oleśnica Mała), who thereby became Silesian landowners.

After the Napoleonic upheavals, Prussia's regional administration was reorganised yet again. In 1816, Silesia became one of ten provinces. It was divided into four *Regierungsbezirke*, or 'governmental districts', centred on Oppeln, Liegnitz, Reichenbach and Bresslau (Reichenbach was dissolved in

1820). In accordance with the King's earlier promise, a Silesian Diet or *Landtag* was called in 1825, which met in Bresslau late in the following year. Elected on a narrow property-based franchise, it was dominated by the landowners and had very little middle-class or urban representation. Given the onset of industrialisation, it was to become increasingly unrepresentative of society. It was to be the scene of growing protests, and received some 300 petitions requesting the establishment of more representative bodies. Heinrich Hoffmann von Fallersleben summed up the apparent futility of Prussian politics in his *Unpolitische Lieder* ('Apolitical Songs', 1841):

> Das Beten und das Bitten ist erlaubt,
> Ja, und erlaubt ist alles überhaupt,
> Was niemals nützt den armen Untertanen –
> Wenn wir an ein Versprechen etwa mahnen,
> Gesetzlich bitten, was wir fordern können,
> Da will man uns das Bitten auch nicht gönnen,
> Man weist uns ab mit kalten Hohn zuletzt:
> Ihr habt die Form verletzt.[101]

> (Prayers and requests are gladly accepted,
> Everything is indeed permitted,
> But what does it help our forsaken subjects –
> When we recount the promises broken
> We politely ask what should be demanded
> And even then, it won't be granted,
> We are dismissed with naked scorn:
> To make demands is just bad form.)

The author was to pay for his sarcasm with his career. But others would fill his place. Bresslau soon gained a reputation, like the Rhineland, as a hotbed of liberal and even Socialist thought. It was to produce Heinrich Simon and Wilhelm Wolff, two of the radicals of the Frankfurt Parliament (see above), and was to be one of the wellsprings of German Socialism.

The presence of the Prussian army in strength acted as a constant counterweight to the local radicals. From 1823, the VI Army Corps was permanently stationed in Bresslau; and it brought some 10,000 troops with it. Its official role was to guard the nearby frontier with the Congress Kingdom of Poland. Unofficially, it served as an effective brake on political passions. If necessary, it was always ready to quell unrest.

After the abortive revolution of 1848–9, the revised Prussian constitution of 1850 gave a modicum of hope to the kingdom's liberals. Virtually all adult males could vote, but the weight of their votes depended on their 'class' – or, more exactly, on their tax liability. Thus each of the three 'classes' chose one-third of the electors. In effect, the electoral weight of the 5 per cent of the population in the first class was equal to the 82 per cent in the third class. Reaction had triumphed. Nonetheless, some semblance of modern politics was allowed to develop. Thanks to the rise of the popular *Fortschrittspartei*, or 'Progressive Party', a bitter wrangle arose and the existing system increasingly came under attack. Then events overtook the Progressive Party itself, when it failed to persuade the working class that their future lay with liberalism. The Progressives were unable to prevent the emergence of a genuine labour movement under the Bresslauer Ferdinand Lassalle.

The son of a prosperous Jewish textile merchant, Lassalle (1825–64) studied at Bresslau and Berlin before being caught up in the turmoil of 1848–9. Escaping the exile imposed on contemporaries such as Karl Marx, he emerged from prison in 1849 an unshakeable champion of the working class. After many struggles, in 1863 he founded the *Allgemeiner Deutscher Arbeiterverein* (ADAV), or 'General German Workers' Association'. A keen orator, agitator and pamphleteer, Lassalle promoted the new party across the country almost single-handedly. Though the ADAV numbered only a few thousand members at the time of his death in a duel in 1864, it was to be a forerunner of the modern German Social Democratic Party (SPD). His home town responded reluctantly to the new party's appeal. In the elections of 1867, the two constituencies of Bresslau East and Bresslau West both returned Progressive Party candidates. Lassalle's tomb, renovated in 1948 by admirers, has been preserved to the present day in the main Jewish cemetery.

Bresslau benefited throughout the nineteenth century from the quality of its administrators. In Frederick von Merckel (1775–1846) and Arthur Hobrecht (1824–1912) it was run by men of genuine ability and ambition, whose careers were to raise its profile and influence. Merckel entered Prussian service aged only twenty-four, as an assessor in the Bresslau Justice Commission. Progressing through the provincial bureaucracy, he headed the *Bresslauer Kammer* in 1804 and became Silesian *Oberpräsident* in 1816. His contribution to the restoration of the Silesian administration after the French invasion was later acknowledged by Frederick William IV. And the Danziger Hobrecht served as *Oberbürgermeister* of Bresslau from 1863 to 1873, when he was especially concerned with the organisation of the education system. He was then called to Berlin, where he served again as *Oberbürgermeister* before being appointed Prussian Minister of Finance.

However, municipal politics in Bresslau were undergoing fundamental change. Administrators like Hoym and Merckel had become anachronisms by the mid-nineteenth century. As archetypal Prussian 'servants of the state', they belonged to another age, when deference ruled supreme and politics was the exclusive playground of the rich and well connected. Their successors operated in an arena where service to the people threatened to replace service to the state, and politics was becoming increasingly participatory. Conservative circles in Berlin were bound to look askance.

＊

In 1741, Bresslau, with a population of approximately 50,000, was still largely confined to the old walled town of the Middle Ages. It suffered no material damage during the Prussian annexation – the only major damage occurring in 1749 when the gunpowder store was struck by lightning and exploded, killing or injuring some 700 people. Frederick II soon began the repair and expansion of the defences. New and improved fortifications were laid out and a permanent garrison was established on the sparsely populated Bürgerwerder (Kępa Mieszczańska). Next to the headquarters building, a sugar refinery was opened in 1772 to obviate expensive imports. Many other dwellings and businesses grew up nearby, thereby hastening the integration of the Bürgerwerder into Bresslau proper. To improve the northern fortifications, the outer Oder arm that surrounded Cathedral Island was drained, thereby depriving the cathedral of its insular position and giving fresh impetus to settlement in the north-east. In a few decades, Frederick's fortifications were surrounded by urban overspill and were rendered militarily useless.

By the late eighteenth century, Prussian Bresslau was fully integrated into an international network of postal and relay services. It featured prominently in one of the very early tourist guides, published in Weimar in French in 1793 by Hans Ottokar Reichard.[102] Indeed, with a declared population of 60,179, Bresslau was presented after Vienna (270,000), Berlin (151,000), Hamburg (120,000) and Prague (84,000) as the fifth city of Germany. Apart from Dresden and Cologne, no other German cities exceeded 50,000; Munich, Frankfurt and Danzig were the only others to exceed 40,000.

Bresslau was connected to all of them, and by extension to the rest of Europe, by a permanent system of posthouses and stagecoaches, which permitted passengers, packets and messages to travel at the 'incredible' speed of 24–9 kilometres per day. Prussia insisted that travellers carried passport letters, which were checked at the city gates; and certificates of good health prevented lengthy investigations by sanitary inspectors. In Bresslau, as in Berlin, the standard charge of three groschen per kilometre covered tips for the postillion and the *Wagenmeister*; twenty-three kilograms of baggage were carried gratis. There were four main routes – west, east, north and south – divided into stages where horses could be watered or changed:

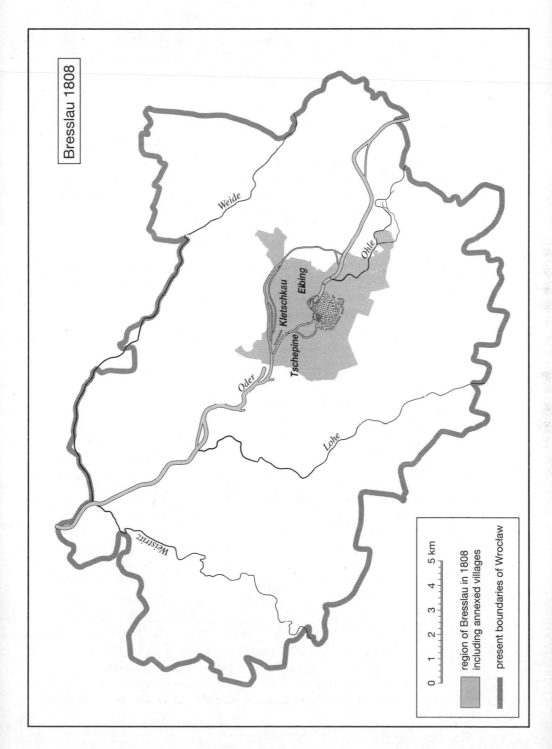

Bresslau 1808

Weide

Ohle

Kletschkau

Elbing

Tschepine

Oder

Lohe

Weistritz

5 km

0 1 2 3 4 5 km

region of Bresslau in 1808
including annexed villages

present boundaries of Wroclaw

			VIENNE
		21	Prague (via Budweis)
	LEIPSICK	11	Reinertz
12½	Goerlitz	1½	Glatz
3	Bunzlau	1½	Frankenstein
1½	Haynau	1	Nimptsch
1	¹IEGNITZ	1	Jordansmühl
2	Neumarkt	1½	Domslau
2	BRESSLAU	1	BRESSLAU
	BRESSLAU		BRESSLAU
2	Oels	2	Neumarkt
2	Wartenberg	1½	Parchwitz
1	Kempten	1½	Lüben
1	Wernscov	1	Polkwitz
1½	Naramici	2	Neustädtel
18	VARSOVIE	1	Wartenburg
		1	Grünberg
		2	Crossen
		1½	Ziebingen
		1½	FRANCFORT/Oder[103]

Reichard's itineraries were accompanied by *observations locales*. Many localities in the environs of Bresslau received favourable mention:

- BUNZLAU: a fine orphanage: St Dorothy's Church: Mr Liebner's flower garden: the mechanical works of Messrs Jacob & Hutting: the brown earthenware pottery, known as 'Bunzlau ware' . . .
- HAYNAU: The Lutheran Church contains several remarkable tombs and a fine library. At Tschetschendorf, 1½ leagues from Haynau there is a beautiful English Park.
- LIEGNITZ: The castle is one of the finest in all Silesia: it was besieged in 1241 by the Tartars . . . At Wahlstadt, the Benedictine Convent built on the site of the battle of 1241 has some good pictures.
- OELS: The castle library with collections of antiquities and natural history: St John's Church, the Catholic Church and the celebrated Public School. The mineral springs at Skarfin lie 3 leagues from the town.
- GLATZ: The ancient castle and fortifications: the fine College of the *ci-devant* Jesuits. The Parish Church keeps a miraculous icon. One should see the picture gallery of Mr Krause and the botanical gardens of his brother, the apothecary.

- NIMPTSCH: The surroundings, including the village of Vogelsang, the park at Iseritz, and the view from the Kassenberg, are remarkable. The village of Kosemitz is famed for the chrysoprases found nearby.
- NEUMARKT: This small town is known for its tourbes and its carriages.
- GRÜNBERG: Here there are some sizeable cloth factories. Over 2,410 vineyards produce only sour wine.[104]

Reichard's description of Bresslau itself runs to nearly three pages. Among the long list of 'remarkable buildings', literary bodies, galleries, entertainments, inns and industries, one also learns about the Silesian Lodge of the Freemasons and, quite wrongly, of the imperial victory at nearby Leuthen thirty-six years earlier (see Appendix).[105]

Opinions about Bresslau at the turn of the nineteenth century varied considerably, but many were unflattering. Goethe's comments (see page 232) have been explained by the fact that he visited following a late summer drought that had raised the bad odours to unusual levels. Nonetheless, he described it as a city from which he hoped 'to be delivered'.[106] A contemporary of his wrote that Bresslau was 'an old, gloomy and cramped fortress . . . One passes under the battlements, across the Oder bridge and through the city gate with a feeling of horror'.[107] Indeed, travellers were informed in advance of the city's shortcomings. The future American President, John Quincy Adams, who passed through in 1804, had been told that Bresslau was 'nothing more than a large, old, and very dirty city . . . containing nothing that deserved the attention of travellers'. Yet, having seen it for himself, he conceded that it contained 'objects of curiosity sufficient to amuse and employ the few days we have devoted to the place'.[108]

For one thing, Bresslau was already adorned with a number of fine palaces. The Spaetgen Palace had been purchased by Frederick II in 1750 to serve as the royal residence. After being extended and refitted, it suffered enormous damage during the Austrian siege of 1760, when many rooms were entirely burned out. It was home to the King during the dark winters of the Seven Years War and was the scene of the muted celebration of his fiftieth birthday in January 1763. The new Hatzfeld Palace was built in 1775, replacing its predecessor, which had been destroyed in 1760. It housed Jérôme Bonaparte. And the classical Wallenberg-Pachaly Palace on the Roßmarkt was completed in 1787. It was built by C.G. Langhans for the Pachaly banking family (it currently houses part of the University Library).

Bresslau was deprived of its fortifications by order of Napoleon himself.

As elsewhere in Germany, the city walls were to be dismantled and the ditches filled, though the gates were to be left standing. In total 2,000 labourers were hired for the task. After the French withdrawal, the King of Prussia was approached for financial aid. He could only donate the land and recommend, as Napoleon had done, that the battlements be turned into promenades. The outer suburbs, which had been damaged during the siege, saw partial renovation under Jerôme Bonaparte. The Schweidnitzer suburb to the south was favoured by the building of attractive boulevards surrounding the new Tauentzien Platz. The General's wish of 1760 was now granted. An elegant marble sarcophagus, designed by C.G. Langhans and J.G. Schadow, was erected at the centre point of the square. Soon afterwards, in 1827, a powerful neo-classical statue of Marshal Blücher was erected on the Salt Market.

In reality, early nineteenth-century Bresslau had much to offer the intelligent visitor, no less in its collections of books and paintings than in its architecture. A Polish princess and collector who recorded her lachrymose impressions during a visit in 1816 found much to see:

We reached [Bresslau] in the early morning; but, because of the Wool Fair, we had to make do with an indifferent inn and bad meal. After that we set off round the town and were most warmly welcomed by the bookseller, Korn. I had neither the time nor inclination to look through his shop, which contains many fine publications . . . So he took us to his private rooms where some beautiful pictures were hanging that he had acquired from Mirabeau. He deals, among other things, in antiques . . . and the word *superbe* never leaves his lips.

The next day, Korn invited us to dinner at his property [in the former abbey] at [Oswitz] on the outskirts of Bresslau. Then, we went to see the Wool Fair . . . In the evening, the German theatre presented a play [*Der Wald bei Bondi*] in which a dog discovers his master's murderer. The poodle, playing the role of the faithful dog, was so adorable that I was moved to tears . . .

In the morning, a Sunday, I went to Mass at the cathedral . . . I observed the ancient vaulting and the Gothic pillars, with respect and emotion. There was once a time when all this belonged to Poland. I didn't realise that tears were rolling down my cheeks as I revelled in the past . . . [Later], entering the Church of the Holy Cross, I heard the lusty singing of the people [which] moved me so deeply as I listened to the same Polish refrains one hears at home . . .[109]

The Princess then left for a tour of the mountain spas. But she was back in Bresslau a few weeks later for another three-day stay, when she lodged at the inn of 'the honest Rautencrantz':

In the evening, I attended ... an interesting new play, *Jolanda, Queen of Jerusalem*. It was about chivalry, and a large part was taken up by the Templars ... [Then] we visited churches. I have always liked the Gothic style. But now I see that it is best suited to divinity ...

I called on Professor Bach [at the School of Fine Arts] who possesses a remarkable collection of paintings. Guido Reini's *Head of Christ* reduced us again to tears ... Another picture by Carracci depicts the Saviour dying in the arms of the Holy Virgin. A third is a Rembrandt of great beauty portraying *The Restraint of Scipio* ...

The next day we went to look at the library house in St Elizabeth's Church ... I didn't notice the books, all German, but was amazed by the manuscripts, above all by a four-volume copy in folio of Froissart [written] on well-preserved pergamon and illustrated by exquisite miniatures. Napoleon ... wanted to take it, and when that failed, he tried to buy it, offering a vast sum of money ... But it remained in [Bresslau]. There's also a very ancient manuscript of Cicero's *De natura deorum*: an *Iliad* in Greek on pergamon, and a very fine Valerius Maximus. The oldest items are four Latin Gospels from the VIIth century ...

On 3 September we left [Bresslau] after breakfast, making for [Oels] where we dined at an inn. Afterwards, we drove to [Groß Wartenberg], which is in the possession of Duke [Gustav] Biron de Courland, whose wife is Countess Maltzan. Both of them were away, enjoying themselves in Dresden. So we spent the night in an excellent inn ...[110]

Bresslau's extensive battlements took several decades to disappear. Though the walls were swiftly demolished, the rubble took longer to remove and the last of the towers did not succumb until 1838. Nonetheless, growing space had been provided beyond the medieval limits and by 1840 the population had grown again by two-thirds of its 1800 level. Those decades saw a flurry of municipal building projects. The neo-classical Alte Börse on the Salt Market dated from 1824, whilst the Neues Rathaus on the Main Square (1863) and the Neue Börse on Graupenstrasse (now Krupnicza) (1867), were fine examples of the neo-Gothic style.

By the mid-nineteenth century, therefore, Bresslau's appearance was a source of pride. For people who had known it earlier, its new look made it virtually unrecognisable:

There are few traces left to suggest that [Bresslau] was once a powerful fortress. The grim fortifications have been exchanged for green gardens and for lively promenades densely planted with trees. On all sides nowadays it is brighter, merrier, and more spacious. The hand of the present is constantly smoothing out the ugly wrinkles of the past. In place of deadly cannon, the three bastions now carry the green tips of trees and innumerable wreaths of flowers ...[111]

According to Gustav Freytag, Bresslau compared favourably to the Prussian capital:

> It was in the autumn of 1836 that I went to Berlin. My friend was . . . much annoyed because I declared that the market-place in Bresslau was more beautiful than the *Gendarmen Markt*, and I would not allow that the statue of the commander-in-chief by the principal barracks was better than our Blücher in the Salt Market. He was very unwilling to allow that the churches in Bresslau were more picturesque than those in Berlin with their great domes. And he got quite angry when I remarked to him that the wide streets of his city looked like a large coat on a small body . . .[112]

Nonetheless, expansion had its problems. The old infrastructure could no longer cope. The condition of the Ohle had long been a source of concern, but by the mid-nineteenth century it had become little more than an open sewer. Hence it was decided in February 1866 to drain it, fill it and pave it, thereby creating a pedestrian zone around the inside of the Old Town. In 1870, the new streets were named Reußenohle, Schloßohle, Altbüßerohle and Kätzelohle.

In this same period, the city acquired the basic utilities of a modern metropolis. New pavements were laid in 1826, and the old oil lamps of the previous century were replaced at the same time by new, larger lamps suspended over the streets. The first gaslights did not appear until 1847 and for many years did not extend beyond the central areas. The process of replacing the ancient wooden water conduits with underground iron pipes went on continuously for fifty years between 1780 and 1830. An attempt made in 1825 to increase the flow by steam-driven pumps was not particularly effective. Great efforts were invested in the renewal of bridges, most of which at the turn of the century were rickety wooden affairs. Stone-built bridges were constructed in front of the Schweidnitz and Ohlau Gates, once the walls had been demolished. And in 1822, an iron bridge, which had been brought in pieces by barge from Gleiwitz (Gliwice), was erected on the site of the former Nikolai Gate. In 1844, a bridge was put in place to link the freshly built Upper Silesian Station with the right-bank suburbs, which at that time were accessible only by ferry.

By mid-century, Bresslau's public face was fast recovering. Around that time, a traveller from Bremen wrote:

> The city does not have an imposing image . . . [but] though cramped and crowded, it gives a homely, pleasant impression. It is not dark, like a medieval city, and neither is it cold from a lack of features, like a modern one. This mixture, this variety is particularly appealing . . . I can

sympathise that Maria Theresa shed tears when this pearl of Silesia was torn from her crown.[113]

A generation later, the spread of the outer suburbs was radically changing Bresslau's overall aspect:

> The temptation to build is growing with every year that passes. There is no space left in the city centre, so it is sought beyond the former line of the walls, where whole streets, and not just individual houses, are springing up like mushrooms. The new suburbs now embrace the Old Town in a vast arc, just as they do in Kraków; and each of them has its own character. The Schweidnitz Suburb is considered to be the seat of affluence and wealth, whilst the Nikolai Suburb, and the others across the river, have taken in industrial factories. Walking among the high chimneys and the howl of machines, it feels as if one were in some factory town in England.[114]

Seen by outsiders, the citizens of Bresslau displayed a particularly dour character:

> Many details reveal that society here on the banks of the Oder has taken *oszczędność* [thrift] as their watchword. Comfort, trade and dealing are the emblems of Silesia's capital. [But] here . . . they do nothing without a piece of chalk at hand [to calculate the costs], not even dances and entertainment . . . [Rich and poor], they all live and dress modestly, with little regard for hospitality. And if anyone here wants to spend some money, they either go abroad or to Berlin so as to avoid a bad reputation in their home town.[115]

As Bresslau expanded, the outlying villages were consumed. In 1868, the population was increased by some 14,000 by the incorporation of the communes of Gabitz, Neudorf, Höfchen, Lehmgruben, Huben, Fischerau and Alt-Scheitnig. By 1871, it had passed the 200,000 mark. Bresslau had long been the second city of Prussia. It would now enter the German Empire as the third city, after Berlin and Hamburg.

The dynamic growth of Bresslau went hand in hand with changes in the surrounding countryside. When the Counts Hatzfeld rebuilt their palace in the city, for example, they equally redesigned their country seat at Trachenberg [Żmigród]. If the Prince-Bishop needed to underline his status with a resplendent new residence on Cathedral Island, he obviously had to match it with a resplendent new summer palace in the mountains of Bohemia.

An earlier episcopal palace had been built in the village of Pöpelwitz near

Bresslau by Bishop Francis Ludwig Neuburg (r. 1683–1732). But it fell into disuse after being sacked and ruined during the Seven Years War. At this point, it was taken over by the robber band of a Silesian 'Robin Hood' called Manduba, who reportedly terrorised the rich and helped the poor. Manduba hailed from Morgenau (now Rakowiec within the city limits of Wrocław) and, like Robin Hood, had a ladyfriend called Maria or Marion. He was said to organise orgies in the new suburb of Scheitnig, and had to be bought off by the City Council. He was killed by a renegade of his own band. As late as the early twentieth century, Polish peasants in the district of Morgenau still called it 'Marianów'.

The Napoleonic Wars probably did more to adorn the Silesian heritage than to damage it. One memento was to be found at Bunzlau (Bolesławiec), where a cast-iron obelisk was raised in 1813 in memory of Field Marshal Kutuzov who died there.

Probably the most dramatic additions to the landscape, however, were to be found in a series of grandiose neo-Gothic piles, which were constructed for the local nobility. A prime example was built at Fürstenstein (now Książ) near Schweidnitz, where the medieval castle was remodelled in 1794. The so-called 'Old Castle' there is, in fact, a modern artificial neo-Gothic ruin designed by C.W. Tischbein. In August 1800, the King and Queen of Prussia took part at Fürstenstein in a mock-medieval tournament, which happened to be witnessed on his travels by John Quincy Adams:

> The carousel was in a style of great magnificence . . . The close adherence to the forms usual in the times when knighthood was in its glory: the pomp and solemnity of the representation: the contrast between the grandeur of the spectacle and the old ruined walls, the relics of five centuries; and [that] between the romantic wildness of the extensive prospect around, and the crowded thousands who were present to see the show: all contributed to produce a pleasing effect.[116]

Several of the old estates and secularised abbeys fell into the hands of the Prussian royal family to be turned into luxurious rural retreats. The Abbey of Heinrichau (Henryków), for instance, was given to Princess Friderike, later Queen of the Netherlands. It then passed into the possession of the Grand Dukes of Saxe-Weimar-Eisenach. In 1832, the estate of Erdmannsdorf (Mysłakowice) was acquired by King Frederick William III, who converted the *Schloss* in imitation English Gothic style by Schinkel and Stüber. A portion of the estate was reserved for a colony of Protestant refugees from the Austrian Tyrol, and a group of Tyrolean-style chalets was built for them. A similar castle at Kamenz (Kamieniec), also designed by

Schinkel, was built in 1838–73 for Prince Albrecht of Prussia and his wife, Princess Marianne of Orange-Nassau.

Of course, Silesia had much more to offer than pseudo-Gothic follies. The railways fuelled a stream of tourists to the mountains as well as to the spas. And several small towns were taken over by local industries. The elegant 'Hotel zur preussischen Krone' at Bad Salzbrunn (Szczawno Zdrój) was the birthplace of the writer Gerhart Hauptmann. The town of Habelschwerdt (Bystrzyca) on the Bohemian border became a centre of the match industry. But Kreisau (Krzyżowa), near Schweidnitz, belonged to the same category as Fürstenstein or Kamenz. It was awarded in 1867 to Field Marshal Helmuth von Moltke for services rendered during the Austro-Prussian War. Needless to say, any traveller heading for Bad Salzbrunn, Habelschwerdt or Kreisau would usually have started from Bresslau.

*

For Central Europe, the Austro-Prussian War of 1866 had consequences far beyond the purely political sphere. It upset the balance not merely of military and political power, but of the cultural and social traditions that 'Austria' and 'Prussia' embodied. Ever since 1741, Bresslau – though ruled by Prussia – had developed in a world where Prussia and Austria were rivals of equal standing, where each of them aspired to lead the 'Greater Germany' that many people believed to be the formation of the future. Yet after 1866, all such assumptions evaporated. Under Bismarck's inspiration, Prussia opted not only to put an end to Austrian rivalry by force, but equally to exclude Austria permanently from the 'Little Germany' that he was planning. Vienna ruled over an empire of a dozen nationalities and was constrained by necessity to reconcile multiple interests. Indeed, in consequence of 1866, she created the 'Dual Monarchy' of Austro-Hungary, which went a considerable way towards multinational federalism and which gave the Magyars and the *Kaisertreuen* – Poles of Galicia (though not the other nationalities) – a place in the sun alongside the Austrian Germans. Berlin, in contrast, moved in exactly the opposite direction. The old Prussian dynasticism was pushed into second place by the new German nationalism. 'Germanity' was to be elevated and everything non-German relegated. Less and less respect was to be paid to the fruitful diversity of the past. For a province like Silesia, which was part German and part Slav – and for a city like Bresslau, whose heritage had Austrian, Bohemian and Polish as well as Prussian layers – the shift was ominous. Bresslau had long been located on the borders of Prussia and Austria. Yet in 1864, when it watched as the Tsarist army finally suppressed the adjacent Kingdom of Poland, the complexities of its position increased. Henceforth, its citizens were to stand on the frontline of the German and Russian Empires. On the one hand, they could draw comfort from joining an enlarged German club and from seeing Prussianism offset by the gentler, more easy-going ambience of southern and western Germany. On the other hand, they were bound to feel anxious at becoming an exposed and vulnerable outpost on the new Germany's eastern frontier. In an age when nationalism was rising on all sides, future conflict was not hard to forecast.

SIX

Breslau in the German Empire,
1871–1918

The German Empire, established through the force of Prussian-led armies, was proclaimed at Versailles in a defeated France in January 1871. It was to experience phenomenal economic and demographic growth, outstripping its rivals, like Great Britain, in many sectors of production and showing an almost 50 per cent growth in population in its first three decades.[1] Seemingly unperturbed by its social and political stresses, the German Empire exuded an unshakeable belief in its own strength. Yet, trapped between a vengeful France and an expansive Russia, it was vulnerable to the international turbulance of the era. Despite more than a generation of peace, it plunged, by the deliberate choice of its leaders, into the maelstrom of the First World War.

The Empire proclaimed in the Hall of Mirrors was not a unitary state. In theory, at least, it was a voluntary association of twenty-five rulers, including four kings, eight princes, six grand-dukes, four dukes and three senates of the free cities. The King of Prussia, who assumed the mantle of Emperor, was merely the first among (nominal) equals. Under this federal system the imperial government in Berlin assumed responsibility for defence, foreign affairs, customs, currency, banking and the criminal and civil codes, while the individual state governments retained control of education, agriculture, justice, religious affairs and local government. The remnants of provincial sovereignty produced some interesting peculiarities. Saxony, Bavaria and Württemberg, for example, all maintained their own diplomatic missions at Vienna, St Petersburg and the Vatican until 1914.

Any residual feeling of independence in the member states was, however, illusory. The German political system was based on the power of Prussia. By far the largest state, with more than 60 per cent of the population, and hosting the imperial capital, Berlin, Prussia dominated from the start. The imperial constitution, drawn up by the Chancellor, Otto von Bismarck, enshrined Prussian supremacy. In the Upper House, the Bundesrat, where representatives of the states met to discuss common action, Prussia (with seventeen out of fifty-eight votes), played the key role. Given that meetings were invariably held in private and in the presence of the Emperor or Chancellor, few representatives of the other states would oppose Prussian proposals. The office of imperial Chancellor also derived its importance from being held in tandem with the Minister-Presidency of Prussia. 'Imperial policy was in effect Prussian policy writ large.'[2]

Moreover, despite the existence of various democratic bodies, the system as a whole was not subject to democratic accountability. The Lower House, or Reichstag, was elected via a free ballot and on the basis of universal male suffrage. As such, it developed a genuine popular legitimacy, yet it was politically rather emasculated. It only rarely initiated legislation and imperial Ministers were not even required to appear before it or to answer its members' questions. It had been deliberately starved of power.[3] But the complaint voiced by the Socialist Karl Liebknecht, that it merely served as a 'fig leaf to cover the nakedness of absolutism',[4] is exaggerated. In practice, if not in theory, the Reichstag had a role to play. Though its remit was limited, it was empowered to discuss all aspects of German legislation, including the annual budget. Even the Chancellor was to some extent dependent on its good will. Though he could only be appointed or dismissed by the Emperor, he relied for the success of his programme on the cooperation and support of the Reichstag. All imperial Chancellors except one were obliged to resign when they lost that support.

The place of Silesia and Breslau in this constellation was relatively simple. As an integral part of the Kingdom of Prussia, Silesia was divided into thirty-four constituencies returning members to the imperial Reichstag. Its capital city yielded two: Breslau East and Breslau West. It was also represented, as previously, with sixty-five seats in the Prussian Chamber of Deputies (*Abgeordnetenhaus*). That body was elected, not by universal male suffrage, but rather by the so-called 'three-class franchise' (see pages 254–5), thereby perpetuating the conservative character of the Prussian administration.

Initially, amid the enthusiasm of a victorious war and the unification of Germany, the peculiarities of the imperial constitution were ignored or overlooked. The Emperor's new subjects were enthused by the new state. The early years of the Empire, known as the *Gründerzeit*, or 'Time of Foundation', were characterised by rapid economic growth and a speculative boom. New businesses sprang up, railways and public works proliferated. Their proprietors' elegant new villas vied for space on the fashionable boulevards with the new ministries. Marion Dönhoff described the *Gründerzeit* as a 'gold rush', a time when the old Prussian values of duty and honour were replaced as the measure of all things by money.[5] Yet the boom was followed by a bust. On 7 January 1873, the National Liberal deputy Eduard Lasker rose in the Reichstag to attack the corruption and mismanagement of the Pomeranian railway. His remarks delivered a body blow to public confidence and loosed a wave of selling, which rapidly dissolved the gains of previous years. That spring, the Vienna stock market collapsed. The low point was not reached for another six years. Commentators spoke of a 'Great Depression',[6] whose effects were all the more severe since it coincided with the rise of anti-Semitism (see below) and with the conflict known as the *Kulturkampf*.

In essence, the *Kulturkampf* was a political conflict over the influence of Catholicism and of the Catholic states within the Empire. Bismarck viewed the supranational allegiances of Roman Catholics with suspicion, especially after the promulgation of the doctrine of Papal Infallibility in 1870. And he was especially worried by the (Catholic) Centre Party, which had been founded the same year and which soon became the second-largest party in the Reichstag, attracting many of the Empire's opponents. His initial legislation was intended merely to clarify spheres of influence. But from 1872, Bismarck sought to subordinate the Catholic Church to the state.

The main body of *Kulturkampf* legislation was drawn up by Adalbert Falk, Prussia's Breslau-educated Minister of Culture. The May Laws of 1873 stipulated a university education for all candidates for the priesthood, subjected all appointments to an examination (*Kulturexamen*) and hence to a state veto, and suspended subsidies in dioceses where the measures were resisted. They provoked a papal encyclical declaring the measures invalid and punishing compliance with excommunication, but the power of the state outweighed that of the Papacy. By 1876, the imprisonment or expulsion of disobedient clergy had left almost one-third of Prussia's Catholic parishes without an incumbent.

Due to its Catholic majority,[7] the province of Silesia was profoundly affected by the *Kulturkampf*. The attempts of the Prince-Bishop of Breslau, Heinrich Förster (1799–1881), to resist resulted in personal fines, the freezing of his income and, in 1875, his deposition. He was forced to retire to Jauernig in Austrian Silesia, which, though part of his diocese, lay beyond the borders of Germany. The initiator of the legislation, Dr Adalbert Falk, was his godson.

Though Förster's successors did much to repair Church–state relations, the *Kulturkampf* was to have lingering effects, especially in Upper Silesia, where the Catholic population represented 88 per cent of the total and was mainly Polish to boot. It served to galvanise the very forces that it had sought to suppress. In 1871, only half of Germany's Catholic electorate had voted for the Centre Party, giving it 18 per cent of the vote. Three years later, the Centre Party vote had risen to 28 per cent.[8] In Upper Silesia, where only one of twelve constituencies had returned a Centre Party candidate in 1871, all twelve returned Centre Party members to the Reichstag a decade later. Over the same period, the proportion of the Centre Party vote in Silesia as a whole rose from 17.7 to 41.9 per cent.[9] The government in Berlin was reaping a harvest of its own making.

As the *Kulturkampf* was drawing to a close, Socialism began to occupy Bismarck's mind. The SPD (Social Democratic Party) was on the rise. After gaining only two seats in 1871, it had gained twelve six years later, with 9 per cent of the vote. After two assassination attempts[10] were made on the Emperor, the new creed's supposed threat to social order was thought to be manifest. The resultant anti-Socialist legislation of 1878 was a curious mixture of coercion and latitude. In a raft of laws, Socialist meetings, Socialist societies and Socialist publications were forbidden, and the authorities were granted special powers to deal with Socialist agitation. Yet Socialists could still stand for election and speak freely in the Reichstag. In the 1880s, further measures were introduced. Known as 'state Socialism'; they included free medical treatment, accident and sickness insurance and state pensions. Such schemes had been planned since the 1850s, and their introduction can be seen as an attempt to wean the working class away from revolutionary Socialism.

Though Bismarck created the first comprehensive welfare system in Europe, his ulterior motive of undermining political Socialism was not achieved. Indeed, as with the *Kulturkampf*, his efforts were largely counterproductive. The Socialist vote fell in 1878, but rose again in 1884, yielding twenty-four seats in the Reichstag. Moreover, far from being crushed, the movement went underground, becoming better disciplined and better organised. In the Gotha Programme of 1875, it successfully reconciled the two rival factions of Lassallians and Marxists. In Silesia, the SPD vote rose from 0.6 per cent in 1871 to 11.7 per cent in 1890. Breslau returned its first SPD MP in 1878 before emerging as a long-standing bastion of Social Democracy. On the eve of the First World War, Breslau and Liegnitz (Legnica) both returned SPD votes of more than 35 per cent, while that of Silesia as a whole reached nearly 28 per cent.

The Bismarckian era cannot be considered an unmitigated success. Outwardly, the new Germany went from strength to strength; inwardly, it was faltering. Bismarck's heavy-handed methods had alienated both the working class and many Catholics, while his pseudo-democratic constitutional system had hampered Germany's political growth. More ominously, his removal in March 1890 left his creation in the hands of elements all too ready to use an aggressive foreign policy to distract internal dissent.

Meanwhile, the ship of state sailed on without its pilot. The conciliatory instincts of the new Chancellor, Leo Caprivi (1831–99), extended the social-welfare system and allowed the anti-Socialist legislation to lapse. The later Bülow government of 1900–9 continued the conciliatory trend by forming a pro-government bloc of parties in the Reichstag. Such moves contributed to a growth in the importance of the Reichstag and to the tentative emergence of a *de facto*, if not *de jure*, constitutionalism. At the same time, more sinister forces were ever more openly at work.

German nationalism became a mass creed in the last decades of the nineteenth century. In a sense, it was necessary to overcome strong regional differences and the federalism of the constitution. But it emerged in a form that depreciated the older Saxon, Prussian or Hanoverian identities and it possessed a particularly ebullient, boisterous, even vulgar flavour:

> Was ist des Deutschen Vaterland?
> Ist's Preussenland? Ist's Schwabenland?
> Ist's, wo am Rhein die Rebe blüht?
> Ist's, wo am Belt die Möwe zieht?
> > O nein, nein, nein!
> > Sein Vaterland muss grösser sein,
> > Sein Vaterland muss grösser sein . . .

> Was ist des Deutschen Vaterland?
> So nenne endlich mir das Land.
> 'So weit die deutsche Zunge klingt
> Und Gott im Himmel Lieder singt,'
> > Das soll es sein, das soll es sein!
> > Das, wackrer Deutscher, nenne dein,
> > Das nenne dein.[11]

> (What is the German's Fatherland?
> Is it Swabia, or the Prussian land?
> Is it the Rhine where the sweet vine blooms?
> Or on the Belt, where the seagull swoops?
> > Oh, no, no, no!
> > His Fatherland must greater be,
> > His Fatherland must greater be . . .

> What is the German's Fatherland?
> Won't you tell me where it can be found?
> 'As far as the German tongue resounds
> And hymns to God in Heaven abound'
> > That shall it be. That shall it be!
> > That, bold German,
> > Is the land for thee!)

Such patriotic songs were very much in fashion. By 1890, the *Deutschland-lied*, which had begun to evoke similar sentiments, had been officially adopted as a national anthem; all the basic emblems of German nationality – flag, anthem and currency – were now in place. In some quarters, the growing nationalism spilled over into chauvinism.

The *Alldeutscher Verband* (ADV), or Pan-German League, was founded in 1891 to promote Germany's 'national-imperial mission'. Though modest in size, it was perhaps the most strident of the nationalist organisations. Concerned mainly with political lobbying and nationalist 'philanthropy', such as the provision of libraries and book clubs, it was relatively weak in conservative eastern Germany, where the colonial question was hardly to the fore. Nevertheless, Breslau was numbered among the three active ADV chapters east of Berlin[12] and hosted the organisation's general meeting in September 1913. Like other such groups, the ADV enjoyed a schizophrenic relationship with central government. Though its extremists were a thorn in the side of responsible politicians, they enabled the German government to pose as the voice of moderation. Their usefulness was acknowledged by an official of the Wilhelmstrasse, who, paraphrasing Voltaire, said, 'if the Pan-German League did not exist, we would have to invent it'.[13]

The *Deutscher Ostmarkenverein* (DOV), or German Society for the Eastern Marches, was of particular relevance to the eastern provinces of Prussia. Known colloquially as the *Hakata*, after its three founders: Hansemann, Kennemann and Tiedemann, it was established in 1894 in reaction to Caprivi's conciliatory policy towards Prussia's Polish community. Despite the violence of its rhetoric, it strictly disclaimed any aggressive designs and preferred to see itself as a club for 'Teutonic Knights in frock coats'.[14] Yet its goal was to promote German resettlement, to strengthen German cultural and economic interests and to undermine the historic Polish population of the East. (Since it was convinced that all parts of Prussia were German by right, it complained of 'Polonisation', as if it were the German element that was under attack.) Though concentrating its efforts in Posnania, it found a great deal of support in Silesia. By 1914, Silesia could count some 12,000 *Hakata* activists; and Breslau maintained a regional secretariat, run by the brothers Fritz and Kurt Voßberg. Under their efforts, impressive growth was achieved, and a measure of autonomy was gained from the headquarters in Berlin. Felix Dahn, popular novelist and Rector of Breslau University (see below), became a renowned speaker at *Hakata* events. But his success was limited. By 1906, it was noted with alarm that neither the landowners nor the working classes were being attracted. In the ensuing campaign, the movement began to concentrate on the Upper Silesian question and found impressive support there.

Somewhat predictably, national consciousness spread among the Poles in proportion to the restrictions imposed upon them. From 1873, strict limitations had been imposed on the use of the Polish language in Prussia's eastern provinces and a state policy had been introduced of purchasing Polish-owned estates for German settlers. In response, a highly effective Polish national movement had organised itself, aided by a Polish-language press. By the turn of the century, Polish and German nationalism were at loggerheads. Some Germans tended to view the Poles as indolent and untrustworthy and to talk condescendingly of 'making human beings out of them'. For their part, the Poles of Prussia watched it change from a haven of relative tranquillity into an oppressor that rivalled Russia. They became famous among Poles elsewhere for their supposedly German characteristics of efficiency, meanness and national assertiveness. In Great Poland, in particular, they beat the German nationalists at their own game, actually increasing their share of landed property and greatly strengthening Polish cultural activities. From 1904, they launched a series of 'school strikes' in protest against the Germanisation of Polish children.

By that time, Germany had become the single most powerful European state. It stretched for more than 1,280 kilometres, from Metz to Memel on the Russian border, and from Emden on the North Sea to Pless (Pszczyna) in the environs of Cracow. Its 65 million population was Europe's most productive, yielding more than 18 million tonnes of steel and 280 million tonnes of coal per annum.[15] The state created by Bismarck in 1871 had been consolidated and nurtured through two generations and now stood at its height. Yet behind the brilliant façade, dark problems festered. Its political system had been explicitly crafted to preserve the influence of the old elites and to exclude genuine mass participation, and it was peculiarly resistant to change. In foreign affairs, its demands for 'a place in the sun' had led to a programme of armament and colonial expansion, which served only to antagonise its European neighbours. Its Emperor, William, was a manic-depressive with an inferiority complex, whose ill-judged speeches and tactless asides caused consternation both at home and abroad. In the prelude to war, Germany's unbridled ambition added a dangerous ingredient to an international crisis marked on all sides by a fatal mixture of pride and complacency. The assassination at Sarajevo of the Austrian Crown Prince, Franz Ferdinand, provided the spark that ignited the fuse. A flurry of mobilisations and declarations of war came hard on its heels.

Challenged in both east and west, the German military had put their faith in the so-called Schlieffen Plan. As Chief of the General Staff before 1905, Alfred von Schlieffen (1833–1913) had been charged with drawing up military preparations for the expected war. He envisaged a swift victory

German Empire 1871

against France, necessitating a rapid sweep through Luxemburg, Belgium and Holland. This would be followed by the rapid transfer of Germany's triumphant forces from west to east for a concentrated offensive against Russia. In this way, it was thought, the nightmare scenario of a drawn-out, two-front war could be avoided. But it was not.

At the turn of the century, Germany was drawn into Europe's growing international crisis. From Berlin's viewpoint, the Franco-Russian Alliance had put Germany at a distinct disadvantage and the only prudent response was to exploit the Empire's new-found industrial might and to launch a major programme of naval and military armament. Breslau, like all cities, was deeply involved, not least in the expansion of heavy industry. But two symbolic moments signalled her involvement. Firstly, in 1911, a fast modern cruiser was named the *Breslau* in her honour; it would number the later Grand Admiral Karl Dönitz among its crew and would be instrumental in bringing the Ottoman Empire into the First World War. Secondly, in September 1906 Breslau was chosen as the headquarters for the annual manoeuvres of the imperial army.

On this latter occasion, Breslau was visited by none other than the young British politician, Winston Churchill. Then aged thirty one, Churchill had recently been re-elected as the Member of Parliament for Manchester North-West and had just been appointed Under-Secretary for the Colonies in the Liberal Government. A soldier, journalist, author and adventurer, whose escapades in the Boer War had made him world-famous, he already cut a figure well in advance of his years. More importantly in German eyes, he was a personal acquaintance of King Edward VII, the Kaiser's cousin, and a habitué of all the highest political circles at court and in the great aristocratic houses. In other words, he was known to be a rising statesman with a worldwide strategic vision and with access to the King's ear. So when Churchill expressed an interest in attending the manoeuvres in Silesia, the German Ambassador in London, Count Metternich, handed him a personal invitation from the Kaiser.

Churchill seems to have been most exercised by what he should wear. He received a letter on this point from the King's Secretary aboard the Royal Yacht at Cannes, who advised that his regimental uniform of the 4th Hussars would be 'quite right'. A second letter from the German Military Attaché in London, Count von der Schulenburg, put all the details in place:

German Embassy

11 August 1906
. . . You have been invited by the Emperor, and during the whole time of your stay in Breslau you will be his guest, and the *Hofmarschallamt* will provide accommodation for you. You have nothing to do but write to the

German Embassy about the exact time of your arrival in Breslau on the afternoon of the 6th September. You will be met at the station by an officer and will find everything arranged for you.

In my opinion, it would not be suitable to wear your diplomatic uniform ... From your military uniform you want the Levée Dress for the review at Breslau and for a State Dinner which will be given, I believe, the same day.

During manoeuvres, you will have to wear Undress Field Service Uniform with sword. There will be no objection that Capt. Guest of 1st Life Guards attends our manoeuvres *privately*. But he must write to your military attaché at Berlin to provide him with a passport and he must procure a horse for himself. The manoeuvres, I suppose, will be far away from Breslau, and you will run down daily by a special train which conveys only the official guests of the Emperor ...

Very sincerely yours
F. von der Schulenburg.[16]

Having kitted himself out with a few sartorial extras, including the plume of Marlborough's hat and a full-dress leopardskin of the Queen's Own Hussars, Churchill set off on a leisurely summer rail journey via Deauville and Paris.

Few details of his stay in Breslau survive. One letter written in the city on 8 September was addressed to his friend Edward Marsh: '. . . After all, I did not wear the leopard . . . not even a whisker – as the parade was changed to a sort of half-manoeuvre order. He [the Kaiser] arrived, however, growling, at the last minute.'[17] A week later, however, from Vienna, Churchill sent his impressions to a governmental colleague:

14 September 1906
. . . I went to Breslau for the manoeuvres, which were indeed impressive. There is a massive simplicity and force about German military arrange-ments which grows upon the observer; and although I do not think they have appreciated the terrible power of the weapons they hold and modern fire conditions, and have in minor respects much to learn from our army, yet numbers, quality, discipline and organisation are four good roads to victory . . .[18]

The letter went on to report that he had met 'with HIM' [i.e. with His Imperial Majesty, the Kaiser] at the Parade Dinner in Breslau, and that they had talked about South Africa. '[The Kaiser] was very friendly and is certainly a most fascinating personality.' A very long account of the conversation was sent directly to the King.

Churchill's more mature reflections were penned three years later when he travelled to Bavaria to attend German manoeuvres for a second time:

This army is a terrible machine. It marches sometimes 35 miles in a day. It is in number as the sands of the sea – and with all the modern conveniences. There is a complete divorce between the two sides of German life – the Imperialists and the Socialists. Nothing unites them. They are two different nations . . . Much as war attracts me and fascinates my mind with its tremendous situations – I feel more deeply every year . . . what vile and wicked folly and barbarism it all is . . .[19]

Nonetheless, his most apposite comment was made when he returned home from Breslau in 1906. 'I am very thankful', he told his aunt, 'that there is a sea between that army and England.'[20]

Breslau's preparations for war began in the autumn of 1912. Materials were assembled for withstanding a siege and plans drawn up to support a minimum of 390,000 people. The state-financed *Kriegsverein*, or 'War Club', and *Spiel und Sportverein*, or 'Games and Sports Club', sought to raise physical and ideological fitness. In 1913, on the centenary of the War of Liberation, a huge propaganda campaign was launched to encourage patriotic enthusiasm. The Kaiser himself attended the VI Army Corps' autumn manoeuvres.[21]

In July 1914, news of the assassination in Sarajevo repeatedly brought Breslau's students on to the streets in support of their Austro-Hungarian ally. On 1 August, the University Rector, the historian Professor G. Kaufmann, summoned a meeting in the Aula Leopoldina to say farewell to staff and students who were leaving to join the colours. War was being imposed on Germany as it had been in 1870, he said, but he believed in the strength of German youth. He was answered by lusty cries of '*Burschen heraus!*'.[22]

In August 1914, the bulk of German forces, including the VI Army Corps based in Breslau, were sent to confront the French and British armies on the Western Front. They enjoyed some successes, notably the surprise attack on Liège and the battle of the Marne, which almost brought them within sight of Paris. But the line held, and the German advance was halted. In mid-September, German forces fell back to the line of the Aisne. The Schlieffen Plan was abandoned, together with all hopes for a rapid conclusion to the war.

The end of the German western offensive left Prussia's eastern provinces dangerously exposed. In Breslau, which was one of the primary targets of a Russian advance, fear was heightened by the absence of the VI Army Corps, and by rumours that the Russian General Staff was about to force the Lower

Silesian border. As the French Ambassador in Petrograd reported, 'The Grand Duke [Nicholas] is determined to advance with full speed on Berlin and Vienna, more especially Berlin, passing between the fortresses of Thorn, Posen and Breslau.'[23] The scare led to the erection of barbed-wire defences to the east of the city and the evacuation of Silesian children to less threatened areas. In the winter of 1914–15, the Russian army camped barely eighty kilometres to the east of Breslau in the direction of Łódż and, to the south, reached the outskirts of Cracow. German frontier positions were strengthened by a rapidly created Silesian *Landwehr* under General Remus von Woyrsch, which, together with Austrian units, faced down the superior Russian forces throughout that first winter. A solitary thrust towards Breslau in mid-December 1914 hinted that the offensive was about to start. But the threat was effectively removed by the German victories at the Masurian Lakes in September 1914 and, above all, at Gorlice in Galicia in August 1915. It did not recur for thirty years.

Nonetheless, Breslau still contributed greatly to the German war effort. The city garrison, incorporated into the German VI Army, had formed the 'pivot' of the Schlieffen Plan, fighting the French in the battle of the Ardennes in August 1914. It would subsequently see action at Verdun in 1916 and in the following year at Passchendaele. Another regiment from Breslau, that of the 1st *Leib-Kürassiere*, was engaged at the battle of the Marne in 1914, before transferring to the Eastern Front in Polesie. Some 10,000 Breslauers of military age lost their lives.

Two military figures connected with Breslau deserve special mention. Manfred von Richthofen, the 'Red Baron' (1892–1918), remains one of the legendary heroes of military aviation. Born in Breslau the son of an officer, he entered the Prussian military academy in Wahlstatt (Legnickie Pole) at the age of eleven. His first love was horses: he had been a regular competitor in horse races around Breslau and served in a cavalry regiment on both fronts in 1914. The following year, he joined the nascent German air force, thereby confirming the theory – widespread at the time – that pilots were the 'cavalrymen of the air'. After only twenty-four hours' training he set off on his maiden solo flight, which finished with a crash-landing. His first 'kill' against the Royal Flying Corps came on 17 September 1916:

> I was so close to my opponent that I was afraid I would ram him. Then, suddenly, his propeller stopped turning. Hit! The engine was shot up and the enemy was forced to land on our side, as it was out of the question for him to reach his own lines. I noticed the machine making swaying movements that indicated something was not quite right with the pilot. Also the observer was no longer to be seen, his machine-gun left pointing

skywards. Therefore, I had hit him and he was lying on the floor of the fuselage.[24]

In his excitement, Richthofen landed nearby and raced to the crash-site. He arrived in time to see the bodies of Flight Lieutenant L.B. Morris and Lieutenant T. Rees being pulled from the wreckage. He was to become the most successful, and probably most famous, flying ace of the First World War, with some eighty victories to his credit. Awarded the prestigious *Pour le Mérite* for bravery, he was appointed commander of the *Jagdgeschwader 1*, or Fighter Wing 1, which became known in the Allied camp as the 'Richthofen Squadron'. Despite numerous injuries and the efforts of the German authorities to ground him, he continued flying. But by the final year of the war, he no longer flew with the carefree insolence of old:

> I am in wretched spirits after every aerial combat . . . When I put my feet on the ground again at the airfield, I go directly to my four walls, I do not want to see anyone or hear anything. I believe that the war is not as the people at home imagine it, with a hurrah and a roar; it is very serious, very grim . . .[25]

Soon afterwards, in April 1918, the 'Red Baron' was shot down and killed near Amiens. The twenty-five-year-old had fallen to a single bullet through the heart. He was buried by the British with full military honours, while an unseemly spat erupted between the Allied units claiming this most prestigious of 'kills'.

Though not originally from Silesia, the Moltke dynasty had settled near Schweidnitz in 1867, when the Kreisau estate was granted to Field Marshal Helmuth von Moltke for distinguished services during the Austro-Prussian War. The Field Marshal's nephew, also Helmuth von Moltke (1848–1916), enjoyed rapid promotion through the ranks, succeeding Schlieffen as German Chief of Staff in 1906. This time, the Moltke name belied its owner's abilities. He was blamed for fatally tinkering with Schlieffen's Plan, weakening the right wing of the German sweep through the Low Countries so as to preserve Dutch neutrality, while needlessly strengthening the German holding forces in the east. After the battle of the Marne, he suffered a nervous breakdown and was relieved of his command. He died in Berlin two years later. The family's reputation would be fully restored by his son (see below).

The wartime tribulations of Germany's civilian population were considerable. Breslau's City Council was immediately ordered to hand over to the *Stellvertretende Generalkommandos der Korpsbezirke* – that is, to the Regional Military Command. A curfew was introduced from 10 p.m. to 6 a.m. Public meetings were banned; the press was heavily censored. Almost from the outset, the British blockade led to shortages of raw materials and foodstuffs. In 1915, a domestic bloodbath mirrored the human one on the Western Front. Germany's nine million pigs were slaughtered as the country could no longer afford to feed them. Despite this, there was soon a shortage of pork. Rationing was introduced for bread, and was extended to meat, milk and butter and even to carrots and turnips. Prices rocketed: potato prices jumped by 200 per cent: eggs by 362 per cent. One of the city's two market halls was closed. Widespread food riots resulted in many cities, including Breslau. The so-called 'turnip winter' of 1916–17 heralded a further deterioration, and a failed potato crop left millions of Germans on the verge of starvation. The daily diet in Breslau in 1917 stood at 1,132 calories compared with 1,750 in Munich. Ersatz became the new watchword, with snail meat and herb tea on the menu. It was estimated, and reported by *The Times* in London, that the British blockade caused more than 750,000 civilian deaths in Germany.[26] At the very end of the war, the municipal authorities of Breslau decreed capital punishment for food-hoarding.[27] Over the four years of conflict, Breslau's trade had fallen by two-thirds. Gas and electricity production fell, too. Cold and disease took their toll. Tuberculosis was rife, claiming more than 8,000 victims. The overall population dropped from 544,000 to 472,000.[28] Russian prisoners joined the wartime landscape. The first group of about 3,500 reached Breslau in 1915 where they were put to work in the big factories. The Linke-Hofmann works benefited from more than 700 POWs.

Once the Schlieffen Plan had failed, Germany was faced with the two-front war that its statesmen and generals had so feared. Thereafter, though largely undefeated, and indeed victorious in the east, she could not realistically win the war. After the entry of the United States, the superior resources of the Entente powers took their toll. Discontent, when it came, was directed mainly at the government and the supreme command. It was also reflected in domestic politics. In 1916, the inter-party *Burgfriede*, or 'political truce', agreed at the onset of hostilities, crumbled. The following spring, spurred on by the fall of the Tsar, German Socialists recovered their voice. The splinter USPD, or Independent Socialists, began calling for genuine parliamentary government and for peace without annexations. One of the many defectors to the USPD was the Reichstag member for Breslau, Eduard Bernstein.

From 1915, the German conquest of Russian Poland and the restoration of the Polish kingdom under German auspices did not pass without a suitable response. Since the German authorities had permitted the celebration of Poland's National Day on 3 May 1916 in Warsaw, they could hardly prevent it a year later in Breslau. The Polish 'Sokol' Youth

Movement revived. But the Commander of the VI Corps drew the line at recruiting for the Polish legions. Breslau's commercial community briefly saw prospects for eastern expansion and a special Eastern Fair was held in Scheitnig Park in August 1918. But defeat on the Western Front put an end to all such plans.

By 1918, four bitter years of war had eroded the trust between ruler and ruled. In the autumn, impending defeat in the west provided the gloomy climate for a breakdown of discipline. The revolution began in Kiel on 29 October, when naval crews mutinied. Civil unrest followed elsewhere in Germany, often inspired by military defectors. In Breslau in early November, the garrison mutinied, liberating convicts from the jails, looting numerous shops and occupying the offices of the *Schlesische Zeitung* in a vain attempt to influence its content. One person freed from Breslau's Kletschkau Prison was the co-founder of the German Communist Party (KPD), Róża Luksemburg (see below). On the same day as the Kiel mutiny, the Emperor left Germany, never to return. His Empire was pronounced dead.

The First World War for Germany finished in practice at the Armistice of 11 November 1918, and in law at the Treaty of Versailles on 28 June 1919. The feelings of humiliation were crushing. In Breslau, a series of meetings was held to remember the dead. On 16 July 1919, Professor Kaufmann, who had sent his students to the front five years earlier, joined the new Rector in saluting their sacrifice. 'The Fatherland', they said, 'will rise again to be a great power.'[29]

*

In the last quarter of the nineteenth century, Wilhelmine Germany enjoyed economic growth that eclipsed its competitors. From being a middle-ranking country, it became an economic powerhouse. Its output of iron ore in the imperial era quadrupled; its production of iron and steel rose tenfold. By 1914 it was producing fully one-quarter of the world's coal. It also experienced a 'second Industrial Revolution', through the creation of chemical, electrical and optical industries.

In the early rush, quality took second place. In the post-1871 boom, 'Germany' was built in a hurry. Businesses, houses and factories were established in short order. In Britain, the epithet 'jerry-built' came to typify all the shoddiness and shortcomings of Germany's early industrial production. At the Philadelphia Fair in 1876, many German exhibits were denounced as 'cheap and nasty'.[30] Yet, in barely a generation, the pejorative term 'jerry-built' would be superseded by the proud words 'Made in Germany' – synonymous with quality and precision. In 1911, the

Encyclopædia Britannica noted ominously that 'in no other country of the world has the manufacturing industry made such rapid strides within recent years as in Germany'.[31] Britain's favourite market had become its most feared competitor.

Yet the imperial period began with a textbook 'boom and bust'. The victory over the French added a five-billion-franc indemnity to government coffers, which was augmented by an extra 762 million marks derived from the currency reform. The large amount of liquid capital in the economy led to a frenzy of expansion and speculation that was typified between 1871 and 1873 by the establishment of some 726 joint-stock companies. This figure compared with 276 for the entire period from 1790 to 1870.[32] The bust, when it came, caused the collapse of many such enterprises. Public confidence, and that of the stock market, was not restored until the 1880s.

Nevertheless, Silesia benefited from the large-scale injection of capital. It was to be a major contributor to the wider success of the German economy, most prominently in its output of coal and iron. Though Upper Silesia produced less coal than the Ruhr, it still exceeded the entire output of France.[33] Moreover, its yield was growing rapidly. Between 1852 and 1913 it increased thirty-fourfold.[34] Iron production rose from 230,000 tonnes in 1871 to 963,000 in 1910.[35] For the remainder of Silesia, progress was slower. Hampered throughout most of the nineteenth century by the protectionist policies of its natural markets in Russia and Austria-Hungary, the province was forced to redirect its efforts towards internal German consumption. Even so, its native industries of woodworking, agriculture, brewing, tobacco and textiles all saw growth. Breslau was their hub.

Breslau formed one of three Silesian industrial areas, including Upper Silesia and Waldenburg (Wałbrzych). In 1871, it had a population of some 208,000, and ranked third in size among the cities of the new German Empire. By 1910, though its population had grown to 512,000, it had been pushed down to seventh position by the still-greater growth of Leipzig, Munich, Dresden and Cologne.[36] Its subsequent development mirrored its economic integration into the Empire. Its traditional role as the marketplace of East and West declined, but it acquired sizeable service and manufacturing sectors.

Breslau's ancient fairs reflected this shift. Though they continued to be held into the early twentieth century, their emphasis changed. They remained generally lucrative, but some sectors, such as agriculture, went into decline. Whereas 2,540 tonnes of wool had changed hands at Breslau's Wool Market in 1850, for example, by 1900 the figure had fallen to just 360 tonnes. Meanwhile, the growth of new sectors was shown by the launch of a machinery fair in the 1880s. By that time, markets for flax, honey, leather, ceramics, horses and cattle already jostled with four annual fairs and a daily food market.

Manufacturing also flourished. Breslau benefited from good communications and from its proximity to the heavy industry of Upper Silesia. Firms such as Archimedes AG, making engineering components, served the mining and iron and steel sectors. The Linke-Hofmann works, one of the city's largest employers, specialised in locomotives. Founded in 1856, it thrived on the expansion of the German railway network. Early in 1871, it became a public company, taking the name of the Breslau Locomotive plc (*Breslauer Aktiengesellschaft für Eisenbahnwagen*). By 1913, it had produced its 1,000th locomotive and had supplied wagons to the imperial court in Berlin. It was to become Europe's largest manufacturer of railway carriages.

By the early twentieth century, therefore, Breslau was a manufacturing centre that was addressing rapidly rising consumption. It possessed, among other firms, 162 distilleries, 32 breweries, 24 leather factories, 23 tobacco manufacturers, 25 sugar refineries and 31 manufacturers of straw hats.[37] Its 81 financial institutions threatened to eclipse Berlin as the chief financial centre of the Empire. Its merchant bankers – Pachaly, Eichborn and Heimann among them – were some of the most important in eastern Germany. In 1900, a dozen large commercial banks were operating.

Breslau experienced parallel progress in the retail sector. Older establishments, such as the Molinari Haus on Albrechtstrasse, were joined by new competitors. The Barasch Store, on the east side of the Main Square, was completed in 1904 with its impressive *Jugendstil* frontage and illuminated globe and rapidly became one of the town sights. It set a trend of combining large-scale retailing and adventurous architecture, which was to continue in the 1920s with the erection of the Wertheim and Petersdorff stores.

The First World War greatly emphasised the importance of Upper Silesia's heavy industry and of cities like Breslau that were connected to it. It also increased the economic role of the state. By 1918, Breslau had become 'the administrative, economic and cultural centre of eastern Germany'.[38]

*

The German Empire had no state religion, and the multi-denominational nature of German society was a well-established fact. The Emperor, in his capacity as King of Prussia, was *summus episcopus* of the state Evangelical Church within Prussia, but he enjoyed no such headship in the Empire as a whole. The overall balance was roughly two to one in favour of the Protestants over the Roman Catholics. Roughly 1 per cent of the population adhered to Judaism. Practised coexistence was the norm.

The Prussian state Church, like the Church of England after the creation of the United Kingdom, enjoyed all the legal and political advantages of 'an established Church', but only in selected parts of the Empire. It was the spiritual arm of the Hohenzollern monarchy, and carried with it all the overtones of patriotism and loyalism that only the monarchical link could bestow. In Breslau, it was heavily dominated by the Lutheran wing of the movement, although members of the smaller Calvinist wing in the *Evangelisch-Reformierte Kirche* had traditionally benefited from royal protection, ever since Frederick the Great granted them the Hofkirche beside the castle in 1750. With the exception of the cathedral, which remained Roman Catholic, it controlled the great majority of the major churches and schools. The organisation of the state Church was bureaucratic and centralised. The Municipal Consistory, whose superintendent acted as the chief ecclesiastical administrator in Breslau, was subordinated to the Silesian Provincial Consistory, whose headquarters were on Castle Square. Yet the Vratislavian branch of the Church retained its own particular outlook and traditions. It had never had strong links with the Pietist movement, which thrived in many parts of Germany; and it held true to the legacy of the Gerhard dynasty of pastors, especially D.G. Gerhard (1734–1808), author of the much-loved *New Evangelical Songbook*, who had preached a liberal and enlightened approach to religion, and C.T. Gerhard (1773–1841), who was a pioneer of Christian youth clubs and social work. Its newsletter, *Das Breslauer Kirchliche Wochenblatt*, which appeared for 125 years until closed by the Nazis, was the oldest of its kind in Germany. Until 1888, it remained under the direct patronage of the City Council, which only reluctantly transferred its legal and financial powers to a local Union of Evangelical Parishes and to the Evangelical Tax Office. Nonetheless, it retained control of a wide network of influential charitable, educational and social institutions. The Evangelical Military Chaplaincy, to which all serving soldiers, officers and their families were required to belong, added a special flavour. St Barbara's served as the garrison church, where many parades started, and was supported outside the town centre by the Church of the Saviour, which served the cavalry barracks of the 1st Silesian Regiment of Cuirassiers, 'Great Elector'. In Wilhelmine Germany, Protestantism, monarchism and militarism overlapped.

The Roman Catholic Church probably experienced the greatest upheavals, many of them attributable to the doctrine of Papal Infallibility as promulgated by Pope Pius IX in 1870. Both the *Kulturkampf* of 1871–7 and the 'Old Catholic' movement were provoked by the new doctrine. The 'Old Catholic' movement saw Papal Infallibility as the culmination of a long drift towards ultramontanism, which had concentrated the authority of the Catholic Church in the papal curia rather than in the national or regional churches. It emerged from the declaration of fourteen German Catholic professors and teachers in 1870 at Nuremberg. Objecting – like the 'German Catholics' years earlier – to numerous Catholic practices, it generated its own profession of faith, the Declaration of Utrecht, and its own Bishop, Joseph Hubert Reinkens (1821–96).

Though born in Aachen, Reinkens had settled in Breslau in 1850 where he lectured in church history, before becoming Rector of the university in 1865. He wrote important monographs on Clement of Alexandria and Martin of Tours. A study trip to Rome in 1867 caused him to have profound reservations about papal circles, which he expressed in numerous books and tracts. Despite the bitter opposition of Bishop Förster, he participated in the Nuremberg Congress and became a leading member of the Old Catholic movement. He consequently lost his permit for religious instruction in Breslau and was excommunicated in 1872. After that, he preferred to stay with fellow Old Catholics, such as J.J.I. von Döllinger in Munich. In 1873 he was elected in Cologne as the first Bishop of the movement before being consecrated in Rotterdam. He had close ties with the Anglo-Catholic wing of the Church of England and launched the Old Catholic movement in Switzerland. His successor in 1896 was to be the Breslau Philosophy Professor, Theodor Weber (1836–1906). By that time their followers numbered some 50,000.

Nonetheless, the Roman Catholic Diocese of Breslau was still the second-largest in the world, caring for more than two million souls. And it continued to struggle with the consequences of the *Kulturkampf*. Bishop Förster died in exile, and was succeeded in 1881 by Robert Herzog (1823–86), who worked closely with his canon and adviser, the Centre Party politician Adolf Franz, to effect a compromise between Church and state and to make up the deficit in Catholic clergy.

Yet it was under Georg von Kopp (1837–1914), Prince-Bishop of Breslau from 1887, that the diocese reached its apogee. As Bishop of Fulda, he had already contributed to the dismantling of the *Kulturkampf* laws and had emerged as a trusted channel between the Prussian government and the Vatican. His appointment to Breslau was highly political, as it carried with it seats in the Austrian Upper House and in the regional parliament of Austrian Silesia. His new bishopric, therefore, assumed 'an importance far beyond Silesia, which, even in the long history of the diocese, had never previously been the case'.[39] Kopp presided over the regeneration of the Breslau diocese, establishing both a theological seminary and a diocesan museum. Even so, he became embroiled in fresh controversies. In 1891, Pope Leo XIII's encyclical *Rerum Novarum* put the Catholic Church firmly in favour of social justice, and in 1899 Catholic workers were granted the right to join Christian trade unions. Together with the Bishop of Trier, Bishop Kopp stood at the head of those advocating a trade-union movement that was exclusively Catholic. The controversy dragged on until the outbreak of war in 1914. Kopp's later years were soured by his gradual alienation from mainstream Catholic thought, and by a dispute over the perceived liberalisation of German society, which he once described as the 'infection of the west'.

Generally speaking, open conflict between Protestants and Catholics was avoided. But a constant current of hostility ran deep in the attitudes of the Protestant majority, who were repeatedly tempted to believe that their Catholic compatriots were unpatriotic. In Breslau, these resentments surfaced most frequently in the affairs of the student corporations. In 1889, for example, the Protestant society, the *Gustav-Adolf Verein*, appealed to its members 'to uphold the Lutheran faith, which is particularly threatened by the Catholic Church in the Silesian Borders'. In 1904–5, the Catholic corporation *Winfridia* had to withstand concerted calls for its closure in a campaign that has been dubbed 'a belated child of the Bismarckian *Kulturkampf*'. It survived, and in the last years before 1914, the number of Catholic organisations was growing.[40]

The Protestant Church did not escape without divisions of its own. The Old Lutheran Church (see above), based on the synod in Liegnitz, went from strength to strength, and an Old Lutheran Theological Seminar was founded in Breslau in 1883. The city had become the focus of the movement, attracting numerous Old Lutheran scholars, such as Rudolf Rocholl, who became a member of the Church Council in 1885. By 1905, the community numbered some 52,000 souls and seventy-five pastors.

German Jewry, in contrast, worked hard to heal its divisions. The split between the Orthodox and Reform Jews had been narrowed in Breslau by the formation of an *Einheitsgemeinde*, or 'United Community', and reconciliation advanced further during the long reign of the Reformed Rabbi, Manuel Joël (1826–90). In 1872, Rabbi Joël joined his Orthodox counterpart, Gedaliah Tiktin, when they jointly consecrated Breslau's New Synagogue. It stood for all to see as proof of the fact that Breslau's Jewry had attained a position of affluence and respect.

From just under 14,000 in 1871, the Jewish community of Breslau passed the 20,000 mark by 1910, becoming the third-largest in Germany. The prime indicator of its new-found confidence can be found in the cemetery on Lohestrasse, which opened in 1856 and is one of the best examples of its kind in Europe. The overwhelming opulence of many of the tombs and sarcophagi, such as those of the Schottländer, Kolker and Heimann families, bears witness to their status in the imperial era. The fact that the vast majority of the inscriptions are in German rather than Hebrew underlines the high level of cultural assimilation.[41]

It is always tempting, of course, to stress the negative. But any objective survey of Jewish life would present a confident, vibrant community that was tackling its problems with energy and intelligence. Under Rabbi Jacob Guttmann (1845–1919), who for two decades headed both Breslau Jewry and the Union of Rabbis in Germany, Breslau was presented as a model for others. The sheer number of social, charitable, cultural and educational organisations was truly impressive. So, too, was the spread of modern trusts and foundations to finance their activities. Older bodies, such as the Theological Seminary or the Infirmary-Funeral Board, were joined by a wide range of societies varying from the Israelite Refuge for the Homeless and the Israelite Hospice for Incurables to the Jewish Youth Clubs, the Peah Organisation for the Unemployed (1907), and the Jewish Nurses' Home (1899). One group of Jewish women were particularly emancipated and enterprising. Led by the Rabbi's wife, Beate Guttmann (1859–?), and Paula Ollendorff (1860–1938), who had worked as a teacher in England, they set up a Boys' Club, a Girls' Club, a Kindergarten, a children's sanatorium in the mountains, a School of Domestic Science and, well in advance of its time, a Home for Single Women and Battered Wives. These people were in the world vanguard of showing what a modern, liberated, assimilated but still entirely Jewish community could do.

In the early twentieth century, the state's fears about Catholicism gave way to fears about Socialism and atheism, which in conservative circles were often confused. In the latter years of his Chancellorship, Bismarck conceded that earlier anxieties about an anti-German Catholic League had been exaggerated and that the rise of the Catholic Centre Party was less of a threat to stability than the rise of the SPD. As a result, he abolished state control of Catholic seminaries, withdrew the *Kulturexamen* for state appointments and allowed the ban on religious Orders to lapse. By the end of the century, most of the banned Orders, with the exception of the Jesuits, had returned. The new atmosphere enabled the Emperor to raise a Bavarian Catholic to the Chancellorship. Prince Chlodwig von Hohenlohe-Schillings-fürst (1819–1901), whose brother was a cardinal but whose mother and sisters were Lutherans, epitomised the religious compromise that lay at the heart of the imperial project, but his seven years in power were noted mainly for the deference shown to his increasingly (and assertively) reactionary master.

In the religious sphere, the Kaiser personally patronised an official drive for the public promotion of morality and Christian values. The policy involved, on the one hand, a flurry of church-building and a number of 'home missions' to deprived districts of Germany's sprawling cities and, on the other, a determined attempt to suppress pornography, homosexuality, prostitution and artistic licence. The positive aspect of the programme achieved some results. Both the state Church and the Roman Catholic Church sought to ensure that new parishes were created to cater for the spiritual needs of the new working class. In Breslau, several large churches, such as St Antony's and St Augustine's, were built for this purpose in the 1890s and 1900s. The negative aspects, in contrast, rapidly ran into trouble. Both the so-called *Umsturz-Vorlage*, or 'Subversion Bill', which made it a criminal offence to undermine the religious beliefs of German soldiers, and the parallel *Lex Heinze* on literary censorship were defeated in parliament. Worse still, the Kaiser's immediate entourage was embroiled in a series of scandals known collectively as 'the Eulenburg Affair'. In the first of these, the case of *Moltke v. Harden*, which ran through three trials between 1907 and 1918, General Kuno von Moltke failed to prove that he and his friend, Philip, Prince zu Eulenburg, had been libelled by allegations of homosexuality. The plaintiff, a scion of the famous military family, was the Commandant of Berlin. Eulenburg was an aide-de-camp to the Kaiser. The defendant, Max Harden, a Jewish editor, successfully relied on the distinction between homosexual practice, which was clearly illegal, and homosexual orientation, which was not. An attempt to enforce morality foundered on the patent hypocrisy of the would-be enforcers.[42]

The imperial establishment had fretted that the new German masses were being brought up to be godless and therefore unpatriotic. They need not have worried. When the troops marched off to the First World War, they were blessed by their bishops and archbishops, including the new Bishop of Breslau, Adolf Bertram. They marched with GOTT MIT UNS on their belts, and they fell in their millions, with very little protest. There were far fewer mutinies in the German army than among their French or Russian adversaries. The great majority of the fallen were conscripts, who had no choice in the matter of whether or not to fight. As shown by their graves in all of Breslau's cemeteries – Protestant, Catholic and Jewish – they died in the service of what most accepted to be their 'Fatherland'.

*

Prussian Silesia was once described as the 'Sleeping Beauty'[43] of German culture. In response, some may say that beauty lies in the eye of the beholder; and that Silesian culture was neither somnolent nor exclusively German. But one can see what was meant. For much of the nineteenth century, Silesian luminaries often found fame and fortune elsewhere in Germany, usually in Berlin. Gustav Freytag, probably the best-read

German author of the era, chose to settle in Leipzig and later in Wiesbaden. Other Vratislavians, such as Adolph Menzel, Willibald Alexis and the *Jugendstil* architect Martin Dülfer, followed the same course. Indeed, in many ways Breslau was still seen by other Germans as a distant and forbidding place. When the economist Lujo Brentano accepted a professorship in Breslau in 1872, he regarded it as a form of 'exile'.[44] Nonetheless, he was to remain for a decade.

By the 1890s, however, the cultural exodus began to be reversed. The prominence of Breslau as a seat of culture and learning rose steadily. It attracted artists and academics of national standing, such as Theodor Mommsen, Hermann Markgraf and Gustav Stenzel. Indeed, in the space of two or three decades, Breslau was transformed from a solid centre of national standing into a cultural star of international splendour.

The arts, too, prospered mightily in Breslau, especially when the comparative conservatism of Berlin forced out many less conventional artists. The old Breslau Art Academy, founded in 1791, moved into its own premises in the former Ziegelbastion in 1868. It attracted the painter Max Wislicenus (1861–1957) and the sculptor Theodor von Gosen (1873–1943), who was a teacher there from 1905. One of its most enthusiastic students was Gerhart Hauptmann (1862–1946), who found there 'youth, hope and beauty' and 'drew, sculpted, drank, wrote poems, made plans and built castles in Spain' within its walls. The academy developed a particular flair for architecture, especially under the directorship of Hans Poelzig (1869–1936) from 1903 to 1916. He presided, along with Richard Plüddemann (1846–1910) and Max Berg (1870–1947), over an explosion of modernist building, which contributed in no small part to the later development of the *Neues Bauen* movement. Among his own contributions, he could count the Pergola and the Pavilion exhibition hall within the *Jahrhunderthalle* complex of 1913.

Breslau's performing arts developed a very strong reputation. Numerous music societies were founded during the nineteenth century. In 1861, the Breslau Orchestral Society (*Orchesterverein*) was formed, which reached prominence in the 1880s under the baton of Max Bruch and under its later director Rafał Maszkowski.[45] The Opera House (Stadttheater) on the Schweidnitzer Strasse was reopened in 1871, having twice been destroyed by fire, and soon began to attract leading performers. It provided an early forum for the tenor Leo Slezak, the artistic director Theodor Loewe and the conductor Wilhelm Furtwängler, and gained renown as a home for Wagnerian nights. The relationship began with a performance of *Tannhäuser* in 1852, and by 1897 it staged its 200th production of *Lohengrin*. It later held the German premières of Verdi's *Othello* (1893) and Mussorgsky's *Boris*

Godunov (1913). The city's musical surroundings would have inspired many Vratislavians, perhaps two in particular: the singer and conductor Isidor Henschel (1850–1934) and the composer and pianist Moritz Moszkowski (1854–1925).

Two personalities in Breslau's musical history stand out. One of them, Johannes Brahms (1833–97), will always be associated with the city through his *Akademische Fest-Ouvertüre*, Op. 80, which he composed in 1879 on the occasion of receiving an honorary doctorate. The overture contains an orchestral treatment of the universal students' song:

> Gaudeamus igitur
> Iuvenes dum sumus.
> Post iocundem iuventutem,
> Post molestam senectutem,
> Nos habebit humus.
>
> (Let us rejoice, therefore,
> So long as we are young.
> After joyful youth,
> And after miserable old age
> The ground will have us.)

It was a fitting tribute to a city whose academic and intellectual community was fast becoming one of the most distinguished in Europe.

Max Bruch (1838–1920) spent seven fruitful years with the *Orchesterverein* in Breslau. When he arrived from his previous appointment as conductor of the Liverpool Philharmonic, he was already a celebrated composer. His Violin Concerto No. 1 in G Minor (Op. 26), which was destined to reach the pinnacle of the classical repertoire, had been released twenty years earlier. He was also the author of an opera (*Hermione*) two oratorios, two symphonies, two concertos, a cycle of Scottish folk songs and a patriotic hymn to the German Kaiser. During his stay at Breslau, Bruch produced, among other items, his Symphony No. 3 in E Major (Op. 51), the Concerto No. 3 in D Minor (Op. 58), a cantata entitled *Das Feuerkreuz*, based on Sir Walter Scott's *Lady of the Lake* (Op. 52), and an Adagio on Celtic Themes for Cello and Orchestra (Op. 56). He left Breslau in 1890 for an extended tour of the USA before returning to Germany as the head of composition at the Berlin *Hochschule für Musik*.

In those years, Breslau reverberated to all sorts of music. There was a professional concert almost every day. Church music was based at the prestigious Royal Academic Institute, while choral music of various timbres was represented by the Breslauer *Singakademie* or the popular *Bohn'scher Gesangverein* created by Professor Emil Bohn (1830–1909). The Viktoria Theater specialised in operetta. And military music was ever-present – in the streets, in the restaurants, on summer afternoons in the parks and aboard the Oder pleasure boats. On the Kaiser's birthday, every 27 January, the band of the VI Army Corps traditionally woke the citizenry with a rousing march through the streets at dawn.

The stage also flourished. The Lobe Theatre, founded by the actor and director Theodor Lobe (1833–1905), opened in 1869 with a performance of Lessing's *Minna von Barnhelm*, which, appropriately, had been written in Breslau. The Deutsche Theater concentrated on a high-brow repertoire not only of German classics, but of Shakespeare and Ibsen. The Thalia Theatre, with its cheaper seats and populist programme, was opened in 1870 to complement its more illustrious rivals by catering for working-class tastes. And leading the way was the Stadttheater under the directorship of Theodor Loewe (1855–1935). In nearly fifty years of service, including more than three decades as head of the Stadttheater, Loewe created a veritable Mecca of dramatic art.[46]

Breslau possessed a circus. In 1889 a permanent site on the Luisenplatz was made home to the *Zirkus Renz*. Under the 'big top' 3,000 Vratislavians enjoyed daily displays of acrobatics and exotic animals. Breslau Zoo offered similar attractions, but with a very particular twist. There, humankind was on display. The 'People Shows' (*Völkerschauen*) began in 1874 with the display of a Nubian tribe from the Sudan. The exhibits lived in enclosures, where they were encouraged to behave and dress as 'normally' as possible and to give displays of tribal dancing and ritual. The show was such a success that numerous other displays followed: Australian Aboriginals in 1882, Sudanese Dinka in 1894, Kalmyks from Astrakhan in 1897, Ashantis from the Gold Coast in 1899 and the Futa people of Guinea in 1906. The high point was reached in 1912, when a Bedouin caravan, complete with sheikh and harem, acted out the kidnapping of a prospective bride.[47] The Vratislavians would have been amazed, titillated and perhaps even repulsed, but, in the Age of Imperialism, their feelings of superiority over the world's non-white races would have been unaffected. The implicit offence of holding such displays in a zoo would never have crossed their minds.

Physical culture found a respected place in the Breslau scene. The old slogan of *mens sana in corpore sano* made great sense to the imperial generations, and the recovery of ancient German prowess through gymnastics was a fundamental principle of the old *Turnvater* Friedrich Jahn. In the imperial era, scores of organisations sprouted. The *Alter Turnverein*, or 'Old Gymnastics Society', had started in 1858. The First Breslauer Rowing Club (EBRV) was founded in 1876. The popular German Cycling Club (DRB) started in 1884, and in 1900 hosted the European championships in Scheitnig Park. The local Swimming Club (BS), which held river meetings during the summer, took possession of its covered *Jugendstil* baths in 1899. Yet that was not half of the matter. Breslau also hosted horseriders, horseracers, hunters, pigeon-fanciers, duck-shooters, anglers, chess-players, climbers and ramblers. As the natural starting point for trips to the *Riesengebirge*, or 'Giant Mountains', Breslau had four separate branches of the Austro-German *Alpenverein* in 1900. An estimated 40–50,000 people reached the summit of the Schneekoppe every year – an average of almost 150 every day.[48]

Yet Breslau's two seats of higher learning, the university and the polytechnic, became the twin powerhouses of the city's cultural precocity. For, quite apart from their own world of study and scholarship, Breslau's academics were equally active in other spheres. The Breslau Polytechnic, or Technische Hochschule, gained full recognition in 1910, when it moved to its splendid neo-Renaissance building on the riverside, one year before the university celebrated its centenary and changed its name. By that time, Breslau University was the fifth-largest in Germany and was home to more than 2,000 students and 189 academic staff.[49] Its library held 300,000 volumes and 7,000 manuscripts. Its medical clinics for dermatology, pathology and gynaecology were all of a first-class standard. With Munich and Berlin, Breslau became one of only three German cities having both a university and a polytechnic. This complex of institutes of higher learning attracted students from throughout Germany and Central Europe and trained many illustrious alumni. Every major subject was represented; and in an age when the drive for universal education and literacy was attaining its goals, the social prestige of the upper tier of education was at its height.

Two features of Wilhelmine student life stand out. One was the prominence of the student corporations, which upheld an inimitable ethos of fraternity, honour and self-help. Uniforms, obscure rituals and duelling were all part of the scene. In Breslau, all the leading corporations – *Borussia*, *Lusatia*, *Silesia*, *Markomannia* and *Vandalia* – possessed their own recreational villas and residences. They were all either Protestant or non-confessional and tended to gang up on the Catholic *Winfridia*. Another feature was the admission of women, who from their initial appearance in 1895 increased to almost 10 per cent of the student body twenty years later. Clara Bender, daughter of the then *Oberbürgermeister*, was a member of the original eleven pioneers. Clara Immerwahr, who obtained a Ph.D. in chemistry in 1900, was the first woman to earn a higher degree. Ewa Remberg, from Warsaw, was the first foreign woman to register, in 1909–10. Women were admitted to the student corporations as auxiliary *Corpsdamen*, but quickly formed their own Protestant and Catholic organisations. Their preferred disciplines were philosophy and medicine.[50]

The list of Vratislavian alumni, and of other scholars and writers with Vratislavian connections, contains a host of distinguished names. It is invidious, no doubt, to mention some and ignore others, but it is slightly better than saying nothing.

Dr August Mosbach (1817–84), for example, a Cracovian who lived all his adult life in Breslau, was a historian who devoted his career to the collection and publication of local archival materials. Owing to the Prussian censorship, his earliest work, *Pomniki dziejów Polski XVII, 1840–2*, had to be published under the pseudonym of 'A. Podgórski'. His achievements complemented those of the Establishment figure, Dr Hermann Markgraf (1838–1906), who directed both the Municipal Archive and the Municipal Library. Together, they furnished all future historians of the city with the tools of their trade.

Professor Georg Kaufmann (1842–1929), another historian of lesser standing, held strong conservative views and ambitions in academic politics. As Rector in 1905–6, he laid plans for the university's centenary five years later and edited the centenary *Festschrift*.

Professor Joseph Partsch (1851–1925), a home-grown scholar born in the Giant Mountains, was educated in Breslau from the age of nine and obtained a Ph.D. in geography at the age of twenty-three. Classicist, ancient historian and biographer as well as geographer, he is best remembered as one of the founders of geopolitics (see Introduction). His younger brother, Professor K.F.M. Partsch (1855–1932), was the long-term director of the Institute of Dental Surgery, but as an enthusiast for mass sport, is best remembered as the founder of the Academic Gymnastic Society.

Father Hermann Hoffmann (1878–1972), pacifist and ecclesiastical historian, graduated from the Catholic Theological Faculty in 1902. Chaplain at the St Matthias Gymnasium, he founded the journal *Archiv für schlesische Kirchengeschichte* ('Archive for Silesian Church History'), which is still in being. Despite his deep devotion to Silesian Catholicism, he was destined to be deported.

Among Breslau's academic writers, none enjoyed greater popularity than Felix Dahn (1834–1912), Professor of Law from 1888. A sentimental pan-German nationalist, Dahn fielded every genre in the literary arsenal – lyric poetry, drama, academic studies and, above all, a vast output of historical novels – to portray his political views. His four-volume *Ein Kampf um Rom* ('A Struggle for Rome', 1876) is a florid account in the style of a typical *Professorenroman*, of the Ostrogothic Kingdom in Italy. As Rector in 1895–6, he welcomed the first student intake containing women with the ineffable sentiment: 'The past and the future of Germany have always demanded masculine characters.'

The Jewish author Micah Berdichevsky (1865–1921) studied in Breslau in the 1890s. A native of Medzhybizh in Ukraine, he moved on to Berlin and wrote in German. His Hebrew works, which include *Me-Otsar ha-agadah* ('From the Treasures of the Haggada', 1913–14) and *Me-Huts le-tehum* ('Out of the Pale', 1922–3), portray Jewish legend and folklore and examine the dilemmas of assimilation. He spent the last decade of his life working as a dentist.

Jan Kasprowicz (1860–1926), an educated Polish peasant from Kujawy, was a contemporary of Berdichevsky. Soon after arriving in Breslau, he was imprisoned for belonging to a secret Socialist society. He began to write a cycle of sonnets while studying philosophy, history and modern languages, and one of his early poems, *Na targu* ('At the Market'), describes Breslau street life. He left the city to become a professor in Lvov in Austrian Galicia, and then to devote himself to poetry in his Tatra retreat. A translator of both Goethe and Shakespeare, and a lyricist of the highest calibre, Kasprowicz sang of nature, love, religion and social justice. But once he addressed a theme that must often have disturbed a Polish patriot educated in a German university at the height of imperial bombast:

> Rzadko na moich wargach –
> Niech dziś to warga ma wyzna –
> Jawi się krwią przepojony,
> Najdroższy wyraz: Ojczyzna . . .
>
> Zboża się złocą dojrzałe,
> A tam już widzimy żniwiarzy,
> Ta dłoń swą na czoło mi kładzie . . .
>
> A nad tą dolą – niedolą
> Poranna nieci się zorza,
> Na pieśń mą, Ojczyzny pełną
> Spływa promienność jej boża.
>
> W mej pieśni, bogatej czy biednej
> Przyzna mi ktoś lub nie przyzna –
> Żyje, tak rzadka na wargach,
> Moja najdroższa Ojczyzna.[51]
>
> (Rarely upon my lips –
> And may those lips today confess it –
> Does that dearest word appear,
> Saturated in blood: Fatherland . . .
>
> The ripened corn turns to gold,
> The harvesters are already in sight

[But] I rest my head on my hand . . .

Yet over the scene of desolation
The rays of the dawn arise;
And my song, so full of the Fatherland
Is bathed in its divine radiance.

In my song, whether rich or poor,
– recognised by someone or not –
There lives, so rarely on my lips,
My dearest Fatherland.)

It would be interesting to know the relationship in the poet's mind between *Ojczyzna* and *Vaterland*.

The example of Kasprowicz underlines an important aspect of Breslau's role in the development of Polish culture. Breslau was more significant as a magnet for bringing in Poles from outside than as a centre for cultivating the language, literature and history of its own small Polish minority. The resultant symbiosis of German and Polish elements is not understood by commentators who persist in regarding 'German' and 'Polish' as separate categories. Of course, the Slavonic Literary Society (TLS) played a role until it was closed down by the authorities in 1886. Of course, the Polish language continued to have its practitioners and promoters, some of them unlikely candidates such as the Protestant pastor from Cieszyn, Jerzy Badura (1845–1911), who published his *Nowiny Śląskie*, or 'Silesian News', in Breslau. Of course, leading Polish writers, such as Adam Asnyk, Teofil Lenartowicz and Maria Dąbrowska, continued to find their way to Breslau for one reason or another. And, of course, later Polish researchers would lionise the role of the devoted Catholic priests, such as Father Norbert Bończyk (1837–93) and Father Konstanty Damrot (1841–83), who regarded the preservation of Polish culture as indivisible from the propagation of the Faith. Yet there is a serious danger of viewing these activities in isolation and out of proportion. The cardinal fact is that Wilhelmine Breslau was a bastion of a peculiarly brash brand of German culture. And all the thousands of Poles who were submerged by it had somehow to find a *modus vivendi*. Some of them simply lost their Polishness. Some found a balance between the two parts of their identity. Others reacted so fiercely against imperial German attitudes that they became militant Polish nationalists. One of the really interesting questions, which no historian appears to have addressed, concerns the extent to which Polish nationalism in Great Poland or Upper Silesia owed its origins to the reactions of a pre-1918 generation who had lived and studied in Germany, especially in Breslau.

It must also be remembered that neither German nor Polish culture in

Breslau was homogenous. Many Silesians thought of themselves quite simply as Silesians; and they often spoke neither standard German nor standard Polish. Right up to 1918 and beyond, two distinct local dialects flourished, each with its social constituency, traditions and literature. The *Schlesische* dialect of German had its own writers and poets, such as Gerhart Hauptmann. The Silesian dialect of Polish, which the Poles called *Śląski* and the Germans *Wasserpolnisch*, had a heavy admixture of Germanic vocabulary and syntax. It too had its promoters, who regarded themselves as the true natives or 'autochthones' and the Poles from elsewhere as foreigners. For them, 'going to Poland' meant crossing the Silesian border and visiting Poznań, Warsaw or Cracow.

Breslau's undoubted forte lay in the development of modern science. The array of achievements is almost too diverse and too copious to summarise. If one conducts a search under 'Breslau' and 'Science' in any good general reference work, one immediately receives a torrent of exciting biographies:

Alois Alzheimer (1864–1905), psychiatrist
Friedrich Bergius (1884–1949), organic chemist
Max Born (1882–1970), physicist
Eduard Buchner (1860–1917), chemist
Ferdinand Cohn (1828–98), bacteriologist
Julius Cohnheim (1839–84), pathologist
Paul Ehrlich (1854–1915), bacteriologist
Adolf Engler (1844–1930), botanist
Abraham Fraenkel (1891–1965), mathematician
J.G. Galle (1812–1910), astronomer
Eugen Goldstein (1850–1930), physicist
Felix Hausdorff (1868–1912), typologist
G.R. Kirchhoff (1824–87), physicist
Robert Koch (1843–1910), bacteriologist
Leopold Kronecker (1823–91), mathematician
Ernest Kummer (1810–93), mathematician
Philipp von Lenard (1862–1947), physicist
Otto Lummer (1865–1925), physicist
Rudolph Minkowski (1895–1976), astrophysicist
Richard Pfeiffer (1858–1945), bacteriologist
Ernst Pringsheim (1859–1917), physicist
Nathan Pringsheim (1823–94), botanist
Wilhelm Roux (1850–1924), embryologist
Julius von Sachs (1832–97), botanist
Franz Eugen Simon (1893–1956), physicist
Otto Stern (1888–1969), physicist
Alfred Stock (1876–1946), chemist

Ludwig Traube (1818–76), pathologist[52]

One can only apologise for the many names that have necessarily been omitted.

Some of Breslau's scientists were involved in research that caused controversy. Professor Fritz Haber (1868–1934), for example, earned the name of Germany's 'Doctor Death'. After studying in Berlin, he returned to Breslau to take over his father's business, but tired of merchant life and opted for an academic career. Though largely self-taught, he lectured at the Technical Highschool in Karlsruhe before being appointed Professor of Physical Chemistry in 1898. In the early twentieth century, he threw himself into the quest to synthesise ammonia and reached his goal in 1909. Two years later he was called to Berlin to head the newly founded Institute for the Advancement of Science. At the outbreak of war in 1914, he placed the institute at the disposal of the government and became involved in the development of chemical weapons. Less than a year later, on 22 April 1915, Haber personally directed the German chlorine gas attack at Ypres. His wife and fellow chemist, Clara Immerwahr, committed suicide in protest at his work, but he pressed on undeterred. He was later to be involved in the development of 'Zyklon B'.

Within science, Breslau's mastery of the medical sciences was especially remarkable. It is clear that one is dealing here not just with a succession of talented individuals, but above all with a formidable scientific community that possessed the organisation, the resources and the intellectual climate for promoting excellence. Breslau saw the birth not just of theories and hypotheses, but of whole new disciplines.

Dr Ferdinand Cohn, for example, is considered one of the pioneers of bacteriology. As director of the Institute of Plant Physiology at the university, he established the journal *Beiträge zur Biologie der Pflanzen* ('Contributions to the Biology of Plants') in 1870 and was instrumental in bringing the then-unknown Robert Koch to Breslau. It was in Cohn's laboratory in 1876 that Koch demonstrated the origin of anthrax.

Dr Paul Ehrlich was likewise a pioneer of immunology. He studied at the Magdaleneengymnasium and at Breslau University before qualifying as a doctor in 1878. He moved first to Berlin, where he worked with Koch at the Institute for Serum Research, and then to the Institute for Experimental Therapy in Frankfurt-am-Main. He was one of the very first researchers to marry medical science with modern chemistry, and was the founder of chemotherapy.

Professor Albert Neisser (1855–1916) was educated, like Ehrlich, at the Breslau Magdaleneengymnasium and the university. He became Professor and Director of the Dermatology clinic there in 1882. Despite his work on leprosy and syphilis, his name is permanently linked with gonorrhoea, or *Neisseria gonorrhoeae*, which he discovered in 1879. Surprisingly, given his field of work, his villa in Scheitnig Park formed the focus of Breslau's polite society, where he entertained, among others, Gerhart Hauptmann, Gustav Mahler and Richard Strauss. His professional colleagues at the university clinic included several notables, such as Alois Alzheimer (1864–1915), the discoverer of the disease that bears his name; Jan Mikulicz-Radecki (1850–1905), a specialist in abdominal surgery and inventor of the oesophagus-scope; and the world-renowned neurologist Otfrid Foerster (1873–1941).

Foerster had several claims to fame. He introduced occupational therapy into psychiatric practice; he invented the technique of chordotomia, since known as the Foerster Method, in neurological surgery; and he wrote the standard textbook of neurology. In 1922–4, he was Lenin's doctor.

In the age of the Nobel Prize, therefore, when the international prizes were first founded as a measure of scientific and artistic excellence, it need not have been a huge surprise to see that a disproportionate share of the early awards went to Breslau. Two of the city's ten Nobel Prize-winners were literary figures, three were chemists and three were physicists. Four of them were actually born in the city; six were employed either in the university or in other Vratislavian institutions; and only one of them was not of imperial vintage:

1902	Theodor Mommsen	Literature	Ancient History
1905	Philipp von Lenard	Physics	Photoelectrons
1907	Eduard Buchner	Chemistry	Fermentation
1908	Paul Ehrlich	Medicine	Immune Systems
1912	Gerhart Hauptmann	Literature	Drama and Prose
1918	Fritz Haber	Chemistry	Synthesis of Ammonia
1931	Friedrich Bergius	Chemistry	Synthetic Fuel
1943	Otto Stern	Physics	Magnetic Momentum
1954	Max Born	Physics	Quantum Mechanics
1994	Reinhard Selten	Economics	Industrial Games Theory

Among the physicists, Stern had worked as Einstein's assistant, while Lenard was one of Einstein's most unbending critics. Haber's award caused an outcry. Selten, whose father was a bookseller from Breslau, was deported as a schoolboy.

The celebrations of 1913 recalled the War of Liberation and incontestably provided the highlight of Breslau's imperial age. Centred on the purpose-built Jahrhunderthalle complex, they started with an exhibition of 7,240 items of Napoleonic memorabilia, including the main attraction, Napoleon's carriage. Their centrepiece was intended to be the *Festspiel in deutschen Reimen*, written by Gerhart Hauptmann and produced by Max Reinhardt. Designed to inaugurate the hall, it contained some memorable exchanges between Blücher and Wellington among the dead and dying on the battlefield of Waterloo:

Blücher: Brother, the task is completed.
Wellington: Without you we would have lost the battle.
              But, my dear Marshal, what is that?
Three superhuman female figures have risen above the battlefield and are directing their furious gaze at the generals. They are holding each other's hands.
Blücher: That's a peculiar trio.
              Hey! Wenches! Are you dumb?
              The devil haunts battlefields:
              But since the Corsican has flown, no devil of Waterloo
              can scare Wellington and Blücher.
              God knows, he who answers not is a cur!
The Women:
With one voice, loud and fearsome.
              We are the voice with which the World screams for
              peace.
              We are always heard – we never cease! Even in the
              thunder of the battery.
              The commandment says: Thou shalt not kill.
              Why do men kill one another?
              We cry into the void, we wail, we lament,
              That Christian brothers torture, burn, stab and kill.
Blücher: Do you hear that, Brother?
Wellington: Oh yes, I do.[53]

Less than a year before the outbreak of the First World War, the pacifist *Festspiel* stressed the importance of Napoleon but failed to mention the King of Prussia. Described by *The Times* as 'most curious',[54] it was quietly dropped from the proceedings.

Over the imperial decades, one of the features of Breslau's cultural life could be observed in the rise of an inimitable Vratislavian intelligentsia. Given the great variety of eccentric individuals, the group is not easily defined, but some of its characteristics are self-evident. For one thing, it was intcnsely proud of its Germanity, in a way that could have applied only among people who could still remember their families' pre-imperial, non-intellectual or non-German roots. For another, it was determinedly secular, not anti-religious, but convinced that religious allegiances (or the lack of them) should play no part in their public acceptance. It was very affluent, since it was born of a society that respected and willingly paid for intellectual brilliance; and, blissfully unaware of the terrors to come, it was unusually self-satisfied. Above all, it was devoted to the full enjoyment of the high civilisation of which it was both the product and the creator. It had few counterparts elsewhere in Europe. It was less radical in tone than its counterparts in France, less insecure than English intellectuals, and far less discontented than the dissident intelligentsia of Poland or Russia. If it resembled anything, it was the cultural elite that was forming in the USA at the same time, and which was destined to absorb many of its survivors and their values. For those who could remember it, it was remembered with fondness:

My Breslau grandfather was one of the ugliest men I have ever known . . . I remember him as a heavy man, with a very large, quite bald head fringed with white wisps, somewhat protruding watery blue eyes, a bulbous nose and a pendulous lower lip . . .

Every afternoon, after school, I would go to the grandparents' nearby apartment and, after dutifully kissing Grossmama's hand and shaking hands with Grosspapa, do my homework and piano practice under her supervision and then . . . copy paintings from their large library of art books, and play games with him on the wide green felt-covered table which served . . . as a writing and reading desk. The games were dominoes, draughts and a German card game called 'Sixty-six'. Incongruously for someone so formal and insistent on good manners in all other respects, he would permit mutual banter in rough language, 'Schweine-hund', 'Mistvieh', and other such German terms of endearment.

Paul Heimann was born in 1857, of old German Jewish families, his father's from Alsace on the border with France, his mother's from Quedlinburg near the Harz mountains. His father had built up an extremely prosperous business selling agricultural machinery in the eastern rural provinces of Germany. Paul, having passed through a classical Gymnasium and acquired a law degree – I remember once seeing a copy of his Dr jur. Thesis, a handsomely printed booklet of barely twenty-five pages – had no taste for business. Soon after his father's death, he liquidated the firm and thereafter, for almost half a century, lived on the income from his investments, designating himself on official forms as 'rentier' . . .

In his early thirties, about 1890, Paul had married an extraordinarily beautiful girl of Polish-Jewish descent, some twelve years younger than himself. Why she had married him . . . I cannot even guess . . . They displayed to each other courtesy rather than affection. They had one daughter, my mother, whom, with ostentatious classicism, they called Julia. They subjected her to a succession of foreign governesses so that at the age of six she had passable Italian, French and English; pushed her through a classical secondary education, Latin and Greek, and launched her on university studies of archaeology from which she fled into marriage with my father at the age of 22.

In their days of affluence before World War I, Paul and Marie lived in style, entertaining lavishly in their large house – strictly, two stories of a three-storey apartment mansion linked by a vast hall and ballustraded staircase. They travelled extensively, especially to Italy and France, would think nothing of taking the train 300km to Berlin for a night at the opera . . . and collected *objets d'art*, with one of the best private collections of miniatures in Germany as the *pièce de résistance*. Their German, like that of most educated middle-class Germans of an earlier generation, was studded with French words, such as *étui, paletot, pince-nez, parapluie, parterre* . . .

Whether Paul had any serious occupations . . . I do not know . . . He devoted himself to unpaid charitable activities, an honorary treasurer of the Jewish orphanage and member of the municipal social welfare committees, and to his two hobbies, the history of art and the history of the Papacy. He had a substantial library in both fields and would spend several hours each day reading large tomes in German, French and Italian – Burckhardt, Ranke, Taine and others. I still possess a leather-bound notebook in which he meticulously recorded, in his neat small sloping hand, with dates over a period of forty years, every serious book he read.

In politics, he was, I imagine, a mildly liberal conservative. Certainly, he took the liberal local paper, the *Breslauer Neuste Nachrichten*, while Grossmama read the arch-conservative *Schlesische Zeitung* . . . I doubt whether he had any religious convictions. I am sure he was not a practising Jew, though he did, I seem to recollect, make periodic donations to the local synagogue.

Each day began when he rose very early, about 5.30 a.m., and with two small dogs, a small white Pomeranian and a large black Chow, took the tram to a park on the other side of the city for breakfast. Two or three mornings a week would be spent at meetings of his charitable organisations. In the afternoon he would read and, for a while, play with us. His only regular social activity was an outing, every Thursday evening, with his cousin by marriage, a judge whom we called Uncle Richard, to drink a glass of beer in a nearby restaurant. Once, I remember, he took me to the huge *Jahrhunderthalle*, a sort of steel-and-glass Crystal Palace built in 1912 [*sic*] to commemorate the centenary of the liberation of Prussia from the Napoleonic yoke, to see the 'six-day' bicycle race which was then a

vastly popular spectator sport. Strangely, now I come to think of it, for a
man of such esoterically cultivated tastes, he did not just go for my
benefit; he himself enjoyed the vulgar spectacle. Very occasionally all three
grandchildren would be invited to a *Konditorei*, that curious German
institution which served chiefly cream cakes and ice cream . . .[55]

Like many educated Breslauers, Paul Heimann would have been thoroughly
familiar with the ending of Felix Dahn's *Ein Kampf um Rom*:

See there, my brother, the enemy army massed on the beach. In honour
they lower their standards and the glowing sun sinks behind Misenum
and the Islands. Purple covers the sea like a broad regal cloak, purple
colours our white sail and gold shimmers on our weapons. See how the
south wind lifts the banner of Theoderic, showing the way north, showing
the will of the Gods. Come, brother Harold, weigh the anchor! Take the
helm, turn the dragon prow! Come, Freya's wise bird – Fly, my falcon!
Show the way – To the north! To the land of Thule! We are bringing the
last Goth home.[56]

Imperial Germans loved to think of themselves as the modern Goths or
Teutons. They could not have known that their own empire, too, was
rushing to an early end.

*

It is sometimes said that Breslau was at its most cosmopolitan during the
Imperial Age. Certainly, the establishment of mass railway travel raised
international mobility to previously unheard-of levels. The opportunities
offered by a burgeoning industrial city acted as a major pull on the
overpopulated rural regions to the east and south. Economic migrants
flocked in from partitioned Poland, from Austria-Hungary and from less-
developed parts of Germany. The ethnic mix of the migrants was rich. The
'melting pot' was set to bubble ever more vigorously.

At the same time, the forces of assimilation were unusually strong. Social
advancement in the rapidly expanding economy was largely dependent on
the acceptance of a German identity. And German identity was being driven
forward day by day, both by compulsory primary education and by universal
male conscription. Schoolchildren could become literate only in German,
and military conscripts were not allowed to leave the imperial army unless
they had mastered the rudiments of German. Most importantly, German-
ness carried great prestige. It was connected with wealth, influence,
modernisation, high culture and power. The pot could be expected to melt
its contents and to leave a smaller residue than ever before.

At this point, it may not be out of place to make a small digression into the nature of ethnicity and national identity. In the age of nationalism, to which imperial Germany made such a formidable contribution, it was largely assumed that the 'nations' were fixed, natural, eternal and essentially unchanging quantities. They were thought to have existed in Europe since time immemorial – hence the interest in prehistory – and to be engaged in modern times in a desperate, Darwinian struggle for survival à outrance. They were also imagined in many quarters as something akin to biological species. The talk was of 'races' and 'tribes' and of 'blood' and 'breeds', as if 'nationality' were an inbuilt element of everyone's genetic make-up. Learned treatises were written about 'national character' as if each member of each nation possessed a preordained set of inborn qualities, both mental and physical. The Welsh were musical. The Scots were mean. The Irish were drunks. The English were born with 'stiff upper lips'. Germans were Germans and Poles were Poles just as 'roses are red and lilacs are blue'. Many such attitudes persisted throughout the twentieth century.

More recently, historians, sociologists and psychologists who study these things have come to realise that ethnicity and nationality are much more complex and ephemeral than was once supposed. Two concepts are vital. Firstly, it is necessary to grasp that national identity can be both invented and superseded. Four hundred years ago, no one claimed to be 'British' or 'American' (except perhaps in the geographical sense). But, thanks to the creation of the United Kingdom and of the United States, millions of people have been persuaded to take on an identity that formerly did not exist. Both 'the British Nation' and 'the American Nation' have been created in modern times from very disparate elements. By the same token, two or three hundred years ago, Prussian identity was an established fact. It was carefully cultivated by the Prussian authorities. Nowadays, it has all but evaporated. It has disappeared through the abolition of the state and the dispersal of the community that had created and sustained it.

Secondly, it is necessary to understand that human beings possess multiple identities, not simple ones. Everyone belongs to a greater or lesser extent to many groups: to a nuclear family, to extended paternal and maternal families, to a birthplace, to a town or district where they grew up, to a linguistic, religious or cultural community, to a political state, to a racial group, even to a continent. Everyone, to varying degrees, accepts or rejects the connections that surround them. And everyone tries to establish their own hierarchy of priorities within the numerous competing layers that claim their loyalty. Some individuals adjust well; others adjust badly and develop 'identity crises'. Some find little difficulty in reconciling their links with more than one nation or state; others find it hard to imagine belonging to anything but one state, one nation, one language and one religion. Yet the real trouble arises when outside authorities attempt to interfere and impose a fixed identity on people who have no wish to accept it.

Understanding all this is essential in order to gauge what was happening in around 1900 in Europe in general, and in imperial Germany in particular. Most governments (though not all) were deploying all the instruments at their disposal to instil the same national identity in the minds of their citizens. The French government was trying to turn 'peasants into Frenchmen'. The British establishment was busy trying to convince the English, the Welsh, the Scots and the Irish – as well as the Australians, Canadians, New Zealanders and South Africans – that they were all 'children of the one great imperial family'. The government of the Kaiser was trying to do the same. It wanted all the Kaiser's subjects to think of themselves with pride as 'Germans' and to reduce all other allegiances to a minimum. That, for the day, was perfectly normal. Only two aspects were somewhat unusual. Firstly, the tempo was furious. The German Empire, founded in 1871, attempted to achieve in decades what some other countries, like Britain, had achieved in centuries. Secondly, the methods, though legal, were not always considerate. Imperial Germany, unlike Tsarist Russia, was a *Rechtsstaat*. It did not operate by brute force or administrative licence, but in a psychological climate where the authorities could boast, browbeat and bully. The individual, vis-à-vis the state, could often feel cowed.

Breslau's position in the process was especially delicate. As a provincial city, it did not enjoy the same degree of latitude that obtained in the capital. As a frontier city, on the edge of the Slavonic world, it was exceptionally sensitive to questions of nationality. Yet, as a city where the German element formed a heavy majority, it could afford to adopt a bullish posture. In short, it was more assertively German than other large cities, like Munich or Cologne, where there were no frontiers or minorities to worry about. And it was less friendly to Poles and Czechs, or to unassimilated Jews, than Berlin was. Despite Breslau's proximity to districts that were solidly Polish, its Polish community was both less numerous and more embattled than its counterpart on the Spree.

Census returns are not very helpful in these regards. The religious categories of the period – Protestant 63 per cent, Catholic 32 per cent, Jewish 5 per cent – have little bearing on ethnicity. And foreign residents were registered by citizenship rather than by nationality. Hence people from Warsaw would most likely appear as 'Russian', and people from Cracow or Lvov as 'Austrian'. Yet, ethnically, they would most likely have regarded themselves as 'Polish', 'Jewish' or 'Ukrainian'.

As always, therefore, the size of the Polish population in Breslau was very difficult to gauge. It was noted in 1874 that most of the right-bank suburbs still spoke Polish, and it was often observed that many of the city's maids, butlers and coachmen were Poles. Certainly Polish names were commonplace, as any glance at old photographs of Breslau will confirm. Yet names are no guide to the current identity of people, and are only relevant to descent on the male side of the family. Polish students were present in considerable numbers, representing 10 per cent of the student body. But they were mainly foreigners. Their organisations included the *Polonia* and *Concordia*, and the Silesian branch of the gymnastic organisation *Sokół*, which also operated out of Breslau. Many of these youngsters would soon become players in the Polish national revival, especially in the Upper Silesian movement.

In this last regard, Wojciech Korfanty (1873–1939) was to be a key figure. Born near Kattowitz (Katowice), he came to Breslau as a student in 1898. Once there, he studied under the economist Werner Sombart (see below), with whom he struck up a lasting friendship.[57] He also joined the university's Upper Silesian Club (*Towarzystwo Akademików Górnoślązaków*) as well as 'Zet', the leading Polish-national secret society. With his fellow students, Jan Kowalczyk and Emanuel Twórz, Korfanty began agitating to win Upper Silesian students for the Polish cause. After failing to complete his studies, at a time when Rector Felix Dahn had banned all Polish student bodies, he became a journalist and travelled extensively. Elected in 1903 as member for Kattowitz-Zabrze, he became one of the first Polish members of the imperial Reichstag, before being elected to the Prussian Landtag in the following year. His later activity as a leader of the Polish Christian Democratic Party, as a participant in the Upper Silesian Risings and as Deputy Prime Minister secured him a lasting place in the Polish historical record. His impact in Upper Silesia was crucial, in Lower Silesia, negligible.

Wilhelmine Breslau saw a steep rise in the Jewish population. Figures quoted state 13,916 (1871), 17,754 (1890) and 20,212 (1910). But similar confusions crop up as they do with the Poles. Jews were regarded exclusively as a religious category, so that the large cohort of non-practising Germans of Jewish origin did not count. Nor did Jewish residents with foreign citizenship.

The rise in Jewish numbers coincided with the crystallisation of a new form of discrimination. The word 'anti-Semitism' was coined in 1879 by the radical author Wilhelm Marr, in *Der Sieg des Judenthums über das Germanenthum* ('The victory of Jewry over Germandom'). It marked a departure from the traditional types of religious or cultural prejudice. It postulated a new secular, racist, irrational form, which found a ready echo with many of those affected by the financial crash. The association of

German Jewry with banking and the stock market had reawakened popular belief in a Jewish conspiracy, which was stoked by numerous nationalist politicians. Many people were alarmed, fearing that the Jews had assimilated all too well and now stood dangerously close to the heart of the body politic. They found solace in Marr's pseudo-scientific racism and his crude stereotyping. The 'Anti-Semitic League' was founded in Berlin soon afterwards and several large Jewish centres witnessed anti-Semitic agitation, which in some cases led to rioting. In Breslau, the dominant pro-liberal sympathies of the Jewish community provoked a hostile reaction from the more nationalistic parts of the press. But violent incidents were rare. Indeed a succession of Jewish politicians, such as Wilhelm Freund, were not prevented from holding the prestigious chairmanship of the City Council, or from being accepted by expressly anti-Semitic councillors.[58] The situation was reflected in a crude piece of doggerel from 1879:

> O Breslau du, O Breslau,
> Du alte Bischofstadt,
> Wo's drinnen so viel Juden
> Und Christenfeinde hat.
>
> Wie ist es denn gekommen,
> Was hast du denn gemacht,
> Daß du es zur Herrschaft
> Der Juden hast gebracht? . . .
>
> Sie sitzen schon im Rathe,
> Fast immer obenan
> Und haben Wort und Stimme
> Der Christ – gehorchen kann.[59]
>
> (Oh Breslau, dear old Breslau,
> You ageing bishop's seat,
> Home to Jews a-plenty,
> And enemies of Christ.
>
> How did it come to be?
> What did you have to do?
> How was it that you brought about
> The mastery of the Jew? . . .
>
> They are sitting in the chamber
> Almost always at the head
> And they have a word and counsel
> That even Christ can heed.)

Twenty years later anti-Semitism emerged once again. Adopted by the

Conservative Party in the 1893 election, it was partly a response to the growing immigration of largely unassimilated and impoverished East European Jews, or *Ostjuden*. Between 1870 and 1914 an estimated two million Jews left their homes in Austria-Hungary, Russia and Romania. Though the majority departed for the New World, a sizeable proportion sought to settle in Germany. Some of them were students driven out by the operation of a *numerus clausus* in Russian universities. Others were economic migrants, or victims of more violent forms of anti-Semitism. By the outbreak of war, almost one-quarter of Germany's Jews were described as 'Eastern' or 'Foreign'. Their presence not only posed a challenge to the authorities, but also aroused the prejudices of established residents, not least among German Jews.[60]

For the *Ostjuden*, Breslau was a popular destination. 30 per cent of them arrived there from Austria-Hungary, and the remainder were internal migrants from Upper Silesia and the province of Posen. They were rarely welcomed with open arms. Though policies further west were less stringent, in Silesia they were required to apply for a permit from the local chamber of commerce as proof of their utility to the state. In general, the municipal authorities of Breslau were more lenient towards applicants than the provincial governor, and most applications were rejected at that higher level. Few such permits were ever issued, and most immigrants were expelled after the two-week stay granted to them as merchants. The city accepted 3,401 *Ostjuden* between 1881 and 1913 and had 1,423 registered in 1910, from a total Jewish population of 20,000.

Breslau's university had a large Jewish student body, some 16 per cent of the total, and two Jewish fraternity organisations. The *Viadrina*, which had been established in 1886,[61] operated along the lines of the traditional *Burschenschaften*, defending Jewish honour by challenging detractors to a duel. Its motto *Nemo me impune lacessit* ('No one provokes me with impunity') demonstrated an enthusiastic bellicosity. But the Christian fraternities refused to duel with its members. A wider (and non-combatant) *Verein Jüdischer Studenten* (Union of Jewish Students) was established in 1899. A decade later, 76 per cent of the estimated 1,100 Russian Jews at German universities were registered at just five institutions – Berlin, Breslau, Königsberg, Leipzig and Munich. In response, a Prussian *numerus clausus* was introduced in 1913, which limited immigrant Jewish students to 900 in total, and to only 100 at the University of Breslau.[62]

Breslau's Jewish Theological Seminary was another attraction. As one of only three such institutions in imperial Germany – the other two being in Berlin and Hildesheim – it engaged large numbers of immigrant students:

38 per cent of students at the Breslau Seminary between 1868 and 1914 were eastern Jews.[63] In the 1880s that figure reached almost 50 per cent.

The presence of the *Ostjuden* raised temperatures. To the German middle class, they often confirmed negative stereotypes – being seen as uncivilised, or as 'half-Asiatic' *Schnorrers*, or 'scroungers'. Even German Jews kept their distance. Many had no desire to be associated with their co-religionists, and referred to them as *Polacken* or even *Polnische Schweine*. One graduate of the Breslau Seminary noted how German Jews found favour over their East European colleagues:

> they were looked upon as the leaders in the seminary, and were treated with special tenderness by the professors. Their claim to special consideration lay in their passports; they were after all Germans, while we others were aliens.[64]

The extent and influence of the immigration of the *Ostjuden* to Breslau should not be overstated, however. The proportion of non-German-speaking Jews in the city never reached even 2 per cent of the total,[65] and both the university and Theological Seminary served as engines of Germanisation. However, the divisions within German Jewry were often lost on the anti-Semites. As one such noted during the First World War, 'There is no eastern Jewish question, only a Jewish question.'[66]

The high rate of assimilation meant not only that significant numbers of Jews converted to Christianity (usually to Protestantism), but also that many of them sought to change their names. In the prevailing climate, it was very much the fashion among Jews both to drop their Old Testament first names and to adopt standard German surnames. A Katz applied in Breslau to become a Kersten; a Herz chose to become a Horst; a Kohn wanted to be Roland, but was prepared to settle for Rohn. Prussian officialdom was not amused, especially when applications were made before the applicants had converted. And paths were not smoothed by a ruling in 1900, which put people who were Jewish by religious practice and those who were Jewish only by origin in the same category. Applicants who sought to drop Polish names did not encounter the same difficulties.[67]

In Breslau, Jews were more integrated than might have been expected. They were able to participate in many realms of social life without jettisoning or compromising their Jewishness. Their academics and literati – Heinrich Graetz, Albert Neisser and Ferdinand Cohn among them – formed the elite not only of Jewish society, but of the city as a whole. Their middle class was generally affluent and increasingly visible in the elegant suburbs. Their politicians played a major role on the municipal stage and formed the backbone of the local Liberal Party. In short, Breslau Jews formed part of a largely inclusive and tolerant society.[68]

It is a mistake, then, to look at Wilhelmine Jewry with hindsight or through the prism of later events as a group heading for disaster. The outlook in 1914 was rosier than it had been for generations. As one historian has pertinently remarked, 'it would have taken a great leap of imagination to nominate Germany as the future perpetrator of genocide against the Jews'.[69]

*

In the imperial era, German society experienced unprecedented change. There was a general shift towards urbanisation. The percentage of the German population living in communities of 100,000 people and over rose from less than 5 per cent in 1871 to more than 21 per cent in 1910.[70] The population of Breslau rose over the same period from 208,000 to more than 512,000. The geographical redistribution was so great that in 1907 little over half of the sixty million Germans still lived in the place of their birth.

Yet mobility within the social order was still limited. Though the shrewd and dynamic could always find ways to succeed, movement between the social strata was not easy. In Breslau, the structure of society remained relatively stable throughout the *Kaiserreich*, with around 30 per cent of males belonging to the middle class and 60 per cent to the working class.[71]

Any impression of universal progress therefore needs to be tempered. Some 30 per cent of households in the German Empire lived in abject poverty. Life for the many thousands housed in Breslau's slums was little improved by the advent of the telephone or the electric tram. They inhabited squalid, overcrowded and antiquated buildings, often five or six storeys high, with inadequate heating and lighting. Their children played barefoot in the narrow alleys and open sewers. The fathers worked ten- or twelve-hour days, six days a week, often in the most unhealthy conditions. More than half of the weekly wage was spent on food; one-quarter on rent. Bismarck's 'state Socialism' provided little more than the most rudimentary social-security net. For such people, social advancement was a distant dream. Most endured their lot in stoical silence. A few were driven to desperation. One of the latter was a Herr Schäfer. In August 1883, it was reported that he had hanged his five young children before taking his own life.[72]

Barely a stone's throw from the elegance of the Main Square, Breslau's poor endured one of the highest mortality rates in Europe. With 30.5 deaths per 1,000 per year,[73] Breslau returned marginally better figures than Munich or Chemnitz, but far worse than the likes of Manchester or Liverpool. Municipal policies did little to ameliorate the hardships. In 1885, Breslau provided the lowest level of spending on poor relief in Germany, allocating a paltry three marks[74] per inhabitant per year. Beneath the imperial veneer, dark problems lurked.

Crime increased as imperial society became ever more polarised. The number of cases heard in Breslau's courts grew year on year, with the largest rise in cases of theft and assault. By the end of the century a new prison building was being constructed in the northern suburbs to house offenders. Kletschkau would serve as the city's main jail until 1945 and is still in use today.

For a time, the chief Prussian executioner was a Breslauer. Lorenz Schwietz had been running a knacker's yard in the city since 1886 and had impressed through his professional attitude and his athletic build. Despite holding a conviction for cruelty to animals, he was appointed by the Justice Ministry in Berlin in June 1900 and carried out his first execution the following August. The official report on his debut makes curious reading. It had much to say about his appearance: his 'calm, secure impression', his 'impeccable posture' and his 'good frock-coat', but was oddly silent on the execution itself. Nonetheless, Schwietz was to enjoy a long career in Prussian service.[75]

Royal visits served to distract attention from the everyday grind. William II was a regular visitor. In 1896, he was present for the unveiling, off the Schweidnitzer Strasse, of a grandiose statue of his grandfather, William I. He had been in Silesia for the autumn manoeuvres and had brought the Russian Tsar to Breslau, so the city was very much on show. The buildings were bedecked with bunting, flags and the imperial arms. The streets, swept and scrubbed, were punctuated by temporary arches bearing eagles, pennants and the initial 'W'. Close to the new monument, an elaborate pergola was draped with gold tassels and topped with an enormous crown. The Emperor sported a silver breastplate and an eagle atop his polished helmet. Official guests could view the spectacle from the comfort of a specially erected grandstand. The remainder of the population jostled for position on street corners and rooftops, in the hope of glimpsing the illustrious visitors.

The Emperor returned for the imperial manoeuvres of 1906. Afterwards, on the parade-ground at Gandau (Gądów), he reviewed a guard of honour selected from the Silesian regiments and the Breslau garrison, whose march-past was attended by the young Winston Churchill (see page 275). One wonders whether the MP for Manchester North-West noticed the contrast between the pomp and the slums, or drew comparisons with his own Edwardian constituency. Within a decade, observers and observed would be at war.

The First World War was a collective disaster for German society. No family emerged from its ravages unscathed. The fate of the von Richthofen dynasty is perhaps instructive. At the outbreak of war, Manfred von Richthofen was already a Lieutenant in the 1st *Ulanen* Regiment based in Ostrowo. His younger brother, Lothar, was at Liegnitz with the 4th Dragoons. On 7 August 1914, within a few weeks of Sarajevo, his sister, Ilse, became a Red Cross nurse. Nine days later, his cousin, Wolfram, was killed serving with the 8th Dragoons near Metz. A month after that, his father, Albrecht, a fifty-five-year-old retired Major, returned to active service, and Manfred's eleven-year-old younger brother, Bolko, entered the military academy at Wahlstatt. The family servant, Gustav Mohaupt, joined the 5th *Hirschberger Jäger.*[76]

The First World War touched the life of every German, from the frontline soldier in the rat-infested trench to the housewife struggling through the 'turnip winter'. Two million lost their lives, and millions more were injured and maimed. But their sacrifices appeared to have been made in vain. Germany emerged half-defeated, humiliated and territorially trimmed. The flower of its youth lay alongside the Allied dead of Ypres, Verdun and countless other slaughters. The eastern enemy had been destroyed and had descended into revolution. But the Western Allies could claim to be the victors, not least morally. The Germans were officially designated as the aggressors, the instigators, the warmongers. They were denied the comfort of '*dulce et decorum est . . .*' Their trauma sufficed to plunge German society into the abyss.

*

Politics in Wilhelmine Breslau took place at four levels – the local, the provincial, the federal and the national. Elections occurred at regular intervals for the City Council, the Silesian Diet, the Prussian Diet and the Reichstag or imperial parliament. Vratislavian politicians buzzed like bees in a hive.

To some extent, Breslau's politics reflected the wider affairs of the German Empire, especially when several of its politicians achieved national or even international status. Yet involvement did not bring tame conformity. Many Vratislavian representatives stubbornly defied convention, shunning the imperial establishment in favour of Socialist democracy.

Breslau's municipal politicians were a mixed bag. The liberal Max von Forckenbeck (1821–92), for instance, was a veteran of 1848 and a former President of the Reichstag. Abandoning national for local politics, he served as Lord Mayor of Breslau from 1872 to 1878. He came to special prominence in 1879 when he called the German middle classes 'to the barricades'[77] in protest at Bismarck's anti-Socialist legislation. Though his call fell on deaf ears, he was described as 'dark red' by the Chancellor, his long-time opponent, but this did not prevent him from moving on to become Lord Mayor of Berlin.

Georg Bender (1848–1924) served as Lord Mayor from 1891 to 1912 and presided over the rapid growth of Wilhelmine Breslau, ensuring that the city's infrastructure kept pace with the rising population. His efforts resulted in the establishment of the Silesian Museum in 1899 and numerous hospices for the care of the poor and sick. He was awarded no fewer than three honorary doctorates by the university.

City Council elections were generally held every five years. In place of universal suffrage, an income threshold was employed to determine the eligibility of the individual to vote. Those thus empowered were, on average, only 7 per cent of the population,[78] and the results reflected the bias. Though the Liberals were always well represented, Social Democratic councillors did not appear until 1900, long after the party's breakthrough in national politics.

The most prominent chairman of the City Council was Wilhelm Freund (1831–1915). Born near Posen (Poznań), Freund came to Breslau as a child and, after studying at the university, established himself as a lawyer in 1862. Moving into politics, he represented Breslau in the Prussian Landtag in 1876–9, and Breslau West in the Reichstag in 1878–81. It was, however, as Chairman of the City Council and adviser to Mayor Bender that he achieved most success – holding that position for almost three decades, from 1886 to 1915. He was described as the personification of Breslau's liberal tradition.

Werner Sombart (1863–1941) was less constant in his convictions. Arriving in 1890 as a professor of political science, he was a man of unusual gifts and unusual temperament. As a city councillor, he was extraordinarily diligent – attending plenary meetings, budget committees, party congresses and filling numerous ancillary posts. As an academic, he was extraordinarily eccentric. He lauded Marxism, yet spoke of the 'barbarism of proletarians'[79] and later flirted unsuccessfully with Nazism. He claimed to have coined the word 'capitalism', but attributed its emergence alternatively to the Jews, for their alleged greed, and to women, for the material demands they make on their menfolk. Like many, he welcomed war in 1914, but saw it as 'psychotherapy for the people', and described it as a conflict between 'tradesmen' (the British) and 'heroes' (the Germans).[80] His unconventional opinions and bombastic style earned him huge acclaim as an author and speaker.

Provincial politics, though a feature of Breslau life for several centuries, have disappeared almost completely from modern historical consciousness. The old Silesian Estates, which had operated in Bohemian and Habsburg times, found a belated successor in the Silesian Landtag, which was constituted by the Prussian government in 1825 and continued to function until 1918. For obvious reasons, the Landtag was dominated by political figures from outside Breslau and, in particular, by the landed gentry. Even so, it was not an insignificant institution, and was one of the many things that tied Breslau not just to the surrounding district, but to the whole of Silesia. In 1898, it received a large dignified building on the Gartenstrasse near the Hauptbahnhof, which still stands virtually untouched, but which few contemporary Vratislavians will ever have noticed.

Reichstag elections, being based on universal male suffrage, allowed a degree of genuinely democratic politics. Prior to the SPD breakthrough of 1878, the middle-class *Fortschrittspartei*, or 'Progress Party', held the two constituencies of Breslau East and Breslau West. The third constituency of Breslau Neumarkt remained under the control of the Conservative Parties, whose long-term dominance was only briefly broken by the election of a Catholic Centre Party candidate in 1890. It was the Reichstag elections that enabled Breslau to develop into a national stronghold of Social Democracy.

Though the honour of sending the first Silesian SPD member to Berlin went in 1874 to the constituency of Reichenbach-Neurode, Breslau's two central constituencies consistently ensured – with the sole exception of the session of 1907–12 – that at least one SPD member was returned. Indeed, they supported several of the most prominent names of German Socialism. The breakthrough of 1878 was achieved through the election of Klaas Peter Reinders (1847–79), who defeated the local businessman Leo Molinari by the narrow margin of 9,771 votes to 9,316. Originally from Emden in northern Germany, Reinders had come to Breslau as an apprentice to visit the birthplace of his idol, Ferdinand Lassalle. Finding the Socialist movement disorganised, he founded the newspaper *Die Wahrheit* ('The Truth'). His early death brought more than 20,000 mourners to his funeral.

Reinders' successor was to be the prominent journalist Wilhelm Hasenclever (1837–89), who, as a chairman of the founding SPD congress at Gotha, was one of the party's pioneers. Cooperating with Wilhelm Liebknecht on the Socialist newspaper *Vorwärts* ('Forward'), he soon increased support. He held the Breslau East seat through three elections before being defeated in 1884 by the Conservative candidate and Silesian regional president Otto von Seydewitz. A lively and combative politician, he was fined six times[81] for his conduct during Reichstag debates.

The constituency of Breslau West followed suit. There, the breakthrough came in 1881 with the election of a former saddler, Julius Kräcker (1839–88), who had worked with Reinders on *Die Wahrheit*. Kräcker found an ingenious way to evade the restrictions of Bismarck's anti-Socialist laws.

Forbidden to produce election placards, he printed a notice, apparently advertising cigars:

> Eine hochfeine Zigarre ZUM Preise von 5 Pfennigen deutscher REICHS-Währung verkaufe ich heute und die folgenden TAGE, soweit der Vorrat reicht. Ich erlaube mir, auf diese Sorte ganz besonders aufmerksam zu machen, und rate, daß jedermann diese Zigarre WAEHLT. KRAECKER, Zigarren- und Tabakverkauf, Altbüßerstraße, 35.[82]

> (Today and for the following days, while stocks last, I am selling a very fine cigar for the price of 5 German pennies. Please allow me to make you especially aware of this brand and to advise that everyone should choose this cigar. Kräcker, Cigar and Tobacco sales, Altbüßerstraße, 35.)

The capital letters carried the message ZUM REICHSTAGE WAEHLT KRAECKER ('Vote Kräcker for the Reichstag'). He held the seat until his death.

Dr Bruno Schönlank (1859–1901) was the next prominent Socialist to hold Breslau West, after the brief Conservative interlude. A journalist of some note, like Hasenclever, he had worked both on *Vorwärts* and as editor-in-chief of the Socialist flagship *Leipziger Volkszeitung*, thereby setting the standard for high-quality Socialist journalism in imperial Germany. He served in the Reichstag for eight years and was instrumental in bringing the SPD Congress to Breslau in 1895.

Breslau's most famous Reichstag member, however, was undoubtedly Eduard Bernstein (1850–1932). Having returned in 1901 from London, where he had been Engels's secretary, Bernstein was known to his friends for his affability and good nature, and to his critics for his adoption of English manners. His fame, or notoriety, derived from his pursuit of 'revisionist Marxism', which he had fostered in the 1890s, and which sparked a furious row within the international Social Democratic movement. He represented Breslau East from 1902 to 1906 and again from 1912 to 1918. Though sometimes considered to be on the right wing of the SPD, he was to join the fledgling USPD in 1917, in protest against the continuation of the war. He returned to the fold in 1920 when the USPD merged with the Communist Party of Germany (KPD).[83]

Bernstein held that Socialism was the product of liberalism, rather than of a revolt against the capitalist middle class. Always practical and undogmatic, he dropped his early belief in capitalism's imminent collapse and did not regard the bourgeoisie as exclusively parasitic or oppressive. In short, he argued that the social and economic climate had changed radically since Marx's day and that a thoroughgoing revision of Marxist tenets was long overdue. As he wrote in 1909:

As soon as the nation has reached a political level, where the laws of the propertied minority have ceased to constitute a serious obstacle to social progress, and where the disadvantages of political action are outweighed by its advantages, then the call for violent revolution has become a meaningless phrase.[84]

He concluded that the prospects for lasting success lay in steady advance rather than in violent upheaval.

Bernstein's revisionism marked an important parting of the ways in the history of the theory and practice of Socialism. Viciously attacked by Parvus in the *Sächsische Arbeiterzeitung* and by Róża Luksemburg, who had taken over at the *Leipziger Volkszeitung*, it drew the ire first of Plekhanov and then of Lenin. But its critique of the 'inevitability' of Socialist revolution provided the essential background for Lenin's seminal work *What is to be done?* (1902) and hence for the precipitation of revolutionary Marxism-Leninism. After Bernstein, there could be no reconciliation between the Socialists who were committed to democracy and the Communists who were committed to violence. Lenin thought that Bernstein was a traitor to the cause. Lenin's commitment to a closed revolutionary elite, which was to lead – not follow – the working class, was incompatible with Bernstein's ideas of democratic, evolutionary Socialism. Yet Bernstein would become the long-term winner. His intellectual demolition of economic determinism in general, and of historical materialism in particular, proved very accurate. His revelations after the First World War, that Lenin had been in the pay of German Intelligence, discredited the Bolsheviks. And his influence after the Second World War, long after his death, when the SPD finally prepared itself for government in West Germany, would be decisive.

Paul Löbe (1875–1967) was a Breslau Socialist whose lifetime spanned the gap between Karl Marx and Willy Brandt. Unlike many of his predecessors, he was a native Silesian, a carpenter's son from Liegnitz. Politically active from the age of fourteen, he became editor of the *Volkswacht* newspaper, where he gave keen support to Bernstein. In his memoirs, he described the atmosphere of the *Volkswacht* offices as a form of proletarian ideal:

In September 1898 I joined the Breslau 'Volkswacht' as a typesetter . . . It had once been run by Liebknecht's son-in-law Bruno Geiser . . . and for decades remained purely a workers' publication, free of academics. The chief was Julius Bruhns, once a cigarette maker from Bremen . . . Alongside him worked the cobbler Ernst Zahn and the bookbinder Emil Neukirch . . . A year later followed the printer Franz Klühs . . . the stone-mason Richard Schiller, the gardener Okonski, the painter Förster, the tailor Reinhold Darf and the failed theologian Georg Kaul.[85]

Löbe's own career took off in earnest in 1919 with the calling of the National Assembly, of which he became Vice-President, and the foundation of the Weimar Republic, in which he served as Reichstag President from 1920 to 1932.

The connections with Breslau of Róża Luksemburg (Rosa Luxemburg) spanned twenty years. Born in Zamość, Poland, in 1871, 'Bloody Róża' first came to Lower Silesia in 1898 to agitate for the SPD among the Polish workers. She was to return under very different circumstances some two decades later. Having been imprisoned in 1915 for her vociferous opposition to the war, she was transferred from the comparative luxury of Wronke (Wronki) near Posen to the harsher regime of Breslau's Kletschkau Prison in July 1917. As she wrote to Mathilde Jacob:

> Here I am leading the existence of a proper convict . . . the difference from Wronke is in every respect a sharp one, though this is not a complaint but merely an explanation if for the time being I do not write letters woven out of the scent of roses, the azure colour of the sky and the wisps of cloud, to which you have hitherto been accustomed.[86]

She confessed of Kletschkau that 'the first impression of my new lodging was so shattering that it took an effort to hold back the tears'.[87] Nonetheless, she was still able to smuggle out letters to her friends in the Spartacist League, and even to write a pamphlet fiercely criticising the Bolsheviks and their conduct during the recent Russian Revolution. Her letter to Luise Kautsky dated 24 November 1917 was extremely pessimistic:

> Are you happy about the Russians? Of course, they will not be able to maintain themselves in this witches' Sabbath, not because statistics show economic development in Russia to be too backward . . . but because Social Democracy in the highly developed West consists of wretched cowards who will look quietly on and let the Russians bleed to death . . .[88]

Her pamphlet dating from September 1918 would be taken in due course as 'a clairvoyant indictment of the Bolsheviks'. While granting that Lenin's party was the only one to have done its 'revolutionary duty', she lambasted almost every aspect of Lenin's policy – on land, on nationalities, on the Constituent Assembly and, above all, on dictatorship:

> Freedom only for the supporters of the government . . . is no freedom at all. Freedom is always and exclusively freedom for the one who thinks differently. Not because of any fanatical conception of 'justice' but because all that is instructive, wholesome and purifying in political

freedom depends on this essential characteristic: and its effectiveness vanishes when 'freedom' becomes a special privilege.[89]

They were fine words. Their author was finally released on 9 November 1918 – the day of the general strike when the last imperial Chancellor handed his office to the Chairman of the SPD and former saddler, Friedrich Ebert. White-haired and physically broken, Róża Luksemburg spoke briefly to the assembled crowds from the balcony of Breslau City Hall before hurrying to board a train for Berlin. Within a month she had co-founded the KPD. Within two months she would be murdered, her battered body thrown into Berlin's Landwehr Canal. But Breslau's Socialist heritage was not forgotten. As a commentator in the 1920s would recall, 'Breslau undoubtedly belongs to those places in Germany, whose Social Democratic workers movement, apart from its present importance, can also claim a historical interest.'[90]

*

Breslau saw its most rapid urban development during the imperial period. The primary impetus can be found in the demographic explosion of the late nineteenth century: the city's population rose by more than 150 per cent between 1871 and 1914. As numbers climbed, the conglomeration spread out to swallow further outlying villages. Kleinburg (Dworek) and Pöpelwitz (Popowice), to the west, were incorporated in 1896; Herdain (Gaj), Dürrgoy (Tarnogaj) and Morgenau (Rakowiec), to the south and east, in 1904; and Gräbschen (Grabiszyn), to the south-west, in 1911. Thanks to regulation of the river, Leerbeutel (Zalesie) (1901) and Karlowitz (Karłowice) (1904) could both be established as modern garden suburbs in the once-marshy valley.

The communication network had to develop to keep pace with the urban expansion. In a spate of bridge-building, old-fashioned or temporary river crossings were replaced by magnificent iron structures. The Lessing Bridge, to the east of the Old Town, was constructed in 1874. The King's Bridge and Wilhelm's Bridge, connecting the Bürgerwerder to the north and south, were erected in 1876. From 1883, the Gneisenau Bridge, formerly the Corpus Christi Bridge, linked the Sand Island to the north bank of the river. And the Cathedral Bridge, joining Sand Island to the (former) Cathedral Island, was completed seven years later. In all, some sixteen major new bridges were built.

Tramways saw marked growth in the late nineteenth century. In 1876, the *Breslauer Straßen-Eisenbahn-Gesellschaft* (BSEG) won the contract to provide a private tram service. And on 10 July of the following year, the intriguing sight of a horse-drawn tram greeted people on the streets. The

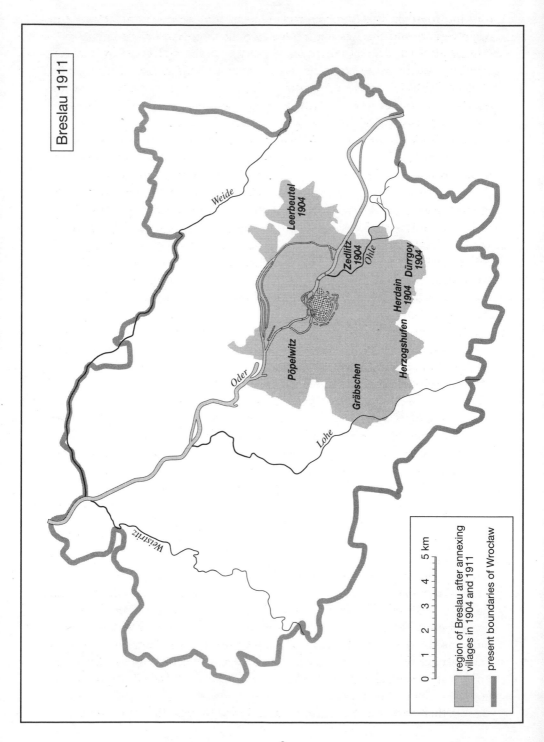

Breslau 1911

Weide

Leerbeutel 1904

Zedlitz 1904

Ohle

Herdain 1904

Dürrgoy 1904

Herzogshufen

Pöpelwitz

Gräbschen

Oder

Lohe

Weistritz

0 1 2 3 4 5 km

region of Breslau after annexing villages in 1904 and 1911

present boundaries of Wrocław

opening route on that summer morning ran from the Königsplatz via the Main Square and the Lessing Bridge to Scheitnig (Szczytniki) in the east. Numerous routes were subsequently added. Some sixteen years later, a small, privately owned electric tram route, the *Elektrische Straßenbahn Breslau* (ESB) joined the city centre with the burgeoning suburbs. All of the horse-drawn routes were electrified in 1902, and by 1914 Breslau possessed a comprehensive tram network serving most districts.

Other improvements followed hard and fast. In 1881, the first telephone and telegraph office was opened, with just sixty-four subscribers. The link to Berlin was completed seven years later, by which time it had some 1,200 users. In 1871, a new waterworks on Am Weidendamm began to supply filtered river water. It was complemented, in 1904, by a further installation using groundwater. Repeated flood damage prompted a plan for a relief canal, which was constructed between 1912 and 1917 and named the Breitenbach. It began near Wilhelmshafen to the east and rejoined the Alte Oder near the Hindenburg Bridge. It turned the suburbs of Scheitnig, Wilhelmsruh (Zacisze), Grüneiche (Dąbie) and Bischofswalde (Biskupin) into an artificial island.

The municipal gas supply was brought on-stream in 1864, and two further gasworks were commissioned before the building of a fourth station in 1904 in Breslau-Dürrgoy, which made the older ones obsolete. By 1914, the extended Dürrgoy gasworks supplied 85 per cent of the city's requirements. Similar advances were made with the electricity supply. An experimental installation on the Lessingplatz gave way in 1888 to a permanent power station on the Kleinen Groschengasse to the south of the Old Town. Growing demand required a second power station, which was opened in 1901 on the Schieben Weg.

Rapid urban growth in this period did not inhibit fine architecture. The victorious war of 1870–1 had brought a marked increase in public spending, which was often dedicated to the erection of statues. The Empress Augusta monument was typical. It was built in 1874 to commemorate the fallen of the Franco-Prussian War. As the centrepiece of the manicured gardens on the left bank of the Oder, it consisted of an elegant neo-Gothic spire with a pair of cannons at its base. Others followed, such as the statue of the Prussian legal reformer Svarez, on the Ritterplatz (1896), the Moltke statue on Kaiser-Wilhelm Strasse (1899) and the statue of the Iron Chancellor, built on the Königsplatz by the *Bismarckverein* (1900). Many new schools and hospitals were also established: the Wenzel Hancke Hospital (1878), the University Hospital complex (1890–1907) and the Elisabeth Gymnasium (1903), to name but three.

Together with the Sternstrasse and Kaiserstrasse, the new suburb of

Scheitnig was typical of the *Gründerzeit* and provided some of the smartest addresses. In the city centre, the Barasch store was a showpiece of *Jugendstil* design as well as a precursor of the consumerist age. Numerous private houses, such as the Haase and Neisser villas, were proof of the extraordinary wealth that was being generated. Such wealth, however, did not always accompany good taste. In 1896, the province of Silesia made a gift to Breslau of a statue of Emperor William I. Cast in bronze, the super-lifesize monarch stood atop a six-metre-high white marble plinth close to the Schweidnitzer Strasse. It was surrounded by figures, friezes, columns and numerous steps. For Emperor William II, it was the height of refinement. The English-woman Daisy Pless, who watched the unveiling, described it as 'a mediocre work, very high with steps leading up to it, and a great marble block on which stands the bronze equestrian statue of the old Emperor'.[91]

The Neue Synagogue of 1872 was opulent, but genuinely imposing. It was designed by the Silesian architect Edwin Oppler (1831–80), whose other works included the synagogues in Schweidnitz (Świdnica) and Hanover. Built in the Byzantine style, it was second only to that in Berlin in size and magnificence. Its sixty-metre central dome was complimented by four lesser octagonal towers and a beautiful rosette window above the main entrance. It dominated the southern suburbs.

Breslau gained a reputation as a home of modernist architecture. Though little innovation can be seen in the Kletschkau Prison (1888) or the Technical Highschool (1910), two successive directors of the Breslau Planning Department can be credited with championing the architectural avant-garde. Richard Plüddemann (1846–1910) exerted a decisive influence between 1885 and 1908. After supervising the construction of numerous public buildings, he crowned his career, in cooperation with F.A. Küster, with the so-called Rittermarkthalle (1908), built on the site of the former Sand Arsenal in the Old Town. Despite a somewhat traditional exterior, the interior employed the innovative use of stressed concrete arches.

Concrete was to be of great significance for Plüddemann's successor, Max Berg (1870–1947), who was born in Stettin (Szczecin) and had trained at the Technical Highschool in Berlin-Charlottenburg, before coming to Breslau in 1909. He is best remembered for the design of the *Jahrhunderthalle*, or 'Century Hall' (1913), which formed the centrepiece of the centennial celebrations. Constructed entirely of stressed concrete, its modernist credentials contrasted sharply with the studied pomposity of the contemporary *Völkerschlacht* monument in Leipzig. It could seat more than 10,000 people and supported a dome, whose span of sixty-seven metres was larger than St Peter's. It would survive all the disasters of the twentieth century, housing all manner of political, cultural and sporting events and receiving all manner of guests – from Adolf Hitler at one end of the spectrum to John Paul II at the other.

Above all, it is only fair to stress that Breslau had grown into a place of considerable beauty. The worst of the slums had been cleared, and the industrial sites did not disfigure the central districts. There were numerous spacious parks, leafy promenades, tree-lined boulevards, flower-filled gardens, extensive riverside vistas, monumental buildings, quaint old corners and fashionable new suburbs. The new blended well with the old. The hundred spires of the city stood tall. The architectural spectrum contained first-class examples of the Gothic, baroque, classical and modernist styles. Few people would have disagreed: Breslau was a good place in which to live.

On the eve of the First World War, Breslau was well connected by railway to all parts of Germany and Europe. In the international railway timetables, it was sufficiently important to be listed as a separate destination on the main 'ABC Routes' from London. Three such routes were advertised, each with a sea crossing and a connection in Berlin. The first route left Charing Cross at 9 p.m., used the night ferry between Dover and Ostend, and reached Breslau the following day after twenty-six hours and 1,430 kilometres. The second route started a Victoria at 10 a.m., took the day boat to Flushing, then proceeded to Breslau over twenty-seven hours, arriving at 2 p.m. on the second afternoon. The third route departed from Liverpool Street at 8.30 p.m. for Harwich, boarded the overnight boat to the Hook of Holland, then caught up with the Ostend passengers to arrive with them on the same late-evening train from Berlin after twenty-six and a half hours. The price of tickets London–Breslau did not vary according to the route taken. First class cost £5 10s. 6d. (single) and £10 7s. 8d. (return): second class cost respectively £3 10s. 4d. and £6 13s. 3d.

From Breslau, travellers could comfortably go to Berlin, Posen or Dresden for the day with ample time for lunch or business. The morning train for Berlin via Kohlfurt (Węgliniec) left the Hauptbahnhof at 6.05 a.m., pulling into the Schlesischer Bahnhof at 10.50 and into Charlottenburg at 11.29. Return trains left Berlin at either 4.57 or 5.30 p.m. arriving back at 9.45 or 11.27. For Posen, one could leave at 7.34 a.m. and arrive in less than two and a half hours at 9.59. The train continued to Stangardt. On the return journey, one could chose between the direct express at 7 p.m., which came in at 9.35, or the late train at 9.38, which had one home on the stroke of midnight. For destinations in Saxony, slower trains left the Freiburger Bahnhof for Görlitz and thence for Zittau or Dresden.[92]

Passengers travelling further afield could cover surprising distances in the space of a single day. By catching the early train to Berlin at 3.30 a.m., one could make connections after 8 a.m. heading for Hamburg, Cologne or Copenhagen. International *wagons-lits* took one overnight in stately stages to Stockholm by 8.49 the next morning, to St Petersburg by 11.35 or to Christiana at midday.[93]

Breslau's connections to the south were equally good. There were express services via Oderberg to Vienna in eight and a half hours, to Budapest in five minutes under twelve hours and to Misskolcz in twelve and a half hours. The Cracow express took almost exactly eight hours. To reach Warsaw was more difficult There was no direct connection and there were two options. One could go either on the line via Krotoschin and Kalisz to Łódź, and thence to Warsaw in about eleven hours, or via Kattowitz in about fifteen hours. The Silesian express sped to Kattowitz in three hours flat. But the rest of the journey, including a halt at the Russian frontier at Granica, could take a further twelve hours.

Breslau's local train services were excellent. There were six trains per day to the mountains at Charlottenbrunn, ten per day to Waldenburg and Hirschberg (Jelenia Góra), and another nine per day to Glatz (Kłodzko) and the Bohemian border at Mittelwalde (Międzylesie):

	a.m.				p.m.				
Breslau	6.15	7.12	10.01	10.30	2.20	3.22	6.04	7.00	12.06
Strehlen	7.15	7.45	10.34	11.20	3.14	*	6.58	7.33	12.59
Camenz	8.13	8.30	11.13	12.15	4.07	4.30	7.56	8.15	1.50
Glatz	9.03	8.57	11.40	12.49	5.09	5.07	8.30	8.38	2.23
Mittelw.	10.12	*	12.31	2.47	6.56	*	9.51	*	*[94]

Breslau's favourite railway, however, ran along the 41.5 kilometres of narrow-gauge track belonging to the *Breslau-Trebnitz-Prausnitzer Kleinbahn*. Opened on 10 July 1897, it started from its own small-scale Gothic station on the Rossplatz, crossed the river on the tramlines of the Gröschel Bridge, turned sharp right into the first halt at Karlowitz (Karłowice), then climbed out of the city into the open countryside to the north. Every hour during the day, a tall-chimneyed tank engine puffed its way along the seventy-five-centimetre track, pulling a mixture of passenger carriages (second- and third-class), closed box cars, open freight wagons and a post van. The journey took one and a half hours, including twenty stops:

1. Breslau – Kleinbahn Pb
2. Breslau – Karlowitz
3. Breslau – Rosenthal
4. Breslau – Lilienthal
5. Weide

6. Hunern
7. Hunern – Simsdorf
8. Kapsdorf
9. Paulskirch
10. Schimmerau

11. Schön Ellguth
12. Wiese
13. Hochkirch
14. Peterwitz
15. Pflaumendorf

16. Trebnitz – Hedwigsbad
17. Trebnitz – Stadtpark
18. Erbenfelde
19. Prausnitz – Ost
20. Prausnitz

At Prausnitz (Prusice), the line joined up with another local railway which went as far as Militsch (Milicz). The initial tariff was fixed at three pfennigs/km for third class, five for second class and eight pfennigs/km/tonne for freight. On Sundays and holidays, special excursion trains ran to Hochkirch (Wysoki Kościoł) and to Trebnitz (Trzebnica). Pilgrims mixed with tourists, with peasants heading for the market, commuters and schoolchildren, clients of the spa and family outings. The 'Trebnitzer Puffer' was to survive two world wars and would not close until finally doomed by neglect in 1967.[95]

Visitors to Breslau had a wide choice of guidebooks. The more discerning would probably have taken their *Baedeker* (see Appendix). The less demanding Briton or American would have carried their copy of Bradshaw's trusty *Continental Guide*:

Breslau – Pop. 512,105.
HOTEL MONOPOL – First Class, on the Palais Platz. Every modern comfort. Suites and single rooms. Rooms from 3M.
VIER JAHRESZEITEN; NORD; KRONPRINZ.
There are four Railway Stations at Breslau – the Hauptbahnhof, on the south side; Oderthorbahnhof, on the north side; the Niederschlesische-Märkischbahnhof and the adjoining Freiburgerbahnhof, on the west side.
TAXIMETER CABS – 1 or 2 persons 1000 meters 50pf., and 10pf. for each additional 500 meters. 3 or 4 persons 750 meters 50pf.
Breslau, the capital of Silesia and the second city in Prussia, is situated in a fertile plain, on both banks of the Oder, at the confluence of the Ohle. It is one of the most important centres of industry and commerce in Germany, engineering is especially prosperous, there are many distilleries, while the country round sends in great quantities of wool, grain, timber, cloth.
To westward from the open space before the Hauptbahnhof runs the Gartenstrasse, and out of this street, the first street north, on right hand, Neue Schweidnitzerstrasse leads right across the city, from south to north, through the Grosse Ring (otherwise Der Ring), the centre of Breslau's street traffic.
Shortly after turning into Neue Schweidnitzerstrasse, and traversing the broad Tauentzienplatz. The old city moat is crossed, and here, right and left, are public buildings; on the right are statue of Emperor William

323

I, and Corpus Christi Church; on the left are Government Offices and Stadt Theater, with, behind, the Palaisplatz, Royal Palace, Kunst Gewerbe Museum, and the Börse (Exchange). A little further north Schweidnitzerstrasse runs into Der Ring.

The noble RATHHAUS is on the south east side of Der Ring, it is of 15th cent.; in the Fürstensaal (princes' hall) are portraits: under the building is the Schweidnitzer Keller, a finely vaulted restaurant; on the east side of building is the Staupsäule (pillory). The Stadthaus adjoins the Rathhaus. In Der Ring are statues of Frederick the Great and Frederick William III; and the west side of Der Ring is a house (1500) once occupied by Kings of Bohemia.

Off the south west corner of Der Ring is Blücherplatz, with a statue of Blücher, and the Alte Börse (now municipal offices). Behind the Alte Börse, in the Ross Markt, is the Savings Bank, where is the City Library of 150,000 vols, 3,600 MSS., and the Civic Archives – open daily. 9.0 a.m. to 2.0 p.m.

Off the north west corner of Der Ring is Elisabethkirche, Protestant, founded 1257, tower 335 ft high; on either side of high altar are portraits of Luther and Melanchthon by Cranach; several interesting tombstones, stained glass windows. Maria Magdalenea Kirche, Protestant, is one street east of Der Ring.

The continuation of Schweidnitzerstrasse from north east corner of Der Ring, leads to a cluster of buildings by the river. Here is the University (2,000 students), then, eastward, the Ursuline Convent and the Law Courts; across the Sandbrücke is the University Library of 350,000 vols. of MSS., and specimens of early printing – an Archaeological Museum is in same building.

The Sandkirche (Church of Our Lady on the Sand), 14th cent., is immediately north of the University Library. Across the Dombrücke, eastward, on the left of Domstrasse, is the Kreuzkirche, 13th cent.; tomb of Duke Henry IV of Silesia before the high altar. At end of Domstrasse is the DOM, or Cathedral of St John the Baptist, 14th cent., the original building dating from 12th cent.; the interior has several monuments, statues and paintings, including, in Chapel of St John, north aisle, Cranach's 'Madonna among the Pines.' The residence of the Prince Bishop is to the south west of the Dom. St Ægidius, oldest church in Breslau, is to the north of the Dom.

A little east of the Dom is the Lessingbrücke, across this, south, on the right, are Government Offices, and, next to them, the Holtei Höhe, and beyond, the Kaiserin Augusta Platz, where is a School of Art. North of the Dom is Botanical Garden.

At the MUSEUM, west of the Hauptbahnhof and south of the Palaisplatz, is a collection of modern paintings and duplicates of old masters. Open daily, except Mon., 10.0 a.m. to 2.0 p.m.; Sun., 11.0 a.m. to 4.0 p.m. In the same building is the Collection of the Silesian Art Union, open 10.0 a.m. to 4.0 p.m.; Sun., 11.0 to 2.0, 1mk.

The principal POST OFFICE is an imposing building at the east end of Albrechtstrasse, near centre of city, due north of Hauptbahnhof.

H.B.M.'s VICE-CONSUL – H. Humbert, Esq.

U.S. CONS. – H.L. Spahr, Esq.[96]

Breslau in 1918 belonged to the part of Germany that felt most betrayed by the terms under which the First World War ended. It was natural that western Germany was particularly sensitive to events on the Western Front, where the Allied armies gained a clear advantage. By the same token, eastern Germany was particularly impressed by the outcome of fighting on the Eastern Front. There, the score was absolutely unambivalent. Breslauers were in the front rank of Germans who had seen the enemy on their doorstep in 1914, and who had then watched as he was driven back 1,600 kilometres and completely defeated. Of course, they could see the implications of the débâcle in the West, like anyone else. But for them, the emotions provoked by falling from the heights of prospective victory to the depths of retreat, revolution and war guilt were unusually bitter. The consequences were to be graver than anyone could have imagined.

SEVEN

Breslau before and during the Second World War, 1918–45

The politics of inter-war Germany passed through three distinct phases. In 1918–20, anarchy spread far and wide in the wake of the collapse of the German Empire. Between 1919 and 1933, the Weimar Republic re-established stability, then lost it. And from 1933 onwards, Hitler's 'Third Reich' took an ever firmer hold. Events in Breslau, as in all German cities, reflected each of the phases in turn.

The German Empire collapsed on 9 November 1918. As the Kaiser departed into exile in the Netherlands, the headless state descended into chaos. Across Europe, numerous parties fought over the remains of four defunct empires. As Churchill wrote, the end of the 'war of the giants' ushered in a 'war of the pygmies'. Germany faced conflict both externally and internally. Fighting broke out on the eastern frontier, while various political groups struggled bitterly to gain the upper hand in government. With Berlin in the throes of revolution and its aftermath, a new republic was planted in the relative tranquillity of the Saxon city of Weimar.

The first years of the Weimar Republic were characterised by extreme political fragility. Despite its impeccable democratic credentials, the young seedling was perpetually under threat. Mutual recriminations abounded. On the right, the myth of the *Dolchstosslegende* – the 'stab in the back' supposedly delivered by the Socialists to the German military – was born. On the left, radical Socialists prepared for a thoroughgoing Soviet-style revolution. In the centre, politicians such as Matthias Erzberger, a warmonger-turned-pacifist, strove to keep the militants apart. Erzberger's signing of the armistice was to cost him his life. He was murdered by right-wing assassins in 1921. Weimar had few champions of its own and survived its infancy only through the efforts of each side to prevent political power falling to their opponents.

The cycle of violence began when the President of the new Reichstag in Berlin, Friedrich Ebert, arranged a pact with the head of the military, General Wilhelm Groener. Overestimating the danger from the Soviet-style

Workers' and Soldiers' Councils, Ebert courted the army, then agreed to accept the support of military circles that were fundamentally hostile to his political aims. By the same act, he diminished the influence of his natural supporters – the largely Socialist councils.

In Breslau, the overthrow of the imperial authorities passed off without major disturbance. On 8 November, a Loyal Appeal for the citizens to uphold their duties to the Kaiser was distributed in the names of the Lord Mayor, Paul Matting, Archbishop Bertram and others. But it had no great effect. The Commander of the VI Army Corps, General Pfeil, was in no mood for a fight. He released the political prisoners, ordered his men to leave their barracks, and, in the last order of the military administration, gave permission to the Social Democrats to hold a rally in the *Jahrhunderthalle*. The next afternoon, a group of dissident airmen arrived from their base at Brieg (Brzeg). Their arrival spurred the formation of 'soldiers' councils' (that is, soviets) in several military units and of a 100–strong Committee of Public Safety by the municipal leaders. The Army Commander was greatly relieved to resign his powers.

The *Volksrat*, or 'People's Council', was formed on 9 November 1918, from Social Democrats, union leaders, Liberals and the Catholic Centre Party. It was led by the Socialist Paul Löbe.[1] Its relations with its opponents were largely peaceful. In its dealings with the officials of the previous administration, it made no attempt to remove them, but merely assigned representatives to facilitate cooperation. It then widened its remit to serve as a central executive for the province of Silesia as a whole. As Löbe noted in his memoirs, the 'revolution' in Breslau was evidently as consensual as possible:

> The coming of the new constellation of power passed in Breslau with surprising calmness, even with celebration ... Three regiments of artillery and infantry, led by the soldiers' councils, marched into the [Jahrhunderthalle]. An endless stream of Breslauers followed ... The powerful organ roared out the Marseillaise ... Then the builder of the hall, Max Berg, dedicated it as a 'Cathedral of Democracy'. Fritz Voigt ... spoke in the name of the soldiers, and I spoke for the Social Democratic Party ... We had brought about a quiet revolution, no human life had been sacrificed and no damage had been done.'[2]

Across Germany, delicate political balancing acts of this sort were soon unsettled by the return of large numbers of demobilised – and often demoralised – soldiers. In Breslau, the *Volksrat* discovered that some 170,000 soldiers and displaced persons were expected to return to a city that could muster emergency quarters for little more than 47,000.[3] The resultant overcrowding radicalised Breslau politics and contributed to the worrying set of social statistics (see below).

It was at this juncture that Ebert had cause to call on the support of the military. In early January 1919 the Spartacist League had taken to the streets of Berlin, hoping to foment Communist revolution and declaring the Ebert government to be the enemy of the working class. At its head stood the communists Karl Liebknecht and Róża Luksemburg, the latter newly released from imprisonment in Breslau. Facing them were the *Freikorps*, irregular bands of volunteers often with violently anti-Communist views, who were called on by a High Command that feared the susceptibility of the regular army to Communist propaganda. Throughout the spring of 1919, the Spartacists were mercilessly suppressed. Many – including Liebknecht and Luksemburg – were shot out of hand. Communist insurrections elsewhere in Germany, from Bremen to Munich and Düsseldorf to Dresden, were dispatched with similar brutality. The working-class movement sustained a blow from which it did not recover.

The unrest in Berlin was mirrored in the provinces and, for a time, appeared to foreshadow the disintegration of the state. In Silesia, economic dislocation, the unresolved national question, the territorial losses sustained in nearby Posnania and the threat of further losses in Upper Silesia were genuine concerns. But, for most people, the prospect of a Communist government was unthinkable. In November 1918, the Breslau *Volksrat* chairman, Paul Löbe, conceded that Silesia would be forced to proclaim itself independent if a Spartacist government were formed in Berlin.[4] Similar sentiments in Upper Silesia inspired a conference in Breslau on 30 December, where representatives of central and local government discussed separation, but fell short of recommending it. Yet the issue of separatism would not go away. In 1919, there were renewed calls for Silesian autonomy and for the inclusion of the province in a future *Oststaat*, which, it was thought, could secede from the Weimar Republic and take the eastern provinces with it.[5] Meanwhile, demands were repeated for the division of Silesia.[6] Despite fears in Berlin that Prussia would unravel, Upper Silesia's request was granted and it became a separate province in October 1919. Breslau was left as the main city of Lower Silesia.

Breslau's strategic location was shifting. Whereas five years before it had been a supply base for the military defences of the frontier with the Russian Empire, it was now the advance post of a very sensitive section of Germany's border with an independent Poland. And Poland, though less powerful militarily than imperial Russia, had stronger political arguments. For the Poles, in line with President Wilson's principles of national self-determination, were laying claim to all districts with a Polish majority.

They were not setting eyes on Breslau itself, but they certainly assumed that Upper Silesia was rightly theirs, together with the eastern districts of Lower Silesia right up to the Vratislavian suburbs on the right bank of the Oder. Moreover, while waiting for the Peace Conference to decide, they showed their determination. In December–January 1918–19, they had driven German troops from the whole of Great Poland. Polish soldiers now occupied trenches so recently occupied by Russians. Breslau's fellow border city of Posen (Poznań) was already in a foreign country. Neighbouring Prague, until recently Austrian, was now the capital of a hostile and previously unknown country called Czechoslovakia. Anxieties spread.

Spartacist rioting in February 1919[7] was a prelude to a long and difficult summer. The uncertainties of the post-war settlement, coupled with the continued presence in office of one of the symbols of the old regime, the Breslau *Regierungspräsident* Traugott von Jagow, contrived to create a powder keg. That summer the fuse was lit. After a wave of crippling strikes, the railway workers forced the authorities to act. On 28 June a curfew was imposed and a programme of forced labour was ordered for the railwaymen. Not surprisingly, the reaction was violent. The next day, a large crowd, led by sailors and Communists, converged on the main railway station. Angry exchanges between the protesters and the police preceded the arrival of the soldiery. In the aftermath, five protesters lay dead and nineteen injured.

Having saved the republic from the Spartacists, the *Freikorps* soon developed into a similar threat themselves. In March 1920, after government attempts to disband two of the most prominent units, disaffected *Freikorps* members marched on Berlin in support of a right-wing journalist, Wolfgang Kapp. The time seemed ripe. The *Reichswehr* declined to resist the putsch and the defence of the republic was left to a much-weakened working class. However, though the Kappists did seize power, they had little idea of what to do with it. They were paralysed by a general strike and the withdrawal of cooperation by the Civil Service. They failed to exploit the widespread presence of sympathetic *Freikorps* units or to coordinate parallel risings in the provinces.

Only in Breslau did Kapp receive any solid backing. When news of the putsch reached Silesia on the morning of 13 March, the unions called a general strike. The trams stopped at noon. Yet the commander of the Military District, General Count Schmettow, declared himself for the putsch, and four of the region's *Freikorps*, headed by Löwenfeld's Third Marine Brigade, marched into the city 'to preserve public order'. The imperial flag flew at the head of their column. They secured the railway station, the main post office and the City Hall, then arrested the municipal government and suspended several newspapers.[8] Their seizure of power was peaceful until the Aulock Corps withdrew to barracks in Karlowitz (Karłowice). At that point their men were fired upon and an arson attack was made on the barracks at Liebichs Höhe.[9] The *Freikorps* were swift and brutally thorough in restoring 'order'. They then waited for the news from Berlin, which never came.

Meanwhile, Traugott von Jagow had been made Minister of the Interior in Kapp's government, and he lost no time in settling scores. He immediately purged his Republican opponents, including the Governor of Silesia, Ernst Philipp, the Breslau Chief of Police, Friedrich Voigt, and the SPD Presidents of Breslau, Liegnitz (Legnica) and Frankfurt an der Oder. After less than a week, however, Kapp's government collapsed and melted back into the *Freikorps* milieu from which it had sprung. On 20 March, legal government returned to Berlin and Breslau's own revolution crumbled. Prisoners were released and the *Freikorps* units withdrew, taking the Kappist administration with them. They had won few admirers. It was said that they had behaved in 'a disgusting fashion', and that they had alienated even the officer corps. An intense campaign of anti-Semitic propaganda had culminated in the brutal murder of the Jewish editor of the *Schlesische Arbeiter-Zeitung*, Bernhard Schottländer.[10] During its retreat, the Aulock Corps massacred eighteen people and wounded scores of others. Seven captured workers disappeared. Hatred of the military was rife.[11]

The Treaty of Versailles stands centre stage in the domestic and foreign affairs of the Weimar Republic. Signed on 28 June 1919, five years to the day after the assassination of Franz Ferdinand in Sarajevo, and forty-seven years after William I's proclamation as German Emperor, it was the defining document of inter-war Germany. A mixture of American idealism, British pragmatism and French *revanchisme*, it contained the seeds of Weimar's discontent and of its ultimate destruction. Its clauses relating to Germany's military emasculation, her territorial truncation, her admission of war guilt and her burden of reparations soured German politics for a generation.

The territorial losses perhaps rankled most. The Germans had reckoned with the forfeiture of Alsace-Lorraine as a consequence of the lost war, and the cession of small regions, such as that of Eupen-Malmédy to Belgium, was not going to cause an outcry. But the losses in the east came as a profound shock. There, in the traditional playground of Prussia, almost 65,000 square kilometres of territory and more than five million inhabitants were to be severed. Danzig (Gdańsk) and Memel were to be handed to international administration, while West Prussia, Upper Silesia and the entire province of Posen were to be surrendered to the reborn Poland.

The loss of Upper Silesia aroused special fears. Without Upper Silesian coal, it was thought that a major part of German industry would grind to a halt. Widespread unrest and even famine were predicted.[12] After the armistice, the political condition of Upper Silesia was extremely precarious. Its municipal politicians saw the admission of Poles to the councils as a prelude to Polish agitation. The tensions were exacerbated by the presence of German paramilitary formations, such as the *Heimatschutz* and the *Freikorps*, whose heavy-handed tactics did little to foster reconciliation.

Matters were not helped by the war of 1919–20 between Poland and Soviet Russia. Western opinion was divided on the merits of the Bolsheviks. But it was united in the belief that the territory of its former Russian ally should remain intact. So when the Poles joined the independent government of Ukraine in driving the Bolsheviks from the Ukrainian capital, Kiev, Western Europe echoed to angry shouts of 'Hands off Russia!' For its part, Communist propaganda played skilfully on German sensitivities. The Bolsheviks were no less hostile to the 'bourgeois' Weimar Republic than they had been to imperial Germany. But they somehow gave the impression that the Red Army was heading for Berlin in order to liberate it and to overthrow the Versailles *Diktat*. Many Germans cheered them. Many joined them in deriding Poland. Such was the enthusiasm that several German newspapers, including some in Silesia, announced in August 1920 that Warsaw had fallen, even when it had not.

Though the draft terms of Versailles had reserved the whole of Upper Silesia for Poland, it was agreed, after German protests, that the issue would be decided by a plebiscite. Tensions were such that the agreement sufficed to spark off the first Polish Silesian Rising of August 1919, which centred on Riebnig (Rybnik) and was brutally suppressed by the *Reichswehr*. A second Silesian Rising in August 1920 coincided with the Polish victory in the battle of Warsaw. It was accompanied by widespread rioting in Breslau, directed mainly against the Inter-Allied Plebiscite Commission, and specifically the French. The Polish Consulate was wrecked, the French Consulate was looted, eight of the Commission's ten cars were destroyed, and the French Consul, M. Terver, was forced to flee.[13] The 'Breslau Incident' soon developed into a full-scale international affair, with angry diplomatic notes being ferried between Berlin, Paris and Warsaw.

The third Silesian Rising proved by far the most serious. In the Upper Silesian plebiscite of March 1921, 59.4 per cent of voters had opted for Germany and 40.5 per cent for Poland. Howls of Polish outrage arose on the grounds that the voting had been distorted by a mass influx of German 'outvoters'. Sensing defeat, the Polish Silesian leader, Wojciech Korfanty, raised a force of some 40,000 Polish volunteers to contest the result. Facing them were the *Freikorps*, the sole military force available after the withdrawal of *Reichswehr* units from the plebiscite zone. All the prominent units of the movement were present: the *Landesjägerkorps*, the *Stahlhelm*, the *Jungdeutsche Orden*, the *Rossbach*, *Reinhard* and *Oberland Freikorps* and Heydebreck's *Wehrwölfe*. Two months of skirmishing followed, including the inconclusive pitched battle of Annaberg (Góry Sw. Anny), until the *Freikorps* were dissolved by Ebert in June.

Breslau students were intimately involved. Those of the 'war generation' had numerous opportunities to revive their martial spirit in the post-war years. In 1918–19, they had flocked to defend the county of Glatz (Kłodzko) from Czechoslovak claims. In the summer of 1919, thousands had participated in the protest meetings against the Treaty of Versailles and in the so-called *Hindenburgkammern*. In March 1920, many of them, especially from right-wing corporations such as the Borussia Corps, had joined groups of armed volunteers supporting the Kapp putsch. In 1921, they joined the mass campaign to organise the German vote in the Upper Silesian plebiscite and the subsequent armed action to defend their victory. The Guttentag and Gogolin battalions of the *Selbstschutz Oberschlesien* consisted mainly of Breslau students who regarded the Polish insurgents as 'bandits'. And, believing that Korfanty's men had been backed by the Polish Army, while they were *not* helped by the *Reichswehr*, they were all too ready to swallow the theory of a renewed 'stab in the back'.[14]

Veterans of the campaign included the Nazi 'martyr' Leo Schlageter, sometime Gauleiter of Silesia, Helmuth Brückner (1896–?) and the later Chief of Police of Breslau, Edmund Heines (1897–1934). In October 1921, a new partition of Upper Silesia was decreed by the Allied Powers: 61 per cent of the province was to remain in Germany, while four-fifths of the industrial installations, most of the coal fields and the cities of Königshütte (Królewska Huta) and Kattowitz (Katowice) were to pass to Poland.

The birth pangs of the Weimar Republic culminated in the crisis year of 1923. The pattern of instability proceeded with the abortive Küstrin (Kostrzyn) putsch by *Reichswehr* elements in February, the establishment of pro-Communist governments in Saxony and Thuringia in March and May, and Adolf Hitler's Beer Hall putsch in Munich in November. The German economy was also deteriorating with astonishing rapidity. The French occupation of the Ruhr at the end of 1922 had begun a spiral of hyperinflation. Taking 1913 as a benchmark, the price index stood at 2.17 in 1918, 4.15 in 1919, 14.86 in 1920 and 19.11 in 1921. After briefly stabilising, it reached 341.82 in 1922, 2,783 in January 1923 and 1,261,000,000,000 by December.[15] For the ordinary citizen it meant financial ruin. Wages could not keep pace with the almost hourly rises in inflation. A wave of strikes and walk-outs swept the country. Rioting broke out in Breslau's commercial centre on 22 July. About fifty large shops were looted by a mob led by

The patriot: Ferdinande von Schmettau donates her hair, 1813.

The Departure of the Volunteers by Adolph Menzel.

Storming the Bakery in the Neumarkt (1846) by Philipp Hoyoll.

Defending the barricades,
7 May 1849.

Kaiser Wilhelm II's
visit, 1906:
Schweidnitzerstrasse.

The opening of the
Jahrhunderthalle, 1913.

The New Market with Neptune fountain.

The City Hall.

The Cathedral.

The New Synagogue (1872).

The Main Square and
St. Elizabeth's Church.

The Main Station (1856).

Blücher Square (otherwise the Salt Market).

Palace Square.

Leni Riefenstahl (1924)
by Eugen Spiro.

Girl and Cat (1937)
by Balthus.

The Gypsy Lovers (1918–19)
by Otto Müller.

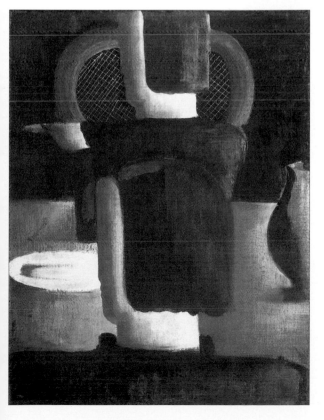

Two Women at the Table (variation)
(1930) by Oskar Schlemmer.

Wojciech Korfanty (1873–1939),
Silesian insurrectionary.

Róża Luksemburg (1871–1919),
Marxist revolutionary.

Fritz Haber (1868–1934),
chemist: 'Doctor Death'.

Manfred von Richthofen (1892–1918),
'The Red Baron'.

Communist agitators. Six looters were killed.[16] Only the currency reform of November 1923 and the introduction of the *Rentenmark* halted the slide.

The mid-1920s brought a modicum of political stability that was mainly the work of Gustav Stresemann (1878–1929). Under his leadership, a 'Great Coalition' of centrist parties formed late in 1923, enabling an element of consensus to creep into German politics. On this basis, he was able to gain some notable successes. Firstly, the introduction in 1924 of the Dawes Plan fixed a timetable for revised reparations payments. It encouraged the German economy to stabilise, and the new Reichsmark was once again tied to the gold standard. Secondly, following the pariahs' Treaty of Rapallo with Soviet Russia of 1922, Stresemann's efforts bore fruit in the Treaty of Locarno (1925) and the reintegration of Germany into the 'polite society' of European nations. He negotiated admission to the League of Nations in 1926 and signed the Kellogg-Briand Pact, outlawing aggressive war, two years later. Yet his agenda was not one of unquestioning compliance. Having formerly supported the Kapp putsch, his own outlook was decidedly revisionist, though he did not pursue his goals by overt confrontation. The terms of the Locarno Pact guaranteed Germany's frontiers in the west, thereby placating France and Britain, but maintained an ominous silence about Germany's borders in the east. Breslauers did not fail to notice. In their eyes, the whole post-war settlement was unjust.

The election results of the Stresemann era in Silesia demonstrated a certain return to normality. There were three electoral regions: Liegnitz and Breslau in Lower Silesia, and Oppeln (Opole) in Upper Silesia. While Lower Silesia maintained a solid Socialist majority in the elections of 1924 and 1928, with one-quarter of the vote going to the nationalist German National People's Party (DNVP), in Oppeln the Catholic Centre Party was dominant. Less than three weeks after its rebirth in Munich in 1925, the Nazi Party (NSDAP) was established in Silesia, when Helmuth Brückner, a veteran of the First World War and the Upper Silesian Risings, wrote to Hitler pledging his 'unconditional support'. Yet since Hitler was forbidden to speak in Prussia, the NSDAP found it very difficult to gain a foothold. In some quarters it was viewed with ridicule when it could not afford to supply the requisite brown shirts and swastikas. Its weakness was demonstrated by the Reichstag results for Silesia in 1928, when it garnered approximately 1 per cent of the vote, well below the 2.6 per cent national average.

Stresemann, the architect of Weimar's brief blossoming, died in October 1929 just a few weeks before the Wall Street Crash, which swept away all his hard work. The German economy – so dependent on short-term US loans – went into meltdown through the collapse of the US stock market. Following

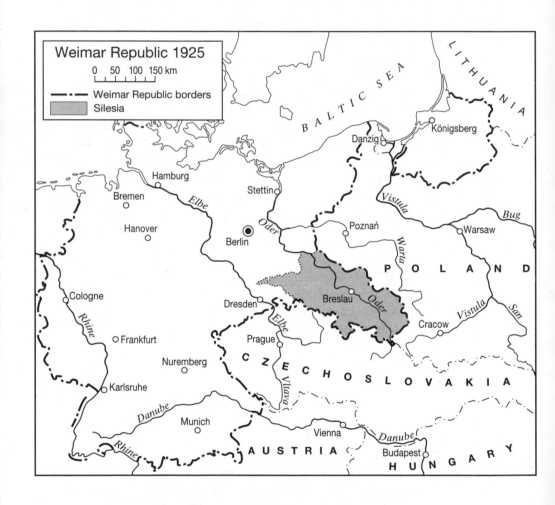

334

a run on the banks, unemployment rose almost exponentially from 1.3 million in September 1929 to three million a year later. It reached six million (one in three of the working population) by the beginning of 1933. The political instability that had so dogged Weimar's early life now returned with a vengeance. In March 1930, normal government was abandoned in favour of a cabinet relying on presidential decree. Thereafter, a series of short-lived governments made increasing use of the President's powers as parliamentary sittings and legislation were marginalised. The suspension of the democratic process only served to weaken public faith in democracy and to strengthen popular support for the anti-democratic parties – above all for the Communists and the Nazis.

The Reichstag election results of September 1930 made shocking reading for democratic politicians. Of the parties that had made up the Weimar coalitions of the 1920s only the Catholic Centre Party emerged unscathed, maintaining its 12 per cent share of the vote. The DNVP vote was halved; the SPD lost 6 per cent, but still emerged as the largest single party. The only main parties to register an increase were the Communist KPD; up from 10 per cent to 13 per cent with seventy-seven seats; and the Nazis, up from 2.6 per cent in 1928 to 18 per cent with 107 seats. One of those seats was won by the Nazi member for Breslau, Helmuth Brückner, returned with 24.2 per cent of the vote.

Weimar was lurching towards its denouement. Despite the success in 1932 of the Hoover Moratorium, which signalled the end of reparation payments, no subsequent government was able to deal with the economic crisis. Nazi and Communist strength continued to grow, apparently in direct correlation with the unemployment figures. In January 1931, hostile demonstrations greeted the Chancellor's visit to Breslau. The words 'death to Brüning' and 'death to the hunger dictatorship' were daubed on many walls.[17] Even the Nazis were impoverished. In February 1931, the SA (Sturmabteilung, or 'stormtroopers') in Silesia was complaining to its chief, Ernst Röhm, that its Breslau company could not turn out for inspection because it completely lacked footwear.[18] Eighteen months later, the Silesian SA Commander, Edmund Heines, noted that 60 per cent of his men were long-term unemployed.[19]

The battles of the Communists and Nazis were played out in towns and streets all over Germany. In June 1931, the annual national rally of the veterans' association, the *Stahlhelm*, was held in Breslau. It was the occasion for violent clashes and equally violent rhetoric. The leader of the *Stahlhelm*, Franz Seldte, made a solemn undertaking:

The life and death struggle of the German nation will be decided here in the east . . . And let this be our vow that we take this [day] . . . that we will never pause, never rest, until all German soil that has drunk of the blood and sweat of numerous German generations has come back to the Reich.[20]

Silesia appears to have been a hotbed of paramilitary activity. Periodic unrest throughout 1932 culminated in the notorious case of the 'Potempa Six'. In the small hours of 10 August, a group of drunken SA men entered a farmhouse near Gross Strehlitz (Strzelce Opolskie) and attacked one of the inhabitants, Konrad Pietzuch, a Pole with Communist sympathies. He was beaten with a billiard cue, kicked and finally shot. The murderers were tried in Beuthen (Bytom) and sentenced to death, but became a *cause célèbre* of the Nazi Party, with Hitler famously declaring that 'German men will never be condemned because of a Pole'.[21] A week after the Potempa murder, a woman in Breslau was arrested for kicking an SA man. She was sentenced to fifteen months imprisonment.[22] The Potempa Six walked free.

That summer, Breslau itself saw spiralling violence. On 23 June, a column of SA men, led by Edmund Heines, was attacked by Communists and eleven were seriously injured. Three days later, a young member of the Socialist self-defence organisation, the *Reichsbanner*, was shot dead. In early August, a police raid on a Nazi safe-house led to the confiscation of a machine-gun, 1,450 rounds of ammunition and twenty-three hand-grenades. On 6 August, grenades were thrown during running battles between left and right. Two days later, another grenade was hurled into the bedroom of a prominent Socialist leader.[23]

Hitler made his first visit to Breslau as part of the campaign for the Reichstag elections of July 1932. He employed startlingly modern election-eering techniques, flying between venues and holding numerous events on any given day. On the evening of 18 April, for example, he gave four speeches: at Beuthen at 6 p.m., at Görlitz two hours later and then two in Breslau. The first, at the Grüneiche Radrennbahn, attracted 6,000 listeners, while at the second, at the *Jahrhunderthalle*, some 10,000 faithful were treated to an embittered attack on the 'Weimar parties':

Meine deutschen Volksgenossen und Volksgenossinnen!
What you see here, and across Germany, is a sign of the rebirth of the German nation. For almost 14 years the ruling parties have promised us the earth and driven us into the ground . . .
Fate gave them 14 years, more than enough. In 14 years Bismarck led Prussia out of despair to the unification of the German Empire, saving the German people from fragmentation and creating that which even we had the honour to experience. In 14 years they have destroyed not only their own efforts, but also the toil of generations . . .

They are now recognised as the greatest incompetents and dilettantes in history!

... I know what they are thinking. They think they can wear us down; that we will tire of the struggle. They are wrong. They can do what they will: deny our propaganda, confiscate our pamphlets, tear down our posters, restrict our newspaper circulation. They can refuse us access to the radio, ban our films, dissolve the SA, the SS and the entire Party. They can terrorise us. They can kill us ...

But we will never surrender.[24]

Hitler spent the night at the Monopol Hotel. His efforts had the desired effect. Against a national average of 37.4 per cent, his party took 43.5 per cent of the Breslau vote. It was the third-highest Nazi return in Germany (after Hanover East with 49.5 per cent and Schleswig-Holstein with 51 per cent) and well above the SPD showing of 24.4 per cent.

By the end of that year, therefore, the Nazis controlled the largest group in the Reichstag. The politicians, who had strenuously avoided asking Hitler to enter government, were finally brought to think the prospect inevitable. On 30 January 1933, Adolf Hitler was appointed Chancellor of Germany at the invitation of President Hindenburg.

The date of 30 January 1933 is conventionally taken to be the opening day of the Third Reich and the last day of democracy. Yet it should not be forgotten that Hitler had been constitutionally appointed head of a coalition government and that the Weimar Republic had been ruled by distinctly undemocratic methods for almost three years. In January 1933, Hitler was still some distance from being an absolute dictator. Yet the process that was to create his dictatorship was put in motion almost immediately. The Third Reich was officially declared seven months later, on 1 September.

The moment in January when Hitler assumed power was recalled by the son of a Breslau doctor, then a seven-year-old boy, who lived in the Kaiser-Wilhelmstrasse and who was looking through the window:

I was sitting with my mother on the edge of the bed and was watching two postal employees who, with an immense effort, were trying to raise a huge flag on the mast of the Post Office [opposite]. A gust of wind suddenly caught the flag and blew it open to full length. It was a flag with the swastika. My mother, who was not usually given to sentimentality, seized my hand as tears of joy ran down her face. She looked at me and told me in a voice quivering with emotion: 'This is a wonderful day, a day that you must always remember. From today, a new era begins for Germany, a better time. At last, the end of the misery and poverty that [has afflicted] so many people, has arrived. Justice will reign once more, and a wonderful future awaits you ...'[25]

At the time, he thought nothing of the fact that his mother's name was Jadwiga Wieczorek, or that his maternal grandfather could not speak German properly. All he knew was that his own father, a former military surgeon, had recently joined the NSDAP with enthusiasm. Nearly seventy years later, he would ask: 'Can one ever tell these things and be understood?'[26]

Breslau supplied a good example of the consolidation of Nazi power in the provinces. SA units and police turned on their opponents as soon as word of Hitler's appointment spread. The planning of a Communist rally was disrupted by the arrival of some 500 SA men, who, with police support, paraded in front of the Communist ranks. Violence inevitably ensued and was brutally crushed by the police. In the subsequent rioting, shots were fired and an unemployed labourer was killed. All Communist rallies were banned as a threat to public order.

After January 1933, the *Gleichschaltung* or 'coordination' of social and political life was rapidly realised. In Breslau, it was completed by the appointments of Nazi Gauleiter Brückner as Lower Silesian *Oberpräsident* and of Silesian SA chief Heines as Breslau Police Chief. Elsewhere in the province it was just as thorough. All fourteen Silesian *Oberbürgermeister* were replaced; and only three of the forty-eight *Landräte*, or regional administrators, survived in office until March.[27] That month Silesia's first concentration camp was established in the Breslau suburb of Dürrgoy (Tarnogaj). Though short-lived, it was to house many of the prominent Socialists of the region, including former Reichstag President Paul Löbe, the former Lower Silesian President, Heinrich Lüdemann, and the former Mayor of Breslau, Karl Mache. In the Reichstag elections that spring Breslau was one of only seven constituencies to return an absolute Nazi majority. Against a national average of 43.2 per cent, it scored 50.2 per cent; Liegnitz scored 54.0 per cent. The election turned out to be the prelude to the Reichstag granting Hitler 'emergency powers' and to the creation of a formal Nazi dictatorship.

Vicious events occurred across Germany. The SA moved against each of its political enemies. Legality was supplied by a rump-Reichstag in Berlin cowed by Nazi stormtroopers. The nationwide suppression of the Communists was completed by the ban in February, which followed the Reichstag fire. The trade unions and the Social Democrats were picked off in turn. The trade-union offices in Breslau were stormed by SA units in March, when two employees were killed.[28] In May the unions were dissolved and were forcibly incorporated into the huge, Nazi-run Labour Front (DAF). The Socialists, having refrained from extra-parliamentary activity, succumbed in June, when they too were outlawed as inimical to the German state and people. In April, SA units raided several Breslau bookshops, confiscating works by Stefan Zweig, Thomas Mann and Emile Zola. Three Polish students at the university were taken to Nazi Party headquarters and severely beaten.[29] In May, a ritual burning of works by 'Jewish and Marxist' authors was held on the Schlossplatz.[30]

Despite such outrages, everyday life for those people left unmolested by the regime actually improved. The domestic economy recovered. In 1935, the level of industrial production of 1928 was restored.[31] The number of unemployed fell. Nationally, unemployment dropped from 4.8 million in 1933 to 2 million in 1935[32] and was practically eliminated by 1939. In Silesia the jobless figure fell from almost 500,000 in 1933 to 154,000 by 1935.[33]

Meanwhile, the limits of Nazi power in 1933-4 can be illustrated by one of President Hindenburg's very last decrees. In July 1934, he ordered that all war veterans who had seen active service under fire should be awarded a medal entitled *Ehrenkreuz der Frontkämpfer*, or 'Frontline Honour Cross'. All such veterans were to be presented with the medal by local officials, together with a certificate signed by Chancellor Hitler. By 1934 many of the officials were Nazis. A proportion of the veterans were Jewish, but they had to be given their medals like everyone else. Dr Alexander Walk, for example, the local physician at Nimkau (Miękinia) near Breslau, got his medal from the *Landrat* of Neumarkt (Środa). It was to save his life.

The darker side of Nazi rule became increasingly apparent. After the elimination of the party's opponents, the summer of 1934 saw an internal party feud – the so-called 'Night of the Long Knives' – in which the 'Socialist' wing of the movement, along with much of the SA, was liquidated.

Already, in April 1933, SPD sources[34] had reported a gun battle on the streets of Breslau between rival units of the SA. They thought it reflected the fundamental social split in the Nazi membership and Hitler's betrayal of working-class interests. The next year, it was clear that the SA's days were numbered. The stormtroopers were considered by the party leadership to be an undisciplined group that took the 'Socialist' element of 'National Socialism' too seriously. Silesia, as a bastion of its power, was to witness the slaughter at first hand. Udo von Woyrsch (1895–1983), *SS-Oberführer* and Himmler's *Sonderkommissar* for Silesia, was to lead the operation. He was ordered to arrest certain SA leaders and occupy the Breslau police headquarters. In fact, he went much further. His men ran amok. The Breslau Police President, Edmund Heines, was summarily executed. His deputy, Hans Engels, was taken to nearby woods and blasted with a shotgun. The one-armed former Silesian *Freikorps* leader, Peter von Heydebreck, died proclaiming 'Long live the Führer!', apparently unaware that the Führer had ordered his execution. The Gauleiter, Brückner, was expelled from the province and stripped of office. In the aftermath, an extended and bloody 'clean-up' operation against the Silesian SA was brought to a close only through Göring's personal intervention.[35]

Having cleared the field for action, the Nazi Party began to move against its alleged racial enemies. Punitive measures against the Jews had been promoted from the outset. A boycott of Jewish shops was attempted in April 1933 and Jews were excluded from the Civil Service and other professions. But the main body of anti-Semitic legislation began in 1935. The Nuremberg Laws decreed racial and genealogical definitions of Jewishness, while depriving the Jewish community of their legal rights. Criminal penalties were imposed on marriages between Jews and Gentiles and on any form of sexual relations. In April 1935, a Breslau woman was pilloried for her relationship with a Jewish man. The fate of her lover is unknown. Much of the Jewish community became 'non-persons' overnight. In due course, the *Reichskristallnacht* of November 1938 underlined the fact that the new Germany had no place for Jews.

The details of how the Breslau SS received and executed their orders on *Kristallnacht* have been reconstructed both from post-war trials in Germany and from the reports of the Polish Consul, Leon Koppens. They make depressing reading. They also suggest a high degree of planning. According to the Consul's report to Warsaw, he was already aware at 8 p.m. on 9 November that the SS had orders for an '*Aktion*'. German records state that the *SS-Oberabschnitt Südost* in Breslau received a message from Berlin at 1.09 a.m. on the 10th, telling their commanding officer, Erich von dem Bach-Zelewski, to place an urgent call to a hotel in Munich, where Reinhard Heydrich was staying. Everything points to a scenario where Heydrich simply gave his final command to execute orders that had been prepared in advance. Heydrich talked of 'the demonstration'. In Breslau, uniformed SS and SA units were on the move within twenty minutes of the call being made. At 2 a.m., *Wehrmacht* sappers put the first explosive charges under the New Synagogue. Compliant journalists were on hand to take notes. The following day, the *Schlesische Tageszeitung* published two articles: one '*Wie Breslau mit den Juden abrechnete*' ('How Breslau got even with the Jews') and the other '*Demonstrationen auch in ganz Schlesien*'('Demonstrations through-out Silesia'). A passer-by remarked, 'I was in the Middle Ages.'[36]

Unusually in relation to the rest of the Reich, where 'Crystal Night' has been described as an urban phenomenon, the Silesian SS targeted every single village and hamlet where Jews were living. They smashed their way through Brückenberg (Bierutowice), Gottesberg (Boguszów) and Habel-schwerdt (Bystrzyca Kłodzka) to Sprottau (Szprotawa), Striegau (Strzegom) and Strehlen (Strzelin) (see below). In Trebnitz (Trzebnica), they forced the

Jews of the village to set the synagogue alight themselves. Then they cut the beards of the men and arrested them; the women were released. A special SS squad from Breslau, under Criminal Commissar Schubert, headed for the Zionist *Auswandererlehrgut* camp at Gross Breesen (Brzeźno), which trained candidates in agriculture and crafts before sending them to Palestine. The staff were arrested, the farm buildings smashed and robbed.

SS-Oberführer Katzmann reported his achievements to Berlin:

> In Breslau alone, 1 synagogue (burned), 2 synagogues (demolished), 1 building of the 'Society of Joy' (demolished), at least 500 shops (completely destroyed), 10 Jewish Inns (demolished), 35 other Jewish enterprises (demolished) and 600 men arrested . . .[37]

Historians who know what the Nazi regime perpetrated in the 1940s are sometimes distracted from making a realistic assessment of the 1930s. Of course, between 1933 and 1939 Hitler was consciously engaged in what he regarded as a preparatory phase for greater things to come. He was laying the foundations for a scheme that he had outlined in *Mein Kampf*, but which he did not expect to mature during his first decade in power. He was preparing for a general war to overthrow the Versailles settlement and to conquer his longed-for eastern *Lebensraum*. But he did not think that Germany would be ready for a general, as opposed to a local, war before 1942-3 at the earliest. So the fact is that in the 1930s many aspects of Nazism were at best latent. In its pre-war peacetime mode, Nazism fell significantly short of its subsequent wartime nadir. What is more, it fell significantly short of the atrocities that Stalin had been perpetrating on a grand scale in the USSR for many years. By 1939, as is now known for certain, the Soviets had already murdered far more human beings than the Nazis would ever do. The Kulak Campaign or the Ukrainian Terror Famine had no parallels in the pre-1939 Reich. The 'Great Terror', which Stalin unleashed against his own party and which consumed up to a million lives, makes the 'Night of the Long Knives' look like a petty disturbance. The Gulag system, which was already twenty years old, completely dwarfed the Nazi KZ (concentration camp) system, which was still in its infancy. By collectivising the land, by nationalising all commerce and industry and by killing the cream of the Red Army officer corps, Stalin had entered on regions of totalitarian control where Hitler would never dare to tread. These considerations have more than a theoretical bearing. They facilitate comparative analysis without which no valid judgements can be made. But to some extent they also enable an understanding of the Nazis' exaggerated hatred of 'Bolshevism', which, though visceral and largely unsubstantiated, was nonetheless used as a central justification for the regime and which many fearful Germans shared.

Racism was the one aspect of theory and practice that set the Nazis apart, not only from the Soviets, but from other Fascists, like Mussolini or Franco. The belief in a racial hierarchy of humanity was absolutely fundamental to the Nazi creed, and it has given them a reputation for surpassing evil. It led them to view the world in terms of 'superhumans' and 'subhumans', of 'desirables' and 'undesirables'. Yet, in the 1930s, the practical applications of Nazi racism were still in gestation. The so-called 'Euthanasia Campaign', which began in August 1939 and would account for 70–80,000 clinical murders in Germany and Austria, was the sole pre-war instance where theoretical schemes for extermination reached the point of execution. Code-named 'T-4 Aktion', from the address at Tiergarten 4 in Berlin, whence the operations were coordinated, it involved much more than the 'mercy-killing' of incurables or the terminally ill. It was a systematic attempt, initiated on the express orders of the Führer, to kill every person in the Reich who was mentally or physically disabled. It spelt an automatic sentence of death on every cripple, every epileptic, every schizophrenic, every spastic, everyone with a genetic deformity, every Down's Syndrome sufferer, everyone diagnosed with Alzheimer's, motor-neurone disease or cystic fibrosis. All these innocent people were condemned to be transported involuntarily to one of six designated death centres to be gassed or lethally injected, to be issued with false death certificates and cremated without trace.

There can be no doubt whatsoever that Breslau was touched by the 'T-4 Aktion', like every other city in the Reich. Indeed, the patients of the university medical clinics, especially in psychiatry and neurology, and of the municipal mental asylum on Einbaumstrasse, would have been automatic targets. The directors of these institutes received Registration Form No. 1 from T-4 HQ, instructing them, for purposes of 'economic planning', to list all persons in their care who suffered from a set of illnesses, who had been designated criminally insane or who had been resident inmates for more than five years. They were told to return the completed form within three to ten weeks. Roving teams of T-4 assessors would then arrive to check the returns against reality. Many victims thereby learned of their fate in advance, and in some instances wrote farewell letters to their families. In due course, the incredibly named 'T-4 Community Patient Transport Service' would send a convoy of trucks or buses to pick up the patients. It took them to the pre-prepared facilities where white-coated 'medics', false shower rooms, extraction of gold teeth, the excision of body parts and incineration awaited. Next of kin would be scrupulously informed within days that their relative had unfortunately died from 'pneumonia', 'a stroke' or 'breathing problems'. The two such facilities closest to Breslau were in the Brandenburg Prison complex near Berlin and at Sonnenstein Castle near

Pirna in Saxony. Sporadic protests were lodged by both Protestant and Catholic clergy. The Führer would later regret that greater secrecy had not been maintained for his solution to 'life unworthy of life'.[38] Cardinal Bertram wrote a protestatory memorial on the matter on 16 July 1941 – but to no effect. The crime had been committed.

Bolstered by a booming economy, by increased armaments production and by labour-intensive public-works projects, such as the construction of *Autobahns*, Germany gained the confidence to reach out for Hitler's primary foreign-policy goal – the dismantling of the Versailles settlement. Germany had withdrawn from the League of Nations in 1933. The return of the Saarland and the introduction of conscription in 1935, as well as the remilitarisation of the Rhineland in 1936, increased the pace of events. In 1938 the *Anschluss* with Austria was achieved. At Munich in September, Germany annexed the Sudeten regions of Czechoslovakia. In 1939, the invasion of Bohemia and Moravia, the creation of a Slovak puppet administration and the seizure of the so-called Memelland from Lithuania completed the first stage of Hitler's foreign campaign. 'Greater Germany' had become a reality, virtually without a shot being fired.

Breslau, which lay immediately to the north-east of the 'Sudetenland', was intimately affected by the disintegration of Czechoslovakia. The Sudeten Germans, who lived on the Bohemian side of the Giant Mountains, were indistinguishable from those who lived on the Silesian side. They formed part of a single, regional community. Their leader, Konrad Henlein, came from the town of Maffersdorf near Reichenberg, which was not twenty kilometres from the Silesian border. Moreover, they had genuine grievances. They had been incorporated into Czechoslovakia without any regard for the principle of national self-determination; they had not been treated as equals by the government in Prague; and they had been suffering the highest rate of unemployment in the country. So, for the Nazis, they constituted a heaven-sent instance of political fodder that was exploited to the full. In all the Nazi-inspired events in Breslau in the 1930s, Sudeten delegations, Sudeten parades and Sudeten costumes were visible at every turn.

Breslau participated to the full in the excitement of the heady days of the 'Munich Crisis'. Breslau Radio was one of three German broadcasting centres that were pumping propaganda into the Sudetenland and transforming Henlein's *Sudetendeutsche Partei* into an instrument of Nazi policy. Breslau was the headquarters of the Army Group, whose tanks and soldiers were manning the frontier with northern Bohemia and threatening to invade. The gap between the Iser and the Giant Mountains seemed to be in their sights. Breslau was the place where all the reports, and rumours and refugees from that northern sector were collected. One of the troublespots was at Reichenberg (Liberec), just twenty-four kilometres from Silesia, whence besieged opponents of Henlein had appealed to Lord Runciman's mission and where serious rioting took place in mid-September. Yet in most frontier settlements the disturbances were not excessively violent. 'In at least fifteen villages and towns in the frontier districts', a British reporter wrote, 'crowds collected in the main squares and streets, sang *Deutschland über Alles* and the Horst Wessel song, and then dispersed. In one or two places, the demonstrators shouted "We want a plebiscite".'[39] When Czechoslovak authorities restored order, the Nazi reaction was hysterical: '. . . the complete lack of control and the wild Hussite spirit of the Czech police and soldiery may produce an extremely grave situation,' roared the *Völkische Beobachter*. 'We know how unbearable it is', thundered Göring, 'that a miserable people – God knows where they come from – should be oppressing a highly civilised people. We know who is backing these ridiculous pygmies in Prague – it is Moscow.' Hitler's thoughts were relayed by radio from the rally at Nuremberg:

> The misery of the Sudeten Germans is without end. The Czechs want to annihilate them . . . I say that if those tortured creatures cannot obtain rights and assistance by themselves they can obtain both from us . . . I demand that the oppression of 3,500,000 Germans in Czechoslovakia shall cease and be replaced by the right of self-determination.[40]

Two weeks later, by international agreement, Hitler was given what he wanted. The *Wehrmacht* occupied the Sudetenland unopposed. The Sudeten Germans and the Silesian Germans who had been politically separated for 198 years were reunited. Five months after that, Hitler was in Prague.

In late 1938, Germany's attention had turned to Poland. German claims to Danzig, to the so-called Polish Corridor, and to Upper Silesia were staked ever more vociferously. The pressure was enormous. Yet the Poles proved far less supine than their neighbours. They refused to yield, rejected all Nazi threats and blandishments and the idea of Soviet assistance. Hitler, emboldened by the hesitations of the West, prepared for a military showdown. The secret protocols of a non-aggression pact with the USSR, signed on 23 August 1939, put the last pieces into place.

When it came, the Second World War began in Silesia. At 8 p.m. on 31 August, German units led by the *Sicherheitsdienst* (SD) carried out a phoney attack on a German radio station in Gleiwitz (Gliwice), close to the Polish border. Among the force were a number of convicted criminals, presumably participating on the promise of remission. After bursting into one of the studios, the attackers broadcast a patriotic announcement in Polish, sang a rousing Polish chorus and departed. The convicts, carefully dressed in

Polish uniforms, were then mown down by the SS. The 'provocation' was complete. Breslau Radio announced that the Reich had been treacherously invaded by Poland. At 4.40 a.m. the next day, 1 September, the German cruiser *Schleswig Holstein* opened fire on the Polish enclave at Westerplatte in Danzig harbour. All along the frontier German forces launched their planned *Blitzkrieg*. Poland fought back. The Second World War had begun.

*

The new era that dawned on 9 November 1918 posed many difficult challenges to the German economy. It brought considerable overcapacity in many areas of wartime production and precipitated large-scale unemployment. It swept away much of the traditional network of suppliers and markets. Most seriously, it left Silesia as an isolated strip of territory squeezed between two hostile neighbours, Poland and Czechoslovakia, whose passion for economic autarky spelt danger.

The first crisis to hit was caused by the cession of eastern Upper Silesia to Poland in 1921. At the stroke of a pen, Germany lost 3,000 square kilometres, rich mineral resources, valuable industrial plants and around 400,000 skilled workers. It lost the industrial cities of Kattowitz, Königshütte, Myslowitz (Mysłowice) and Tarnowitz (Tarnowskie Góry). It lost fifty-three of the province's sixty-seven coal mines, 75 per cent of its pig-iron production and a majority of its zinc mines.[41] Many of these concerns had formerly been supplied and supported by the manufacturing and service industries of Breslau. The consequences were necessarily serious.

The expected unemployment arrived. The decade of inflation that culminated so disastrously in 1923 was coupled with a demographic crisis of demobilised soldiers and refugees, which threatened severe social unrest. In 1919, Breslau alone accounted for some three-fifths of Silesia's unemployed, while Upper Silesia showed relatively low levels of unemployment. Furthermore, the official figures were dwarfed by the legions of 'unofficial jobless'. In May 1919 the municipal Labour Exchange noted that 6,280 people were looking for work, while only some 3,856 were receiving benefit.[42] Thereafter, a wave of strikes affected the railways and the metallurgical industry, not least the Linke-Hofmann works.

The years of crisis came to a head in 1923, when the inflation that had been endemic in the German economy since 1913 ran completely out of control. By December of that year the Reichsmark was in freefall at more than a billion times its former value. In Breslau, a litre of milk cost 240,000,000,000 marks; an egg, 246,000,000,000.[43] The Linke-Hofmann works, mindful of the recent unrest, brought freshly minted banknotes from

Berlin to distribute wages twice a day, in a vain attempt to counteract their almost instantaneous depreciation.

The political stabilisation of the mid-1920s brought substantial improvements to the socioeconomic conditions, but Breslau still languished at the wrong end of Germany's major statistical indices. Unemployment continued to rise. In January 1925, the city had 6,672 persons unemployed and receiving support; a year later, the figure had almost trebled to 15,444. By late 1929, it had reached 23,978, with only Chemnitz returning worse figures.[44] Poverty was widespread. Per capita income in Breslau was less than half that of Frankfurt-am-Main, while 6.8 per cent of Breslau families lived on welfare support compared to 2.9 per cent in Leipzig and 2.5 per cent in Dresden. In such conditions, health inevitably suffered. The rate of infant mortality in Breslau, for example, at 12.9 per cent of all live births, was worse than all comparable German cities.[45] Local government did little to ease the situation. In 1929 it earmarked only 3.5 Reichmarks per capita for health care, while Berlin set aside 10.1, Frankfurt 8.6 and Cologne 5.3.[46] Poor housing stock served to compound these factors. In 1925, 17 per cent of apartments in the Silesian capital consisted of a single habitable room. This compared to 4.5 per cent in Berlin and 2.4 per cent in Chemnitz. Overcrowding was commonplace. More than two-thirds of all Breslauers lived in apartments with fewer than three habitable rooms.[47]

Breslau's industrial companies spent several years in the doldrums. In the 1920s Linke-Hofmann was sold twice, once to the Lauchhammer concern and then to Busch of Berlin. The Archimedes works joined up for a time with Linke-Hofmann before going into business with a couple of firms from Chemnitz. Vratislavian industry was repeatedly driven to seek outside assistance – in 1925 from the *Sofortprogramm* and in 1930–2 from the *Osthilfe*, or 'Eastern Aid'.

By the time of the worldwide economic crisis of 1929, the Breslauers were espousing radical solutions to their predicament. One in six was unemployed; recruitment to the ranks of the Nazis or Communists was simple and brought with it a sense of belonging and a sense of purpose. At the very least in part, the conversion of a once solidly Social Democratic city to the cause of Nazism must be seen as a thoughtless reaction to the unprecedented economic troubles of the day.

Business picked up after 1932. The installation of the Nazi regime was indubitably a factor, especially when military orders began to be placed. The Linke-Hofmann factory, now called FAMO (*Fahrzeug und Motorenwerke*), did well from its tractors, and even more so from its tanks, building (among other things) versions of the Panzer Mk II and Mk III. In the 1930s

Archimedes trebled its workforce. By 1939, the number of active factories in Breslau was growing, but it still had not returned to the pre-slump position.

Breslau undoubtedly benefited from the first peaceful years of the Third Reich, but its economy was slow to recover. In 1936, in a nation where unemployment was becoming a thing of the past, Breslau still returned figures of 10.4 per cent, the worst in Germany. By 1939, export output was only one-fifth of its 1914 level, while water-borne traffic had fallen by a half. Only through the outbreak of war, and the concerted efforts of local and national government, did Breslau begin to share fully in the boom that the rest of Germany was enjoying. By then, Breslau had benefited from the building of the *Autobahn*, and was slowly regaining its traditional role as a commercial centre for East-Central Europe. Progress was facilitated by the establishment of the *Süd-Ost Messe*, or 'South-East Fair', in 1935. Renamed the *Breslauer Messe* two years later, it made a great impact on restoring fortunes.

*

In the first half of the twentieth century, religious life in Germany underwent several upheavals. After 1918, all the churches were criticised for the unashamedly patriotic attitudes that were adopted during the First World War and brought no known benefit. They were seen as a prop of the conservative order that had served Germany so badly. Consequently the churches became very defensive. The Weimar Republic was often denounced as ungodly; anti-Semitic statements from the clergy were not uncommon; and, on the fringes, both 'Nordic Christianity' and even neo-paganism made their appearance. In the late 1920s, the growing support for both Communists and Nazis was to some extent connected to the anti-religious stance of the rival totalitarian groups. But many were more than ready to listen to rants about religion being 'the opium of the people' or about the clergy being 'traitors to the nation'.

German Christianity was already in crisis, therefore, before Hitler took power. But the rise of the Nazis posed special problems. In essence, the Nazi regime was fundamentally hostile to traditional religion. Hitler's 'philosopher', Alfred Rosenberg, was totally opposed to Christianity, and his influence was seen in many of the chants and refrains of the Hitler Youth and the SA: 'We follow not Christ', the Nazis sang, 'but Horst Wessel'; or 'Hang the Jews and put the priests against the wall'. Hitler himself was a lapsed Catholic, who had severed all links with the practices of his childhood. Many of his colleagues, like Himmler, dabbled in neo-paganism; all the symbols and rituals of Nazism, from the sign of the swastika to the cult of torchlights, were non-Christian in origin. The Nazis had no time for

Christian saints, while worshipping ancient Germanic heroes and Wagnerian heroines.

Christians were forced either to resist or to accommodate the new
political climate. The great majority chose accommodation. The Prussian
state Church, which commanded the allegiance of the largest Protestant
community in Silesia, found itself in a singularly awkward dilemma. On the
one hand, it was trained to pay respect and deference to the state. Its
traditional slogan had been 'Throne, Altar and Nation'. And from 1924, it
was intimately linked in Breslau to the municipal authorities, when the Lord
Mayor and City Treasurer were made ex officio members of the local
Evangelical Consistory. On the other hand, when the state was overrun by
godless Nazis, its distaste was manifest, yet it could not bring itself to rebel.
It preferred pastoral humility to open confrontation, thereby leaving the
Nazis free to do their worst. In the reforms of 1938, it lost its rights in the
parishes and the Protestant Theological Seminary, and was subjected to an
'Evangelical Deaconry'. Despite such hindrances, the Protestant Church
continued to serve its flock. Pastor Konrad Müller (1884–1967), for
example, worked undisturbed as minister of Breslau's St John the Baptist
Church from 1918 to 1945. He was to become chaplain to the defendants of
the Nuremberg Tribunal. His younger colleague, Pastor Joachim Konrad
(1903–79) was deprived by the Nazis of his preaching licence, but was
nonetheless able to act in 1940–5 as the last Protestant priest of St
Elizabeth's Church. After the war, he was to serve in West Germany as
Chairman of the Association of Silesian Protestants in exile.

The *Deutsche Christen* (German Christian movement), in contrast, was
formed not by 'trimmers', but by active collaborators. Founded in 1932, it
adopted the Führer principle through the election of a 'national bishop',
inserted numerous 'Aryan paragraphs' into its constitution and subordinated itself totally to the NSDAP. Some of its luminaries even sought to
repudiate the Old Testament because of its Jewish authorship. One of the
founders of the *Deutsche Christen* was the Silesian Wilhelm Kube
(1887–1943), later Gauleiter of 'White Ruthenia' and would-be Gauleiter of
Moscow.

The *Bekennende Kirche*, or 'Confessing Church', was alone in its single-
minded determination to resist the regime and counteract the complicity of
the *Deutsche Christen*. It was formed in 1933 with Pastor Niemöller's
'Provisional Pastoral Union', and was crystallised in 1934 at the Synod of
Barmen, where its theological and administrative organisation was established. It bravely denounced Nazi 'paganism' and the 'Führer Cult', and
opposed the Nazi-inspired trend for 'deconfessionalisation'. In Silesia, it
grouped itself around a network of 'Fraternal Councils'. But in Breslau it

endured a painful split. In 1935, one group under Bishop Otto Zänker (1876–1960), the last of the senior Protestant leaders to stay clear of the 'German Christians', signed a declaration of loyalty to the Third Reich. This approach attracted a majority of Vratislavian pastors, but was weakened by Bishop Zänker's forced retirement in 1939. The minority 'Neustadt Programme' was left as the sole independent Protestant voice. Its chairman, Ernst Hornig (1894–1976), Pastor of St Barbara's Church, led prayers for peace during the Munich Crisis and was to survive the Siege of Breslau. One of its female ministers, Katherine Staritz (1903–53), who dared to assist fugitive Jews, was sent to Ravensbrück concentration camp.

The Vratislavian theologian Dietrich Bonhoeffer (1906–45) was one of the Confessing Church's martyrs and the inventor of the concept of 'Christianity without Religion'. He had left Germany in 1931 to work in the International Ecumenical Movement, yet returned to fight the Nazis' 'contempt for humanity'. Despite being briefly arrested in 1937 and later banned from preaching, he never wavered from the position taken in a broadcast for Radio Berlin in February 1933, when he warned that the Führer (Leader) would become a *Verführer* (a seducer). Active in the resistance circle around Admiral Canaris and the *Abwehr*, he was arrested again in April 1943 and imprisoned in Berlin. Documents linking him to the *Kreisau* conspirators led to his execution in Flossenbürg concentration camp in April 1945. Much was made of his return to Germany from the safety of exile. He had no regrets:

> I want to assure you that I have not regretted coming back for a moment . . . I knew quite well what I was doing, and I acted with a clear conscience. I have no wish to cross out of my life anything that has happened since . . . I resolved to play a part in Germany's fate. It is with no reproach that I look back on the past and accept the present.[48]

The majority of German Catholics were no less apprehensive about the regime than the Protestants were. They saw the power and dangers of the Nazi propaganda machine, yet hesitated to make a stand. The position taken by Cardinal Adolf Bertram, Prince-Bishop of Breslau (1858–1945), was perhaps typical. As Chairman of the Bishop's Congress in Fulda from 1919 and head of the largest diocese in Germany, Cardinal Bertram was hugely influential. Yet his political statements were often ambivalent. He claimed to champion the Poles among his flock, but advocated the pro-German cause during the Upper Silesian plebiscite. Prior to 1933, he criticised the demagoguery of Nazism but not specifically its anti-Semitism. After Hitler's seizure of power, he ordered the public reading of Pope Pius XI's twin encyclicals – *Mit brennender Sorge* and *Divine Redemptoris* – which ruled that Nazism and Communism were both incompatible with Christianity. He protested in private to Berlin on numerous topics, including educational policy, Church policy, euthanasia and the treatment of non-Aryan Catholics, especially Poles. Yet he stopped there. As a contemporary noted in 1935, Cardinal Bertram feared a rupture between the Church and the state, since 'the fidelity of many Catholics towards the Church might fail the test'.[49] So he preferred to parry direct attacks on the Church, but not to fight from principle.

Many people, therefore, deprived of decisive leadership, attempted to combine their allegiance to Christianity with service to the Third Reich. Conflicts inevitably ensued. The Gauleiter and *Oberpräsident* of Silesia in 1934–40, Josef Wagner (1899–1945), was one who came unstuck. A Lorrainer and former official in Westphalia, Wagner had belonged to the first group of twelve Nazi MPs in 1928. Yet as a devout and practising Catholic, he sought to blunt anti-religious legislation and frequently complained about the activities of the SS. As Gauleiter in Breslau, he sent his daughter to the Ursuline School and was himself a frequent communicant at Cathedral Masses. In 1940, he was accused of disclosing classified information to the 'Catholic Action' society. Removed from his posts, he was tried before the Supreme Party Tribunal in January 1942 and, though found not guilty, was jailed and sent to a concentration camp. He was probably shot by the Gestapo in Plötzensee Prison in Berlin.[50]

The fighter-ace Werner Mölders (1913–41) was another example of a man who tried to serve two masters. A veteran of the Spanish Civil War, he was given the highest awards for bravery and appointed 'General Inspector of Fighter Pilots', aged only twenty-eight. Yet, as a committed Catholic, he was regularly shadowed by the Gestapo, who kept a lengthy file on him. When he died in a crash-landing at Breslau-Gandau (Gądów), he left a cache of letters that expressed his horror at Nazi killings and called for Catholics to be considered fully fledged Germans. The Gestapo denounced his correspondence as a forgery and Bormann offered a reward of 100,000 marks for information on its 'author'.

The complex currents of religious belief in inter-war Germany are perhaps best illustrated in the inspiring life and death of Edith Stein (1891–1942). Born in Breslau into an Orthodox Jewish family, and a graduate of the University of Breslau, where she studied German philology, history and psychology, Stein was a woman of extraordinary intellectual, spiritual and moral powers. Taking an interest in philosophy, she moved to Göttingen, and after an interval as a volunteer nurse in the Austrian army, obtained a Ph.D. summa cum laude at Freiburg in 1916. At that stage she regarded herself an atheist, and worked as an assistant to Edmund Husserl, the father of phenomenology. She also returned to lecture in Breslau. At this point, having read the autobiography of St Teresa of Ávila, she converted to Catholicism. It was the last step on a road that had begun several years before, when the widow of a young professor killed during the war told Stein that 'his death had helped her to walk the Way of the Cross of her master'. 'For the very first time,' she wrote later, 'I saw with my own eyes the victory of the Church over . . . death, born from the redemptive suffering of Christ . . . My faithlessness was broken; Judaism faded; and Christ shone forth in the mystery of the Cross.'

The middle years of Edith Stein's life were taken up by secular scholarship and religious studies. The young academic made an intensive study of St Thomas Aquinas, flitting between conferences in Germany and abroad. She repeatedly tried to be accepted for habilitation, but several universities, including Breslau, rejected her because she was a woman. She finally took a teaching post in the Dominican School at Speyer. Paradoxically, her interest in Judaism returned, and on regular visits to her mother in Breslau she attended the synagogue.

In 1933, in Cologne, Stein entered the closed Order of the Carmelites and took the monastic name of Sister Teresa Benedicta of the Cross. On Maundy Thursday that year, she recorded a mystical vision. 'I conversed with the Saviour', she wrote, 'and I told him I knew His Cross would be placed on the Jewish people . . . when the service ended I felt certain inside me that I had been listened to. But what exactly that carrying of the Cross implied, I did not yet know.' From then on, she devoted herself to contemplation, study and writing. Her principal works were *Temporal and Eternal Existence* and the unfinished *Knowledge of the Cross*. In 1938, to escape Nazi persecution, she moved to the Carmelite Convent at Echt in the Netherlands.

Edith Stein, in the view of the Nazis, belonged to the pseudo-category of 'non-Aryan Christians'. In other words, she was Jewish by race and Christian only by religion. It was a sentence of death. She intended to move yet again to Switzerland, but was caught with her sister in a Nazi round-up of Dutch Jews, which was deliberately activated in response to a protest of the Catholic bishops against Nazi atrocities. She was arrested at Echt on 2 August 1942. Seven days later she perished in the gas-chamber at Auschwitz. She was beatified in 1987 and canonised in 1998 as a co-patroness of Europe – not without a vociferous outcry from various American Jewish circles. According to a pamphlet with the imprint of the German Catholic hierarchy: 'It is historically fair to say that Edith Stein was killed as a Jew, although, it is equally fair to believe her own words, when she declared that by this act, she wanted to carry the Cross of Jesus'[51] (see page 482).

As amply shown by the nature of the attacks on Breslau Jewry (see below), the Nazis were no more interested in Judaism than they were in Christianity. They were interested only in their own phoney ideas on race. Non-Jewish converts to Judaism (who were not unknown) were not in danger from the Nuremberg Laws, and so long as Jews were allowed to live, they were free to practise their religion. The Jewish Theological Seminary continued to function normally until closed down in 1938. The old Stork Synagogue in Breslau stayed in use as long as there were Jews to use it. Breslau's New Synagogue, close to Tauentzien Platz, was filled with daily worshippers until *Reichskristallnacht* in November 1938, when it was blown to smithereens.

The last of the liberal rabbis of Breslau, Dr Vogelstein, stayed on when most of his flock were leaving, as Walter Laqueur recalled:

> Dr Vogelstein was one of the most cultured men I've ever known and one of the friendliest. He had written an erudite book on Roman history and kept one of the largest private libraries in town. Many's the time I saw him in the bookshops when he would apologise with a smile: 'I'm sure that I have the blessed book somewhere, but for the moment I just can't find it.' The last time I visited him, in 1938, he was a broken man. He was a solid German patriot who had decided to reject all traces of Jewish nationalism. So now his whole world was in ruins. It was the time of Hitler's greatest success, and hence of an unknown future. He was a gentle person, yet there was in him no less the fire of an Old Testament prophet. He quoted for me the passage from Isaiah about the coming Day of Vengeance and – as befits a liberal Rabbi – St Paul's Letter to the Romans, xii, 19. Just as I was about to leave, he presented me, as with a parting gift, with the lines of Friedrich von Logau:

> > Gottesmühlen mahlen langsam,
> > Mahlen aber trefflich klein;
> > Ob aus Langmut Er sich säumet,
> > Bringt mit Schärf' Er alles ein.[52]

> > (The mills of God they grind so slow,
> > They grind so slow, they grind so fine
> > Though He may tarry in His patience
> > He will not miss a single grain.)

Needless to say, Friedrich von Logau (1604–55), whose rhyming epigrams were written as an antidote to the horrors of the Thirty Years War, was – like Dr Vogelstein himself – a Silesian and a stoicist.

*

In its cultural development, the Weimar Republic was widely infused with liberal attitudes and modernist styles. Many of the trends had their origins before the First World War, but the political collapse of 1918 brought about a widening of intellectual horizons in a flourishing cultural scene, where conservative criticism mingled with, and tempered, the wilder manifestations of modernism. Having been in the ranks of the avant-garde in imperial Germany, Breslau was well placed after 1918 to strengthen its position.

The Breslau Osteuropa-Institut, established in the summer of 1918, added variety to the scene. Originally intended to assist German exploitation of the lands gained by the Treaty of Brest-Litovsk, it lost its ostensible *raison d'être* through Germany's withdrawal from the East. Nevertheless its five departments, including East European law, economics and history, did not become redundant. In conjunction with partner institutes in Danzig (Gdańsk) and Königsberg, it addressed a growing demand for knowledge about Europe's turbulent, eastern half.[53] In subsequent years it would be ever more closely identified with German industrial and nationalist circles, and provided support for the realisation of Nazi expansionist aims. (Like SSEES at the University of London, it was a pioneer of what would later be called 'Area Studies'.)

The Academy of Arts lay at the centre of Breslau's cultural world. Reorganised by Hans Poelzig prior to the outbreak of the war, it reached its creative zenith between 1925 and 1931 under the directorship of Oskar Moll (1875–1947). In one view it can be regarded, through its concentration on workshop practice, as 'a predecessor of the first (Weimar) *Bauhaus*'.[54] Its links with the Bauhaus were intimate. Poelzig had wanted Walter Gropius to succeed him, and many of the Bauhaus artists and designers also taught in Breslau.

The stage designer Oskar Schlemmer (1888–1943), for example, came to the Breslau Academy in 1929 after nine years of teaching at the Bauhaus. The abstract artist Georg Muche (1895–1987), who had worked with Schlemmer on the very first Bauhaus exhibition of 1923, came in 1931. Indeed, between them, the lecturers and students of the Breslau Academy represented almost all of the main artistic trends of the Weimar period. The 'Munich New Secession', a protest against Impressionism, was co-founded by Alexander Kanoldt, who taught in Breslau in the late 1920s, and by Otto Mueller, a celebrated painter of nudes and gypsies. Kanoldt went on to become one of the stars of *Neue Sachlichkeit*, or 'New Objectivity', a reaction against Expressionism, which was associated with names such as Otto Dix, Georg Grosz and Carlo Mense. Among its students, the academy trained Expressionist artists like Alexander Camaro, Willy Jaeckel and Ludwig Meidner, and the sculptor Joachim Karsch. Many years later, from the safety of exile, the graphic artist Johannes Molzahn, who had been Oskar Moll's pupil and colleague, wrote to Moll's widow Margarethe:

> Everything that I have seen and experienced since those Breslau years has only strengthened my earlier conviction, that the Academy under Oskar Moll was a classic example of an artistic-educational institution in the contemporary world.[55]

Two of Breslau's most famous artists of the inter-war period had little connection to the academy. The first was Eugen Spiro (1874–1972), who studied for just two years in Breslau before continuing his studies in Munich in 1894. He went on to become a leading member of the 'Berlin Secession' movement. alongside fellow Vratislavian Willy Jaeckel. After working as a sketch artist for the General Staff during the First World War, Spiro became a noted portrait painter. Perhaps his most famous sitter was Leni Riefenstahl (b.1902), the former dancer and actress who would later make her name as director of the Nazi propaganda films *Triumph des Willens* ('Triumph of the Will', 1936) and *Olympia* (1938). Spiro emigrated to France in 1935 and, from 1941, spent the remainder of his life in the USA.

Count Balthazar Klossowski de Rola, or 'Balthus' (1908–2001), was the other. Self-taught, enigmatic and controversial, Balthus was for some 'the last great painter of the 20th century'. His depictions of pubescent girls brought him fame and notoriety, with one critic noting sourly that 'he is to little girls what Stubbs is to horses'. Nonetheless, his pictures featured in numerous international exhibitions and even graced the private collection of Picasso, who described him as 'a real painter'. On his private life he was deliberately silent. Though Balthus spent his early life in Paris, it has been suggested that he was born in Breslau. The fact that his native tongue was German might seem to support this contention, but the artist himself was less than forthcoming: 'Balthus is a painter about whom nothing is known,' he once said, before adding, 'Now, let us look at the pictures.'[56]

The efforts of two Breslau academics in other fields, Otfrid Foerster and Fritz Haber, offer an interesting reflection of Weimar politics. Professor of Neurology in Breslau since 1909, Foerster was called to Moscow in 1922 to advise the team that was treating Lenin. The choice of a German doctor to treat a Soviet leader was an interesting one. It may be seen as an assertion of the 'Rapallo Spirit', whereby the two pariah nations of Europe had resumed relations and had waived reparations.

Haber's post-war activities illustrate Germany's economic frailty. After his controversial Nobel Prize (see above), he set to work on a project which, by extracting gold from sea water, sought to ease Germany's payment of reparations. His seemingly hare-brained scheme – which extended the concept of panning for gold in rivers – involved him in a series of experimental Atlantic crossings by specially adapted liners.[57] In 1928, thoroughly disillusioned, he was forced to conclude that gold-panning in the ocean was not going to fill Fort Knox.

The Vratislavian literary community, which came to the fore after 1918, had strong links with the pre-war period. The leading literary journal, *Der Osten* ('The East'), had been launched in 1902 and became the vehicle of the 'Breslau School of Poets'. The leading personality, Carl Hauptmann (1858–1921), Gerhart's brother, died at the start of the 1920s, but exerted a strong influence on younger writers. Among the latter was Walter Meckauer (1889–1965), whose debut with *Die Bergschmiede* (1916) dealt with the themes of Silesian nature and *Heimat* popularised earlier by Gerhart Hauptmann. His *Josche zieht ins Feld* (1931) revealed sympathies for the Russian Revolution. Two other writers stand out, both inspired by sentimental 'Silesianism'. Will-Erich Peuckert (1895–1969) was an ethnographer, whose *Schlesischer Volkskunde* (1928) was a standard work. His novel *Luntross* (1924) was written in the same cosy spirit. Paul Keller (1873–1932), who edited the monthly *Die Bergstadt*, was one of the most successful writers in Germany. His early novel, *Waldwinter* (1902), treated the subject of the flight to nature by modern city dwellers. His entertaining *Drei Brüder suchen das Glück* (1929) closed a career in which he had sold five million books. His grave in Breslau survives.

Breslau's formidable musical establishment continued to attract some of the biggest names. Gustav Mahler (1860–1911) had met both triumph and disaster in Breslau – disaster with the ill-received IV Symphony in 1903 and triumph with his presentation of the V Symphony (1905) and III Symphony (1906). But the strong Mahlerian tradition was upheld after the composer's death by the chief conductor of the Breslau Orchestra, Georg Dohrn, who worked in the city for more than thirty years up to 1933. Wilhelm Furtwängler (1886–1954), whose career had started as a reserve conductor in 1905–6, returned on numerous occasions between 1925 and 1940 with his Berlin Philharmonic. Richard Strauss (1864–1949), whose opera *Salome* had been premièred in Breslau in 1906, reappeared frequently both as a conductor and accompanist until the mid-1930s.

Yet the halcyon days of Weimar were to be short-lived. The advent of the Third Reich subjected all aspects of academic and cultural life to severe strictures. The effect on the art world was immediate. The Führer's tastes did not match those of the Breslau Academy. Wholesale academic dismissals preceded a Nazi offensive against art, which culminated in the confiscations of October 1936, when the Breslauer Otto Mueller had the honour of being put on the same 'degenerate' list as Kokoschka, Picasso and Van Gogh. The resultant Munich 'Exhibition of Degenerate Art' attracted some two million visitors and was the most popular exhibition ever staged in the Third Reich.[58] The fate of 'degenerate' artists was rather more serious. Those who remained in Germany faced escalating penalties. Most, like Schlemmer, had to survive as best they could. He was removed from the Breslau Academy in 1933, and all his works were removed from German galleries. One of the leading artists of his day was thus reduced to camouflaging the municipal gasometer in Stuttgart. It is said that he died in 1943 from 'grief at not being allowed to paint'.[59]

Once the staff were suitably tamed, academic life could be bent more energetically to the purposes of the Nazi regime. In 1939, for example, a group of Breslau academics was commissioned to examine the historical preconditions for 'large-scale settlement policy in the eastern territories'. It included the Professor of German Folklore, Walter Kuhn (1903–83). Born in Bielitz (Bielsko-Biała), Kuhn was a specialist on the German linguistic enclaves of eastern Poland and was involved as an adviser in the resettlement of the Volhynian Germans.[60] He was to become one of the leading lights of *Ostforschung* or 'Eastern research'.

Other projects followed. After the September campaign, a number of professors were engaged by the Ministry of Education to supply 'proof' that the Polish areas annexed to the Reich were culturally German. Three scholars from Breslau were selected: the art historian Dagobert Frey, and the prehistorians Ernst Petersen and Martin Jahn. Frey delivered his first contribution in 1941: a lavishly illustrated book on the city of 'Krakau'. In it, he contrived to avoid all mention of the Jewish community, which had made up about one-quarter of the pre-war population and had been extremely influential in its cultural history. He also refused to identify the ancient capital of the Kingdom of Poland as a Polish city. The following year, he published a guide to Lublin, which showed a similar degree of objectivity.[61] Breslau University itself was given a broader task to fulfil. In a speech in November 1941, the President of the German Academy outlined the demands of German culture:

> [In order for us] to possess a space . . . it must be won spiritually. [To this end] the Reich University in Posen, together with the old eastern universities in Königsberg and Breslau shall form a consolidated Eastwall of German spirit which shall forever watch and prevent any Slav inroads.[62]

Anthropology was an academic discipline that lent itself to the ideological requirements of the times. The 'Breslau School'[63] had been established in 1929, when Egon Freiherr von Eickstedt was appointed Professor of Anthropology and launched a number of overseas expeditions. His work to establish a typology of racial and behavioural characteristics culminated in

Die rassischen Grundlagen des deutschen Volkstums ('The racial basis of Germanity, 1934), which identified five 'germanic races' – Nordic, Dinaric, Mediterranean, Alpine and East Baltic. Supported by collaborators such as Ilse Schwidetzsky, the school became a leading centre for the study of Nazi theories of race, so beloved by the likes of Heinrich Himmler. Surprisingly perhaps, it was to survive the death of its Nazi sponsors, publishing journals such as *The Mankind Quarterly* and turning itself into a scientific base for modern, right-wing race theories.

After 1933 literature became intensely political. An established figure like Professor Paul Merker (1881–1945), who had the chair of Modern Literature in Breslau, held on by specialising in Renaissance studies and by maintaining a bland, apolitical façade. But many succumbed to the pressure for nationalistic and locally patriotic writing. Hans Christoph Kaergel (1889–1946), for example, followed an early work called *Volk ohne Heimat* (1922), with a later one called *Hockewanzel* (1933), which was openly contemptuous of Poles and Czechs. As editor of an anthology of German Silesian verse, he qualified to be chosen in 1940 as the *Landesleiter*, in effect the wartime dictator, of the provincial Literary Board. Gerhart Pohl (1902–66) wrote plays and novels on subjects such as the Waldenburg (Wałbrzych) coal basin and the romance of the Silesian railways. Wolfgang Schwarz, whose first collection of poems was entitled *Das neue Lied der Heimat* (1941), was an officer in Germany's Cossack Brigade. Others paid heavily for their views. Walter Steinberg (1913–92) was a Communist writer, who spent three years in Kletschkau Prison, having been handed over to the Nazi authorities by the USSR. Arthur Silbergleit (1881–1941) was a Catholic priest of Jewish descent, who died in Auschwitz.

Emil Ludwig (1881–1948) was one intellectual who refused to compromise. The son of the Breslau eye specialist Hermann Cohn, he trained as a lawyer before gaining international fame in the 1920s with his biographies of, among others, Goethe, Napoleon and Bismarck. He was forced into exile in Switzerland in 1932 and subsequently to the US, where he became an adviser to President Roosevelt, whose biography he also wrote. His highly readable books were very diverse: *Three Titans* (1930) on Michelangelo, Rembrandt and Beethoven; *The Nile: Lifeportrait of a river* (1936), and his autobiographical *Geschenke des Lebens* (1931). His hatred of the Nazi regime was expressed in numerous bitterly anti-Fascist pamphlets for the American authorities. In his 'How to treat the Germans' (1943), he expounded on the arrogance, brutality and intolerance of his compatriots:

> The Germans do not even have a word for 'fair', just as they have no word
> for 'gentleman'. Both of these words were incorporated into the rich

German language in their English forms. The Germans, trained to be soldiers, lack the Anglo-Saxon sportive spirit and joy in games; they are a nation without hobbies.[64]

Ludwig never returned to Breslau after 1932. But his memories of the district of his youth were not bitter ones:

> The Stadtgraben [the old moat] was a quiet spot. Thirty houses stood there; some were villas with gardens, others were arranged as flats for letting but had been for decades in the hands of the same old families . . . It was a sort of aristocratic Corso, along which the carriages of the rich would drive now and then . . . Once the walls had been destroyed and peace nominally established . . . a comfortable commercial town had taken the place of the truculent fortress, and all seemed quiet on the hillside; rarely was music to be heard there, and even the moat, broad as a river and bordered with the green of drooping willows and dense alder trees, was never enlivened by a passing boat, its character being more fitly indicated by the presence of a few swans.[65]

The inter-war period in Germany was notable for the advent of mass culture. In Breslau, as elsewhere, cinema, radio and, of course, sport, grew in popularity. Weimar presided over the revolution in cinema – the era of Fritz Lang, G.W. Pabst and Kristina Söderbaum. It brought a spate of innovative building including the Deli Cinema of 1926, designed by Hans Poelzig. By 1939, Breslau possessed thirty-seven cinemas, of which only ten survived the war. Radio, too, was the product of technological advance, becoming another staple of cultural life. Breslau's radio tower (1925) and Berlin's Haus des Rundfunks (1930) were both designed by Poelzig. From then on, 'Breslau' was to figure on radio dials throughout the world, as one of the most powerful radio stations in Europe.

Cycling and football were the most popular pursuits of inter-war Breslau. Based on the track at Grüneiche and, later, at Lillienthal, cycling numbered some twenty-four clubs by 1939 and many stars, such as Richard Scheuermann and the Heidenreich brothers. Its popularity was exceeded only by that of football. Yet Breslau enjoyed two fairly glory-free decades in the German League. Its leading clubs, *Schlesien Breslau*, *SC Breslau 08* and *Sportfreunde Breslau*, never managed to reach a final of the German Cup or Championship competition and won no silverware. The closest they came was in two semi-final appearances, one for *Sportfreunde Breslau* in 1920, and one for *SC Breslau 08* in 1929. There was more success on the international stage. Five football internationals were played in Breslau, where the German national team remained unbeaten with two draws and three victories. One of those victories, in May 1937, was a monumental 8–0 thrashing of Denmark. The team – Jakob, Janes, Münzenberg, Kupfer, Goldbrunner, Kitzinger,

Lehner, Gellesch, Siffling, Szepan and Urban – went on to win the following ten games. They came to be known as the 'Breslau Eleven'.

The highlight of the inter-war sporting record, however, must undoubtedly be found in the XIIth *Deutsche Turn und Sportfest*, or German Sports Festival, held in Breslau in July 1938. In the presence of the Führer, the athletes and sportsmen and sportswomen of the Reich competed in all imaginable disciplines before a total audience of some 600,000 spread over nine days. Hitler's appearance in Breslau was later described by a teenager who saw his Führer for the one and only time in his life. As he later recalled with some embarrassment, Hitler was treated with 'the deference due to a God':

It was a Sunday of sunshine, benefiting from what Germans at the time called *Führerwetter*. The Sports and Gymnastics Festival had brought thousands of visitors into Breslau from all over the Reich . . . At the time, Hitler had reached the peak of popularity. Even his most determined critics admitted that in a free referendum he would have won 80% support. The Sudeten Crisis had already begun, and week by week, the pressure on Czechoslovakia was being tightened . . . Yet there was no thought of a new war, which Germans, especially in the East, feared like the plague.

That day, I was carrying a flag of the German youth movement, and was standing somewhat at an angle to the Führer's rostrum, at the opposite side of the open space where he was reviewing the march-past of the gymnastic groups. From a distance of about a hundred metres, I could see him very well and I never took my eye off him. Obviously, we were all overexcited; around us, tension, anticipation and joy reigned. A band was playing marching music and heated up the atmosphere.

Suddenly, a far-off noise was heard coming from the streets near the square. It got louder and louder, until it seemed like a hurricane . . . It approached us in a rising wave, reaching skywards and ready to sweep us away. I've never since experienced such a sensation, simultaneously terrified and fascinated. Seeking support, I latched onto a heavy pole from which a black flag with a lightning sign was waving. Hitler turned towards the noise with a tense look. But I also noticed that one group was standing at their posts with stoical ease. These were the Führer's bodyguard from the SS Adolf Hitler, gigantic men over two metres tall wearing black uniforms and black steel helmets. They surrounded the rostrum, and, at the sign from an officer, closed ranks . . .

Then it happened. A marching column of six rows emerged from the Schweidnitzerstrasse, all dressed alike in grey suits and Tyrolean hats. They were the front of the huge delegation from the Sudeten Gymnastic Association in Czechoslovakia. It was the crowning point of the march-past, and a propaganda performance carefully thought out by the manipulators of Goebbels' ministry (as I later realised) . . .

When the flag-bedecked head of the procession came level with the Führer, he stepped forward, stood at the edge of the balustrade, raised his right arm, and greeted the Sudeten Germans' banners . . . At that moment, I felt as if the whole Schlossplatz and the thousands of spectators would explode like a colossal bomb. The roar of enchantment became unbearable.

. . . Of course, I was screaming like everyone else with all my strength. The wonderment carried me away. Apart from that, one can't escape from mass hysteria. I myself wanted to participate, to be at one with that wonderful company.

Suddenly, one could distinguish a new sound amidst the shouting, a sharp staccato whose meaning I could not immediately grasp. The words passed from mouth to mouth until finally in an ever more insistent rhythm they were voiced by the whole crowd, as if by one enormous throat: Ein Volk, Ein Reich, Ein Führer (One People, One State, One Leader). And then, once again, drowning itself in a hypnotic emotion of unlimited power.

It took people out of their daily routine, away from their humdrum existence, from their isolation. It gave them a convincing sense of belonging to a magnificent whole, a feeling of victory and strength. For a few brief moments, it promised the unattainable, a glimpse of immortality . . .

Girls and young women, dressed in folk costume, were the first to advance on the Führer's stand, pushing aside the giant SS-men, who clearly had orders not to intervene. Hitler leaned over the barrier and, smiling, shook the hands stretched out to him. Women wept with joy.

Hitler's private photographer, Heinrich Hoffmann, was circling around. He had a monopoly on the Führer's official pictures, and made a fortune from them . . . 35 years later, when I was doing research in the photographic archives in Washington and London, those shots taken that day in Breslau in 1938 were still there . . . [66]

Hitler aimed to make German youth as 'tough as leather, as swift as whippets and as hard as Krupp steel',[67] and thereby prove the superiority of the Aryan race. In this regard, one is reminded of the old Polish joke: 'as slim as Göring, as tall as Goebbels, and as blond as Hitler'.

Breslau's Polish culture slipped steadily downhill between 1918 and 1945. It enjoyed the backing neither of the Church hierarchy nor of the state. In the 1920s, paradoxically, it suffered from the re-establishment of an independent Poland. The proliferation of Polish institutions in nearby Poznań, from the creation of the Adam Mickiewicz University to the expansion of a Polish cultural infrastructure of theatres, schools, libraries, bookshops and societies, attracted many people who before 1918 might have been drawn to Breslau. After 1933, under Nazi rule, the picture of decline faded into one of terminal crisis. An early signal was emitted when a group of students at the university was set upon by stormtroopers and severely thrashed, simply for speaking Polish. Since Nazi ideology put the Poles into the category of *Untermenschen*, it followed that no case existed for preserving – let alone for respecting – Polish language, literature, art or history. Such things, quite officially, were declared to be inferior. The Nazis had far more radical plans than the old *Hakatists* (see above), but they put the *Hakatist* programme into effect.

The post-war *Encyclopaedia of Wrocław* (2000) lists no single Polish writer who was active in Breslau in the 1920s and 1930s. The only Polish books to be published for local consumption were devotional booklets and newsletters issued by the diocesional office. There was no Polish bookshop. All Polish students were expelled from the University of Breslau in 1939. A resolution passed in the Aula Leopoldina declared, 'We are profoundly convinced that no Polish foot will ever cross the threshold of this German University again.'[68]

*

Between 1918 and 1945, Breslau's 'Germanity' was manifested with unequalled intensity. Not only did Germans represent an overwhelming numerical majority, but they were in the grip of an ugly public mood, where all signs of otherness at the very least provoked frowns and, at the worst, blows. Both in the 1920s (in the days of the hyperinflation, the *Freikorps* and the Upper Silesian Risings) and even more so in the 1930s (the days of mass unemployment, street warfare and Nazi gangsterism) it was very uncomfortable not to be a German. Discrimination increased. The ethnic minorities dwindled, and by 1939 had been virtually eliminated. The Poles were made well aware of the danger early on. The Jews, who were very largely German by language and culture, could have little inkling of the virulent hostility brewing against them.

The Polish community in Breslau dropped from a meagre 4–5,000 in 1918 to a statistically insignificant residue two decades later. After the First World War, Polish Masses were resumed in St Ann's Church, and from 1921 in St Martin's. A Polish Consulate was opened on the Main Square, and a tiny Polish school was established by a devoted teacher, Helena Adamczewska. But the omens were not favourable. The creation of the Polish Republic drew off most of the educated people who might have given communal leadership. On 26 August 1920, a German mob broke away from a plebiscite meeting to demolish both the Polish Consulate and the Polish

School. The Polish Library was burned to the ground, together with several thousand books.

Matters improved briefly in the mid-1920s, and the Polish Consulate, School and Library reopened. The Union of Poles in Germany (ZPN), whose membership was strongest in Berlin and on the Ruhr, launched a branch in Breslau. A minuscule Polish People's Party won a total of 250 votes in the election of 1924. A 'Polish House' was established in 1928 on the Heinrichstrasse as a focus for cultural and educational activities. A Polish scout troop was formed. And the Polish 'Harmonia' Choral Society supported three choirs. But the numbers simply did not match the dedication of the activists. And the onset of mass unemployment cut Breslau off from the traditional stream of work-seekers from its Polish hinterland.

All hopes for a lasting Polish revival in Breslau were dashed after 1933. What is more, the advent of the Nazis coincided with a marked influx of students from the Polish districts of German Upper Silesia, who were no longer permitted to study in Poland. A clash was therefore inevitable. The creation of a Polish Student Union in 1933 came at the very time when the Gestapo was beginning to investigate Polish students as an undesirable element. During the compulsory registration of all students by the police, Poles and Jews were issued with the same distinctive yellow identity cards. Polish students were later able to exchange their yellow cards for standard brown ones marked *Polnische Minderheit*, or 'Polish minority'. But then the restrictions began. In 1937, all Polish scout and student uniforms were banned. In 1938, the Polish House was ransacked by the police, and all activities ceased. In March 1939, a last defiant and illegal parade was held under the banner of *Wiara Ojców*, 'the Faith of our Fathers'. Community leaders were arrested, and casually sent to the concentration camps. In the first half of 1939, while emigration was still possible, many of the remaining Polish families in Breslau simply packed their bags and left for Poland. The very last Polish Mass in German Breslau was celebrated in St Martin's Church on 17 September 1939,[69] the day of the Soviet invasion of Poland. Polishness appeared to have been eliminated for good.

The attacks on Breslau's Jewry passed through similar stages. A curious sign of the changing times was seen in the local Breslau branch of the *Alpenverein*. In 1881, the branch had voted to exclude members who wanted to keep out the Jews. In 1921, it voted to exclude the Jews. The initial violence of the immediate post-war years blew over, but it returned in the 1930s with a vengeance. In 1933–5, anti-Jewish discrimination was patchy and disorganised. After the Nuremberg Laws of 1935, it became thorough and systematic. In 1938–9, after *Reichskristallnacht*, it was unrestrained and life-threatening. But it could not yet be described as exterminatory.

After 1918, a sea-change occurred in attitudes towards Breslau's Jewish community. New groups, such as the German Freedom Party, were established with explicitly anti-Semitic programmes. The Kapp putsch of 1920 provided the first victims (see above). Later that year, a Jewish-owned store and a hotel housing *Ostjuden* were attacked by a mob. In July 1923, a demonstration against inflation and unemployment turned into a riot that blamed the Jews for the nation's ills. The success story of Wilhelmine assimilation was evaporating.

Nonetheless, for many Breslau Jews life continued much as before. An elementary school was founded in 1921 and a secondary school two years later. A home for the aged and a youth institute were opened in 1930. The younger generation of Jews saw anti-Semitism as incomprehensible. Their parents prayed that it would be a passing phase.

Fewer than half of Breslau's highly assimilated Jews practised their former religion. Most of them did not even think of themselves as Jewish. The son of such a family, which had returned to Breslau after spending the war years abroad, recalled the 1920s:

It was the Germany of the Weimar Republic. I remember being shifted from the bedroom to the hall one night during the week of the Kapp Putsch, when machine-gun bullets came through the window of our suburban apartment . . . I remember being sent shopping with bread ration stamps. I remember discussing the latest dollar rate with other boys during the great inflation. I remember the presidential elections of 1925 when General Hindenburg, the war hero already nearing his dotage, defeated the candidates of the disunited left and centre.

Politics did not occupy centre stage at home. My father was a scientist, proud of being a citizen of the free city of Hamburg . . . and consciously anglophile. He was much less nationalistic than most of his academic colleagues but shared their class prejudices . . . He rejected socialism on free-trade grounds, and the Social Democrats as the party of the uneducated. My mother was completely unpolitical. Beautiful, determined and out to enjoy life . . . she left my father to marry an old Prussian nobleman when I was 12 . . .

Three of my four grandparents were Jewish by descent though no longer by religion . . . But of all this Jewish background we were as children barely aware. It did not affect our lives in any way . . . except that we enjoyed occasional holidays with our rich Polish uncle . . . Both my parents were Protestants, and I was baptised and confirmed in the Lutheran Church. But this, too, was a matter of social convention . . .

My last three years of secondary school were also the last three years of the Weimar Republic. Politics became inescapable . . . One after the other my classmates at school joined the Nazi organisations. I increasingly attached myself to the small band of active anti-Nazis in the class, one of whom was an artistically gifted boy who called himself a socialist. Another became a clergyman ... and briefly succeeded Willy Brandt as Burgomaster of Berlin. A third [became] conductor of the opera at Bremerhaven. We sat for our leaving exam in January 1933, and went off with our headmaster on the traditional [top] form ski-ing tour. When we got back, the Third Reich had broken out ...[70]

The advent of Hitler's chancellorship made the threat to German Jewry more explicit. Two Breslau diarists, Walter Tausk (1890–1941) and Willy Cohn (1888–1941), bore witness to the growing persecution. The former, who was an ex-soldier and a convert to Buddhism, chronicled Jewish life between 1933 and 1940. Cohn's diaries document the terminal phase in 1941.

To begin with, Tausk was reasonably positive. He noted as late as 1935 that there was 'no anti-Semitism in Breslau', talking instead of 'rather an openly expressed hatred of this [Nazi] government'.[71] It is difficult to say whether he was poorly informed or simply hoping against hope. For the Nazis were not biding their time passively. They were not ready for the mass violence that would break out shortly. But they were constantly spreading the threats and the smears. Julius Streicher's paper, *Der Stürmer*, for instance, published a long series of articles in 1934, each exposing the alleged misdeeds of Jews in a given German city. One week's article was devoted to Breslau, where, it was said, Jews practised the ritual murder of German children.

Very few people, in fact, knew what was really happening in Germany. Yet, as would be revealed only many decades later, the Nazis were secretly arming themselves with the means to give practical application to their racial theories. In particular, they wanted to find ways of identifying lines of Jewish descent in the population, irrespective of whether or not the individuals concerned were aware of their genealogy. To this end, the Nazis desperately needed two things which, on gaining power, they had not possessed. Firstly, they needed automated machines that were capable of extracting and cross-referencing detailed genealogical information from millions and millions of census returns. Secondly, they needed skilled demographers, who could develop the requisite techniques. The machinery was supplied by the American firm of IBM, whose 'punch-card system' was ideally suited for the purpose and whose German subsidiary, Dehomag, signed a contract on 8 January 1934 for manufacturing the system under licence in Germany. The demographers were found by trial and error:

On July 2 1936, several Nazis met in a Breslau inn to discuss the services of Fritz Arlt, a Leipzig statistician. Arlt had created a cross-referenced card file on every Leipzig Jewish resident, down to the so-called quarter Jews. What made Arlt's expertise desirable was that his cards also listed which ancestral Polish towns their families originated from. At the Breslau meeting, Arlt was assigned to work with the security offices of the [SS] *Auslandsorganisation*. His groundbreaking Polish demography was deemed so pivotal, [he] was asked to journey to Berlin to assist Eichmann's *Referat* II, 112, with expenses to be paid by the SD.[72]

In retrospect, one can see that this step was absolutely critical in the Nazi preparations for their campaign of genocide against the Jews. It gave them the confidence not only to identify the racial profile of every Jew in Germany, but to extend their information base to Europe's main reservoir of Jewish settlement in Poland. The concept of Germany's eastern *Lebensraum* moved from the realm of vague rhetoric to that of practical implementation. In due course, Arlt was destined to head the 'Population and Welfare Administration' (*sic*) of the wartime General Government.[73]

Once the Nuremberg Laws were instituted, therefore, the predicament of the prospective victims deteriorated overnight. The Nuremberg Laws, and their application, require some explanation. There were two main decrees: one was the *Reichsbürgergesetz*, or 'Citizenship law'; the other was the *Schutz des deutschen Blutes und der deutschen Ehre*, or 'The defence of German blood and German honour'. Every single person in Germany had to submit an application to the police and was then issued with an identity card, which had to be carried at all times. 'Aryan citizens' received brown cards. Jewish non-citizens, and various other categories, received yellow cards to make them instantly recognisable on inspection of their documents. From then on, discrimination was formalised and legalised. In the previous phase, as happened in Breslau, Jews lost their jobs as lawyers or doctors when Nazi thugs simply appeared in their offices and threw them out. But they could often find alternative employment or even return discreetly to their posts once the thugs had left. After 1935, no such ruses were possible. So-called 'Aryans' were themselves liable to prosecution if they broke the law, either by allowing Jews to work in forbidden categories of employment or by engaging with a Jewish person in sexual relations. The definition of Jewishness was exclusively determined by biological kinship.

At a stroke, therefore, Germany's Jews were disenfranchised, driven from the professions and from public office and stripped of their nationality. All relations between Jews and non-Jews were forbidden. In Breslau, six women were sent to the concentration camps for the new crime of *Rassenschande*, or 'Racial disgrace'. By 1939, all Jews had to adopt the names 'Israel' for men and 'Sara' for women. Their passports were marked with the red letter 'J'. If they applied to emigrate, their property was confiscated. There was no point protesting that one did not regard oneself as Jewish.

Reichskristallnacht proved a further turning point. The wave of mayhem, engineered by Goebbels, was supposed to be a popular response to the assassination, by a Jewish youth, of the German Ambassador in Paris. Nationwide, it cost ninety-one lives. Thousands of Jewish businesses, apartments and synagogues were looted and destroyed; 30,000 persons were arrested and many committed suicide. One eye-witness in Breslau was the fourteen-year-old John Najmann:

> That morning I left for school as usual. As I walked out of our building I saw my teacher rushing along with his hat pulled down and his collar up. I spoke to him but he whispered to me to go away, to leave him alone. 'There will be no school today,' he said. I continued on my way, past the small department store. All its windows were smashed, and German storm-troopers were throwing clothing and household goods from the upper floors onto the street. Police holding hands formed a cordon to stop the crowd being hit by the flying objects. When the store had been emptied of stock, the police stepped back and the spectators took armfuls from the huge pile. I saw a tram pass and the conductor and passengers got off to help themselves to whatever they could carry . . . I walked on and passed the prayer rooms where my family worshipped on the ground floor of a block of flats. The scrolls of our Torah had been taken out, dumped on the pavement and were burning there. I went back later and stuffed my pockets with the ashes and charred scraps . . . When I got home . . . my mother and I wept. It was the first time I had seen her cry.[74]

One Breslauer who escaped the horrors of *Reichskristallnacht* was Dr Alfons Lasker, father of the famed cellist Anita Lasker-Wallfisch. He was spared through the bravery of his Gentile friend, Walter Mehne:

> Mehne . . . was not a Jew, and he deliberately ignored the fact that the streets were crawling with members of the Gestapo looking for Jews. He climbed the stairs to our flat, took my father with him, and drove him around the town in his car for the rest of the day . . . The courage of a man like Mehne is all the more noteworthy since he was a well-known figure in Breslau. His premises were situated on the first floor of a building on the Tauentzien Platz, right in the centre of the town . . . The Mehnes were steadfast in their refusal to hang up a picture of Hitler . . . they also refused to hang out a swastika on the various 'flag days'. It made them instantly suspect. But they did not yield an inch. They disapproved of what was happening and were not afraid to show it. Both father and son conducted themselves in a manner which can only be called exemplary.[75]

Walter Tausk's recollections of *Kristallnacht* make harrowing reading. He noted that the mayhem 'was only stopped with a lot of effort. It had already degenerated into the looting of flats, strangulation, lynchings and man-slaughter.'[76] Later that year he wrote, 'those arrested go to Buchenwald, where the majority of the arrested Jews from Breslau are . . . or rather, were'.[77] His account was confirmed by a man called Rosten,[78] who was one of around 3,000 Jewish males from Breslau, from a total of some 10,000, who were sent to Buchenwald in the so-called 'November Action'. After weeks of maltreatment, in which an average of thirty inmates died daily, he was released because he was a First World War veteran and had promised to start emigration proceedings. By the end of 1938, two-thirds of Breslau's 30,000 Jews had left.

The exodus of Breslau's Jews took place in three or four distinct phases, each phase being less voluntary than the preceding one. In the first wave, people who saw the implications of Hitler's rise to power, and who had good contacts abroad, were free to board a train and go. In the course of 1933, between 2,000 and 3,000 people took this opportunity:

> My father had been dismissed from his chair at Breslau University under the 'Aryan Laws' and had been invited to a research appointment at Oxford. Together with his second wife and my younger sister, he moved to Oxford in August, and I followed six weeks later. On October 10 1933, I crossed the Channel from Calais to Dover and travelled straight through to Oxford. The next morning, the Rector of Lincoln College inducted me into the college; and the Vice-chancellor performed the matriculation ceremony in the Divinity School. I was distressed by my inability to understand a word he was saying. It was only sometime later [I learned] it had been Latin . . .[79]

Another curious case came to light after the war, when a lady briefly returned to Breslau to see if her house had survived. According to a man who met her then, she had been the Jewish wife of a German engineer who wanted to join the Nazi Party. Since Nazi Party members were forbidden to have Jewish spouses, the husband took his wife by train to the Swiss border, waved her goodbye, and returned to Breslau. She survived. He did not.[80]

In the second wave, which began after the implementation of the Nuremberg Laws, would-be emigrants faced much greater difficulties. For one thing, they had usually lost their main source of income. They were often forced to sell their assets at knock-down prices in order to cover the costs of emigration, and every step of the proceedings was closely watched by the Gestapo. Max Silberberg, for instance, had been co-owner of the Weissenberg Company in Breslau, which produced magnesite for the steel industry. He was also the founder of the priceless private art collection that bore his name. In 1934, after his company had been forcibly 'Aryanised' without compensation, he decided to sell his pictures. He entrusted them to a Jewish auctioneer, Paul Graupe, who was still in business and who placed them, in 1935, in a run of four auctions, duly marked as 'non-Aryan property'. Van Gogh's *L'Olivette* was bought by the National Gallery in Berlin. A Cézanne found its way to the Hermitage in Leningrad. And Pissarro's *Boulevard Montmartre, Printemps* disappeared into the art market, to surface in 1997. Graupe then left safely for New York. Silberberg's son, Alfred, and his daughter-in-law, Gerta, fled to Britain. Silberberg himself was held in a concentration camp from which he was never released.

In May 1938, the eighteen-year-old Walter Laqueur had just completed his secondary schooling and was preparing to study abroad:

I had just finished school and my future lay in the hands of various committees, organisations and consulates. I had a lot of free time and went almost every morning to the *Südpark*. I remember I read Céline's *Voyage au bout de la nuit* there. I don't know what it was that fascinated me about this story of cynicism and desperation, perhaps I had an inkling that another journey to the end of the night was about to begin. Or is it wrong to attribute the gift of prophecy to an 18-year-old? I remember how I met a former teacher of mine on one of those mornings. He was not a Nazi. He had been forced to retire early. He was deeply pessimistic about the future and advised me most strongly to leave the country as soon as possible. He spoke of the hard times to come, and that he envied me the opportunity to get out. Finally he asked that I should return when the worst was over. Then he bade me farewell, but suddenly appeared to remember something and said: 'You know that I tried, not always with success, to explain the *Niebelungenlied* to you? Have another look at the story of Hagen!'

That was the last time that I saw Dr U., as he left the park with his ebony walking stick. There is no trace of him, no less of the other teachers. I looked at the story of Hagen, but I'm not sure what he meant. Perhaps it was Hagen's last words, before his final battle, [where he says that] everything had turned out as he had predicted (. . . *es ist auch so ergangen, wie ich mir hatte gedacht*). For a while, I was fascinated by another part of the *Niebelungenlied*: As Hagen is on the way to the court of Attila, he crosses the Danube with King Gunther's escort. There, a group of nymphs prophesy that they will all be killed, with the sole exception of the priest. Hagen laughs and pushes the clergyman into the swollen river to punish the nymphs for their lies. But the priest is swept to the opposite bank, whilst Hagen and his companions are killed in a battle, which they had brought upon themselves.[81]

In the third wave, which began amid the panic of *Reichskristallnacht*, thousands of Breslau Jews, who had previously opposed emigration, fled in terror, in imminent fear of their lives. One family's story must suffice:

We lived in a small town called Strehlen, a town of about 15,000 people about 20 miles south of Breslau . . . We were quite well to do . . . My great-great-grandfather had come to the town as a peddler in the early 1800s. He became wealthy and the money stayed in the family . . . My parents had a brick factory and a farm. We lived in a 200-year-old farmhouse.

It was 1936 when I can remember the first incidents of anti-Semitism. As a youngster, I didn't really believe it. There was a boy from my class that was not allowed to come and see me any more. He had to join the *Jungvolk*, the Hitler Youth . . .

In 1938, it became nasty . . . Crystal Night was November 9th 1938 . . . They hit us at about 6.00 in the morning, black shirts, stormtroopers . . . they sent the stormtroopers from Strehlen to another little town . . . so the home boys would not be inhibited. They came just before dawn . . . They took my mother and father out of bed, left us children alone with grandmother . . . Of course, we were terribly upset . . . All the three of us boys could hear was the noise of breaking glass, of turning over furniture and breaking things. About 7.30 or 8.00, I ran downstairs and asked one of the men 'When are my parents coming back?' And he said *'Geh' rauf oder ich gebe dir 'ne Ohrfeige!'* ('Get upstairs or I'll give you a smack') . . . [But] then they went to the next Jewish home. We were the first ones to be hit, lucky because they became drunk later.

They took our car with them. We went downstairs and saw that the ground floor was completely demolished. Every window was broken . . . They had taken a knife through every picture . . . though we had some pictures of Frederick the Great. They didn't touch those . . .

That same afternoon . . . an honest policeman came and took my father away. He told my father: 'Mr Stargardter, I suggest you take a lot of money . . . you may be gone for a long time.' He was part of the establishment, not Gestapo. My father did take a lot of money. Turns out he stayed for about 10 weeks in Buchenwald . . . Later that day, the stormtroopers vandalised the synagogue and poured cow urine all over the Torah and inside the building. It was not burned however. As a matter of fact there was no burning in Strehlen.

The people in Strehlen, the day after the house had been vandalised [everyone] came to look at the house, like looking at a car accident . . . Most just shook their heads and said 'My God, what has happened here?' There were a very few who shook their fists and yelled 'Damned Jews!' or something. [But] most people were completely indifferent or they were afraid to say anything . . . They didn't have enough guts to stand up and say 'This is wrong' . . .

[My father] told us that when they were admitted into the camp, they walked through a line of attendants or whatever those animals were . . . and they were hit with sticks . . . [Yet] the worst thing that happened to him is that . . . he got scarlet fever . . . He came back after 9 or 10 weeks because he had been decorated as a soldier in World War One with the Iron Cross. In those days, it was a reason for letting Jews out of concentration camps; I don't think it lasted long.

My mother at that time was in the process of selling the properties . . . We were required to sell everything within a certain amount of time. It was November 1938 . . . and we stayed another 6 months or so . . . We could travel anywhere as far as I know . . . There was no requirement for permits; there weren't any badges. Some stores and restaurants had signs 'Jews stay out'. We left [Strehlen] two months before the war. I wasn't there for the worst . . .

I remember my father saying 'They're not going to touch us. The government is doing business with us.' The brick factories were selling bricks to the German Air Force to make underground hangars. They weren't going to touch us. That was the attitude. And, of course, the people who waited the longest never got out . . .

Mother lived through all this and I don't really think that she was bitter. She was more German than Jewish right to her death in 1981. [Indeed] two of her best friends were Germans . . . Tante Anita was a German woman in Strehlen, an employee of the German Railroad. She came to our house the day we left, even though she had been threatened that she could lose her job . . .

We were forced to sell our property, and in August 1939 my parents, my grandmother, my two brothers and I left Germany on a German ship, with something like $10.00 apiece . . . The final sale of our properties was conducted by an uncle after we left. In 1940, he wrote a letter to Guatemala stating that he had managed to send a large sum of money to a bank in Switzerland. In spite of many efforts to retrieve it, the money is still there.[82]

Of course, these were the lucky ones. They lived to write their memoirs. They had money, and diamonds to hide in their baggage. They had relatives abroad. Their experiences cannot fairly be compared either to the mass atrocities that were already taking place in the Soviet Union or to the genocide that the Nazis were to perpetrate in the coming years.

In the final wave of departures, which took place under the shadow of war in 1939, a prominent episode was that of the *Kindertransporte*. Jewish parents, who could not leave themselves, made arrangements to send their children to freedom. They were helped by foreign charities, which undertook to organise the trains and take care of their charges. Altogether some 10,000 children were saved. From Breslau, they often went to Prague, where refugee camps had operated for several years, and thence to Switzerland, France or Britain. They were permitted to leave Germany on payment of a bond that they would not return. They were loaded on to trains, often in the dead of night and with very few possessions. One such train left the Hauptbahnhof in Breslau in late July 1939. On it was nine-year-old Ella Feldmann:

> I had already said good-bye to my father and was standing at the window of the train, which was just about to leave. Suddenly the door was flung open by a woman with tears streaming down her face. With her were two toddlers, a boy and a girl screaming and howling. She just managed to ask me my name, and to [have me] promise her to look after them, when the guards blew the whistle and the train pulled out.[83]

The stowaways were four-year-old twins: Hanna and Jochi Najmann. They had been too young to qualify for the *Kindertransport*, but, in desperation their mother had pushed through the lines and thrust them into the carriage. From then on, they were on their own.

*

Breslau's municipal politics mirrored the trends of the Weimar Republic and the Third Reich, passing through successive phases of imperial collapse, democracy, stagnation and Fascist extremism. Breslau was exceptional, however, in its enthusiasm for the revolution of 1918. As Paul Löbe noted, the fall of the Kaiser was greeted in Breslau with celebrations and a large measure of popular support. Universal suffrage was introduced for communal elections and the city's *Volksrat* governed from the start with a firm consensus.

To begin with, many things continued in the pre-war vein. The Social Democrats maintained their majority and held a commanding share of municipal offices in the early years. However, the new political forces were not slow to show themselves. The left liberals, who had dominated the city's municipal politics, fell victim to the widespread popular disenchantment with democratic politics. By 1924, they numbered just four seats in the City Council. On the right, new nationalistic and anti-Semitic parties prolifer-ated. One of them was the *Deutscher Bismarckbund*, founded in Breslau by Wilhelm Kube (1887–1943). A former journalist, Kube was prominent among the right-wing splinter groups of German politics. After joining the Nazi Party in 1927, he enjoyed his greatest political success before being assassinated by partisans in 1943 (see above).

On the left, the Communist movement took similar flight. In 1919–24, it grew from a fringe group with sixty members in Breslau to a mass party many thousands strong. It drew strength from a merger with the Independent Socialist Party (USPD), who were by far the stronger partner. Its press organ was the *Schlesische Arbeiter Zeitung*. In 1924–5, it was delegalised and its local secretary, A. Oelsner, imprisoned. But it revived in good time to enter with gusto the street-fighting of 1929–33 and, in the early stages, to confront the Nazis on more than equal terms. Its local activists included Alfred Hamann (1882–?), who was exposed as a police informer; Erich Hausen (1900–?), who fell out with the party leadership and emigrated to the USA; Ernst Wollweber (1898–1967), who created a Soviet spy-ring in Breslau before disappearing to the USSR; and Augustin Sandtner (1893–1944), whose career alternated between the Prussian Landtag and various prisons. In April 1933, Sandtner was arrested and sent to Sachsenhausen.

As national politics became increasingly polarised, municipal politics became increasingly violent. In November 1930, the Breslau City Council, long hamstrung by intra-party strife, was superseded by a 'municipal dictatorship'.[84] Politics was played out in physical confrontations on the streets, where Nazi stormtroopers brawled with Socialists and Communists. By 1933, the Nazis had emerged victorious. The Silesian SA leader Edmund Heines was appointed Police President that May. Hitler's bull-necked poacher had turned gamekeeper.

The Reichstag ceased to function normally in 1934, and the democratic façade was dropped. Nonetheless, Reichstag members for Breslau made up a bouquet of Nazi notables. Erich von dem Bach-Zelewski (1899–1972), for example, though born in Pomerania, always had close connections to Silesia. He had served with the 1st Silesian Infantry Regiment during the First World War, then with the *Freikorps* and then with a local border-protection unit. He joined the NSDAP and SS in 1930. He was returned as Reichstag member for Breslau in July 1932 and held the position until the last days of the Third Reich. After a spell in Königsberg, he headed the south-eastern SS sector, based in Breslau, between 1936 and 1941. Von dem Bach was to achieve notoriety as the commander of anti-partisan activities on the Eastern Front and later in the suppression of the Warsaw Uprising. At Nuremberg, he would be denounced by Göring as a *Schweinehund* and a *Verräter* (pigdog and traitor) for cooperating with the Allies: a policy that the former *Reichsmarschall* described as 'selling his soul to save his stinking neck'.

Baldur von Schirach (1907–1974) was another fine specimen. The future Gauleiter of Vienna, founder of the Nazi Students' Association and head of the Hitler Youth had an American mother and spoke fluent English. He fell in love with Hitler having heard him speak, and began his Nazi career as a very youthful Reichstag member for Breslau in 1932. By his own admission, he was a man who 'simply believed' in Nazism, but became increasingly disillusioned by its realities. In 1938 he forbade any Hitler Youth participation in the 'criminal action' of *Kristallnacht*.[85] Thereafter a persistent critic of Nazi racial policy, he testified at Nuremberg, describing Hitler as a 'murderer a million times over'.

At the local level, the Nazi Party took charge of affairs through its network of party leaders or Gauleiter. The first of these in Breslau was Helmuth Brückner (1896–1945?). Born at Peilau (Piława) near Nimptsch (Niemcza), he served in the First World War and in the *Freikorps* before entering right-wing political circles. As a member of the Breslau City Council and editor of the radical *Völkisches Wochenblatt für Schlesien*, he effectively established the NSDAP in Silesia. On 15 March 1925, he wrote to Hitler in Munich:

> Dear, honoured Herr Hitler,
> The undersigned leaders of the former 'National Socialist Freedom Movement' hereby declare their membership of the 'National Socialist German Workers' Party' and place themselves at the disposal of Adolf Hitler. Behind them stands the overwhelming majority of the former members of the 'National Socialist Freedom Movement' in Silesia. Inspired by an unshakeable belief in the victory of the German will for freedom, they bring to you, man of destiny and great leader Adolf Hitler . . . a triple Heil![86]

Brückner was rewarded with the post of Gauleiter, which he held in concert with those of *Oberpräsident* of Silesia, representative in the Prussian Landtag and *Gruppenführer* in the SS. His connection with Röhm's faction, however, led to him being stripped of all offices and honours. He is thought to have ended his days working on a Heinkel production line in Rostock.

Josef Wagner (1899–1945) was Brückner's successor. A Lorrainer and former schoolteacher, he had belonged to the first twelve Nazi MPs of 1928 and had been instrumental in establishing the NSDAP in the Ruhr. He was appointed Gauleiter in Breslau in 1935 when he was still Gauleiter of Westphalia. He reached the peak of his career four years later, by which time he had collected the additional titles of Vice-President of the Prussian *Staatsrat*, Reich Commissioner for Price Setting and Reich Commissioner for the Defence of Silesia. Yet, as a practising Catholic, Wagner was under surveillance and his fall was swift (see above).

Karl Hanke (1903–45) was another schoolteacher, but a man of a different stamp. A protégé of Goebbels, he had risen through the ranks, becoming Under-Secretary in the Reich Ministry of Information and Propaganda in 1937 and an admirer of his mentor's wife, Magda, whom he entertained in private in his Berlin flat. The ensuing scandal forced him to withdraw to the ranks of the *Wehrmacht*, where he participated in the Polish and French campaigns before being promoted by Hitler to the post of Gauleiter of Lower Silesia in early 1941. Nonetheless, Hanke was not popular with the people of Breslau. A party 'yes' man, unlike Wagner, he was nicknamed *Spitzbart*, or 'Goatee', on account of his beard and was disliked because of his overbearing manner and his abuse of office. Appointed *Reichsverteidigungskommissar*, or Reich Commissioner for Defence, in November 1942, he expanded his remit to include responsibility for all armaments production and defence preparation in Silesia. In this capacity he must bear responsibility for the destruction of Breslau at the end of the war. His blind belief in Nazi propaganda and in the hopeless *Festung* policy, and his fatal delays in ordering the civilian evacuation, would make the city's end as violent and painful as possible.

In true totalitarian manner, however, the Nazis (like the Communists) ran a dual system of parallel party and state authorities. The party ruled; the state acted under party orders as the subordinate administrative branch of government. At the local level, this meant that the City Council was allowed to function as before, but under the strict supervision of Nazi officials. The office of Lord Mayor continued, but was subordinated to that of the Gauleiter. The local elections of March 1933 gave a commanding lead to Nazi candidates, whose representation on the council jumped from three seats to forty-five. The SPD scored nineteen; the Catholic Centre thirteen and the Communists six. But at the first meeting of the council, the Socialist and Communist councillors were unceremoniously excluded. Several were taken straight to the camp at Dürrgoy. One of these was the local SPD secretary, Karl Mache (1880–1944), who had served as Lord Mayor from 1928 to 1933. His fate underlines the extraordinary reversal of fortune that came about under the Nazis. Cast into Dürrgoy in 1933, he lasted eleven years, before dying in Gross Rosen (Rogoźnica) just before the end of the war. From 1933 to 1944, his former office of Lord Mayor was filled by 'an old Party comrade', Dr Hans Fridrich.

From then on, the 'New Order' reigned undisturbed. On 10 May 1933, the first of several book-burnings was organised. Official parades took place on almost any pretext – the Führer's birthday, National-Socialist Labour Day, Mother's Day and to celebrate the visits of each and every Nazi dignitary. Speaking Polish in public on such occasions was treated as an offence.

*

Population growth had been the prime engine of Breslau's urban development during the imperial period. However, by the early twentieth century, it had slowed considerably. Between 1910 and 1939, Breslau grew by only 23 per cent (to 629,000), whereas Dortmund, for example, enjoyed growth of 153 per cent.[87] With the primary dynamic effectively removed, urban expansion slowed throughout the inter-war years, though urban change and renewal were still important themes.

Following the rapid growth of the nineteenth century, Breslau saw the principal urban challenge as the improvement of social conditions and of housing stock. It was blighted by some of the worst social statistics in Germany (see above), which were addressed, at least in part, by an architectural competition for expansion plans, the *Stadterweiterungswettbewerb* of 1921. Entries fell into two competing categories: the building of high-rise blocks versus the laying out of new suburbs.

Max Berg, as head of the Planning Department, was the primary exponent of the high-rise option. The success of his *Jahrhunderthalle* project gave him great prestige. He was enthused by the 'high-rise fever' of the post-war period and submitted numerous plans for the centre of Breslau. He was the first German architect to link his designs to the requirements of the housing shortage. In 1920, he argued for office and business blocks to free up residential areas of the city.[88] He viewed communal living in skyscrapers as the embodiment of the new democratic society. Among his submissions were plans for a high-rise shopping centre at the Freiburger Bahnhof, for an office block on the Lessingplatz and, most controversially, for several variants of a tower block next to the Gothic Rathaus on the Main Square. Unfortunately for Berg, the council was not ready for such designs. The only blocks to be built in Berg's preferred style were the Postcheckamt of 1928 and the Sparkasse (on the Main Square) of 1929. Neither was by Berg himself.

The city fathers encouraged the development of Breslau's suburbs and the incorporation of more surrounding villages. On 1 April 1928, the area of the city more than trebled overnight from 4,962 hectares to 17,509. An intensive construction programme then concentrated on the development of Pöpelwitz (Popowice), Westend, Gräbschen (Grabiszyn) and Zimpel (Sępolno).

The suburb of Zimpel is an interesting example of this approach. Intended as a garden suburb, similar to Bourneville in Birmingham or Margarethenhöhe in Essen, it was begun soon after the First World War according to plans by the Breslau architects Paul Heim and Hermann Wahlich. In the 1920s, 3,000 flats and 250 spacious detached houses were constructed around a central grassed area – the *Zimpeler Wiese*. In 1932, the Protestant Gustav-Adolf Gedächtniskirche was added to complement the

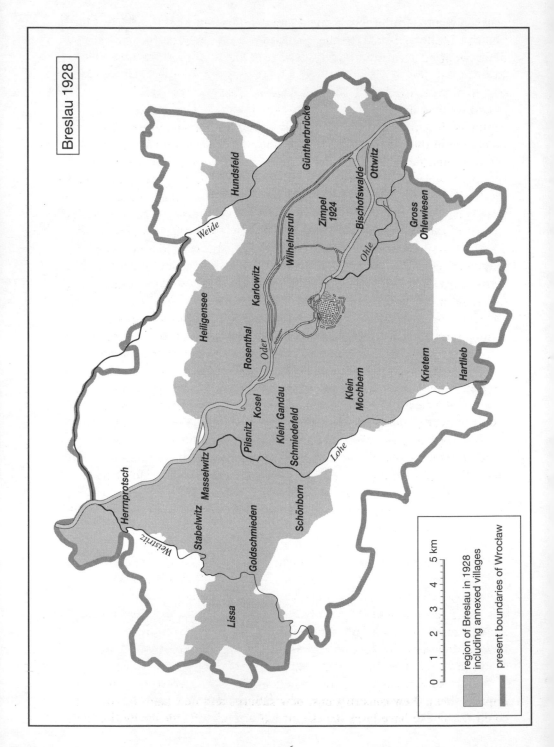

Breslau 1928

region of Breslau in 1928 including annexed villages

present boundaries of Wrocław

5 km

0 1 2 3 4

existing Catholic Church of the Holy Family and the Friedrich Ebert School. Ideally situated beside Scheitnig Park, Zimpel became a very desirable place to live and by 1939 housed some 11,000 residents. Its streets were named after birds: Amselweg, Drosselweg, Falkenweg, Sperlingsweg and Elsterweg (Blackbird, Thrush, Falcon, Sparrow and Magpie).

Breslau was no stranger to progressive projects. The Breslau Academy continued to attract and produce many of the leading architects of the era. Its alumni in the 1920s included Adolf Rading, a collaborator with Mies van der Rohe and Gropius at the Bauhaus; Hans Scharoun, later the creator of Berlin's magnificent Philharmonic; and Heinrich Lauterbach, who organised the *WuWa* exhibition in the summer of 1929. The *Wohnung und Werkraum Ausstellung*, or *WuWa* (Home and Workplace Exhibition), established in the suburb of Grüneiche (Dąbie), was intended as a showpiece of modernism. The thirty-seven designs, many using innovative techniques such as reinforced concrete and flat roofs, loosed a storm of argument between conservative and progressive architects. But it is now regarded as a milestone in the history of German architecture.

The innovative work of Max Berg was consolidated by the appointment of his former colleague, Richard Konwiarz, as head of the Planning Department. Konwiarz, who had collaborated with Berg on the *Jahrhunderthalle*, presided over Breslau's greatest inter-war construction project – the stadium complex. Built between 1926 and 1928, close to Zimpel and Leerbeutel (Zalesie), the complex comprised a main athletics arena and football pitch, the *Schlesier Kampfbahn*, which could hold 60,000 spectators, and the neighbouring *Jahn Kampfbahn* which offered tennis courts, a firing range, a gymnastics hall, a boxing ring and a fifty-metre swimming pool. It was completed by the *Friesen Wiese*, an open area of 140,000 square metres, with grandstands and some twenty football pitches. The Breslau Sports Stadium was rewarded with the bronze medal for architectural design at the Los Angeles Olympic Games in 1932. It formed the centrepoint of a rich network of some thirty sporting facilities, which were sufficient to attract the National Sports Festival of 1938 and the Hitler Youth Games of 1942 and 1943. In 1938 it was renamed the 'Hermann Göring Sportsfield'.

The Nazis added little to Breslau's beauty. The ostentatious Party House was built for the NSDAP on the Gartenstrasse in 1933. Another large administrative complex appeared near the Lessing Bridge in 1937 (now the Urząd Miejski). The clearance of several dilapidated districts in the city centre gave rise to solid workers' apartment blocks, or *Volkswohnungen*.

Visitors to Breslau in the late 1930s would have seen several things to impress them. New constructions, new suburbs and new names apart, they could not fail to have been struck – if not actively offended – by the huge swastika banners draped on the front of every major building, and by the gigantic political slogans stretched across the streets. But they would also have been given food for thought by the extraordinary improvement in all branches of travel and communication. If they had travelled to Breslau from Berlin, they would have passed the 310-metre-high mast of the wireless station of the German Post Office at Königs-Wusterhausen, and the long-wave and short-wave masts of *Deutsche Welle* at Zeesen. If they came by motor car, they would have cruised at ease on the *Autobahn* or would at least have seen it under construction. If they had landed at Gandau Aerodrome, eight kilometres to the west of the city centre, they would have arrived in one and a quarter hours and would have seen that Breslau had daily commercial air links with eight German cities, including Cologne, Stuttgart, Gleiwitz and Stettin (Szczecin). If they stayed at the first-class Monopol Hotel, they would have found that forty of the fifty rooms were now fitted with en-suite bathrooms. The loudspeakers on every street corner were a nuisance. But the streets were thronged with modern cars: the elegant Horch, the massive twelve-cylinder Maybach, the sleek Mercedes and, by 1939, an occasional Volkswagen. And the choice of restaurants was wide:

Monopol, Schloss-Platz	*Traube*, Schweidnitzer Strasse
Savoy, Tauentzien Platz	*Würzburger Hofbrau*
Haase-Gaststätte	*Philippi & Co.*, Albrechtstrasse
Pschor Brau	*Siechen*, Junkern Str.
Schloss Restaurant	*Kissling*, Junkern Str.
Ratsweinkeller, Ring	*Baeker & Braetz*, Kaiser Wilhelm Str.
Schweidnitzerkeller, Ring	*Fahrig*, Zwinger Platz.[89]

In the summer, tourists and trippers were well catered for in a number of open-air garden restaurants at the Liebichs-Höhe, at Zum Dominikaner, at the Terrassen-Gaststätte by the Jahrhunderthalle, and at the Schweizerei in Scheitnig Park. For people with good appetites and no political conscience, there was much to offer.

In the turmoil of political change in the inter-war period, streets, bridges and entire towns and villages were renamed. In their eagerness to dismantle the symbols of the imperial regime, Breslau's ruling Socialists in 1920 demanded the rechristening of the Kaiserbrücke as Freiheitsbrücke, or 'Freedom Bridge', and of Kaiser Wilhelm Platz as Reichspräsidentenplatz. Within a few years, another wave of name-changing arrived. During the Third Reich, Freiheitsbrücke reverted to Kaiserbrücke and Reichspräsiden-tenplatz was rechristened Hindenburgplatz. Then the Nazis added their own brand of nomenclature. Kaiser Wilhelm Strasse became Strasse der SA, Menzelstrasse became Göringstrasse, Grüneiche Weg became Horst Wessel

Strasse and, predictably, Friedrich Ebert Strasse became Adolf Hitler Strasse. To mark the expansion of the Reich, the Schweitzer Strasse was turned into Revaler Strasse and the old Piasten Strasse into Memelland Strasse. In 1936 the names of a large number of towns and villages of the Breslau region, which were considered 'too Polish', were Germanised. Thus, among many others, Pawelwitz adopted the more 'German'-sounding Wendelborn (now Pawłowice), Boguslawitz became Schwarzaue (now Bogusławice), and Wilschkowitz, Wolfskirch (now Wilczkowice). The Breslau suburbs of Pöpelwitz, Karlowitz (Karłowice) and Zedlitz (Siedlec) somehow survived unchanged. It was clear that even town planning was not immune to the strictures of the new, integral German nationalism. (And it was a game that the Communists would play with equal relish, but rarely with a full understanding of what had gone before. When the post-war regime was to modify the Oppelner Strasse to Ulica Opolska, they were presumably unaware that the Nazis had chosen Oppelner as a replacement for the Karl Marx Strasse of Weimar days.) The ultimate accolade was bestowed during the *Sportsfest* of 1938, when Breslau was officially designated 'Adolf Hitler's Most Faithful City'.[90]

By far the most exciting plans for Nazi Breslau were the ones that were never realised. At the many 'Brown Fairs' and 'South-Eastern Fairs' staged by the party in Breslau between 1933 and 1942, numerous projects were launched. At the South-Eastern Fair of 1936, for example, a plan was unveiled that envisaged the construction of a canal between the Oder in Upper Silesia and the Danube at Bratislava, thereby creating a network of waterways linking the Baltic and the Black Sea.[91] Others soon followed. On 19 November 1938, following the Munich Agreement, a treaty was signed between the Third Reich and Czechoslovakia for the construction of a superhighway between Breslau and Vienna with German extra-territorial rights. A second treaty provided for the construction of a major Oder–Danube canal. Perhaps the most ambitious scheme, however, was to put Breslau at the focus of an *Autobahn* network linking Calais with Sofia and, ultimately, Istanbul. Other branches were foreseen linking Kiev, Odessa, Lvov, Cracow and Bucharest with the Reich. Peculiarly, the plan made no mention of the sovereign rights of Poland, Romania or the USSR: the lands through which the motorway would actually be built.

*

The war that Hitler unleashed on 1 September 1939 was not the war that he had been anticipating. It bore little resemblance to the scenario presented to his generals two years earlier and summarised in the Hossbach Memorandum. It was in fact a piece of last-minute political, as well as military, opportunism. Despite his constant ranting about Germany's eastern *Lebensraum*, Hitler, like many Germans of his generation, despised Poland without ever having bothered to go there. He was furious that the Polish leaders had spurned his advances for an anti-Soviet alliance and, being totally ignorant of Polish history, could not understand why the Poles remained steadfastly unimpressed by Nazism. He probably thought in any case that the Western powers would dump the Poles as they had recently dumped the Czechs. Yet Hitler was right on one key matter. He guessed correctly that Stalin would happily join him in destroying Poland and carving up Eastern Europe. So he thought that the risks were small. Once Ribbentrop and Molotov had signed the Nazi-Soviet Pact, Hitler hesitated once or twice and then cast caution aside. Briefing his military staff on the eve of the invasion, he was in a savage mood:

> Genghis Khan had millions of men and women killed by his own will and with a gay heart. History only sees him as a great state-builder . . . I have sent my Death's Head Units to the East with the order to kill without mercy men, women and children of the Polish race or language. Only in such a way will we win the *Lebensraum* that we need. Who, after all, speaks today of the annihilation of the Armenians?[92]

German Breslauers were fearful, as everyone was, of another world war. But many of them felt that a limited expedition against Poland was well justified:

> In the [autumn] of 1939, the military attack on Poland enjoyed considerable public support in eastern Germany. The adult generation had not been able to overcome the pain caused by the defeat of 1918, by the loss of the Prussian province of Posen and by the aggressive activities of Korfanty's Polish insurrectionaries in Upper Silesia. The majority of [German] Silesians did not like the new hostile neighbour in the East, they [cared little] for a Polish state, which, as they thought, had never previously existed. In the view of many Germans, the replacement of Poland by the 'Reichsgau Wartheland' and the 'General Government' was simply restoring the previous state of affairs.[93]

So much, one is tempted to comment, for the level of historical education in interwar Germany about its neighbours.

Owing to its proximity to Poland, Breslau was thrown in September 1939 into the frontline of military operations. Situated just forty kilometres from the frontier beyond which the major Polish troop concentrations had been deployed, it inevitably played a crucial role in the *Wehrmacht*'s offensive. It lay at the centre of the springboard area for von Rundstedt's Army Group

South, whose initial headquarters were at Glogau (Głogów). Von Blasko-witz's 8th Army started from Trebnitz, while Reichenau's 10th Army started from Schweidnitz (Świdnica). General Hoepner's 16th *Panzer* Corps was poised to cross the frontier beyond Kreuzburg (Kluczbork).

On the Polish side, the Army of Łódź under General Juliusz Rómmel, a distant relative of the more famous German officer, Erwin Rommel, was deployed on either side of Sieradz. Its task was to hold the line of the Rivers Warta and Widawka. Three infantry divisions – the 10th, 28th and 30th – were flanked by two cavalry brigades: the Border Cavalry Brigade (KrBk) to the north and the Volhynian Cavalry Brigade (WBK) to the south. An independent cavalry regiment of the Frontier Corps (KOP) with a battery of artillery was based in advanced positions around Wieluń. The 2nd Legionary Division was held behind the front around Lask, while another, the 44th, was still in transit from the central reserve. Rómmel's personal preference had been for a pre-emptive attack on Breslau – a suggestion described by the Chief of the General Staff as 'a complete absurdity'.[94]

General Rómmel, however, ordered his troops to assume positions well forward of the defence line, thereby exposing them to the initial German onslaught at dawn on 1 September. The weight of the attack fell in the southern sector, aiming to pierce the junction between the Army of Łódź and the adjacent Army of Cracow. Here, the principal battle on the first day took place near the village of Mokra, where the Volhynian Cavalry Brigade lost more than 500 men and the 4th *Panzer* Division more than 100 armoured vehicles, including many tanks. The Poles successfully used heavy artillery from an armoured train, while the Germans called up warplanes. On the second day, other German units crossed the southernmost stretch of the Warta near Działoszyn, gaining the critical breakthrough. Thereon, the 16th *Panzer* Corps surged forward, and within seven days formed one of the advanced German columns approaching Warsaw. Elsewhere, the Army of Łódź was fully engaged in a fighting retreat to its defence line, until overtaken on the 6th by the heart-breaking order – necessitated by disasters on other fronts – for a general withdrawal eastwards to the Vistula. After that, the German 10th, 11th and 13th Corps, which had all marched from starting points to the east of Breslau, were drawn into the desperate, extended battle on the River Bzura, where the Poles staged a spirited counter-offensive that was not contained until 17 September. On that day, Stalin's Red Army finally honoured its secret obligations under the Ribbentrop-Molotov Pact and, by rapidly overrunning eastern Poland, rendered all Polish defence plans useless. As for General Rómmel, despite a contradictory account in his memoirs,[95] he seems to have abandoned his troops on the morning of the 6th following an air raid on his headquarters at

Julianów and, leaving three gendarmes in charge, to have driven off for Warsaw with his entire staff. Having disappeared for a couple of days, he resurfaced in the capital in time to be given command of the improvised 'Army of Warsaw', which held out heroically for a further three weeks. He personally conducted the capitulation of Warsaw to General Johannes von Blaskowitz on 27 September.

Breslau was no less important for the operations of the *Luftwaffe*.[96] While it housed the permanent command centre of *Luftkreis* 8, nearby Reichenbach (Dzierżoniów) was made the operational headquarters of *Luftflotte* 4, which was moved from Vienna to provide air support for Army Group South. The 676 aircraft of this one Air Fleet, commanded by General Alexander Lohr, easily outnumbered the total of 398 serviceable aircraft available to the entire Polish air force. They flew to their forward airfields on 24 August in readiness for Göring's order of 31 August to launch Operation *Ostmarkflug* at 4.45 the next morning. The fighter group J676 and the bomber group K676 were both based near Breslau, at Breslau–Schöngarten and Zipers–Neudorf, while similar formations were based at Liegnitz, Oels (Oleśnica), Ohlau (Oława), Brieg, Reichenbach, Oppeln, Langenau (Czernica) and Neisse (Nysa). Good weather in the south permitted *Luftflotte* 4 to open the air war with a dawn bombing raid on Cracow conducted by 60 Heinkel 111s of K64 from Langenau. Shortly afterwards, the very first dogfights of the Second World War took place. In one of them, Sgt Frank Neubert, flying a Junkers 87B out of Neisse, shot down a Polish fighter as it took off from the Balice Field near Cracow. In another, S–Lt (Pilot-Officer) Władysław Grys of the 122nd Squadron, Army Cracow – who would later serve under RAF command during the Battle of Britain – destroyed two Dornier 17E bombers of K677, which were returning from Cracow to Oppeln. Both Dorniers crashed in the village of Żurada, south of Olkusz – the first German air losses of the war.

Of course, the *Luftwaffe*'s vast superiority soon made itself felt. After swiftly neutralising Poland's air defences in the south, *Luftflotte* 4 took an active part both in the rapid advance of the 16th *Panzer* Corps and in the containment of the Polish counter-offensive on the Bzura. Having moved its machines on to bases inside Poland, it also made a major contribution to the mass air raids of 24–5 September on Warsaw, which finally surrendered three days later. In this the *Luftwaffe* was assisted, as were all German operations, by radio beams that had been specially broadcast from a Soviet station in Minsk since the first day of the war. In all, 333 Polish aircraft were lost, compared to 258 German losses. But numerous Polish pilots escaped to fight for the Allied cause in France and Britain.

Naturally, once the frontier of the Greater Reich was pushed far to the east, Breslau ceased to be a frontline city. Indeed, it would not be directly involved in the fighting until the final months of the war in 1945 (see Prologue).

Poland, of course, formed the core of the Nazis' *Lebensraum*, whose population consisted largely of 'subhumans' and was destined to be racially cleansed. Polish society was to be reduced to a residue of illiterate helots. All educated Poles who were not judged fit for 'Germanisation' and every single Jew were somehow to be eliminated. They were to be replaced by German colonists, who were brought in from wherever the Nazis could find them. Some months later, Heinrich Himmler gave an address in the Breslau Jahrhunderthalle. His audience consisted of around 12,000 ethnic Germans, mainly from Bukovina and Bessarabia:

> In spite of the war, you will be sent, week by week and train by train, to your new homeland. You are returning to a German east, but to a German east which does not lie beyond Germany's border, but which forms a part of the mighty German Reich. In the coming weeks and months, you will travel to your new homes . . . in the General Government . . . This will involve some hardship, but also much joy and happiness for you Germans.[97]

From the outset, therefore, the war in Poland was characterised by gratuitous brutality. It was not merely a military operation, but 'a racial struggle'. On the eve of the Polish campaign, five special units, or *Einsatzgruppen*, were formed. Each numbered around 500 SS and SD men, and was attached to one of the German armies. They were numbered I–V and were named after the cities in which they were mustered: Vienna, Oppeln, Breslau, Dramburg (Drawsko) and Allenstein (Olsztyn). Heinrich Himmler summed up their purpose as 'the radical suppression of Polish resistance . . . using all available means'.[98] 'Resistance' carried a very broad definition.

One of the most infamous of these units was led by Udo von Woyrsch, who had been a Reichstag member for Breslau in the early 1930s and had organised the bloody suppression of the Silesian SA. In 1939, he was given command of an additional *Einsatzgruppe*, which was to operate in Upper Silesia. On 7 September his unit moved into the area of Kattowitz. Its dispatches were brutally brief: 'insurgents arrested . . . rebels shot . . . synagogue set on fire . . . more on-the-spot executions . . . 4 Jews and 3 Poles shot . . . 18 Jews shot . . .'.[99] Its actions spread into western Galicia and into the rear of the 14th Army, whose commander, General List, was not amused. He complained to his superiors of 'illegal activities' and 'mass shootings', and noted 'an open ill-feeling' on the part of his men 'towards anybody wearing an SS uniform'.[100] Woyrsch's unit was withdrawn on 22 September and disbanded at the end of November.

The first years of the war went well for Germany. The swift victories in Poland, Denmark, Norway, the Low Countries and France exorcised the ghosts of the First World War. By mid-1941, after less than two years of warfare, Hitler controlled most of Western and Central Europe. But Operation Barbarossa was to change everything. The German-Soviet campaigns, which were to decide the future of Eastern Europe and which were fought with unparalleled ferocity, gave the *Wehrmacht* an initial advantage. But they dragged on. In 1943, they produced astonishing victories for the Soviets at Stalingrad and Kursk. And in 1944–5, they saw the Red Army rolling westwards in an unstoppable tide bound for Berlin.

The stark realities of the fighting can be demonstrated by the fate of units raised in Breslau. In 1939, some 10,000 Breslauers were conscripted and drafted principally to the 8th, 18th and 28th Infantry Divisions. They fought in all theatres of the war. But the fate of the 18th Infantry is especially illuminating. Sent in the first instance to Poland and then to France, it was re-formed in October 1940 as the 18th Motorised Infantry Division, which served in Yugoslavia. Moved to the Eastern Front, it fought at Donetsk and Kharkov, but in July 1944 it was virtually wiped out at Bobruisk. Hastily re-formed for a second time, it defended the approaches to eastern Prussia before being decimated yet again. That winter, it was reconstituted a third time and posted to Berlin, where it was finally destroyed.[101] Germany's material and human losses on the Eastern Front, totalling 5.5 million military and civilian casualties, were horrifying. And Breslauers paid their share of the blood toll.

Soldiers born in, or connected with, Breslau fought on all the fronts in which the German armed forces were engaged in 1939–45. Two in particular deserve mention – one a high-ranking *Luftwaffe* officer, the other the most celebrated of all *Panzer* commanders.

Colonel-General Baron Wolfram von Richthofen (1895–1945) was a cousin of the 'Red Baron' in whose squadron he had flown in 1917–18 (see pages 278–9). Described as a 'hard-faced, intelligent and arrogant man', he was the inventor of 'carpet-bombing' long before Bomber Harris adopted the concept. As commander of the Condor Legion in Spain, he had been directly responsible for the destruction of Guernica in 1937, and as commander of the 8th Air Corps he executed the raid on Belgrade in April 1941 that killed 17,000 civilians. During Operation Barbarossa, he was the *Luftwaffe*'s chief operational officer on the Eastern Front.

The legendary Hyazinth, Count von Strachwitz von Gross Zauche und Camminetz (1892–1968?), the *Panzer-Graf*, was a scion of an ancient

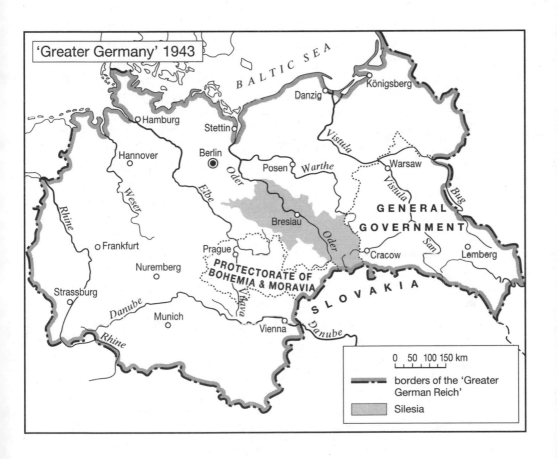

'Greater Germany' 1943

BALTIC SEA

Danzig
Königsberg
Hamburg
Stettin
Hannover
Berlin
Posen
Warthe
Warsaw
Oder
Vistula
Vistula
Elbe
Weser
Breslau
GENERAL
GOVERNMENT
Rhine
Frankfurt
Prague
Cracow
San
Lemberg
Oder
Bug
PROTECTORATE OF
BOHEMIA & MORAVIA
Nuremberg
Strassburg
Danube
SLOVAKIA
Munich
Vltava
Vienna
Danube
Rhine

0 50 100 150 km

━ ━ borders of the 'Greater
German Reich'

Silesia

Silesian family whose roots went back to the battle of Liegnitz (see pages 69–70). He was renowned for his dashing courage and for his uncanny 'nose', which repeatedly saved him from impossible scrapes. Thirteen times wounded, and laden with decorations, he was one of the handful of German soldiers ever to receive the prestigious 'Diamonds to the Knight's Cross'. In September 1914, aged twenty-two, he had commanded a Germany cavalry troop which, having circumvented French defences on the Marne, rode far enough behind the lines to catch sight of Paris. In August 1942, aged forty-nine, as commander of the leading 16th *Panzer* Division, he led the first group of German soldiers to gaze on the Volga at Stalingrad:

> The German spearhead pushed on for the last few miles. At about four in the afternoon, just as the August sunlight was softening, they reached Rynok north of Stalingrad, and 'there the soldiers of the XVI Panzer gazed on the Volga, flowing past right before their eyes'. They could hardly believe it. 'We had started early in the morning on the Don,' recalled one of Strachwitz's company commanders, 'and then we were on the Volga.' Somebody in the battalion produced a camera and they took photographs of each other standing on the backs of their vehicles, gazing through binoculars at the far shore. These were included in the Sixth Army HQ records with the caption 'The Volga is reached'.[102]

One of the younger captains, who would soon take command when von Strachwitz was flown out of Stalingrad, recalled the scene as he stood atop his tank on the high western bank of the river. 'We looked at the immense, immense steppe towards Asia,' he remembered, 'and I was overwhelmed.'[103] They were 1,925 kilometres almost due east from Breslau.

Breslau's soldiers were mainly conscripts. They fitted no pattern and were often wrenched from occupations that they would have preferred to pursue. One was a young priest from the seminary at Trebnitz taken into the SS. His particular struggle was not to fight the enemy, but somehow to convince his comrades that true Christian principles were not to be confused with Nazi ideology. He survived to tell the tale.[104] So, too, did a seventeen-year-old Breslauer who was drafted straight from the *Hitlerjugend* into the 13th Battalion of the [Silesian] *Panzer* Brigade. When he reported for training at Neisse in the spring of 1944, he was in for several surprises:

> We soon realised that almost half our battalion consisted of Poles belonging to the so-called 'Group III' which the Nazis had invented. The only criterion was to have some sort of German ancestor; and, since the German war-machine was starting to crack through the loss of manpower, these 'looted Teutons', as we called them, were taken into the Wehrmacht.

As things turned out, it was all quite favourable for them, since their families now became relatives of a soldier and could claim certain privileges . . .

We all took the oath: 'I SWEAR BEFORE GOD ALMIGHTY TO GIVE UNCONDITIONAL OBEDIENCE TO ADOLF HITLER, LEADER OF THE GERMAN REICH AND NATION AND COMMANDER-IN-CHIEF OF THE WEHRMACHT: ALSO, AS A BRAVE SOLDIER, TO BE READY TO GIVE MY LIFE FOR THIS OATH' . . . It never entered anyone's head that we had not sworn our oath to the Fatherland, to Germany, or to the constitution. [In fact], we had sworn allegiance to one single man, Adolf Hitler, as if he were God. After that, he could do what he wanted with us . . .

Our instructor was a Rhinelander, Corporal Schwalge, who considered our Polish recruits to be 'eastern trash' and who spared no opportunity to persecute them mercilessly. He exploited their poor knowledge of German to make fun of them and to humiliate them. He was a young sadist, who enjoyed tormenting the people in his charge . . .

Suddenly, before our training was finished, we were ordered to join an emergency unit at the front and we took our instructors with us. Corporal Schwalge's [belated] attempts to turn himself into our comrade-at-arms didn't save him. Our Polish colleagues had their revenge. Schwalge was one of the first to die a hero's death . . . The bullet entered through his shoulders and came out through his chest . . . Both we and the Poles were content to have rid ourselves of that nasty guy . . .

I set foot on Polish soil for the first time in the winter of 1944–45 at Schwersenz to the east of Poznań. There was a beautiful Polish girl, who helped in the kitchens . . . Of course, it was a hopeless affair. But I decided to make my private peace treaty with the Poles. Never again would I talk of our *Lebensraum* in the east, or tell those stupid jokes, or sing those silly songs about dirty Polish villages . . .

The courage of our Polish comrades [impressed us], as did their resilience and their willingness to help. Each of us [Germans] was more than happy to have one of them beside him on the frontline. But now, they're all dead, every single one of them, Poles and Germans. The whole battalion perished, shot to pieces by the Red Army in the loop at Budapest . . .[105]

Behind the front, the whole panoply of Nazi repression was quickly assembled. German-occupied Poland had the eternal misfortune to be chosen as the chief laboratory of Nazi racial science, but the network of Gestapo prisons, labour camps, SS concentration camps and death camps put out new tentacles both in the 'Old Reich' and the 'New Reich', especially in the General Government. Breslau itself had six forced-labour camps and five concentration camps, the largest being the ZAL (forced-labour camps) at Breslau-Gross Masselwitz (Maślice), Markstädt (Lasko-wice) and Rattwitz (Ratowice) and the KZ (concentration camps) at Breslau-Deutsch Lissa (Leśnica) and Breslau-Fünfteichen (Meleswice).[106] These were established in the early 1940s to supply a cheap workforce for the city's growing military-industrial sector.

Breslau's Kletschkau Prison was both to hold and interrogate local prisoners and, in the early period when there was a marked shortage of capacity, to guard prisoners in transit to Dachau or Buchenwald. For a few days in November 1939, for example, it housed the entire academic staff of the Jagiellonian University in Cracow, who had been rounded up en masse by the SS and condemned without trial to incarceration in Sachsenhausen.[107]

Maria (Maruška) Kudeřikova (1921–43) was one of countless victims of the Gestapo who died in Kletschkau Prison. Barely adult, she belonged to a Communist group and was suspected of disseminating hostile propaganda in her native Moravia. She was sent to Breslau from Prague and succeeded in writing a memoir, *Fragments of Life*, before she was guillotined on 21 March 1943. She could not have known, but only three years were to elapse before her Communist comrades would be killing another young woman of exactly the same age, in the same place and for the same offence (see below).

Forced labourers were a common sight in wartime Breslau. They came in four main categories. One group, recruited by the German *Arbeitsdienst*, was officially described as volunteers. In reality, they were often the product of round-ups and quota-collections, where the element of choice was minimal. Mainly Poles, but later Balts, Ukrainians, Serbs and others, they were sent to Germany for designated jobs, accommodated in private homes or hostels and paid a pittance. Usually young men and women, they were directed to menial jobs as domestic servants, unskilled factory workers or farmhands. The second group enjoyed no pretence of voluntary recruitment. Directed to hard labour as a form of punishment for offences either real or imagined, they were subjected to rigorous discipline, housed in barracks and maintained at subsistence level. The third group were essentially slaves. Housed in sub-camps of the KZ system, organised in brigades and placed entirely at the disposal of the SS, they regularly worked till they dropped. The fourth group were foreign prisoners of war, mainly Frenchmen and Belgians, who were brought to Germany under the clauses of the capitulation of June 1940.

In the course of the war, the numbers of all categories of workers in Breslau climbed steeply. Up to 200,000 German workers were transferred from the western parts of the country, together with their enterprises. The official tally of forced labourers rose to 43,950 in 1943 and 51,548 in 1944; and of (Western) POWs from 5,538 (1941) to 9,876 (1944), of which 2,857 were British. Overall, the population headed for the one-million mark. The native Breslauers felt themselves to be overrun by a flood of Czechs, Poles, Ukrainians, French and Soviets. The Jewish presence, though publicly unacknowledged, was still prominent in the slave brigades from the camps.

Life for the top class of forced labourers seemed relatively benign compared with that of the less fortunate. Shelter, food and pay (though very poor) was guaranteed. Yet, as a Polish woman from Jarocin recalled, the list of prohibitions was endless:

> We were obliged to wear an armband marked 'P', and we were not allowed to ride on the trams, to enter a church, theatre, restaurant, opera or circus, or even to visit the zoo or botanical garden. We could not participate in any sports, speak Polish in the street, listen to the radio, or read the press. We were not even free to sit on the park benches, which were marked with the words: FÜR POLEN UND JUDEN SITZEN VERBOTEN. We were not permitted to study, or to get married . . .[108]

Any transgression of these rules was treated as a 'breach of contract' and risked immediate investigation by the Gestapo.

Life for the lowest class – slave workers – meant a daily confrontation with death. Nothing except maltreatment was guaranteed. A Jewish camp doctor, Hans-Werner Wollenberg, who was interned at ZAL Brande in Upper Silesia, recorded the arrival on 13 January 1943 of a transport of 100 sick 'workers' from Breslau-Markstädt. In driving snow, they had been forced to disembark at a nearby station and to endure a three-hour wait for a connecting train. Fifteen-year-old Itzek Feldbaum had frozen to death, despite the efforts of his friend to revive him. Another two prisoners, both sixteen-year-olds, died on the short journey back to Brande. Itzek Feldbaum's brother David died from wounds sustained in Markstädt.[109] Though predominantly young, few members of that one transport pulled through.

Poles formed by far the largest contingent of non-Germans in wartime Breslau. Ironically, as soon as the Nazis had boasted in 1939 that they had cleared the city of Poles, they began to re-import them in droves. There were Polish 'volunteer workers', Polish 'compulsory workers', Polish 'slave workers', Polish POWs and, of course, a huge contingent of Polish Jews. When the first wartime Poles began to appear, the German Eastern League (BDO) printed leaflets with the message: GERMANS – REMEMBER THAT NO POLE IS YOUR EQUAL. Those among them who were free to move around outside work hours often ate Sunday lunch at the Schubert tavern or attended the (illegal) Polish Mass that was held on Sundays at the cemetery chapel of St Roch behind the Breslau-Nikolai station. Once, on 11

November 1944, they sang the Polish hymn, *Boże coś Polskę*, defying arrest. Many of them were housed in the vast camp at Breslau-Burgweide (Sołtysowice). An enormous influx occurred in late 1944 when civilians rounded up during the Warsaw Rising were sent to Breslau en masse. Estimates of the numbers range between 30,000 and 60,000.

Complications arose from the fact that a proportion of Poles of mixed ancestry were classed as *Volksdeutsche*, or 'ethnic Germans', who received special privileges and higher rations. Not surprisingly, relations between Poles who had signed the *Volksliste* and those who had not were strained. And unpleasant incidents were common. A Polish woman called Marta Hübner, for example, was put on the *Volksliste* because of her German-sounding surname. When she heard another Polish girl saying that 'no-one knows how the war will end', Hübner reported her to the Gestapo for defeatism. As it happened, the accused spoke better German than her accuser and was supported by her employer, Georg Birg, a Schindler-like figure who was known as a '*Polen- und Judenfreund*' and who said that the two silly women had a spat.[110] But it was a close shave. Informers like Hübner could easily get people sent to a concentration camp, and there were Gestapo informers in every single group.

The Nazi concentration camps were initially set up along the lines of the prototype at Dachau to remove political offenders from circulation. Their inmates had no rights and no hope of release. They were fed on starvation diets, clothed in ragged, striped uniforms, housed in huts, covered in lice and subject to every form of physical and psychological abuse. Drawn from every single nationality of German-occupied Europe, they were the victims of the policy, well known to their counterparts of the Soviet Gulag, of 'extermination by labour'. Their lot was symbolic of Nazi ideology, which stated without shame that 'the master race' held the absolute right of life and death over inferior breeds. Groß Rosen, near Schweidnitz, was the nearest major concentration camp outside Breslau. Established in 1940, it is estimated to have housed some 160,000 inmates during its existence, of whom perhaps 100,000 died. It was fed by many sub-camps, including several workcamps (AL), in Breslau itself. AL Breslau I existed to supply workers to FAMO, AL Breslau II to Linke-Hofmann. AL Breslau-Hundsfeld (Psie Pole) was a camp for women prisoners employed in the Rheinmetall-Borsig works. In January 1945, Groß Rosen received the remnants of the 'death-march' of evacuees from Auschwitz, only to send off its own columns of evacuees on another death-march in the direction of Buchenwald. Wojciech Dzieduszycki (b.1912), who was to feature prominently in the post-war life of Breslau/Wrocław, was prisoner no. 7821 at Groß Rosen. He was once made to stand in front of a firing-squad in one of the daily executions, but was saved by the German director of the camp orchestra, who shouted, 'Don't you kill my best violinist!'

The clutch of concentration camps at Auschwitz (Oświęcim) formed the largest and most infamous such complex in the Reich. It was the brainchild of the head of the Breslau *Sicherheitsdienst*, Arpand Wigand. It was located on the old frontier of Silesia and Galicia, on the edge of a small town that was a stop on the railway line between Breslau and Cracow. In the post-war years, when accurate information was in short supply, it would gain the false reputation of a death-camp for Jews where four million died. In reality, it was made up of three different types of camp. KZ Auschwitz I, which was opened in the summer of 1940 for Polish undesirables, was a standard concentration camp. KZ Auschwitz III–Monowitz was essentially a punitive labour camp, servicing the adjacent fuel factory. KZ Auschwitz II–Birkenau was a vast hybrid, which started as an extension of the original concentration camp, but was supplemented in time by purely exterminatory installations more akin to the dedicated 'death-camps' at Treblinka, Bełżec or Sobibor. The largest groups among its inmates were Polish Catholics, Jews and Soviet POWs; but the absolute majority among its 1.5–1.7 million casualties were Jews who never set foot in the camp, walking straight from the arrival ramp to the gas-chambers.

By an odd coincidence, the very first penal inmate of Auschwitz was destined to live after the war in the city where the idea of the camp had been conceived. In 1940, Stanisław Ryniak was a twenty-five-year-old Polish apprentice at the Building School in Jarosław, arrested by the Gestapo on suspicion of underground conspiracy. He was sent to Auschwitz from Tarnów Prison on 10 June 1940 with the very first trainload of prisoners, and was tattooed on the arm with '31' (numbers 1–30 having been allocated to German convicts working as auxiliaries for the original SS guard). Ryniak was a member of the workgang that built the first huts and erected the perimeter fence. He survived everything from floggings, typhus and the starvation bunker to a spell in the underground quarries. He walked free after a record 1,691 days, attributing his remarkable survival to 'good luck, mental and physical stamina, and the help of colleagues'.[111]

The 'Holocaust' is an unhistorical term for an all-too-historical episode, namely the systematic genocide by the German Nazis of about six million European Jews. The term was invented after the war to replace the only existing alternative – the 'Final Solution of the Jewish Question', which was the Nazis' own euphemism. It was the product of a deliberate decision to murder every man, woman and child who fitted the Nazi criteria of Jewishness. Qualitatively distinct from the various forms of persecution that had been inflicted earlier, the genocidal campaign was executed in 1941–5, mainly in SS camps built in German-occupied Poland. It is rightly considered to be the lowest pit in the history of man's inhumanity to man.

The scale of Breslau's involvement in the Holocaust was relatively small, for the simple reason that perhaps 75 per cent of Vratislavian Jews had fled before it started. Even so, the horrors border on the indescribable. The Nazis built no formal ghetto in Breslau, though in 1939–41 the remnants of the Jewish community were clustered in the district around the Storch Synagogue. Jewish organisations were closed, and special transit camps were prepared for the elderly at Tormersdorf (Predocice), Grüssau (Krzeszów) and Riebnig. Jewish numbers actually rose in those years from about 6,000 to 12,000, owing to an influx of refugees from other places.

Exceptionally, in the first months of the war, a few well-connected Jewish families passed through Breslau on their road to freedom. Richard Pipes was among them. His father had been a high official in Poland's Ministry of Foreign Affairs in Warsaw, who was helped by Italian diplomatic colleagues to obtain a set of Bolivian passports. In October 1939, the family travelled by train from Warsaw to Breslau. They stayed at the Four Seasons Hotel on the Gartenstrasse, their baggage following them on a porter's truck from the nearby Hauptbahnhof. The next day, they headed for Switzerland and a new life in America.

The shadowy existence of Jews in Breslau in 1939–41 was described in several surviving eye-witness accounts. The Jews were barred from public parks, public benches and playgrounds, forbidden to have a haircut or drive a car and allowed into certain shops only at certain times and for items on the Jewish ration card. They were obliged to work, clearing snow or collecting household refuse, for example, for which they were paid one Reichsmark per day, though their treatment by their superiors was described as 'almost without exception impeccable'.[112] The diarist Willy Cohn attempted to lead as normal a life as possible, continuing his research in the University Library. At first he was optimistic and was touched by the generosity and kindness of his Gentile former colleagues and of his neighbours. He considered that the attitude of the Breslauers towards the Jews was 'in general one of sympathy' and he doubted that the German people would allow themselves to be incited by the government and the press. On 25 July 1941, however, he was informed by a colleague that '12,000 Jews had been shot in Lemberg'[113] (Lwów), apparently by the SS. Three weeks later he wrote that: '50 young Jewish people . . . have died in a camp in Linz from "heart failure"'; 'murder is everywhere'.[114] One month after that entry, he received notice from the authorities that he and his family would have to leave their flat on 30 September, whereupon they would be *verschickt*, or 'sent away'. Two days after that notice, on 17 September, the diary entries end.

The deportation of Jews from Breslau seems to have been carried out in successive operations between July 1941 and June 1943. The sources sometimes conflict on the exact details, but once Gauleiter Hanke had set the first *Judenwohnungsaktion*, or 'Jewish Housing Action', in motion, the dates and destinations of the main movements have been well established:

25.11.1941	Kaunas (Lithuania)	2,000
3.5.1942	Tormersdorf, Riebnig, Grüssau	517
3.5.1942	Izbica, Sobibor, Bełżec, Majdanek	1,000
26.7.1942	Tormersdorf, Riebnig, Grüssau	424
27.7.1942	Theresienstadt	1,100
30.8.1942	Tormersdorf, Riebnig, Grüssau	500
31.8.1942	Theresienstadt	1,065
24.2.1943	Theresienstadt	102
5.3.1943	Auschwitz, Sobibor	1,405
2.4.1943	Theresienstadt	277
9.6.1943	Theresienstadt	39
11.6.1943	Theresienstadt	161
16.6.1943	Theresienstadt	18
9.1.1944	Theresienstadt	73
11.1.1944	Theresienstadt	3
25.4.1944	Theresienstadt	18
8.11.1944	Theresienstadt	1 [115]

Breslau's Jewish cemetery on Lohestrasse registered its last funeral on 12 August 1942. A year later, the SS Inspector of Statistics declared Silesia '*Judenrein*' – 'cleansed of Jews'. At the same time, he noted that 50,570 stateless and foreign Jews were 'engaged in camp activity' in the Breslau region alone. He was not confused: in his mind, people 'engaged in camp activity' did not officially count as part of the population. On 10 June 1943, a Gestapo official in Breslau reported that arrangements for the Jewish community had, for all practical purposes, been completed.

The procedures of deportation were attended by extraordinary bureaucratic punctiliousness and by the ubiquitous absurdities of Nazi jargon. Official notices talked of *Umsiedlung*, or 'Resettlement', and *Arbeitseinsatz*, or 'Work Duty'. So-called *Sammelstellen*, or 'Assembly Points', were designated at a police sub-station beside the Breslau-Odertor Station and in the former Jewish 'Friends' House' besides the Storch Synagogue. Deportees were properly informed in advance and by post:

At the request of the Breslau Gestapo (Department IIB) and in accordance with the information already given, you are informed that you must gather at your area Police Headquarters on Thursday 9th April 1942 at 7.30 a.m. sharp. Upon presentation of this notification, you and your family members with their baggage will be prepared for resettlement or work duty abroad. You must understand that any resistance to this order will result in police counter-measures, and that attempts to avoid resettlement will result in forced evacuation. It is expected that all demands will be met with punctuality and calmness.[116]

SS officers supervised the final selection at the assembly points. Medical notes and pleas for exemption were examined in all seriousness, as if they really made a difference. For the victims, ignorance could be bliss:

Next on the list for deportation was my grandmother, and I remember getting her ready and hanging a bag around her neck with all the various medications in it that she was supposed to take. She did not really understand what was happening to her – thank God – but she retained her pride and dignity to the end. I took her to the assembly point and stood by her side until her name was called for registration; and I was treated to a most impressive spectacle by this proud old lady. A Gestapo man sat at a table reading out names, and the people who were called had to walk past the table to the other side of the yard. When he called 'Lasker', my grandmother walked past the table, but not without stopping in front of the Gestapo man. She looked him straight in the face, and said very loudly: 'Frau Lasker to you.' I thought he would hit her there and then, but not a bit of it. He just said simply: 'Frau Lasker', I was extremely proud of her.[117]

The experiences of millions can hardly be comprehended. But the story of individuals can illustrate the collective tragedy. Laura Goldschmidt had been born in Breslau on the last day of August 1867. A widow, living on the elegant Kaiser Wilhelm Strasse, she was ordered to the Breslau Police Presidium in May 1942. She was permitted to take only what she could carry, although additional items could be delivered for a fee. Aged seventy-four, she was taken in a locked freight wagon to the former labour camp at Riebnig some forty kilometres distant. There she was housed, with 517 other Breslau Jews, in a camp without lavatories, cooking facilities, water supplies, lighting or heating. On 7 September 1942, Laura Goldschmidt died. The costs of her cremation were covered by the confiscation of her assets held at the Breslau City Savings Bank.[118]

By an extraordinary coincidence, the last recorded sighting of Edith Stein occurred in Breslau. On 7 August 1942, a military train was taking on water at a depot near the Hauptbahnhof, when a freight train with Dutch markings drew up alongside. A military postal worker called Johannes Wieners watched as the guards threw open the doors of the wagons, packed to bursting with people, revealing the sight and stench of indescribable human degradation. When a woman in nun's clothing appeared in the open door, he was able to engage her in a brief conversation. 'It's awful,' she said, 'we have no containers.' Then, looking around, she added, 'This is my beloved home town. I will never see it again. We are riding to our death.' Wieners asked if the others knew. The answer came: 'It is better that they don't know.'[119]

The departure of the Jews opened the way for the terminal plunder of their property. The medical equipment of the Jewish Hospital was particularly sought-after and the local office of the Siemens firm offered to buy it from the City Treasury for 2,000 Reichsmarks. But it was handed over to the Silesian Board of Social Welfare (*Volkswohlfahrtamt*).

Yet two categories of Jews had not departed. One of them consisted of Jews married to Aryans, the other of so-called *Mischlinge*, or 'persons of mixed parentage'. In 1943, the New Jewish Association (NJV) was formed to care for them. Its *Vertrauensman*, or 'agent', in Breslau was Erich Ludnowsky. But it lasted less than a year. In January 1944, one of the final transports took over seventy Jews to Theresienstadt. Only around twenty remained. A lady called Elina Strużyna applied for exemption on the grounds that her soldier son had been seriously wounded at the front. She was classed as a *Geltungsjude*, a Jew only 'in the eyes of the law'. The records do not reveal whether her application was accepted. Probably not.[120]

Yet even the last transport was not the end. The Gestapo were still not satisfied with their performance. They knew that their documentation was not perfect and that some Jews were still alive in hiding, so they continued their work to the very final day of the war. Karla Wolff, a young nurse, was one they never caught. She had not waited to be arrested, but slipped out of her lodging in the middle of the night and disappeared until May 1945. She was one of Breslau's 160 Jewish survivors.

Breslau played its part in another appalling policy of Nazi racism – namely the mass kidnapping of Polish children for the purposes of planned breeding. During his very first visit to occupied Poland in 1939, Himmler had noticed the abundance of fair-haired, blue-eyed boys and girls, and he immediately set up a system for seizing his human loot. Orphanages throughout Poland were combed for likely candidates. Specially trained teams of brown-suited women from the Nazi welfare organisation, the *National Sozialistische Volkswohlfahrtsamt* (NSV), the feared 'Brown Sisters', toured towns and villages enticing youngsters with sweets and promises.

Gestapo snatch-squads also operated. Racial experts waited in the collecting centres to screen the victims. German names and false biographies were provided for children who passed the pseudo-scientific tests and who were then transferred either to German adoption agencies or to the stud-farm brothels of the SS *Lebensborn* organisation. The 'unusables' were never returned to their parents, but were summarily shot, sent to the concentration camps or, if they were lucky, put to work on German farms. Numbers are impossible to calculate, but an international commission searched for several years for an estimated 200,000 lost Polish children still thought to be alive in post-war Germany. If this estimate was correct, and if, as calculated, only 10 per cent of the kidnapped were judged 'usable', the total number of victimised children must have approached two million.[121]

A camp located near the station at Brockau (Brochów) on the outskirts of Breslau acted as one of the principal collecting centres. It was most active in 1940, when the Warthegau was being 'cleansed', and again in 1943, when the Zamość region was being cleared for German settlement. In one six-week period in the summer of 1943, 12,000 children were transported from Lublin to Brockau by lorry. At full steam, the camp could cope with several hundred children per day:

> The children's heads, bodies, arms and legs were measured, as well as the pelvis in the case of girls and the penis in the case of boys, and they were divided into three groups: a) those representing a desirable addition to the German population; b) those representing an acceptable addition to that population; and c) the unwanted.[122]

One of many children to pass through Brockau was Ilona Helena Wilkanowicz, born at Pabianice near Łódź on 28 March 1931. At the age of twelve, she had been evacuated from the local orphanage and sent in a large group to the SS Ilenau School at Achern in Baden, where many of the girls were branded and injected with hormones. Renamed Helen Wilkanauer, she worked for a fruit farmer, Frau Fruh, until the end of the war. She was still living in Achern, married with three children, when she was eventually tracked down and interviewed in the 1970s:

> I was kidnapped in Poland, at Pabianice. Three SS men came into the room and put us up against the wall. There were about a hundred children altogether. They immediately picked out the fair children with blue eyes, including me ... I was twelve years old at the time. My father, who tried to stop my being taken away, was threatened ... But I have no idea what happened later because we were taken immediately to the

children's reception camp at Brockau. In November 1943, we were brought here to . . . Achern.

The unsuitable children were sent away from the school and liquidated. They threatened to send us to a concentration camp at every opportunity. Somehow, I managed to survive. Perhaps it was because I'm a blonde, I don't know.[123]

The Allied authorities in post-war Germany decided not to give priority to the rights of wronged Polish parents and a mere 15 per cent of the lost children were ever repatriated.[124]

The Third Reich ran regular POW camps only for prisoners from the Western powers: those from Britain, France, Poland and the USA were properly treated. Soviet prisoners were not. The *Wehrmacht* and the *Luftwaffe* tended to guard their opposite numbers and conditions were infinitely better than they were in civilian camps run by the SS. Owing to its distance from the Western Front, Silesia became a common location. A group of camps near Sagan (Żagań) was destined to become famous due to a couple of celebrated escapes that would provide the true basis for popular post-war films.

The Wooden Horse relates to an episode in 1943, from *Stalag Luft III*, which held more than 1,000 Allied airmen. Many of the inmates took escaping as their duty, and their efforts were aided by the sandy soil of Lower Silesia, which was ideal for tunnelling. An ingenious scheme was thought up whereby a tunnel was dug from a hole in the middle of the parade-ground by diggers concealed in a wooden gymnastic vaulting horse. For four and a half months, the horse was daily carried back and forth to the same spot under the noses of the 'goons', ferrying both the diggers and their loads of soil. Eventually, the time came when the tunnel was deemed to have passed under the perimeter fence. Two men made the break on the night of 29 October:

> Peter stuck his head out of the tunnel. He looked towards the camp. It was brilliantly floodlit . . . The high watch-towers were in darkness and he could not see whether the guards were looking into the camp, or in his direction. He pulled out his kitbag, wriggled out of the hole and dragged himself full-length across the open ground and into the ditch. He expected every second to hear the crack of a rifle and to feel the searing impact of its bullet in his flesh. He lay, out of breath, in the shallow ditch and looked up . . .
>
> The diversion in the huts reached a new crescendo of noise. There were men blowing trumpets, men singing My Brother Sylvester, men banging the side of the huts and yelling at the top of their voices. 'They're

overdoing it,' John whispered. 'The silly bastards'll get a bullet if they're not careful.' . . .

Once they reached the shelter of the trees they walked slowly on, away from the wire. Peter could feel his heart thumping inside his chest. He wanted to run, but forced himself to walk . . . carefully, feeling with his feet for the brittle dry branches and pine cones that lay among the needles on the forest floor. His tunnelling clothes were wet with perspiration and the keen night air cut through them . . .

'Let's get out of these combinations,' John said. 'Get cleaned up and dressed like human beings.'

'Not yet. Lay the trail away from the railway station. We'll hide them near the road to Breslau . . .'[125]

The ruse worked. Posing as French workers, the two escapees bought train tickets from Sagan to Frankfurt, changed for Küstrin, reached the harbour of Stettin and, with the help of a Danish seaman, sailed for Sweden as stowaways on the good ship SS *Norensan*.

The Great Escape relates to a later episode at *Stalag Luft III* the following year, when a much larger network of tunnels called 'Tom, Dick and Harry' was established. The longest of them, 'Harry', was equipped with a workshop, air pumps and a miniature railway to transport the soil. It stretched for some 104 metres before exiting beyond the wire. On the night of 24 March 1944, it provided the escape route for seventy-six Allied prisoners. When the alarm was raised, the largest manhunt of the war was organised by the head of the Gestapo in Breslau, Max Wielen. Within days, most of the escapees had been captured, many as far away as Saarbrücken, Flensburg or Danzig. Only three, a Dutchman and two Norwegians, managed to escape to Britain. The remainder faced retribution. By orders of Hitler, fifty of their number were executed; of the fifty, twenty-seven were killed by the Breslau Gestapo. Wielen was to face trial in Hamburg in 1946 and was sentenced to life imprisonment.

Nearly two million French soldiers were made prisoner in Germany in 1940, and many were sent to work in Silesia. Marcel Neveu (1907–2001) was one of them. A military radio officer, who came from the village of Sancheville (Eure-et-Loir) near Chartres, he was captured in Belgium and sent to Sagan, where he was held in the intervals between long spells of agricultural labour on German farms. He worked for a *patron* called Henschel, and for another called Kupke. (In appearance, Neveu bore a striking resemblance to Karol Wojtyła.) In his later years, he repeated his war stories ad infinitum to the point where his family decided to record them on tape. He knew of 'The Great Escape', for example, although he was out of the camp at the time, and he had much to say about the conditions among the prisoners of various nationalities on those Silesian farms.

Talking to his granddaughter forty years later, Neveu was at pains to stress that the post-war films made about Sagan bore little relation to reality. '*Pas pareil*,' he would say, '*pas pareil*' – 'not the same thing.' He also had a colourful description of the moment when the tunnellers were discovered by a guard. 'This [guard] came down from his watchtower and went for a pee beside a fir tree, and saw this guy coming out like a mole from a hole.' On another occasion he got himself into trouble when he stood between a group of Polish girls, whom the farmer had been beating, and called him '*un sale Nazi*' ('a dirty Nazi'). Fortunately, the farmer did not report him. By the autumn of 1944, Neveu talked to his boss more boldly: 'When the Russians come, you are "kaputt".' To which the boss replied, 'The Russians are never coming here.'

The Russians arrived in February 1945. If farmer Henschel had still been there, 'the Poles would have wrung his neck'.[126] Oral history is a great source of knowledge, but like all subjective sources – it must be handled with care.

*

Religious life in wartime Breslau proceeded in the darkening shadow of Nazi atrocities. Generally speaking, Christian leaders were no more inclined to make a stand after 1939 than they had been beforehand. Yet one must not rush to judge people who lived under totalitarian pressures. The Nazi Party employed officials to oversee ecclesiastical affairs. Even so, occasions *did* arise when consciences were roused to action. In 1939–40, for example, Cardinal Bertram, Archbishop of Breslau, was made aware of mass repressions taking place in the adjacent Warthegau, not least against Polish Catholic clergy. In towns and cities such as Poznań, churches were being forcibly closed, while priests were being arrested, tortured and murdered in droves – 4,000 Polish priests were cast into Dachau alone. In his capacity as Chairman of the German Catholic episcopate at Fulda, Bertram appealed to the Vatican for protection.[127] His appeal was ignored. For whatever reason, Pope Pius XII was not willing to intervene. Nothing was ever done by the Vatican to help the three million Polish Catholics who were killed during the war. A couple of years later, when the Pope ignored similar appeals to intervene against the Holocaust, he attracted accusations of anti-Semitism. Such accusations are, however, misplaced unless they are accompanied by similar charges relating to all categories of victim neglected by the Vatican. Pope Pius XII did not regard it as his Christian duty to condemn the Nazis for anything, or to express public compassion for anyone.

In due course, Cardinal Bertram was to have detailed information about the Holocaust. In August 1943, he received a letter from an unidentified Jew who was startlingly well informed. The letter claimed that four million Jews had already been murdered. It detailed the activities of the *Einsatzgruppen* in occupied Poland, and the establishment and liquidation of the ghettos – especially that of Cracow, whence the letter appeared to have come. The correspondent even knew of the existence of the extermination camp at Bełżec. He concluded, 'The German people who gave birth to a devil will perish through him.'[128] It is not known what Cardinal Bertram's reaction was, but he and his circle could not have pleaded ignorance.

The Protestant and Catholic clergy of Breslau stayed at their posts until the evacuation of January 1945. Even then, a delegation of priests persuaded the Gauleiter to allow some of their number to stay. Among them were Ernst Hornig and Dr Joachim Konrad, whose pleas would eventually move the *Festung* commander to capitulate (see page 34). But Paul Peikert (1884–1949) was to achieve more lasting fame. Priest of the Catholic parish of St Mauritius in Breslau since 1932, he had been arrested by the Gestapo in August 1937. Yet he managed to return to his position and to remain during the siege. From the start, he set out to record the death of Breslau for posterity. He risked his life to collect German and Soviet propaganda leaflets; he noted the opinions of his parishioners; and he recorded daily events in his *Chronik über die Belagerung Breslaus* ('Chronicle of the Siege of Breslau'). An increasingly embittered critic of the Nazi regime, Peikert provided an honourable coda to an otherwise unedifying period in the history of his co-religionists. He concluded, 'May this diary show future generations what we had to endure and may God in his mercy keep them from a similar fate.'[129]

*

The shift from *Blitzkrieg* to 'Total War' made progressively greater demands on the German economy. Silesia was required to respond to the pressures of Allied bombing in the west of the Reich. In March 1942, Hitler decreed that a weapons factory be established in Breslau, beyond the range of even the most determined Allied pilots. Later that month, the building department of Albert Speer's huge empire swung into action, using Jewish forced labour for the construction of what became known as the Krupp 'Berthawerk' near Markstädt.[130] With a floorspace of 120,000 square metres and seven large halls, the 'Berthawerk' was designed to produce artillery pieces and anti-tank guns using the steel of the Markstädt steelworks and the labour of the Fünfteichen concentration camp. At its peak in 1944, it was employing just under 10,000 predominantly Czech workers and producing more than 400 Le F.H. 18/40 Field Guns per month. Ironically, given the endemic unemployment in preceding decades, its managers cursed the lack of German labour and their necessary reliance on the less productive concentration-camp inmates. The lack of enthusiasm of the latter was understandable. On arrival at the Fünfteichen concentration camp, they were given clothing and a pair of wooden clogs. Each morning they would be mustered at 4.30 a.m. for a five-kilometre forced march to the factory. There they averaged twelve hours a day at lathes, mills and grinders. Often drenched in oil and burned by hot fragments of metal, they would then return to the camp, where food consisted of a thin, indistinct soup. Medical care was rudimentary and brutality arbitrary. Only the youngest and fittest would survive.[131]

According to the conservative estimates of the British Ministry of Economic Warfare, the forty-one economic targets in the Breslau area employed almost 60,000 workers.[132] Linke-Hofmann at its peak employed nearly 5,000 workers and, in addition to its staple railway wagons, produced the propulsion systems for the V2 rocket.[133] FAMO employed a similar number, building tanks, self-propelled guns and submarine and aero-engines. Junkers at Gandau assembled, among other things, Ju 87 'Stuka' divebombers. And in a state-of-the-art, air-conditioned factory at Hunds-feld, Rheinmetall-Borsig employed 2,000 workers manufacturing bomb components. The so-called 'Y' fuse, which was specifically designed to kill Allied bomb-disposal officers, was one of its most sinister products. Fitted into a conventional bomb, it consisted of a chain of timers and mercury switches, which stopped bombs from exploding until they had hit the ground, come to rest and been tampered with. To further frustrate efforts to make such bombs safe, it was deliberately mislabelled.[134]

As the war progressed, however, no amount of new factories, slave labourers and relocations could make Germany's war economy keep pace with its enemies. After the initial setbacks, Soviet military production recovered to outstrip its German rival. And, in the US, Hitler had taken on an industrial superpower that was in a league of its own. Allied bombing nullified the small advances made. The RAF and USAAF steadily overtook the *Luftwaffe*'s failing efforts. By 1944, Allied tonnage dropped on the Reich reached a peak of 663,000 tonnes, dwarfing the *Luftwaffe*'s total for that year of 9,334. Indeed, the Allied monthly average for 1944 (77,743) even exceeded the total tonnage dropped by the *Luftwaffe* on the UK during the entire six years of the war (75,655).[135]

Breslau was listed as a 'target of primary importance' in the RAF 'Bomber's Baedeker' of January 1943.[136] Its marshalling yards and power station were prioritised. So, too, were the Junkers, FAMO, Rheinmetall-Borsig and Linke-Hofmann factories. Yet as the main bomber fleets never flew much beyond Dresden, Breslau was spared. The same could not be said when it came into the sights of Soviet ground artillery.

*

Resistance to the Nazi regime came in various guises. It ran a huge gamut of attitudes from people who decided on internal migration, living their lives as if the Nazis did not exist, to those who risked their lives by collecting intelligence, sabotaging the German war effort or even conspiring to kill the Führer. In Silesia, it was complicated by the dual presence of German and Polish resistance groups. One should not pretend that either of them was specially effective.

The so-called *Kreisauer Kreis*, or 'Kreisau circle', takes pride of place in Breslau's role of honour. Named after the Moltke estate near Schweidnitz where most of its meetings took place, it formed the hub of German resistance to Hitler, and many of its members bore close links to the Silesian capital. The owner of Kreisau (Krzyżowa), Count Helmuth James von Moltke, was the son and grandson of two Field Marshals. His friend and co-conspirator, Graf Peter Yorck von Wartenburg, came from Klein Oels to the north-east of Breslau and had worked in 1936–41 in the Breslau Presidium. Their Commander-in-Chief designate (in case they assumed power) was the Breslauer General Field Marshal, Erwin von Witzleben, who had led the victorious French campaign of 1940. The conspiracy also included Dr Hans Lukaschek, former *Oberpräsident* of Silesia, and Fritz Voigt, former Police President of Breslau and Reichstag deputy. When Schenk von Stauffenberg's assassination attempt at the Führer's lair in East Prussia (with which the Kreisau circle was closely connected) failed in July 1944, the conspirators were discovered and arrested. Their leaders were hanged from meat-hooks in a Gestapo execution chamber, filmed for the Führer's pleasure.

Count Michael von Matuschka (1888–1944) was also rounded up in the general blood-letting of that summer. Born in Schweidnitz, he had been schooled at the St Matthias Gymnasium in Breslau. As an advocate of the restoration of normal Germano-Polish relations during the insanity of Nazism, he was condemned to leave few marks on the historical record, but is nonetheless commemorated at his former school. He was hanged in Plötzensee Prison in September 1944.

The remarkable Rudolf-Christoph von Gersdorff (1905–80) was one conspirator who escaped Nazi retribution. Born in Lüben (Lubin) in 1905, he had risen through the ranks, being stationed for much of his time in Breslau, to join the General Staff in 1937. Yet, disillusioned by the Nazis, he used his position to plan an audacious assassination attempt. On 21 March 1943, when Hitler was due to attend a ceremony at the Berlin Armoury, he prepared to execute a 'suicide bombing'. Wired with two British-made 'clam charges' he was thwarted only when the Führer cut the tour short. Nonetheless, Gersdorff maintained sufficient composure to return the explosives safely to his brother's house in Breslau and to avoid subsequent detection. He survived his intended victim by some thirty-five years.

The Polish underground resistance movement was the largest in Europe. Its principal organisation, the Home Army (AK), controlled by the Polish government-in-exile, was an umbrella for numerous lesser bodies that represented all the democratic orientations. (It was approximately 100 times larger than the corresponding Communist movement, the 'People's Guard' (AL), which after the war would monopolise all the credit.) Throughout the war, it ran a secret underground state, replete with judicial, educational, propaganda and intelligence departments. Its Sabotage Division, the *Kedyw*, was particularly efficient, being armed and funded by the British. What is more, since the western half of Poland was annexed to the Greater Reich, it was able to move around all parts of Germany with relative ease. Lower Silesia was often targeted, but with no special success. In 1940, a group called the *Związek Odwetu* (ZO), or 'Union of Revenge', was formed to sabotage the German economy and transport network, but its cells in Kattowitz, Warsaw, Cracow, and Lower Silesia were broken by the Gestapo. An espionage network called *Stragan*, or 'Market Stall', operated in Silesia, Poznań and west Prussia for three years. Its agents, who were specially sent by the AK command in Warsaw, worked in the FAMO factory and were rounded up in January 1943. Others were undeterred. Late in 1942, Breslau military intelligence noted the continued existence of numerous resistance organisations, among them *Jaszczurka*, the *Polska Organizacja Polityczna* and the *Siła Zbrojna Polski*.[137]

The Olympus Group was made up of native Vratislavians who met in the apartment of the Wyderkowski family. Their connections with Warsaw were slight, but their aims were very clear. They sought to recruit Polish workers to their cause in Breslau's factories; to sow sabotage and 'go-slows'; and to collect economic and political intelligence. Fifty-eight of their members were arrested on 5 June 1942 after two years' work. They were sent either to Auschwitz or Groß Rosen. Their liaison officer with the AK was Stanisław Grzeszewski.

Much of the information about Breslau, which has been preserved in the files of former Polish army intelligence in London, probably originated with the Olympians. It includes detailed lists of every industrial enterprise in Breslau; an outline guide for visiting spies; a list of all Nazi Party officers in Breslau, replete with names, addresses and telephone numbers; and a remarkable (undated) summary of 296 military units and sites present in Breslau and its district.[138] From the latter one learns, for instance, that the

Wehrkreis-Kdo VIII (Command of Military Region VIII) was stationed at Gabitzstrasse 122–8 (tel.82081); that the *Luftgau Kommando VIII* (Regional Air Command) was located at Matthiasstrasse 1, and the *SS Oberabschnitt Südost* at Eberschen-Allee 17/19 (tel.82411). The Military Interpreters Company was based at the Woyrsch Barracks in Breslau-Karlowitz; the Chief Army Hospital at Werderstrasse 88; the Lutheran Military Chaplaincy at Memelstrasse 65; and the *Hitlerjugend Gebiet Schlesien* at Ohlauer Stadtgraben 17–18 (tel.52241). The military airfield at Gandau housed the *Flugzeugführer-Schule 'E': Strachwitz*, an aerodrome and, near the village of Kuhnau (Kunow), Stalag VIIIC. Visiting resistance fighters had no excuse to get lost.

The British Special Operations Executive (SOE) constantly sought to spur on anti-Nazi resistance. In November 1944 it launched 'Operation Fleckney'.[139] A British-trained Pole by the name of Paul Penczok was parachuted into Germany on a mission to organise sabotage and subversion in Breslau. Unfortunately the SOE file is ominously silent on Penczok's performance.

By late 1944, the prospect of a German defeat and the continued advance of the Soviets had sown alarm in the eastern provinces of the Reich. Rumours of the permanent detachment of Germany's eastern provinces were dismissed as a sick joke, but the proximity of the Red Army gave ample reason for concern. The Soviets had crossed the border of east Prussia into the 'Old Reich' in August 1944, and tales of atrocities against the civilian population multiplied. That winter the frontline ran from Memel on the Baltic through Warsaw, where the Soviets had allowed the rising to be crushed by the SS, and on to Budapest. Yet any feeling of optimism on the German part, resulting from the Soviets' pause on the Vistula, was sorely misplaced. Soviet strategists were planning to cover the 320 kilometres from the Vistula to the Oder in a mere fifteen days. For the first time since 1813, Breslau would find itself engulfed by the frontline of conflict.

Breslau's experience in those last months of the war was doubtless repeated in other parts of eastern Germany. Designated a *Festung*, or 'fortress' – as was Glogau – despite the patent lack of anything resembling fortifications, it was to be held by a motley collection of under-age *Hitlerjugend*, elderly *Volkssturm* ('territorial reservists') and battle-hardened *Waffen SS* veterans. The first Soviet air raids struck on 18 January 1945. They were followed two days later by the evacuation of civilians and non-combatant personnel. On the first day alone, in deep snow and freezing temperatures, some 60,000 women and children are thought to have left on foot, taking with them only what they could carry. By the time the Soviet siege closed in mid-February, just 200,000 people remained. The Breslau garrison held the besiegers at bay, but failed to delay the Soviet advance. When Hitler committed suicide on 30 April, it continued to resist. It surrendered at six o'clock on the evening of 6 May, half an hour before General Jodl's general capitulation at Rheims (see page 35). Breslau had experienced its *Götterdämmerung*, or 'Twilight of the Gods'. The most prominent long-term victim was to be its German character. German Breslau, like Jewish Breslau, would cease to exist.

*

One or two days before the civilian evacuation began, a young, wounded soldier returned home to Breslau on leave in order to recuperate. He found that his mother and sisters were about to depart, but that he and his father – like all men of military age – were under orders to stay. Ulrich Frodien was just eighteen years of age. His evocation of the terrors of a dying city, from which he risked his life to escape, is unsurpassed.

When Frodien set off on a reconnaissance of the snowbound city streets, he ran into a desperate crowd of panic-stricken refugees, who had crossed the Lessing Bridge from the empty eastern suburbs and who were following the blaring instructions of wayside loudspeakers: 'WOMEN AND CHILDREN TO MAKE THEIR WAY ON FOOT IN THE DIRECTION OF OPPERAU AND KANTH.' The crowd suddenly stopped on hearing contradictory instructions. Lost children wailed. Old people collapsed. When Frodien entered the apartment of a neighbour, he found that the old man and his housekeeper had hanged themselves. Inspecting an improvised barricade with his father, they decided that the Soviet tanks would take just fifteen minutes to demolish it – '14 minutes for the tank crew to stop laughing, and one minute to brush it aside'. When he turned a corner, he was faced with the terrifying sight of the 'Chained Dogs', the German military police, and quickly took cover. 'The military police', he recalled, 'were more dangerous for me than the whole of the Red Army.' They carried heavy metal shields on their chests, heavy metal chains to leash their snarling dogs, guns at the ready and no human feelings whatsoever. They had strict orders to shoot without warning at suspected deserters and at the looters who were busy in the abandoned houses.

The Frodiens' plan of escape was a gambler's throw. It reads like historical fiction, but is a good example of history lived under stress and later relived (necessarily) with subjectivity. At all events, the plan worked. Ulrich's father dressed up in his military surgeon's uniform from the First World War, suitably bedecked with medals. Ulrich himself was bandaged dramatically round the head with stained cloths and wore his distressed army overcoat. They had revolvers, but no valid documents. As they walked out of their apartment on the Strasse der SA for the last time, the father said, 'Take a look: you'll never see your homeland again.' He went on, 'From now on, you call me "Captain" and stand to attention.'

The Hauptbahnhof was surrounded by scenes 'from the lowest ring of Dante's Inferno'. Despite eighteen degrees of frost, it was besieged by a baying mob held back by a cordon of sullen soldiers. These were the Breslauers who had left it too late. No more civilian trains were leaving. But an army hospital train was standing at the nearby freight station. Ulrich's father suddenly appeared with a line of eleven walking wounded who had all been told to limp and moan. Reaching his son, he barked out, '*Gefreiter!* [Private!] Take your bag. By the right, quick march!' He then pushed his way through the crowd, waved a piece of paper under the noses of the military police, saluted them and led his charges on to the platform. 'None of those swine', he muttered under his breath, 'even murmured about documents.'

Waiting for the hospital train to move seemed like an eternity. Night fell. Hours passed. There was a fearsome stench of stale sweat and iodine. The temperature rose. No one talked. The silence was broken only by snores and screams. Nurses rushed along the train's corridors; torches flashed in the darkness. Men were dying, and orderlies carried off the dead to the mortuary wagon. But the *Wehrmacht* could still serve up clean sheets, bean soup and a glass of water. Ulrich fell asleep on the carriage floor. He awoke to the rhythmic clatter of the train's bogies riding along the track – 'the most beautiful music in the world'. They were heading for Prague. 'We had left and lost Breslau,' he later wrote. 'But Breslau itself survived everything. Today, it is alive and flourishing again, though under its new name – Wrocław.'[140]

EIGHT

Wrocław: Phoenix from the Ashes, 1945–2000

At about six o'clock on the evening of 6 May 1945, the last commander of *Festung* Breslau, General Niehoff, was driven to the Villa Colonia in the southern suburbs, to sign the act of capitulation. The ruins passed under the control of the Soviet Army, and of the Soviet Army's controllers, the NKVD. The next morning, lines of haggard German soldiers threw down their arms at designated points in front of the Market Hall or on the Königsplatz. They then marched off to the unknown destinations of Soviet captivity from which many would never return. Their fur-capped conquerors stood guard at every street crossing with fixed bayonets, surrounded by the mountains of rubble. White flags hung from gaping windows.

Bewildered civilians crept nervously from their underground hiding places. One young woman described the experience:

> In front of the house a small group of Soviet soldiers was standing, with medals on their chests. One of them asked if anyone could translate and explain that German women had to go with them and prepare food. So I volunteered. In the company of several German girls, I went to the cellars where the soldiers had set up their quarters. I didn't even notice that I'd been separated from the rest and that I was on my own with an officer. He told me to wash some glasses, filled them up with either wine or vodka, and ordered me to drink. I refused. He then pushed me onto some sort of a bed for obvious purposes. I stood up, but he'd already pushed me down again when three other officers came in ... The soldiers laughed when I couldn't find the exit. Terribly upset, I ran home, wrapped myself in a long skirt and covered my head with a scarf ... My brother said, 'That won't help you.'[1]

She was not even German. At least she had escaped the life-threatening gang rapes that were the Red Army's *forte*.

The first organisation to be set up was one of several designed to hunt down Nazi sympathisers. On 7 May, after a meeting with Soviet political officers at the prison on Kletschkaustrasse, the German Anti-Fascist Freedom Movement, or *Antifa*, began to operate led by Hermann Hartmann. It had its own security apparatus and was divided into twelve sections, each with its own food station. Soon afterwards, the *Antifa* raided the house of the woman who had just escaped the Soviet soldiery. Those German Communists were looking 'for my boss's brother-in-law,' she recalled, 'a fervent Nazi. They were burning for revenge, for a reckoning for everything they had suffered. But they didn't catch him, and went away with nothing.'[2] The true irony of the story was revealed a couple of months later, when the *Antifa* was summarily closed down. The staff of its central office had turned out to consist almost entirely of ex-members of the NSDAP.[3] The German Social Democrats then came to the fore – in so far as one can talk of any effective German politics.

Once in full control, the occupying Soviets put the ruined city to the torch. From 7 May, the shattered wreck of Breslau was deliberately set alight. Gangs of looters ran from street to street, ransacking the war-damaged houses, driving out the cowed inhabitants, spilling petrol and starting fires that raged for days and smouldered for weeks. Whole districts blazed. On 10 May, the priceless book collection of the University Library, stored in the Church of St Anne for the duration of the siege, went up in flames. On 15 May, huge conflagrations reduced the Museum in Castle Square to ashes, and triggered an explosion that demolished the twin towers of Mary Magdalene's Church. For two days, a pitched battle flared between rival Soviet units fighting over the former German foodstores on the Sternstrasse. The idea that Breslau had been completely destroyed by the siege was a post-war fiction.

In the midst of the mayhem, the Soviet Army held a victory parade. While smoke drifted over the city, the triumphant troops of Lieutenant-General Gluzdovsky's 6th Army filed past a saluting-base on the airfield at Pilczyce (Pilsnitz).[4] Beside the tribune hung a banner:

ДА ЗДРАВСТВУЕТ ПАРТИЯ БОЛЪШЕВИКОВ
РУКОВОДИТЕЛЪ ПОБЕДЪ НАД НЕМЕЦКО-ФАШИСТКИМ ИГОМ

(Long live the Party of Bolsheviks,
Leader of the Victory over the German Fascist Yoke)

Taking the salute alongside Gluzdovsky were his two deputies: the chief political officer, Major-General Vasily Klokov, and Major-General Kvash-nievsky. Both Gluzdovsky and Kvashnievsky were Soviet officers of Polish descent.

Arson, rape, robbery and systematic looting proceeded unrestrained.

After some time, however, the pattern changed. Once the larger Soviet units were withdrawn, most criminal violations were left to individual deserters and freebooters, and the Soviet authorities turned their energies to dismantling any installation that caught their fancy. On 1 June, Soviet troops dismantled Breslau's principal power station in the suburb of Siechnica (Kraftborn). From there, they moved on to the two FAMO factories, from which all undamaged machines were removed, and thence to the Linke-Hofmann works, which were similarly stripped. Railway tracks, street lights and overhead cables were carried off regardless. Freight trains were marshalled at Psie Pole (Hundsfeld) ready to transport anything and everything to the USSR. They were also used by hordes of private looters:

> Hundreds of railway wagons of every shape and size stood in a vast marshy meadow amidst pools of knee-deep water. As soon as one group of passengers alighted from a train another group would clamber aboard with their sacks of loot, pictures, bedding and anything else they could lift.[5]

Most descriptions of Soviet plunder emphasise the insatiable hunger for watches, women, window frames and wheelbarrows. Bicycles were also in great demand. But there was another obsession:

> Oh yes, pianos were a real Soviet speciality. They are expensive, beautiful and elegant. In any case, the Russians are a musical nation. In our tenement, there were five pianos, one for every family . . . Then one day, a Soviet truck drew up. *Davai!* [Hand them over!] We beg them: 'Leave us just one.' But it's *Niet, Niet, Niet.* Then my father hit a keyboard to show it wasn't working. So they left us that one. And that's how I remember it: a forlorn piano lying on the street amid the ruins.[6]

From time to time, armed patrols of the NKVD, and later of the Polish Internal Security Corps (KBW), would conduct a trawl in order to trap looters and marauders. They did not try very hard.

On 8 May, 'Peace in Europe' was declared. In Breslau it was an irrelevance. And for the Soviet occupiers, plundering proceeded apace. For them, '*Stunde Null*' or 'Zero Hour' meant nothing. For the German civilians, there was no relief in sight. Yet on the very next day, an unexpected event occurred. An advance party of thirteen Polish administrators arrived without warning, took over an undamaged house at 25/7 Blücherstrasse and ceremonially fixed the Polish state emblem over the door. They had been appointed by the 'committee of puppets', whom Stalin had put in charge of Soviet-occupied Poland; and they had been charged with laying claim to the capital of Lower Silesia. On the 10th, they were joined by a further group of self-appointed colleagues, including the 'City President' Bolesław Drobner (1883–1968), and by a taskforce of the feared, Communist-run Office of Public Security (UBP). Their presence was anomalous, to say the least. Indeed, in terms of international law, it was downright improper. As yet, Poland had no internationally or internally sanctioned government, and there had certainly been no official change in either Germany's or Poland's frontiers. The induction of Poland's Provisional Government of National Unity (TJRN), as envisaged by the Yalta Agreement, was still seven weeks away. The Interallied Conference at Potsdam, which was to determine Germany's future, would not convene for nearly three months. So the Polish administrators who laid claim to Breslau on 9 May 1945 were arranging a classic fait accompli. Acting on orders from their political masters, they were aiming to ensure that Breslau was safely in Polish hands before the victorious Allies could even discuss it. What is more, they had not managed to clear their démarche with the Soviet military authorities. Temporary arrangements were agreed at a meeting on 11 May with three Soviet colonels. But it was not until a delegation headed by Bolesław Drobner had travelled on 13 May to Marshal Koniev's head-quarters at Żagań (Sagan) that Soviet acquiescence was properly secured. For the time being, the in-coming Polish administration would coordinate its activities with the offices of two parallel Communist-appointed figures – the Plenipotentiary for Lower Silesia of the Temporary Polish Government, Stanisław Piaskowski, and the superior Plenipotentiary General for the so-called 'Recovered Territories', Edward Ochab. In order to boost its influence with the German population, it recognised one of the rival anti-Fascist groups, the DVA, to whom it distributed identity cards. Yet the precarious position of the Polish administrators cannot be overstated. When President Drobner organised a second military parade on Castle Square on 26 May, the march-past of troops from the Second Polish Army, which had taken part in the capture of Berlin and was now being posted to Silesia, was watched largely by people in Soviet uniform. Polish infantry, artillery and cavalry marched across Castle Square (now renamed Plac Wolności, or 'Freedom Square') in a conscious re-enactment of the victory parades held there by the Nazis in 1939 and 1940 – only now the swastika standards, which had once waved overhead, were enthusiastically trampled underfoot.

Remarking on the events of those days, many ill-informed commentators have said that 'the Poles' seized Breslau and that many of the offences and injustices that ensued were committed 'by Poles'. This sort of statement requires refinement. It is important to clarify which Poles one is accusing. Of course, there can be no doubt that Bolesław Drobner and most of his associates were Polish, and never thought of themselves as anything else.

Drobner had once fought with Piłsudski's Legions, had served the left wing of the Polish Socialist Party (PPS) for decades and would work for years in the local government of his native Cracow. On the other hand, it is absolutely essential to realise that all the political organisations of post-war Poland, which men like Drobner ran, were almost completely devoid of popular support. They were set up in 1944–5 on instructions from Moscow and were entirely dependent on the none-too-subtle backing of Soviet forces. They were servants of a foreign power, which had overrun Poland in much the same way as it had overrun half of Germany. In the eyes of the great majority of the Polish nation, they were traitors and oppressors or, at best, time-servers. They were not legitimate Polish representatives.

As a matter of fact, Drobner had been a prisoner in the Soviet Gulag only a couple of years earlier. So, too, had been his close colleague, Alexander Zawadzki, who had been put in charge of Upper Silesia and who, in 1952, would become President of the Polish People's Republic. These men were living under licence and were bound by invisible chains. They would be discarded as soon as their services were no longer required. They belonged to a higher class of bureaucratic slave overseeing the general mass of helots. Having no solid native backing, they naturally turned either to unscrupulous careerists or to the dregs of society to do their bidding. Drobner himself aired a scheme for creating a moneyless economic system and for dividing the city into German and Polish sections. It was nicknamed 'The Drobner Republic' and ensured that his days in Silesia were numbered.

It is also essential to realise that no one in the early post-war years could have established a fully fledged Communist regime in Poland. Stalin likened the task to 'putting a saddle on a cow'. For one thing, Communism had always been deeply unattractive to Catholic Poles, and doubly so after Soviet misconduct in 1939–41. For another, Stalin had made the bad mistake of murdering virtually the entire *actif* of the pre-war Polish Communist Party in the Great Purge of 1937–9. As a result, less than a decade later there were not enough trained Polish Communists alive to run a factory, let alone a country of thirty million people. Three years would have to pass before the revived Polish Communist movement could pull in enough recruits to think of taking power and creating a Soviet-style 'People's Democracy'. In the meantime, Stalin had to make do with an endless series of phoney front organisations, which pretended to be 'Polish', 'Popular' and 'Democratic' but were nothing of the kind. He introduced a dictatorship of stooges.

Finally, one must realise that the Polish claim to the so-called 'Recovered Territories', of which Breslau was the jewel, was almost entirely the product of Soviet policy. It had very little to do with the Poles' own aspirations. Prior to 1939, no responsible Polish political party or leader had ever laid explicit claim to Breslau.[7] The Polish government-in-exile had discussed the issue in the context of a proposed Polish–Czechoslovak Confederation, but it was never formalised. It had also been proposed by a number of nationalistic circles in pre-war Upper Silesia, such as the one that gathered around Father Karol Borgieł (alias Milik, 1892–1976), a military chaplain who had published a famous postcard showing a map with Breslau and Szczecin (Stettin) on the Polish side of the frontier. But it was never adopted by public opinion as a whole. Prior to the Potsdam Conference, not even the pro-Soviet elements that were running Poland had openly admitted to the claim for which Moscow was secretly rehearsing them. By the twentieth century, Breslau's links to the so-called Piast legacy had almost completely disappeared from Poland's national imagination. The idea of transferring well-established German cities and provinces to Poland would never have taken root except for intensive Soviet propaganda and the realisation that the Soviet annexation of Poland's own eastern provinces could not be reversed. If Poland had not been forced to abandon Wilno (Vilnius) and Lwów, it is unlikely – despite the immense anger caused by the Nazi atrocities – that many Poles would have cared to claim as they did. Oppeln, Danzig and Allenstein, yes; but Stettin, Grünberg and Breslau, no.

As it was, the battered and doubly defeated Polish nation was in desperate straits. The Soviet authorities were again busy cleansing ethnic Poles from the provinces seized by the USSR, exactly as they had done in 1939–41. Poland's need for territorial compensation was acute, and Moscow's ancient plan to compensate the Poles with German land had already been sold in principle to the Western powers. It had been mooted as long ago as 1914,[8] had been secretly agreed by 'The Big Three' at Tehran in 1943 and had been publicly unveiled at Yalta in February 1945. In May 1945, when Drobner and co. moved in, there were no Poles in Breslau to greet them, save a community of ex-slave labourers, a gang of railwaymen and a detachment of special police. Yet Vilnius and Lvov and many other eastern Polish cities had been held by the Soviets for more than a year. Polish expellees from the East were already on the road. It was only a matter of time before they and millions of their dispossessed countrymen would be persuaded that Breslau was theirs by right. Even those who resisted the propaganda could admit that Breslau should be theirs by necessity.

The Polish expellees from the Soviet Union were euphemistically called 'repatriants'. The term conveniently masked the involuntary nature of their resettlement and the foreign nature of their destinations. But their initial numbers were insufficient to upset the ethnic balance of Breslau's population. The Polish Repatriation Board (PUR) set up one reception point at Hundsfeld in May 1945 and another in the city on Pauliner Strasse in

July. The first Polish child to be born in post-war Breslau – a boy – was safely delivered on 11 June. The first trainload of 800 German expellees, principally members of the discredited *Antifa*, pulled out on 6 July. Breslau also saw vast numbers of refugees in transit. The main categories consisted of Polish displaced persons returning from Germany, and Sudeten Germans fleeing from Bohemia, where specially savage expulsions had already started.

In the three months separating the end of the siege and the start of the Potsdam Conference many social activities, municipal services and institutions were revived:

12 May, a Polish Mass at St Antony's Church
16 May, the Post Office on Matthias Strasse
18 May, a surgical ward at the All Saints Hospital
20 May, the District Court (*Sąd Grodzki*)
27 May, the Popular Theatre on Gartenstrasse
29 May, at the Civil Registry, the first Polish marriage
31 May, the City Committee of the Polish Socialist Party (PPS)
10 June, *Nasz Wrocław*, the first Polish newspaper
16 June, Cinema Warsaw: the film *Majdanek*
25 June, the first city bus line: to Karłowice (Karlowitz)
29 June, a concert by the City Symphony Orchestra
12 July, a branch of the Polish National Bank
19 July, the Widau River Railway Bridge
21 July, in the Municipal Theatre (Opera), a recital of *Pan Tadeusz*

At this juncture, no retail shops were open for business. The Reichsmark had been declared invalid, but Polish currency was not yet circulating officially.

The stupendous task of clearing the debris of war was undertaken with little help from the Soviet Army and with no hope of rapid progress. All German civilians were ordered to report for duty in work brigades. As often as not, they worked with their bare hands. Thousands of rotting corpses had to be buried. Thousands of mines had to be defused. Piles of fallen masonry had to be moved to make pathways through blocked streets. Buildings in danger of collapse had to be pulled down. Broken sewers, water pipes, tramlines and cables had to be patched up. A few factories were still operating, manned by a mixture of Germans, ex-slave labourers and prisoners of war, but most had been requisitioned by the Soviets, who waited until June before handing over forty-five major installations. The engineer who was charged at a slightly later date with restarting the city's flour mills recalled the absurdity of his predicament. One day a Soviet commandant burst in, shouting that he needed flour. When told that no flour could be produced, since Soviet troops had recently removed all the machinery, he shrugged. When asked where the machinery had gone, the commandant replied, '*Za Ural*' 'Beyond the Urals'. A couple of weeks later, a detachment of the commandant's men delivered a consignment of assorted milling machines presumably plundered from elsewhere in Germany.[9]

One of the gaps in our knowledge of those first post-war months concerns the fate of tens of thousands of POWs and other prisoners, whom the Nazis had forced to work for them in Breslau throughout the siege. Exact numbers are impossible to ascertain, but quite a few individuals, especially Poles, did survive and have recorded accounts of their maltreatment.[10] One also hears that a sizeable contingent of ex-prisoners was taken off by the Soviets to man the mines at Wałbrzych (Waldenburg). Even so, there would seem to be many who simply disappeared. Few questions were asked in 1945, when tides of war-torn humanity were flowing in all directions. But nowadays inquiries are necessary. If the SS had shot their prisoners at the end of the siege, traces would have been left of a large-scale, last-minute massacre. If the SS did not shoot them, they must have fallen into the hands of the NKVD. And what then? Short of definite information, one must fall back on the knowledge of Stalin's general policy in such circumstances, which was to demand the return of all of 'his' own people who had been abroad, and then to shoot them or to send them to an almost certain death in the camps.[11] It is entirely possible, therefore, that the lines of German soldiers who were marched out of Breslau under Soviet guard were accompanied by similar lines of their former prisoners: former Soviet POWs, who were being marched home to be killed.

Another 'blank spot' concerns the fate of Polish people who inhabited districts which in early 1945 had not yet been assigned to Poland. Numerous such areas lay in Pomerania, and others in both Upper and Lower Silesia. On the order of the NKVD, many tens of thousands of men and women were rounded up by the Soviet authorities and deported to the Gulag. They were caught up in the paranoid policy of 'securing the rear', to pre-empt disruption by civilians in districts adjacent to the frontline. A partial inquiry conducted in the 1990s produced 30,000 names from Silesia alone. Many of them died. The survivors were brought back from Russia in 1946–7 to Frankfurt an der Oder, where they were issued with documents (falsely) recording their release *from captivity in Germany*. Those among them who already possessed death certificates for friends or relatives who had died in Russia were reissued with certificates (falsely) stating the place of death as somewhere in Poland.[12]

Political tensions heightened as the Potsdam Conference approached. On

9 June, after exactly one month in office, Bolesław Drobner was told to resign. He was replaced by Alexander Wachniewski, a member of the Communist Polish Workers' Party (PPR), who announced that his party was taking control. None of these announcements carried much weight, since the Soviet military authorities were still supporting a German City President, whom they had appointed in parallel and who ran his own force of *Ordnungspolizei*. The Soviets were hedging their bets.

The Potsdam Conference delivered its verdict on 2 August. Three decisions were of particular relevance to Breslau's fate. Firstly, the three heads of government reaffirmed their opinion that 'the final delimitation of Poland's western frontier should await the peace settlement'. 'Delimitation' was a diplomatic term for 'minor changes'. No general peace conference, however, was ever held, and no final peace settlement was ever reached. Secondly, 'Pending the final determination of Poland's western frontier, the former German territories east of a line running from the Baltic Sea . . . and thence along the Oder River . . . and along the western Neisse River to the Czechoslovak frontier . . . shall be under the administration of the Polish state.' The Oder–Neisse Line left Breslau wholly on the Polish side. But 'under the administration of' was clearly intended to stop short of 'legal annexation'. From the legal point of view, the transfer of Breslau to Polish rule was provisional. Finally, the Potsdam Agreement declared that 'the transfer to Germany of German populations, or elements thereof, remaining in Poland, Czechoslovakia and Hungary, will have to be undertaken . . . Any transfers that take place should be effected in an orderly and humane manner.'[13]

So much is common knowledge. It is not always recognised, however, that Breslau – as distinct from other parts of the 'Recovered Territories' was transferred to Poland only as the result of a last-minute change of heart. Both Churchill and Truman went to Potsdam having planned 'to leave Stettin and Breslau on the German side of the frontier'.[14] Their view of 'the Oder Line', as they originally called it, foresaw a frontier running along the Oder and the Eastern Neisse. In this case, Breslau would have been divided in two, with the main part of the city in Germany and only the right-bank suburbs in Poland. Churchill in particular was anxious that Poland should not be overloaded. 'It would be a great pity', he had remarked at Yalta, 'to stuff the Polish goose so full of German food that it died of indigestion.'[15] Truman, for his part, 'did not like the way that the Poles had occupied this area without consulting "The Big Three" '. So when Stalin first mentioned the Western Neisse on the afternoon of the Sixth Plenary Session on 22 July – in the immediate aftermath of the Americans learning about the successful

A-bomb test in New Mexico – Churchill rejected the proposals as unacceptable.

It was Churchill who then suggested that Polish government leaders should present their case in person. The subsequent meeting on 24 July, between Churchill and a Polish delegation headed by Bolesław Bierut, bordered on the farcical. Churchill had little grasp of Polish realities, and was clearly oblivious to the fact that, in addition to being Chairman of Poland's National Homeland Council (KRN), Bierut was a Soviet career officer who had risen through the Comintern. Churchill's lecture on 'Polish independence', 'friendship with Soviet Russia', 'territorial moderation' and 'multi-party politics' was, therefore, a total waste of time. 'I do not take the view', he said, 'that only Communists are democrats.' Wisely, Bierut made no reply, except on the territorial issue. He later told Churchill that Poland's development 'would be based on the principles of Western democracy' and on 'the English model'. Of his own controllers, he said, 'the NKVD plays no part in Poland at present'. The Polish elections would be 'even more democratic than those in England'. The very next day Churchill flew to London, where he learned of his defeat in the general election. At Potsdam, the American delegation was left without its British partner. On 29 July, Truman vainly proposed the Eastern Neisse once again. That evening, Stalin told the Polish delegation to accept the River Queiss (Kwisa) – a very minor concession. But in the morning of the 30th the Americans settled for the Western Neisse without demur. Only then was it certain that Breslau would pass to Poland. 'I would never have agreed to the Western Neisse', Churchill wrote later, 'and was saving it up for a final show-down.'[16] But the final show-down never came. One has to wonder if the doughty British statesman was swayed by his visit to German Breslau thirty-nine years earlier (see pages 275–7).

The detailed provisions for implementing the Potsdam Communiqué were contained in a message from the Interallied Control Council in Berlin:

. . .

(2) The entire German population to be moved from Poland ($3\frac{1}{2}$ million persons) will be admitted to the Soviet and British zones of occupation in Germany . . .

(4) It is considered possible . . . to proceed . . . in accordance with the following schedule:
    During December 1945 at the rate of 10 percent of the total number
    During January and February 1946, at the rate of 5 percent . . .
    During March 1946 at the rate of 15 percent . . .
    During April 1946 at the rate of 15 percent . . .
    During May 1946 at the rate of 20 percent . . .

> During June 1946 at the rate of 20 percent . . .
> During July 1946 at the rate of 10 percent . . .[17]

Further refinements to the plan had to be made. But 95 per cent of the Germans living inside Poland's new borders were scheduled to be expelled by August 1946. The fate of the remaining German Breslauers had been sealed by fiat of the Allied powers.

Once the Potsdam decisions were announced, the Polish authorities could operate in the 'Recovered Territories' with much greater assurance and – more importantly – with the undivided support of the Soviet military. In practice, they acted as if the Potsdam Conference had created a permanent settlement, and they left it to others to mark relevant parts of the map with the cautionary words 'Under Polish Administration'. They insisted that Breslau now be referred to exclusively as 'Wrocław', and they made it the centre of a new administration district that included the towns of Oława (Ohlau), Środa (Neumarkt), Wołów (Wohlau), Trzebnica (Trebnitz), Oleśnica (Oels) and, with some delay, Legnica (Liegnitz). Conveniently, Legnica was designated as the seat of the Soviet Army Command in Poland. In law, however, the Recovered Territories did not belong to Poland in any definitive sense for forty-six years (see page 494). Throughout those decades, Wrocław was to suffer from the rarely mentioned, but palpable, climate of impermanence.

The Roman Catholic Church reacted even more quickly to the changed circumstances than the Polish government did. Armed with the requisite documents from the Vatican, the Polish Primate, Cardinal August Hlond, arrived in Wrocław unannounced on 12 August 1945. He told the German clerics that he was assuming control of the diocesional administration. He made his move four days before an agreement could be concluded between the Polish Republic and the USSR for the transfer of all German state property. By the end of the month, none other than Father Karol Milik had taken up residence in the cathedral as the Polish diocesional administrator. The stage was set for a season of Polish-German cohabitation in Wrocław's churches and for a long game of cat and mouse between Church and state. Under Father Milik, the Church was committed to oppose Communism, but also to bang the nationalist drum.

*

In 1945–7, the ethnic composition of the city was transformed. In less than two years, German Breslau faded away as Polish Wrocław came into view. In the summer of 1945, the residual pool of Germans was actually increased by the influx of people seeking their pre-war possessions. But soon thereafter the rising tempo of organised German expulsions was matched by

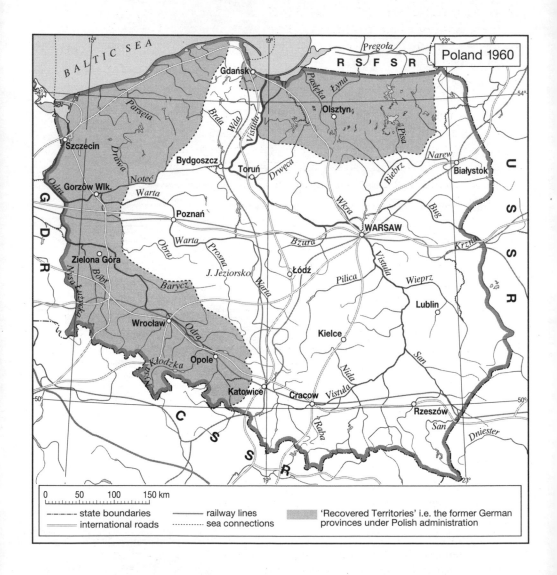

Poland 1960

the accelerating rate of Polish arrivals. The statistics speak for themselves. At the end of December 1945, only 33,297 Poles were registered in Wrocław, compared to more than five times that number of Germans. Nine months later, the positions had been almost exactly reversed: 152,898 Poles as against 28,274 Germans. By March 1947, Wrocław counted 214,310 inhabitants, of whom 196,814 were Poles and only 17,496 Germans. Owing to the demand for skilled labour, the final phase of German expulsions proceeded slowly.

The plight of German civilians was, to any decent observer, heart-rending. Leaderless, defenceless and penniless, they consisted mainly of elderly men, women and children, and they were subjected to extremes of both deprivation and humiliation. Starving, sick and stupefied, they bore the full brunt of the pent-up collective anger and contempt that Soviets and Poles alike had harboured through the long years of total war (surprisingly, they included a sizeable contingent of German Jews). As a sober witness wrote in July 1945:

> Already 300 to 400 people die in Breslau every day ... Now the same methods of extermination are applied to us as we applied to other peoples, only that ... the Russians and the Poles do not murder senselessly as did our *Waffen SS* and *Gestapo*. But if one considers the intention, it amounts to the same thing.[18]

Extreme distress fostered warped human relationships. Most German civilians behaved like a defeated people: passive and non-confrontational. But more than one report talked of their extraordinary self-abasement. 'The servility of all Germans towards the representatives of the Red Army is hard to describe,' one official wrote; 'and the prostitution of German women arouses nothing but disgust. It's not German women who are raped by Soviet soldiers but, on the contrary, Soviet soldiers who come under attack from prostituted German women.'[19]. It is tempting to wonder whether some disillusioned members of a community that had been taught to see itself as the master race did not automatically assume a degrading, slave-like stance towards their conquerors following their defeat. But absolving the Soviet Army of blame is hardly appropriate.

Indeed, in some cases the Soviets were prepared to aid German civilians. Some reports claim that field kitchens were set up to feed the starving. A twelve-year-old German boy recalled how he would sing and dance for the soldiers, to receive a share of their rations:

> I used to mix with the soldiers. Some would swear at me or chase me away. But some accepted me, perhaps being reminded of their own

children. I would sit in the middle of the mass of soldiers and sing German folksongs. After each one, I would hold out my hand and then swiftly hide the booty in my knapsack. The Russians seemed to have their fun. They made requests, and the vodka bottle was passed around. I spun around like a dancing bear, reeling to the sound of the balalaika . . . Finally, I collapsed from sheer exhaustion. My knapsack was full of black bread and a piece of bacon that had belonged to the Russians. With my last strength I struggled home, full of pride, but I couldn't understand why my mother burst into tears.[20]

Poles were also taken aback by the obsequiousness of some Germans. On the other hand, they could be very critical of their own people. A young Polish eye-witness would later recall his own feelings:

The Polish newcomers played and preyed on the remaining Germans in a most disgusting fashion. Exploiting the locals' penury . . . they spared them no crude reminder of what their own compatriots had suffered at the hands of Nazi Germany. At the time I was a young sensitive lad, but I realised what [a horror] collective guilt can become, even if applied for very real crimes.[21]

The most acute conditions prevailed in the summer and autumn of 1945. In the new rationing system, Germans received only half to one-third of the food allowed to others, and at all the distribution points they were forced to wait at the end of the queue. In July, the złoty currency replaced the Reichsmark at the punitive rate of 1 zł = 2 RM. But many Germans were made to work for no pay, thereby driving them to strike, to protest and increasingly to live from begging, from selling their possessions or from prostitution and crime. Incoming Poles often evicted German families unceremoniously from their homes. This led the authorities to resettle the homeless in earmarked streets, thereby creating an informal type of ghetto. Two or three German families would be obliged to share one apartment. Overcrowding bred disease, and deaths from typhus or diphtheria and from suicide multiplied. Children succumbed most readily. Immunisation shots were given free to Poles; Germans were charged 100 złoty. Households infected by contagious disease were required to hang a black flag from the window. According to some reports, Germans were made to wear a white band with the letter 'N' for *Niemiec* (German) on the left arm. The first train carrying German expellees was scheduled to leave the Main Station on 1 October and was eagerly awaited. Preference was given to 'Anti-Fascists'.[22]

Amid the common suffering, one expulsion was especially poignant. The playwright Gerhart Hauptmann (1862–1946) had lived at Haus Wiesenstein in the village of Jagniątów (Agnetendorf) since 1902. He had spent his last years in 'internal migration', barely tolerated by the Nazi regime. In 1945, sensing his own end, he had expressed the desire to be buried in his native Silesia. But the new Silesia could not grant his wish. In the spring of 1946, Hauptmann was offered a comfortable relocation to Dresden. He refused. In April, the Soviet authorities visited him again, stressing that he must leave 'for his own safety'. He prevaricated. He wanted to make a last appeal to the German people – a call for optimism, fearlessness and unity – but a relapse robbed him of consciousness. On 3 June, he uttered his last words: no grand appeal to humanity, rather a plaintive '*Bin – ich – noch – in – meinem – Haus?*' ('Am I still in my house?'). Three days later, he died. It was a perfect epitaph for the tragedy of his people. A clod of Silesian earth was placed in the coffin in which the Nobel Prize-winner was then expelled. He was finally laid to rest on Hiddensee near Rügen.[23]

For the majority, the journey of expulsion to the West took place in two or three stages. The expellees were usually gathered at short notice in the square of their village or city district. They were permitted to take with them only what they could carry. From there, they were taken to a transit camp, which for Wrocław would have been either at the Świebodzki (Freiburg) Station or at Węglowice (Kohlfurt). After that, they were packed into bolted freight cars and transported to one of the Allied zones of occupied Germany. Each stage held its special terrors.

A man from the village of Brochów (Brockau) near Wrocław described the first stage:

One day at the beginning of January . . . we were ordered to line up outside the town hall early in the morning. Despite the weather being bitterly cold, we were kept waiting . . . until the late afternoon [when] the order was given for the trek to set off . . . By the time we reached Breslau it was dark and we were completely exhausted. We were then taken to a camp, namely a filthy building, formerly used as a school . . . We spent the night in the yard, guarding our baggage . . . After a couple of days, the Poles 'checked' us, during which the Polish customs officials took most of our belongings and our money from us. Finally, after waiting what seemed an endless age, we were taken to the Freiburg Station in Breslau. On the way, we were repeatedly molested and robbed by a rabble. At about midnight, they put us into cattle-trucks, which were dark and cold, and the train set off westwards . . .[24]

Polish officials freely admitted their inability to protect their charges. The expellees were usually moved at night so as not to attract attention, but there were only two or three guards for contingents several hundred strong. At the station, even the railwaymen resorted to robbery. But then the railwaymen themselves often had no food or housing.

A German priest who witnessed the arrival of the expellees in Germany, described what he saw:

> The people, men, women, and children all mixed together, were tightly packed in the railway cars, these cattle wagons themselves being locked from the outside. For days on end, the people were transported like this, and in Görlitz the wagons were opened for the first time. I have seen with my own eyes that out of one wagon alone ten corpses were taken and thrown into coffins which had been kept on hand. I noted further that several persons had become deranged . . . The people were covered in excrement, which led me to believe that they were squeezed together so tightly that there was no longer any possibility for them to relieve themselves at a designated place.[25]

The British military authorities, who accepted more than a million expellees into their zone, called it 'Operation Swallow'. In April 1946, they protested at the prevailing conditions; in August, they scaled down the rate of acceptances; and in December, they stopped them altogether. After that, no expellee trains could go beyond the Soviet zone.

As the rate of departures increased, the number of remaining Germans decreased; and so did their security. They were easy game for the gangs in Wrocław, which were by now running out of control. Life in one street in February 1946 sets the scene:

> On February 6th, at seven o'clock in the morning, Renata B, a girl of fifteen, who was on her way to the children's mass in St Sebastian's chapel in the Church of St Mary's-on-the-Sand, was stopped by a Polish militiaman. He dragged her into a demolished building, raped her, and stole her clothes . . . On February 10th, at two o'clock in the middle of the night, armed marauders entered the house at No. 8 Cathedral St, which was inhabited by the cathedral organist. They first raided the ground-floor apartment belonging to a teacher, and robbed him . . . of his last pair of shoes and trousers . . . Then, they proceeded to loot the apartment of Mr L, the schoolmaster . . . On February 13th at eleven o'clock at night, marauders raided the house at No. 9 Cathedral Street in which were located the offices of Dr S., a member of the cathedral chapter . . . One of the marauders forced the Prelate to sit on the floor, threatened him with a revolver . . . [and] hit him on the head with a whip . . . In the meantime, the rest of the marauders ransacked the house . . . and took all the things away on a lorry. They even raped the 60-year-old wife of Dr V., to whom the Prelate had given accommodation. On February 15th, despite the door

and windows being barricaded, Polish marauders managed to enter No. 7 Cathedral St through a window that faced the yard [and] subjected [the inhabitants] to the same treatment . . . On February 16th, at ten o'clock at night, a crowd of thirty marauders assembled in front of the statue of St John Nepomuk by the Church of the Holy Cross, then proceeded to loot the nearby vicarage after the terrified inhabitants had fled. On February 24th, marauders attired in Russian and Polish uniforms but speaking only Polish, broke into the house of the Sisters of Charity at No. 4, Kapitelweg . . . In addition, the cathedral had been raided and looted on February 10th, as well as the tiny chapel of St Aegidius . . . where marauders stole the tabernacle.[26]

This was a sworn deposition. Its accuracy cannot easily be verified, but it leaves a strong impression that the fearful marauders were none other than off-duty militiamen. If so, it reflects the type of person whom the Communist Militia was then recruiting.

In the view of some Germans, the Polish Communist Militia (MO) 'behaved even worse than the Russians'.[27] Though the killings in Wrocław and its district did not reach the horrendous levels reported in Upper Silesia, notably at the camps at Łambinowice (Lamsdorf) and Świętochłowice (Schwientochlowitz),[28] the cruelty and abuse were manifest. One report among thousands came from Trebnitz (Trzebnica):

We were arrested by Polish militia and an OGPU officer one afternoon in October 1945 . . . When they arrested us, they stole all the things that took their fancy. When we reached [Trzebnica], they took me to No. 17 Breslau Street, formerly the house of Mr Schitkowsky, the choirmaster, but now the militia HQ. They locked me up in a cellar for six weeks . . . We were crowded together like so many animals. We never once received water for a wash. Swarms of lice ran around . . . There was no electric light . . . The stench from the bucket was overpowering . . . The militia guards, most of them youths, took a special delight in tormenting their poor prisoners either beating or kicking them or setting the dogs at them. They were highly amused whenever one of the prisoners got bitten . . .[29]

Conditions on Kleczkowska (Kletschkau) Street in 1945–6 were reminiscent of the Gulag. A jail designed for 500 inmates contained 8,000. Six men, Poles and Germans together, would share a cell of eight square metres. They had no heating, no utensils and no medical treatment. They had to live off one mug of watery barley broth per day. Beatings were routine, and one inmate reckoned that one-third of the men died before release. The dead were interred in mass graves without coffins. Once a fortnight, each man could receive a 2.7-kilogram parcel:

As they were not allowed to travel by train, the women used to travel to the prison on foot . . . Some of them walked sixty miles and more . . . from Lueben, Glogau and Hirschberg. When they handed over the parcels to the Poles in the prison post-office, they were usually beaten . . .[30]

Prisoners who understood no Polish were in for a specially bad time:

We always had to call out our names and number in Polish when we lined up in the prison-yard . . . On one occasion, one of the prisoners who did not know any Polish called out the wrong number instead of thirty. He thereupon received thirty strokes in the face . . .[31]

According to official figures, twenty-seven Germans were executed at Kleczkowska Street.[32] One may be sure that this was not an overestimate.

It is obvious that the MO was not much interested in fighting crime or in protecting Germans:

The south-east district . . . behind the Main Station was a veritable inferno. Numerous gangs of marauders lived in the ruined buildings in this quarter, and not a night passed without houses in the vicinity being raided or some German being shot. One of the inhabitants of St Henry's parish was stabbed in the neck with a bayonet in broad daylight in his own garden, whilst his sixteen-year-old son was beaten to death with the butt-end of a rifle . . . Night after night cries for help resounded through the streets . . . The inhabitants who were in danger of being raided made a terrific din by beating pan lids together in the hope of driving the marauders away . . . Marauders broke into St Dorothy's Cemetery . . . and actually removed gold teeth from the dead. The south district of [the city] as far as Stone St had been part of the fighting zone, and as a result there were still a large number of mines in the streets. In the Parish of St Henry's alone, about 200 persons either lost their lives or . . . were taken to St Anne's Hospital with lacerated limbs . . .[33]

The last substantial groups of German expellees departed from Wrocław in the spring and summer of 1947. The Catholic Sisters of the Good Shepherd, whose convent had operated on Plac Grunwaldzki (Kaiser Street) since 1859 and who specialised in the reformation of delinquent girls, received their marching orders on 18 April. They had suffered terribly from typhus. They had sheltered numerous fugitives. Their Mother Superior had been sent to prison on charges of espionage; their house had been ransacked by militiamen before being claimed by a group of uninvited Polish Salesian priests; and they had handed their convent over to some Polish nuns in order to keep the priests out. They now celebrated Mass for the last time and walked out on to the street at two in the afternoon. They were to join a convoy carrying 2,984 persons:

> At about five o'clock, we were taken to the station . . . and crowded into three trucks . . . At about one o'clock in the middle of the night three Polish militiamen wrenched open the door of the truck . . . and proceeded to rob us of various belongings . . . and food. Finally, at five o'clock in the morning, the train set off, and we sang the hymn 'Dear Lord, we thank thee' in gratitude for being spared. Three days later we reached Elsterhorst in the Russian Occupied Zone. We spent the night in the train but were taken along to a camp . . . next day . . . All new arrivals had to take a shower, women and children all together in one room – completely naked . . . After lengthy negotiations, we nuns were spared the ordeal of the shower, and they sprayed us with a disinfectant powder instead . . . Those weeks in the camp were almost like a little holiday. On one occasion a baptism was held in our shed. The child had been born during the journey . . .
>
> And now the time came for us to part. As we did not receive our official permits for the Western Occupied Zones, we were obliged . . . to go to Eisenach and . . . [cross] the frontier illegally in fear and trembling of being caught by the Russians. [We] finally reached Bebra at the end of May 1947 . . . I very often think of Silesia, and I hope and pray that all the Silesians may some day be able to return to their beloved country . . .[34]

As the German expellees left, the Polish repatriants arrived. Their ordeals had been every bit as harrowing and had lasted much longer. The provinces of eastern Poland from which they came – then being reorganised as eastern Lithuania, western Belorussia and western Ukraine – had been ravaged by the very worst experiences of the Second World War. The multi-ethnic communities of those parts – Polish, Jewish, Belorussian, Ukrainian and German – had been violently torn apart by military action, social engineering, successive genocides, ethnic cleansing, political purges and plain banditry. In 1939–41, they had been annexed by the Soviet Union. The landowners were dispossessed, the peasants collectivised and the rest classed as 'bourgeois enemies'. The Poles among them (about six million) were viewed with intense suspicion, being collectively seen either as *Pany*, or 'landlords', or as lackeys of the *Pany*. Statistically, they were predominantly peasants, but the reality did not matter. More than two million were deported to oblivion in the depths of Russia, either as exiles or as prisoners of the Gulag and other punitive settlements. The officer class was wiped out by mass killings at Katyń and elsewhere. In 1941–4, these same territories had been fought over, twice, in the titanic struggle between the Soviet Army and the German *Wehrmacht*. Civilian casualties, through collateral damage and reprisals, were enormous. But this time the racial engineering of the Nazis was added to the mix. Around two million Jews were murdered in cold blood by the *Einsatzgruppen*, while several hundred thousand Poles were butchered or displaced by the terrorist bands of the nationalist Ukrainian UPA. The German settlements, mainly in Volhynia and Galicia, were 'relocated' to the General Government. In 1944–5, when the Soviets returned, yet another reign of terror was unleashed. It was directed against 'nationalists' (that is, people who did not welcome rule by Stalin), 'saboteurs' (people who did not work with excessive enthusiasm), 'recidivists' (people who bad-mouthed the previous spell of Soviet management) and so-called 'collaborators' (people who could not explain to the NKVD how they failed to be killed by the Nazis). Vicious campaigns were fought in the forests and, once again, the convoys of cattle wagons rolled eastwards to 'the Great White Bear' – Siberia.

In such circumstances, anyone who could join a convoy rolling westwards, *out* of the USSR, could only thank God for the chance. According to official statistics, the authorities handled some 1.5 million migrants in 1944–8, though the total number of refugees – whether legal or illegal – was undoubtedly much higher. These were the desperate remnants of a community on the brink of extinction. Their homes lay in districts that were still being contested by the Soviet Army and anti-Soviet partisans. They were selected by Soviet rules that ignored pre-war Polish citizenship, and which used the Polish language and the Roman Catholic religion as the twin criteria for Polishness. (Notwithstanding the fact that the vast majority had been born in pre-1939 Poland or in pre-1918 Tsarist Russia or Austria, they were all given papers bearing the fiction 'born in the USSR'.) Jews were not normally eligible, though they could often get through by joining one of the Polish Communist organisations. Lithuanians, Belorussians and Ukrainians were banned from leaving. Poles from Vilnius were generally sent to Gdańsk or Toruń; Poles from Lvov and other southern locations went to Silesia.

The journey from the East began at collecting centres, where the wait could last for weeks and where local robbers and gangsters had a field day. It was overseen by brutal soldiers and hostile Soviet bureaucrats, who normally treated a request to leave the Soviet Union as a crime and who persecuted the would-be migrants for having exceptional permission to depart. It was complicated by the presence of domestic animals, which some of the migrants were allowed to take with them, and was characterised by filth, hunger, thirst, inhuman overcrowding, interminable delays and frequent death. For, unlike the German expellees, who spent on average three to four days in the cattle wagons, the Polish 'repatriants' spent an average of three to four weeks. Their only consolation was the fact that for the tens of thousands of their compatriots who had been deported five years earlier to Kazakhstan and eastern Siberia, the journey had lasted three to four months.

The memory of the journey would stay with the 'repatriants' for the rest of their lives. Michał Sobków was one who, being well provisioned, made it in relative comfort:

We left our home in Koropiec in September 1945 with fear and foreboding. Poland is a fine word . . . but we were going off into the dark. It was not easy to say good-bye to the faithful Ukrainian who had agreed to take care of things until we returned . . . Mother was already an old lady. My sister had been ill for several years . . . and I was barely 17-years-old, and knew nothing except for very basic farm work.

The cart was loaded with our few possessions, with a horse and cow tethered behind . . . I went to the stable to see my chestnut foal for the last time, and begged to be forgiven . . .

The collecting point was at Pyszkowice about 30 km away. There was no station, just a dead-end railway line . . . and straw covered tents on either side of the tracks. At the Evacuation Committee, they told me to go to the forest and cut myself a decent staff in case of attack by bandits . . .

We waited for two months, but others waited much longer. The camp was overcrowded. Food was running out. The livestock was dying. Our supervisor was constantly drunk . . . One day, he said that we might have a chance of getting a few wagons from the Soviets if we club together and buy a pair of fancy boots for the requisite dignitary. It started to rain . . .

They gave us two hours to move our things into the open cars, which had stopped in a deep cutting. Shouts, screams and bellows rang out as people and animals slithered down the slope to get aboard. Then the train started with no warning, taking only half the cars with it. A blast of the whistle, and we thank God that we have put that stage behind us . . .

At Kopczynce, there's a surprise. Railwaymen come to tap the wheels, then order the wagon to be uncoupled. They say we're overloaded. Arguments fail, until I jump down and hand them a couple of bottles of vodka. 'Too little . . .' So I give them a third. It's the same at the next station . . .

Many people had eaten no food since Pyszkowice. We had a little dry macaroni, but we didn't dare let anyone see us eating it. Our mare miscarried. Lack of water and fodder was killing off the animals. More and more frequently we passed a wooden cross beside the tracks, crudely made from wagon boards, to show where a repatriant had been buried . . .

At one station, I ran over to a guard who was standing there with an automatic rifle on his shoulder:

– 'Where are we?' I call from a distance.

– 'In the "Recovered Territories" . . . '
– 'And do you know where they're taking us?'
– 'To the "Recovered Territories",' he answered with a smile . . .

The journey of more than a month ended for us at Brochów near Wrocław. Many people can't find their things . . . We're told that we can spend the night in a multi-storeyed building across the tracks. It's completely empty, just bare walls. But I fall asleep under a proper roof for the first time in weeks . . .

For three days we've no idea what's happening . . . [Then] we are driven across Wrocław in carts, and on the other side of the Grunwald Bridge, we come to a square crowded with thousands of people. I've never seen anything like it. There are goods for sale everywhere. Our guide says it's the Szaberplatz. A banner hangs on the wall: 'PIONIER BUDUJE – SZABROWNIK RUINUJE' (The Pioneer builds, the Shabrovnik destroys). I ask what 'Shabrovnik' means. I'm told – 'criminals' . . .

At our destination, we're welcomed by a sign that reads GROSS MOCHBERN . . . We pass some lovely houses, only to be told that they have been reserved for people from Central Poland . . .[35]

For someone freshly released from the Soviet Union, Wrocław's Szaberplatz offered a store of unimaginable wealth.

Many 'repatriants' had left their homes years before. Krystyna P., for instance, had fled from Łódź with her family in September 1939 as a four-year-old. Captured by the Red Army in eastern Poland, she was deported to a camp in Arctic Russia, which she later left in the company of other Polish escapees who sailed away on a raft, singing the national anthem *Jeszcze Polska nie zginęła* and defying the guns of the Soviet guards. Resettled at Kangur in the Urals, she learned that her father had been arrested for a second time by the NKVD and murdered. Having attended a Russian school for four years, she finally managed to leave with her Jewish mother, kissing the Polish earth at the frontier and reaching Wrocław in April 1946. She later became a Professor of Medicine. Her one souvenir from the Gulag was a small wooden picture of Red Riding Hood, carved for her by a German POW. Her future husband, then a boy of five, had been driven out of his home at Lisowce on the Dniester by the 'ethnic-cleansing' operations of the UPA. His Polish-Ukrainian family spent seven winter months camping out for safety in the vicinity of a military transport camp, and five weeks on one of the first repatriation trains. Throughout that journey, they lived with their cow under a makeshift roof of branches and ferns. On arrival at Brochów in May 1945, they were kept cooped up in their mobile home for ten agonising days, before being shunted eastwards again to Kluczbork (Kreuzburg). They spent another year on an abandoned farm, before being assigned a permanent place of residence near Sobótka (Zobten) in the summer of 1946. On the final stage, the boy fell off the moving train and was pulled unconscious from the track. He survived, and grew up to become a distinguished historian.[36]

The city of Lvov – in Polish, Lwów – deserves special mention. Though now claimed by Ukrainians as the capital of western Ukraine, it had been a prominent Polish metropolis since the fourteenth century. In other words, it was a close counterpart to German Breslau – a city whose identity was about to be transformed through no fault of its own. Its motto was Semper Fidelis, reflecting a loyalty to the Polish cause that had remained unshaken in terms of language and culture throughout the 145 years of Austrian rule (1773–1918). Its pre-war population of 318,000 was more than 50 per cent Polish Catholic, about 30 per cent Jewish and less than 10 per cent Ukrainian. The Jan Casimir University, founded in 1661, was a bastion of Polish learning. The Ossolineum Institute, founded by Count Josef Maksymilian Ossoliński in 1817 to preserve Polish culture under foreign rule, housed the largest collection of Polish literary and artistic treasures in the world. For obvious reasons, therefore, any Polish *Lwowianin* who sought to escape Soviet rule tried to head for Wrocław. Those Lwów professors who had survived the murderous Nazi purge of 1941 moved en bloc there. A special train carrying a selection of the Ossolineum's library and art collection pulled into the station of Wrocław-Brochów on 27 July 1946. The old Ossolineum was given a new home in the building of the St Matthias Gymnasium, which had once housed the crusading Order of the Red Star. Most of the *Lwowianie* arrived in a compact body, which was able to retain its sense of identity. They were intensely patriotic, deeply resentful of their fate and thoroughly disenchanted with Communism even before they arrived. They brought with them their lilting border accent, together with many of their traditions and institutions. They provided the backbone of the Polish University of Wrocław, which opened its doors in September 1945, and they filled the ranks of Wrocław's depleted professions of doctors, lawyers and engineers. For a generation at least, the name of Lwów was one that the Communist regime dreaded.

Among the 'repatriants', there arrived the scattered remnants of a very special group of refugees, the 'Katyń families'. Six years earlier, in 1940, Stalin had ordered the mass murder of some 22,000 imprisoned Polish reserve officers. The victims were the cream of the bourgeois 'class enemy' – professors, doctors, lawyers, teachers and engineers – whose destitute widows and children were turned overnight into social pariahs. Many of the families were forcibly deported by the Soviets to Central Asia, unaware of their menfolk's fate. Many who had lost their homes in eastern Poland chose at the end of the war to settle in Silesia. Most would be forbidden to work except in menial jobs, to draw pensions or to enter higher education. None would be allowed to talk in public of the true cause of their misfortune. Aleksander Rysyński, for instance, reached Księżenice near Wrocław in December 1945, aged seventeen. He and his younger brother were the orphaned sons of a missing Polish army captain, who, as Aleksander would learn much later, had been murdered by the NKVD. Deported as a child to Kazakhstan, he had buried both his mother and grandmother on the steppe with his own hands. He was one among thousands of survivors who could not pay tribute to his parents until the 1990s. He never forgot the chilling words of the NKVD officer on the day of his deportation. When his mother had asked, 'Where are you taking us?', she was told, 'Don't weep, woman. You are going to join your husband.'[37]

The reaction of Polish refugees arriving in Silesia ranged from euphoria to the deepest disillusionment. Anyone who had imagined that the ruins of Wrocław could necessarily provide the milk and honey of a promised land was due for a rude shock. And yet the Communist government was running a huge propaganda campaign to attract settlers from all over Poland. Posters were hanging in railway stations:

FRONTEM NA ZACHÓD
To racja stanu, to ostatni bój o dziedzictwo po Piastach
ZACHODNIE ZIEMIE
Eldorado
Żolnierz polski krwawym trudem wyzwolił prastare ziemie polskie
Polska ziemia dla Polaków
5,000 samochodów Przeznaczone dla Rozwozenia
osadników na Zachodzie[38]

(FACING WESTWARD. It's our *raison d'être*: the last fight for the legacy of the Piasts. WESTERN TERRITORIES. Eldorado. By his bloody labours, the Polish soldier has liberated the ancient Polish lands. Polish Land for Poles. 5,000 trucks have been reserved for taking settlers to the west.)

Special efforts were made to recruit ex-soldiers and skilled workers:

JESZCZE CZAS POLEPSZYĆ
SOBIE WARUNKI BYTU
Przed zblizającą się zimą
ZACHÓD CZEKA
Wielkie połacie ziem nad Odrą
i Nyssą wzywają
rolników – na gospodarstwa wiejskie

fachowców – do przemysłu
rzemieślników – do warsztatów
pracowników umyłowych – do administracji
PUR daje przejazd ulgowy i pomoc w podróży[39]

(STILL TIME TO IMPROVE YOUR STANDARD OF LIVING before the coming winter. THE WEST AWAITS. Huge swathes of land by the Odra and Nysa are calling farmers to the farms, specialists to industry, craftsmen to the workshops, and white-collar workers to the administration. The Repatriation Board offers subsidised travel and help with the journey.)

The propaganda posters flatly denied the popular wisdom on the subject. Poles widely talked of Wrocław as 'the forbidden city', and it was said to be 'a nest of bandits'. Everywhere one heard the same stories about 'hordes of robbers stripping people on the streets in broad daylight', or about the underground Nazi *Wehrwolf* organisation that was 'murdering Polish settlers every night'.[40] Post-war Wrocław's reputation was not much higher in Warsaw or Cracow than it was in Berlin or Hamburg.

Finding somewhere to live was the major problem for all arriving migrants. Basically, they could either apply to the Municipal Housing Office for an official allocation, and wait; or they could go house-hunting on their own. In the early period most people chose the latter. It was a strange, exciting and often dangerous exercise. Gangs were operating and squatters were everywhere. The utilities were down. The houses were predominantly derelict, looted or damaged. Until one investigated, it was often impossible to tell whether or not they were inhabited.

One family, which was to keep its house in Krzyki (Krietern) for the next half-century and more, chose it because it was empty and because Mother liked the roses in the garden. Father, who was an aristocrat, thought a suburban villa to be something of a come-down from his hereditary palace at Jezupol in the Ukraine. But, having just been released from a Nazi concentration camp, he was glad of anything. The front of the house had been completely blown off by a bomb or shell, and it looked uninhabitable. But the back was intact, and provided shelter while the rest of the structure was being patched up. And it soon became clear that everything in the East had been lost for ever, so they stayed. The wife of the German owner showed up after several weeks, but all she wanted was to collect a few souvenirs and to depart for western Germany. She was to remain in touch with the family until she died several decades later.[41]

The trickiest part for many migrants was to negotiate with the Germans who were still in residence. Of course, Communist officialdom had no respect for private property and showed no compunction in throwing

German residents on to the street. Individual Polish predators were quite capable of doing the same, and organised gangs even more so. But there was room for manoeuvre. If German residents insisted on keeping their homes to themselves, the chances were that someone would pick on them. If they could find a decent Polish family to share the premises, then they could hope to remain *in situ*, at least temporarily. A Polish refugee from the East, who arrived in late 1945, described how it worked:

> After much searching, I found a small house on a side street, with a useful outhouse . . . but I realised that Germans were living there . . .
>
> A tall elderly German opened the door. I didn't speak German, although I had studied it a little . . . and to my surprise, we understood each other perfectly. A middle-aged woman joined us.
>
> Before crossing the threshold, I stated that I was a Pole and a repatriant from the East, and that tomorrow I was going to bring my family to their house. For the time being, all I wanted was a night's lodging. They took me in somewhat icily, which is hardly surprising . . . But the atmosphere thawed, and I even heard that they were pleased that my family would be moving in . . .
>
> I learned that the old man was called Paul Grosser. His daughter-in-law Emma had a husband who so far had not returned from the war and two teenage sons, Werner and Michael.
>
> I could see that repatriants did not have the best of reputations with the German community. Yet [our hosts] were resigned to sharing the destiny of a defeated nation even though, as they told me, they couldn't be held guilty for Hitler's crimes . . . For my part, I saw that both sides were somehow joined by the same miserable fate. We [Poles] had been driven from our native soil by the [Ukrainian] bands, and they [the Germans] were paying for a war that had been started by a devil . . . Despite the language barrier, our relations developed in a friendly fashion.[42]

Employment was the second priority. Fortunately, Wrocław was short of everything except jobs. Antoni Zięba (1894–1986) was one man for whom the ruined city provided a golden opportunity. A trained teacher from Upper Silesia and a veteran of both the Polish-Soviet War and the September Campaign, he had escaped from Soviet captivity only to be recaptured by the Germans during the Warsaw Rising and thrown into a camp. He travelled to Wrocław in July 1946 with his wife and three children because they were homeless. Crossing Grunwald Square on the day of his arrival, he ran into a pre-war colleague from Wilno, also a teacher, who asked him:

– What are *you* doing here?

– I've been staying at Jędrzejów, where we ended up after the Warsaw Rising.

– Well, I'm the departmental director in the Educational Board. Perhaps you could organise a third *Gymnazium* for me here in Wrocław. We have one in operation; and a second is in preparation, but a third will soon be necessary . . . I should warn you that at present we can't guarantee you either a building or teachers or any financial credits . . .

– *Bagatela* [he thought], 'a minor detail' . . . [43]

'This was no time for moaning or wringing one's hands,' Zięba recalled. 'It was a time for rolling up one's sleeves.'

On other occasions, bold initiative paid off. Another teacher, Cyryl Priebe, who lived in Poznań, weighed up his prospects at the end of the war and thought of a way of becoming an instant headmaster. He took the train to Wrocław in May 1945 to visit his brother-in-law, who had already found a job as deputy *Starosta* of Strzelin (Strehlen). From there, Priebe undertook a series of trips to the surrounding towns and villages until he found what he was looking for in Drezdenko (Driesen). The little town was full of 6,000 Italian POWs and their Soviet guards, but there was also a burnt-out German schoolhouse. Moreover, there was a Pole called Ferenstein who had taken over the flour mill and who, having three daughters in need of an education, was ready to organise the repair of the school. Priebe then played his master card – a piece of paper from the Education Board in Poznań, obtained through acquaintances, stating that he was a suitable candidate for headmaster. He opened his new school on 1 October. [44]

Conditions for the 'repatriants' who were sent to the countryside were particularly difficult. In many cases, they were allocated farms where the German owners were still resident but not inclined to help. Unlike their counterparts in the city, they were completely isolated, unable to communicate and often in considerable personal danger. One such rural repatriant would later recall the scenes that he watched as a seven-year-old boy in a village near Sobótka. His father set to work in a field, virtually with his bare hands. The unfriendly soil required the tools that his German neighbours had hidden. At first, they laughed in derision at his efforts, but he persisted. And they slowly came round to the idea that the two families might run the farm better than one. They were greatly influenced by the fact that the newcomers, like themselves, were Catholics. They began to walk to church together on Sundays, and then to work together. The Germans produced the tools and proudly showed off their machines. Harvest-time turned out to be the happiest of romps. There were twice the number of hands for the reaping. The children played with no inhibitions.

Poles and Germans regaled each other with their harvest songs. When the time came for the German family to leave, they were genuinely missed.[45] Thirty years later, when a British visitor called at the farm, he could not fail to notice the primitive state of agriculture. But he also noticed that the grave of the German family's grandmother, who had died from old age during the months of cohabitation in 1946–7, was still being tended with freshly picked flowers.

Poles who came to Wrocław immediately after the war remember the experience in various ways. A young man who would later make an extremely prominent academic career recalled the gradual process of assimilation:

When I arrived in Wrocław in June 1946, the town and its inhabitants, which I saw through the window of the tram ... appeared completely alien. I looked at the buildings whose architecture differed entirely from what I had known in Kielce or Kraków ... After some time, I realised that the majority of those buildings were windowless façades which concealed the burned-out shells behind them. For years, perhaps for more than a decade, these scorched buildings were to accompany the daily journeys to my home in Oporów [Opperau]. Slowly, however, I learned to savour the charm of Tumski Island, the Baroque University and the Gothic churches. With time, that same Wrocław, which had once felt so strange, became peculiarly close to me ...[46]

That same witness, who was a trained historian, later remarked how mistaken scholars are who try to reconstruct the essence of post-war Wrocław from official records:

In the press [of the period], one finds lying information about the wide popular support for the authorities and about mass participation for activities which ... in reality were inspired by the PZPR [Polish United Workers' Party], if not organised with physical compulsion. Similarly, the most one can say about official papers is that they convey only a partial view of the truth since they were usually prepared with a view to supplying what the authorities wanted to hear. Party materials and reports by the Security Office, which were supposed to inform the authorities about social moods and attitudes, were fixed in the same way. If one adds to that the frailties of human memory, which fifty years later as so-called 'oral history' would constitute the only source of reasonably reliable knowledge about the post-war years, it is not surprising to note [the poor results]. Recent historical works concerning post-war Wrocław, and more generally on post-war Poland, are often very far from the reality, or rather, from the picture of the times which eye-witnesses recall ...[47]

Impressions of a different order were preserved by people whose childhood was passed in post-war Wrocław. A woman who would rise to high positions in Poland's diplomatic service remembers the ruins with great affection. 'We children had enormous fun playing in the rubble,' she recalled. It was the perfect playground for hide-and-seek, with endless nooks and cellars for exploring. Every day was a treasure hunt that produced a magical array of rusty helmets, playing cards, badges, bullets, broken pots, bayonets, bric-a-brac and broken machines:

> We lived in fear of the war. I had constant nightmares about Germans killing my parents, digging holes in the living room, or throwing grenades into the cellar . . . Evidently, the War was still in the air. Every house in our district had a bunker; and there was an anti-aircraft gun in the neighbouring garden . . . The helmet which we found had a hole right through it with sharp edges. We had wonderful games with it. It must have belonged to the corpse of a German soldier in the garden whom Mama arranged to have buried in the nearby cemetery . . .
>
> Everything that surrounded me as a child was 'post German', for we brought nothing with us from Jezupol, except for a few pictures . . . In our cellar, there was a wash-house with a big brass boiler, an enamel tub and a wringer . . . No-one had anything like that . . . Everything of better quality was German: bicycles, coffee-mills, mincing-machines, lawn-mowers, electric irons, or such tremendous luxuries like metal cigarette boxes or cake tins. We had a post-German croquet set . . . and a post-German piano, which Father bought off a German in the next street. (To buy a piano one needed special permission from the Ministry of Culture . . . but somehow our piano stayed with us.)
>
> Germans weren't mentioned much at school. They were officially defined as *okupanci*, 'occupiers' of the Piast lands . . . One year, on All Saints' Day, my history teacher took the whole class to a German cemetery and ordered us to light candles in front of graves with Polish-sounding names. I remember, being obstinate, that I lit my candles in front of some German names, because it seemed wrong to treat the dead unequally . . .[48]

For the fraction of German Breslauers who had contrived to remain, post-war memories could be especially poignant. Such *Zurückgebliebene*, or 'stay-behinds', lived a curious and often schizophrenic existence. Fearful of being discovered, they adopted Polish norms to the point where their true identity would be kept concealed from all but the most trusted friends. Fellow 'stay-behinds' might be suspected through a careless aside or a linguistic lapse, but the question was rarely asked. Despite the hardships, some, like Eva Maria Jakubek, grew to be proud of their Polish 'veneer':

Ich lebe in zwei Dimensionen
der Sprache:
die eine – vertraut,
in die Wiege gelegt,
die andere – erkämpft
im Zwange des Alltags.
Die eine – geliebt –
die andere – verhaßt ...
solange ich sie nicht kannte.
Dann stieß sie mir auf die Tür
zu der anderen Welt,
die ich staunend betrat ...
wie anders die Sitten,
die Kunst, die Kultur,
die Geschichte –
Wer bin ich,
Sie zu verachten?
Ihre Helden und Mythen,
die Traditionen –
nun so vertraut
im Fliehen der Jahre.
Ich lebe in zwei Dimensionen –
nicht nur der Sprache:
hin und her schwebe ich
auf unsichtbarem Steg –
zuhause jetzt
hier und dort.[49]

(I live in two dimensions
of speech:
the one – familiar,
learned in the cradle,
the other – hard won
in the daily grind.
The one – adored –
the other – despised ...
as long as it escaped me.
Then it threw open the door
to the other world,
which I entered with amazement ...
How different the customs
the art, the culture,
the history –
Who am I,
to hold it in contempt?

Its heroes and myths,
the traditions –
now so familiar
after all these years.
I live in two dimensions
not only of speech:
I float to and fro
on an invisible line –
at home now
both here and there.)

The children of mixed Polish–German families often found life hard. One woman, whose German father had helped the Polish underground during the war and had married his Polish wife in Poznań, nonetheless nursed very ambiguous feelings about her post-war schooldays in Wrocław. She spoke perfect Polish and yet was not fully accepted by all her classmates. She had a German surname, but so did many of the others. She could not see whence the suspicions arose, and paid for her worries with much soul-searching. Only in time, and with the help of sympathetic friends, did she come to understand her predicament better. They eventually told her how odd it was for them, on visiting her house, to see the Christmas tree dressed with silver strips of lametta, or to be asked to wear felt slippers.

In normal times, bilingualism and dual identity can be a great advantage. But post-war Vratislavian society was not normal. It was dominated by uprooted people who had lost one homeland and were not yet sure that they had found another. Such people were desperate not only to be Polish themselves, but to believe that everything and everyone around them was purely Polish. They belonged to the generation which proclaimed that 'every stone in Wrocław speaks Polish'. They were not interested in nuances. And they could actively resent those who reminded them that reality was rather more complex.[50]

From the historian's viewpoint, several large questionmarks hang over the post-war migration of Germans and Poles. The first issue is purely technical and concerns railway freight. The movement of about six million human beings from the USSR to Poland and from Poland to Germany required administrative expertise of the sort attributed to Adolf Eichmann, and logistical planning on a scale at least twice as large as anything attempted during the Holocaust. Where, in 1945–7, did the rolling stock come from? Where, and by whom, was the operation coordinated? And were the two parts of the operation separate or linked? In the particular case of Wrocław, one could pose the last question in a more specific way. Were the cattle trucks that rolled into Wrocław from the East sent straight back to the

USSR for more repatriants? Or were those same trucks emptied of their Polish cargo at one of the stations of the eastern suburbs and then sent round to Wrocław-Świebodzice to collect their German cargo?

Secondly, as evidenced by all the literature, German and Polish accounts of the migration have been strictly sealed within separate compartments. Germans recall German suffering, and stereotypically blame 'the Poles' or 'the Russians' or both. Poles recall Polish suffering, and stereotypically blame 'the Russians' or 'the Germans' or both. What exactly has prevented both Germans and Poles from seeing the obvious truth that their particular sorrows had much in common?

Thirdly, though the necessary materials have become available, the overall history of the largest series of human migrations in modern European history has never been written. How long will it take before German, Polish and Russian specialists put their heads together to produce the definitive account?

It would be wrong to assume, however, that the majority of Wrocław's growing post-war population came exclusively from the East. The 'Wild West' of the new Poland attracted all sorts, from many parts. Several distinct categories deserve mention:

- landless peasants seeking vacated ex-German farms
- young people, especially from Wielkopolska, seeking factory employment
- landowners dispossessed by the agrarian reform of 1946
- anyone seeking a new start after wartime disasters, broken marriages or shattered dreams
- Ukrainians displaced by the resettlement programme in south-east Poland
- Jewish refugees, especially from the USSR
- political dissidents, especially members of the wartime resistance, on the run from Communist persecution
- foreign immigrants accepted for resettlement by the Polish government
- drifters, carpet-baggers and criminals.

In October 1945, the Wrocław authorities made a formal complaint to the government after a train pulled in from Cracow carrying a huge consignment of Cracovian 'undesirables' – convicts, speculators and habitual alcoholics. No response came from Warsaw on that issue. But an effort was made to direct different categories to different locations. Zgorzelec on the Neisse frontier, for example, was earmarked for Greek Communist refugees displaced by the civil war in Greece. Wałbrzych, a mining town, received a large injection of Polish miners from Belgium and France. And Dzierżoniów (Reichenbach) became home to 50,000 Jews.

For many reasons, the extraordinary story of the Jewish settlement at Dzierżoniów has never been properly told. But the outlines can be gleaned from the memoirs of Jakub Egit, the Zionist leader who ran the experiment from 1945 to 1948 after serving in the Soviet Army. 'I was haunted by the thought', he wrote, 'that here in this land, which the Germans had cultivated for so many years, the Jews could exact retribution and justice . . . by making this former German territory a Jewish settlement.' His plan was to set up a *Yishuv* – an autonomous Jewish district within Poland. On visiting the Minister for the Recovered Territories, Edward Ochab, he claims to have been told, 'You go to it, whether it pleases anyone or not . . . We shall support you in all your endeavours and with all the forces at our disposal.' And so, for three years, all went well. Starting with a small group of *Kazettlers* – KZ survivors – the community swelled rapidly. It supported schools, hospitals, *kibbutzim*, orphanages and a publishing house in Wrocław. According to Egit, by-laws were passed to require all remaining Germans to wear white armbands, to raise their hats to Jews on the streets and to step off the pavement if a Jew approached. Then, in 1948, it all came to an end. The Communist regime changed its policy (see page 448); Jakub Egit headed for a Communist jail, while most of his supporters headed for Israel.

Similar happenings occurred in nearby Bolków (the former Bolkenhain). In this case, a training camp was established for members of the Zionist *Hagana*, the core of the future Israeli army. Military instructors were supplied by the Soviet and Polish armies. Recruits came in and went out through the frontier-post at Kudowa Zdrój (Bad Kudowa) and numbers reached 2,500. But again, in 1948, it all stopped.[51]

The Jewish presence in Wrocław was less focused, but somewhat more durable. Numbers rose to about 20,000, before declining in the 1950s and ending almost completely in 1968. The principal dividing line within the community ran between the majority who were always preparing to leave for Palestine and a minority who intended to stay. Among the latter were Bundists and Communists. A local Jewish committee was also very active in cultural and municipal affairs, several Jewish newspapers circulated and a Yiddish Theatre operated from mid-1945, receiving its own new building in April 1949. Jewish demonstrations were a common sight. One, on 7 July 1946, in the week of the Kielce Pogrom, saw 6,000 Jewish protesters denounce the jailing of Zionists by the British in Palestine. Another, on 24 May 1947, saw the Zionist politician, Adolf Berman – brother of the chief of Poland's Communist Security Police, Jakub Berman – expressing his gratitude for Polish and Soviet backing of the Zionist cause at the United Nations.

Like Egit's *Kazettlers*, a number of Jewish migrants to Wrocław had somehow survived in occupied Poland. Maria A., for example, had been born to a Christian family of mixed Polish-Jewish descent in Lwów just before the war. During the Soviet occupation of 1939–41, her father had gone into hiding for fear of the NKVD. During the Nazi occupation, her Jewish mother had chosen to volunteer for hard labour in Germany, rather than await detection by the Gestapo. The infant daughter was consigned to the care of a peasant woman and was then handed on to an acquaintance who had recently miscarried and who could pass Maria off as her own. The child was baptised and was brought up under the name of Maria Korzeniewicz with her (unacknowledged) adoptive parents. At the end of the war, her mother returned safely from Germany, settled in Wrocław – as many Lvovians did – and reclaimed her child without a word of thanks. The adoptive parents had taken care of the child in the full knowledge that they were risking instant death for themselves and their nearest relatives. They had no other children.

Another Jewish fellow, who would later wish to be identified only as 'Jerzyk', had fled Poland for the USSR and had worked as a ship's stoker on the Caspian Sea. He came back in the ranks of the Soviet-led Kościuszko Division, settling first in Gdańsk and then in Wrocław. His main claim to fame was to have been a prize-winner in a pre-war short-story competition organised by the legendary Polish-Jewish writer, Janusz Korczak. The subject was 'How the world will look in 1950'. The entry of the fourteen-year-old Jerzyk had been uncannily prophetic:

> The war broke out. As usual, everything started from a trivial matter, and barely a week had passed when the entire planet was in flames. I am not going to dwell on it. I only need to say that nearly one-twentieth of all the inhabitants of the Earth died, which is one hundred million. People returned to the Stone Age, just trying to win as soon as possible and to save their lives . . .
>
> [After the war] tens of millions of soldiers, acquainted with technology, felt out of place. Everything went to pieces. A thousand gangs moved to the east and spontaneously settled down on the smouldering ruins . . . And although the downfall of life was great, it was revived in a much better form.[52]

The comfortable re-establishment of a viable Jewish community in post-war Poland was inhibited by three interrelated factors. Among the Jews, there was a significant rise in militant Zionism, and hence in the desire to depart for Palestine. Among the Poles, strong resentment was felt against the Zionists, who were seen to find fault with Poland at every turn and were not disposed to help rebuild the war-torn country. Most evidently, there was a marked tendency among Communist and pro-Communist Jews to join the very worst organs of the Stalinist state machine. The vengeful philosophy of anti-Fascism carried considerable attractions in the immediate aftermath of the Holocaust. As several studies have shown, Holocaust survivors were not always immune to imitating the bestial methods of their erstwhile tormentors.[53] And for many years the subject was taboo and it was hotly denied both by Polish Communists and by Jews abroad. Yet it was confirmed by the best-qualified witness of all, Jakub Berman, when he finally opened his mouth many decades later.[54]

Given the heavy concentration of Jewish immigrants in post-war Silesia, the role of Jewish recruits in the Wrocław branch of the Office of Public Security (UBP) was particularly sensitive. They were prone to prey not only on obvious opponents of the regime, like the Peasant Party or the Catholic Church, but on Jewish organisations as well. What is more, as Berman confirmed, they were often under special orders to change their names and their accents, and hence to conceal their origins; and they often occupied senior positions. Of course, their role should not be exaggerated. The UBP employed all sorts of people. The published list of 337 UBP operatives in Wrocław in 1945 contains only a handful of persons who were obviously of Jewish descent.[55] Equating policemen with Jews, or Jews with policemen, is plainly ridiculous. But it is also ridiculous to pretend that there was no problem to discuss. The matter rankled at the time, and it is still vividly remembered. When a small group of students called a public protest in 1946, for example, because the Soviet Army had raided yet another power station and they were having to study in darkness, they were challenged by a high-ranking officer of the UBP: Major Rubinsztajn, who told them, 'You are *bydło* [animals]'. According to the most recent estimate, Jews in the upper echelons of the security apparatus reached 13 per cent,[56] while constituting well under 1 per cent of the population. 'The over-representation of Jews in the security apparatus is a fact.'[57]

The fears and dangers of that era, as seen through Jewish eyes, do not always match what others remember. A certain Mr D., who was interviewed in Wrocław fifty years later, confirmed the high profile of Jews in the security apparatus, but approved of it. 'Those Jews who worked in the police, in the Security Office,' he commented, 'should not be criticised, because thanks to them Wrocław was not like Kielce or other places. People were scared of doing anything, because the Public Security and the police had orders that there was no anti-Semitism. They were scared until 1956.'[58] He described how the premises of the Jewish Committee on Włodkowica Street were watched, day and night, by armed guards:

These were hired guards, paid. They stood with guns at the gate. And it wasn't the Germans we were afraid of . . . we were afraid of Poles who wanted to make a pogrom. In those days, I went neither to the Committee, nor to the synagogue, nor to the community. I kept aside. I was afraid of assemblies that could end in a pogrom . . . I worked all day long, and went to bed at night in a sort of hiding place, like a mouse. At that time, I was afraid of my very shadow. Everyone who survived the occupation was mentally scarred.[59]

There was no pogrom in post-war Wrocław.

Henryk Traller (b.1919) was one of those who were recruited by the Stalinist police. Having received an orthodox Jewish education in pre-war Łódź, attending *cheder*, Talmud Torah and *yeshiva*, he joined the Communist KZMP youth organisation. After the war, he joined the Communist Party, graduated from the party school and was then called to the party committee:

'Wouldn't I like to join Security?' I said, 'I'm absolutely sure I don't.' 'How about the police then?' Well, I thought, the police take care of criminal matters, let it be . . . Later, I was reassigned to Wrocław, to the special tasks department . . . I said goodbye to them [in June 1954]. When Gomułka came to power, I noticed that something was wrong. In 1957, I registered to leave.[60]

In fact, Traller did not leave and remained on Włodkowica Street for the rest of the century. Neither he nor Mr D. thought to spell out what the Stalinist police actually did. Most curiously, they both thought that after 1956, when conditions vastly improved for the mass of the population, life was not so good for them.

Progress in the rural townships and villages of the Wrocław region was no better than in the city. Indeed, 'limited progress' would be a less accurate description than 'drift, depression and decrepitude'. Sociological studies, which could be published only after the collapse of Communism, showed that the first two generations of post-war Polish settlers in the countryside of Lower Silesia failed to prosper.[61] The migrants had not simply lost their eastern homeland. They had walked into an empty, alien and unwelcoming environment where a brutal Communist regime ruled supreme and where, in the late 1940s, the collectivisation campaign had robbed them of both land and hope. They were not impressed in the least by Silesia's natural beauties. They disliked the large, brick-built German farmhouses, which they did not bother to repair. They resented the relative infertility of the soil, which was not suited to their traditional skills. And, until 1970 at least, they believed their Silesian sojourn to be temporary. 'They lived with packed suitcases', among piles of uncollected rubbish. They drank excessively. They let drains and heating systems collapse, then suffered in their damp rooms from high rates of rheumatism. They watched with indifference as heaps of discarded farm machinery rusted away in their leaking barns. They were sealed off by the Iron Curtain from their western neighbours, but found no 'Promised Land' in place of their imagined 'Paradise Lost' in the East. Whenever possible, they told their children to leave for central Poland. Objectively speaking, their fate was just as tragic as that of the German expellees, whose land and property they had so reluctantly inherited. It can only be summarised by the terms apathy, alcoholism and alienation. One of the hardest burdens to bear was created by the education system and the censorship of the Communist regime, which insisted that the Poles' former homeland in the East had never been theirs. This was the equivalent of Breslauers arriving in West Germany and being told officially, by teachers and administrators, that Breslau had never been German.

A detailed study of the small town of Lubomierz reveals social conditions that were as absurd as they were harsh. Set in charming wooded foothills some ninety-six kilometres west of Wrocław, the former Liebenthal had been largely resettled in 1946–7 by a group of Polish migrants from Czortków in the Ukraine. It was first renamed Miłosna, and later Lubomierz. (It would never have been allowed to call itself 'New Czortków' and it never quite regained its pre-war population of about 1,500.) In 1946, it had possessed a solid infrastructure of services and installations: six bakeries, four butcher's shops, nine tailors, four hairdressing salons, four forges, three bookshops, seven food stores, two pharmacies, six restaurants, a cinema and a hotel. There was a plumber, a car mechanic, a watchmaker, several joiners, metal-workers, furriers and saddle-makers. The local agricultural industry was supported by a dairy, a cheese factory, a sugar refinery and a complex of fish ponds. Further employment was provided by a large building firm, a farm-machinery business and by wholesale distributors specialising in soap, household products, tobacco and textiles. The health service was run by two doctors, an orthopaedist, a veterinarian, three dentists and the forty-four-bed hospital of the Benedictine convent. Within a decade, most of this infrastructure had disappeared. The post-war campaign against German culture saw the destruction of municipal records, including the plans of the town's drainage and water systems. As a result, broken sewers and water pipes could not easily be repaired. Many cellars were permanently flooded. And the fish ponds reverted to a swamp. In 1949 the Stalinist 'Struggle for Trade' was to finish off all private workshops and businesses and drive out all private professionals and employees. Most social and economic institutions were replaced with huge delay, by highly inferior state-run centres. A State Machinery Repair Point opened only in 1951. A Municipal Demolition Committee, for removing wartime rubble, was not convened until 1956. The first post-war industrial complex, an Agro-Industrial Combine, did not start production until 1976. Under Communist rule, Lubomierz never received back its cinema, its hotel or its residential hospital.

The effects of the local politics of Lubomierz were, by any standards, dire. The only figure with genuine authority, Father Bernard Pylik, who had migrated with his parishioners from Czortków, was jailed in 1950 for opposing collectivisation. All subsequent parish posts were filled by nonentities appointed with Communist Party approval. After the rigged elections of 1947, no independent person could stand for local office, all positions being distributed among party time-servers. The outcome was a strange Communo-clerical diarchy through which the town Secretary of the PZPR, simultaneously Director of the Agro-Industrial Combine, ran virtually everything in partnership with the long-serving parish priest. (One can only imagine a Polish Clochemerle in which the republican mayor and the reactionary curé had miraculously joined forces.)

*

Political developments in Wrocław were running far ahead of physical and economic reconstruction, but not necessarily in the healthiest of directions. In the first years after the war, many competing political parties were established – the Polish Peasant Party (PSL), the Polish Socialist Party (PPS), the Communist Polish Workers' Party (PPR) and numerous Jewish parties of various complexions. The authorities laid great emphasis on symbolic events such as an All Saints' Day gathering at the Soviet Cemetery and the May Day Parade. For the time being, no attempt was made to prevent celebrations of Poland's National Day on 3 May, though the Corpus Christi procession of 1946 was stopped from entering the city centre. Yet the regime attracted little spontaneous support. Membership of the PPR stayed humiliatingly low, and the real results of the falsified Referendum of 30 June 1946 were deeply disappointing to the authorities. Although the party declared a comfortable win for their platform of 'Three Times Yes', most people knew that a clear majority of Vratislavians had voted against Communist advice, with 'Three Times No'.[62] In the background, one of the most perfidious political campaigns in European history was being unleashed. Under Soviet guidance, the Communists set out to demonstrate that all their democratic opponents had been Nazi collaborators. On 22

January 1946, they announced the execution of a captured Nazi called Edgar Dickmann, who had murdered some ninety prisoners twelve months earlier. On 18 July, they shot twenty-two-year-old Helena Motykówna for belonging to a group inspired by the non-Communist, i.e. democratic, wartime resistance movement.[63] She was the first of hundreds to be consumed in similar manner by Kleczkowska Prison.

After much delay, considerable effort and ingenuity were directed at 'de-Germanisation'. All swastikas had been removed in the first hours after the siege, but their ghostly outlines persisted for many a year on many an unpainted wall. All streets, squares and districts were given Polish names, often with a discordant political flavour. The main street leading to the Central Station was renamed after General Świerczewski, a Communist hero of the Spanish Civil War. The Dominikanerplatz was graced with the name of Feliks Dzerzhinsky, founder of the Soviet Secret Police. The district of Wilhelmsruh became, more appropriately, Zacisze – literally, 'Quiet'. The district of Krietern became Krzyki – literally, 'Shouts'. All German monuments were either demolished or replaced. The statue to Frederick the Great, which had stood for ninety-eight years on the Main Square, was carried off. An empty plinth, which had formerly housed the statue of Frederick William III, was eventually toppled in 1956 by the figure of the Polish poet, Alexander Fredro, recovered from Lvov. The statue to Kaiser Wilhelm I was toppled during a Socialist meeting on 21 October 1945. 'The downfall of this little Fritz', an orator proclaimed, 'is a symbol of the downfall of the whole Nazi-Prussian regime, which will never rise again.' All former German citizens, mainly the children of mixed marriages, who wished to claim Polish nationality were obliged to register by 1 July 1946. But they were pressed to change their names. So a Helmut would become a Kazimierz; and a Hilda, a Halina. Surnames were sometimes changed, too. Polonisation was being pushed into the most intimate corners of identity.

Economic mobilisation was painfully slow. Although an operational group of the National Economic Commission (KERM) had been in existence since May 1945 and a Municipal Plan since January 1946, the results were meagre. The production of the first coal wagons at the Pafawag works called for a visit on 26 January 1946 from Vice-Premier Gomułka and Industry Minister, Hilary Minc. But many factories remained in Soviet hands. The rubble was hardly diminishing, no major building programme had been started, and the labour market was in chaos. In November 1945, Father Milik lodged a protest against the security police's habit of rounding up people during Mass to fill the compulsory work brigades.[64]

Living standards had fallen far below wartime levels. Official ration cards provided a near-starvation diet. The rationing system operating in September 1946 recognised four categories of recipients. The top category received a small amount of the bare essentials, including 8.5 kg of bread, 0.02 kg of tea and 0.964 kg of tinned meat per week. The fourth category received nothing but 4 kg of bread, 0.5 kg of barley meal and 0.4 kg of salt.[65] Housing conditions were disastrous. No materials were available for repairs. Unwashed people were crammed into the limited supply of undamaged rooms, often in the company of pigs and poultry. Contagious diseases raged. Crime flourished and murder – especially infanticide – increased. Daylight robbery and night-time burglary were a constant menace. Few criminals were caught. The *Szabrownicy*, or 'looters', and black marketeers were ubiquitous. The Szaberplac, or 'Plunder Square', was the main centre of commerce. Power cuts occurred every day and the darkened city remained under curfew from 8 p.m. to 5 a.m.

Given such an appalling environment, the creation of a thriving Polish cultural life from scratch was nothing less than miraculous. Yet music and poetry could clearly feed the heart even if the stomach was empty. And the thirst for education after six years of war was limitless. A group of cultural-scientific experts had reached Wrocław with President Drobner in May 1945; and their achievements outshone those of all their colleagues. The number and quality of dramatic, symphonic and operatic performances, often in half-ruined auditoria, was truly amazing. Much was done by visiting artists and companies from Cracow; but local initiatives counted for more. At the première of Moniuszko's *Halka* on 8 September 1945, the Opera was packed. At the première of *The Barber of Seville* in December, the lights went out for two hours. But no one left their seat. Schools started teaching with forty pupils to a class. Football clubs, boxing matches and popular cabarets sprang up from nowhere. The sheer determination of the early years would bear a much greater cultural harvest later on. Yet one cannot deny that the passion for Polish culture was driven in part by the very un-Polish character of the setting. Poles reciting Mickiewicz in post-war Wrocław were like Englishmen staging *A Midsummer Night's Dream* in Calcutta and pretending that they were in Stratford. As the writer Maria Dąbrowska recorded in 1947, 'One reason why one always feels so bad in Wrocław is that nostalgia hangs in the air: as if one were in exile, infinitely far from one's own people.'[66]

In 1947–8, as reconstruction languished, the pace of political change accelerated. The general election of 19 January 1947 gave a comfortable victory to a Government Bloc led by the PPR and the PPS. As the director of the Communist Party's 'department of electoral mathematics' would later confess, the results had been blatantly rigged. In Wrocław, all posters put up by the opposition PSL had been torn down; all PSL candidates were physically harassed; and individual voters had to wait for hours while organised groups were bussed in by the authorities. Thereafter, three official policies came to the fore. Firstly, the government launched an ideological campaign based partly on vulgar Marxism and the emulation of Soviet norms and partly on extreme Polish chauvinism. Claims to the Recovered Territories, for instance, were to be buttressed by nationalistic and elaborate pseudo-historical arguments. Secondly, the twin parties of the Government Bloc were to be prepared for merger and for the resultant establishment of a one-party state. Thirdly, the opposition was to be subjected to a mounting reign of terror.

The ideological turn took many forms, but was best observed in a series of show events, all of which were staged in, or near, Wrocław. For a season, Wrocław became 'the political capital of Poland'. In September 1947, for instance, the Polish government played host to the founding meeting of the Communist Information Bureau (Cominform), which was held in the unlikely setting of the tiny mountain resort in Szklarska Poręba (the former Schreiberhau). The meeting, which was strictly confined to the most senior comrades of the Communist elite, was attended by dignitaries from all countries of the Soviet Bloc. One of its aims was to coordinate propaganda against the Marshall Plan, which Moscow had forbidden its clients to touch. Another was to advertise the Polishness of the province to which the delegates were invited.

In contrast, the Exhibition of the Recovered Territories (WZO) of 1948 was designed for the masses. Invented by Poland's chief ideologist, Jerzy Borejsza, it was located on the site of the *Jahrhunderthalle* in the garden suburb of Sępolno (Zimpel) – now renamed the Hala Ludowa, or People's Hall – and consisted of a light-hearted funfair combined with heavy political propaganda, housed in some fifty pavilions. It was adorned with socialist-realist statues of heroic workers and peasants, with faces turned to a sky dominated by a soaring ninety-six-metre steel needle. The emphasis was switched at the last minute from anti-imperialism to technical progress and Polish-Soviet brotherhood. The huge historical section drew extensively on an exhibition prepared, but never actually presented, in Poznań called 'A Thousand Years of Polish-German Struggle'. It promoted four main themes: the struggle of Slavonic tribes in prehistory; Polish-German conflict over ten centuries; the return of Poland to its 'Piast Path'; and 'Our Immemorial Right to the Recovered Territories'. In all, in the hundred days of its existence, the WZO welcomed more than 1.5 million visitors. It certainly gave them a well-needed rest, some cheap food and the sense of belonging that so many of them lacked. The opening on 21 July was attended by Bolesław Bierut, already President of the Republic, but not by the Minister of Recovered Territories, Władysław Gomułka, who had fallen from grace. (It was nearly ruined by a broken panel which, under the slogan 'The Rightful Owner returns to his Land', was supposed to display a Polish peasant, but in fact showed a helmeted German soldier.) The closing ceremony on 31 October, which included a speech about the 'people's assumption of power', ended with a concert by the Wrocław Philharmonic.[67]

One pavilion, which never saw the light of day, had been prepared by Jakub Egit and his local Jewish Committee. Two weeks before the WZO opened, the pavilion was inspected by Soviet and municipal officials. They did not like Chaim Hanft's statue of a Jewish miner, and they did not approve of Jewish achievements being presented as separate from everything else. 'Comrade Egit, you must think you are in Israel,' one of the inspectors observed. There was no appeal. The pavilion was handed over to the Polish Western Society.[68]

The 'International Congress of Intellectuals in Defence of Peace' took place in the Wrocław Polytechnic for four days in August 1948. Attended by a galaxy of celebrities from forty-five countries, including Irène Joliot-Curie, Graham Greene, Pablo Picasso, Ilya Ehrenburg, Mikhail Sholokhov, Salvatore Quasimodo, Bertolt Brecht, Harold Ould, Jorge Amado, Kingsley Martin and Julian Huxley, it was supposed to lend respectability to the foreign policy of the Soviet Bloc. But its methods proved all too transparent. The delegates were irritated by the constant attentions of Secret Service agents. The Polish group, which featured some distinguished names, such as Tadeusz Kotarbiński, Hugo Steinhaus, Władysław Broniewski and Antoni Słonimski, was frankly embarrassed. 'When we entered the Congress Hall,' Maria Dąbrowska wrote in her diary, 'we were searched no less than seven times, and the headquarters of the Congress was packed with secret servicemen.'[69] A message from Albert Einstein was blatantly doctored, while a speech by the Soviet academician Alexander Fadeyev attacked modern Western culture indiscriminately, likening the works of 'your Millers, Eliots, Malraux and other Sartres' to the 'creations of jackals and hyenas'. It all caused great offence. Huxley departed. The British historian A.J.P. Taylor bravely voiced a lonely protest. Jakub Berman phoned the Kremlin in desperation.

A.J.P. Taylor's intervention showed great strength of character. He was a prominent if eccentric British Socialist, the most popular historian of his generation and, as a suspected fellow traveller for the USSR in the 1930s, an unlikely champion of anti-Soviet discontent. (As the modern-history tutor at Magdalen College, he would become the chief mentor of numerous future historians, including Norman Davies.) Several members of the British delegation, such as Professor J.B. Haldane and the 'Red Dean' of Canterbury, Dr Hewlett Johnson, urged him to desist. And the organisers asked him to submit his text in advance. He ignored them:

It is a long journey from London, [he began] and I – for one – did not make that . . . journey in order to listen to commonplaces or to read slogans which seem to have been left over from the World Meeting of Democratic Youth. We intellectuals are not children; and most of us came here for . . . the purpose of securing co-operation between intellectuals of all countries . . . We can't work unless we have free movement . . .

As intellectuals, we must have some common standards; and I fear that these standards are still lacking. In my opinion, it is our duty . . . to preach tolerance, not to preach hate. In America, and now in England too, more and more people say that there is nothing to choose between the Soviet Union and Nazi Germany, that both want to conquer the world. Many intellectuals, in America as well as in England, have fought against this view. And now, when we come here, what do we find? The same views in reverse. The same bogeys; here it is called American Fascism, over there it is called Russian Bolshevism. We intellectuals, instead of inflating these bogeys, should be trying to bring peoples of both sides to their senses.

If we intellectuals are to work together, it must be on the basis . . . of truth. As an historian, I cannot sit silent when I listen to history being remade. On this Polish soil an Englishman has the right and duty to say this; we and the French were the only peoples who went to war against Nazi Germany without waiting to be attacked, we and the French alone entered this war in order to liberate Poland. A more flagrant . . . example of this historical distortion was when Mr Fadiejew recited the countries which had resisted Hitler . . . One country was missing: yet Yugoslavia had a record of resistance second to none. Now, in order to suit the convenience of a political party, Yugoslav resistance is blotted out. Under this banner of dishonesty I, for one, will not march . . .

Ah yes, but what are we for? I know what I'm for – for a single humanity, not for British culture, not American culture, not Soviet culture, but for a single human culture. We intellectuals belong to the country of Voltaire and Goethe, of Tolstoy and Shakespeare. But if it must be something less, then Europe – the Europe that is neither Communist nor American . . .

I – if alone – am for the freedom of the mind – freedom for the artist to create as he wishes, freedom for the scientist to research, freedom for the writer to express his own ideas. Unless we meet on this basis, we can meet on none . . . All peoples ask for freedom from oppression – freedom from arbitrary arrest, freedom from a secret police, freedom to speak their opinion of their own government as well as of others. If we defend this, we defend also the peace of the world and we offer the people of the world what they want. But even if I spoke only for myself, I would still say: without intellectual freedom, without love, without tolerance, the intellectual cannot serve humanity. And in short, here I am, here are my opinions. I could have no others.[70]

According to Taylor's latest biographer, 'Taylor caused an uproar. The Communists were furious. The Poles were delighted, and he was lionised . . .' He even went over to one of his acquaintances in the audience and whispered, 'I've been dreaming of giving a speech like that since God knows when!' Most importantly for the outside world, a woman reporter left Poland immediately and sent the story to the *New York Times*. 'Taylor became the man who had spoken for freedom behind the Iron Curtain.'[71]

The British press, too, was duly agitated. The left-wing *Daily Herald* printed a front-page report detailing how Taylor had told the congress that 'it was for war, not peace'. The liberal *Manchester Guardian* took a similar line under the heading 'Stench of Decay'. *The Times*'s report was headed 'Soviet Claptrap'. On 4 September, the *New Statesman* published a long article on 'Hyenas and Other Reptiles', and appended a letter from Taylor himself and six other colleagues:

> We the undersigned members of the British group at the Wrocław Congress regret that we are unable to accept the resolution passed there as the whole truth . . . Two ways of life are in conflict throughout the world and it should be the task of intellectuals to resolve the conflict by peaceful means. We feel the implication of the resolution that one side alone is to blame to be a waste of a great opportunity. We believe that, though we were in a minority at the Congress, we represent the majority of men and women throughout the world.
>
> | A.J.P. Taylor | Edward Crankshaw |
> | Felix Topolski | Richard Hughes |
> | A.G. Weidenfeld | Denis Seurat |
> | Olaf Stapledon[72] | |

Only the Communist *Daily Worker* failed to mention the controversy. On 1 September, it published an interview with the leader of the Soviet delegation, Eugene Tarle, who dutifully denounced US warmongering.[73] The British Foreign Office was well pleased. Its file on the Wrocław Congress opened with remarks about 'our "intellectuals" making fools of themselves'. It closed with praise for A.J.P. Taylor, '[whose] views are so notoriously unorthodox as to make it clear he is not just an official spokesman'.[74] Nonetheless, on the final day of the Congress, 337 of 357 participants passed a resolution condemning 'the war preparations of a handful of greedy profiteers in Europe and America who have adopted . . . the ideas of racial superiority from Fascism'. Such a manifest mockery only proved that intellectuals are more malleable than most.[75]

One month later, Wrocław hosted the General Assembly of the Polish Historical Society; 600 delegates attended. They were told by the Minister of Education that it was 'essential to create a Marxist School of History'.[76] They also heard how the leaders of post-war Poland were 'heirs to the Piasts' and how the detestable Jagiellons had cared only for the East. Much was made of the centenary of the Springtime of Nations of 1848.

Meanwhile, the path towards a one-party state was undertaken in two stages. To begin with, the pro-merger group within the socialist PPS had to take full control of their party and purge the independent elements. For this purpose the XXVII Congress of the PPS was called to Wrocław for 14–17 December 1947 with 1,300 delegates from all over Poland. Orchestrated by Józef Cyrankiewicz, who was destined to take a leading position in subsequent Stalinist regimes, it was also attended by the most prominent figures of the government – General Rola-Żymierski, Władysław Gomułka and Jakub Berman. The rank-and-file were dead set against fusion. They cheered Cyrankiewicz when he told them with effortless cynicism that 'the Polish Socialist Party is, and *will be* necessary to the Polish Nation'. The proposals of the platform 'for eventual merger' were listened to in silence. But they were backed up by a 'spontaneous parade' of 60,000 workers on Grunwald Square. The Congress resulted in emergency powers being granted to Cyrankiewicz, who was then able to effect the merger at his leisure.[77]

After that, the Communist PPR had to put its own house in order. A more conformist brand of Marxist-Leninism was demanded. In August, accusations of rightist deviation were levelled against Gomułka and his followers – hence his absence from the WZO and the expulsion of some 150 'rightists' from the party organisation in Wrocław alone. Bolesław Bierut, who since 1944 had posed as a 'non-party man', suddenly emerged as the party's all-powerful General Secretary. In December 1948, at Warsaw, he shepherded the obedient comrades into the fold of the Polish United Workers' Party (PZPR), which was to rule Poland for the next forty-two years. In Wrocław, the merger at the top was reflected in a merger of the local Socialist and Communist press to found a united *Workers' Gazette*. On 16 December, its first number reported, 'The First Congress of the PZPR is debating with joy and enthusiasm.' A week later, on Stalin's birthday, it commented, 'The whole of proletarian Wrocław has paid its respects to Josef Stalin, the guardian of the working masses of the whole world.'

None of this manipulative politics would have been possible without the parallel use of coercion and terror. In 1947, the pressure steadily mounted on all non-controlled elements. In February, the Jewish Bund was still able to hold a national conference, and in March the local branch of the PSL held its last free AGM. In April, the last Soviet garrison left Wrocław, but it was soon replaced by a strong garrison of the Internal Security Corps (KBW), which returned from active service in the ethnic cleansing of Ukrainian districts during 'Operation Vistula'. The premises of the opposition PSL were repeatedly raided, their newspaper closed down, and their local Chairman put on trial. Much of the year passed under the shadow of the amnesty – a dubious promise of immunity for any armed opponents of the regime who laid down their arms. Sermons in several Wrocław churches urged acceptance of the amnesty; and about 2,000 people did so. But on 27 November 1947 three members of the 'Freedom and Independence' group were demonstratively shot in Kleczkowska Prison in the company of a Nazi murderer from the Baranowicz Ghetto. In 1948, though May Day saw 130,000 marchers, the 'Third of May' was banned.

At the same time, the Communist security services in Wrocław were liquidating the wartime leadership of the Home Army (AK), many of whom had sought refuge in Silesia. In July 1948, immediately before the WZO, the security forces launched 'Action X' throughout Lower Silesia. They arrested about 800 people, many of them former AK members from Vilnius. The following January, they sent the body of Stanisław Odyński, head of the AK in Lithuania, to the University Department of Anatomy for surgical practice by medical students.

Only in retrospect could one see the true horror of the emerging Stalinist regime. The number of political executions was mounting. On 10 August 1948, during the WZO and just before the Congress of Intellectuals, three men were sentenced to death by the military court in Wrocław. Major Ludwik Marszałek, thirty-seven, was an AK officer from Dębica. Władysław Cisek, twenty-seven, a former AK soldier, was a student of the Wrocław Polytechnic, who had joined 'Freedom and Independence'. Stanisław Dydo, twenty-six, was a law student at Wrocław University, whose father had died in Auschwitz. They were all shot on 27 September. Before they died, they wrote their farewell letters:

– My darling wife, Wanduś [Wanda]! I loved you enormously. Forgive me for any wrong I did you. I bless you, and beg God that we may meet again in the life hereafter. Ludwik.
  – My little daughter Marysia! I bless you. Be happy. Look to heaven so that we may live in eternal bliss. Daddy.
  – My little son Chris! I give you my blessing for a happy life. Pray, work, be a good Pole, and may God allow that we meet in Heaven. Your father.[78]

Two of the three letters were found in the archives in 1995 – unposted.

The Chief Military Procurator of Poland's Stalinist regime, Helena Wolińska (Brus), came to Wrocław in August 1949 to supervise the prosecution of Ignacy Marczak, charged with sabotage. She did not tarry for his execution, but in several instances she extended the terms of interrogation of prisoners. (Fifty years later, she would face trial in Warsaw on charges of judicial murder, and requests for her extradition from Great Britain.)[79] But Wolińska had more important matters to attend to. And she had plenty of zealous colleagues and deputies. Most of the top military prosecutors in post-war Poland were camouflaged as Soviet officers on secondment. A few of them, surprisingly, had once been members of the pre-war Polish Army, who were put to work to repress their former comrades. Such was Captain Jan Kołodziej (1912–67), who somehow managed during the war to join the AK and work for the German-run District Court in Cracow, and in April 1945 to volunteer for the People's Army. He served as a military judge in Wrocław in 1950.[80]

In those immediate post-war years, Wrocław was observed by many foreign visitors. They were mainly, though not exclusively, Western Communists and other left-wing sympathisers, who wanted to view 'the gains of Socialism'. They included Maurice Thorez, the French Communist leader, and a long procession of Britons from Cecily Chesterton to Connie Zilliacus, John Silkin and Denis Healey. It is not easy to learn what they thought, not least because the systematic mendacity of Soviet-style regimes was not yet common knowledge. Like Thorez, who visited in November 1947, they were shown round the war-scarred Tumski Island and told of the Piast legacy, which had somehow been bequeathed to the Communists; and they were invited to reflect on the unimaginable scale of the human and physical damage, which was all the fault of the Fascists.

Denis Healey, 'the best Prime Minister Britain never had', was far better informed than most. Having turned in anger against the puerile Communism of his student days, he was now the International Secretary of Britain's ruling Labour Party, and in late 1947 made a tour of Hungary, Czechoslovakia and Poland to watch the process of the Socialist-Communist 'fusion' that was everywhere afoot. Well briefed in London by Adam Ciołkosz, the exiled leader of the true PPS, he knew about Stalin's misconduct in Poland; he knew about Katyń; and he knew in outline what the Communists were trying to do. Yet when Healey came to Wrocław to attend the PPS Congress, it is clear from his later account that he did not quite grasp what was happening. For one thing, he thought that Wrocław had formed part of East Prussia. For another, he clearly entertained the possibility that Cyrankiewicz was fighting a tough rearguard action against the prospect of a merger. He even repeated the bon mot that someone told him about Cyrankiewicz bringing Gomułka to the conference, while Cyrankiewicz's wife, a film actress, brought her film director. '*A chacun son régisseur!*' the joke went ('Everyone is following orders from someone'). Unfortunately, Healey did not realise just how true the joke really was.[81] Foreigners were not alone in imagining that something more than political shadow-boxing was possible. Cynical jokes were absolutely appropriate.

Some people were better equipped to judge the direction of events. Dr Feliks Mantel, for example, travelled to the PPS Congress at Wrocław from Vienna, where he was serving as Poland's minister plenipotentiary. A Jewish lawyer and lifelong Socialist, he had worked in 1945 as Bolesław Drobner's deputy and, as vividly described in his memoirs, was the official who had taken possession of Auschwitz from the Soviet military. Like Drobner, Mantel was a child of the Gulag. Nonetheless, he had consistently called for cooperation between Socialists and Communists. In 1931, he had penned articles in *Robotnik* ('The Worker'), the organ of the pre-war PPS, calling for the decriminalisation of the KPP. And again in 1945, he had put his name to an appeal urging the post-war PPS to cooperate with Gomułka. Yet by the end of 1947, he saw that the game was up. The Communists' understanding of cooperation was not tolerable to democratic Socialists. Mantel's suspicions were confirmed by the Communist coup in Prague in February. His trip to Wrocław proved to be his last visit to Poland. He travelled back to Vienna, crossed secretly into the American zone and entered a life of exile spent first in Argentina and then in Paris.[82]

*

Stalinism in Poland, which lasted from 1949 to 1956, was nasty, brutish and mercifully short. It involved much more than the obligatory cult of Joseph Stalin. In politics, it required the universal adoption of Marxist-Leninist ideology, the unwavering imitation of the USSR and the imposition of Soviet-style 'democratic centralism', where the ruling party enjoyed a complete monopoly of dictatorial power. In economics, it demanded nationwide central planning and a strong preference for military production, heavy industry and collectivised agriculture. In the social sphere, while giving nominal control to workers and peasants and eliminating all 'social enemies', it raised the comrades of the party *nomenklatura* into a super-class. In culture, it made social realism the sole acceptable doctrine. In order to function, it relied on preventative censorship, elaborate propaganda, innumerable enforcement agencies, ubiquitous police surveillance, the myth of foreign danger and the exclusion of the outside world. Above all, it created a violent, mystical mindset best likened to the tyranny of an extreme religious sect, where the true believers acted out their fancies and the ordinary people lived in fear. It began in Poland with the creation of the PZPR; it faltered after Stalin's death in 1953; and it slowly dissolved in the years preceding Khrushchev's 'Secret Speech' in March 1956 into something rather milder.

Stalinism hit Wrocław as it hit all the cities of the Soviet Bloc. The outward manifestations were everywhere apparent. A purpose-built Party House was erected on Wojciech Cybulski Street for the Voivodship Committee of the PZPR – the new seat of power. The City Presidency was abolished. All employees, high and low, were verified for political reliability. All workers were given 'norms' to fulfil. The bookshops filled up with a million copies of *The History of the All Union Soviet Communist Party (Bolsheviks)*. The streets filled up with parades and propaganda posters, but were emptied of private shops. Many of them changed their name for the second time in five years. Stalin Street ran north of the Main Square; Stalingrad Street to the south. The old Kürassierstrasse, for five years 'Benedikt the Pole Street', now became 'The Street of Leading Workers'. Entertainment in 1949 was provided by a Russian choir (preceded by a lecture on materialism in music), the film *Lenin in October*, an Albanian folk-dance group and a visiting Chinese poet. The intense centralisation of power in Warsaw left all other Polish cities feeling intensely provincial. Wrocław gave the impression of 'a vast, extended village',[83] where the only sign of urban life were the trams covered in cheap blue paint. People kept pigs and goats in their basements or on their balconies. Gardens were turned into allotments. 'We were ruled by idiots,' wrote a Silesian poet, 'in a provincial outpost of a Soviet colony.'[84] He was thinking of Cracow, which had survived the war intact. How much more bitter this sentiment was in crippled Wrocław!

Wrocław, however, was not a fertile ground for ideological indoctrination. For one thing, many of the work-seekers who had recently migrated from the Polish countryside were deeply religious. A party campaign in 1948–9 to remove all religious emblems from the workplace backfired badly amid shouts of '*My chcemy Boga*' ('We want God'). Though the percentage of party membership among workers was now high, it had only been achieved by making it an unofficial prerequisite for employment. For another thing, especially among educated people, the solid block of 'repatriants' from the eastern borders would simply not swallow the slogans. In the combined University and Polytechnic, for example, where the teaching body was dominated by senior professors from Lwów, both staff and students were hostile to the regime. They did not rejoice one bit when their institution was dedicated to Bolesław Bierut. As a former academic recalls, 'the staff was split down the middle between the Party appointees and their non-Party opponents'. The Rector from 1945 to 1952, Professor Stanisław Kulczyński (1895–1975), a botanist of international repute, had been Rector of the University of Lwów in the 1930s, when he had honourably resigned over the discrimination against Jewish students. During the war, he had worked for the Polish government in London and served in the AK. He now belonged to the minority who joined the Communist regime in the hope of moderating its excesses.[85]

The Voivodship Committee of the PZPR in Wrocław was an important local cog in the streamlined, conveyor-belt dictatorship that was now running. It took its secret orders, usually by telephone, from the Politburo in Warsaw and applied them to all the lower rungs of the machine within its jurisdiction. Towards its superiors, it adopted a posture of slavish deference. Towards everyone else, it acted with tyrannical impunity. Among other things, its power derived from its absolute control of all appointments within the city, from that of important officials in the municipal administration to the lowliest positions of authority in youth clubs, trade unions and cultural societies. Prior to the compromise of 1956, it even controlled the appointment of the clergy. Its first Secretary, Władysław Matwin (b.1916), was a professional Communist, who had spent the war years in the USSR and who would return to Wrocław in 1957–63 after a spell as editor-in-chief of *Trybuna Ludu*, Poland's chief Communist newspaper. His replacements in the intervening years – Witaszewski, Kuligowski and Kowarz – were figures of such distinction that they do not merit entries in the 1,000-page *Encyclopedia Wrocławia* (2000). Nonetheless, they were the chief spiders in the Communist web of social control and political repression.[86]

One might think that Wrocław was close to the hearts of the central planners in distant Warsaw. It might have looked like an ideal *tabula rasa* on which their utopia could be built. In reality, the ideal was a mirage. The new society of Poland's 'Wild West' was highly atomised: labour discipline was low, illegal private enterprise flourished and the 'Western Bonus' ensured that sacked workers could easily find employment elsewhere. The role given to Wrocław in the Six Year Plan (1949–55), was less prominent than that of more promising areas like Upper Silesia. It did not extend beyond the repair and relaunching of the main heavy factories – Domel, Hutman, Archimedes, WSK and, above all, Pafawag. (The WSK works, which produced electrical machinery, was renamed after Felix Dzerzhinsky.) As a result, the Stalinist years in Wrocław have been labelled 'The Years of Stagnation'. No major project similar to the model industrial suburb of Nowa Huta in Cracow was attempted. Reconstruction flagged. Although many of the city's trams had been sent to Warsaw, no new buses were delivered until 1954. And although the population continued to rise, from 300,000 in December 1948 to 370,000 in 1955, it did not increase nearly as fast as that of the other major centres of industrialisation.

Nothing better illustrates Wrocław's predicament than the sad story of 'The Exploitation of Bricks' and the resultant 'Mondszajn Affair'. In 1949, the Directorate of Municipal Reconstruction (DOM) was closed down and replaced by the Municipal Demolition Enterprise (MPR). The directors of DOM, who were sent to Nowa Huta, had been accused of favouring private enterprise and the rebuilding of churches. So instead of being rebuilt, Wrocław was to be knocked down in the most calculated and cynical way. The aim was to collect undamaged bricks for the reconstruction of Warsaw. The targets, therefore, were not the lingering piles of rubble, but buildings that had somehow survived intact and which could otherwise have been repaired. The methods were barbaric. They coincided with the party's other obsession of eliminating the last traces of German culture. In 1949, for example, the Renaissance Wlast Gateway, near the Salt Market, was torn down for its bricks. Soon the magnificent General Post Office succumbed, together with hundreds of modern villas in the outer suburbs. In 1949, the tally was 140 million bricks; in 1951, 165 million. Yet as reconstruction of the cathedral approached completion, work on the City Hall was suspended for lack of funds. As Warsaw's Old Town rose again, Wrocław's Old Town was still in tatters. Mondszajn was the director of MPR and his activities in Wrocław became legendary, not least through his attempt to flee the country for Israel, allegedly with a solid-gold frying pan in his baggage. Accused of corruption after the Stalinist period, he was committed to prison in 1958.

The regression was no less marked in the cultural sphere. Many of the artists who had revitalised the city simply left. Others, like the patriotic sculptor and ex-KZ inmate, Antoni Mehl (1905–67), were dismissed. Several key institutions, such as the Wrocław Philharmonic, were closed down. In the face of aggressive censorship and of authorities who demanded pictures of heroic workers, it became an act of bravery to produce an innovative play or to recite a thoughtful poem. Ironically, the State Jewish Theatre under the famous Ida Kamińska enjoyed greater freedom and patronage than its counterparts. And in a climate where the populace was fully occupied in meetings and petitions denouncing 'Anglo-Saxon aggressors' or 'capitalist machinations', energies had to find new outlets. One was sport: the international cycling 'Peace Tour' was very popular. Literature saw a retreat into the classics. In the worst years of Stalinism, the publication of Polish favourites, or the production of classic plays, was relatively safe and immensely comforting. For the most part, however, philistinism ruled. It followed the example of a local party secretary, who ordered the pulping of much of the University Library's irreplaceable collection of German-language books – 'which would not be needed'. For his services, he became Minister of Culture of the People's Republic.

The Roman Catholic Church came under direct attack. Although Wrocław saw no show trials, the clergy was severely harassed. Anti-clerical meetings were staged in the factories. 'The Polish nation has won true freedom,' roared the *Workers' Daily* (GW) on 23 March 1949, 'not that of a colony or of slaves. We won't give it up just because that's what the Bishops want.' A parallel campaign was launched against the Vatican after a papal letter to the German bishops (1948) seemed to imply less than total support for the new frontiers. In 1951, the Apostolic Administrator, Father Milik, was expelled, several weeks before the inauguration of the reconstructed cathedral. He was replaced by a politically subservient priest. The first post-war Bishop of Wrocław, Bolesław Kominek (1903–74), received the *sacra* in 1954, but was prevented from taking up the see for two years.

Meanwhile, the spasmodic arrests and executions of the post-war years swelled into a systematic reign of terror. The jails were filled with political prisoners. Police informers penetrated all walks of life, and a body of spurious laws enabled criminal procurators to accuse almost anyone of 'Fascist–Hitlerite crimes'. The civil courts concentrated on the elimination of so-called 'speculators' and 'saboteurs' – who were generally nothing of the sort – while the military courts targeted the remnants of wartime resistance, whom they usually classified as 'bandits' or 'terrorists'. In good Soviet style, the machine began to devour its own servants. More than 1,400 militia and intelligence agents were arrested. So, too, was General Marian Spychalski, one of Gomułka's associates, who in 1950 was lying low in Wrocław working as an architect when he was arrested by Berman's deputy, Anatol Feigin. Police archives that were opened forty years later revealed a scandalous picture of universal official depravity. Interrogations were routinely accompanied by beatings and torture. Fanciful accusations were pursued in the full majesty of the 'People's Law'. Defendants died without explanation, disappeared, committed suicide or were condemned in a mass of meaningless verbiage:

In a period when the toiling masses of Poland have proceeded to the building of the foundations of Socialism and the construction of a creative human life in the framework of the Six Year Plan, reactionary underground groups directed by the agents of American imperialism, recruited from elements of the former Home Army and other pro-Fascist organisations, and moved by hatred for People's Poland, are endeavouring to prevent the Polish Nation from achieving the economic and cultural goals through the use of terrorist-sabotage operations . . .[87]

In the end, automated judges passed extreme sentences of hard labour, life imprisonment and death. Appeals were rejected, sometimes by Bierut in person. Executions in Kleczkowska Prison were carried out casually, sometimes carelessly:

> One of the most terrible sights was that of an officer who was shot three times. He had survived the camp at Auschwitz, but having fought the Communists he was arrested and sentenced to death. At the first salvo, only one rifle fired and the bullet missed him. [At the second attempt] two rifles fired, but the bullets did not cause fatal injury. Finally, the commander approached the man, prostrate in a pool of blood, drew a revolver and shot him in the head . . .[88]

Unmarked graves were waiting in special plots at the Osobowice (Oswitz) Cemetery. A captive press, if it talked at all, talked only of the elimination of convicts, deserters and *Volksdeutsche*.

In their paranoiac obsessions with political conformity, the Stalinist police investigated every last nook and cranny of people's lives. Foreigners were especially vulnerable. Petro Damovsky (1901–59), for example, was a Bulgarian citizen of Macedonian nationality who had fought for the Communist partisans during the Greek Civil War and had been resettled in Międzygórze (Wölfelsgrund) in Lower Silesia in 1949. Soon afterwards, he was denounced by his Communist comrades as a 'nationalist' and 'Titoist provocateur', was arrested by UBP agents and formally accused of 'spreading hostile, whispered propaganda'. He had been a member of an Emigrants' Committee, and it turned out that his real offence was to have demanded that Macedonian refugee children should receive lessons in the Macedonian language, as well as in Greek and Polish. This was magnified into the charge that the accused had been spreading malicious lies about the Polish state using terrorist methods to Polonise Macedonian children. His temerity cost him two years in jail, two trials – one in the Regional Court in Wrocław and another in the Supreme Court in Warsaw – and an endless series of interrogations concerning his activities in Bulgaria, Yugoslavia, Greece and Poland (interrogations in that era routinely involved torture). Meanwhile his file at the Wrocław branch of the UBP bulged with the statements of informers, policemen, lawyers and translators, all struggling with the minutiae of Balkan politics. Who gave the orders, for instance, to murder the headman of the village of Bukowik (Oksia) in 1947? Apart from a document recording the termination of investigations in March 1952, the file does not reveal the prisoner's ultimate fate. But according to information supplied by his family, Damovsky was sent home to Bulgaria, re-arrested and sent to a camp, whence he was only released to die. His was just one case among thousands. But it illustrates the lengths to which political terror was applied, not least among Communists.[89]

The full toll of Polish Stalinism has yet to be established, but the recent examination of tens of thousands of cases, and hundreds of death sentences in Wrocław alone, leaves no doubt about the murderous nature and vast scale of the phenomenon. Still harder for outsiders to understand is the calculated treachery. Major Wiktor Komorowski (b.1879), for example, was 'the Nestor of the Polish Air Force and a veteran of the Polish–Soviet War'. Recalled to service in 1939, he escaped abroad and served with the RAF in Britain. After the war, he returned to Poland and settled at Bierutowice (Brückenberg) near Jelenia Góra. He possibly had some sort of low-level connection with the intelligence services either of the United Kingdom or of the Polish government-in-exile. Arrested with his wife and three sons on charges of spying, together with fifty-five other people in the village, Komorowski died after interrogation in Kleczkowska Street on 16 April 1951. One son, Richard, received a prison sentence, another, Jerzy, received the death sentence; and the third, Bogdan, escaped, but surrendered on a promise of mercy for his brother and his father (who was already dead). Jerzy and Bogdan Komorowski were shot together on 6 August 1954.

One of the last victims of Stalinist judicial murder in Wrocław was Włodzimierz Pawłokowski (d.1955), who had been the PSL candidate in the elections of 1947. Persecuted by the Communist police, he went into hiding, forming an underground group called *Rzeczpospolita Walcząca*, or 'The Fighting Commonwealth', and avoided capture until 1953. Caught in possession of the Peasant Party standard, he was found guilty of treason and executed.

Many strange facts about Stalinist Silesia could not be revealed for decades. At the time, they were kept secret through sheer terror. The extraordinary story of the mines at Miedzianka was a case in point. Miedzianka was the post-war name for an old town on the River Bobr, some sixty-five kilometres south-west of Wrocław. It had previously been known, through the rich mineral deposits nearby, as Kupferberg. Some time after the Soviet Army arrived, they found that the mines could yield an ore that was far more valuable than copper. The German inhabitants were expelled, the NKVD took over the entire town and Soviet engineers ran all operations. Miners were hired at five or even ten times the average local wage. They were not given any protective clothing, and they were not told what they were extracting. They slaved beside a slogan: *'Pracuj, nie oszczędaj*

Dr Edith Stein (1891–1942),
murdered by the Nazis.

Helena Motykówna (1924–46),
executed by the Communists.

Tadeusz Różewicz (b. 1921),
poet.

Władysław Frasyniuk (b. 1954),
Solidarity activist.

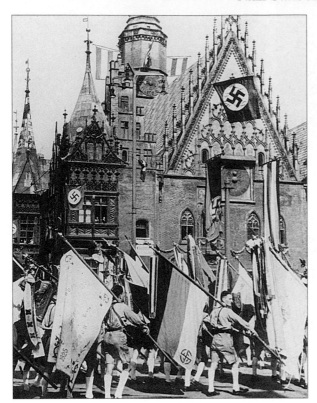

The City Hall bedecked, 1938.

Adolf Hitler adored, 1938.

The besieged: Gauleiter Hanke marshals the *Volkssturm*.

The besiegers: Soviet infantry attack.

Cathedral Island without roofs, May 1945.

Friedrich-Wilhelm-Strasse with a T-34, May 1945.

Polish 'repatriants' arriving from the East.

German 'expellees' departing for the West.

Picasso at the Stalinist 'Congress of Intellectuals', 1948.

The *Panorama Racławicka* (1893–4), rescued from Lwów.

Polish Army tanks on patrol during martial law, 1982.

Paddling across Świdnicka Street during the flood of 1997.

The Cathedral Bridge, renovated.

The main Jewish cemetery, intact.

Pope John Paul II in Wrocław, 1997.

się, twoim dzieciom będzie lepiej' ('Work, don't hold back, your children will have a better life'). And then they began to fall ill. They had no proper medical care; those who inhaled the dust, or left it on their bare hands, weakened and died. But they and their families dared not talk. For talkers disappeared and informers were everywhere. No one was arrested. Suspects and offenders were simply beaten to death or thrown down an empty mine shaft. Men died for losing their pass, for muttering a comment about Stalin or for leaving a nugget in their boots. On the surface everything looked normal – there was no barbed wire. As one of the survivors remarked some fifty years later, 'This Gulag was inside of people, in their souls, in their heads. Everyone knew that it was not permitted to speak, to think or even to remember.'[90] Then it stopped. Uranium-mining was abandoned in 1953. The Soviets left, internal security troops moved in and wiped Miedzianka from the map. The galleries were sealed with concrete, the church was dynamited; houses and streets were razed without trace. The hillside reverted to nature. At the end of the century, a few people in the neighbouring village would tell what they knew. And an old woman of uncertain origin was heard to exclaim: '*Und damit Schluss!*' ('And that's the end of it').

It is very difficult to imagine the fearful atmosphere of the Stalinist years or to guess how much people knew. One of the characteristics of the Stalinist terror was that it was completely unpredictable. It paralysed resistance because no one could tell where it would strike next. Yet all the evidence points to the conclusion that it never took the same hold in Poland as it did in Russia or elsewhere in the Soviet Bloc. Moreover, there are many signs that Polish culture was not prepared to submit. The popular singer Maria Koterbska (b. 1924), for example, would recall the time in the early 1950s when she was supposed to sing about girls falling in love with bricklayers and when her unlicensed performances of dangerous 'American Swing' landed her with a total ban on performing. A crowd of fans who gathered in front of her home in Bielsko (Bielitz) had to be dispersed by her husband with the words 'You're going to get us all into prison'. But Koterbska belonged to a group that was determined to do it their way. Together with the conductor of the Silesian Radio Orchestra, Jerzy Harald, and his wife, the songwriter Krystyna (Eugenia) Wnukowska, she built up a repertoire of intimate lyrics that made a direct appeal to people's genuine emotions. At a concert in the Hala Ludowa in Wrocław in 1953, she sang a catchy melody that brought the house down and was destined to become the city's theme song. First called the 'Tramway Song', it became known as the 'Wrocław Waltz'.

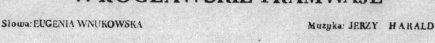

WROCŁAWSKIE TRAMWAJE

Słowa: EUGENIA WNUKOWSKA

Muzyka: JERZY HARALD

Mkną po szynach niebieskie tramwaje
przez wrocławskich ulic sto.
Tu przechodnia uśmiechem witają
dzieci, kwiaty i każdy dom.

Na przystankach nucą słowiki,
dźwięczy śpiewem stary park,
Przez Sempolno, Zalesie i Krzyki
niesie melodie wrocławski wiatr.

Wieczór zapada, już noc niedaleko, już gwiazdy migocą na niebie,
Srebrzy się Odra, najmilsza ma rzeka i płynie z pioszenka do ciebie,
Mkną po szynach niebieskie tramwaje przez wrocławskich ulic sto.
Tu przechodnia uśmiechem witają dzieci i kwiaty, i każdy dom.
Na przystankach nucą słowiki, dźwięczy śpiewem stary park.
Przez Sępolno, Zalesie i Krzyki niesie melodię wrocławski wiatr.
A kiedy rankiem fabryczne syreny dzień dobry powiedzą znów miastu
Słonko jak jaskier wykwitnie z zieleni, dziewczyna zaśpiewa przy pracy
Mkną po szynach niebieskie tramwaje . . .

(The twilight is falling, and night-time approaching; the stars are twinkling
  above,
The Odra flows silver: the dearest of rivers is bringing this song to my love.
The sky-blue tramcars glide along the tramlines on a hundred Wrocław
  streets.
Flowers and children greet them with a smile, like every house on the way.
The wind blows the melody off through the suburbs, to Sępolno, Krzyki,
  Zalesie.
And when factory sirens tell the city 'Good Morning' at each and every
  dawn,
The sunlight will break through the leaves like buttercups; and a girl will
  break into song:
'The sky-blue tramcars glide along the tramlines . . .')

To an outsider, the words must have sounded excruciatingly sentimental
and banal. But Vratislavians loved them. For people living grim lives in a
still ruined city, they were heart-warmingly welcome, exactly because they
were so outrageously unreal. What is more, given the Party's own
propensity for overblown propaganda, they had more than a touch of
subversive satire. After all, the Party Committee had recently decreed that
all their tramcars must be painted red.[91]

*

In the four decades between Khrushchev's not-so-'Secret Speech' of 1956
and Gorbachev's domestically disastrous policies of glasnost and perestroika,
the Soviet empire moved inexorably towards collapse. Although armed with
the world's biggest arsenal of (unusable) nuclear weapons, it was incapable
of satisfying the basic needs of its captive nations and lurched ever more
unsteadily towards the moment of reckoning. Within the Soviet camp, the
Polish People's Republic, while gaining an ever greater degree of autonomy,
followed the same general trajectory. Under Gomułka (1956 to 1970), it
reached an uneasy *modus vivendi* between a defiant nation and a still-
ambitious Party. Under Edward Gierek (1970 to 1980), it risked its

prosperity on an unorthodox economic experiment that failed. Under General Wojciech Jaruzelski (1981 to 1990), who used brute force to rescue the party from the initial triumph of Solidarity, it saw a half-hearted dictatorship edging ever less reluctantly towards final surrender.

For much of the time after 1956, Wrocław played only a minor role in political developments. It had other priorities. Although echoes were heard of each of the country's major crises – in October 1956, March 1968, December 1970 and June 1976 – it was not until 1980 that Wrocław emerged as a prominent national player. In the meantime, maximum use was made of the limited 'thaw' to rebuild the city, to create a sense of purpose in the city's new society and, above all, to unleash a magnificent surge of cultural energy.

A City Plan for Wrocław was drawn up in 1954, but by the end of the Stalinist regime little had been achieved. A showpiece quarter in Stalinist style, the KDM, was tiny in comparison to the equivalent in other cities and was not ready until 1958. A State Plan for the Reconstruction of Wrocław was not passed until July 1956. Only then, eleven years after the war, could systematic rebuilding begin. The airport at Strachowice was opened in 1958; the old Lessing Bridge was finally replaced by the modern Peace Bridge in 1959. Yet the emphasis was necessarily placed on the rapid realisation of a programme of mass housing. For in 1957–62, the population of Wrocław increased twice as fast as the population in the country as a whole. A housing complex near the New Market appeared first. Another at Gajowice (Gabitz) to the south, completed in the early 1960s, was the herald of numerous high-rise housing estates in the suburbs. These were utilitarian necessities. Less forgivable was the construction of the East–West Route – a modern throughway which carved a grotesque gash through the heart of the Old City, permanently disfiguring the cityscape, in order, or so it was said, to provide direct access to the Party House.

In 1956, when nearby Poznań broke into open revolt, Wrocław contented itself with street demonstrations, genuine factory meetings and a mutiny in the Communist Youth Movement (ZMP). Calls were heard for the return of Wilno and Lwów, for an official statement about Katyń, for the release of Cardinal Wyszyński, for the support of Budapest and for the withdrawal of all Soviet post-holders in Poland, including the Russian General commanding the Silesian Military Region. Wrocław's factories reverberated to discussions about workers' self-government. A crowd pulled down the plates STALIN STREET, and painted their own signs for THE STREET OF HUNGARIAN HEROES (which was duly changed by the authorities into NATIONAL UNITY STREET). Poland's subsequent political settlement, which saw Khrushchev's wrath tamed as Gomułka was re-installed at the head of

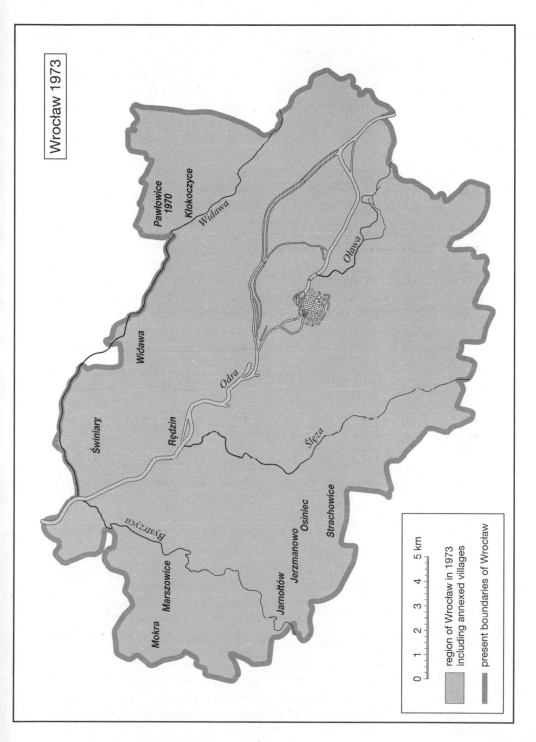

Wrocław 1973

Pawłowice 1970
Kłokoczyce
Widawa
Oława
Widawa
Odra
Świniary
Rędzin
Ślęza
Bystrzyca
Strachowice
Osiniec
Mokra
Marszowice
Jarnołtów
Jerzmanowo

0 1 2 3 4 5 km

region of Wrocław in 1973
including annexed villages

present boundaries of Wrocław

the ruling party, involved a thorough purge of Stalinist elements, the 'repatriation' of numerous Soviet 'advisers' and a fundamental agreement for cooperation between Church and State. Though the party dictatorship continued, the terror evaporated.

The year of 1956 finished off Stalinism. But it had different effects in different places. Gomułka's Poland was not the same as Kadar's Hungary or Khrushchev's Soviet Union. Indeed, Poland allowed the 'thaw' to proceed further than anywhere in the Soviet Bloc. But then again, Wrocław was not in the same position as Warsaw or Cracow. Wrocław's Stalinist team was disbanded. Hilary Chełchowski (1908–83), a politicised carpenter who had run Poland's disastrous collectivisation campaign and had been rewarded with the task of running Lower Silesia, was sent back to Warsaw. General Sergei Grokhov (alias Stanisław Popławski, 1902–73), a Russian in disguise, who had been commander of the Silesian Military Region, an honorary citizen of Wrocław and a deputy in the national Sejm, was sent back to Moscow. Having risen to be Deputy Minister of Defence, his last job before leaving was to crush the Poznań Rising. The new party team gave out mixed signals. On the one hand, it was headed by Władysław Matwin (b. 1916), who, as a former editor of *Trybuna Ludu*, could not be regarded as a liberal. On the other hand, it was sincerely determined to put an end to the 'Years of Stagnation'.

Shortly after the 1956 troubles, the British Ambassador in Warsaw drove down to Wrocław 'to see what sort of success the Poles are making of a formerly flourishing German city'. Sir Eric Berthoud was not the sharpest of diplomats and his report betrays no awareness of Wrocław's special difficulties. But it does reveal the very low starting point from which Wrocław's coming revival had to begin. 'Polish youth', Sir Eric observed, is 'anchorless and basically demoralised', 'strongly anti-Russian and a-moral' and 'allergic to Communist clichés'. He noted that a road accident, in which a Polish girl had been killed by a Soviet army truck, had almost sparked a riot. In his eyes, Wrocław presented 'a lamentable and depressing picture' and 'a general atmosphere of apathy, dirt and neglect'.[92]

In the 1960s therefore, Wrocław's economy was modernised and diversified. Pafawag, the largest employer, moved production from coal wagons to electric locomotives, and Dolmel specialised in generators for export. Consumer products appeared, notably motorcycles, fridges and washing machines from firms such as Predom and Polar. Jelcz buses, built on the site of the former Krupp 'Berthawerk' at Laskowice, appeared in 1954. In a town where many roads still needed rolling, the Fadroma factory came up with a world-famous road-roller. From 1959, the Elwro factory launched Poland's electronic industry in conjunction with the polytechnic.

In the same year, the Odra Dockyard (WPR) launched the first boat of a river fleet that would exploit the water link with Germany and would assume a dominant position in Poland's river trade. Overall, by the early 1970s, Wrocław was producing 2.8 per cent of Poland's GDP – a slice twice as large as its population actually justified. And the population was still growing. From 400,000 in 1958, it passed 600,000 in the late 1970s. By that time, Wrocław was ceasing to be Poland's 'Wild West'.

Once the German population had left, Wrocław's religious life was overwhelmingly dominated by the Roman Catholic Church and by Polish Catholic clergy. Most of the city's churches, which had been in Protestant hands since the Reformation, were restored to Catholic ownership. In the 1960s, when the reforms of the Second Vatican Council gave preference to services in the vernacular, the Polish character of Vratislavian Catholicism increased. What is more, the wholesale influx of Catholic Orders, both secular and monastic, caused a marked shift in the spiritual and intellectual climate of Catholic circles. The Dominican Order, for example, which had once played a very prominent role in city life but had been absent since 1810, regained St Wojciech's Church in 1957 and re-established an influential presence. Until 1989, it had to bear the indignity of living at an address in Feliks Dzerzhinsky Square. The Jesuits, the Franciscans, the Capuchins, the Salesians, the Bonifraters, the Ursulines and others also reappeared, though not the Benedictines or Premonstratensians.

Yet the Roman Catholics by no means enjoyed a monopoly. The Communist authorities were eager to promote any religious organisation that would undermine the people's traditional beliefs. They introduced the Polish-Catholic Church from America, which had broken with Rome, and fostered a split in the Roman ranks by sequestrating the 'Caritas' and 'Pax' organisations. In the 1950s, they regularly removed clergymen from the scene by conscripting them into the army. A representative of the Polish Evangelical-Lutheran Church reached Wrocław on 9 May 1945 in the company of Bolesław Drobner, and was given the former Calvinist Court Church, renamed the Church of Divine Providence. Another former Lutheran parish was re-established at St Christopher's for the Methodists, Adventists and various fundamentalist sects who had no previous links with the city, either among Germans or Poles. Orthodox Christians were catered for after 1963 when the former Church of St Ann became the autocephalous church of Sts Cyril, Methodius and Ann. (Greek-Catholics, who were quite numerous among repatriants to Wrocław, but who were regarded as traitors to Russian Orthodoxy, were not yet officially recognised. And a much-reduced Jewish community remained after 1968 around the White Stork Synagogue and community centre in Włodkowica Street.)

The Roman Catholic hierarchy faced constant official harassment and ill will when it tried to establish or extend educational or pastoral institutions. Permission was repeatedly refused to reopen the Theological Faculty at the university. In its place, Bishop Kominek opened the Polish Theological Society in 1957 and the Papal Theological Faculty in 1968. The latter was fully recognised by the Vatican, but not by the Polish authorities.

Perhaps in reaction to the sterility of the preceding years, Wrocław's cultural life burst into bloom in the late 1950s with remarkable energy, clocking up a number of world-famous achievements. The state controls were not lifted, but local party leaders exercised them with effective restraint. In film, for example, there was no native tradition. Yet there was plenty of space, and plenty of ruins for war-film sets. As a result, all the leading Polish film-makers came to Wrocław – among them Andrzej Wajda, Wojciech Has and Sylwestr Chęciński. Wajda's searing adaptation of Jerzy Andrzejewski's *Ashes and Diamonds* (1948), which explored the sensitive subject of post-war disillusionment and collaboration, was particularly well matched to Wrocław's own experience. Later, a sad tale was compounded by the death of the film's leading actor, Zbigniew Cybulski, in an accident at Wrocław Station.

Henry Tomaszewski's Pantomime Group had nothing whatsoever to do with the ruling party's cultural programme. Its avant-garde approach, combining classical subjects with totally original, silent interpretations, did not belong to any established genre. It started its career in November 1956 with productions of Hugo's *The Hunchback of Notre Dame* and Gogol's *The Overcoat*. From 1958, it set off to general acclaim on a series of Europewide tours, which culminated in a spectacular success at the Théâtre des Nations festival in Paris. The Paris of Jean-Louis Barrault was, in fact, its spiritual home.

Jerzy Grotowski's Laboratory Theatre, which had been operating since 1959 in Opole (Oppeln), came to Wrocław five years later at the invitation of the City Council. It was a tiny, elitist outfit presenting occasional, experimental productions to an absolutely minimal audience. Indeed, it only ever succeeded in launching three premières: *Książę Niezłomny* (The Fearless Prince, 1965), *Apocalypsis cum Figuris* (1968) and *Akropolis* (1969). Yet Grotowski's credo, as contained in *Towards a Poor Theatre* (1968), won him global recognition, putting him in the pantheon of Modern Theatre alongside Stanislavsky, Meyerhold and Brecht. 'The rhythm of life in modern civilisation', he wrote, 'is characterised by pace, tension, a feeling of doom, the wish to hide our personal motives and the assumption of a variety of roles and masks ... In our search for liberation, we reach biological chaos.'[93] Theatre, therefore, has 'a therapeutic function'. In an introduction for new actors, Grotowski outlined ten principles:

- The actor's performance, [which we call 'a total act'] . . . is an invitation to the spectator [and] could be compared to an act of genuine love between two human beings . . .
- Through shock, through the shudder which causes us to drop our daily masks and mannerisms, we are able, without hiding anything, to entrust ourselves to something we cannot name but in which live Eros and Caritas.
- Art cannot be bound by the laws of common morality or by any catechism . . . The actor must have the courage . . . to reveal himself.
- The director, whilst guiding and inspired by the actors, cannot dictate to them. It is a question of freedom, partnership, discipline and respect for the autonomy of others.
- A creative act of this quality is performed in a group, and therefore, within certain limits we should restrain our creative egoism.
- We must never privately exploit anything connected with the creative act.
- Order and harmony . . . are essential conditions without which a creative act cannot take place . . . We demand consistency . . .
- Creativity . . . is boundless sincerity, yet disciplined i.e. articulated through signs . . . For what we here call 'the method' is the very opposite of any sort of prescription.
- An actor should not try to acquire any sort of recipe or build up a 'box of tricks' . . . The centre of gravity in our work pushes the actor towards an inner ripening which expresses itself in a willingness to break through barriers, to search for 'a summit', for totality.
- There can be no total act if the actor dissipates his creative impulse, even away from the theatre . . . as a means of furthering his own career.[94]

The Laboratory Theatre closed in 1982. Grotowski left for the USA soon afterwards and died abroad in 1999.

Success bred success. In the 1960s, Wrocław built up an impressive range of cultural institutions – schools, higher academies, festivals of theatre, of opera and of music, museums and the monthly journal *Odra* (from 1961), which gained national standing. Seeing that it had declared an end to illiteracy in only the previous decade, this was no mean feat. In 1968, the poet, dramatist and novelist, Tadeusz Różewicz (b.1921) took up residence in Wrocław. He was to become one of its most respected figures. He well understood the echoes of the past:

Chciałem opisać
opadanie liści
w parku południowym

pięć białych łabędzi
stojących na zamglonym lustrze
wody . . .

myslałem o poetach
krainy środka
posiedli oni wiedzę
pisania doskonałych utworów
ale światło ich wierszy
dociera do mnie
po tysiącach lat

liść dotknął ziemi

zrozumiałem
płaczące obrazy
milczenie muzyki
tajemnicej okaleczonej poezji[95]

(I wished to describe
the falling of the leaves
in the South Park

five white swans
standing on the misted mirror
of the water . . .

I thought of the poets
of the middle land
they possessed the craft
of writing perfect compositions
but the light of their verses
is reaching me
after a thousand years

a leaf touched the earth

I understood
the weeping pictures
the silence of the music
the secret of crippled poetry)

His work inspired 'a letter from Breslau to Wrocław':

Lieber Tadeusz Różewicz, sie leben
in Wrocław, ich bin in Breslau geboren.
Die Samenflüge, die Flockenfälle,
die Jahreszeiten, die ehrwürdigen Steine
begegnen uns, den Passanten, freundlich.
Aber die Stadt nennt uns Kinder.

Ostrów Tumski erinnert mit Glocken
dass Codex Maioris Poloniae Deutschen
und Polen als Nächstverwandte beschworen.
Da sah ich die grausam verheerte Stadt
in neuer Würde, von Polen gerettet
aus den Trümmerwusten des Jahrhunderts.

Sei gegrüsst Wratislavia
und du, grausilberne Oder,
walderbesetzte Babuschka!
Sang mit dir deutsch und polnisch,
und träumte in deinen alten Geschichten
am Feuerchen unter der Eisenbahnbrücke . . .

Im Marmorschatten Wilhelms des Ersten
hab ich mein erstes Mädchen geküsst,
Elisa, sie schmeckte nach Veilchenpastillen.
Der Mond, irissilberne Säule, schwankte
im Stadtgrabendunkel. Der alte Preusse
ist abgewrackt. Der Kuss hat gehalten . . .

Lieber Tadeusz Różewicz, wir beide
sind Cives Wratislavienses, Gott will es.
Die Stadt hat uns beide in ihre Geschichte
genommen. Die heraklitische Oder
umfriedet Ihre und meine Jahre.
Wir müssen uns leiden. Oder wir sterben.[96]

(Dear Tadeusz Różewicz, you live
in Wrocław, I was born in Breslau.
The seeds float, the flake falls,
the seasons and the venerable stones
greet us, passers-by, in friendly fashion.
Yet the city calls us its children.

Ostrów Tumski reminds us by its bells
That Codex Maioris Poloniae conjures
Pole and German alike, as closest kindred.
There I saw the devastated city
in its new dignity, salvaged by the Poles

471

from the wreckage of this century.

Hail Vratislavia,
and you, silver-grey Oder,
beforested Babushka!
German and Polish I sang along with you
and dreamed amidst your old stories
by the fire under the railway bridge . . .

In the marble shadow of William the First
I stole my first kiss,
Elisa, she tasted of violet pastilles.
The moon, iris-silver pillar, quivered in the
darkness of the moat. The old Prussian
has gone for scrap. Yet the kiss still lingers . . .

Dear Tadeusz Różewicz, we are both
Cives Vratislaviensis, it's God's will.
The city has taken us both into her history.
The Heraclitic Oder enfolds your years
and mine alike. We must bear
with one another – or else we shall die.)

The poetic letter-writer was Heinz Winfried Sabais (1922–81).

In several fields, Wrocław's academic life gained considerable prestige. Most of the professors of Lwów's world-famous School of Mathematics, for example, had not survived – Stefan Banach died from a Nazi medical experiment – but there were enough of them left in Wrocław to preserve the tradition, among them Banach's partner, Professor Hugo Steinhaus (1887–1972). The botanist Professor Stanisław Tołpa (1901–96) was an equally popular and much-decorated figure. In the humanities, many potential talents were held back. Promotion depended on publishing and publication was subject to the dead hand of the Communist censors. Safety could most easily be found in harmless or obscure disciplines, such as seventeenth-century history, the field of Professor Władysław Czapliński (1905–81).

Lwów lived again in innumerable ways. One was in the tradition of publishing historical and geographical atlases. Another was in the music hall, where Wojciech 'The Count' Dzieduszycki (b.1912) burst on to the scene after 1956. An aristocrat from the East who had lost everything, he had trained before the war as a violinist and opera singer, and could turn his hand to the music hall with gusto. His revue *Dymek z papierosa* ('Cigarette Smoke'), with its inimitable mixture of humour, pre-war music and Lvovian dialect, was fêted both in the national media and abroad.[97]

Political relaxation bore fruit in many unexpected ways. Polish sport, for example, could not flourish so long as athletes were not permitted to travel freely. A young mountaineer from Wrocław, Wanda Rutkiewicz (née Błaszkiewicz, 1943–92), showed the way. A product of the local Climbers' Association, which practised in the peaks of the Sudety, she was able to move in the 1960s to the Alps and thence to the Himalayas, revealing a world-class talent. In 1973, she became the first woman to conquer the north face of the Eiger, and in 1978, the first European woman to reach the summit of Everest.

Once installed, Bishop Kominek proved a tower of strength both to the Church and to the wider community. Raised to the rank of archbishop and then cardinal, he was one of the authors of the famous open *Letter to the German Bishops* (1965), which sought not only to reconcile Poland with Germany, but also to persuade Poles to confess their own faults. 'We forgive, and we ask for forgiveness' was not a sentiment to endear him with the Communist authorities. For several years they prevented him from visiting Rome. He was certainly one of the principal figures who prepared the way for a change in German attitudes and for Chancellor Willy Brandt's historic visit to Poland in 1970. At the same time, the Bishop was firmly attached to Poland's claim to the 'Recovered Lands'. He persuaded the Vatican to accept Polish claims and published a book entitled *In the Service of the Western Territories* (1977).

Of course, the ruling party had good reason to treat Bishop Kominek with immense suspicion. Like the Polish Primate, Cardinal Wyszyński, and like Wyszyński's number two, Archbishop Karol Wojtyła of Cracow, Kominek had mastered the art of taking a principled stand against Communism without ever descending to the Communists' own language of deceit and invective. He accompanied the Primate to Rome in October 1970, on their key mission to persuade the Vatican to restore Poland's full diocesional structures. He was duly rewarded. In June 1972, the papal bull *Episcoporum Poloniae coetus* formally reorganised, among others, the metropolitan status and territory of the Archbishopric of Wrocław. In 1973, Pope Paul VI raised Archbishop Kominek to the College of Cardinals. Vratislavians heard the good news via Radio Free Europe. So, too, did the Archbishop's staff, who were thereby engaged in a desperate scramble to find the late Cardinal Bertram's biretta. Only when suitably attired could the recipient appear to accept the congratulations of the populace.

Cardinal Kominek had only one successor during the rest of the century. Appointed to the Archbishopric of Wrocław in 1976, Henryk Gulbinowicz (b.1928) proved to be a pastor of exceptional warmth and humanity. Born in distant Lithuania, he had lived under the shadow of Communism since childhood, and he behaved as if the whole great city was his chosen parish.

He, more than anyone, led his flock unerringly from the dark days of his early years to the quiet waters of the new millennium. He was raised to the cardinalcy in 1985. 'Wrocław', he once remarked, was a '*miejsce pojednania*' – 'a place of reconciliation'.

*

Unlike the city, the surrounding countryside did not enjoy a sense of revival. After 1956, Poland dropped compulsory collectivisation, but the farmers of Lower Silesia were still suffering from alienation and did not react with the same alacrity as elsewhere. In a town like Lubomierz (see above), the Party Secretary and his partner, the parish priest, were not unduly disturbed. The chronicle of their nefarious economic activities over a period of nearly thirty years speaks volumes about the scandalous impunity of officialdom that Communism encouraged. The corrupt comrade and the corrupt churchman kept regional dignitaries happy by organising luxurious hunting parties in the nearby forest. Reverend A quickly earned himself the unheard-of luxury of a VW Golf by fencing stolen goods and by specialising in the lucrative trade of pre-war German books. Comrade B set up a modern fish-shop on the market square, replete with white-aproned staff and an armoured cash-register. It failed miserably, through lack of cooperation with the adjacent food co-operative. The fish shop had a freezer, but no transport. The co-operative had a refrigerated truck, but no freezer. So no fish ever arrived. Yet Comrade B was unconcerned, since all his investments were state-funded. In any case, he had many other schemes up his sleeve:

> For instance, he apparently set up a pheasant farm, from which all the birds escaped. So he replaced the pheasants with Merino sheep, which had caught his attention during a trip to Bulgaria. However, this type of sheep did not wish to be acclimatised and all the animals perished . . . [Later], he was supposedly considering the establishment of a llama stud, since suitable conditions for it might have existed in the mountains. Fortunately, the political changes of the late 80s put an end to such joyful activities.[98]

Still more discreditable was an enterprise invented by the ever ingenious Secretary and his priestly partner in 1970–2. They systematically demol-ished the unused Lutheran cemetery, in order to sell off its valuable gravestones. When they had finished, they covered the former cemetery with an all-weather tennis court – all the more remarkable since no one in Lubomierz played tennis.

*

In the more relaxed atmosphere after 1956, German expellees began to trickle back to view their old homes. Many were confused and disoriented by the 'new' city before them. Many sought the landmarks of their youth, in vain. Henry Kamm, now Special Correspondent to the *New York Times*, visited on several occasions. In 1966, he was struck principally by the transformation of 'German Breslau' into 'a vigorously Polish city'. 'One city has died,' he wrote. 'In its place, and in its stones, there lives another.'[100] The nostalgia is strong. The Nos 9 and 16 trams 'still go to the stadium – Hermann Göring Stadium then, Olympic Stadium now.' In 1973, Kamm reported on the fragile remnants of Jewish life. He blamed 'the officially instigated nationwide outburst of anti-Semitism in the spring of 1968'. He noted anti-Semitic graffiti and anti-Semitic hooligans. He visited the neglected Jewish Cemetery on Legnica Street, which contained one remaining German war memorial – to perhaps 200 Jews 'who gave their lives for Germany in World War I'.[101] He did not notice that, while the Jewish Cemetery had been preserved, all the city's German cemeteries had disappeared.

Visitors from West Germany, who could not travel direct and who had no diplomatic representation in Poland, nonetheless came in ever-increasing numbers. They stayed in the Monopol, 'the only building to have kept its pre-war name'; they were puzzled by many things, not least the statue to 'Hr Fredro'; they approved of the restoration of the cathedral and the Rathaus; they disapproved of the uncleared rubble, the rude shop girls, the universal black market and the peasant carts on the streets. They were offended by the state of the cemeteries. They looked in vain for German signs, and sometimes – in typical pre-war fashion – they looked down on '*typische Ostpolen*'. With difficulty they sought out the few remaining Germans, not always with a friendly response. One such reporter, by now a Canadian citizen, Charles Wasserman, provoked a vigorous reply to his book from the local press. Another, August Scholtis, was considered more objective. Two themes recurred, neither of them to Wrocław's credit. Firstly, it was noted that similar wartime damage to West German cities had been cleared up long since. Secondly, after only cursory contact with the locals, it was realised how poorly Polish workers were remunerated. In 1957, a crane-driver clearing rubble in Wrocław asked a visitor from Tübingen how many months he must work in West Germany to earn the equivalent of a Volkswagen. The answer was ten. The crane-driver had to work for fifty-two. But then, there were no VWs for sale. On one thing the visitors were all agreed: they were seeing 'The German East'.[102]

For some, it was a taxing experience. The philosopher and anti-nuclear activist Günther Anders (1902–92) revisited the city of his birth in the summer of 1966. He was struck by the disturbing mixture of familiarity and profound otherness felt by many returning *Vertriebene*:

> Before I've even realised and before I've identified the street we're driving down or the area we're passing through, we're there ... Something appears before me, something very familiar: the silhouette of Cathedral Island with its many church spires ... But although familiar, something about the silhouette is not right ... From here, one would never have seen this complex of churches; between here and there, which is now empty or a mass of rubble, there had been suburbs which blocked the view. My God ... I can recognise the Church of St Elisabeth ... but I still can't find my way. After checking the map I realise that I've been going round in circles in exactly the same district that I used to hang about in almost every day between 1909 and 1915 ... [103]

The theatre director Peter Schumann (b.1935), who had started a new life in the USA, left Breslau as a nine-year-old boy in 1944 and returned forty-three years later with his Russian wife and his American daughter. He, too, had trouble getting his bearings:

> – Peter, do you recognise anything?
> – Nothing. Let's go to the railway station. I'll find my way from there. The station at Brochów is a pleasant, clean little building. Recently restored. It looks astonishingly bright in the gloomy November landscape.
> – It's not far from here, Peter says. Every afternoon I used to ride on a large bicycle to the station to meet my father, who commuted to the town by train. I could hardly reach the pedals. Father would greet me and then ride home on the bicycle with me running behind ...
> – Straight on, then right to the bottom of that little street between the avenue of high trees. They're chestnuts. Pity that you can't see them in springtime.
> At the end of their garden stood a number of dark, medium-sized villas, each slightly different.
> – Stop, it's here, Peter ordered, but our house has gone. There's another one standing in its place, for sure on our foundations.
> We left the car by a newly-built corner house with an ugly flat roof. Most of the old surrounding houses were intact.
> – Further down our neighbours kept a cat, which once robbed us of a grilled duck. And the owner of the house opposite hanged himself just before our departure. Our street was called *Parkstrasse*. We used to play 'Cowboys and Indians' in the nearby park. When our arrows got stuck in the branches, we used to shin up the trunks of the trees ...
> – What was it like living here? Elke asks.
> – It was so German and old-fashioned. Manicured gardens, polished

windows, clipped hedges. But not all that much has changed. In the house over there with the step roof, Kästner, the poet, lived – not the famous Kästner – but another one, whom the entire district was proud of, because he was our own . . .

Elke takes pictures. Peter by the fence. Peter under the chestnut. Further pictures next to the obelisk commemorating Soviet soldiers . . . Elke translates the tablet for her daughter, pronouncing the Russian words beautifully . . .

. . . The streets are empty. A few children play in the gardens. A couple of curious girls follow us to the edge of a wide open heath where Peter as a toddler had chased pheasants with his spear, and as a 9-year-old, had watched aeroplanes circling overhead as buildings near the station burned . . .

. . . Peter remembered nothing about the war except the fires and the constant anxiety about his father's coming home safely. But he remembers their flight perfectly. The train was overcrowded with refugees . . . They sat on their belongings piled to the ceilings. Father was supposed to take the family to an aunt in Hamburg and then return. But he never did . . . Their aunt was worried to death about a son who hadn't returned from the Front . . . and soon afterwards she killed herself . . .

We return. A cat jumps out of the hedge, blinks its eyes and watches us. 'Hey you – moggie!' Peter cries, 'What are your roots? Was it your great-granddad who stole that grilled duck from the Schumanns?'[104]

The year of 1968 is generally regarded as a year of disgrace in Poland. A feud within the ruling party spiralled out of control until it turned into a general attack, not only on the democratic opposition, but often on the country's few remaining Jews. The feud had broken out some years earlier between two extreme and opposite party factions, one fired by virulent nationalism, the other by its attachment to the discredited practices of Stalinism. The former group, known as 'the Partisans', was led by an ex-Ukrainian Communist called Denko, who had now been transformed into General Mieczysław Moczar, Minister of the Interior. The latter group, targeted by Moczar, centred round former employees of the disbanded Ministry of Security. It was dominated by ill-starred Communist agents who had largely been sent from Russia to Poland by Beria in 1944–5, and who included a disproportionate number of ex-Jews, also with changed names. Moczar made his bid for power in the wake of the Arab-Israeli War in 1967, of student protests and of the 'Prague Spring'. In the process, he unleashed a purge, that, though originally directed at his unrepentant Stalinist comrades, was soon affecting every Jewish person in the land – real or imagined, guilty or innocent. It was a witch-hunt. (Ironically, the one man it did not remove was Jakub Berman.) There was no overt violence. By mid-1968, Jewish families were being called in by Moczar's police and given one-way travel documents to leave the country. Poland's Jewish community shrank from about 30,000 to perhaps 5,000. Wrocław was no different from other Polish cities. The Vratislavian press joined in the 'anti-Zionist campaign', and the Jewish Theatre was sequestrated. But the purge did produce one creditable moment. Professor Edward Marczewski (1907–76) was a mathematician, sometime Rector and a former combatant of the Warsaw Rising. Originally called Szpilrajn, he was arbitrarily dismissed from the university, but as soon as the Moczarite faction had faded, he was awarded an honorary doctorate as a mark of his colleagues' esteem.

Official politics, however, carried on regardless. And two events that fleetingly put Wrocław in the world headlines amply illustrated the outlook of the Soviet Bloc. In September 1969, a colossal military parade was staged in Wrocław to mark the end of the Warsaw Pact manoeuvres codenamed 'Odra-Nysa 69'. Troops from the Soviet Union, Poland, Czechoslovakia and East Germany proudly demonstrated their gosling-steps before the pact's commander, Soviet Marshal Ivan Yakubovsky. In a speech at the Olympic Stadium, a member of the PZPR's Politburo made a fatuous statement about 'the time ripening for an all-European security system'. Anything further removed from reality would have been hard to invent. For the previous year those same Warsaw Pact troops had invaded Czechoslovakia in order to crush the 'Prague Spring' in the bud. And they were back a year later to ensure that the anniversary would not be exploited for any sort of independent demonstration. The crushing of Czechoslovakia had been justified on the totally false pretext that NATO had been planning an invasion of its own. As usual, Soviet-led aggression was wrapped up in a sickening package of 'peace-loving' verbiage. The idea that anyone in the free world could have felt any security in the company of such brutes and hypocrites was purely fanciful. It could only have been conceived by men who were blissfully unaware of the similarly hypocritical verbiage that had been spouted in the very same stadium just thirty years before.

Another stage-managed performance of breathtaking deceit was laid on in Wrocław on 10 October 1978 in the second so-called International Intellectuals' Conference. It was a deliberate attempt to rerun the farce of 1948 (see page 448), of whose true proceedings the delegates were kept entirely in the dark. This time, the chief host was none other than Józef Cyrankiewicz who had spent much of the preceding decades as Prime Minister of the People's Republic, but who was now presented in his latest guise as 'Chairman of the All-Poland Committee of Peace Defenders'. His chief partner was Ramesh Chandra, Chairman of the World Peace Council. What Cyrankiewicz really thought about his return to Wrocław, where he had betrayed the Polish Socialist movement in 1947, was not recorded. Nor can one say whether Chandra had any real knowledge of Cyrankiewicz. At all events, the delegates warmly applauded the speeches praising 'the struggle against all forms of repression and the fight against neo-colonial exploitation and racism'. They would never have guessed that many thoughtful Vratislavians considered themselves to be the victims of neo-colonial exploitation.

In the 1960s and 1970s, when the PRL was functioning with a modicum of success, Wrocław established itself as one of Poland's leading cities. For the first time since the war, it found a modest place in the higher politics of the ruling party. At one time, it was a place of exile for failed dignitaries banished from Warsaw. But it gradually emerged from the shadows. Among the party-sponsored representatives to the state Sejm, for example, Władysław Gomułka had been the only prominent name to appear on the Wrocław list in the immediate post-war years. (Tellingly, one of Gomułka's fellow deputies from Wrocław had been General Grokhov, alias Popławski.) But from 1957 to 1969, the Wrocław list improved. It included both Adam Rapacki, sometime POW, Foreign Minister and author of the Rapacki Plan, and Tadeusz Mazowiecki, a member of the non-party (but party-sponsored) Catholic Znak Group, who three decades later would emerge as Prime Minister. From 1972 to 1985, it was headed by General Wojciech Jaruzelski, the sometime powerful Secretary of the party's Military-Political Committee and chief link-man with the KGB, who in 1981 would emerge first as General Secretary and then as Poland's military dictator.[105]

*

There are several good reasons why the Solidarity movement was born in the former German city of Gdańsk rather than in the former German city of Wrocław. Wrocław did not possess the same overseas connections that existed in the Gdańsk shipyards, and it had not experienced the same traumas that had accompanied the bloody suppression of strikes in the Baltic cities in 1970. Minor disturbances occurred in 1968 and again in 1976, but the Party had little trouble in calling out its legions to protest against 'Zionists' and 'dissidents'. When the real testing time came in the summer of 1980, however, Wrocław stood shoulder to shoulder with Wałęsa's men in Gdańsk. Minor strikes had already occurred in Wrocław in July, directed against the food shortages and savage price rises that had not been seen since the Retail War of 1949. But on 26 August, at the VII Bus Depot on Grabiszyn Street, driver Tomasz Surowiec and mechanic Czesław Sławicki led the call 'to go out and stay out' until all the justified demands of the Gdańsk workers had been met. Within three days, a hundred strike committees in and around Wrocław had committed their support. A huge field Mass was celebrated at Grabiszyn (Gräbschen). Uncensored brochures proliferated. The authorities wavered; and in Gdańsk they capitulated. It was on the initiative of a delegate from Wrocław, the historian Dr Karol Modzelewski, that on 17 September the nationwide protest movement adopted the name of Solidarność (Solidarity).

In the sixteenth months during 1980–1, when Solidarity first operated legally, Wrocław was enthused by the spirit of liberty. The alliance between the intellectual and the proletarian wings of the movement was well matched, with dynamic committees dominating both the seats of higher learning and all the major factories. A quarter of a million Vratislavians joined, including 86 per cent of all employed people. So, too, did one-third of the PZPR's *actif*, thereby paralysing the local authority. Local leaders emerged: the twenty-six-year-old Władysław Frasyniuk, Jerzy Piórkowski, Piotr Bednarz, Józef Pinior, Marek Muszyński, Tomasz Wojcik, and Wrocław's first delegate to the All-Polish Solidarity Congress in Gdańsk, the historian Adolf Juzwenko. In a period of acute economic crisis, with queues and shortages on every hand, Solidarity became the universal social arbiter. Wrocław headed the Solidarity region of Lower Silesia. Marches and Masses were held to celebrate and to protest – not least against the assassination attempt on the Pope. But the bounds began to be felt. In October 1981, employees of the Fadroma works held a referendum and called for free elections to the Sejm and an end to the Party's constitutional 'leading role'. The chairman of the Solidarity committee in the factory was immediately arrested. The limits of official tolerance had been breached.

At dawn on Sunday, 13 December – as in all other Polish cities – tanks replaced the trams on Wrocław's streets. Around 400 Solidarity leaders were interned. The ZOMO security police devastated Solidarity's regional headquarters. A 'state of war' had been declared by General Jaruzelski, whose positions as Polish Premier and Party Secretary masked his more important role as a senior figure in Moscow's international network of military commissars. For three days, Jaruzelski's troops battered down the gates of resisting factories and clubbed the striking workers until they would sign 'statements of loyalty'. One young man died from such treatment in the polytechnic. A curfew descended amid the snow. But Frasyniuk and others had escaped the net and further resistance was prepared. The slogan circulated: 'The Winter is yours, the Spring will be ours!'

In these trying circumstances, a very heart-warming phenomenon arose. Thanks to the widespread admiration for Solidarity in Germany, many German towns and cities generously undertook to twin themselves unofficially with a partner in Poland. Moral support, expressions of sympathy and, in due course, food parcels and whole convoys of supplies flowed from west to east, strengthening the spontaneous links. German communes supported Polish communes; German churches helped Polish churches; German schools adopted Polish schools. Wrocław was adopted by Dortmund. Nothing could have done more for German-Polish rapprochement.[106]

From 1982 to 1989, Wrocław lived through the unreal world of confrontation between 'us' and 'them'. For a time, militancy prevailed. The militant offshoot 'Fighting Solidarity' came into the open. Violent clashes recurred on the 'Gaz-Platz' of Perec Square and the 'ZOMO-strasse' of Ulica Grabiszyńska. In 1983, the strikes subsided and martial law was suspended. But the Solidarity underground persevered in Wrocław, not least after the arrest and belated imprisonment of its fugitive leaders. Samizdat publishing flourished. The Church provided shelter for dissident voices. The local Party, shaken to its roots and shorn of its most energetic members, engaged in all the hopeless experiments of political and economic tinkering that would gradually convince the government in Warsaw that the Communist system had no future.

In July 1982, Pope John Paul II visited Wrocław during his second tour of Poland and celebrated an open-air Mass before 700,000 rapturous people in the Partynice hippodrome. The local Party department of ideology urged its agents to polemicise with the Pope's statements 'without mentioning names'.

In June 1985, the *Panorama Racławicka* was finally opened to the public in Wrocław after forty years of official chicanery. Mounted inside a purpose-built rotunda facing Tumski Island, the 116-metre canvas painted in 1893 by Wojciech Kossak portrayed Kościuszko's victory over the Russians at Racławice. Brought after the war from its original home in Lwów, it had been prepared for exhibition several times but always rejected. From the viewpoint of Communist politics, it was horribly incorrect.

At this juncture, the political impasse looked complete. Political arrests, sackings and verifications were the order of the day. The authorities had lost their authority. But the underground opposition had lost its will to oppose actively. It simply refused to approve Communist initiatives. After the 'amnesty' of 1984, the most prominent protest group, 'Freedom and Peace', staged Gandhi-like marches in front of Polish and Soviet barracks. After Chernobyl, it turned increasingly to ecological issues.

Yet in the autumn of 1987, there first appeared Wrocław's most original contribution to the popular cause – the Orange Alternative. In a city that already had a reputation for the Theatre of the Absurd, a doughty student of art history and self-styled 'Major', Waldemar Frydrych (b.1953), hit on the idea of undermining the dictatorial authorities by making them look ridiculous. He was the author of the choicely named *Manifesto of Socialist Surrealism* (1981) His first (illegal) 'happenings' filled the city centre with young people dressed as broken pots or garden gnomes. Another event had assistants handing out tiny samples of the most sought-after consumer item of the day – toilet paper. On Army Day, a line of floats appeared headed by a cloth tank marked 'Hitler Kaput', followed by a Battleship *Potemkin* and a troupe miming the storming of the Winter Palace – all under the slogan of 'The Warsaw Pact – Avant-Garde of Peace'. The police stations were filled with people dressed up as Soviet sailors or Red Cossacks. On St Nicholas's Day, the city was invaded by an army of Father Christmases. This time, the police stations filled up not just with red coats and reindeer, but with almost anyone dressed in red or carrying a sack. On the 'Day of the Child', thousands of people appeared wearing nappies. The end was truly nigh. Shortly afterwards, the Regional Committee of Solidarity, headed by a newly released Frasyniuk, began to operate once again in the open.

In 1987, Wrocław also learned of the beatification of its first modern candidate for sainthood – St Teresa Benedicta of the Cross. This, too, was a sign of the times. For forty years, Communist propaganda had endeavoured to conceal the Jewish element in Poland's wartime suffering. Edith Stein was regarded as a figure who could reconcile Catholic and Jewish memories (see page 351.)[107]

The parliamentary elections of 4 June 1989 were viewed in Wrocław as a straightforward contest between the *nomenklatura* list of the ruling Party and the Citizens Committee (WKO) of Dr Adolf Juzwenko. In every seat that was open to a free vote, all the WKO candidates won hands-down. Figures such as Barbara Labuda and Radosław Gawlik, who until recently had been fugitives, were to be Wrocław's representatives in parliament. Roman Duda, who had recently been fired as the university's Dean of Mathematics, and Karol Modzelewski, were to be Wrocław's senators. They went to join a Sejm that was to appoint the Soviet Bloc's first non-party Prime Minister and, with some delay, to insist on free presidential elections. When Lech Wałęsa finally emerged in November 1990 as Poland's first legitimately elected President since 1939, Poland and Wrocław could rightly feel that liberation had finally arrived.

*

During the forty years that separated the post-war resettlement campaigns from the fall of the Iron Curtain, the former German expellees and Polish repatriants were doubly or trebly alienated. With very few exceptions, they never returned to their old homes. Yet they were inevitably treated as foreigners and intruders as they struggled to build a new life in a new environment. If only they could have seen it, the destitute Breslauers who arrived in a war-torn Essen or Hamburg had to undergo the same heavy experiences that awaited the destitute *Kresowcy*, or 'Eastern Borderers', who arrived in war-torn Wrocław. They were a recognisable minority with their own sorrows, their own needs and their own accents; and they were not always welcome. Their children grew up in completely new surroundings, with new friends, new attitudes and new allegiances, which as often as not created barriers between them and their parents.

In post-war West Germany, the *Vertriebenenverbände*, or organisations of expellees, were swift to establish themselves. Many groups formed around the churches, as mutual aid societies or as a political lobby for the rights of those dispossessed by the loss of the eastern territories. Though banned in the GDR, they represented a powerful influence in West German politics. A ministry for *Vertriebene* was established under Chancellor Adenauer and the voice of the *Landsmannschaften*, like that of Herbert Hupka of Silesia, was commonly heard in the German media. The *Bundesvereinigung der Breslauer* was founded in 1953 as a subdivision of the larger *Landsmannschaft Schlesien*. Officially, the *Vertriebenenverbände* limited their activities to the cultural sphere. In this, they were aided by a system of patronage agreements, through which, for example, Cologne became a patron city of Breslau and Lower Saxony the patron of Silesia. They thereby secured the chance to preserve the cultural heritage of the lands lost in 1945. But their lot was not a happy one. Although their charter spoke of the establishment of a free and united Europe and of an end to the cycle of revenge, many expellees understandably continued to harbour hopes of a restoration of former German property in the East and of a revision of the Oder–Neisse frontier. They perceived themselves as the only Germans to have atoned for the crimes of Hitler, yet they were increasingly viewed by the rest of German society as backward-looking, even crypto-Fascist. Such frustrations were compounded by a feeling of dislocation, which often permeated even the younger generation. The singer/songwriter Heinz-Rudolf Kunze put their feelings to music:

> Ich wurde geboren in einer Baracke
> Im Flüchtlingslager Espelkamp,
> Ich wurde gezeugt an der Oder–Neisse Grenze,
> Ich hab nie kapiert, woher ich stamm.[108]

> (I was born in a barrack-block
> In the refugee huts at 'Espelkamp',
> I was conceived on the Oder–Neisse line,
> I've never understood where I come from.)

By the early 1970s, with their numbers in decline, the *Vertriebene* were on the wane. Through the introduction of Willy Brandt's *Ostpolitik*, they were actively sidelined. Almost at a stroke the Oder–Neisse line was recognised, the ministry for *Vertriebene* was dissolved and dialogue with the expellees was replaced by direct dialogue with Poland. Yet the expellees could still make the news. In 1985, the annual meeting of the *Landsmannschaft Schlesien* hit the headlines with its controversial choice of motto – '*Schlesien bleibt unser!*' ('Silesia still belongs to us'). Its Chairman, Herbert Hupka, offended Polish sensitivities by paraphrasing their national anthem with the slogan: '*Noch ist Schlesien nicht verloren, solange wir leben . . .*' ('Silesia has not perished yet, so long as we still live . . .'). Another *Vertriebene* spokesman proclaimed, 'I would rather have a fourth or fifth partition of Poland than [accept] that Breslau will stay Polish for ever.'[109]

Yet, with the reunification of Germany and the emergence of a democratic Poland, the 'hawks' have mellowed and the 'doves' have been given their day. Indeed, even the hawks became distinctly dovish. At the annual meeting of the *Landsmannschaft Schlesien* in Nuremberg in July 2000, 100,000 former Silesians heard the same Herbert Hupka, now an honorary citizen of his home town of Racibórz, call for the introduction of bilingual road signs and intensified German teaching in ethnically mixed districts of Silesia. Cultural and educational exchanges have largely replaced the trading of insults, and a few individuals have ventured back to repair their dilapidated estates and 'do their duty'.[110]

Over half a century after their expulsion, the connection to 'home', or *Heimat*, was still a strong one. The *Bundesvereinigung der Breslauer*, based in Bonn, had some 6,000 members and maintained the *Breslauer Sammlung* archive in Cologne. The newspaper *Der Schlesier – Breslauer Nachrichten* had a circulation of around 18,000, of which some 500 readers belonged to the various Silesian clubs in the USA and Canada.

Jews also felt the pull of the old city. The largest of their organisations was the 1,200-strong *Verband ehemaliger Breslauer in Israel*, or the 'Association of Former Breslauers in Israel', run by Moshe Goldstein in Tel Aviv. A sister organisation existed in London in the 'Association of Jewish ex-Berliners and ex-Breslauers'. Best known among them was the cellist Anita Lasker-Wallfisch (b.1926), a survivor of Auschwitz and Bergen-Belsen and a founder member of the English Chamber Orchestra.[111]

Former Breslauers, who for fifty years gained great comfort from their associations and from their associations' publications, might have spared a thought for their counterparts in Wrocław, who enjoyed no such luxury. While the *Vertriebene* in West Germany were free to organise, protest and publish, those in post-war Poland were not. The remnant of German

Breslauers who contrived to remain behind formed a *Deutsche Sozial-Kulturelle Gesellschaft* (DSKG) as early as 1957, with the primary aim of preserving the German language and culture. For a time they enjoyed the patronage of the GDR, but life caught between the rock of apathy and the hard place of political hostility was difficult. Only in 1991 did their fortunes improve. Now the largest of the German societies in Lower Silesia, the DSKG has more than 1,000 members and runs a lively cultural and educational programme.

For the *Kresowcy* life in post-war Poland was no easier. There was no such thing as an 'Association of Repatriants', let alone a *Landsmannschaft* of Galicia or a *Vereinigung der Lemberger*. Such things were simply not permitted. There were plenty of candidates in Wrocław who would willingly have spoken up for Lwów as Herbert Hupka spoke up for Breslau. But they were forced to keep their mouths shut on pain of imprisonment, or, in the early 1950s, of worse. If they wanted, as they so passionately did, to sit together and to talk of 'the good old times in the East', they could do so only in small groups and in private. They could hold no rallies. They had no access to radio and television. And they had no voice in local or national politics. The Society of Lovers of Lwów and of the South-East Borders (TML), which was founded in Wrocław in 1989, could not have been formed earlier. Its journal was entitled *Semper Fidelis*.

In this connection, homage should be paid to the heroic individuals who defied the threat of repression and kept the candle of memory burning. One story must suffice. Roman Aftanazy (b.1914) had worked as a young man in Lwów, in the Ossolineum. His hobby at that time was photography; and he spent his vacations cycling round the country roads of Galicia and Volhynia and taking pictures of the great aristocratic palaces and gentry houses of the region. It was a perfectly normal thing to do. Yet when he arrived in Wrocław as a 'repatriant' in 1946, Aftanazy realised that his collection of pre-war pictures was virtually unique. So he devoted the rest of his working life to expanding and completing it. Much of the art and architecture that he had recorded in the 1930s had been destroyed during the war. And the Soviet authorities were de-Polonising their 'Recovered Territories' with the same ruthless philistinism that the Polish Communists used to de-German-ise theirs. Wherever Polish castles and palaces were still standing east of the Bug, their fabric had been vandalised, their contents stripped and their inhabitants expelled. And no one could protest. Yet Roman Aftanazy had the iron will to pull triumph from disaster. For forty years, while continuing his work as a harmless-looking archivist, he systematically garnered every surviving picture and every piece of relevant information. He wrote more than 40,000 letters – that is, three per day for four decades – contacting every surviving resident or owner and compiling a card-index of similar proportions. His life's work was ready for publication as soon as Communism collapsed. His astonishing fourteen-volume, lavishly illustrated work, *Dziejów rezydencji na dawnych kresach Rzeczypospolitej* (The History of the Great Houses in the Former Borderlands of the Polish Commonwealth, 1991–7)[112] has won him many prizes. And quite rightly so. No one has done more, or against greater odds, to preserve the memory of his eastern *Heimat*.

In those same decades, former Breslauers were making their way in the world; and some were becoming famous. An exceptional number were academics. Ernst Alfred Cassirer (1874–1945), for instance, was a distinguished philosopher who had left Breslau as a boy. A Jewish refugee who fled to an unwelcoming Oxford and then to Columbia (New York), he applied neo-Kantian criticism to a wide range of subjects. His first major work, the *Philosophie der symbolischen Formen* (1928–9) appeared during his stay in Hamburg. His last one, *The Myth of the State* (1946), was published posthumously.

Norbert Elias (1897–1990), one of the pioneers of historical sociology, stayed long enough in his native Breslau to complete both his schooling and his medical studies. Driven out of Germany, like Cassirer, by the Nazis, he had the misfortune to publish his masterwork *Über den Prozess der Zivilisation* (1939) in German and in an obscure Swiss edition, at the very outbreak of war. As a result, he did not gain his academic post in England until he was near retiring age, and did not gain worldwide recognition until his prolific retirement. He is considered the founder of 'Figurational Studies'. As befits an exile and a sociologist, the established anthology of his works is prefaced by his own verse:

> How strange these people are
> How strange I am
> How strange we are.[113]

Contrary to rumour, however, at the turn of the millennium not all ex-Breslauer academics were dead. Dr Joachim Meisner (b.1933) was Archbishop of Cologne. Dr Heinz Wolfgang Arndt (b.1915) was Professor Emeritus of Economics at the ANU in Canberra. Walter Laqueur (b.1921) was one of the leading lights of contemporary history, unusual in the USA for being as principled in his abhorrence of Communism as of Fascism. Laqueur's authorship list was running to eighty-one titles in his eighty-first year. They ranged from *Communism and Nationalism in the Middle East* (1956) and *A History of Zionism* (1972) to *Fascism: A Reader's Guide* (1976), *The Political Psychology of Appeasement* (1980) and, also on the Soviet

Union, *The Dream that Failed* (1994). His most popular work, which has been repeatedly updated, was *Europe since 1945*.

Fritz Stern (b.1926), Professor at Columbia – whose godfather is stated to have been the Vratislavian chemist Fritz Haber – has stayed with German history. He started with *The Politics of Cultural Despair* (1961), continued, on Bismarck, with *Gold and Iron* (1977), and followed up with *Dreams and Delusions: The Drama of German History* (1987). This last contains more than one memorable paragraph:

> National Socialism needs to be remembered – and not only in scholarly monographs or trashy films – but in the moral consciousness of all of us. There is an appropriate epitaph for it, as for the Stalinism which evoked Nadezhda Mandelstam's outcry: 'Silence is the real crime against humanity.'[114]

Oddly enough, the index of *Dreams and Delusions* does not carry a single entry for 'Breslau'. But it is hard to believe that Stern's work, like that of Laqueur, does not carry Breslau between every line on every page.

Reinhard Selten (b.1930) left Breslau as a schoolboy. Forty years later he was Professor of Economics at the University of Bonn. In 1994, he was a co-laureate of a Nobel Prize in recognition of his work on 'the analysis of equilibria in the theory of non-cooperative games'.

Ewa Stachniak (b.1952) belonged to a Vratislavian generation that had not been born when the German Breslauers left. She studied English at Wrocław before emigrating to Canada in the early 1980s. Like many others who chose to leave Poland during the Solidarity era, she had a strong sense of guilt. It was like jumping ship when one ought to have been helping the hard-pressed crew. Her first novel, *Necessary Lies* (2000), centres on the mental processes of emigration. It starts with the words 'Peter would have said that she had betrayed Poland.' Peter is the child of a German woman who walked out of Nazi-ruled Breslau in 1945. Anna, the heroine, with whom he falls in love, is a Polish girl who (like the author) walked out of Communist-ruled Wrocław. The main theme is forgiveness:

> My novel is not a prescription for forgiveness, but an attempt to define what can be forgiven and what one can only try to forget . . . One of the characters, Peter's mother, chooses the path of silence in order to avoid lying about the past and to protect her son from her experiences. I think that Anna is seeking a position where forgiveness is possible, whilst also stating convincingly that such a position may prove impossible to attain.[115]

Not everyone with Vratislavian connections, however, was well informed of their origins. Mark Burdajewicz (b.1938), for example, an engineer who was brought up in the Poznań region, emigrated to Australia in 1967 and became a prominent figure in Polish Australian circles. His father had told him 'fantastic fables' about 'somebody from my family who had gone to the most distant country in the world, long, long ago'. But Mark never thought he would be able to, check them, because all contact with his family had been lost during the war. So he did nothing until Australia was celebrating its bicentenary and lots of people were tracing their ancestors. He advertised in all the major Australian newspapers and immediately received two relevant replies. His father had *not* been fantasising. Franciszka Balbina Burdajewicz (1814–1902), a Roman Catholic girl from Leszno, had married Johann Gottfried Kühnel (1814–1902), a Lutheran from Breslau, in about 1840 and, possibly for religious reasons, they had decided to leave Silesia. They sailed from Bremerhaven in June 1846 on the *Paulina*, arriving in Port Adelaide on 27 September after a voyage of fifteen weeks. They had five children in addition to the son who had travelled with them, and twenty grandchildren. Their youngest son, William, founded a thriving piano and organ business in Rundle Street, Adelaide, and was sufficiently prosperous to have taken a display to the Berlin Exhibition of 1900. Ninety years later, the Kühnels' descendants had only the vaguest notion of their common ancestors. 'One lady told us', Mark noted, 'that she always knew that Balbina was Polish or from some other North European country, because she had inherited her grandmother's beautiful complexion'.[116]

*

Ten years is not much time in which to recover from six decades of war, dictatorship and neglect. Common sense suggests that it could take as long to repair the ravages of Communism as it took to inflict them.

In the initial transition from Communism to democracy, Wrocław passed through the same ambiguous phase as Poland as a whole. Just as Mazowiecki's Solidarity government was installed in Warsaw in 1989, while overall control was maintained by institutions subject to General Jaruzelski's Presidency, so the top offices of local government in Wrocław passed into Solidarity hands in 1990, *before* the Communist Party had abandoned its hold on other parts of the machine. The local elections of June 1990 brought a second clean sweep of the broom. Solidarity candidates again swept the board. The newly elected Chairman of the City Council described the state of the city as 'bad'. The new President of the city, Bogdan Zdrojewski (b.1957), used the adjective 'tragic'. At any earlier point during the PRL, such officials would have been drawn from a closed party-run list, and would have been subordinated to the local PZPR hierarchy. Indeed, the last Secretary of the PZPR in Wrocław, B. Kędzia, hung on to office into 1990, though his voice no longer counted. Nonetheless, one cannot say that the new order had fully emerged until the PZPR had completely closed down. In Warsaw, General Jaruzelski clung to the Presidency until November 1990. In Wrocław, the historic day came in January when, like rats leaving the sinking ship, the comrades packed up their belongings in the Party House and left. (The Party House, for which the party had no title deeds, became a university building.) After that, Bogdan Zdrojewski, the city's Chief Executive, had an open road before him. Twice re-elected, he was to dominate local politics until the start of the new millennium. He was the chief 'mover and shaker' of liberated Wrocław.

The new order called for two fundamental changes – the establishment of a free-market economy, and the creation not just of democratic institutions but of a democratically minded civic society to run them. Wrocław, though deep in the doldrums, was less inhibited in these tasks than many other cities moulded by the Communist system. For one thing, it was not too constrained by the dinosaurs of heavy industry, possessing a broad range of more modern enterprises that could justify accelerated investment. For another, as had been shown by the remarkable resilience of Wrocław Solidarity, it possessed that most valuable of commodities: a young, dynamic and skilled population that was not unduly burdened by the old official culture. Also, being located close to both the Czech Republic and to the newly reunited Germany, it enjoyed the prospect of playing its part in the growth of a heretofore underdeveloped European region. Sooner or later, the proximity to liberated Prague and liberated Berlin would reap vital and unforeseen dividends.

Economic recovery depended partly on local initiative, especially in the modernisation of a dilapidated infrastructure, and partly on attracting foreign investment. An important advance was made with the balancing of the city's budget, which, after the chaos of hyperinflation and financial restructuring in 1991–2, fell largely under the city's own control. A measure of discipline and self-help was generated by the fact that the proportion of income derived from state funds remained disproportionately low.

The break-up of Solidarity after the collapse of Communism was unavoidable. A movement designed to oppose a totalitarian regime could not forego the necessary fragmentation of competing interests that normal democratic life requires. It was a painful lesson. In Wrocław, the usual proliferation of ephemeral groupings could be observed in such groups as Frasyniuk's ROAD (which merged with the Freedom Union) and the Freedom Party (which derived from 'Fighting Solidarity'). One part of Solidarity reverted to being purely a trade-union organisation, while most of its former supporters went their different ways. As elsewhere, the splintering and fusing slowed after two or three years. But the right wing remained divided until the appearance of the Solidarity Electoral Alliance (AWS) in 1997. Meanwhile, the left-of-centre SLD made strides under the guidance of semi-reconstructed ex-Communists.

Important symbolic changes were made. Already in June 1990, the municipal coat of arms was returned to the form once granted to the city by the Emperor Charles V. A street-name commission set to work once again, abolishing the names of Soviet dignitaries or Communist nonentities and replacing them with the previously forbidden names of Piłsudski, Dmowski, Anders, Okulicki and 'the Eaglets of Lwów'.

Long-forgotten memorials began to appear as soon as Communist censorship collapsed. The west wall of St Elizabeth's Church was a favourite site for such memorial tablets, all of which were dedicated – either individually or collectively – to people murdered by the Soviet or Polish Communist authorities:

- to 'the "Jaworniacy", youthful victims of Stalinist Terror, 1944–56'
- to 'soldiers and miners, tortured and killed, 1949–59'
- to the 'Grey Ranks' (Boy Scouts), killed and tortured 1939–56
- to 'Poles: murdered and tortured in Wrocław, 1945–56'
- to 'Home Army and WiN, 27.IX.48' victims
- to the Peasant Battalions, 1940–56
- to the Polish Forces in the West
- to 'the National Armed Forces (NSZ): victims of two occupations'
- to the Soldiers of the Underground Resistance and Prisoners of the Communist regime
- to Maciej Kalenkiewicz-Kotowicz: last OC, AK Nowogródek
- to Aleksander Krzyżanowski (1895–1951): last OC, AK Wilno

A specially unpleasant problem arose with regard to the Osobowicki Cemetery. The unmarked 'prison plots' of people executed in the 1940s and 1950s for political offences had been laid out in close proximity to the *Aleje Zasłużonych*, or 'Comrades' Row', reserved for deceased party dignitaries. Thanks to the sympathy of cemetery staff, relatives of the executed 'politicals' knew where the graves of their loved ones lay. But they had been helpless when, late in the 1980s, the prison plots were unceremoniously bulldozed to make way for an extension of Comrades' Row. The Communists were as dismissive of the dead as they were of the living.

Another problem arose over a monument set up by the Odra to the memory of Poles murdered by 'Ukrainian Nationalists' during the war. The monument was thought by some to bear a tasteless inscription and did not have official permission to be erected. It still stands, albeit with crudely erased wording.

Liberated Poland took exceptional interest in the neglected areas of its history. In Wrocław, which had special ties to the eastern borders, much of that interest was directed to a re-examination of Poland's mournful relations with Russia and the Soviet Union. But there was also concern for a more open approach to Silesia's multinational past, to the catastrophes of Communism and to the sensitive questions of the city's German and Jewish legacies. In one of the few articles where Wrocław made the front page of the *New York Times*, historical revision was the focus. 'We have turned 180 degrees,' commented one informed Vratislavian. 'There is no more schizophrenia. We can research and present the true history of Breslau . . . No history was free, but in contemporary history there was direct Party interference . . . either pure and simple lies, or pure and simple silence.'[117]

Several local institutions took an energetic lead. The Museum of History, whose director, Dr Maciej Łagiewski, had been very active in the German and Jewish fields,[118] stood at the forefront of the new approach. The university's historians were energetically exploring and analysing the records of blank spots in the city's history, notably in the post-war and Stalinist periods.[119] They were preparing a full-scale survey of the university's own magnificent, but largely non-Polish, history. The Ossolineum Institute launched a new journal devoted to local history, the *Rocznik Wrocławski*.[120] The city's leading publisher, the Dolnośląskie, promoted a number of colourful books of a type that had been sorely missed earlier. They included a complete historical guidebook, an excellent tourist guide,[121] a high-class survey of the city's past from the earliest times to 1997 and the *Encyclopedia Wrocławia* (2000).[122] 'We wished to present Wrocław', declared the authors of the survey, 'as the common heritage of those who co-created its cultural, economic and political fabric.'[123] Amen.

In this regard, the collapse of Communism removed yet another barrier that had long separated Poland from Czechoslovakia. The closure of the frontier in 1968 along the Sudety mountains had been the latest in a long series of events that kept Poles and Czechs apart, self-absorbed in their separate cages. The Czech writer Vladimiř Macura (1945–99) made a conscious effort to bridge the gap. He launched a cycle of five 'Silesian' novels, all set in the Čelakovský circle in mid-nineteenth-century Breslau. The first novel, *Informátor* (1993), was followed by *Komandant* (1994) and *Guvernantka* (1997). Interviewed by a Polish critic, Macura explained that the historical setting was 'secondary'. Breslau's 'Springtime of Nations' in 1848 was being used as a semi-fictional substitute for the Prague Spring of 1968: 'We ourselves are the historical figures in my novels.' Yet he was well aware of the isolation that the Iron Curtain had encouraged, not least between neighbours within the Soviet Bloc. 'In former times', he remarked, 'Prague was closer to Vienna than Wrocław.'[124] A passage in *Guvernantka* makes the point more explicitly.

> We travel through the open fields, among the hot blackened stubble still smelling of the harvested corn. I look through the carriage window at Vratislav, anchored behind us like a great ship with billowing sails. We walk round the lake in the park, where the swans are swimming as they do in the city moat . . . From the mound of the summerhouse, we look towards Bohemia. It's clear; and we can make out the silhouette of the mountains. As always, we wonder if Bohemia lies on the other side. But we're afraid to ask. They would tell us 'No!', that the land of the Czechs is much, much further away.[125]

Nothing served to remind Vratislavians more of the unsettled historical scores than the constant stream of press articles on subjects from which they had long been protected. Claims for the return of art treasures carried off by the Communist authorities for the benefit of Warsaw's museums enjoyed general approval. They concerned, among many other items, the fifteenth-century Wartenburg Triptych, taken from the cathedral, and decorated medieval shields made for the municipal guard.[126] Claims for the return of property once belonging to Jews, in contrast, could easily cause bewilderment. After all, the majority of Vratislavians were the descendants of people who themselves had lost virtually everything during the war; and they had no hope whatsoever of recovering their property. Yet Peter Koppenheim (b. 1931) of Manchester was not deterred. His family mansion in Breslau was lost in February 1939 when he and his relatives fled Germany after being terrorised by the Gestapo. According to the account that he obtained from a Wrocław taxi-driver, it was destroyed by the Russians in 1945. So Koppenheim was now pressing a multimillion-pound claim against the present Polish government, which, he was reported as saying, 'for 54 years' had pursued 'a policy of ethnic cleansing . . . and the murder of thousands of Polish Jews'.[127]

No less disturbing, and somewhat more realistic, were calls for a re-examination of consciences over Polish-German relations in general and the post-war expulsion of innocent Germans in particular. This was an episode that was ordered by a joint decision of the Allied Powers (see page 412), but which was executed by the Communist authorities and by large numbers of Polish civilians.[128] As it happened, it was Krzyżowa (Kreisau) near Wrocław, the former mansion of the von Moltke family and scene of the plot to kill Hitler (see page 402), which was chosen in November 1989 for the meeting of symbolic reconciliation between Prime Minister Mazowiecki and Chancellor Kohl (the meeting being interrupted by news from Berlin of the fall of the Wall). At the time, Krzyżowa housed a derelict collective farm (PGR). Soon afterwards, handsomely rebuilt, it became a residential youth centre for the propagation of international understanding.[129]

A small bone of Polish-German contention which emerged in 1992, but which was not resolved, concerned a historical document more than 700 years old. The State Department in Washington DC had revealed that a 'Vellum' donated to the Library of Congress by a US veteran sometime after 1945 had been identified as a bull of Bishop Anselm, originating from St Vincent's Monastery in Wrotizla. Dated 19 May 1263, the document records a papal grant of forty days' indulgence to the Monastery's guests. At first, American officials misattributed it to 'Bratislava'. But now they intended its return to its rightful owners. But who *were* the owners? Polish archivists, citing the principle of archival territoriality, argued for the Vellum's return to Wrocław. They were able to point out with some force that in 1263 Wrotizla had been in Poland. German regulations, in contrast, supported the claim of the Prussian Cultural Heritage Foundation in Berlin. Stalemate ensued.

An important step at this time was the change in status of the Ossolineum, from being state-dependent to a legally independent foundation. Not everyone grasped the significance. Nor did they all approve when the Ossolineum's director dared to purchase the manuscript of *Pan Tadeusz*, which had been on deposit in the institute for more than a hundred years. To minds formed under the old regime, everything belongs to everyone (especially to the Party) and nothing belongs to anybody. In reality, in the new law-based society, the heirs of the family who had made the original deposit had every right to question the use of their property and a settlement was necessary. In any case, it was important to show that cultural institutions need not share the immobile mentality that characterises state bureaucracy. The Ossolineum had been in state hands for more than half a century. When still in Lwów, it had been confiscated in 1940 by the Soviet authorities and transferred to the Academy of Sciences of the Ukrainian SSR. Its director at that time was Jerzy Borejsza (alias Goldberg, 1905–52), who was to become post-war Poland's chief Communist ideologist and who was the brother of Jacek Różański, Berman's future deputy at the UBP. During and immediately after the war, its priceless collections were plundered, both by the Nazis and by the Soviets. As a result, barely 30 per cent of the pre-war holdings were transferred to Poland in 1946, when the collection was divided and one part of it relocated in Wrocław (see p. 429). The lion's share, including the institute's archives, remained in Ukraine.[130]

It was a nice irony that the Ossolineum's first director under the democratic system, Dr Adolf Juzwenko (b.1939), came to Wrocław as a 'repatriant' refugee from the lands which Borejsza's circle had striven to hand to the Soviet Union for ever.

The Jewish community in Wrocław revived. It was a bare shadow of its former self, but numbers rose from a mere forty in 1993 to about 200 by the end of the century. A youth group appeared and the Stork Synagogue underwent lengthy restoration. The district around Włodkowica Street, which also contained Protestant and Orthodox churches, was declared a Zone of Tolerance.[131]

A comprehensive plan for urban development was drawn up in 1990. It was given a good start by the rapid completion of several existing large-scale building projects using the so-called *plomby* or 'tooth-filling' method, which avoided major demolition work. It included a general reorganisation of commercial structures, a thorough repair of the antiquated road system and, at long last, the final stage of reconstruction and refurbishment in the city centre. The commercial restructuring involved the separation of wholesale and retail markets, the abolition of the 'Goliath', a giant bazaar in a circus tent on Grunwald Square, the licensing of numerous small private and specialised shops and the first generation of out-of-town hypermarkets – 'Marino', 'Hit' and 'Billa'. The reordering of the roads and communications started with an in-depth repair of water, gas, electric and drainage facilities and resurfacing work; and it looked forward to the activisation of a motorway network that had been first envisioned in the 1930s. The refurbishment of the city centre focused on the complete recobbling of Main Square and the careful renovation of all its unrestored or half-restored buildings. By the late 1990s, Wrocław could look forward to having a finely finished hub, which had taken fifty years to complete, but which had avoided the overhasty modernisation of many of its counterparts in Germany. The city could now provide a spacious, graceful and lively focus for municipal life, and could present itself as a fitting partner for Cracow and Prague on the grand tour of Central Europe.

The year following Chancellor Kohl's visit to Krzyżowa, the German Federal Republic finally recognised the Oder–Neisse frontier *de iure*, which thereby guaranteed Wrocław's permanent legal inclusion in Poland. The long-postponed decision had been made a condition of the USA's formal acceptance of a united Germany and was widely attributed to the influence of the US presidential adviser on Polish affairs, Jan Nowak-Jeziorański (b. 1913). A war hero and sometime director of Radio Free Europe, Nowak had close ties with Wrocław. He was a member of the Ossolineum's board of governors, and was the only person ever to receive both an honorary degree at the university and honorary citizenship.

In 1993, Wrocław's freedom and security were further bolstered by the evacuation of the former Soviet Army command base in Legnica. The vast garrison of the base, which was the outward sign of Poland's dependence and the watchdog of the still-larger garrison in East Germany, had been set up on Stalin's orders in 1945. For nearly half a century it had thrown a shadow over the whole province, reminding people of Soviet domination, failing to fraternise with the local population and casting the Polish troops of the Silesian Military Region into the role of auxiliaries. Over the decades, the base had welcomed successive political masters from Brezhnev to Gorbachev, and from time to time, such as in 1969, it had staged some impressive shows of strength. But with the death of the Soviet Union, it became redundant. For a year or two, the soldiers of what had now become the Russian Army kicked their heels, stole cars, took menial jobs and waited to go home. Then they left. They packed their own equipment, and any items of domestic furnishing that they could strip, hack off or unscrew. They left Legnica an ecological disaster area. Few people in Silesia shed tears at their departure.

Wrocław had a long tradition of music festivals. But in 1991, a new type of initiative emerged, first in Brzeg (Brieg) and then in Wrocław and other Silesian cities. Supported by a foundation called 'Our Silesia – Our Europe', the International Silesian Music Festival was specifically designed to create 'bridges of understanding' between the nations of Central Europe. It took the title *Porozumienie – Verständigung*, or 'Understanding'. Its chief patron, a native of Brzeg, was Maestro Kurt Masur, Chief Conductor of the New York Philharmonic.

In May 1997, Pope John Paul II paid his second visit to Wrocław. The occasion was the opening of the International Eucharistic Congress, attended by 7,000 faithful, including the Orthodox patriarchs of both Constantinople and Moscow. The accent was distinctly ecumenical. All members of the Polish Ecumenical Council were represented. A Jewish delegation was warmly applauded. The central theme of the Holy Father's homily on the *Statio Orbis* was 'Freedom'. 'Especially here, in this part of Europe,' he declared, 'the very word of freedom makes the heart beat stronger.' And he continued, 'We know the taste of slavery, war and injustice. So too do those countries which like us have survived the tragic experience of the loss of freedom, both personal and collective. Today we rejoice for the recovered freedom [which] cannot be simply possessed . . . It must be constantly won through the exercise of Truth.'[132] In Legnica, the Pope was welcomed by another huge congregation, which awaited him on the former Soviet airfield.

All the progress of a decade, however, was put at risk by the Great Flood of July 1997. In a summer of exceptional rains in the Sudety mountains, where precipitation of 415 millimetres in a four-day period represented 250 per cent of the average total for July, the retaining reservoirs overflowed and a vast muddy tide moved slowly down the Odra valley. It submerged large tracts of land in the Czech Republic and Upper Silesia before approaching Wrocław on 12 July. (It only made world news when it overtook German territory near Berlin towards the end of the month.) At Oława, above Wrocław, the river was ten kilometres wide and about nine metres deep. The only way of stopping or reducing it was to dynamite the dykes and release as much water as possible into farmland polders before it entered the city. But the key points on the dykes were occupied by protesting villagers, and the post-Communist authorities did not know how to deal with them. So Wrocław went under for eight days. Soldiers and volunteers filled sandbags. In those institutions, like the Ossolineum, which moved fast enough, valuables were carried to the upper floors. The Main Square and its immediate surroundings remained dry. Yet many of the streets to the south, on the islands and in the suburbs, were submerged. Thousands of houses were inundated up to the first or second floors. Still more thousands of cars were overwhelmed, some with their lights still shining eerily underwater. The huge estate of Kozanowa, foolishly built in the 1960s on the northern floodplain that had been prepared in German times, was ten metres below the water. Gas and electricity supplies were cut. Traffic in the unaffected areas was blocked by sandbag barricades. Movement, in many places, was only possible by boat, dinghy, army amphibian and helicopter. Emergency rations were distributed. By general consent, the central government failed miserably, while the local authorities acted with speed and efficiency. The damage was astronomic, not least since private-property insurance was not yet widely practised and people in the poorer quarters would have to live for months surrounded by damp and decay. But, amazingly, no one died. And the psychological effects were not all negative. Vratislavians realised how much they had to lose.[133] In July 1997, the cost of repairs was estimated at 709,486,000 złoty – the almost exact equivalent of the city's annual budget.[134]

The historian has other reflections. Why was Wrocław so unprepared? After all, the Odra had delivered many similar disasters over the centuries, most recently in 1854 and 1903. Everyone was blaming the Communist planners (who were not blameless). But there was another explanation. Unfortunately, the Polish population of Wrocław could draw on no collective memory prior to 1945, and consequently could not even imagine the full fury of the Odra aroused.

The affairs of contemporary Wrocław, therefore, are divided into the time before and the time after the flood. Recovery was mercifully swift, and a report prepared by a young American academic in November 1998 struck a decidedly optimistic note.[135] Economically, Wrocław was successful in attracting foreign capital. More than 1,000 joint partnerships had been formed, two-thirds of them in manufacturing. German companies accounted for the largest number of ventures – 290. But, in terms of total capital investment, the United Kingdom came first, Germany second, and Sweden third. Wrocław's landscape was dotted with famous foreign names – Cadbury, Siemens, Pilkington, Adtrans, Daimler Benz, Ikea, Deutsche Bank, Tesco . . .

The Lower Silesian Chamber of Commerce had established special links with Wiesbaden and Dresden (Germany), Breda (Netherlands), Poitiers (France) and Charlotte (North Carolina). These links mirrored parallel cultural exchanges. An exhibition on Konrad Adenauer at the Ossolineum in 1997 reflected new attitudes to Germany. The multi-sided 'Festival of Saxon Days in Breslau' (June 1998) was inspired by the Wrocław-Dresden Exchange, which, though founded in 1959, had now acquired a voluntary character. The stated goal of its sponsors was 'to build our part of the common European House'. Similar sentiments underlay the wider provincial links between Berlin-Brandenburg and Silesia, as reflected in the bilingual joint publication *Wach auf, mein Herz, und denke / Przebudź się, serce moje, i pomyśl.* ('Wake up, My Heart, and Think'). Given Germany's federal structure, the interprovincial approach was proving fruitful. On the vital question of the city's identity, it was observed that Wrocław 'was becoming a European city rather than being just Polish, [or] just Polish with a German background'. One respondent talked of 'Europolis – a centre stimulating the development of a large region'.[136] Wrocław had reached the position, unimaginable only ten years before, of preparing its bid to host the World Fair, Expo 2010.[137]

*

Saturday, 24 June 2000, St John the Baptist's Day: on the feast of its patron saint, Wrocław celebrated the millennium 'of the Bishopric and of the City'. To be exact, the celebrations marked the thousandth anniversary both of the foundation of a bishopric (which in 1929 had become an archbishopric) and of the entry into the historical record of a city, that was in reality much older. They took place under the joint sponsorship of the Cardinal Archbishop, Henryk Gulbinowicz, and of the City President, Bogdan Zdrojewski. As the climax of many other festivities – concerts, exhibitions, publications, film shows, fireworks, discussions and historical lectures – an open-air High Mass was celebrated in the Market Square. The principal celebrant was the papal legate, Cardinal Edmund Szodek, an American prelate born in Grand Rapids, Michigan. A giant crane held a large cross over the square. A huge stage carried the altar, flanked by rows of distinguished guests. Seven leading churchmen occupied seven thrones beside the altar – among them the Legate, the Primates of Gniezno and Prague and the Greek-Catholic Metropolitan. Behind them sat the mitred ranks of the country's entire episcopate. To the right sat the assembled dignitaries of city and state, including the President and Premier of the Republic, the City Council, honorary citizens, mayors and palatines. To the left sat the representatives of non-Catholic denominations – Orthodox, Protestant, Jewish – and delegations of sister cities: from Dresden, Poitiers, Breda and Charlotte. In front sat the packed representatives of the professions, the universities, the armed services, the city offices, guilds and fraternities. The blaze of colour was matched only by the feast of sound. Gold capes and red skullcaps glistened among mountains of flowers, banks of coloured spotlights and forests of coats of arms. A line of blue headdresses marked a company of nuns; while the politicians stood meekly in their charcoal suits. Black marked the serried rows of secular clergy. A block of pure white located the concelebrant priests, each carrying a pure-white umbrella. Ermine stoles and gold chains identified a regiment of rectors. Massed choirs competed with an orchestra, an organ and soloists, boosted by towering electronic speakers. They started with the hymn 'God is Love', followed by *Gaude Mater Poloniae* and the song of John the Baptist, 'Herald of the Rising Sun':

> Tyś jest głos co woła wa puszczy
> Przygotujcie drogę Panu.
>
> (You are the voice that cries in the wilderness
> 'Prepare Ye the Way of the Lord'.)

Every moment of the next three hours was filled with fervour, emotion and striking symbolism. During the preparatories, the congregation sang the ancient anthem *Bogurodzica Dziewica* ('O Virgin Mother of God'), once sung before the battle of Grunwald in 1410. The liturgy was accompanied by the soaring music of Mozart's Coronation Mass in C (K317). During the homily, the Legate appealed to the legacy of the Piasts. During his own address, the Cardinal Archbishop struck a complementary note, praising the contribution to 'the Vratislavian reality', not only of Poles and Germans but of Jews, Czechs, Hungarians and Austrians. Later in the day, he was to pay homage to his predecessor, the first Bishop – 'a man of unknown nationality'. During the Confession of Faith, distinguished non-believers kept their lips sealed. During the collection, a cardinal dozed. During the Preface, a wayward mobile phone embarrassed the episcopal ranks. The *Pater Noster* was notable for almost full participation. The Sacrament of Peace saw the Cardinal Archbishop come over to greet his Orthodox and Protestant counterparts and, by coincidence, a shining row of novice nuns and even a visiting historian. During communion, a press photographer rudely jumped a line of bishops so as not to lose his niche on the platform to a rival camera crew. At the very end, after the command to 'Go in Peace', the stage emptied to the blast of trumpets and the chorus from Handel's *Joshua*:

> Trumpets sound the triumphal chord:
> Sing the heart-felt hymn of adoration.
>
> (Trąby grajcie triumfalny zew
> z głębi serc śpiewajcie uwielbienia śpiew.)

Pride, pomp and piety were all on parade – as no doubt they were a thousand years before, when the first bishop was consecrated. Some people would say that some things had changed little – least of all human nature. But Wrocław's new-found self-confidence was there for all to see. Fifty-five years after the death of Breslau, the capital of Silesia was once again free, dynamic and open to the world. 'The Flower of Europe' had bloomed once more.

APPENDICES

The Piast Dynasty 990–1370

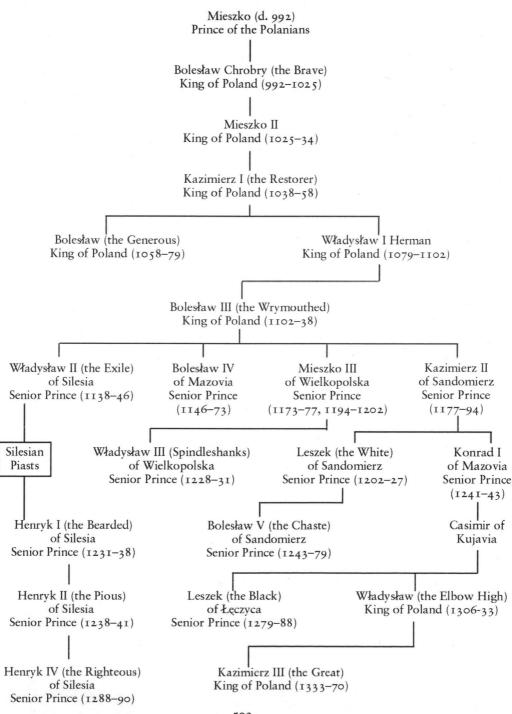

Mieszko (d. 992)
Prince of the Polanians

Bolesław Chrobry (the Brave)
King of Poland (992–1025)

Mieszko II
King of Poland (1025–34)

Kazimierz I (the Restorer)
King of Poland (1038–58)

Bolesław (the Generous)
King of Poland (1058–79)

Władysław I Herman
King of Poland (1079–1102)

Bolesław III (the Wrymouthed)
King of Poland (1102–38)

Władysław II (the Exile)
of Silesia
Senior Prince (1138–46)

Bolesław IV
of Mazovia
Senior Prince
(1146–73)

Mieszko III
of Wielkopolska
Senior Prince
(1173–77, 1194–1202)

Kazimierz II
of Sandomierz
Senior Prince
(1177–94)

Silesian
Piasts

Władysław III (Spindleshanks)
of Wielkopolska
Senior Prince (1228–31)

Leszek (the White)
of Sandomierz
Senior Prince (1202–27)

Konrad I
of Mazovia
Senior Prince
(1241–43)

Henryk I (the Bearded)
of Silesia
Senior Prince (1231–38)

Bolesław V (the Chaste)
of Sandomierz
Senior Prince (1243–79)

Casimir of
Kujavia

Henryk II (the Pious)
of Silesia
Senior Prince (1238–41)

Leszek (the Black)
of Łęczyca
Senior Prince (1279–88)

Władysław (the Elbow High)
King of Poland (1306–33)

Henryk IV (the Righteous)
of Silesia
Senior Prince (1288–90)

Kazimierz III (the Great)
King of Poland (1333–70)

The Piast Dukes of Silesia
1138–1335

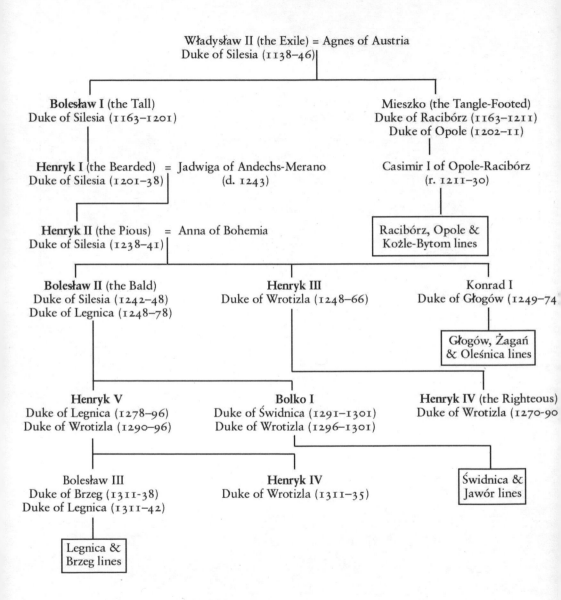

Władysław II (the Exile) = Agnes of Austria
Duke of Silesia (1138–46)

Bolesław I (the Tall)
Duke of Silesia (1163–1201)

Mieszko (the Tangle-Footed)
Duke of Racibórz (1163–1211)
Duke of Opole (1202–11)

Henryk I (the Bearded) = Jadwiga of Andechs-Merano
Duke of Silesia (1201–38)   (d. 1243)

Casimir I of Opole-Racibórz
(r. 1211–30)

Henryk II (the Pious) = Anna of Bohemia
Duke of Silesia (1238–41)

Racibórz, Opole &
Koźle-Bytom lines

Bolesław II (the Bald)
Duke of Silesia (1242–48)
Duke of Legnica (1248–78)

Henryk III
Duke of Wrotizla (1248–66)

Konrad I
Duke of Głogów (1249–74)

Głogów, Żagań
& Oleśnica lines

Henryk V
Duke of Legnica (1278–96)
Duke of Wrotizla (1290–96)

Bolko I
Duke of Świdnica (1291–1301)
Duke of Wrotizla (1296–1301)

Henryk IV (the Righteous)
Duke of Wrotizla (1270–90)

Bolesław III
Duke of Brzeg (1311–38)
Duke of Legnica (1311–42)

Henryk IV
Duke of Wrotizla (1311–35)

Świdnica &
Jawór lines

Legnica &
Brzeg lines

(The rulers of Wrotizla are marked in bold)

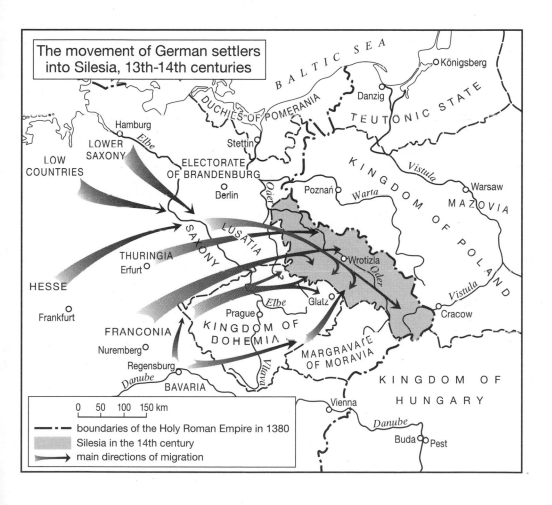

The movement of German settlers into Silesia, 13th-14th centuries

0 50 100 150 km

— · — boundaries of the Holy Roman Empire in 1380

Silesia in the 14th century

→ main directions of migration

The Luxemburg and Jagiellon Dynasties
1335–1526

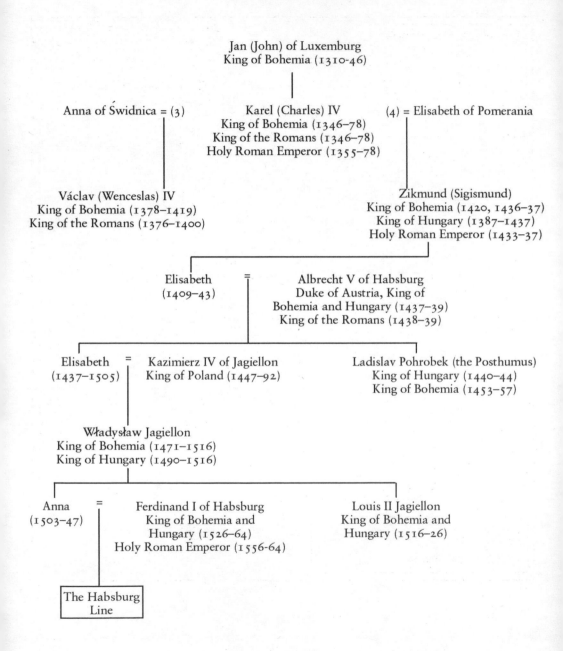

Jan (John) of Luxemburg
King of Bohemia (1310-46)

Anna of Świdnica = (3)

Karel (Charles) IV
King of Bohemia (1346–78)
King of the Romans (1346–78)
Holy Roman Emperor (1355–78)

(4) = Elisabeth of Pomerania

Václav (Wenceslas) IV
King of Bohemia (1378–1419)
King of the Romans (1376–1400)

Zikmund (Sigismund)
King of Bohemia (1420, 1436–37)
King of Hungary (1387–1437)
Holy Roman Emperor (1433–37)

Elisabeth
(1409–43)

Albrecht V of Habsburg
Duke of Austria, King of
Bohemia and Hungary (1437–39)
King of the Romans (1438–39)

Elisabeth
(1437–1505)

Kazimierz IV of Jagiellon
King of Poland (1447–92)

Ladislav Pohrobek (the Posthumus)
King of Hungary (1440–44)
King of Bohemia (1453–57)

Władysław Jagiellon
King of Bohemia (1471–1516)
King of Hungary (1490–1516)

Anna
(1503–47)

Ferdinand I of Habsburg
King of Bohemia and
Hungary (1526–64)
Holy Roman Emperor (1556-64)

Louis II Jagiellon
King of Bohemia and
Hungary (1516–26)

The Habsburg
Line

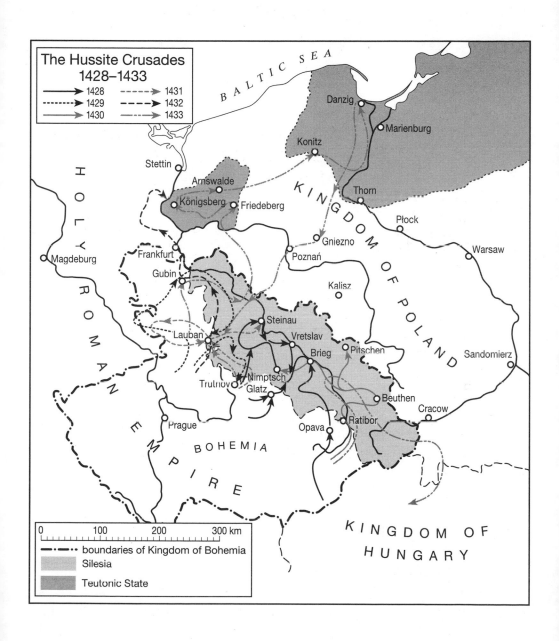

The Hussite Crusades
1428–1433

→	1428	⇢	1431
→	1429	⇢	1432
→	1430	⇢	1433

BALTIC SEA

Danzig
Marienburg
Konitz
Stettin
Thorn
Arnswalde
Königsberg
Friedeberg
Płock
KINGDOM
Magdeburg
Frankfurt
Gubin
Gniezno
Poznań
Warsaw
Kalisz
OF
Lauban
Steinau
POLAND
Vretslav
Brieg
Pitschen
Trutnov
Nimptsch
Glatz
Sandomierz
Prague
Opava
Ratibor
Beuthen
Cracow

HOLY
ROMAN
EMPIRE

BOHEMIA

KINGDOM OF
HUNGARY

| 0 | 100 | 200 | 300 km |

— · — boundaries of Kingdom of Bohemia

Silesia

Teutonic State

Bishops of Vratislavia

1. Johannes/Jan   1000
2. Hieronymus   1046–1062
3. Johannes/Jan I   1063–1072
4. Petrus/Piotr I   1073–1111
5. Siroslaus/Żyrosław I   1112–1120
6. Heimo   1120–1126
7. Robert I   1127–1142
8. Robert II   1142–1146
9. Johannes/Jan II   1146–1149
10. Walter   1149–1169
11. Siroslaus II   1170–1198
12. Jaroslaus/Jarosław   1198–1201
13. Cyprian   1201–1207
14. Lorenz   1207–1232
15. Thomas I   1232–1268
16. Thomas II   1270–1292
17. Johannes/Jan III Romka   1292–1301
18. Heinrich von Würben   1302–1319
19. Oksa Nanker   1326–1341
20. Przecław von Pogarell   1342–1376
21. Wenzel von Liegnitz   1382–1417
22. Konrad von Oels   1417–1447
23. Peter II Nowag   1447–1456
24. Jodocus von Rosenberg/Jodok z Różomborku   1456–1467
25. Rudolf von Rüdesheim   1468–1482
26. Johannes/Jan IV Roth   1482–1506
27. Johannes/Jan V Thurzó   1506–1520
28. Jakob Salza   1520–1539
29. Balthasar von Promnitz   1540–1562
30. Kaspar von Logau   1562–1574
31. Martin Gerstmann   1574–1585
32. Andreas Jerin   1585–1596

33.	Paul Albert	1599–1600
34.	Johannes VI von Sitsch	1600–1608
35.	Karl von Habsburg	1608–1624
36.	Karol Ferdynand Waza	1625–1655
37.	Leopold Wilhelm von Habsburg	1656–1662
38.	Karl Joseph von Habsburg	1663–1664
39.	Sebastian von Rostock	1665–1671
40.	Friedrich von Hessen	1671–1682
41.	Franz Ludwig zu Neuburg	1683–1732
42.	Philipp Ludwig Sinzendorf	1732–1747
43.	Philipp Gotthard Schaffgotsch	1747–1795
44.	Joseph Christian Hohenlohe-Bartenstein	1795–1817
45.	Emanuel Schimonski	1824–1832
46.	Leopold Sedlnitzky	1836–1840
47.	Joseph Knauer	1843–1844
48.	Melchior von Diepenbrock	1845–1853
49.	Heinrich Förster	1853–1881
50.	Robert Herzog	1882–1886
51.	Georg Kopp	1887–1914
52.	Adolf Bertram	1914–1945
	(Karol Milik [apostolic administrator]	1945–1951)
	(Kazimierz Lagosz [curate]	1951–1956)
	(Bolesław Kominek [curate]	1956–1972)
53.	Bolesław Kominek	1972–1974
54.	Henryk Gulbinowicz	1976–

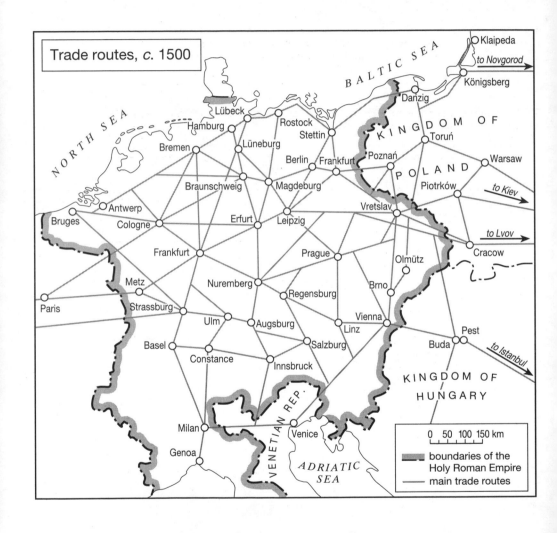

Trade routes, _c._ 1500

BALTIC SEA

NORTH SEA

to Novgorod

Klaipeda

Königsberg

Danzig

Lübeck

Hamburg

Rostock

Stettin

Lüneburg

KINGDOM OF

Toruń

Bremen

Berlin

Frankfurt

Poznań

Warsaw

Braunschweig

Magdeburg

POLAND

Piotrków

to Kiev

Antwerp

Erfurt

Leipzig

Vretslav

Bruges

Cologne

to Lvov

Frankfurt

Prague

Olmütz

Cracow

Metz

Nuremberg

Brno

Paris

Strassburg

Regensburg

Vienna

Pest

Ulm

Augsburg

Linz

Buda

to Istanbul

Basel

Salzburg

KINGDOM OF

Constance

Innsbruck

HUNGARY

Milan

Venice

Genoa

VENETIAN REP.

ADRIATIC
SEA

0   50 100 150 km

boundaries of the
Holy Roman Empire

main trade routes

The Habsburgs
1526–1740

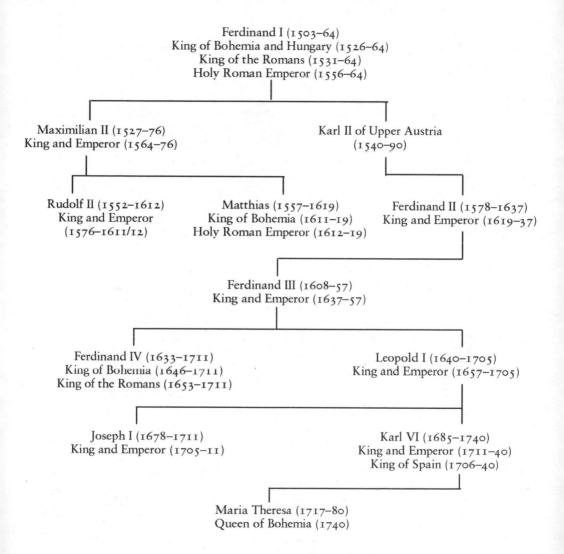

Ferdinand I (1503–64)
King of Bohemia and Hungary (1526–64)
King of the Romans (1531–64)
Holy Roman Emperor (1556–64)

Maximilian II (1527–76)
King and Emperor (1564–76)

Karl II of Upper Austria
(1540–90)

Rudolf II (1552–1612)
King and Emperor
(1576–1611/12)

Matthias (1557–1619)
King of Bohemia (1611–19)
Holy Roman Emperor (1612–19)

Ferdinand II (1578–1637)
King and Emperor (1619–37)

Ferdinand III (1608–57)
King and Emperor (1637–57)

Ferdinand IV (1633–1711)
King of Bohemia (1646–1711)
King of the Romans (1653–1711)

Leopold I (1640–1705)
King and Emperor (1657–1705)

Joseph I (1678–1711)
King and Emperor (1705–11)

Karl VI (1685–1740)
King and Emperor (1711–40)
King of Spain (1706–40)

Maria Theresa (1717–80)
Queen of Bohemia (1740)

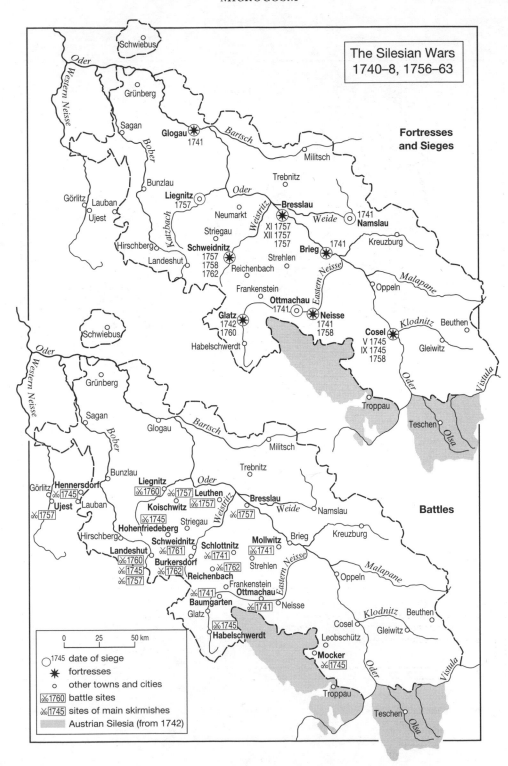

The Silesian Wars
1740–8, 1756–63

Fortresses
and Sieges

Schwiebus

Oder

Western Neisse

Grünberg

Sagan

Glogau ✳
1741

Bartsch

Militsch

Bunzlau

Görlitz
Lauban
Ujest

Liegnitz ◎
1757

Neumarkt

Oder

Trebnitz

Katzbach

Weistritz

Bresslau ✳
XI 1757
XII 1757
1757

Weide

1741 ◎
Namslau

Striegau

Hirschberg

Landeshut

Schweidnitz ✳
1757
1758
1762

Reichenbach

Strehlen

Brieg ✳
1741

Kreuzburg

Frankenstein

Ottmachau
1741 ◎

Eastern Neisse

Oppeln

Malapane

Glatz ✳
1742
1760

Habelschwerdt

Neisse ✳
1741
1758

Cosel ✳
V 1745
IX 1745
1758

Klodnitz

Beuthen

Gleiwitz

Oder

Vistula

Schwiebus

Oder

Western Neisse

Grünberg

Sagan

Bober

Glogau

Bartsch

Militsch

Bunzlau

Trebnitz

Görlitz
Hennersdorf
⚔1745
Ujest
⚔1757
Lauban

Liegnitz
⚔1760
⚔1757 **Leuthen**
⚔1757

Koischwitz
⚔1745
Striegau

Bresslau
⚔1757

Weide
Namslau

Battles

Hirschberg

Hohenfriedeberg

Weistritz

Landeshut
⚔1760
⚔1745
⚔1757

Schweidnitz
⚔1761

Burkersdorf
⚔1762

Reichenbach

Schlottnitz
⚔1741

⚔1762
Strehlen

Mollwitz
⚔1741

Brieg

Kreuzburg

Frankenstein
Ottmachau
⚔1741

Eastern Neisse

Neisse

Oppeln

Malapane

Baumgarten
⚔1741
Glatz

Habelschwerdt
⚔1745

Cosel

Leobschütz

Klodnitz

Beuthen

Gleiwitz

Oder

Vistula

Mocker
⚔1745

Troppau

Teschen
Olsa

0 25 50 km	

◎ 1745 date of siege
✳ fortresses
○ other towns and cities
⚔1760 battle sites
⚔1745 sites of main skirmishes
▨ Austrian Silesia (from 1742)

Troppau

Teschen
Olsa

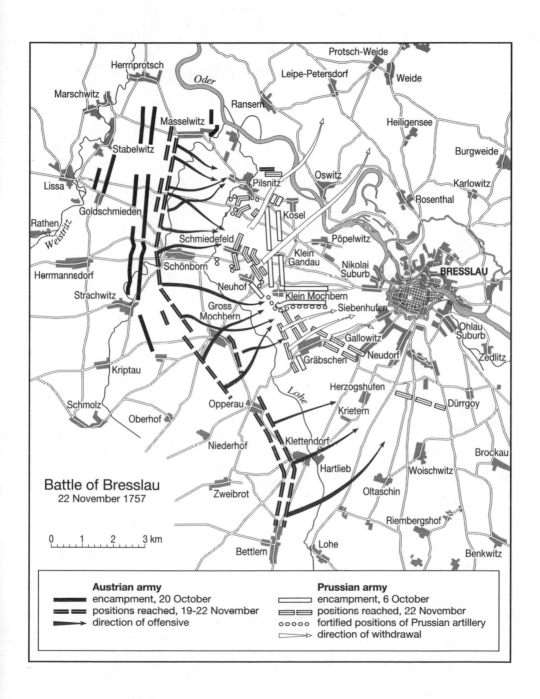

Battle of Bresslau
22 November 1757

0 1 2 3 km

Protsch-Wejde
Leipe-Petersdorf
Weide
Herrnprotsch
Oder
Marschwitz
Ransern
Heiligensee
Masselwitz
Burgweide
Stabelwitz
Pilsnitz
Oswitz
Karlowitz
Lissa
Kosel
Rosenthal
Goldschmieden
Pöpelwitz
Rathen
Weistritz
Schmiedefeld
Klein
Gandau
Nikolai
Suburb
BRESSLAU
Herrmannsdorf
Schönborn
Neuhof
Klein Mochbern
Strachwitz
Gross
Mochbern
Siebenhufen
Ohlau
Suburb
Kriptau
Gallowitz
Neudorf
Zedlitz
Gräbschen
Herzogshuten
Schmolz
Opperau
Lohe
Dürrgoy
Krietern
Oberhof
Niederhof
Klettendorf
Brockau
Hartlieb
Woischwitz
Zweibrot
Oltaschin
Riembergshof
Bettlern
Lohe
Benkwitz

Austrian army
— encampment, 20 October
= = positions reached, 19-22 November
➤ direction of offensive

Prussian army
☐ encampment, 6 October
▱▱ positions reached, 22 November
ooooo fortified positions of Prussian artillery
➱ direction of withdrawal

Extract from *Guide de l'Allemagne* (*1793*)
by Hans Ottokar Reichard

Breslau. Population 60,191 (in 1787).

Notable buildings. Curiosities. The Augustin church (the main altar is a masterpiece) – the Premonstratensian chapel – the convent of the Order of St. Clair – St. Matthew's chapel – the church of the Holy Cross – the bishop's palace – the Lutheran church of St. Elizabeth (the bell is one of the largest in existence) – the church of St. Mary Magdalene – the reformed church – the town hall – the arsenal – the customs house – the market – the exhibition rooms – the Hatzfeld palace – the college of the former Jesuits – the academic buildings – the island called *Dom-Insel* – the hydraulic machine.

Literary and other establishments. The college or *Gymnasium* – the *Realschule* – the *Gymnasium* of Mary Magdalene – the anatomy theatre – the botanical garden – the patriotic and economic society – lecture societies.

Entertainments. Public and private concerts: balls and dances: picnics: promenades on foot or by carriage in the gardens of Fiebig and Fink; in the English garden of Prince Hohenlohe at Scheitnig; in the gardens at Kriechen: the changing of the guard: the grand military review in August: pleasure trips on the water at Skarfine.

Art collections. The libraries of the Augustins, the Canons Regular of the Holy Cross, the Bishop's Gallery, the churches of St. Elizabeth, St. Mary Magdalene and of St. Bernhard, the Jesuits and the 'War and Domains Chambers' (where there is a model of the *Riesengebirge*). Collections of coins, prints and natural history, in the churches of St. Matthew, St. Elizabeth and St. Mary Magdalene.

Masonic Lodges. The provincial lodge of Silesia: the 3 Skeletons, the Column and the Bell: (system of the Grand Lodge of Germany).

Inns. The Golden Goose, the Golden Eagle, the Blue Stag.

Factories. Manufactures: serge, needles, pencils, fine fabric, leather. Sugar refineries; bleachers of wax; dyers for Turkish thread; fine liqueurs at the Hensel distillery etc.

Fairs. Two considerable fairs.

Surroundings. The battle of 1757 between the Empire and the Prussians in favour of the former. The battle-field lies 3 leagues from Breslau, between Lissa and Leuthen, on the road to Liegnitz. *Sybillen-Ort* and the gardens of the Duke of Brunswick-Oels.

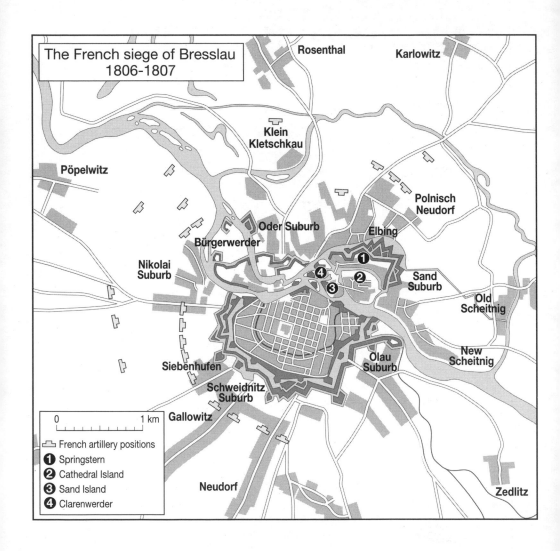

The French siege of Bresslau
1806-1807

Rosenthal
Karlowitz
Klein
Kletschkau
Pöpelwitz
Polnisch
Neudorf
Oder Suburb
Elbing
Bürgerwerder
Nikolai
Suburb
❶
❹
Sand
Suburb
❷
Old
Scheitnig
❸
New
Scheitnig
Siebenhufen
Olau
Suburb
Schweidnitz
Suburb
Gallowitz
Zedlitz
Neudorf

0   1 km

French artillery positions
❶ Springstern
❷ Cathedral Island
❸ Sand Island
❹ Clarenwerder

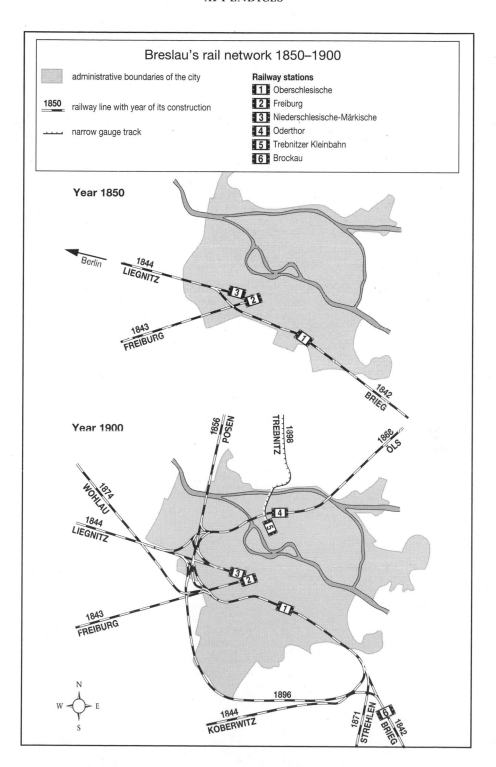

Breslau's rail network 1850–1900

The Hohenzollerns
1740–1918

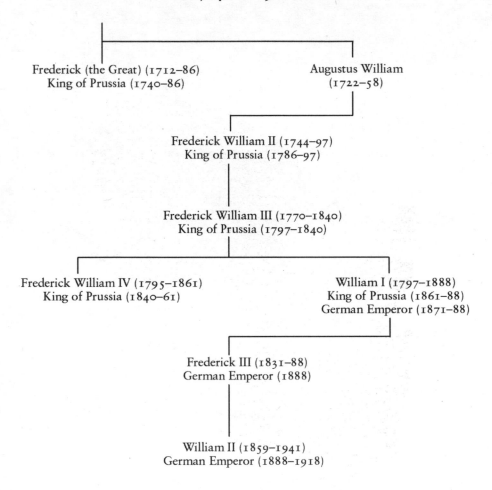

Frederick (the Great) (1712–86)
King of Prussia (1740–86)

Augustus William
(1722–58)

Frederick William II (1744–97)
King of Prussia (1786–97)

Frederick William III (1770–1840)
King of Prussia (1797–1840)

Frederick William IV (1795–1861)
King of Prussia (1840–61)

William I (1797–1888)
King of Prussia (1861–88)
German Emperor (1871–88)

Frederick III (1831–88)
German Emperor (1888)

William II (1859–1941)
German Emperor (1888–1918)

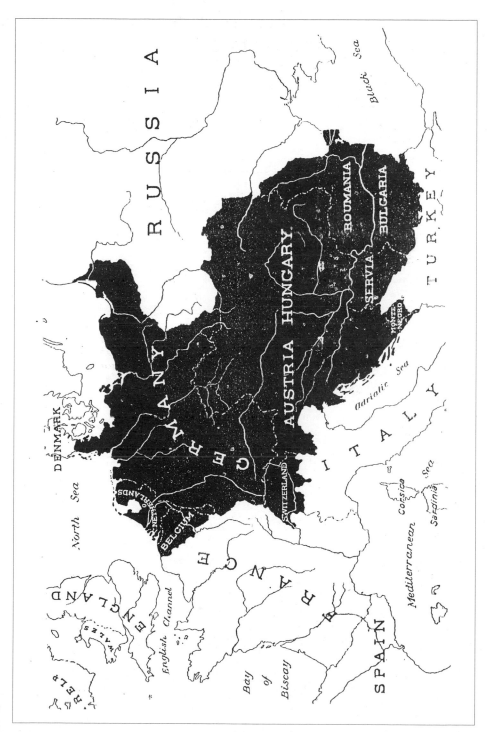

Joseph Partsch's vision of 'Mitteleuropa', 1903

Extract from Baedeker's Guide (1904)

33. Breslau

Railway Stations. Breslau has four railway stations: 1. *Central Station* . . . for the Upper Silesian, Posen, Glatz, and Zobten railways, and for some trains of the 'Niederschlesisch-Märkisch' line. 2. *Märkisch Station* . . . for the remaining trains of this line and for all the trains of the Right Bank of the Oder Railway. 3. *Freiburg Station* . . . for the Freiburg, Schweidnitz and Reppen lines. 4. *Oder-Tor Station* . . . to the north of the town, for Trebnitz, Oels, Gnesen, Upper Silesia, Warsaw, etc.

Hotels. MONOPOL, Wall-Str. 7, with lift and restaurant; WEISSER ADLER, Ohlauer Str. 10; . . . RESIDENZ, Tauenzien-Platz 16, no restaurant.

Chief Attractions (1 day). Forenoon: Ring, Rathaus, St. Elizabeth's, Blücher-Platz, Schweidnitzer-Str., Museum of Industrial Art, Museum of Fine Arts. – Afternoon: Promenades (Liebichs-Höhe, Holtei-Höhe), Cathedral, Zoological Garden, and Scheitnig (or Wilhelmshafen or South Park).

Breslau . . . the second city in Prussia, the capital of Silesia and seat of government for the province, the headquarters of the 6th Army Corps, and the residence of a Roman Catholic prince-bishop, with 423,000 inhab. (157,000 Rom. Cath., 20,000 Jews, 5,900 soldiers), lies in a fertile plain on both banks of the *Oder*, at the influx of the *Ohle*. The islands formed here by the Oder are connected with the banks by numerous bridges. The city consists of the *Altstadt* and five continually increasing suburbs.

Breslau, Lat. *Wratislavia*, Pol. *Wrocław*, a town and episcopal see as early as the year 1000, is of Slavonic origin, and with Silesia belonged to Poland down to 1168, after which it became the capital of the independent Duchy of Silesia. In 1261 Duke Heinrich III introduced the municipal law of Magdeburg. On the extinction of the dukes in 1335 it was annexed to Bohemia and became subject to the emperors of the Luxemburg family, who took the city under their special protection, so that, in spite of the storms of the Hussite wars and of the following centuries, an independent German element was strongly developed.

At this period also Breslau received its architectural character. The latest style of Gothic architecture, and that of the earliest Renaissance, were zealously cultivated here. The finest Gothic church is the elegant Church of St. Elizabeth, and the handsomest secular building in that style is the Rathaus. Here, as in all Slavic and semi-Slavic countries, the Renaissance gained ground at a remarkably early period. The new style appears to have been applied to portals and to monuments, but works of greater magnitude were unfortunately never attempted. To the Jesuit style the town is indebted for its imposing University.

In 1523 the citizens embraced the Reformation, and in 1527 they fell under the Austrian supremacy. In 1741 Frederick the Great marched into Silesia and took Breslau by surprise. In 1757 the town was again occupied by the Austrians, but was recaptured by Frederick after the battle of Leuthen. In 1760 Tauenzien repelled an attack by Loudon. In 1806-7 the town was besieged by Vandamme, who took it and levelled the fortifications. In March, 1813, Breslau was the scene of an enthusiastic rising against the French, on which occasion Frederick William III issued his famous appeal 'An mein Volk'. Since then the city has rapidly increased.

Breslau is now one of the most important commercial and industrial places in Germany. The principal manufactures are steam-engines, railway-carriages, beer, liqueurs and spirits. The staple commodities are linen and cotton goods, iron-work, coal, glass-ware, oil, mill-products, and sugar.

Vratislavian Nobel Prize Laureates

1902 Literature

Theodor Mommsen (1817–1903), for historical writing, with special reference to the monumental work, *A History of Rome*.

1905 Physics

Philipp Lenard (1862–1947) for work on cathode rays.

1907 Chemistry

Eduard Buchner (1860–1917) for biochemical researches and the discovery of cellfree fermentation.

1908 Medicine

Paul Ehrlich (1854–1915) in recognition of work on the immune system (awarded jointly with Ilya Ilyich Mechnikov).

1912 Literature

Gerhart Hauptmann (1862–1946) in recognition of fruitful, varied and outstanding production in the realm of dramatic art.

1918 Chemistry

Fritz Haber (1868–1934) for the synthesis of ammonia from its elements.

1931 Chemistry

Friedrich Bergius (1884–1949) in recognition of contributions to the invention and development of chemical high-pressure methods (awarded jointly with Carl Bosch).

1943 Physics

Otto Stern (1888–1969) for contributions to the development of the molecular ray method and the discovery of the magnetic moment of the proton.

1954 Physics

Max Born (1882–1970) for fundamental research in quantum mechanics, especially for statistical interpretation of the wave function.

1994 Economics

Reinhard Selten (1930–   ) for the pioneering analysis of equilibria in the theory of non-cooperative games (awarded jointly with John C. Harsanyi and John F. Nash).

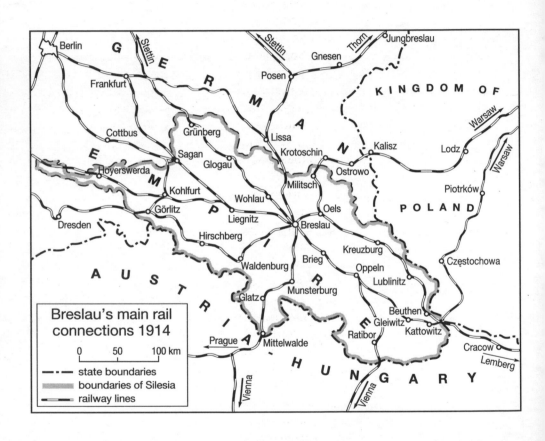

Berlin

G E R M A N Y

Stettin

Frankfurt

Cottbus

Grünberg

Sagan

Glogau

Hoyerswerda

Kohlfurt

Görlitz

Dresden

Wohlau

Liegnitz

Hirschberg

A U S T R I A

Stettin

Posen

Gnesen

Thorn

Jungbreslau

KINGDOM OF

Lissa

Krotoschin

Kalisz

Warsaw

Lodz

Warsaw

Ostrowo

Militsch

Piotrków

POLAND

Oels

Breslau

Kreuzburg

Częstochowa

Waldenburg

Brieg

Oppeln

Lublinitz

Glatz

Munsterburg

Beuthen

Prague

Mittelwalde

Gleiwitz

Ratibor

Kattowitz

Cracow

Lemberg

Vienna

Vienna

H U N G A R Y

Breslau's main rail
connections 1914

0   50   100 km

— · — state boundaries
▨ boundaries of Silesia
━ railway lines

Archbishopric of Breslau 1930

0   50   100   150 km

BALTIC SEA

ARCHBISHOPRIC OF OSNABRÜCK

BISHOPRIC OF BERLIN

BISHOPRIC OF WARMIA

○ Frauenburg

ARCHBISHOPRIC OF PADERBORN

Vistula

○ Schneidemühl

Warta

○ Berlin

Oder

A R C H B I S H O P R I C

○ Gniezno

○ Warsaw

BISHOPRIC OF MEISSEN

Meissen ○

O F   G N I E Z N O

○ Breolau

Wurta

(to Silesian Diocese)

ARCHBISHOPRIC OF PRAGUE

Oder

Vistula

○ Prague

ARCHBISHOPRIC

(to Silesian Diocese)

Olomouc ○

OF OLOMOUC

Archbishopric of Breslau

boundaries of Schneidemühl (Piła) prelacy

Silesia

Breslau on the Eve of War, 1939

One man, who watched the last weeks of pre-war Breslau with professional care, was a young Polish intelligence officer, who worked at Poland's Consulate-General at Charlottenstrasse 24 (Ulica Krucza) between 10 July and 1 September 1939. Despatched by the Second Bureau in Warsaw to strengthen the small intelligence-observation unit, code-named 'Adrian', which had been operating in Breslau since 1936, Lt. Marian Dlugolecki was ordered to report on the progress of German mobilisation. Playing a game of cat-and-mouse with the Gestapo and the local police, he nonetheless managed to discern the tell-tale signs of coming war. He observed night trains loaded with tanks moving south to Upper Silesia, and the same empty flat-cars returning in daytime for new consignments. He saw convoys of troops on the *Autobahn* which had been closed to civilian traffic, and a dust-covered group of regimental *Wehrmacht* officers from western Germany arriving on the Schweidnitzerstrasse. And in a city blissfully unaware of the preparations, he checked for military movements both at the Hauptbahnhof and at Strachwitz aerodrome.

Then suddenly, in mid-August, he found himself completely alone in an empty building. One of his colleagues was arrested. His boss departed in haste to Poland. The Consulate-General was surrounded by a police cordon. And the consular staff stopped coming to work. In those last ten days, he made one overnight train journey to Berlin, and a final courier run to Rawicz in Poland, when he saw the growing tensions at the frontier. After that, he waited at his post until the day came to burn the cipher book and to be offically expelled:

> Friday – 1 September 1939. It was already after midnight . . . I can't stand waiting for hour after hour . . . I made a pretty big fire in the kitchen grate mainly from newspapers, because I preferred not to use the chemicals for destroying documents which had been provided. The cipher book lay on one side together with the latest telegrams . . . I shaved . . . And then went to bed with the radio turned down but not switched off . . . In the early

hours, I heard a loud voice and the end of a communiqué. At first I didn't quite comprehend. But when the communiqué was repeated, I grasped its significance. THE WAR HAD STARTED.

I ran quickly to the other room and opened the window. Perhaps I would hear some shots or something . . . [But] Charlottenstrasse was still sleeping. A draught of balmy air entered the house, announcing another hot day. It was hard to reconcile the fact that, while fighting would already have started on the frontier, here [in Breslau] nothing was happening . . .

At six o'clock, there was loud banging on the front door . . . The police! . . . I lit the fire, and waited till it was burning fiercely before going down to open up . . . My driving instructor had come to collect the money for my last lesson . . .

At eight o'clock, there was more knocking at the door. I recognised 'Grubas' [the Consulate caretaker] who had brought me some food . . . We embraced warmly, not without a tear . . . I watched him disappear round the corner of the street . . .

At ten o'clock, the Swedish Consul, small and balding, arrived to take possession of office . . . When I opened the safe and he saw the revolver, he said 'I don't want to see that' . . .

At eleven o'clock, two motor-cars drew up. It was the Consul with two German police officers . . . The conversation was very short . . . One of the officers announced that the entire consular staff would be leaving by convoy in two hours time for Dresden . . .

Our departure did not arouse the least interest. The street was empty.[1]

Eating supper in a Dresden hotel, the interned Dlugolecki was to hear the first news bulletins from the Front. 'General Gasiorowski taken prisoner, the 7th Infantry Division dispersed near Czestochowa'. A thunderbolt! This was Dlugolecki's own division. He returned to his room, then asked permission of the duty sergeant to pace the corridor. The sergeant wanted to talk:

'Listen, I know how you feel. I was a soldier in the last war. Everything was fine at first. But how did it end? Now it's starting again in the same way. We were four brothers, and all served in the war. I alone am left, and an invalid. And they've dragged me back to the service . . . Today, my own sons are in the Army. My wife can't stop weeping. We may never see them again.[2]

'I never imagined', Dlugolecki wrote, 'that in those first days of the war, a German would show me a little humanity.' In due course, he was expelled to neutral Sweden whence he began a lifetime of exile spent first in Paris and eventually in Edinburgh.

[1] Marian Dlugolecki, *Ostatni Raport*, Wrocław, 1995, pp. 112 15
[2] Ibid., pp. 118–19

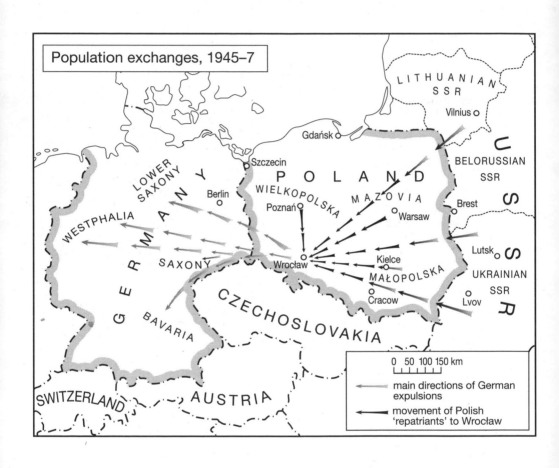

Population exchanges, 1945–7

LITHUANIAN SSR

Vilnius

Gdańsk

Szczecin

POLAND

LOWER SAXONY

Berlin

WIELKOPOLSKA

Poznań

MAZOVIA

Warsaw

BELORUSSIAN SSR

Brest

WESTPHALIA

GERMANY

SAXONY

Wrocław

Kielce

MAŁOPOLSKA

Lutsk

UKRAINIAN SSR

Lvov

BAVARIA

CZECHOSLOVAKIA

Cracow

SWITZERLAND

AUSTRIA

0 50 100 150 km

main directions of German expulsions

movement of Polish 'repatriants' to Wrocław

Place-Name Directory

German–Polish

Agnetendorf	Jagniątów	– Herdain	– Gaj
Albendorf	Wambierzyce	– Heernprotsch	– Pracze Odrzańskie
Allenstein	Olsztyn	– Heiligensee	– Poświętnie
Auschwitz	Oświęcim	– Herrmannsdorf	– Jerzmanowo
Bad Kudowa	Kudowa Zdrój	– Herzogshufen	– Borek
Bad Landeck	Lądek Zdrój	– Huben	– Huby
Bad Salzbrunn	Szczawno Zdrój	– Kanth	– Kąty
Bad Warmbrunn	Cieplice Zdrój	– Karlowitz	– Karłowice
Bernstadt	Bierutów	– Kawallen	– Kowale
Beuthen	Bytom	– Klein Gandau	– Gądów Mały
Bielitz	Bielsko	– Kleinburg	– Dworek
Boguslawitz	Bogusławice	– Klein Ohlewiesen	– Księże Małe
Bolkenhain	Bolków	– Kletschkau	– Kleczków
Breslau	Wrocław	– Klettendorf	– Klecina
– Bartheln	– Bartoszowice	– Kosel	– Kozanów
– Benkwitz	– Bieńkowice	– Kraftborn	– Siechnica
– Bettlern	– Bielany	– Krietern	– Krzyki
– Bischofswalde	– Biskupin	– Kriptau	– Krzeptów
– Brockau	– Brochów	– Leerbeutel	– Zalesie
– Bürgerwerder	– Kępa Mieszczańska	– Lehmgruben	– Glinianki
– Burgweide	– Sołtysowice	– Leipe Petersdorf	– Lipa Piotrowska
– Dom Insel	– Ostrów Tumski	– Lissa	– Leśnica
– Dürrgoy	– Tarnogaj	– Lohe	– Ślęza
– Elbing	– Ołbin	– Marschwitz	– Marszowice
– Gabitz	– Gajowice	– Masselwitz	– Maślice
– Glockschütz	– Kłokoczyce	– Mochbern	– Muchobór
– Goldschmieden	– Złotniki	– Morgenau	– Rakowiec
– Görlitz	– Zgorzelisko	– Muckerau	– Mokra
– Gräbschen	– Grabiszyn	– Neudorf	– Nowa Wieś
– Gross Ohlewiesen	– Księże Wielkie	– Neuhof	– Nowy Dwór
– Grüneiche	– Dąbie	– Niederhof	– Mokronos Dln.
– Güntherbrücke	– Swojczyce	– Oberhof	– Mokronos Grn.
– Hartlieb	– Partynice	– Oltaschin	– Ołtaszyn

– Oswitz	– Osobowice	Glogau	Głogów
– Ottwitz	– Opatowice	Gnesen	Gniezno
– Pilsnitz	– Pilczyce	Goldberg	Złotorjya
– Pirscham	– Bierdzany	Görlitz	Zgorzelec
– Pöpelwitz	– Popowice	Goschütz	Goszcz
– Protsch-Weide	– Pracze Widawskie	Gottesberg	Boguszów
– Ransern	– Redzin	Gröditzberg	Grodziec
– Rathen	– Ratyn	Gross Bressen	Brzeżno
– Riembergshof	– Radomierzyce	Gross Peterwitz	Piotrkowice
– Rosenthal	– Różanka	Gross Rosen	Rogoźnica
– Sacrau	– Zakrzów	Gross Strehlitz	Strzelce Opolskie
– Sand Insel	– Wyspa Piaskowa	Gross Wartenberg	Syców
– Schebitz	– Świniary	Grottkau	Grodków
– Scheitnig	– Szczytniki	Grünberg	Zielona Góra
– Schmiedefeld	– Kuźniki	Grüssau	Krzeszów
– Schmolz	– Smolec	Habelschwerdt	Bystrzyca Kłodzka
– Schönborn	– Zerniki	Haynau	Chojnów
– Siebenhufen	– Siedem Łanów	Heinrichau	Henryków
– Stabelwitz	– Stabłowice	Hirschberg	Jelenia Góra
– Strachwitz	– Strachowice	Hohenfriedeberg	Dobromierz
– Tschepine	– Szczepin	Hundsfeld	Psie Pole
– Vorderbleiche	– Wyspa Słodowa	Jägerndorf	Strzelniki
– Weide	– Widawa	Jauer	Jawor
– Wendelborn	– Pawłowice	Jordansmühl	Jordanów Śląski
– Wilhelmsruh	– Zacisze	Kamenz	Kamieniec
– Woischwitz	– Wojszyce	Kammin	Kamień
– Zedlitz	– Siedlec	Kattowitz	Katowice
– Zimpel	– Sępolno	Kentschkau	Karńcza Góra
– Zweibrodt	– Zabrodzie	Klein Bresa	Brzezinka Średzka
Brieg	Brzeg	Klein Oels	Oleśnica Mała
Brückenberg	Bierutowice	Kohlfurt	Węglowice
Bunzlau	Bolesławiec	Kolberg	Kołobrzeg
Bunzelwitz	Bolesławice	Königsberg	Kaliningrad (Rus)
Cosel	Koźle	Königshütte	Chorzów
Danzig	Gdańsk	Konstadt	Wołczyn
Dramburg	Drawsko	Kreisau	Krzyżowa
Driesen	Drezdenko	Kreuzburg	Kluczbork
Dyhernfurth	Brzeg Dolny	Krieblowitz	Krobielowice
Erdmannsdorf	Mysłakowice	Krossen	Krosno
Falkenberg	Niemodlin	Kuhnau	Kunow
Frankenstein	Ząbkowice Śląskie	Kunersdorf	Kunowice
Freiburg	Świebodzice	Kupferberg	Miedzanka
Freiwaldau	Gozdnica	Küstrin	Kostrzyn
Fünfteichen	Meleświce	Lamsdorf	Łambinowice
Fürstenstein	Książ	Landshut	Kamienna Góra
Glatz	Kłodzko	Langenau	Czernica
Gleiwitz	Gliwice	Lauban	Lubań
Glofenau	Głównin	Lebus	Lubusz

Leobschütz	Głubczyce	Sagan	Żagań
Leubus	Lubiąż	Sankt Annaberg	Góra Św. Anny
Leuthen	Lutynia	Schmograu	Smogorzów
Liebenthal	Lubomierz	Schreiberhau	Szklarska Poręba
Liegnitz	Legnica	Schweidnitz	Świdnica
Lissa (Pr. Posen)	Leszno	Schweinitz	Świdnica
Löwenberg	Lwówek	Schwientochlowitz	Świętochłowice
Lüben	Lubin	Sprottau	Szprotawa
Lublinitz	Lubliniec	Strehlen	Strzelin
Lubowitz	Łubowice	Steinau	Ścinawa
Markstädt	Laskowice	Stettin	Szczecin
Militsch	Milicz	Striegau	Strzegom
Mittelwalde	Międzylesie	Tarnowitz	Tarnowskie Góry
Mollwitz	Małujowice	Teschen	Cieszyn
Münsterberg	Ziębice	Thorn	Toruń
Myslowitz	Mysłowice	Tormersdorf	Predocice
Namslau	Namysłów	Trachenberg	Żmigród
Neisse	Nysa	Trebnitz	Trzebnica
Neukirch	Nowy Kościoł	Wahlstatt	Legnickie Pole
Neumarkt	Środa Śląska	Waldenburg	Wałbrzych
Neustadt	Prudnik	Weigelsdorf	Ostroszowice
Nimkau	Miękinia	Wilschkowitz	Wilczkowice
Nimptsch	Niemcza	Wohlau	Wołów
Oberglogau	Głogówek	Wohnwitz	Wojnowice
Oels	Oleśnica	Wölfelsgrund	Międzygórze
Ohlau	Oława	Wollin	Woliń
Oppeln	Opole	Würben	Wierzbna
Oppcrau	Oporów	Ziegenhals	Głuchołazy
Ottmachau	Otmuchów	Zobten	Sobótka
Parchwitz	Prochowice	Zobtenberg	Ślęża
Patschkau	Paczków	Zottwitz	Sobocisko
Pawelwitz	Pawłowice	Zülz	Biała
Peilau	Piława		
Peterwitz	Stoszowice		
Peterswaldau	Pieszyce		
Pitschen	Byczyna		
Plagwitz	Płakowice		
Pless	Pszczyna		
Posen	Poznań		
Prausnitz	Prusice		
Radlowitz	Radłowice		
Ratibor	Racibórz		
Rattwitz	Ratowice		
Reichau	Zarzyce		
Reichenbach	Dzierżoniów		
Reimswaldau	Rybnica Leśna		
Riebnig	Rybnik		
Ritschen	Ryczyn		

Polish–German

Biała	Zülz	Kamienna Góra	Landshut
Bielsko	Bielitz	Karńcza Góra	Kentschkau
Bierutów	Bernstadt	Katowice	Kattowitz
Bierutowice	Brückenberg	Kłodzko	Glatz
Bogusławice	Boguslawitz	Kluczbork	Kreuzburg
Boguszów	Gottesberg	Kołobrzeg	Kolberg
Bolesławice	Bunzelwitz	Koźle	Cosel
Bolesławiec	Bunzlau	Kostrzyn	Küstrin
Bolków	Bolkenhain	Krobielowice	Krieblowitz
Brzeg	Brieg	Krosno	Krossen
Brzeg Dolny	Dyhernfurth	Krzeszów	Grüssau
Brzezinka Średzka	Klein Bresa	Krzyżowa	Kreisau
Brzeźno	Gross Breesen	Książ	Fürstenstein
Byczyna	Pitschen	Kudowa Zdrój	Bad Kudowa
Bystrzyca Kłodzka	Habelschwerdt	Kunów	Kuhnau
Bytom	Beuthen	Kunowice	Kunersdorf
Chojnów	Haynau	Lądek Zdrój	Bad Landeck
Chorzów	Königshütte	Łambinowice	Lamsdorf
Cieplice Zdrój	Bad Warmbrunn	Laskowice	Markstädt
Cieszyn	Teschen	Legnica	Liegnitz
Czernica	Langenau	Legnickie Pole	Wahlstatt
Dobromierz	Hohenfriedeberg	Leszno	Lissa (Pr. Posen)
Drawsko	Dramburg	Lubań	Lauban
Drezdenko	Driesen	Lubiąż	Leubus
Dzierżoniów	Reichenbach	Lubin	Lüben
Gdańsk	Danzig	Lubliniec	Lublinitz
Gliwice	Gleiwitz	Lubomierz	Liebenthal
Głogów	Glogau	Łubowice	Lubowitz
Głogówek	Oberglogau	Lubusz	Lebus
Głownin	Glofenau	Lutynia	Leuthen
Głubczyce	Leobschütz	Lwówek	Löwenberg
Głuchołazy	Ziegenhals	Małujowice	Mollwitz
Gniezno	Gnesen	Meleświce	Fünfteichen
Góra Św. Anny	Sankt Annaberg	Miedzanka	Kupferberg
Goszcz	Goschütz	Międzygórze	Wölfelsgrund
Gozdnica	Freiwaldau	Międzylesie	Mittelwalde
Grodziec	Gröditzberg	Miękinia	Nimkau
Grodków	Grottkau	Milicz	Militsch
Henryków	Heinrichau	Mysłakowice	Erdmannsdorf
Jagniątów	Agnetendorf	Mysłowice	Myslowitz
Jawor	Jauer	Namysłów	Namslau
Jelenia Góra	Hirschberg	Niemcza	Nimptsch
Jordanów Śląski	Jordansmühl	Niemodlin	Falkenberg
Kaliningrad (Rus)	Königsberg	Nowy Kościoł	Neukirch
Kamień	Kammin	Nysa	Neisse
Kamieniec	Kamenz	Oława	Ohlau

Oleśnica	Oels	Toruń	Thorn
Oleśnica Mała	Klein Oels	Trzebnica	Trebnitz
Olsztyn	Allenstein	Wałbrzych	Waldenburg
Opole	Oppeln	Wambierzyce	Albendorf
Oporów	Opperau	Węglowice	Kohlfurt
Ostroszowice	Weigelsdorf	Wierzbna	Würben
Oświęcim	Auschwitz	Wilczkowice	Wilschkowitz
Otmuchów	Ottmachau	Wojnowice	Wohnwitz
Paczków	Patschkau	Wołczyn	Konstadt
Pawłowice	Pawelwitz	Woliń	Wollin
Pieszyce	Peterswaldau	Wołów	Wohlau
Piława	Peilau	Wrocław	Breslau
Piotrkowice	Gross Peterwitz	– Bartoszowice	– Bartheln
Płakowice	Plagwitz	– Bielany	– Bettlern
Poznań	Posen	– Bieńkowice	– Benkwitz
Predocice	Tormersdorf	– Bierdzany	– Pirscham
Prudnik	Neustadt	– Biskupin	– Bischofswalde
Prusice	Prausnitz	– Borek	– Herzogshufen
Psie Pole	Hundsfeld	– Brochów	– Brockau
Pszczyna	Pless	– Dąbie	– Grüneiche
Racibórz	Ratibor	– Dworek	– Kleinburg
Radłowice	Radlowitz	– Gądów Mały	– Klein Gandau
Ratowice	Rattwitz	– Gaj	– Herdain
Rogoźnica	Gross Rosen	– Gajowice	– Gabitz
Rybnica Leśna	Reimswaldau	– Glinianki	– Lehmgruben
Rybnik	Riebnig	– Grabiszyn	– Gräbschen
Ryczyn	Ritschen	– Huby	– Huben
Śinawa	Steinau	– Jerzmanowo	– Herrmannsdorf
Ślęża	Zobtenberg	– Kąty	– Kanth
Smogorzów	Schmograu	– Karłowice	– Karlowitz
Sobocisko	Zottwitz	– Kępa Mieszczanska	– Burgerwerder
Sobótka	Zobten	– Klecina	– Klettendorf
Środa Śląska	Neumarkt	– Kleczków	– Kletschkau
Stoszowice	Peterwitz	– Kłokoczyce	– Glockschütz
Strzegom	Striegau	– Kowale	– Kawallen
Strzelce Opolskie	Gross Strehlitz	– Kozanów	– Kosel
Strzelin	Strehlen	– Krzeptów	– Kriptau
Strzelniki	Jägerndorf	– Krzyki	– Krietern
Świdnica	Schweidnitz	– Księże Małe	– Klein Ohlewiesen
Świdnica	Schweinitz	– Księże Wielkie	– Gross Ohlewiesen
Świebodzice	Freiburg	– Kuźniki	– Schmiedefeld
Świętochłowice	Schwientochlowitz	– Leśnica	– Lissa
Syców	Gross Wartenberg	– Lipa Piotrowska	– Leipe Petersdorf
Szczawno Zdrój	Bad Salzbrunn	– Marszowice	– Marschwitz
Szczecin	Stettin	– Maślice	– Masselwitz
Szklarska Poręba	Schreiberhau	– Mokra	– Muckerau
Szprotawa	Sprottau	– Mokronos Grn.	– Oberhof
Tarnowskie Góry	Tarnowitz	– Mokronos Dln.	– Niederhof

– Muchobór	– Mochbern	Ząbkowice Śląskie	Frankenstein
– Nowa Wieś	– Neudorf	Żagań	Sagan
– Nowy Dwór	– Neuhof	Zarzyce	Reichau
– Ołbin	– Elbing	Zgorzelec	Görlitz
– Ołtaszyn	– Oltaschin	Ziębice	Münsterberg
– Opatowice	– Ottwitz	Zielona Góra	Grünberg
– Osobowice	– Oswitz	Złotoryja	Goldberg
– Ostrów Tumski	– Dom Insel	Żmigród	Trachenberg
– Partynice	– Hartlieb		
– Pawłowice	– Wendelborn		
– Pilczyce	– Pilsnitz		
– Popowice	– Pöpelwitz		
– Poświętne	– Heiligensee		
– Pracze Odrzańskie	– Heernprotsch		
– Pracze Widawskie	– Protsch-Weide		
– Radomierzyce	– Riembergshof		
– Rakowiec	– Morgenau		
– Ratyń	– Rathen		
– Rędzin	– Ransern		
– Różanka	– Rosenthal		
– Sępolno	– Zimpel		
– Siechnica	– Kraftborn		
– Siedem Łanów	– Siebenhufen		
– Siedlec	– Zedlitz		
– Ślęża	– Lohe		
– Sołtysowice	– Burgweide		
– Smolec	– Schmolz		
– Stabłowice	– Stabelwitz		
– Strachowice	– Strachwitz		
– Świniary	– Schebitz		
– Swojczyce	– Güntherbrücke		
– Szczepin	– Tschepine		
– Szczytniki	– Scheitnig		
– Tarnogaj	– Dürrgoy		
– Widawa	– Weide		
– Wojszyce	– Woischwitz		
– Wyspa Piaskowa	– Sand Insel		
– Wyspa Słodowa	– Vorderbleiche		
– Zabrodzie	– Zweibrodt		
– Zacisze	– Wilhelmsruh		
– Zakrzów	– Sacrau		
– Zalesie	– Leerbeutel		
– Zerniki	– Schönborn		
– Zgorzelisko	– Görlitz		
– Złotniki	– Goldschmieden		

NOTES

Foreword

1 1 October 2000: at the International Writers' Meeting in Vilnius, as reported in *Rzeczpospolita*, Warsaw 40 (406), 7 October 2000: C. Miłosz, 'Aby duchy umarłych zostawiły nas w spokoju', ibid., +Plus—Minus, D1–2
2 Ibid., D1
3 Günter Grass, *Przekleństwo i Łaska* ('Curse and Grace'), ibid., D2

Introduction

1 Joseph Partsch, *Central Europe*, London, 1903, p. 333
2 Ibid.
3 Ibid., p. 336
4 Ibid., p. 340
5 See Jacques Le Rider, *La Mitteleuropa*, Paris, 1994, pp. 92–6
6 Theodor Heuss, *Friedrich Naumann*, Stuttgart, 1949; see also P. Theiner, *Sozialer Liberalismus und deutsche Weltpolitik; Friedrich Naumann in Wilhelminischen Deutschland*, Baden-Baden, 1983
7 See H. & C. Seton-Watson, *The Making of a New Europe: R. W. Seton-Watson and the Last Years of Austria-Hungary*, London, 1981
8 See P. S. Wandycz, *The Price of Freedom: A History of East Central Europe from the Middle Ages to the Present*, London, 1992; also Alan Palmer, *The Lands Between: A History of East-Central Europe since the Congress of Vienna*, London, 1970, and Richard Crampton, *Eastern Europe in the Twentieth Century*, London, 1994. See also Jerzy Kłoczowski, *East Central Europe in the Historiography of the Countries of the Region*, Lublin, 1995
9 Odette Keun, *Continental States: Marches of Invasion, Valley of Conquest, Peninsula of Chaos*, London, 1944
10 See V. Havel et al., *The Power of the Powerless*, London, 1985, G. Konrád, *Antipolitics: An Essay*, New York, 1984, A. Michnik, *Letters from Prison and Other Essays*, Berkeley, 1985
11 Josef Kroutvor, *Poliže s. dejinami*, (*c.*1978), trans. as *Europa Środkowa – anegdota i historia*, Izabelin, 1998
12 Timothy Garton Ash, 'Does Central Europe Exist?', in *The Uses of Adversity: Essays on the Fate of Central Europe*, London, 1999, pp. 161–91.
13 Ibid.

Prologue

1 *Schlesische Tageszeitung*, 20 January 1945
2 Horst Gleiss, *Breslauer Apokalypse 1945*, vol. 1, Wedel, 1986, p. 204

3 Ibid., vol. 1, p. 204

4 Paul Peikert, *'Festung Breslau' in den Berichten eines Pfarrers*, K. Jońca and A. Konieczny (eds), Wrocław, 1997, pp. 25–6

5 Gleiss, op. cit., vol. 1, p. 211

6 Sebastian Siebel-Achenbach, *Lower Silesia from Nazi-Germany to Communist Poland 1942–49*, New York, 1994, p. 60

7 Bundesarchiv (Koblenz) Ost-Dok. 2, no. 171, pp. 123–5

8 See Nerin E. Gun, *Eva Braun – Hitler. Leben und Schicksal*, Velbert-Kettwig, 1968, pp. 237–8. With thanks to Antony Beevor.

9 Gleiss, op. cit., vol. VII, p. 357. It is probable that the KZ inmates of Dyhernfurth were shot because of the sensitive nature of the work they had been doing. Dyhernfurth was an I. G. Farben factory for the production of the nerve gas 'Tabun'

10 David Irving, *The Destruction of Dresden*, London, 1985, p. 84

11 *Schlesische Tageszitung*, 22 January 1945

12 Paul Adair, *Hitler's Greatest Defeat*, London, 1994, p. 181

13 I.C.B. Dear and M.R.D. Foot (eds), *The Oxford Companion to the Second World War*, Oxford, 1995, p. 445

14 John Erickson, *The Road to Berlin*, London, 1983, p. 447

15 Ibid., p. 429

16 Ibid., p. 472

17 Joachim Konrad, *Das Ende von Breslau*, Vierteljahrshefte für Zeitgeschichte, 1954, vol. 4, p. 389

18 Gleiss, op. cit., vol. VII, pp. 1167–9

19 Albert Seaton, *The Russo-German War*, London, 1971, pp. 560–1

20 Hugo Hartung, *Schlesien 1944/45*, Munich, 1956, p. 280

21 Siebel-Achenbach, op. cit., p. 28

22 Gleiss, op. cit., vol. V, p. 279

23 For example, *Wehrmacht* estimates from 24 March 1945 of 143,000 (quoted in Gleiss, op. cit., vol. III, p. 787) or the commonly quoted figure of 180,000–200,000 (among others, *Breslau 1945 – Zerstörung einer Stadt*, Marzena Smolak, Wrocław, 1995). Joachim Rogall puts the figure at 200–300,000 (Rogall, *Schlesien und die Schlesier*, Munich, 1996, p. 164)

24 Erickson, op. cit., p. 472

25 Ivan Koniev, *Year of Victory*, Moscow, 1969, p. 56

26 Ibid., p. 55

27 Irving, op. cit., p. 90. Also quoted in Alexander McKee, *Dresden 1945*, London, 1983, p. 103

28 Martin Gilbert, *Second World War*, London, 1989, p. 639

29 R.E. Dupuy and T.N. Dupuy, *The Collins Encyclopedia of Military History*, Glasgow, 1993, p. 1225

30 *Schlesische Tageszeitung*, 2 February 1945, pp. 1, 2

31 Gleiss, op. cit., vol. II, p. 100A

32 Peikert, op. cit., p. 39

33 Aleksandr Solzhenitsyn, *The Gulag Archipelago*, London, 1974, quoted in Richard Overy, *Russia's War*, London, 1997, p. 262

34 RGASPI 17/125/314. Quoted by Antony Beevor in *Berlin: The Downfall, 1945*, to be published, London, 2002

35 Oppeln Incident: KA-FU, E1:18, vol. 6, quoted by Beevor, op. cit.

36 Solzhenitsyn, op. cit., p. 240, quoted by Beevor, op. cit.

37 Gleiss, op. cit., vol. VII, p. 1605

38 Ibid., vol. VII, p. 1605

39 Peikert, op. cit., pp. 153–4

40 SS-Hauptsturmführer W. Scholz (SS Besslein Regt) quoted in Gleiss, op. cit., vol. IV, p. 651

41 H. von Ahlfen and H. Niehoff, *So kämpfte Breslau*, Stuttgart, 1978, pp. 77–8

42 Gleiss, op. cit., vol. III, p. 910

43 Hugo Hartung, 'Der Abschied', *Merian* 3, 1 July 1950, p. 69

44 Gleiss, op. cit., vol. IV, pp. 1113–14: Hendrik Verton, *Gruppenführer* in the SS Besslein Regiment

45 Ibid., vol. III, p. 828

46 Peikert, op. cit., p. 147

47 Fritz Morzik, *Die deutschen Transportflieger im Zweiten Weltkrieg*, Frankfurt am Main, 1966, pp. 223–4. Though the records are incomplete, the missing section – from 25 March to 6 April – is not critical

48 Gleiss, op. cit., vol. IV, p. 935

49 PRO London, ref: HWI/3539, document ref. CX/MSS/T469/7

50 Quoted in Christopher Duffy, *Red Storm on the Reich*, London, 2000, p. 260

51 Gleiss, op. cit., vol. III, p. 651

52 K. Jońca, A. Konieczny, *Upadek Festung Breslau*, Wrocław, 1963, p. 28

53 Ibid.

54 Hartung, *Schlesien*, op. cit., p. 321

55 Hugo Hartung, 'Ostern 1945', in *Breslau – Geliebt und Unvergessen*, Herbert Hupka (ed.), Leer, 1990, p. 73

56 This would appear to disprove the widely held belief that the only aircraft to use the Kaiserstrasse airstrip was that used in Gauleiter Hanke's escape

57 Gleiss, op. cit., vol. IV, p. 500

58 Ibid., vol. IV, p. 644

59 Quoted by the *Guardian*, 2 May 1945

60 Gleiss, op. cit., vol. V, p. 35

61 Ibid., vol. V, p. 130

62 PRO London, Ref: WO 309/1294

63 Peikert, op. cit., p. 202

64 Gleiss, op. cit., vol. III, p. 797

65 Ibid., vol. VIII, p. 730

66 Stanisława Marciniak, 'Dane mi było przeżyć, in *Niewolnicy w Breslau, Wolni we Wrocławiu*, Wrocław, 1995, pp. 119–22

67 Konrad, op. cit., p. 390

68 Johannes Kaps, *Die Tragödie Schlesiens 1945–6*, Munich, 1952, p. 122

69 Gleiss, op. cit., vol. V, p. 231

70 Ibid., vol. VIII, p. 1300

71 Many myths surround Hanke's flight on 5 May 1945. Albert Speer claimed that Hanke left Breslau in a prototype helicopter, but this is not corroborated

(Dan van der Vat, *The Good Nazi, The Life and Lies of Albert Speer*, London, 1997, p. 218). Hanke's ultimate fate is contested. Like many Nazis he was widely suspected of escaping to South America, though numerous reports mention his death at the hands of Czech partisans near Komotau in the Sudetenland. A PRO file shows British Military Prosecutors hunting Hanke in Garmisch, Austria, in the autumn of 1946

72 Gleiss, op. cit, vol. V, p. 233
73 Hartung, *Schlesien*, op. cit., p. 355
74 Quoted in Duffy, op. cit., p. 267
75 Seaton, op. cit., p. 561
76 Gleiss, op. cit., vol. V, p. 1094
77 Seaton, op. cit., p. 561

1. Island City: Archaeology and Prehistory to AD 1000

1 In the modern suburb of Krzyki (Krietern), at Skarbowców Street, discovered in 1996
2 At Osobowice (Oswitz)
3 At Partynice (Hartlieb)
4 At Zakrzów (Sacrau)
5 'Na ziemiach nadodrzańskich życie na moment jakby zupelnie zamarło.' M. Kaczmarek et al., *Wrocław: dziedzictwo wieków*, Wrocław, 1997, p. 11
6 The 'Giant Mountains' – *Krkonoše* in Czech, *Karkonosze* in Polish and *Riesengebirge* in German
7 The 'Snowy Head' – *Sněžka* in Czech, *Śnieżka* in Polish and *Schneekoppe* in German
8 The 'Cats Hills' – *Kocie Góry* in Polish and the *Katzengebirge* in German
9 *Ślęża* in Polish, *Zobten* in German
10 Marianna Bocian, 'Na Moście Tumskim we Wrocławiu', *Lyrisches Breslau*, Wrocław, 1996, p. 126
11 Siegfried Herbst, 'Mittag am Fluß', ibid., p. 140
12 (ed.) Jerzy Duma, *Zuflüsse zur unteren Oder und zur Ostsee bis zur Persante*, vol. 4 of *Hydronymia Europaea*, Stuttgart, 1988, p. 68
13 *Encyclopaedia Britannica*, 11th edition, Cambridge 1911, vol. XXV, p. 90, under 'Silesia'
14 J. MacKillop, *Dictionary of Celtic Mythology*, Oxford, 1998, p. 309; see also J. Rozwadowski, *Studia nad nazwami wód słowiańskich*, Cracow, 1948, p. 259ff.; H. Krahe, *Unsere ältesten Flussnamen*, Wiesbaden, 1964, pp. 41, 102; J. Udolph, *Die Stellung der Gewässernamen Polens innerhalb der alteuropäischen Hydronymie*, Heidelberg, 1990, pp. 204–11
15 *Tacitus on Britain and Germany*, H. Mattingly (trans.), Baltimore, 1948, p. 138
16 Jordanów (Jordansmühl) and Wolfskirch (Wilczkowice)
17 Grabiszyn (Gräbschen), Gądów Mały (Klein Gandau) and Dąbie (Grüneiche)
18 Jordanów
19 *The Neolithic in Poland*, Tadeusz Wiślanski (ed.), Krystyna Kozłowska (trans.), Wrocław, 1970, p. 131
20 Barry Cunliffe (ed.), *Oxford Illustrated Prehistory of Europe*, Oxford, 1994, p. 257
21 Biskupin
22 See Martin Jahn, *Die Kelten in Schlesien*, Leipzig, 1931; J. Filip, *Keltové ve středni Europě*, Prague, 1956; Zenon Woźniak, *Osadnictwo Celtyckie w Polsce*, Wrocław, 1970; Janina Rosen-Przeworska, *Spadek po Celtach*, Wrocław, 1979; J. Kostrzewski, *Pradzieje Śląska*, Wrocław, 1970

23 Karńcza Góra (Kentschkau): Woźniak, op. cit., table 1
24 At Sobocisko (Zottwitz) ibid., passim
25 At Brzezińka-Sredzka (Klein Bresa) ibid., passim
26 At Głownin (Glofenau) and Radłowice, ibid., passim
27 At Sobótka (Zobten), near Wrocław, ibid., pp. 65–6
28 Ibid., pp. 65–75, tables XVI, XVII
29 J. Rosen-Przeworska, op. cit.
30 Sites include Książ (Tschansch), Osobowice and Kosanów (Kosel)
31 *Tacitus*, op. cit., p. 139
32 Magdalenea Maczyńska, *Die Völkerwanderung*, Zurich, 1993, p. 71. The finds from the Zakrzów site were partly lost during the Second World War
33 Fritz Geschwendt, *Breslau in der Urzeit*, Breslau, 1922, p. 22
34 For example, Zakrzów
35 Heinrich Bartsch, *Geschichte Schlesiens*, Würzburg, 1985, p. 10
36 Michał Parczewski, *Die Anfänge der frühslawischen Kultur in Polen*, Vienna, 1993, p. 141
37 Konrad Jażdżewski, *Poland*, London, 1965, Glyn Daniel (general ed.), figure 21, Dobrodzien (Guttentag) Culture
38 Felix Dahn, 'Gotentreue', in *Das Oxforder Buch der Deutscher Dichtung*, H.G. Fielder (ed.), Oxford, 1930, pp. 472–3. English translation by Dr Cyril Edwards
39 J. Słowacki, *Dzieła wszystkie*, J. Kleiner (ed.), Wrocław, 1972, XVI, p. 358 (from *Król-Duch*, Rhapsody II, Song I, lines 9–12)
40 Ibid, XVI, p. 365 (from *Król-Duch*, Rhapsody II, Song II, lines 1–16)
41 Dimitri Obolensky, *The Byzantine Commonwealth*, London, 1971, p. 86
42 Francis Dvornik, *The Slavs: Their Early History and Civilisation*, Boston, 1956, p. 26
43 Norman Davies, *God's Playground*, vol. 1, Oxford, 1981, p. 45
44 Jörg Hoensch, *Geschichte Böhmens*, 3rd edition, Munich, 1997, p 39
45 Johannes Chrząszcz, 'Die Einführung des Christentums in Schlesien und die Gründung des Bistums Breslau (1000)', in *Oberschlesien*, vol. 13, no. 5, August 1914, p. 2
46 An exhibition to this effect was displayed in the porch of the Uniat Church (the former St Ann's chapel) in 2001
47 A.P. Vlasto, *The Entry of the Slavs into Christendom*, Cambridge, 1970, p. 115
48 *The Annals of Jan Długosz*, abridged by Maurice Michael, Chichester, 1997, pp. 2–4
49 Paweł Jasienica, *Piast Poland*, Alexander Jordan (trans.), Miami, 1992, p. 29
50 *Schlesisches Urkundenbuch*, vol. 1, Historische Kommission für Schlesien (ed.), edited by Heinrich Appelt, Cologne, 1963, p. 3, (translated from the Latin by Dr Paul Smith)
51 Norman Davies, *Adalbert or Wojciech: Gdańsk or Danzig: A Multinational Millennium, 997–1997*, SSEES occasional papers, no. 37, London, 1997
52 Lutz E. von Padberg, *Die Christianisierung Europas im Mittelalter*, Stuttgart, 1998, p. 256
53 Jazdzewski, op. cit., p. 126
54 Bolko von Richthofen, *Die ältere Bronzezeit in Schlesien*, Berlin, 1926, p. 127
55 T. Sulimirski, *The Sarmatians*, London, 1970, Glyn Daniel (general ed.), p. 166
56 'Chodzi bowiem o to, że dopiero we wczesnym średniowieczu można dowodnie stwierdzić obecność ludności slowiańskiej na ziemiach polskich.' Kaczmarek, op. cit., p. 12
57 *Tacitus*, op. cit., pp. 139–40
58 Davies, op. cit., vol. 1, p. 47

2. *Wrotizla between the Polish, Czech and German Crowns, 1000–1335*

1 Thietmar of Merseburg, vol. IV, p. 45. Polish version as *Kronika Thietmara*, Marian Jedlicki (ed.), Poznań, 1956. Translated by Dr Paul Smith

2 *The Annals of Jan Długosz: Annales seu cronicae incliti regni Poloniae*, abridged and edited by Maurice Michael with a commentary by Paul Smith, Chichester, 1997. Hereafter referred to as 'Długosz'. See also Gerard Labuda, *Zaginiona Cronica w Rocznikach Jana Długosza*, Poznań, 1983

3 Długosz, op. cit., p. 86

4 The development of the town of Hundsfeld appears to have been intimately involved with the imperial invasion of 1109. In one interpretation the name of the town is thought to have come from the aftermath of the battle, in which wild dogs feasted on the fallen. Another holds that the imperial forces were encamped at Hundsfeld and were forced to bear the insults of the locals. A less colourful account holds that the town developed on the site of a settlement of the Duke of Silesia's dog handlers. Hugo Weczerka (ed.), *Schlesien*, Stuttgart, 1977, p. 201

5 Długosz, op. cit., p. 70

6 Ibid., p. 71

7 Ibid., p. 178

8 R.E. Dupuy and T.N. Dupuy, *The Collins Encyclopedia of Military History*, 4th edition, Glasgow, 1993, p. 379

9 See 'Die Familie Strachwitz', Arthur, Graf Strachwitz, *Wie es wirklich war – Errinerungen*, Dülmen, 1991, pp. 406–47

10 Długosz, op. cit., p. 181

11 See R.A. Skelton, Thomas E. Marston and George D. Palmer, *The Vinland Map and the Tartar Relation*, New Haven and London, 1995, map following p. 130

12 At the battle of Dürnkrut in 1278, where Otakar was defeated and killed by Rudolf of Habsburg, fully one-third of the Bohemian force was made up of Silesians. Bruce Boswell, 'Territorial Division and the Mongol Invasions', *The Cambridge History of Poland* (to 1696), W.F. Reddaway, J.H. Penson, O. Halecki, R. Dybowski (eds), Cambridge, 1950, p. 99

13 Długosz, op. cit., AD 1238, p. 175

14 Ibid., AD 1290, p. 234

15 Ibid., AD 1293, p. 238

16 Joachim Bahlcke, *Schlesien und die Schlesier*, Munich, 1996, p. 27

17 Weczerka, op. cit., p. 201

18 K. Wutke, 'Schlesiens Bergbau und Hüttenwesen, 1136–1528', in *Codex Diplomaticus Silesiae*, vol. XX, Breslau, 1900

19 Długosz, op. cit., p. 97

20 Heinrich Bartsch, *Geschichte Schlesiens*, Würzburg, 1985, p. 18

21 St Luke, chapter 3, v. 4–5

22 The results of Czesław's activities are disputed. Some maintain that a great storm drove the invaders away, others that the appearance of a column of light disturbed them. The conventional interpretation holds that fire drove the Mongols out of Wrotizla, however. Modern scholarship can attribute this 'miracle' to two possible sources. Either the fires around Wrotizla itself spread to the Mongol camp, or it was an accident of their own making through their use of 'Greek fire' or even gunpowder

23 See entry on St Ceslaus in *The Catholic Encyclopedia*, New York, 1913

24 Fritz Enderwitz, *Breslauer Sagen und Legenden*, Breslau, 1922, p. 17

25 R.J. Loenertz, *Une Ancienne Chronique des Provinciaux dominicains en Pologne*, Archivum Fratrum Praedicatorum, vol. XXI, Rome, 1951, pp. 5–50

26 See Paul Smith, 'Crusade and Society in Eastern Europe: The Hospital and the Temple in Poland and Pomerania, 1145–1370', University of London, unpublished Ph.D. thesis, 1994

27 Willy Lorenz, *Die Kreuzherren mit dem roten Stern*, Königstein/Ts., 1964, p. 134

28 Walter Kuhn, *Beiträge zur Schlesischen Siedlungsgeschichte*, Bad Windsheim, 1971, pp. 106–30

29 Hartmut Boockmann, *Der Deutsche Orden*, Munich, 1981, p. 78

30 Eric Christiansen, *The Northern Crusades*, London, 1997, p. 155

31 See P. Górecki, *Parishes, tithes and society in early medieval Poland, 1100–1250*, Philadelphia, 1993

32 Ferdinand Seibt, 'The Religious Problems', in *Eastern and Western Europe in the Middle Ages*, Geoffrey Barraclough (ed.), London, 1970, p. 107

33 Norbert Conrads (ed.), *Schlesien*, Berlin, 1994, p. 85

34 After Długosz, op. cit., p. 227

35 See Paul Smith, op. cit.; also Appelt-Irgang, *Schlesisches Urkundenbuch*

36 Długosz, op. cit., p. 210

37 Gustav Bauch (ed.), *Geschichte des Breslauer Schulwesens vor der Reformation*, Breslau, 1909, p. 6

38 W. Irgang, W. Bein and H. Neubach, *Schlesien – Geschichte, Kultur und Wirtschaft*, Cologne, 1995, p. 65

39 Bartsch, op. cit., p. 40

40 For the modern German text, see *Die Minnesänger*, Karl Pannier, Görlitz, 1881, p. 291. For Middle High German, see *Deutsche Liederdichter des 13. Jahrhunderts*, Carl von Kraus (ed.), Tübingen, 1952, pp. 160–1. English translation by Dr Cyril Edwards

41 Benjamin Arnold, *Medieval Germany, 500–1300*, London, 1997, p. 9

42 Alexandra Ritchie, *Faust's Metropolis*, London, 1998, p. 18

43 See Herbert Ludat, *Legenden um Jaxa von Köpenick*, Leipzig, 1936

44 Długosz, op. cit., p. 10

45 See Zygmunt Świechowski, *Architektura na Śląsku do połowy XIII wieku*, Warsaw, 1955

46 Adolf Weiss, *Geschichte der Stadt Breslau von der ältesten bis zur neuesten Zeit*, Breslau, 1889, p. 33

47 Charles Higounet, *Die deutsche Ostsiedlung im Mittelalter*, Berlin, 1986, p. 175

48 Klaus Zernack, 'Polnische Bevölkerung und Neustammbildung in Schlesien', p. 90, from *Die Rolle Schlesiens und Pommerns in der Geschichte der Deutsch-Polnische Beziehungen im Mittelalter* – XII deutsch-polnische Schulbuchkonferenz der Historiker von 5–10 Juni 1979, in Allenstein/Olsztyn, Braunschweig, 1980, Rainer Riemenschneider (ed.)

49 F.R.H. Du Boulay, *Germany in the Later Middle Ages*, London, 1983, p. 120

50 Reddaway et al., *Cambridge History of Poland*, op. cit., pp. 56–7

51 See, for example, Bartsch, op. cit., p. 21

52 Benedykt Zientara, 'Schlesien im Piastenstaat bis zur Wende des 13. Jahrhunderts', p. 50, in Riemenschneider, op. cit.

53 Geoffrey Barraclough, *The Origins of Modern Germany*, New York, 1984, p. 253

54 Alexander Gieysztor, 'The beginnings of Jewish settlement in the Polish lands', p. 15, in *The Jews in Poland*, C. Abramsky, M. Jachimczyk and A. Polonsky (eds), Oxford, 1986

55 Leszek Ziątkowski, *Die Geschichte der Juden in Breslau*, Wrocław, 2000, p. 8

56 G. Scheuermann, *Breslau Lexicon*, vol. 1, Dülmen, 1994, pp. 703, 709

57 After M. Wodziński, *Hebrajskie inskrypcje na Śląsku, XIII–XVIII wieku*, Wrocław, 1996, p. 169

58 L. Ziątkowski, *Dzieje Żydów we Wrocławiu*, Wrocław, 2000, p. 10

59 Friedrich Heer, *The Medieval World – Europe 1100–1350*, London, 1974, p. 312

60 Hermann Uhtenwoldt, *Peter Wlast – Graf von Breslau – Ein Wikinger auf ostdeutschen Boden*, Breslau, 1940

61 'Rathslinie von 1287', in the *Breslauer Stadtbuch, Codex Diplomaticus Silesiae*, vol. XI, Breslau, 1882

62 Ibid.

63 Henricus Pauper, 'Rechnung des Stadt Breslau von 1299–1355' in *Codex Diplomaticus Silesiae*, vol. II, Bresslau, 1861, p. 1

64 Ibid., p. 3

65 O. Meinardus, *Das Neumarkter Rechtsbuch . . .* Breslau, 1906

66 See *Breslau als Garnison und Festung 1241–1941*, Günther Gieraths, Hamburg, 1961

67 S. Wormell (ed.), *Pallas – Poland*, London, 1994, p. 594

68 Ibid., p. 595

69 Długosz, op. cit., p. 271

3. Vretslav in the Kingdom of Bohemia, 1335–1526

1 Norman Davies, *Europe: a History*, London, 1997, p. 428

2 The 'Golden Bull' derived its name from the golden seal (Latin *bulla*) with which it was authenticated

3 Lord Bryce, *The Holy Roman Empire*, London, 1875, p. 238

4 A. Weiß, *Chronik der Stadt Breslau von der ältesten bis zur neuesten Zeit*, Breslau, 1888, p. 147

5 Długosz, op. cit., (see note 3 in Chapter 3), p. 274

6 C. Edmund Maurice, *Bohemia*, London, 1922, p. 123

7 J.M.D. Meiklejohn, *A New History of England and Great Britain*, London, 1903, p. 184

8 František Kavka, 'Politics and Culture under Charles IV' in *Bohemia in History*, Mikuláš Teich (ed.), Cambridge, 1998, p. 59

9 G. Scheuermann, *Das Breslau Lexicon*, vol. I, Dülmen, 1994, p. 727

10 Nikolaus Pol, *Jahrbücher der Stadt Breslau*, vol. I, J.G. Bürsching (ed.), Bresslau, 1813, p. 125

11 Norbert Conrads, *Schlesien*, Berlin, 1994, p. 144

12 G. Elze, *Breslau: Biographie einer deutschen Stadt*, Rautenberg, 1993, p. 24. Wenceslas was referred to by the Electors of Mainz, Cologne, Trier and the Palatinate as the '*unnütze König*'.

13 R. Heck, E. Maleczyńska (eds), *Ruch husycki w Polsce: wybór tekstów źródłowych*, Wrocław, 1953, no. 40, p. 57

14 Pol, op. cit., vol. I, p. 174

15 Peter Eschenloer, *Geschichte der Stadt Breslau 1440–1478*, vol. I, Breslau, 1827, p. 38

16 Robert Bruckner and J. Stein, 'Sitten und Unsitten im späten Mittelalter', in *Breslau – Ein Lesebuch*, Diethard H. Klein (ed.), Husum, 1988, p. 28

17 Jörg Hoensch, *Geschichte Böhmens*, 3rd edition, Munich, 1997, p. 160

18 See R. Koebner, *Der Widerstand Breslaus gegen Georg von Podiebrad*, Breslau, 1913

19 Frederick Heymann, *George of Bohemia – King of Heretics*, Princeton, 1965, p. 232

20 Elze, op. cit., p. 32

21 Friedrich August Wenzel, *Mathias Corvinius oder die Belagerung von Breslau im Jahre 1474*, in *Deutsche Schaubuehne*, vol. II, Augsburg and Leipzig, 1811

22 Pol, op. cit., vol. II, p. 45

23 Barthel Stein, 'Beschreibung von Schlesien und seiner Hauptstadt Breslau – 1512–13', in Heinrich Trierenberg (ed.), *Breslau in alten und neuen Reisebeschreibungen*, Düsseldorf, 1991, p. 23

24 Ibid., p. 24

25 Hoensch, op. cit., p. 134

26 František Kavka, 'Politics and Culture under Charles IV' in Teich (ed.), op. cit., p. 67

27 Heinrich Wendt, *Breslauer Bier* in Klein, op. cit., p. 137

28 *Encyclopaedia Britannica*, 11th edition, vol. XII, Cambridge, 1910, p. 930

29 Barthel Stein, *Descripcio Vratislaviae*, quoted in Hugo Weczerka, 'Breslaus Zentralität im ostmitteleuropäischen Raum um 1500' in *Metropolen im Wandel*, E. Engel, K. Lambrecht and H. Nogossek (eds), Berlin, 1996, p. 249

30 Bernhard Brilling, *Geschichte der Juden in Breslau von 1454 bis 1702*, vol. III of *Studia Delitzschiana*, K.H. Rengstorf (ed.), Stuttgart, 1960, p. 9

31 Długosz, op. cit., p. 288

32 Ibid., p. 290

33 Ibid., p. 373

34 See T.A. Fudge, *The Magnificent Ride: the First Reformation in Hussite Bohemia*, Aldershot, 1998

35 A. Stenzel (ed.), *Scriptores rerum Silesiacarum*, vol. I, pp. 251–2, in R. Heck, op. cit., no. 5, pp. 8–9

36 Fudge, op. cit., pp. 87–8

37 František Šmahel, 'The Hussite Movement: an anomaly of European history?' in Teich (ed.), op. cit., p. 87

38 Fudge, op. cit., p. 88

39 Archiv Česky III, 213ff, Heck, op. cit., no. 43 (1420), pp. 59–60

40 S. Belch, *Paulus Vladimir*, vol. I, The Hague, 1965, pp. 24–5

41 Heck, op. cit., no. 41, (1420), 'Inkwizycja w sprawie herezji w stosunku do biedoty wrocławskiej'

42 Pol, op. cit., vol. II, p. 3

43 Jakub Kostowski, 'Die Verehrung des Hl. Johannes Capistrano in Schlesien', in *Heilige und Heiligenverehrung in Schlesien*, Joachim Köhlmer (ed.), Sigmaringen, 1997, p. 149

44 'De Sermonibus Wratislaviensibus', L. Łuszczki O.F.M., *De Sermonibus S. Ioannis A Capistrano*, Rome, 1961, pp. 147–73

45 W. Urban, *Studia nad dziejami Wrocławskiej Diecezji w pierwszej połowie XV wieku*, Wrocław, 1959, pp. 246–51, 280–87, quoted by Łuszczki, op. cit., p. 147

46 Quoted in Elze, op. cit., p. 31

47 Fudge, op. cit., passim

48 See Karen Lambrecht, 'Breslau als Zentrum der gelehrten Kommunikation unter Bischof Johann V. Thurzó (1466–1520)', in *Archiv für schlesische Kirchengeschichte*, 58, (2000)

49 Kavka, in Teich (ed.), op. cit., p. 70

50 Joachim Bahlcke, *Schlesien und die Schlesier*, Munich, 1996, p. 282

51 Ibid., p. 304

52 Joseph Neuwirth, *Peter Parler von Gmünd*, Prague, 1891, p. 105

53 Jakub Kostowski, in *Rocznik Wrocławski*, no. 4 (1997), pp. 283–95

54 J.A. Barth, *Geschichte der seit dreihundert Jahren in Breslau befindlichen Stadtbuchdruckerei*, Breslau, 1804

55 See Peter Wörster, 'Breslau und Olmütz als Humanistische Zentren vor der Reformation' in *Humanismus und Renaissance in Ostmitteleuropa vor der Reformation*, W. Eberhard and A.A. Strnad (eds), Cologne, 1996

56 Gustav Bauch, *Caspar Ursinus Velius*, Budapest, 1886, p. 34

57 L. Corvinus, *Hortulus Elegantarum*, Bodleian Library, 4Bl(8) Th. Sheldon

58 Quoted in Weczerka, *Zentralität* . . . , op. cit., p. 260

59 Bahlcke, op. cit., p. 38

60 Conrads, *Schlesien*, op. cit., p. 164

61 See Karen Lambrecht, 'Aufstiegschancen und Handlungsräume in ostmitteleuropäischen Zentren um 1500. Das Beispiel der Unternehmerfamilie Thurzó', in ZfO, 47, 1998, vol. 3

62 Pol, op. cit., vol. I, p. 112

63 Excavation of the foundations of the City Hall, in the nineteenth century, unearthed one of the oldest Jewish gravestones in Vretslav, that of the Rabbi Chaim Ben Levi, dating from 1246

64 See Alfred Haverkampf (ed.), *Zur Geschichte der Juden im Deutschland des späten Mittelalters und der frühen Neuzeit*, Stuttgart, 1981

65 Leszek Ziątkowski, *Die Geschichte der Juden in Breslau*, Wrocław, 2000, p. 14

66 Marcus Brann (1849–1920), *Geschichte der Juden in Schlesien*, Breslau, 1896–1917 (journal); *Geschichte des jüdisch-theologischen Seminars*, Breslau, 1904; *Heinrich Graetz*, Vienna, 1917

67 Brann, *Geschichte der Juden*, p. 62

68 Długosz, op. cit., p. 310

69 Susslin of Ehrfurt, quoted by Brann, op. cit., p. 63

70 Hermann Markgraf, *Geschichte Breslaus*, Breslau, 1913, p. 18

71 Eschenloer, op. cit., vol. I, p. 253

72 Ibid., p. 253

73 Karen Lambrecht, *Hexenverfolgung und Zaubereiprozesse in den Schlesischen Territorien*, Cologne, 1995, p. 15

74 Ibid., p. 321

75 Pol, op. cit., vol. II, p. 161

76 Dieter-Lienhard Döring, *Alt-Breslau in Sage und Bild*, Leer/Ostfriesland, 1982, pp. 16–17. English translation by Dr Cyril Edwards

77 Lambrecht, *Hexenverfolgung*, op. cit., p. 321

78 Scheuermann, op. cit., p. 1460

79 W.-E. Peuckert, *Schlesische Sagen*, Jena, 1924, p. 51

80 Pol, op. cit., vol. I, p. 159

81 Weiß, op. cit., pp. 364–5

82 Breslauer Stadtbuch, in *Codex Diplomaticus Silesiae*, vol. XI, no. 41; also Heck, op. cit., no. 39

83 Pol, op. cit., vol. I, p. 125

84 See Jan Trzynadlowski, *The Wratislavian Town Hall*, Wrocław, 1997
85 Scheuermann, op. cit., vol. I, p. 531
86 This curious name celebrates the obscure legend of St Ursula and her Maidens. St Ursula was apparently a fourth-century British princess, who was martyred with her entourage in Cologne by the Huns. How the figure of her companions arrived at 11,000 is uncertain. See D. Attwater and C.R. John, *The Penguin Dictionary of Saints* (3rd edition), London, 1995, pp. 347–8

4. Presslaw under the Habsburg Monarchy, 1526–1741

1 Werner Marshall, *Geschichte des Bistums Breslau*, Stuttgart, 1980, p. 67
2 Gerhard Scheuermann, *Das Breslau Lexicon*, vol. 1, Dülmen, 1994, p. 466
3 Ibid., p. 466
4 R.J.W. Evans, *Rudolf II and his World – a study in intellectual history 1576–1612*, Oxford, 1973, p. 198
5 Erich Fink, *Geschichte der landesherrlichen Besuche in Breslau*, Breslau, 1897, pp. 75, 79–80
6 Jean Bérenger, *A History of the Habsburg Empire 1273–1700*, London, 1994, p. 236
7 Scheuermann, op. cit., p. 469
8 Sir Henry Ellis (ed.), *Original Letters Illustrative of English History*, First Series, vol. III, London, 1969, pp. 112–13
9 Nikolaus Pol, *Jahrbücher der Stadt Bresslau*, vol. V, Bresslau, 1824, pp. 219, 221
10 Norbert Conrads (ed.), *Schlesien*, Berlin, 1994, p. 277
11 C.V. Wedgwood, *The Thirty Years War*, London, 1938, p. 448
12 Gustavus III, King of Sweden, *Eulogy of Torstenson*, Stockholm, 1892, p. 8
13 See Lars Tingsten, *Fältmarshalkarna Johan Baner och Lennart Torstenson*, Stockholm, 1932
14 G. Schulz (ed.), *German Verse*, London, 1961, p. 13. English translation by Dr Cyril Edwards
15 Nikolaus Pol, quoted in Scheuermann, op. cit., vol. II, p. 1778
16 See Robert Chenciner, *Madder Red*, London, 2000
17 Johann Friedrich Zöllner, 'Die Türkische Garnfabrik', in *Breslau: Ein Lesebuch*, Diethard H. Klein (ed.), Husum, 1988, p. 140
18 Quoted in Hugo Weczerka, *Breslaus Zentralität im ostmitteleuropäischen Raum um 1500* in E. Engel, K. Lambrecht and H. Nogossek (eds), Berlin, 1996, pp. 256–7
19 Charles Ingrao, *The Habsburg Monarchy 1618–1815*, Cambridge, 1994, p. 90
20 Joachim Bahlcke (ed.), *Schlesien und die Schlesier*, Munich, 1996, p. 228
21 Ingrao, op. cit., p. 128n.
22 Paul Konrad, *Die Einführung der Reformation in Breslau und Schlesien*, Breslau, 1917, p. 2
23 H. Hillebrand (ed.), *The Oxford Encyclopedia of the Reformation*, vol. 2, Oxford, 1996, p. 234
24 Conrads, op. cit., p. 209
25 Ingrao, op. cit., p. 29
26 R.J.W. Evans, *The Making of the Habsburg Monarchy 1550–1700*, Oxford, 1979, p. 15
27 Adolf Herthe, *Die Lutherkommentare des Johannes Cochlaeus*, Münster, 1935, pp. 219–20
28 Martin Spahn, *Johannes Cochlaeus – ein Lebensbild*, Berlin, 1928, p. 321
29 Scheuermann, op. cit., vol. II, p. 1779
30 *The English Hymnal with Tunes*, London, 1933, no. 484, p. 631

31 Ingrao, op. cit., p. 63

32 Bahlcke, op. cit., p. 62

33 Evans, *Habsburg Monarchy*, op. cit., p. 120

34 H. Hoffmann, 'Die Jesuitenmission in Breslau, 1581–95', in *Zeitschrift des Vereins für die Geschichte Schlesiens*, vol. 69, 1935, p. 179

35 Ks. Z. Lec, 'Apostolstwo Słowa . . . we Wrocławiu, 1581–95, 1638–1776', in *Jezuicka Ars Educandi*, Cracow, 1995, pp. 131–40

36 Ingrao, op. cit., p. 97

37 Scheuermann, op. cit., vol. II, p. 1469

38 Bahlcke, op. cit., p. 60

39 Quoted in ibid., p. 66

40 Walter Goldstein, *Tausend Jahre Breslau*, Darmstadt, 1974, p. 247

41 Scheuermann, op. cit., vol. II, p. 1039

42 Günther Dippold, 'Der Humanismus im städtischen Schulwesen Schlesiens', in *Humanismus und Renaissance in Ostmitteleuropa vor der Reformation*, Eberhard and Strnad (eds), Cologne, 1996, p. 234

43 'Thomas Rehdiger' entry by Arthur Biber, in *Schlesische Lebensbilder*, vol. IV, Breslau, 1931, pp. 113–24

44 Wrocław, Biblioteka Uniwersytecka, syg. 550758. The Rehdiger Collection was transferred to the new City Library in 1865 and to the University Library in 1945

45 Hugo Weczerka (ed.) *Schlesien*, Stuttgart, 1977, p. 287

46 Dippold, 'Humanismus . . .', in Eberhard and Strnad, op. cit., p. 242

47 S. Kiedroń and P. Poniatowska, *Śląsk-Niderlandy: Złoty Wiek 1550–1650*, Wrocław, 1998, p. 49

48 Acknowledgement is due to Prof. Ian Maclean of All Souls College, Oxford

49 See Jacobus Horstius, *De aureo dente maxillari pueri silesii . . .* Helmstedt, 1595

50 Martin Opitz, *Gesammelte Werke*, vol. I, George Schulz-Behrend (ed.), Stuttgart, 1968, p. 132. English translation by Dr Cyril Edwards

51 H.G. Fielder (ed.), *Das Oxforder Buch der Deutscher Dichtung*, Oxford, 1930, p. 35. English translation by Dr Cyril Edwards

52 Andreas Gryphius, *Carolus Stuardus*, act V, Hugh Powell (ed.), Leicester, 1955, p. 83. English translation by Dr Cyril Edwards

53 Kiedroń and Poniatowska, op. cit., p. 53

54 H. Watanabe-O'Kelly (ed.), *The Cambridge History of German Literature*, Cambridge, 1997, p. 134

55 J.G. Robertson, *A History of German Literature* (6th edition), Dorothy Reich (ed.), London, 1970, p. 207

56 Conrads, op. cit., p. 297

57 Ibid., p. 332

58 W. Węgrzyn-Klisowska, 'Działalność muzyczna teatru miejskiego we Wrocławiu . . .' in *Rocznik Wrocławski*, IV, 1997, pp. 225–42

59 Ibid.

60 K. Matwijowski, *Uroczystości, obchody i widowiska w barokowym Wrocławiu*, Wrocław, 1969

61 W. Długoborski, J. Gierowski et al., *Dzieje Wrocławia do roku 1807*, Warsaw, 1958, p. 292

62 Ibid., p. 504

63 Leszek Ziątkowski, *Die Geschichte der Juden in Breslau*, Wrocław, 2000, p. 19

64 *Encyclopedia Judaica*, vol. IV, Jerusalem, 1972, p. 1345

65 Quoted by J. Bąkowa, *Szchlachta województwa krakowskiego wobec opozycja Jerzego Lubomirskiego w latach 1661–67*, Cracow, 1974, p. 177

66 See Polski Słownik Biograficzny

67 H. Gautier-Villars, *Le mariage de Louis XV*, Paris, 1990, p. 192

68 Charles Wogan, *Female Fortitude . . .* London, 1722, p. 4, Bodleian Library, Oxford

69 Scheuermann, op. cit., vol. II, pp. 1224–5

70 Fritz Enderwitz, *Breslauer Sagen und Legenden*, Breslau, 1921, pp. 49–51

71 Karen Lambrecht, *Hexenverfolgung und Zaubereiprozesse in den Schlesischen Territorien*, Cologne, Weimar, Vienna, 1995, pp. 319–20

72 Scheuermann, op. cit., vol. I, p. 593

73 Enderwitz, op. cit., p. 86

74 Lambrecht, op. cit., p. 320

75 D. Pickering, *A Dictionary of Witchcraft*, London, 1996, p. 108

76 Christine van Eickels, *Schlesien im Böhmischen Standestaat*, Bohlau, 1994, p. 482

77 Bahlcke, op. cit., p. 51

78 See Karen Lambrecht, 'Stadt und Geschichtskultur – Breslau und Krakau im 16. Jahrhundert', in *Die Konstruktion der Vergangenheit. Geschichtsdenken, Traditionsbildung und Selbstdarstellung in den ostmitteleuropäischen Ständegesellschaften (1500–1800)*, Joachim Bahlcke and Arno Strohmeyer (eds), Berlin, 2001

79 See Gustav Türk, 'Lateinische Gedichte zum Lobe Breslaus', in *Zeitschrift des Vereins für Geschichte und Alterthum Schlesiens*, 36, Breslau, 1901

80 Nicolaus Henel von Hennenfeld, *Breslographia, hoc est: Vratislaviae Silesiorum metropoleos noblissimae brevissima*, Frankfurt, 1613, pp. 6–7. Translated from the Latin by Dr Paul Smith

81 Scheuermann, op. cit., p. 464

82 Quoted in Herbert Hupka (ed.), *Breslau beliebt und unvergessen*, Leer, 1990, p. 54. English translation by Dr Cyril Edwards

5. Bresslau in the Kingdom of Prussia, 1741–1871

1 R.E. Dupuy and T.N. Dupuy, *The Collins Encyclopedia of Military History*, 4th edition, Glasgow, 1993, p. 734

2 Joachim Bahlcke, *Schlesien und die Schlesier*, Munich, 1996, p. 75

3 Friedrich der Grosse, *Gedanken und Erinnerungen*, Woldemar von Seidlitz (ed.), Essen, (n.d.), p. 413

4 *Encyclopaedia Britannica*, 11th edition, vol. 11, Cambridge, 1910, p. 53

5 Thomas Babington Macaulay, 'Frederick the Great', in *Critical and Historical Essays*, London, 1907, vol. II, pp. 131–3

6 Ibid. passim

7 Ibid. passim

8 Adolf Weiß, *Chronik der Stadt Breslau*, Breslau, 1888, p. 1015

9 Döblin was subsquently rewarded for his actions by Frederick the Great with 2,000 louis d'or, which he apparently spent in Bresslau's public houses. Scheuermann, *Das Breslau Lexicon*, vol. 1, Dülmen, 1994, p. 215

10 Macaulay, op. cit., pp. 131–3

11 Christopher Duffy, *Frederick the Great – a military life*, London, 1988, p. 26

12 Colmar Grünhagen, *Friedrich der Große und die Bresslauer – 1704–41*, Breslau, 1864, p. 79. Also quoted in Friedrich der Grosse, op. cit., p. 414

13 Duffy, op. cit, p. 28

14 *Breslauisches Tagebuch von Johann Georg Steinberger, 1740–42*, Eugen Träger (ed.), Breslau, 1891, p. 291

15 Macaulay, op. cit., pp. 133–4

16 E.J. Feuchtwanger, *Prussia: Myth and Reality*, London, 1970, p. 63

17 Duffy, op. cit., p. 66

18 Ibid., p. 147

19 Dupuy and Dupuy, op. cit., p. 734

20 Friedrich der Grosse, op. cit., p. 539

21 Günther Elze, *Breslau: die Geschichte einer deutschen Stadt*, Leer, 1993, p. 69

22 Friedrich der Grosse, op. cit., p. 550

23 Feuchtwanger, op. cit., p. 67; also Friedrich der Grosse, op. cit., p. 580

24 Bahlcke, op. cit., p. 86

25 Scheuermann, op. cit., p. 358

26 J. Stein, *Geschichte der Stadt Breslau im 19. Jahrhundert*, Breslau, 1884, p. 7

27 *Breslau, geliebt und unvergessen*, Herbert Hupka (ed.), Leer, 1990, p. 56. Karl von Holtei, '1806 – Die Franzosen belagern Breslau'

28 Scheuermann, op. cit., p. 357

29 Elze, op. cit., p. 81

30 Stein, op. cit., pp. 43–4

31 *Corpus Iuris Confoederationis Germanicae – Staatsacten für Geschichte und öffentliches Recht des Deutschen Bundes*, P.A.G. Meyer and H. Zöpfl, Frankfurt-am-Main, 1858, Band 1, pp. 147–9

32 *Allgemeine deutsche Biographie*, vol. 31, Leipzig, 1890, p. 640

33 From *The Memoirs of General the Baron de Marbot*, 1929, O.C. Colt (trans.), chapter 23

34 Elze, op. cit., p. 82

35 *Gazeta Warszawska*, no. 52 (1813), in Andrzej Zieliński (ed.), *Wrocławskie Aktualności sprzed lat . . .* , Wrocław, 1979, p. 31

36 H.W. Koch, *A History of Prussia*, London, 1978, p. 197

37 J.J. Sheehan, *German History 1770–1866*, Oxford, 1989, p. 444

38 *The Times*, 27 March 1848, p. 6

39 *The Times*, 12 May 1849, p. 6

40 See E. Eyck, *The Frankfurt Parliament 1848–49*, London, 1968, and Bahlcke, op. cit.

41 Friedrich Engels, in Wilhelm Wolff, *Die Schlesische Milliarde*, Hottingen-Zurich, 1886

42 Bahlcke, op. cit., p. 98

43 Geoffrey Wawro, *The Austro-Prussian War, 1866*, Cambridge, 1996, p. 61

44 Quoted in Giles MacDonogh, *Prussia*, London, 1994, p. 112

45 Friedrich der Grosse, op. cit., p. 420

46 Francis Carsten, *A History of the Prussian Junkers*, Aldershot, 1989, p. 66

47 Bahlcke, op. cit., p. 230

48 Olwen Hufton, *Europe: Privilege and Protest 1730–1789*, London, 1980, p. 206

49 Carsten, op. cit., pp. 63–4

50 Ibid., pp. 77–8

51 Hermann Schöler, in *Schlesische Lebensbilder*, vol. II, Breslau, 1926, p. 232

52 Gerhart Hauptmann, *The Weavers*, act 2, Frank Marcus (trans.), London, 1980, p. 28

53 Konrad Fuchs, *Die Auswirkungen der 1848er Revolution in Breslau, Schlesien*, vol. IV, no. VIII, pp. 217–20

54 *The Times*, 13 March 1852, p. 8

55 Conrads, op. cit., p. 490

56 W.-E. Peuckert, *Schlesische Sagen*, Jena, 1924, p. 58

57 Weiß, op. cit., p. 1046

58 Friedrich der Grosse, op. cit., p. 430

59 See 'Scheibel, Johann Gottfried', in *Biographisch-Bibliographisches Kirchenlexicon* at www.bautz.de/bbkl

60 There are said to be areas of South Australia where Silesian dialect can still be heard

61 See 'Ronge, Johannes' in *Biographisch-Bibliographisches Kirchenlexicon*, op. cit.

62 Dr Abraham Geiger, *Judaism and its history*, New York, 1866, passim

63 Andreas Brämer, *Zur Professionalisierung des Rabbinerberufs. Gründung und Anfangsjahre des Jüdisch-Theologischen Seminars in Breslau (1854–1862)*, unpublished conference paper, courtesy of the author

64 From the Dziennik Poznański, no. 52 (1860), *Wrocławskie Aktualności*, op. cit., p. 129

65 Joseph von Eichendorff, 'Das zerbrochene Ringlein' and 'Abschied'. German text from *Das Oxforder Buch Deutscher Dichtung*, Oxford, 1930, pp. 261–2. Translated by the authors

66 See Lutz Tittel, *Philipp Hoyoll Zerstörung eines Bäckerladens 1846*, Regensburg, 1998

67 Friedrich der Grosse, op. cit., p. 516

68 Friedrich von Sallet, 'Echtes Deutschtum', in *Gedichte*, 3rd edition, Hamburg, 1845, p. 382

69 *Gedichte von Moritz, Graf Strachwitz*, Bresslau, 1864, 'Heimkehr', pp. 377–8

70 'Germania', ibid., p. 249

71 Gustav Freytag, *Soll und Haben*, Munich, 1957, p. 27

72 See 'Adolf Anderssen' in *Schlesische Lebensbilder*, vol. I, Breslau, 1922, pp. 92–4

73 Maria Wirtemberska, *Niektóre zdarzenia, myśli uczucia doznane za granicą*, Warsaw, 1978, pp. 91–3

74 J. Słowacki, *Listy*, Warsaw, 1932, p. 234

75 Quoted in Roland Gehrke, *Der polnische Westgedanke bis zur Wiedererrichtung des polnischen Staates nach Ende des Ersten Weltkrieges*, Marburg, 2001, p. 54 fn. Translated by Wanda Wyporska

76 Kurier Warszawski, *Gazeta Wielkiego Księstwa Poznańskiego* in *Wrocławskie Aktualności*, op. cit., under '1829'

77 Koch, op. cit., p. 117

78 J.M. and M.J. Cohen, *The Penguin Dictionary of Quotations*, London, 1960, p. 163

79 Koch, op. cit., p. 136

80 Meyer and Zöpfl, op. cit., pp. 147–9

81 Mieczysław Pater, *Historia Uniwersytetu Wrocławskiego Do Roku 1918*, Wrocław, 1997, p. 297

82 Karl Herlossohn, in H. Trierenberg (ed.), *Breslau in alten und neuen Reisebeschreibungen*, Düsseldorf, 1991, p. 119

83 Quoted in MacDonogh, op. cit., p. 315

84 Stanislaus S——i, *Ein Wort an die Breslauer Bürger*, University Library, Wrocław, Gabinet Śląsko-Łużycki, 1862, III.

85 Jürgen Matoni, 'Die Juden in Gustav Freytags Werken', in *Oberschlesisches Jahrbuch*, H.-L. Abmeier, P. Chmiel, N. Gussone and W. Zylla (eds), vol. VIII, 1992, p. 109ff.

86 Gustav Freytag, *In Breslau*, Breslau, 1845, pp. 1–4. Translated by Dr Cyril Edwards

87 Dr Otto Henne am Rhyn, *Ritter's Geographisch-Statistisches Lexicon*, Leipzig, 1874, p. 221

88 J.I. Kraszewski, *Listy z podróży* (1860), quoted in Z. Antkowiak, *Wrocław od A do Z*, Wrocław, 1997, p. 215

89 Friedrich der Grosse, op. cit., p. 633

90 Carsten, op. cit., p. 56

91 Ibid., p. 51

92 David Blackbourn, *The Long Nineteenth Century, The Fontana History of Germany 1780–1918*, London, 1997, p. 107

93 Richard J. Evans, *Rituals of Retribution*, Oxford, 1996, p. 295

94 Ibid., p. 295

95 Ibid., p. 257

96 Quoted in ibid., p. 220

97 Grünhagen, op. cit., pp. 171–2

98 Koch, op. cit., p. 117

99 Bahlcke, op. cit., p. 83

100 Nancy Mitford, *Frederick the Great*, London, 1970, p. 192. German text in Friedrich der Grosse, op. cit., p. 658

101 Quoted in Conrads, op. cit., p. 480

102 H.O. Reichard, *Guide de l'Allemagne*, vol. VII, Weimar, 1793, reprinted in Paris, 1971

103 Ibid., Routes 44, 53, 54, 76

104 Ibid.

105 Ibid.

106 *Goethes Briefe*, vol. II, Hamburg, 1964, p. 130

107 Elze, op. cit., pp. 75, 77

108 John Quincy Adams, *Letters on Silesia*, London, 1804, pp. 219–20

109 Izabela Czartoryska, *Dyliżansem przez Śląsk: Dziennik podróży do Cieplic w roku 1816*, Wrocław, 1968, pp. 44–9

110 Ibid., pp. 115–31. (Whatever it was, the *Restraint of Scipio* was *not* a Rembrandt.)

111 J.M. Fritz, *Illustrierte Wochenzeitung*, no. 381, 1867, in A. Zieliński (ed.), *Wrocławskie Aktualnoski Sprzed lat*, Wrocław, 1979, p. 158

112 Gustav Freytag, *Reminiscences of my life*, Catherine Chetwynd (trans.), London, 1890, pp. 150–1

113 Herlossohn, in Trierenberg, op. cit., pp. 118–29

114 *Tygodnik Illustrowany* (Cracow), no. 303, 1865 – *Wrocławskie Aktualności*, op. cit., pp. 151–2

115 *Journal of Parisian Fashions*, no. 17 (1847), ibid. p. 63

116 J.Q. Adams, quoted by S. Wormell (ed.) *Pallas-Poland*, London, 1994, p. 596

6. *Breslau in the German Empire, 1871–1918*

1 *Encyclopaedia Britannica*, 11th edition, vol. XI, Cambridge, 1910–11, p. 808. 41,058,792 in 1871 and 60,641,278 in 1905, thus a 47.6 per cent increase

2 William Carr, *A History of Germany 1815–1985*, 3rd edition, London, 1987, p. 121

3 David Blackbourn, *The Long Nineteenth Century 1780–1918*, *The Fontana History of Germany, 1780–1918*, London, 1997, p. 267
4 Carr, op. cit., p. 120
5 Marion Gräfin Dönhoff, *Preußen – Maß und Maßlosigkeit*, Berlin, 1998, p. 77
6 Heinrich August Winkler, *Der lange Weg nach Westen*, vol. I, Munich, 2001, p. 226
7 Heinrich Bartsch, *Geschichte Schlesiens*, Würzburg, 1985, pp. 262–3. Figures are given for Silesia in 1895 as being 44.7 per cent Protestant and 53.6 per cent Catholic. This compares with Prussian figures for 1900 of 63 per cent Protestant and 35.1 per cent Catholic
8 Statistics taken from table 79 in Volker Berghahn, *Imperial Germany 1871–1914*, Oxford, 1994, p. 335
9 Statistics taken from tables 5 and 6 in Joachim Bahlcke, *Schlesien und die Schlesier*, Munich, 1996, pp. 104–5
10 Though neither of the assassins, Max Hödel and Karl Nobiling, was attached to the Socialist Party, their actions were exploited to clamp down on the SPD
11 Ernst Moritz Arndt, *Was ist des Deutschen Vaterland?*, 1812
12 Roger Chickering, *We men who feel most German – A Cultural Study of the Pan-German League 1886–1914*, London, 1984, p. 138
13 Blackbourn, op. cit., p. 430
14 William Hagen, *Germans, Poles and Jews: The Nationality Conflict in the Prussian East – 1772–1914*, Chicago and London, 1980, p. 266
15 Statistics taken from table 9 in Volker Berghahn, *Modern Germany*, Cambridge, 1982, p. 260
16 Schulenburg to Churchill, in Randolph Churchill, *Winston S. Churchill*, vol. II, London, 1967, p. 195. In 1934–41, Schulenburg was to be German Ambassador to Moscow and hence a witness of the Nazi-Soviet Pact. See also ibid., companion vol. 1 to vol. II, pp. 558–9
17 Ibid., p. 196
18 Ibid., p. 196, WSC to Lord Elgin
19 Ibid., p. 225
20 Ibid., p. 196
21 R. Gelles, *Wrocław w latach wielkiej wojny, 1914–18*, Wrocław, n.d., pp. 36–41
22 K. Popiński, 'Ideowe i polityczne postawy studentów, UWr we latach 1911–21', in *Studia Historica Slavo-Germanica*, vol. XXI, 1996–7, pp. 41–58
23 M. Paleologue, quoted by Martin Gilbert, *The First World War*, London, 1994, p. 45
24 Quoted in Peter Kilduff, *The Red Baron*, London, 1994, p. 52
25 Ibid., p. 198
26 Martin Gilbert, *The Routledge Atlas of the First World War*, London, 1994, p. 77
27 *The Times*, 30 November 1918, p. 7
28 Gelles, op. cit., passim
29 Popiński, op. cit., p. 47
30 Blackbourn, op. cit., p. 313
31 *Encyclopaedia Britannica*, op. cit., vol. XI, p. 811
32 Gordon A. Craig, *Germany 1866–1945*, Oxford, 1978, p. 81
33 Blackbourn, op. cit., p. 320
34 Bahlcke, op. cit., p. 234
35 Ibid., p. 236

36 Statistics quoted in Blackbourn, op. cit., p. 200

37 Norbert Conrads, *Schlesien*, Berlin, 1994, p. 569

38 Bahlcke, op. cit., p. 237

39 Werner Marschall, *Geschichte des Bistums Breslau*, Stuttgart, 1980, p. 145

40 K. Popiński, 'Religijno-światopoglądowe aspekty Kulturkampfu wśród studentów Uniwersytetu Wrocławskiego', in *Rocznik Wrocławski*, no. 4, 1997, pp. 272–81

41 See Maciej Łagiewski, *Der alte jüdische Friedhof in Wrocław*, Wrocław, Bonn, 1988

42 J.D. Steakly, 'Iconography of a Scandal', in M.B. Dubermann et al. (eds), *Hidden from History: Reclaiming the Gay and Lesbian Past*, London, 1991, pp. 233–63

43 Beate Störtkuhl, 'Die Breslauer Moderne 1900–1933', in *'Wach auf, mein Herz, und denke'* *Zur Geschichte der Beziehung zwischen Schlesien und Berlin-Brandenburg von 1740 bis heute*, Berlin/Oppeln, 1995, p. 144

44 Manfred Hettling, *Politische Bürgerlichkeit*, Göttingen, 1999, p. 37

45 Krzysztof Popiński, *Breslaus Musik- und Theaterleben an der Wende vom 19. Zum 20. Jahrhundert*, in *Rocznik Wrocławski*, vol. III, Wrocław, 1996

46 W. Meckauer (ed.), *Das Theater in Breslau und Theodor Loewe, 1892–1917*, Breslau, 1917

47 Scheuermann, *Das Breslau Lexicon*, vol. II, Dülmen, 1994, pp. 1865–6

48 K. Popiński, 'Rekreacja Fizyczna Mieszkanców Wrocławia . . .', in *Ślaski Lobirynt Krajoznawczy*, 6/1994, pp. 113–20

49 *Encyclopaedia Britannica*, op. cit., p. 823

50 K. Popiński, 'Pierwe kobiety na studiach na UWr', in *Studia i materialy z dziejów Uwr*, vol. IV, pp. 187–201

51 J. Kasprowicz, 'Rzadko na moich wargach', S. Grochowiak, J. Maciejewski (eds), *Poezja polska: antologia*, Warsaw, 1973, II, pp. 7–9

52 After Hutchinson's *Multimedia Encyclopedia*, London, 1999

53 Gerhart Hauptmann, *Sämtliche Werke*, Hans-Egon Hass (ed.), vol. IX, Berlin, 1969

54 *The Times*, 19 June 1913, p. 7

55 H.W. Arndt, 'Occupation Rentier', in *Quadrant*, Canberra, Jan.–Feb. 1982, pp. 90–1

56 Felix Dahn, *Ein Kampf um Rom*, vol. III, Leipzig, 1910, p. 438

57 Sigmund Karski, *Albert (Wojciech) Korfanty*, Bonn, 1990, p. 42

58 Till van Rahden, 'Mingling, Marrying, and Distancing. Jewish Integration in Wilhelmine Breslau and its Erosion in Early Weimar Germany', in *Jüdisches Leben in der Weimarer Republik*, Wolfgang Benz (ed.), Tübingen, 1998, p. 204

59 Leszek Ziątkowski, *Die Geschichte der Juden in Breslau*, Wrocław, 2000, p. 85

60 Jack Wertheimer, *Unwelcome Strangers. East European Jews in Imperial Germany*, Oxford, 1987, p. 180

61 The authors are indebted to Lisa Swartout of the University of Berkeley for information on the *Viadrina*

62 Wertheimer, op. cit., p. 69

63 Ibid., p. 155

64 Ibid., p. 156

65 Leszek Ziątkowski, *Ludność Żydowska we Wrocławiu w latach 1812–1914*, Wrocław, 1998

66 Wertheimer, op. cit., p. 181

67 See I.D. Bering, *Der Name als Stigma: Antisemitismus im deutschen Alltag*, Stuttgart, 1987

68 See van Rahden, op. cit.

69 Blackbourn, op. cit., p. 437

70 Berghahn, *Modern Germany*, op. cit., p. 253, table 2

71 Hettling, op. cit., p. 39
72 *The Times*, 21 August 1883, p. 3
73 Richard Evans, *Death in Hamburg*, London, 1987, p. 181
74 Ibid., p. 77
75 Richard Evans, *Rituals of Retribution*, Oxford, 1996, pp. 385–6
76 See Kilduff, op. cit.
77 Hettling, op. cit., p. 164
78 Ibid., p. 381, table 39
79 Blackbourn, op. cit., p. 368
80 Winkler, op. cit., p. 339
81 Scheuermann, op. cit., p. 520
82 Ibid., pp. 841–2
83 See Peter Gay, *The Dilemma of Democratic Socialism*, New York, 1952
84 Quoted in Winkler, op. cit., p. 291
85 Paul Löbe, *Erinnerungen eines Reichstagspräsidenten*, Berlin, 1954, pp. 29–30
86 J.P. Nettl, *Rosa Luxemburg*, 2 vols, Oxford, 1966, vol. II, p. 687
87 *The Letters of Rosa Luxemburg*, Stephen Bonner (ed.), Boulder, 1978, p. 221
88 Nettl, op. cit., vol. II, p. 426
89 R. Luxemburg, *Die Russische Revolution*, Berlin, 1922. English translation by Bertram Wolfe, Ann Arbor, 1961, quoted by Nettl, op. cit., p. 434
90 Theodor Müller, *Die Geschichte der Breslauer Sozialdemokratie*, Breslau, 1925, pp. 400–1
91 Giles MacDonogh, *The Last Kaiser*, London, 2000, p. 233
92 *Bradshaw's August 1914 Continental Guide*, reprint with introduction by J.H. Price, Newton Abbot, 1972, tables 179A, 218A, 180. Prussian State Railways, mid-Europe time
93 Ibid., ABC routes, p. 10
94 Ibid., p. 219
95 Janusz Gołaszewski, 'Stulecie Kolejki Wrocławsko-Trzebnicko-Prusickiej', in *Rocznik Wrocławski*, vol. V, 1998, pp. 133–67
96 *Bradshaw's*, op. cit., p. 468

7. Breslau before and during the Second World War, 1918–45

1 T. Hunt Tooley, *National Identity and Weimar Germany*, Lincoln and London, 1997, pp. 54–5
2 Paul Löbe, *Erinnerungen eines Reichstagspräsidenten*, Berlin, 1949, p. 49
3 Richard Bessel, *Germany after the First World War*, Oxford, 1993, p. 86
4 Günther Doose, *Die separatische Bewegung in Oberschlesien nach dem Ersten Weltkrieg (1918–1922)*, Wiesbaden, 1987, p. 13
5 See Hagen, Schulze, 'Der Oststaat Plan 1919', in *Vierteljahrshefte für Zeitgeschichte*, vol. 18, no. 2, 1970
6 Dietrich Orlow, *Weimar Prussia 1918–25*, Pittsburgh, 1986, p. 102
7 *The Times*, 15 February 1920, p. 8
8 *The Times*, 16 March 1920, p. 15
9 Edgar von Schmidt-Pauli, *Geschichte der Freikorps 1918–1924*, Stuttgart, 1936, pp. 246–9
10 Till van Rahden, 'Mingling, Marrying and Distancing: Jewish Integration in Wilhelminian Breslau and its Erosion in Early Weimar Germany', in *Jews in the Weimar Republic*, Wolfgang Benz (ed.), Tübingen, 1998, p. 208

11 F.L. Carsten, *The Reichswehr and Politics 1918–1933*, Oxford, 1966, p. 85

12 F.L. Carsten, *Revolution in Central Europe 1918–19*, London, 1972, p. 281

13 *The Times*, 28 August 1920, p. 9

14 K. Popiński, 'Ideowe I postawy studentó uczelni wrocławskich w latach 1911–21', in *Studia Historica Slavo-Germanico*, vol. XXI, 1996–7, pp. 41–58

15 Figures taken from Detlev J.K. Peukert, *The Weimar Republic*, R. Deveson (trans.), London, 1991, pp. 62–4

16 *The Times*, 23 July 1923, p. 12

17 *The Times*, 12 January 1931, p. 11

18 Conan Fischer, *Stormtroopers – A Social, Economic and Ideological Analysis*, London, 1983, pp. 46–7

19 Ibid., p. 47

20 *The Times*, 1 June 1931, p. 13

21 Richard J. Evans, *Rituals of Retribution*, Oxford, 1996, p. 617

22 *The Times*, 18 August 1932, p. 9

23 *The Times*, 24 June, 27 June, 4 August, 8 August 1932

24 Klaus A. Lankheit (ed.), *Hitler: Reden, Schriften, Anordnungen, Feb. 1925–Jan. 1933*, vol. V, Munich, 1996, pp. 69–76

25 Ulrich Frodien. Text published in *Karta*, no. 31, Warsaw, 2000

26 Ibid.

27 Joachim Bahlcke, *Schlesien und die Schlesier*, Munich, 1996, p. 138

28 *The Times*, 10 March 1933, p. 13

29 *The Times*, 15 March 1933, p. 14

30 *The Times*, 6 May 1933, p. 11

31 V.R. Berghahn, *Modern Germany*, Cambridge, 1982, p. 258

32 Ibid., p. 266

33 Bahlcke, op. cit., p. 140

34 Fischer, op. cit., p. 196

35 See Heinz Höhne, *The Order of the Death's Head – The Story of Hitler's SS*, London, 1969

36 K. Jońca, 'Noc Kryształowa i casus Grynszpana', Wrocław, 1992, pp. 178–92

37 Ibid., p. 186

38 Michael Burleigh, 'Medical Mass Murder', in *The Third Reich: A New History*, London, 2000, pp. 382–404

39 Alexander Henderson, *Eyewitness in Czechoslovakia*, London, 1939, p. 179

40 Joachim C. Fest, *Hitler. Eine Biographie*, Frankfurt am Main, 1973, p. 265 passim

41 Bahlcke, op. cit., p. 24

42 Bessel, op. cit., p. 130n

43 Figures taken from *Die Not in Breslau*, published by the Statistisches Amt der Stadt Breslau, Breslau, 1924, p. 11

44 See *Statistisches Jahrbuch für das Deutsche Reich*, Berlin, 1926, 1930

45 See *Statistisches Jahrbuch deutscher Städte*, vol. 22, Leipzig, 1926–7, p. 352

46 See *Statistisches Jahrbuch für das deutsche Reich*, Berlin, 1930

47 See *Die Wohnungsnot in Breslau*, Breslau, 1927, p. 66

48 René Marlé, *Bonhoeffer – The Man and His Work*, Rosemary Sheed (trans.), London, 1968, pp. 31–2

49 Richard Grunberger, *A Social History of the Third Reich*, London, 1971, p. 558

50 Sebastian Siebel-Achenbach, *Lower Silesia from Nazi Germany to Communist Poland, 1942–49*, London, 1994, p. 20

51 Hanna Gerl-Falkowitz, *Unerbittliches Licht: Edith Stein. Philosophie, Mystik, Leben*, Mainz, 1998; see also Waltraud Herbstrith, *Edith Stein: A Biography*, London, 1985; 'Vatican Rushes to Canonise a Catholic Jew', *Sunday Times*, 11 October 1998; Ewa Czaczkowska, 'Pierwszy kanonizowany filzof XX wieku' ('The first canonised philosopher of the twentieth century), *Rzeczpospolita*, Warsaw, no. 238, 10 October 1998

52 Walter Laqueur, *Wanderer wider Willen: Erinnerungen 1921–51*, Berlin, 1995, pp. 24–5

53 London University's School of Slavonic and East European Studies was marginally senior to the Breslau Osteuropa-Institut, being founded in 1915

54 J.M. Richards (ed.), *Who's Who in Architecture*, London, 1977, p. 256

55 Hans Winglcr (cd.), *Kunstschulreform 1900–1933*, Berlin, 1977, p. 219

56 *The Times*, obituary, 19 February 2001

57 Morris Goran, *The Story of Fritz Haber*, Norman, 1967, pp. 91–8; and Dietrich Stoltzenberg, *Fritz Haber – Chemiker, Nobelpreistraeger, Deutscher, Jude*, Weinheim, 1998, pp. 487–500

58 Grunberger, op. cit., p. 536

59 Ibid., p. 546

60 See Michael Burleigh, *Germany turns Eastwards – A study of* Ostforschung *in the Third Reich*, Cambridge, 1988

61 Max Weinreich, *Hitler's Professors*, New Haven and London, 1999, p. 193

62 Ibid., p. 128fn

63 Thomas Mielke, *Die Breslauer Schule der Anthropologie – Eine ideologische Vererbungslehre*. Http://www.verwaltung.uni-mainz.de/archiv/html/breslau.htm.

64 Emil Ludwig, *How to treat the Germans*, London and New York, 1943, p. 17

65 Emil Ludwig, *Gifts of Life – a Retrospect*, London and New York, 1931, p. 17

66 Frodien, op. cit.

67 Grunberger, op. cit., text plate 8

68 E. Achremowicz, T. Żabski, *Towarzystwo Słowiańskie w Wrocławiu*, Wrocław, 1973, p. 15

69 W. Urban, 'Ostatnie kazanie polskie w kościele św. Marcina', in *Sobótka*, Wrocław, XVI, no. 1, pp. 101–3

70 H.W. Arndt, 'Three Times 18: an essay in political Autobiography', in *Quadrant*, Canberra, May–June 1969, pp. 18–19

71 Walter Tausk, *Breslauer Tagebuch 1933–40*, Berlin (East), 1976, p. 127

72 Meeting Minutes of the Breslau Party comrades, 2 July 1936: quoted by Edwin Black, *IBM and the Holocaust: the Strategic Alliance between Nazi Germany and America's most powerful Corporation*, London, 2001, pp. 174–5; after Götz Aly and Roth, *Die restlose Erfassung*, Berlin, 1984

73 Black, op. cit., pp. 184–5

74 John Najmann, *The night our sorrow began . . .* in the *Evening Standard*, 7 November 1988

75 Anita Lasker-Wallfisch, *Inherit the Truth*, London, 1996, p. 19

76 Tausk, op. cit., p. 194

77 Ibid., p. 210

78 Mr P. Rosten (EW 1 968–975), ref PIId No. 52, Wiener Library, London

79 Arndt, op. cit., pp. 19–20

80 Interview with W. Dzieduszycki, 25 June 2000

81 Laqueur, op. cit., pp.14–15
82 Hans Stargardter (b. 1927) of Bloomfield, CT, USA. 'My experiences in Hitler's Germany', unpublished typescript, October 1986, updated March 1997
83 With thanks to Hanna Nyman for the testimony of Ella Feldman
84 *The Times*, 29 November 1930, p. 11
85 Joachim Fest, *The Face of the Third Reich*, London, 1970, p. 343
86 Helmut Neubach, *Parteien und Politiker in Schlesien*, Dortmund, 1988, p. 205
87 Statistics from Volker Berghahn, *Modern Germany*, Cambridge, 1982, p. 254
88 Beate Störtkuhl, 'Hochhäuser für Breslau vor dem Hintergrund des "Hochhausfiebers" in Deutschland um 1920', in *Hochhäuser für Breslau 1919–1932*, Jerzy Ilkosz and Beate Störtkuhl (eds), Braunschweig, 1997
89 K. Baedeker, *Germany*, Leipzig, 1936, pp. 140–5
90 T. Kruszewski, 'Zmiany nazw ulic we Wrocławiu w latach Trzeciej Rzeszy', *Acta Universitatis Wratislaviensis*, no. 1860, 1996, pp. 243–55
91 A. Kamiński, 'Targi w Nazistowskim Wrocławiu', in *Rocznik Wrocławski*, vol. IV, 1997, pp. 81–128
92 Quoted in Norman Davies, *Europe: A History*, London, 1997, p. 909
93 Frodien, op. cit.
94 W. Stachiewicz, *Wierności Dochować Żołnierskiej*, Warsaw, 1998, p. 525
95 J. Rómmel, *Za Honor I Ojczyna*, Warsaw, 1958
96 J.B. Cynk, *The Polish Air Force at War, 1939–45*, Atglen PA (1998), 2 vols: vol. I, chapter 1, 'The Lonely Fight with the Luftwaffe September 1939', pp. 58–93; also vol. II, appendix 3, 'The Luftwaffe Order of Battle, 1939', and appendix 5, 'Summary of the LW's War Effort and Losses, September 1939'
97 Götz Aly, *Endlösung*, Frankfurt-am-Main, 1998, pp. 223–4
98 Helmut Krausnick, *Hitlers Einsatzgruppen*, Frankfurt-am-Main, 1985, p. 42
99 Ibid., pp. 42–3
100 Ibid., p. 44
101 James Lucas, *German Army Handbook 1939–1945*, London, 2000, pp. 112, 200
102 Antony Beevor, *Stalingrad*, London, 1998, p. 107
103 Ibid., p. 108
104 Gereon Goldmann, *In the Shadows of His Wings*, London, 2000
105 Frodien, op. cit.
106 From *Verzeichnis der Haftstätten unter dem Reichsführer SS 1939–45*, International Tracing Service, Arolsen, Germany
107 Stanisław Pigoń, *'Sonderaktion Krakau': Erinnerungen aus Sachsenhausen 1939–40*, Vienna, 1988
108 Czesława Ziembowa, 'Zacisnąć zęby i przetrwać', in *Niewolnicy w Breslau, wolni w Wrocławiu*, Wrocław, 1995, pp. 55–6
109 Hans-Werner Wollenberg, ... *und der Alptraum wird zum Alltag – Autobiographisches Bericht eines jüdischen Artztes über NS-Zwangsarbeiter in Schlesien (1942–45)*, Manfred Brusten (ed.), Pfaffenweiler, 1992, pp. 90–1
110 Ziembowa, op. cit., pp. 58–9
111 'Numer 31', *Polityka* (Warsaw), no. 25 (2250), 17 June 2000
112 'Jüdisches Leben in der Provinz Schlesien und in Breslau 1940–41', ref: P III a, no. 619, Wiener Library, London
113 Willy Cohn, *Als Jude in Breslau, 1941*, pp. 45–6

114 Ibid., p. 51
115 Maciej Łagiewski, *Breslauer Juden 1850–1944*, Wrocław, 1996, p. 210; and Alfred Konieczny, *Tormersdorf, Grüssau, Riebnig. Obozy przejściowe dla Żydów Śląska z lat 1941–1943*, Wrocław, 1997
116 Połomski, pp. 92–93.
117 Lasker-Wallfisch, op. cit., p. 49
118 See Konieczny, op. cit.
119 Edith Stein, *Life in a Jewish Family: An Autobiography*, in *Collected Works*, vol. I, L. Gelbe (ed.), Washington, DC, 1986, p. 434
120 Połomski, op. cit., p. 116
121 C. Henry and M. Hillel, *Children of the SS*, London, 1975
122 Ibid., p. 153
123 Ibid., pp. 239–40
124 See J. Wnuk, *Losy dzieci polskich w okresie okupacji hitlerowskiej*, Lublin, 1980
125 Eric Williams, *The Wooden Horse* (1949), London, 1979, pp. 129–32
126 M. Marcel Neveu, recording *c*.1981. By kind permission of Mme Hélène Neveu-Kringelberg
127 J. Garliński, *Poland in the Second World War*, London, 1985, p. 85; see also collected documents, *Le Saint-Siège et la situation réligieuse en Pologne . . . 1939–45*, Rome, 1967, vol. I, pp. 392–8
128 Letter relating to the fate of Jews from Breslau, Germany, 24 August 1943. United States Holocaust Memorial Museum, Washington, DC, ref: RG-14.012
129 Paul Peikert, *Festung Breslau: in den Berichten eines Pfarrers – 22. Januar bis 6. Mai 1945*, Karol Jońca and Alfred Konieczny (eds), Wrocław, 1997, p. 248
130 See Krupp Archive, Imperial War Museum, London, ref: 128c, 'Monatsberichte der Krupp Berthawerk AG – 08/43–06/44'
131 William Manchester, *Arms of Krupp*, London, 1969, pp. 576–80
132 'Bomber's Baedeker' kindly supplied by the Air Historical Branch, Ministry of Defence, London
133 Siebel-Achenbach, op. cit., p. 22
134 See Melanie Jappy, *Danger UXB*, London, 2001
135 Statistics from *Oxford Companion to the Second World War*, I.C.B. Dear and M.R.D. Foot (eds), Oxford, 1995, pp. 1071, 1074; and H. Kinder and W. Hilgemann, *Penguin Atlas of World History*, vol. II, London, 1978, p. 200
136 Bomber's Baedeker, op. cit.
137 Włodimierz Borodziej, *Terror und Politik: Die deutsche Polizei und die polnische Widerstandsbewegung im Generalgouvernement 1939–44*, Mainz, 1999, pp. 170, 181, 212
138 Polish Institute and Sikorski Museum, London, AXII 83/137
139 PRO London, file HS 6/666, 'Acts of Sabotage and Subversion in the region of Breslau'
140 Frodien, op. cit.

8. Wrocław: Phoenix from the Ashes, 1945–2000

1 Stanisława Marciniak, 'Dane mi było przeżyć' ('I was allowed to survive'), *Niewolnicy w Breslau, Wolni we Wrocławiu*, Wrocław, 1995, p. 122
2 Ibid., p. 123
3 Jakub Tyszkiewicz, *Od Upadku Festung Breslau do Stalinowskiego Wrocławia: Kalendarium, 1945–50*, Wrocław, 2000, p. 23

4 As seen on contemporary photographs

5 J. Konopińska, quoted by Tyszkiewicz, op. cit., p. 17

6 Irena Strauss, in 'To było piękne miasto' ('It was a beautiful city'), in *Res Publica*, no. 6 (1990), p. 8

7 General Sikorski's memorandum of December 1942 referred very imprecisely to 'The Oder ... and its tributaries down to the Czech frontier'. E. Wiskemann, *Germany's Eastern Neighbours*, Oxford, 1956, p. 71

8 K. Rosen-Zawadzki, 'Karta Buduszczej Europy' (The Map of Future Europe), *Studia z dziejów ZSRR i Środkowej Europy*, Wrocław, 1972, viii, 141–5 with map

9 W. Dzieduszycki, private interview, 25 June 2000

10 See note 1

11 See Nicholas Tolstoy, *The Victims of Yalta*, London, 1976; *The Minister and the Massacres*, London, 1986

12 As shown in the TV documentary series, *Mała Ojczyzna: 'Końca Wojny nie było'*, TV Polonia, 22 January 2001

13 *Poland, Germany and European Peace: Official Documents, 1944–48*, Polish Embassy Press Office, London, 1948, p. 114

14 Martin Gilbert, *Never Again: Winston Churchill, 1945–65*, London, 1988, p. 88; ibid., pp. 60–1174 for all references to Churchill at Potsdam

15 Wiskemann, op. cit., p. 84

16 Gilbert, op. cit., p. 117

17 Ibid., pp. 115–16

18 Peikert, quoted in Sebastian Siebel-Achenbach, *Lower Silesia from Nazi Germany to Communist Poland, 1942–49*, London, 1994, p. 127

19 Z. Romanow, quoted by Tyszkiewicz, op. cit., p. 20

20 Friedhelm Mondwurf, 'Als Bettelmann in Breslau', in Herbert Hupka (ed.), *Letzte Tage in Schlesien*, Munich and Vienna, 1981, p. 179

21 Dr Andrzej Biernacki (Warsaw), 'Kartka ze Wspomnień Wrocławskich', private letter to Norman Davies, 13 March 2000

22 J. Tyszkiewicz, *Od upadku Festung Breslau do stalinowskiego Wrocławia Kalendarium, 1945–50*, Wrocław, 2000, p. 29.

23 Ekkehard Kuhn, *Schlesien: Brücke in Europa*, Berlin, 1997, pp. 54, 56–7

24 Johannes Kaps, *The Tragedy of Silesia*, Munich, 1952, p. 379

25 Conrad Gröber, quoted by de Zayas, op. cit., pp. 140, 142

26 Kaps, op. cit., Report no. 119, 'Breslau', pp. 361–2

27 Kaps, op. cit., p. 278

28 See John Sack, *An Eye for an Eye: The Untold Story of Jewish Revenge against Germans in 1945*, New York, 1993

29 Kaps, op. cit., no. 195, p. 537

30 Ibid., no. 191, pp. 530–1

31 Ibid., p. 531

32 K. Szwagrzyk, *Golgota Wrocławska 1945–56*, Wrocław, 1996

33 Kaps, op. cit., no. 120, pp. 363–4

34 Ibid., no. 121, pp. 364–7

35 After M. Sobków, 'Do Innego Kraju' ('To Another Land'), *Karta*, Warsaw, no. 14, 1994, pp. 57–68. Koropiec was a village in south-western Ukraine in the district of Tarnopol. 'Recovered Territories' – the Soviet authorities used the same term for the

provinces taken from Poland that the Polish authorities used for the lands taken from Germany. Gross Mochbern (now Muchobór) lay outside the city limits in 1945

36 Private conversation with Dr A. Juzwenko and Prof. K. Orzechowska-Juzwenko, Wrocław, 22 April 2001

37 A. Ryzyński, 'Olega Ryzyńska', in *Pisane Miłością Losy Wdów Katyńskich*, Gdynia, 1999, pp. 369–76.

38 M. Sobków, 'Do Innego Kraju', op.cit., p. 55

39 Z. Żaba, 'Wrocław Nasz' ('Our Wrocław'), *Karta*, Warsaw, no. 14, 1994, p. 70

40 Ibid., pp. 69–78

41 Dzieduszycki, see note 9

42 Sobków, op. cit., pp. 60–1

43 Antoni Zięba, *Pamiątnik Pedagoga*, Wrocław, 1988, pp. 15–16

44 C. Priebe, 'Szkoła z szabru' (A School from Loot), *Karta*, Warsaw, no. 14, 1994, pp. 79–91

45 Dr Adolf Juzwenko, see note 36

46 Prof. J.A. Gierowski, Rector Emeritus of the Jagiellonian University, in M. Lubieniecka (ed.), *Pięćdziesiąt lat duszpasterstwa akademickiego we Wrocławiu*, Wrocław, 1999, p. 33

47 Ibid., pp. 34–5

48 Letter from Mrs Małgorzata Ziemilska-Dzieduszycka, 26 June 2000

49 Eva Maria Jakubek, 'Zwei Dimensionen', in *Schenkt mir keine Orchideen: Gedichte aus Schlesien 1990–99*, Wrocław, 1999. English translation by Roger Moorhouse

50 Interview with Joanna Schmidt, May 2000; see also Jerzy Korczak, *Teodor Müller – Das Schicksal eines deutschen Polen*, Cologne, 2000

51 B. Szaynoch, 'Żydowscy żołnierze z Bolkowa,' *Odra*, 9/1999, 22–6

52 *Mały Przegląd*, Warsaw, spring 1939. Quoted in *The Best of Midrasz*, 1998, Warsaw, pp. 6–9

53 See Sack, op. cit.; also J. Plaskoń, 'Niczego się nie boję' *Polityka*, 32 (2257), 5 August 2000

54 'Jakub Berman', in Teresa Torańska, *Oni: Stalin's Polish Puppets*, London, 1987, pp. 203–354

55 See K. Szwagrzyk, *Golgota Wrocławska, 1945–56*, Wrocław, 1996

56 Alina, Cała, H. Danter-Spiewak, *Dzieje Żydów w Polsce, 1944–68*, Jewish Historical Institute, Warsaw, 1997

57 Jarosław Lipszyc, 'A Failed Rebirth: Stopover in Lower Silesia', *Midrasz*, 7–8 (15–16), July–August 1998. English translation in *The Best of Midrasz, 1998*, Warsaw, 1996, pp. 6–11

58 Ibid., p. 10

59 Ibid., p. 10

60 Ibid., p. 11

61 Zdzisław Mach, *Niechciane miasta* ('Unwanted Towns'), Cracow, 1998

62 Or 'Once Yes and twice No'. See 'Pierwszy rok powojennego Wrocławia', *Rocznik Wrocławski*, 2 (1995), p. 115

63 See Szwagrzyk, op. cit.

64 Tyszkiewicz, op. cit., p. 36

65 Ibid., p. 76

66 Ibid., p. 100

67 J. Tyszkiewicz, *Sto Wielkich Dni Wrocławia*, Wrocław, 1997

68 Jakub Egit, *Grand Illusion*, Toronto, 1991, p.98; Tyszkiewicz, op. cit., *Kalendarium*, pp. 112–17

69 *Dziennik*, I, p. 275, quoted by J. Tyszkiewicz, *Kalendarium*, p. 156

70 'Speech of Professor Taylor at the Intellectuals' Congress' in the possession of Eva Haraszti-Taylor; quoted by Kathleen Burk, *Troublemaker: the Life and History of A.J.P. Taylor*, London, 2000, pp. 193–4. The heading of the text cannot possibly be Taylor's own since he took great pride in *not* being a professor

71 Ibid., pp. 194–5

72 *New Statesman* (London), 4 September 1948

73 *Daily Herald*, 27 August 1948; *Manchester Guardian*, 26, 27, 28, 31 August 1948; *The Times*, 27 August 1948; *New Statesman*, 4 September 1948; *Daily Worker*, 1 September 1948

74 PRO London, FO1110/108, 271

75 M. Urbanek, 'Co rośnie na wierzbie', *Polityka* 31 (2152), 1 August 1998

76 J. Tyszkiewicz, *Kalendarium*, op. cit., p. 159

77 Adam Ciołkosz, 'Poland', in *Social Democracy in post-war Europe*, London, 1951, pp. 34–60; see also L. & A. Ciołkosz, *Zarys dziejów socijalizmu polskiego*, London, 1966

78 Szwagrzyk, op. cit., p. 707

79 'Helena Wolińska, 1919– ', in K. Szwagrzyk, *Zbrodnie w majestacie prawa, 1944–55*, Warsaw, 2000, pp. 181–3

80 Ibid.

81 See Denis Healey, *The Curtain Falls: The Story of the Socialists in Eastern Europe*, London, 1951

82 Feliks Mantel, *Wachlarz Wspomnień*, Paris, 1972

83 Teresa Suleja, *Universytet Wrocławski w okresie centralizmu stalinowskiego, 1950–55*, Wrocław, 1995, p. 214

84 Adam Zagajewski, 'My Krakow', *New York Review of Books*, 10 August 2000

85 S. L. Kulczyński (1895–1975), *Uczeni Polscy*, Warsaw, 1995, vol. II

86 No entries on PZPR leaders appear in Z. Antkowiak, *Wrocław od A do Z*, Wrocław, 1997

87 Szwagrzyk, *Golgota*, op. cit.

88 Ibid.

89 Archive of the Regional Court (Sąd Okręgowy) in Wrocław: under IIK 1950, IVK 1952; ibid.

90 Michał Mońko, 'Gulag Miedzianka', *Odra*, no. 3, March 2000, pp. 33–9

91 Wanda Dybalska, 'Jak powstała Wrocławska Piosenka', *Gazeta Dolnośląska*, no. 104, 5 May 2000

92 Sir Eric Berthoud, 10–12 April 1957, PRO London, FO371/128804 & NP1015/45

93 J. Grotowski, *Towards a Poor Theatre*, London, 1975, pp. 211–18

94 Grotowski, 'Statement of Principles', ibid.

95 T. Różewicz, 'Wiersz', *Wrocław liryczny*, op. cit., pp. 99–100

96 H. W. Sabais, ibid., pp. 104–8

97 A. Hannowa, *Miesiące mojego życia*, Wrocław, 1999

98 Mach, op. cit., pp. 112–13

99 H. Kamm, 'The Past Submerged', *New York Times*, 19 February 1966

100 H. Kamm, 'Polish City, Once German, Retains Only Trace of Vibrant Jewish Life', *New York Times*, 7 December 1973

101 K. Ruchniewicz, 'Wrocław w relacjach Niemców z RFN', *Rocznik Wrocławski*, no. 4, 1997, pp. 129–56

102 Günther Anders, *Besuch im Hades; Auschwitz und Breslau 1966*, Munich, 1979, pp. 50–1

103 *Teatr* (monthly), Wrocław, February 1987

104 R. Gelles (ed.), *Historia Wrocławia w datach*, Wrocław, 1996, pp. 153–5

105 Andreas Bornholt, *Solidarität von Gemeinde zu Gemeinde und Schule zu Schule: Breslau – Dortmund, 1981–89*, Dortmund, 1990

106 Edith Stein, *Life in a Jewish Family: An Autobiography*, translated by J. Koeppel, in *Collected Works of Edith Stein*, L. Gelbe (ed.), Washington, DC, 1986, vol. I, p. 434; entry of 7 August 1942

107 Song by Heinz-Rudolf Kunze in Albrecht Lehmann, *Im Fremden ungewollt zuhaus – Flüchtlinge und Vertriebene in Westdeutschland 1945–90*, Munich, 1991

108 Walter Becher, quoted in Dietrich Strothmann, ' "Schlesien bleibt unser": Vertriebenen-politik und das Rad der Geschichte', in *Die Vertreibung der Deutschen aus dem Osten*, Wolfgang Benz (ed.), Frankfurt, 1995, p. 274

109 *Der Spiegel*, 46/1999, 'Getanzt, getrunken und geweint', pp. 238–43

110 Anita Lasker-Wallfisch, *Ihr sollt die Wahrheit erben. Breslau – Auschwitz – Bergen-Belsen*, Bonn, 1997

111 Roman Aftanazy, *Dzieje rezydencji na dawnych kresach Rzeczypospolitej* (2nd edition), Wrocław, 1991, 11 vols.

112 *The Norbert Elias Reader*, J. Goudsblom, S. Mennel (eds), Oxford, 1997, frontispiece

113 Fritz Stern, *Dreams and Delusions*, New York, 1987, p. 146

114 Ewa Stachniak, *Necessary Lies*, Toronto, 2000; see also 'Kanadyjski debiut', *Gwiazda Polarna*, no. 24, 18 November 2000

115 Letter: Mark Burdajewicz to Norman Davies, 8 April 1999

116 Prof. Karol Modzelewski, quoted in H. Kamm, 'Poland Reawakens to its History as Communism's Mirror Shatters', *New York Times*, 26 January 1995

117 See 'Wratislavia – powrót sławy: Rozmowa z Maciejem Łagiewskim', 1998. See M. Łagiewski, *Macewy mowi*, Wrocław, 1991, and *Wrocławscy Żydzi*, Wrocław, 1994 (*Breslauer Juden*, 1996)

118 On academic history, see especially W. Wrzesinski, T. Suleja; on the Stalinist period, K. Szwagrzyk, M. Ordyłowski; on Jewish matters, S. Bronsztejn, Bożena Szajnok, E. Waszkiewicz; on the post-war years, T. Kulak, J. Tyszkiewicz; and on opposition politics, W. Suleja [Stefański], A. Grocholski. Wrocław's leading journals of historical interest include the *Acta Universitatis Wratislaviensis*, the *Prace Historyczne, Sobótka, Odra, Rocznik Wrocławski*. The opening in 2000 of a Wrocław branch of the Institute of National Memory (IPN) greatly facilitated independent research on the post-war period

119 *Rocznik Wrocławski* (The Wrocław Annual), Towarzystwo Przyjaciół Ossolineum, Wrocław, 1994–

120 Janusz Czerwiński, *Wrocław*, Wrocław, 1997

121 T. Kulak, *Wrocław: przewodnik historyczny* (1997); J. Czerwiński, *Wrocław: przewodnik turystyczny*, 1997; M. Kaczmarek, M. Goliński, T. Kulak, W. Suleja, *Wrocław: dziedzictwo dziejów*, 1997; J. Harasimowic et al (eds), *Encyklopedia Wrocławia*, Wrocław, 2000, p. 988

122 M. Kaczmarek, M. Goliński, T. Kulak, W. Suleja, *Wrocław: dziedzictwo wieków*, Wrocław, 1997, 'Wstęp', p. 5

123 Zofia Tarajło-Lipowska, 'Wrocław był bliżej Pragi', *Odra*, no. 3, March 2000, pp. 56–9

124 V. Macura, *Odra*, ibid., p. 55

125 J. Tyszkiewicz, 'Kto kocha Wrocław, kocha Warszawę', in *Gazeta Dolnośląska*, no. 140, 16 June 2000

126 '11 Żydów skarży Polskę', *Gazeta Wyborcza*, 3 August 1999; 'Holocaust Survivor sues Polish Government', *Independent* (London), 4 August 1999

127 'Rachunek Krzywd' ('A Reckoning of Injury'), *Wprost*, 30 July 2000

128 Fundacja 'Krzyżowa' dla Porozumienia Europejskiego (Krzyżowa Foundation for European Understanding). c/o W. Ofiar Oswięcimskich 7/13, 50–069, Wrocław, PL; also www.aede.org

129 Dr Maciej Matwijów, Librarian, Ossoliński Foundation, Wrocław. Report: 'The Case of a Dispersed Library', 1997

130 Bożena Szajnok, 'Żydzi we Wrocławiu po II wojnie światowej', in *Rocznik Wrocławski*, no. 4, 1997, pp. 173–90

131 'Keeping Safe', M. Maliński, in *Gość w dom, . . . Jan Pawel II W Polsce 1997*, Cracow, 1998, pp. 32–4

132 'Wrocławskie Powodzie' ('Wrocław Floods'), *Rocznik Wrocławski*, 5, 1997, pp. 8–130, with German summaries

133 W. Wrzesiński (ed.), *Wrocławska Kronika Wielkiej Wody*, Wrocław, 1997, p. 139

134 Dr Alison T. Millett, University of Virginia. Report submitted for the Wrocław Project, November 1998. For current information, see www.wroclaw.com

135 From *Wrocław Economic Review*, published by the City Council, Wrocław, 1998

136 K. Bzowska, 'Expo 2010 we Wrocławiuz?', *Dziennik Polski* (London), 21 November 2000

INDEX